Fodor's 6th Edition

W9-CEN-345

Florence, Tuscany, and Umbria

The Guide
for All Budgets

Completely
Updated

Where to Stay, Eat,
and Explore

On and Off
the Beaten Path

When to Go,
What to Pack

Maps, Travel Tips,
and Web Sites

Fodor's Travel Publications • New York, Toronto, London, Sydney, Auckland
www.fodors.com

Fodor's Florence, Tuscany, and Umbria

EDITOR: Chris Swiac

Editorial Contributors: Peter Blackman, Andrew Collins, Satu Hummasti, Jennifer Paull, John Rambow, Ann Reavis, Patricia Rucidlo
Editorial Production: Ira-Neil Dittersdorf
Maps: David Lindroth, *cartographer;* Rebecca Baer and Robert Blake, *map editors*
Design: Fabrizio La Rocca, *creative director;* Guido Caroti, *art director;* Jolie Novak, *senior picture editor;* Melanie Marin, *photo editor*
Cover Design: Pentagram
Production/Manufacturing: Colleen Ziemba
Cover Photo (Rape field in Tuscany): Wolfgang Meier/FPG International/ Getty Images

Copyright

Sixth Edition

ISBN 1-4000-1108-6

ISSN 1533-1628

Important Tip

Although all prices, opening times, and other details in this book are based on information supplied to us at press time, changes occur all the time in the travel world, and Fodor's cannot accept responsibility for facts that become outdated or for inadvertent errors or omissions. So **always confirm information when it matters,** especially if you're making a detour to visit a specific place.

Special Sales

Fodor's Travel Publications are available at special discounts for bulk purchases for sales promotions or premiums. Special editions, including personalized covers, excerpts of existing guides, and corporate imprints, can be created in large quantities for special needs. For more information, contact your local bookseller or write to Special Markets, Fodor's Travel Publications, 1745 Broadway, New York, NY 10019. Inquiries from Canada should be directed to your local Canadian bookseller or sent to Random House of Canada, Ltd., Marketing Department, 2775 Matheson Boulevard East, Mississauga, Ontario L4W 4P7. Inquiries from the United Kingdom should be sent to Fodor's Travel Publications, 20 Vauxhall Bridge Road, London SW1V 2SA, England.

PRINTED IN THE UNITED STATES OF AMERICA

10 9 8 7 6 5 4 3 2 1

CONTENTS

ON THE ROAD WITH FODOR'S

A trip takes you out of yourself. Concerns of life at home completely disappear, driven away by more-immediate thoughts—about, say, what marvels will beguile the next day, or where you'll have dinner. That's where Fodor's comes in. We make sure that you know all your options, so that you don't miss something around the next bend just because you didn't know it was there. Mindful that the best memories of your trip might have nothing to do with what you came to Tuscany and Umbria to see, we guide you to sights large and small all over the region. You might set out to tour Florence's famous Duomo or climb Pisa's Leaning Tower, but back at home you find yourself unable to forget a perfect day spent strolling in the hill towns of Umbria. With Fodor's at your side, serendipitous discoveries are never far away.

About Our Writers

Our success in showing you every corner of Tuscany and Umbria is a credit to our extraordinary writers. Although there's no substitute for travel advice from a good friend who knows your style, our contributors are the next best thing—the kind of people you would poll for travel advice if you knew them.

After completing his master's degree in art history, **Peter Blackman** settled permanently in Italy in 1986. Since then he's worked as a biking and walking tour guide, managing to see more of Italy than most of his Italian friends put together. When he's not leading a trip, you'll find Peter at his home in Chianti, reading, writing, listening to opera, and planning his next journey.

In 1997, **Ann Reavis** decided to put her career as a trial lawyer in the San Francisco Bay area on hold for a nine-month sojourn in Tuscany. She's been living in Florence ever since. A freelance writer and tour guide, Ann has been writing a murder-mystery series based in Tuscany.

Florence-based **Patricia Rucidlo** has two master's degrees, in Italian Renaissance history and art history. When she's not extolling the virtues of the colors to be found in a Pontormo masterpiece or defending the Medici, she's either leading wine tours in Chianti, catering private dinner parties, or working on a cookbook.

You can rest assured that you're in good hands—and that no property mentioned in the book has paid to be included. Each has been selected strictly on its merits, as the best of its type in its price range.

How to Use this Book

Up front is Smart Travel Tips A to Z, arranged alphabetically by topic and loaded with tips, Web sites, and contact information. Destination: Florence, Tuscany, and Umbria helps get you in the mood for your trip. Subsequent chapters are arranged regionally. The Florence chapter begins with exploring information, with a section for each neighborhood (each recommending a good tour and listing sights alphabetically). All regional chapters are divided geographically; within each area, towns are covered in logical geographical order, and attractive stretches of road between them are indicated by the designation En Route. To help you decide what you'll have time to visit, all chapters begin with our writers' favorite itineraries. (Mix itineraries from several chapters, and you can put together a really exceptional trip.) The A to Z section that ends every chapter lists additional resources. At the end of the book you'll find Background and Essentials, including a chronology, a Books and Movies section, and an Italian vocabulary section.

Icons and Symbols

★ Our special recommendations
✕ Restaurant
🏠 Lodging establishment
✕🏠 Lodging establishment whose restaurant warrants a special trip
⚑ Campgrounds
🧸 Good for kids (rubber duck)
☞ Sends you to another section of the guide for more information
✉ Address
☎ Telephone number
🕐 Opening and closing times
💰 Admission prices (those we give apply to adults; substantially reduced fees are almost always available for children, students, and senior citizens)

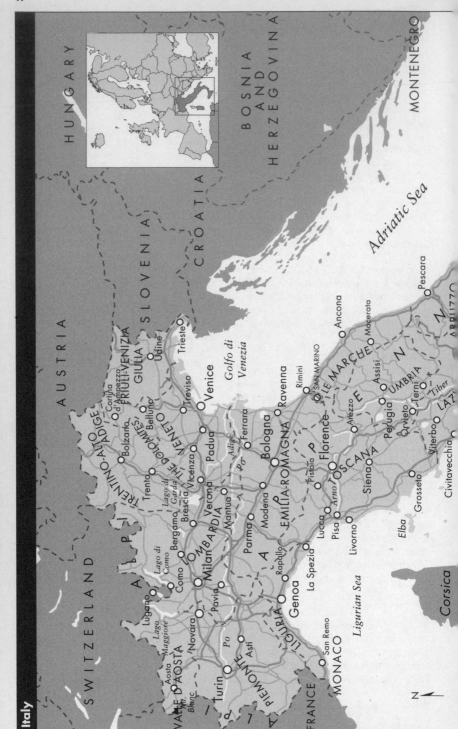

Italy

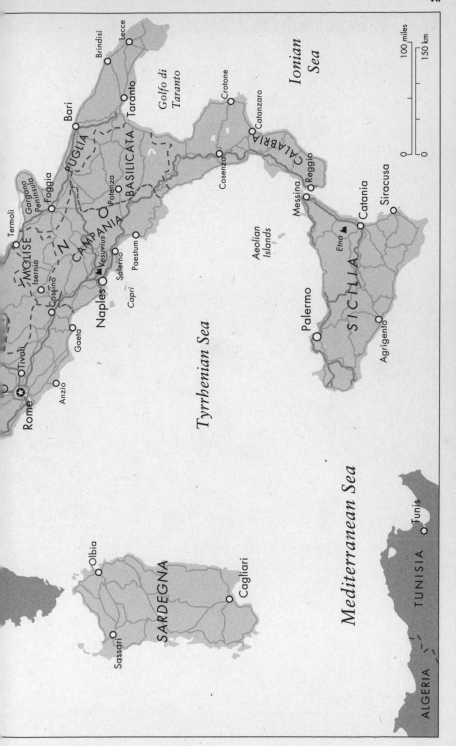

Lecce

Brindisi

Bari

Taranto

Golfo di Taranto

Crotone

Catanzaro

CALABRIA

Cosenza

PUGLIA

Foggia

Gargano Peninsula

Termoli

MOLISE

Isernia

Cassino

Gaeta

Anzio

Tivoli

Rome

BASILICATA

Potenza

CAMPANIA

Vesuvius

Naples

Salerno

Paestum

Capri

Ionian Sea

100 miles

150 km

Messina

Reggio

Siracusa

Catania

Etna

Aeolian Islands

SICILIA

Palermo

Agrigento

Tyrrhenian Sea

Olbia

SARDEGNA

Cagliari

Sassari

Mediterranean Sea

Tunis

TUNISIA

ALGERIA

LIGURIA

Pontremoli

Villafranca
in Lunigiana

Lunigiana

A15

S63

S62

Fivizzano

GARFAGNANA

S486

S12

S324

Lévanto

Cinque
Terre

Monterosso al Mare

Vernazza

Corniglia

Manarola

Riomaggiore

La Spezia

Sarzana

Lérici

Portovénere

Carrara

Massa

Castelnuovo
di Garfagnana

ALPI APUANE

S445

Fornacci
di Barga

Abetone

San Marcell
Pistoies

S12

Prunetto

Bagni
di Lucca

S1

A12

Forte dei Marmi

Marina di Pietrasanta

Lido di Camaire

Viareggio

Pietrasanta

Lucca

Pescia

Collodi

S12

A11

Monteca
Terme

A11

S435

A12

S12

Pisa

Cascina

S439

S4

Marina
di Pisa

Tirrénia

A11

S206

S67

San M

Pontedera

Castel

Livorno

A12

S439

Ligurian Sea

Castiglioncello

S1

S68

Cécina

ITALY

San Vincenzo

S1

S329

S398

Capraia

Piombino

Portoferraio

Cavo

Rio Marina

Porto Azzurro

Castiglion
della Pescai

Elba

N

Pianosa

0 ——— 20 miles

0 ——— 30 km

Tyrrhenian Sea

Gigli

Umbria and the Marches

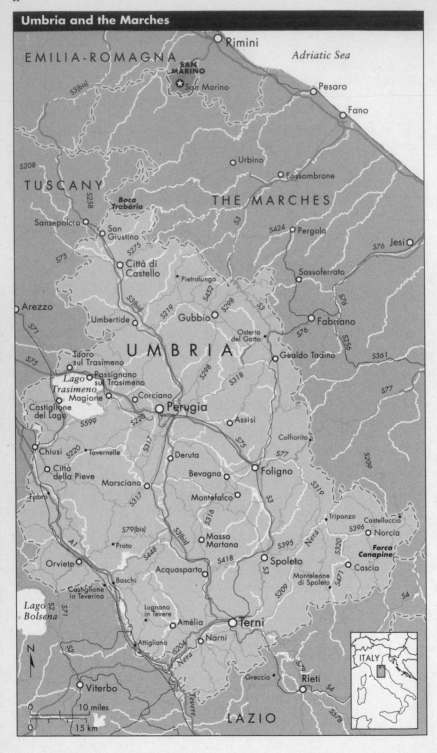

EMILIA-ROMAGNA

Rimini

Adriatic Sea

SAN MARINO
★ San Marino

Pesaro

Fano

S3(bis)

S208

TUSCANY

Urbino

Fossombrone

THE MARCHES

Boca Trabária

S258

Sansepolcro

San Giustino

S275

S573

Città di Castello

Pietralunga

S424   Pergola

S76   Jesi

Sassoferrato

S76

S219   S452   S298

Arezzo

S71(bis)

Umbertide

Gubbio

Osteria del Gatto

UMBRIA

Fabriano

S76

S256

S361

Tuoro sul Trasimeno

Passignano sul Trasimeno

S298   S318

Gualdo Tadino

S71

S75

Lago Trasimeno

Magione

Corciano

Perugia

Assisi

Colfiorito

S77

Castiglione del Lago

S599

S220

S317

S75

S77

S209

Chiusi   S220   Tavernelle

Deruta

Foligno

Città della Pieve

Bevagna

S3

S319

Fabro

Marsciano

S317

Montefalco

S316

Triponzo   Castelluccio

S396   Norcia

Forca Canapine

S79(bis)

Prato

S3(bis)

Massa Martana

Nera   S320

S395

A1

Orvieto

S448

Acquasparta

S418

Spoleto

Cascia

S471

Castiglione in Teverina

Baschi

Monteleone di Spoleto

S2

S71

Lago Bolsena

Lugnano in Tevere

Amélia

Narni

S209

S4

N

Attigliano

S204

Terni

Nera

Greccio

S79

Rieti

Tevere

S3

A1

Viterbo

0   10 miles
0   15 km

LAZIO

S4

S578

ITALY

Numbers in white and black circles ③ ❸ that appear on the maps, in the margins, and within the tours correspond to one another.

For hotels, you can assume that all rooms have private baths, phones, TVs, and air-conditioning unless otherwise noted and that all hotels operate on the European Plan (with no meals) if we don't specify another meal plan. We always list a property's facilities but not whether you'll be charged extra to use them, so do ask what's included. For restaurants, it's always a good idea to book ahead; we mention reservations only when they're essential or are not accepted. All restaurants we list are open daily for lunch and dinner unless stated otherwise; dress is mentioned only when men are required to wear a jacket or a jacket and tie.

Look for an overview of local dining-out habits in Smart Travel Tips A to Z and in the Pleasures and Pastimes section after each chapter introduction.

Don't Forget to Write

Your experiences—positive and negative—matter to us. If we have missed or misstated something, we want to hear about it. We follow up on all suggestions. Contact the Florence, Tuscany, and Umbria editor at editors@fodors.com or c/o Fodor's, 1745 Broadway, New York, NY 10019. And have a fabulous trip!

Karen Cure

Karen Cure
Editorial Director

ESSENTIAL INFORMATION

Addresses in Italy are fairly straight-forward: the street name is followed by the street number. However, you might see an address with a number plus "bis" or "A"—for instance, "Via Verdi 3/bis" or "Via Mazzini 8/A." This indicates that 3/bis and 8/A are the next entrance or door down from Via Verdi 3 and Via Mazzini 8, respectively. Addresses with a number followed by "r" (e.g., Via Santo Spirito 35/r) refer to *rosso* (red), the color of the number painted on the wall. "Red" addresses are always businesses.

In rural areas, some addresses give only the route name or the distance in kilometers along a major road (e.g., Via Fabbri, Km 4.3), or sometimes only the name of the small village in which the site is located.

AIR TRAVEL

Air travel to Italy is frequent and virtually problem-free. Sometimes, however, airport- or airline-related union strikes may cause delays of a few hours. These delays usually are reported in advance. Alitalia, Italy's national flag carrier, has the most nonstop flights to Rome and Milan. Frequent nonstop flights link London with Pisa (British Air, Ryanair). More-frequent flights are available from the United States and Canada; these stop once in Europe before continuing on to Florence or Pisa.

BOOKING

When you book **look for nonstop flights** and **remember that "direct" flights stop at least once.** Try to avoid connecting flights, which require a change of plane. Two airlines may operate a connecting flight jointly, so ask if your airline operates every segment of the trip; you may find that the carrier you prefer flies you only part of the way. To find more book-ing tips and to check prices and make on-line flight reservations, log on to www.fodors.com.

CARRIERS

When flying internationally, you must usually choose between a domestic carrier, the national flag carrier of the country you are visiting, and a foreign carrier from a third country. You may, for example, choose to fly Alitalia to Italy. National flag carriers have the greatest number of nonstops. Domestic carriers may have better connections to your hometown and serve a greater number of gateway cities. Third-party carriers may have a price advantage.

Alitalia—in addition to other major European airlines and smaller, privately run companies such as Meridiana and Air One—also has an extensive network of flights within Italy. Ask your domestic or Italian travel agent about discounts.

On international flights, Alitalia serves Rome, Milan, and Venice. The major international hubs in Italy are Milan and Rome, served by (in addition to Alitalia) Continental Airlines, Delta Air Lines, American Airlines, United Airlines, Northwest Airlines, US Airways, and their European code-sharing partners.

Alitalia and British Airways provide direct service from Heathrow and Gatwick. From Manchester, there are direct British Airways flights daily to Milan and Rome. Meridiana has direct flights daily to Florence throughout the year. Lower-priced charter flights to a range of Italian destinations also are available throughout the year.

Alitalia and Air Canada have the most flights connecting Canada and Italy. Qantas flies to Rome from various cities in Australia, via Bangkok. Alitalia and Air New

Zealand fly from Aukland to Rome with a stop in London.

➤ MAJOR AIRLINES: **Air Canada** (☎ 888/247–2262, 0870/524–7226 in the U.K., 800/919091 in Italy, WEB www.aircanada.com). **Air New Zealand** (☎ 0800/352–266 in New Zealand, 800/876126 in Italy, WEB www.airnz.com). **Alitalia** (☎ 800/ 223–5730, 800/361–8336 in Canada, 0990/448–259 in the U.K., 1300/ 653–747 in Australia, 06/65641 in Rome, 848/865641 elsewhere in Italy, WEB www.alitalia.it). **American Airlines** (☎ 800/433–7300, 06/ 66053169 in Rome, WEB www.aa. com). **British Airways** (☎ 800/247– 9297, 0845/773–3377 in the U.K., 02/8904–8800 in Australia, 09/356– 8690 in New Zealand, 199/712266 in Italy, WEB www.britishairways.com). **Continental Airlines** (☎ 800/231– 0856, 800/296230 in Italy, WEB www. flycontinental.com). **Delta Air Lines** (☎ 800/241–4141, 08705/074–074 in the U.K., 1300/303–744 in Australia, 800/864114 in Italy, WEB www. deltaairlines.com). **Northwest Airlines** (☎ 800/225–2525 or 800/441–1818, WEB www.nwa.com). **Qantas** (☎ 06/ 52482725 in Rome, WEB www.qantas. com). **United Airlines** (☎ 800/241– 6522, 02/69633707 in Milan, WEB www.unitedairlines.com). **US Airways** (☎ 800/428–4322, 848/813177 in Italy, WEB www.usairways.com).

➤ SMALLER AIRLINES: **Air One** (☎ 8488/48880 in Italy, WEB www. flyairone.it). **Meridiana** (☎ 020/ 7839–2222 in London, 199/111333 in Italy, 055/2302314 in Florence, WEB www.meridiana.it). **Ryanair** (☎ 0870/ 156–9569 in London, 199/114114 in Italy, WEB www.ryanair.com).

CHECK-IN AND BOARDING

Airports in Italy have been ramping up security measures, which include random baggage inspection and bomb-detection dogs.

Always **ask your carrier about its check-in policy.** Plan to arrive at the airport about two hours before your scheduled departure time for domestic flights and 2½ to 3 hours before international flights. Assuming that not everyone with a ticket will show up, airlines routinely overbook planes. When everyone does, airlines ask for volunteers to give up their seats. In return, these volunteers usually get a certificate for a free flight and are rebooked on the next flight out. If there are not enough volunteers, the airline must choose who will be denied boarding. The first to get bumped are passengers who checked in late and those flying on discounted tickets, so **get to the gate and check in as early as possible,** especially during peak periods.

Always **bring a government-issued photo I.D. to the airport;** even when it's not required, a passport is best.

CUTTING COSTS

The least expensive airfares to Italy are priced for round-trip travel and must usually be purchased in advance. Airlines generally allow you to change your return date for a fee; most low-fare tickets, however, are nonrefundable. It's smart to **call a number of airlines and check out their Web sites**; when you are quoted a good price, **book it on the spot**—the same fare may not be available the next day. Always **check different routings** and look into using alternate airports. Also, price off-peak flights, which may be significantly less expensive than others. Travel agents, especially low-fare specialists (☞ Discounts and Deals), are helpful.

Consolidators are another good source. They buy tickets for scheduled international flights at reduced rates from the airlines, then sell them at prices that beat the best fare available directly from the airlines. Sometimes you can even get your money back if you need to return the ticket. Carefully read the fine print detailing penalties for changes and cancellations, purchase the ticket with a credit card, and **confirm your consolidator reservation with the airline.**

➤ CONSOLIDATORS: **Cheap Tickets** (☎ 800/377–1000 or 888/922–8849, WEB www.cheaptickets.com). **Discount Airline Ticket Service** (☎ 800/576– 1600). **Unitravel** (☎ 800/325–2222, WEB www.unitravel.com). **Up & Away Travel** (☎ 212/889–2345). **World Travel Network** (☎ 800/409–6753).

ENJOYING THE FLIGHT

State your seat preference when purchasing your ticket, and then repeat it when you confirm and when you check in. For more legroom, you can request one of the few emergency-aisle seats at check-in, if you are capable of lifting at least 50 pounds—a Federal Aviation Administration requirement of passengers in these seats. Seats behind a bulkhead also offer more legroom, but they don't have under-seat storage. Don't sit in the row in front of the emergency aisle or in front of a bulkhead, where seats may not recline.

If you have dietary concerns, **ask for special meals when booking.** These can be vegetarian, low-cholesterol, or kosher, for example. It's a good idea to pack some healthy snacks and a small (plastic) bottle of water in your carry-on bag. On long flights, try to maintain a normal routine, to help fight jet lag. At night, **get some sleep.** By day, **eat light meals, drink water** (not alcohol), and **move around the cabin** to stretch your legs. For additional jet-lag tips consult *Fodor's FYI: Travel Fit & Healthy* (available at bookstores everywhere).

Smoking policies vary from carrier to carrier. Many airlines, including those that fly to Italy, prohibit smoking on all of their international flights; others allow smoking only on certain routes or certain departures. Smoking is prohibited on flights within Italy. Ask your carrier about its policy.

FLYING TIMES

Flying time is 8½ hours from New York, 10–11 hours from Chicago, 11½ hours from Dallas (via New York), 11½ hours from Los Angeles, 2 hours from London (to Milan), and 23½ hours from Sydney to Rome.

HOW TO COMPLAIN

If your baggage goes astray or your flight goes awry, complain right away. Most carriers require that you **file a claim immediately.** The Aviation Consumer Protection Division of the Department of Transportation publishes *Fly-Rights,* which discusses airlines and consumer issues and is available on-line. At PassengerRights.com, a Web site, you can compose a letter of complaint and distribute it electronically.

➤ AIRLINE COMPLAINTS: **Aviation Consumer Protection Division** (✉ U.S. Department of Transportation, Room 4107, C-75, Washington, DC 20590, ☎ 202/366–2220, WEB www.dot.gov/airconsumer). **Federal Aviation Administration Consumer Hotline** (☎ 800/322–7873).

RECONFIRMING

Check the status of your flight before you leave for the airport. You can do this on your carrier's Web site, by linking to a flight-status checker (many Web booking services offer these), or by calling your carrier or travel agent. Always **confirm international flights** at least 72 hours ahead of the scheduled departure time.

AIRPORTS

The major gateways to Italy include Rome's Aeroporto Leonardo da Vinci (airport code FCO), better known as Fiumicino, and Milan's Aeroporto Malpensa 2000 (MIL). Flights to Florence make connections at Fiumicino and Malpensa; you can also take the FS airport train to Rome's Termini Station or a bus to Milan's central train station (Centrale) and catch a train to Florence or Perugia.

Alitalia and other European carriers fly into the smaller airports. Florence is serviced by Aeroporto A. Vespucci (FLR), which is also called Peretola, and by Aeroporto Galileo Galilei (PSA), which is about a mile outside the center of Pisa and about one hour from Florence. The train to Florence stops within 100 ft of the entrance to the Pisa airport terminal.

When you take a connecting flight to Florence and Pisa, be aware that your luggage might not make it onto the second plane with you. The lost-luggage service is efficient, however, and your delayed luggage is usually delivered to your hotel or holiday rental within 12 to 24 hours.

➤ AIRPORT INFORMATION: **Aeroporto A. Vespucci** (FLR; ✉ 6 km [4 mi] northwest of Florence, ☎ 055/30615), also called Peretola. **Aeroporto Galileo Galilei** (PSA; ✉ 2 km [1 mi] south of Pisa, 80 km [50 mi] west of Florence, ☎ 050/500707,

WEB www.pisa-airport.com). **Aeroporto Leonardo da Vinci** (FCO; ✉ 35 km [20 mi] southeast of Rome, ☎ 06/5953640, WEB www.adr.com), better known as Fiumicino. **Aeroporto Malpensa 2000** (MIL; ✉ 45 km [28 mi] north of Milan, ☎ 02/74851, WEB www.sea-aeroportimilano.it).

BIKE TRAVEL

The number of travelers touring Tuscany and Umbria by bicycle has been on the rise. The back roads provide gorgeous scenery, and the Tuscan and Umbrian hills are challenging to even the best-conditioned riders. The greatest hazards to bikers are the fast cars and big trucks that travel the back roads and the lack of shoulders on the roads. Rather than ride alone, most bikers join organized tours. On your own, you can rent various types of bikes for €12 to €18 a day.

BIKES IN FLIGHT

Most airlines accommodate bikes as luggage, provided they are dismantled and boxed; check with individual airlines about packing requirements. Airlines sell bike boxes, which are often free at bike shops, for about $15 (bike bags can be considerably more expensive). International travelers often can substitute a bike for a piece of checked luggage at no charge; otherwise, the cost is about $100. Domestic and Canadian airlines charge $40–$80 each way.

BOAT AND FERRY TRAVEL

Ferries connect the mainland with the Tuscan islands, including Elba, Capraia, Pianosa, Giglio, and Giannutri. To many destinations there is also hydrofoil (*aliscafo*) service, which is generally twice as fast as ferries and double the price. Service is considerably more frequent in summer months. Passenger and car ferries travel to Elba. If you're traveling in July or August, try to make reservations at least a month ahead.

The Toremar and Moby Lines ferry (*traghetti*) companies accept major credit cards and cash, but not traveler's checks.

➤ BOAT AND FERRY INFORMATION: **Moby Lines** (✉ Piazzale Premuda, Piombino, ☎ 0565/221212, WEB www.mobylines.it). **Toremar** (✉ Piazzale Premuda 13/14, Piombino, ☎ 0565/31100, WEB www.toremar.it).

BUSINESS HOURS

Business hours vary from region to region in Italy. In Florence businesses can be open between 7 AM and 10 PM, but they cannot be open more than 13 hours a day. They must close on Sunday, except for the last Sunday of the month, and on national holidays. Many businesses stay closed Monday morning but open in the afternoon. In August places shut down for two to four weeks.

BANKS AND OFFICES

Banks are open weekdays 8:30–1:30 and 2:45–3:45. Post offices are open Monday through Saturday 9–12:30; central and main district post offices stay open until 6 PM weekdays for some operations, 9–12:30 on Saturday. On the last day of the month, post offices close at midday.

CHURCHES

Most churches are open from early morning until noon or 12:30, when they close for three hours or more; they open again in the afternoon, closing about 7 PM or later. Major cathedrals and basilicas, such as the Duomo in Florence, are open all day. Note that sightseeing in churches during religious rites is discouraged.

GAS STATIONS

Gas stations are generally open Monday through Saturday 7–7 with a break at lunchtime. Gas stations on toll roads are open around the clock.

MUSEUMS

Museum hours vary and often change with the seasons. Many museums are closed one day a week, often Monday. Small private museums may close for lunch. Always check locally.

PHARMACIES

Most pharmacies are open 9–1 and around 3:30–8. Cities such as Florence have two or three all-night pharmacies; signs usually posted in pharmacy windows provide information about the nearest one.

SHOPS

Most shops are open 9–1 and 3:30–7:30 Monday through Saturday. Barbers and hairdressers, with some exceptions, are closed Sunday and Monday. Some tourist-oriented shops in the larger cities and towns may be open all day, as well as on Sunday, as are some department stores and supermarkets.

BUS TRAVEL

Italy's bus network is extensive, although buses aren't as attractive an option as in other European countries, partly because of the low cost and convenience of train travel. Schedules often are drawn up with commuters and students in mind and may be sketchy on weekends. Regional bus companies often provide the only means (not including car travel) of getting to out-of-the-way places. Even when this isn't the case, buses can be faster and more direct than local trains, so it's a good idea to **compare bus and train schedules.**

Most of the major cities in Tuscany and Umbria have urban bus services. These buses are inexpensive, but they can become jammed, particularly at rush hours. Bus service outside cities is organized on a regional level and often operated by private companies. SITA operates throughout Italy; Lazzi Eurolines operates in Tuscany and central Italy. Inter-city buses are clean, air-conditioned, and comfortable. Neither city nor private buses permit smoking.

CLASSES

Both public and private buses offer only one class of service. Cleanliness and comfort levels are high on private buses. Neither the private nor the public bus lines accept reservations.

CUTTING COSTS

Public bus lines offer student and monthly passes. Private lines offer one-, three- and six-month passes. Children under 3 ft in height ride free if they're traveling with an adult and don't require their own seat.

TICKETS AND SCHEDULES

You may purchase tickets for city buses with cash from a machine at the station, at newsstands, or at tobacco shops. You must validate the bus ticket in the machine on the bus. For the private lines, tickets may be purchased with cash or a major credit card at the bus station, on the bus, or at travel agencies bearing the bus line's logo. Be sure to validate the ticket either at the bus station or on the bus as soon as you board.

➤ Bus Information: **ATAF** (✉ Stazione Centrale di Santa Maria Novella, Florence, ☎ 055/5650642 or 055/5650222, WEB www.ataf.it). **Lazzi Eurolines** (✉ Via Mercadante 2, Florence, ☎ 055/363041, WEB www.lazzi.it). **SITA** (✉ Via Santa Caterina da Siena 17/r, Florence, ☎ 055/214721).

CAMERAS AND PHOTOGRAPHY

Tuscany is one of the world's premier spots for art and nature photography. For most purposes, an ISO 200 speed film is sufficient, although ISO 400 is a bit more versatile—and better for low-light situations. For action shots and lower light, you may want to choose a higher-speed film. Digital cameras, which have improved dramatically in the past few years, increasingly are being used by both amateur and professional photographers.

Not everyone appreciates being photographed, particularly in smaller towns where locals have sometimes been exploited by photographers. Always ask for permission before taking a photograph of someone. Many museums and churches don't allow flash or tripods and may restrict cameras altogether.

The *Kodak Guide to Shooting Great Travel Pictures* (available at bookstores everywhere) is loaded with tips.

➤ Photo Help: **Kodak Information Center** (☎ 800/242–2424, WEB www.kodak.com).

EQUIPMENT PRECAUTIONS

Don't pack film and equipment in checked luggage, where it is much more susceptible to damage. X-ray machines used to view checked luggage are becoming much more powerful and therefore are much more likely to ruin your film. Try to **ask for hand inspection of film,** which becomes clouded after repeated exposure to airport X-ray machines, and **keep videotapes and computer disks away from metal detectors.** Always **keep film, tape, and computer disks out of the sun.** Carry an extra supply of batteries, and **be prepared to turn on your camera, camcorder, or laptop** to prove to airport security personnel that the device is real.

FILM AND DEVELOPING

All major brands (Kodak, Polaroid, Fuji) of film are available in Tuscany and Umbria. Expect to pay between €4 and €5.25 for a roll of 36-exposure color print film. One-hour and 24-hour developing are readily available in cities; midsize towns usually have 24-hour and three-day developing available. The cost of 24-hour development of a roll of 36-exposure print film is about €8 to €12.

VIDEOS

While VHS videotapes and players are common, be forewarned that Italy, like other countries in Europe, uses a different video system than the one used in the United States. This means you won't be able to play the videotapes you bring from home on Italian equipment, and tapes purchased in Italy won't work in an American VCR.

Videotape for camcorders is readily available throughout Tuscany and Umbria (the international Pal/Secam standards apply). A 90-minute tape (Fuji) costs about €12.50–€13.50. Four-hour VHS tapes cost about €4.50; mini DVDs (60-minute) cost about €10.50.

CAR RENTAL

Renting a car is essential for exploring the countryside, but not if you plan to stick to city travel. Major car-rental companies offer boxy Ford-type cars (such as Astras) and Fiats in various sizes and in good condition, all with air-conditioning. The local rental companies provide good service and, depending on the time of year, they may have greater availability than the well-known international companies.

Because most Italian cars have standard transmissions, automatics are more expensive and must be reserved in advance. Mileage is usually unlimited, but certain offers limit mileage to 150 km a day.

Hiring a car with a driver can come in handy, particularly if you plan to do some wine tasting. Ask at your hotel for recommended drivers, or inquire at the local tourist information office. Typically, drivers are paid by the day, and are usually rewarded with a tip of about 15% on completion of the journey.

➤ MAJOR AGENCIES: **Alamo** (☎ 800/522–9696, WEB www.alamo.com). **Avis** (☎ 800/331–1084, 800/879–2847 in Canada, 02/9353–9000 in Australia, 09/526–2847 in New Zealand, 0870/606–0100 in the U.K., WEB www.avis.com). **Budget** (☎ 800/527–0700, 0870/156–5656 in the U.K., WEB www.budget.com). **Dollar** (☎ 800/800–6000, 0124/622–0111 in the U.K., where it's affiliated with Sixt, 02/9223–1444 in Australia, WEB www.dollar.com). **Hertz** (☎ 800/654–3001, 800/263–0600 in Canada, 020/8897–2072 in the U.K., 02/9669–2444 in Australia, 09/256–8690 in New Zealand, WEB www.hertz.com). **National Car Rental** (☎ 800/227–7368, 020/8680–4800 in the U.K., WEB www.nationalcar.com).

CUTTING COSTS

Most major U.S. car-rental companies have offices or affiliates in Italy, but the rates are generally better if you make a reservation from abroad rather than from within Italy. Each company's rental prices are uniform throughout Italy, so you won't save money by, for example, picking up a vehicle from a city rental office rather than from an airport location. For a good deal, **book through a travel agent who will shop around.**

Do **look into wholesalers,** companies that do not own fleets but rent in bulk from those that do and often offer better rates than traditional car-rental operations. Prices are best during off-peak periods. Rentals booked through wholesalers often must be paid for before you leave home.

➤ LOCAL AGENCIES: **Program** (✉ ☎ 055/282916 in Florence, 050/500296 in Pisa).

➤ WHOLESALERS: **Auto Europe** (☎ 207/842–2000 or 800/223–5555, FAX 207/842–2222, WEB www. autoeurope.com). **Destination Europe Resources** (DER; ✉ 9501 W. Devon Ave., Rosemont, IL 60018, ☎ 800/ 782–2424, WEB www.dertravel.com). **Europe by Car** (☎ 212/581–3040 or 800/223–1516, FAX 212/246–1458, WEB www.europebycar.com). **Kemwel** (☎ 800/678–0678 or 800/576–1590, FAX 207/842–2124, WEB www.kemwel. com).

INSURANCE

When renting a car you're generally responsible for any damage to or loss of the vehicle. All car-rental agencies operating in Italy require renters to buy theft-protection policies. When considering other coverage, before you leave home see what you already have under the terms of your personal auto-insurance policy and credit cards.

REQUIREMENTS AND RESTRICTIONS

In Italy your own driver's license is acceptable. An International Driver's Permit is a good idea; it's available from the American and Canadian automobile associations, and, in the United Kingdom, from the Automobile Association or Royal Automobile Club. These international permits are universally recognized, and having one in your wallet may save you a problem with the local authorities. In Italy you must be 21 years old to rent an economy or subcompact car, and most companies require customers under age 23 to pay by credit card. Upon rental, all companies require credit cards as a warranty; to rent bigger cars (2,000 cc or more), you must often show two credit cards. There are no special restrictions on senior-citizen drivers. Book car seats, required for children under age 3, in advance. The cost is generally about €36 for the duration of the rental.

SURCHARGES

Before you pick up a car in one city and leave it in another, **ask about drop-off charges or one-way service fees,** which can be substantial. Note, too, that some rental agencies charge extra if you return the car before the time specified in your contract. To avoid a hefty refueling fee, **fill the tank just before you turn in the car.** The cost for an additional driver (spouse included) is €4.50–€6.

CAR TRAVEL

Tuscany and Umbria have an extensive network of *autostrade* (toll highways), complemented by equally well maintained but free *superstrade* (expressways). The ticket you are issued upon entering an autostrada must be returned when you exit and pay the toll; on some shorter autostrade, mainly connecting highways, the toll is paid upon entering. Viacards, on sale at many autostrada locations, make paying tolls easier and faster. A *raccordo* is a ring road surrounding a city. *Strade statali* (state highways, denoted by *S* or *SS* numbers) may be single-lane roads, as are all secondary roads; directions and turnoffs aren't always clearly marked.

Signs on country roads are usually pretty good, but be prepared for fast and impatient fellow drivers.

EMERGENCY SERVICES

Autostrade have emergency telephones at regular intervals. Automobil Club Italiano (ACI) offers 24-hour road service. Dial 803/116 from any phone at any time to reach the ACI dispatch operator. ACI also has a multilingual service to answer travelers' questions (cost: 57 European cents a minute). Many international car-rental companies also provide emergency service or information. Check your paperwork or ask when renting.

➤ CONTACTS: **Automobil Club Italiano** (ACI; ☎ 803/116 emergency service, 166/664477 multilingual travelers' service, WEB www.aci.it).

GASOLINE

Gas stations are located at frequent intervals along the main highways and autostrade. Usually on the periphery of towns and cities, they're rarely found in the center of municipalities. Gas stations on autostrade are open 24 hours. Otherwise, gas stations generally are open Monday through Saturday 7–7 with a break at lunchtime. Many stations have automatic self-service pumps that accept only bills of 5, 10, 20, and 50 euros and don't give a receipt (*ricevuta*). It's not customary to tip the attendant when full service is provided.

Gas (*benzina*) costs about €1.10 a liter. It's available in unleaded (*verde*) and super unleaded (*super*). Many rental cars in Italy take only diesel (*gasolio*) which costs about 84 European cents a liter; **ask about the fuel type before you leave the rental place.**

PARKING

Parking space is at a premium in most towns and cities, but especially in the *centri storici* (historic centers), which are filled with narrow streets and restricted circulation zones. It's advisable to **leave your car only in guarded parking areas.** In Florence such indoor parking costs €18–€26 for 12–24 hours; outside attended parking costs about €8–€18. Parking in an area signposted ZONA DISCO (disk zone) is allowed for limited periods (from 30 minutes to two hours or more—the limit is posted); if you don't have the cardboard disk (inquire at the local tourist office) to show what time you parked, you can use a piece of paper. The *parcometro*, the Italian version of metered parking in which you put coins into a machine for a stamped ticket that you leave on the dashboard, has been introduced in many cities.

Parking regulations are strictly enforced both in the cities and small towns. Fines run as high as €50 (more for taking a space designated for people with disabilities) and towing is possible in Florence. In Tuscany and Umbria vandalism and theft of cars is rare. Nevertheless, **don't leave luggage or valuables in your car,** especially in cities and large towns where thieves target rental cars.

ROAD CONDITIONS

Driving on the back roads of Tuscany and Umbria isn't difficult as long as you're on the alert for bicycles and passing cars. In addition, street and road signs are often missing or placed in awkward spots, so a good map and patience are essential. Autostrade are well-maintained, as are most interregional highways. The condition of provincial (county) roads varies, but road maintenance at this level is generally good in Italy. In many small hill towns, the streets are winding and extremely narrow; consider parking at the edge of town and exploring on foot.

Most autostrade have two lanes in both directions; the left lane is used only for passing. Italians drive fast and are impatient with those who don't, so tailgating is the norm here; the only way to avoid it is to get out of the way.

ROAD MAPS

Michelin and Touring Club Italia, which has shops in major Italian cities, produce good road maps. You can also get free street maps for most Tuscan and Umbrian towns at local information offices.

RULES OF THE ROAD

Driving is on the right. Regulations are largely as in Britain and the United States, except that the police have the power to levy on-the-spot fines. In most Italian towns the use of the horn is forbidden in certain, if not all, areas; a large sign, ZONA DI SILENZIO (silent zone), indicates where. Speed limits are 130 kph (80 mph) on autostrade and 110 kph (70 mph) on state and provincial roads, unless otherwise marked. Enforcement of these limits varies from region to region. Fines, however, are stiff: 10 kph over the speed limit can prompt a fine of up to €500; over 10 kph and your license could be revoked. Penalties for driving after drinking are heavy, too, including license suspension and the additional possibility of six months' imprisonment. The relevant blood-alcohol level is 0.05.

Right turns on red lights are forbidden. Headlights aren't compulsory when it's raining and snowing, but it's always a good idea to turn them on. Seat belts are required for adults, and infant and children's car seats are compulsory for babies and toddlers weighing up to 20 pounds and 38 pounds, respectively.

Many towns have central zones where only taxis and buses are permitted; rental cars may be allowed for pick-ups or drop-offs at central hotels.

CHILDREN IN TUSCANY
AND UMBRIA

It's a good idea to provide older children who are allowed to wander on their own with a copy of their passport and the address and phone number of your hotel or rental apartment.

Although not widespread, discounts for children do exist in Italy. Always ask about a *sconto bambino* (child's discount) before purchasing tickets. Children under a certain height ride free on municipal buses and trams. Children under 18 who are European Union citizens are admitted free to state-run museums and galleries, and there are similar privileges in many municipal and private museums.

If you are renting a car, don't forget to **arrange for a car seat** when you reserve. For general advice about traveling with children, consult *Fodor's FYI: Travel with Your Baby* (available in bookstores everywhere).

FLYING

If your children are two or older, **ask about children's airfares.** As a general rule, infants under two not occupying a seat fly at greatly reduced fares or even for free. When booking, **confirm carry-on allowances** if you're traveling with infants. In general, for babies charged 10% of the adult fare you are allowed one carry-on bag and a collapsible stroller; if the flight is full, the stroller may have to be checked or you may be limited to less.

Experts agree that it's a good idea to use safety seats aloft for children weighing less than 40 pounds. Airlines set their own policies: U.S. carriers usually require that the child be ticketed, even if he or she is young enough to ride free, because the seats must be strapped into regular seats. Do **check your airline's policy about using safety seats during takeoff and landing.** Safety seats are not allowed everywhere in the plane, so get your seat assignments as early as possible.

When reserving, **request children's meals or a freestanding bassinet** (not available at all airlines) if you need them. But note that bulkhead seats, where you must sit to use the bassinet, may lack an overhead bin or storage space on the floor.

FOOD

In restaurants and trattorias you may find a high chair or a cushion for a child to sit on, but rarely is a children's menu offered. Order a *mezza porzione* (half-portion) of any dish, or ask the waiter for a *porzione da bambino* (child's portion). Casual establishments such as trattorias usually are good choices for eating out with children. It's best to take only exceptionally well behaved children to higher-end restaurants; indeed, it's rare to see Italian children in them.

Although you won't find spaghetti and meatballs on menus, approximations to it, such as spaghetti *al pomdoro* (spaghetti with tomato sauce) are suitable substitutions. Italian children are fond of spaghetti with Parmesan, and even if it's not on the menu, most chefs are happy to prepare it. Other foods likely to find favor include pasta with butter (*pasta al burro*), fried or roast chicken (*pollo fritto* or *pollo arrosto*), french fries (*patate fritte*), and ice cream (*gelato*). McDonald's is an option, too; the chain is found throughout Tuscany and Umbria; Florence has four branches.

LODGING

Most hotels in Italy allow children under a certain age to stay in their parents' room at no extra charge, but some do charge for them as extra adults; be sure to **find out the cutoff age for children's discounts.** Some five-star hotels and *agriturismi* are off limits to children.

Many hotels provide cots or cribs with prior arrangement; four- and five-star hotels normally have these on hand. Baby-sitting isn't found as easily, especially at budget hotels. Pools in city hotels are a rarity, and video games virtually unheard of. If you stay at a hotel with satellite TV, you'll have access to some English-language news programs, but little more. Even *The Simpsons* is dubbed into Italian.

PRECAUTIONS

Although safe to drink, Italian tap water is heavily chlorinated, which is one reason most Italians drink bottled water. Apple juice (*succo di mele*) is readily available in most bars and supermarkets, as are other fruit juices and popular soft drinks.

Mosquitoes can be pesky in warm weather. Travel with your usual brand of children's insect repellant. There are several Italian brands—Autun, for instance—that also do the trick. They're available in pharmacies and supermarkets.

SIGHTS AND ATTRACTIONS

Places that are especially appealing to children are indicated by a rubber-duckie icon (☺) in the margin.

SUPPLIES AND EQUIPMENT

Baby formula and disposable diapers are available in all pharmacies; supermarkets also sell disposable diapers. The cost of diapers in Italy is similar to that in other countries, but American brands such as Pampers and Huggies cost slightly more here than in the United States. COOP, a reliable local brand, runs about €11 for 50 diapers, while Pampers cost about €9 for 20 and Huggies go for about €9.70 for 34.

American brands of baby food aren't widely available. Italian baby formula (premixed and powder) generally contains more vitamins than its American counterparts; Plasmon is a good brand. Italian bottles are identical to American ones, but no-spill glasses for toddlers are hard to find so bring a couple with you. Jars of baby food and boxes of cereal are sold in grocery stores (local brands are Plasmon and Mellin).

COMPUTERS ON THE ROAD

Getting on-line in Italian cities isn't difficult: public Internet stations and Internet cafés, some open 24 hours, are becoming more and more common. Prices differ from place to place, so spend some time to find the best deal. This isn't always readily apparent: a place might appear to have higher rates, but if it belongs to a chain, it might not charge you an initial flat fee again when you visit a branch in another city. Some hotels have in-room modem lines, but, as with phones, using the hotel's line is relatively expensive. Always check

modem rates before plugging in. You may need an adapter for your computer for the European-style plugs. If you are traveling with a laptop, carry a spare battery and an adapter. Never plug your computer into any socket before asking about surge protection. IBM sells a pea-size modem tester that plugs into a telephone jack to check whether the line is safe to use.

CONSUMER PROTECTION

Whether you're shopping for gifts or purchasing travel services, **pay with a major credit card** whenever possible, so you can cancel payment or get reimbursed if there's a problem (and you can provide documentation). If you're doing business with a particular company for the first time, **contact your local Better Business Bureau and the attorney general's offices** in your state and (for U.S. businesses) the company's home state as well. Have any complaints been filed? Finally, if you're buying a package or tour, always **consider travel insurance** that includes default coverage (☞ Insurance).

➤ BBBs: **Council of Better Business Bureaus** (✉ 4200 Wilson Blvd., Suite 800, Arlington, VA 22203, ☎ 703/276–0100, ℻ 703/525–8277, 𝗪𝗘𝗕 www.bbb.org).

CUSTOMS AND DUTIES

When shopping abroad, **keep receipts** for all purchases. Upon reentering the country, **be ready to show customs officials what you've bought.** If you feel a duty is incorrect, appeal the assessment. If you object to the way your clearance was handled, note the inspector's badge number. In either case, first ask to see a supervisor. If the problem isn't resolved, write to the appropriate authorities, beginning with the port director at your point of entry.

IN AUSTRALIA

Australian residents who are 18 or older may bring home A$400 worth of souvenirs and gifts (including jewelry), 250 cigarettes or 250 grams of tobacco, and 1,125 ml of alcohol (including wine, beer, and spirits). Residents under 18 may bring back A$200 worth of goods. Prohibited items include meat products. Seeds, plants, and fruits need to be declared upon arrival.

➤ INFORMATION: **Australian Customs Service** (Regional Director, ✉ Box 8, Sydney, NSW 2001, ☎ 02/9213–2000, FAX 02/9213–4000, WEB www. customs.gov.au).

IN CANADA

Canadian residents who have been out of Canada for at least seven days may bring in C$750 worth of goods duty-free. If you've been away fewer than seven days but more than 48 hours, the duty-free allowance drops to C$200; if your trip lasts 24 to 48 hours, the allowance is C$50. You may not pool allowances with family members. Goods claimed under the C$750 exemption may follow you by mail; those claimed under the lesser exemptions must accompany you. Alcohol and tobacco products may be included in the seven-day and 48-hour exemptions but not in the 24-hour exemption. If you meet the age requirements of the province or territory through which you reenter Canada, you may bring in, duty-free, 1.5 liters of wine *or* 1.14 liters (40 imperial ounces) of liquor *or* 24 12-ounce cans or bottles of beer or ale. If you are 19 or older you may bring in, duty-free, 200 cigarettes and 50 cigars. Check ahead of time with the Canada Customs and Revenue Agency or the Department of Agriculture for policies regarding meat products, seeds, plants, and fruits.

You may send an unlimited number of gifts (only one gift per recipient, however) worth up to C$60 each duty-free to Canada. Label the package UNSOLICITED GIFT—VALUE UNDER $60. Alcohol and tobacco are excluded.

➤ INFORMATION: **Canada Customs and Revenue Agency** (✉ 2265 St. Laurent Blvd. S, Ottawa, Ontario K1G 4K3, ☎ 204/983–3500, 506/636–5064, 800/461–9999, WEB www. ccra-adrc.gc.ca/).

IN ITALY

Travelers from the United States, Canada, the United Kingdom, Australia, and New Zealand should experience little difficulty clearing customs at any airports in Italy.

Of goods obtained anywhere outside the EU, the allowances are (1) 200 cigarettes or 100 cigarillos (under 3 grams) or 50 cigars or 250 grams of tobacco; (2) 2 liters of still table wine or 1 liter of spirits over 22% volume; and (3) 50 milliliters of perfume and 250 milliliters of toilet water.

Of goods obtained (duty and tax paid) within another EU country, the allowances are (1) 800 cigarettes or 400 cigarillos (under 3 grams) or 200 cigars or 1 kilogram of tobacco; (2) 90 liters of still table wine or 10 liters of spirits over 22% volume or 20 liters of spirits under 22% volume or 110 liters of beer.

There is no quarantine period in Italy, so if you want to travel with Fido or Fifi, it's possible. Contact your nearest Italian consulate to find out what paperwork is needed for entry into Italy; generally, it is a certificate noting that the animal is healthy and up-do-date on its vaccinations. Keep in mind, however, that the United States has some stringent laws about reentry: pets must be free of all diseases, especially those communicable to humans, and they must be vaccinated against rabies at least 30 days before returning. This means that if you are in Italy for a short-term stay, you must find a veterinarian or have your pet vaccinated before departure. (This law does not apply to puppies less than three months old.) Pets should arrive at the point of entry with a statement, in English, attesting to this fact.

➤ INFORMATION: **Ministero delle Finanze, Direzione Centrale dei Servizi Doganali, Divisione I** (✉ Via Carucci 71, Rome 00143, ☎ 06/50242117). **Dogana Sezione Viaggiatori** (✉ Aeroporto Leonardo da Vinci, Rome 00054, ☎ 06/65954343).

IN NEW ZEALAND

All homeward-bound residents may bring back NZ$700 worth of souvenirs and gifts; passengers may not pool their allowances, and children can claim only the concession on goods intended for their own use. For those 17 or older, the duty-free allowance also includes 4.5 liters of wine or beer; one 1,125-ml bottle of spirits; and either 200 cigarettes, 250 grams of tobacco, 50 cigars, *or* a combination of the three up to 250 grams. Meat products, seeds, plants, and fruits must be declared upon arrival to the Agricultural Services Department.

➤ INFORMATION: **New Zealand Customs** (✉ Head Office, The Customhouse, 17–21 Whitmore St., Box 2218, Wellington, ☎ 09/300–5399, WEB www.customs.govt.nz).

IN THE U.K.

If you are a U.K. resident and your journey was wholly within the European Union, you probably won't have to pass through customs when you return to the United Kingdom. If you plan to bring back large quantities of alcohol or tobacco, check EU limits beforehand. In most cases, if you plan to bring back more than 200 cigars, 800 cigarettes, 10 liters of spirits, and/or 90 liters of wine, you will have to declare the goods upon return.

➤ INFORMATION: **HM Customs and Excise** (✉ Portcullis House, 21 Cowbridge Rd. E, Cardiff CF11 9SS, ☎ 029/2038–6423, 0208/929–0152, or 0845/010–9000, WEB www.hmce. gov.uk).

IN THE U.S.

U.S. residents who have been out of the country for at least 48 hours (and who have not used the $800 allowance or any part of it in the past 30 days) may bring home $800 worth of foreign goods duty-free; the duty-free allowance drops to $200 for fewer than 48 hours.

U.S. residents 21 and older may bring back 1 liter of alcohol duty-free. In addition, regardless of your age, you are allowed 200 cigarettes and 100 non-Cuban cigars. Antiques, which the U.S. Customs Service defines as objects more than 100 years old, enter duty-free, as do original works of art done entirely by hand, including paintings, drawings, and sculptures. You may also send packages home duty-free, with a limit of one parcel per addressee per day (except alcohol or tobacco products or perfume worth more than $5). You can mail up to $200 worth of goods for personal use; label the package PERSONAL USE and

attach a list of its contents and their retail value. If the package contains your used personal belongings, mark it PERSONAL GOODS RETURNED to avoid paying duties. You may send up to $100 worth of goods as a gift; mark the package UNSOLICITED GIFT. Mailed items do not affect your duty-free allowance on your return.

➤ INFORMATION: **U.S. Customs Service** (for inquiries and to register equipment, ✉ 1300 Pennsylvania Ave. NW, Washington, DC 20229, WEB www.customs.gov, ☎ 202/354–1000; for complaints, ✉ Customer Satisfaction Unit, 1300 Pennsylvania Ave. NW, Room 5.4D, Washington, DC 20229).

DINING

The restaurants we list are the cream of the crop in each price category. Properties indicated by an ✕🏠 are lodging establishments whose restaurant warrants a special trip. Not too long ago, restaurants tended to be more elegant and expensive than trattorie and osterie, which serve more-traditional, home-style fare in an atmosphere to match. But the distinction has blurred considerably, and an osteria in the center of town might be far fancier (and pricier) than a ristorante across the street. Although most restaurants in Tuscany and Umbria serve traditional local cuisine, you can find Asian and Middle Eastern alternatives in Florence, Perugia, and other cities. Menus are posted outside most restaurants (in English in tourist areas); if not, you might step inside and ask to take a look at the menu (but don't ask for a table unless you intend to stay).

Italians take their food as it is listed on the menu, seldom if ever making special requests such as "dressing on the side" or "hold the olive oil." If you have special dietary needs, however, make them known; they can usually be accommodated. Although mineral water makes its way to almost every table, you can order a carafe of tap water (*acqua di rubinetto* or *acqua semplice*) instead, but keep in mind that such water is highly chlorinated.

Wiping your bowl clean with a (small) piece of bread is considered a sign of appreciation, not bad manners. Spaghetti should be eaten with a fork only, although a little help from a spoon won't horrify locals the way cutting spaghetti into little pieces might. Order your espresso (Italians don't usually drink cappuccino after breakfast time) after dessert, not with it. Don't ask for a doggy bag.

The handiest and least expensive places for a quick snack between sights are probably bars, cafés, and pizza *al taglio* (by the slice) spots. Bars in Italy are primarily places to get a coffee and a bite to eat, rather than drinking establishments. Most have a selection of *panini* (sandwiches, often warmed up on the griddle, or *piastra*) and *tramezzini* (sandwiches served on triangles of untoasted white bread). In larger cities, bars also serve prepared salads, fruit salads, cold pasta dishes, and yogurt around lunchtime. Most bars offer beer and a variety of alcohol, as well as wines by the glass (sometimes good but more often mediocre). A café (*caffè* in Italian) is like a bar but usually with more tables. If you place your order at the counter, ask if you can sit down: some places charge extra for table service. In self-service bars and caffès, cleaning up your table before you leave is considered good manners. Note that in some places you have to pay before you place an order and then show your *scontrino* (receipt) when you move to the counter. Pizza al taglio shops are easy to negotiate. They sell pizza by weight: just point out which kind you want and how much. Very few pizza al taglio shops have seats.

MEALS AND SPECIALTIES

The Italian breakfast (*la colazione*) is typically a cappuccino and a sweet roll served at the local bar. For a larger breakfast, consider dining rooms of large hotels. For lunch Italians may eat a couple of small panini while standing at a local bar or self-serve caffè. A more substantial lunch (*il pranzo*) consists of one or two courses at a trattoria. Dinner (*la cena*) out is likely to be two or three courses at a restaurant or trattoria or pizza and beer at a pizzeria.

Menus separate dishes into *antipasti* (starters), *primi piatti* (first courses), *secondi piatti* (second courses), *contorni* (side dishes), and *dolci* (desserts). At restaurants, trattorie, and osterie, you're generally expected to order at least a two-course meal: a *primo* and a *secondo*; an antipasto followed by either primo or secondo; or, perhaps, a secondo and a *dolce*. Italian cuisine is still largely regional, so ask what the local specialties are and, by all means, have *crespelle* (savory crepes) when in Florence and Tuscany.

In an *enoteca* (wine bar) or pizzeria, it's not inappropriate to order one dish. An enoteca menu is often limited to a selection of cheese, cured meats, salads, and desserts; if there's a kitchen, you may also find soups, pasta, meat, and fish. Most pizzerias don't offer just pizza, and although the other dishes on the menu are supposed to be starters, there's no harm in skipping the pizza. Typical pizzeria fare includes *affettati misti* (selection of cured pork), simple salads, and various kinds of bruschetta and *crostino* (similar to bruschetta, sometimes topped with cheese and broiled). All pizzerias have fresh fruit, ice cream, and simple desserts. But pizza at a caffè is to be avoided—it's usually frozen and reheated in a microwave oven.

MEALTIMES

Breakfast is usually served 7–10:30, lunch 12:30–2, and dinner 7:30–9:30 or 10. In Florence, however, lunch generally is served 1–2:30 (many places don't start serving until 1 PM), dinner 8–10:30; peak times are about 1:30 for lunch and 9 for dinner. Enoteche also are open in the morning and late afternoon for a snack at the counter. Most pizzerias open at 8 PM and close around midnight or 1 AM, or later in summer and on weekends. Most bars and caffès are open 7 AM–8 or 9 PM; a few stay open until midnight or so.

Unless otherwise noted, the restaurants listed in this guide are open daily for lunch and dinner.

PAYING

Major credit cards are widely accepted in Italian eating establishments, though cash is usually the preferred, and sometimes the only, means of payment—especially in small towns and rural areas. (More restaurants take Visa and MasterCard than American Express.) When you've finished your meal and are ready to go, **ask for the check** (*il conto*); unless it's well past closing time, no waiter will put a bill on your table until you've requested it. Prices for goods and services in Italy include tax. The price of fish dishes is often given by weight (before cooking), so the price you see on the menu is for 100 grams of fish, not for the whole dish. (An average fish portion is about 350 grams.) Tuscan *bistecca fiorentina* is also often priced by weight.

Most restaurants charge a separate "cover" charge per person, usually listed on the menu as *pane e coperto* (or just *coperto*); this charge is not for the service. It should be a modest charge (€1–€2.50 per person), except at the most expensive restaurants. Some restaurants instead charge for bread, which should be brought to you (and paid for) only if you order it. A charge for service (*servizio*) is likely to be included either as part of the menu prices or the total bill; if it is, tipping is unnecessary. It is customary to leave a small tip (a euro or two) in appreciation of good service. Tips are always given in cash. Whenever in doubt, ask about the servizio and pane e coperto policies upon ordering to avoid unpleasant discussions about payment later.

When you leave a dining establishment, take your meal bill or receipt with you; if you don't have one, the Italian finance (tax) police can fine you and will fine the business owner for not providing the receipt. The measure is intended to prevent tax evasion.

RESERVATIONS AND DRESS

Reservations are always a good idea in restaurants and trattorie, especially on weekends and holidays. We mention them only when they're essential or not accepted. Book as far ahead as you can, and reconfirm as soon as you arrive in town. (Large parties should always call ahead to check the reservations policy.) Pizzerias and enoteche usually accept reservations only for large groups. We mention dress only when men are required to wear a jacket or a jacket and tie. But unless they're eating outdoors at a sea resort and perfectly tanned, Italian men never wear shorts or running shoes in a restaurant—no matter how humble—or in an enoteca. Shorts are acceptable in pizzerias and caffès. The same "rules" apply to women's casual shorts, running shoes, plastic sandals, and clogs.

WINE, BEER, AND SPIRITS

The grape has been cultivated in Italy since the time of the Etruscans, and Italians justifiably take pride in their local product. Though almost every region produces good-quality wine, Tuscany is one of the most renowned areas. Wine in Italy is considerably less expensive than almost anywhere else, so it's often affordable to order a bottle of wine at a restaurant rather than to stick with the house wine (which, nevertheless, may be quite good). Many bars have their own *aperitivo della casa* (house aperitif); Italians are imaginative with their mixed drinks, so you may want to try one.

You may purchase beer, wine, and spirits in any bar, grocery store, or enoteca, any day of the week. Italian and German beer is readily available, but it's more expensive than wine.

There's no minimum drinking age in Italy. Italian children begin drinking wine mixed with water at mealtimes when they are teens (or thereabouts). Italians are rarely seen drunk in public, and public drinking, except in a bar or eating establishment, isn't considered acceptable behavior. Bars usually close by 9 PM; hotel and restaurant bars stay open until midnight. Brew pubs and discos serve until about 2 AM.

DISABILITIES AND ACCESSIBILITY

Italy has begun to provide facilities such as ramps, telephones, and restrooms for people with disabilities, but such arrangements remain the exception, not the rule. Travelers' wheelchairs must be transported free of charge, according to Italian law, but the logistics of getting a wheelchair on and off trains and buses can make this requirement irrelevant. Seats are reserved for people with disabilities on public transportation, but few buses have lifts for wheelchairs. High, narrow steps for boarding trains create additional problems. In many monuments and museums, even in some hotels and restaurants, architectural barriers make access difficult. The Italian Government Tourist Board (ENIT; ☞ Visitor Information) can give you a list of hotels that provide access and addresses of Italian associations for travelers with disabilities.

Contact the nearest Italian consulate about bringing a Seeing Eye dog into Italy. This requires an import license, a current certificate detailing the dog's inoculations, and a letter from your veterinarian certifying the dog's health.

➤ INTERNET RESOURCES: **Access-Able Travel Service** (WEB www.access-able. com.com); **Accessible Europe** (WEB www.accessibleurope.com); **Consorzio Cooperative Integrate** (WEB www.coinsociale.it).

RESERVATIONS

When discussing accessibility with an operator or reservations agent, **ask hard questions.** Are there any stairs, inside *or* out? Are there grab bars next to the toilet *and* in the shower/tub? How wide is the doorway to the room? To the bathroom? For the most extensive facilities meeting the latest legal specifications, **opt for newer accommodations.** If you reserve through a toll-free number, consider also calling the hotel's local number to confirm the information from the central reservations office. Get confirmation in writing when you can.

SIGHTS AND ATTRACTIONS

Getting around in Italy with a wheelchair is difficult but not impossible, as many of the top sights and attractions are accessible. In Florence, the Uffizi, Palazzo Pitti, Duomo, Baptistery, and the Accademia are all accessible. Local tourist offices provide maps and lists, rated on degrees of ease and difficulty, of banks, supermarkets, sights, hotels, and restaurants.

TRANSPORTATION

Most buses in Italy cannot accommodate wheelchairs; only a few have special ramps, so check with the private bus lines when planning a trip. All of Italy's airports are accessible to people who use wheelchairs. Except for the Pisa airport and Florence, most train stations rely on stairs and few have elevators or accessible passageways between tracks; contact the ticket or information office or the uniformed trackside employees for assistance crossing the tracks. Rental cars with hand controls aren't available in Tuscany and Umbria.

➤ COMPLAINTS: **Aviation Consumer Protection Division** (☞ Air Travel) for airline-related problems. **Departmental Office of Civil Rights** (for general inquiries, ✉ U.S. Department of Transportation, S-30, 400 7th St. SW, Room 10215, Washington, DC 20590, ☎ 202/366–4648, FAX 202/366–9371, WEB www.dot.gov/ost/docr/index.htm). **Disability Rights Section** (✉ U.S. Department of Justice, Civil Rights Division, Box 66738, Washington, DC 20035-6738, ☎ 202/514–0301 or 800/514–0301, for ADA inquiries; WEB www.usdoj.gov/crt/ada/adahom1.htm).

TRAVEL AGENCIES

In the United States, the Americans with Disabilities Act requires that travel firms serve the needs of all travelers. Some agencies specialize in working with people with disabilities.

➤ TRAVELERS WITH MOBILITY PROBLEMS: **Access Adventures** (✉ 206 Chestnut Ridge Rd., Scottsville, NY 14624, ☎ 716/889–9096, dltravel@prodigy.net), run by a former physical-rehabilitation counselor. **CareVacations** (✉ No. 5, 5110–50 Ave., Leduc, Alberta T9E 6V4, Canada, ☎ 780/986–6404 or 877/478–7827, FAX 780/986–8332, WEB www.carevacations.com), for group tours and cruise vacations. **Flying Wheels Travel** (✉ 143 W. Bridge St., Box 382, Owatonna, MN 55060, ☎ 507/451–5005 or 800/535–6790, FAX 507/451–1685, WEB www.flyingwheelstravel.com).

➤ TRAVELERS WITH DEVELOPMENTAL DISABILITIES: **New Directions** (✉ 5276 Hollister Ave., Suite 207, Santa Barbara, CA 93111, ☎ 805/967–2841 or 888/967–2841, FAX 805/964–7344, WEB www.newdirectionstravel.com).

DISCOUNTS AND DEALS

Be a smart shopper and **compare all your options** before making decisions. A plane ticket bought with a promotional coupon from travel clubs, coupon books, and direct-mail offers or purchased on the Internet may not be cheaper than the least expensive fare from a discount ticket agency. And always keep in mind that what you get is just as important as what you save.

DISCOUNT RESERVATIONS

To save money, **look into discount reservations services** with Web sites and toll-free numbers, which use their buying power to get a better price on hotels, airline tickets, even car rentals. When booking a room, always **call the hotel's local toll-free number** (if one is available) rather than the central reservations number—you'll often get a better price. Always ask about special packages or corporate rates.

When shopping for the best deal on hotels and car rentals, **look for guaranteed exchange rates,** which protect you against a falling dollar. With your rate locked in, you won't pay more, even if the price goes up in the local currency.

➤ AIRLINE TICKETS: ☎ 800/AIR–4LESS (WEB www.air4less.com); Best Fares (WEB www.bestfares.com); Europe By Air (WEB www.europebyair. com); Expedia (WEB www.expedia.com); Lowest Fare (WEB www.lowestfare. com); Priceline (WEB www.priceline. com); Travelocity (WEB www. travelocity.com).

➤ HOTEL ROOMS: Hotel Reservations Network (☎ 800/964–6835, WEB www.hoteldiscount.com). International Marketing & Travel Concepts (☎ 800/790–4682, WEB www. imtc-travel.com). Steigenberger Reservation Service (☎ 800/223–5652, WEB www.srs-worldhotels.com). Travel Interlink (☎ 800/888–5898, WEB www.travelinterlink.com). Turbotrip. com (☎ 800/473–7829, WEB www. turbotrip.com).

PACKAGE DEALS

Don't confuse packages and guided tours. When you buy a package, you travel on your own, just as though you had planned the trip yourself. Fly/drive packages, which combine airfare and car rental, are often a good deal. If you **buy a rail/drive pass,** you may save on train tickets and car rentals. All Eurail- and Europass holders get a discount on Eurostar fares through the Channel Tunnel.

ECOTOURISM

Tuscany and Umbria have recycling programs in place. If you rent a house or apartment, ask the manager about the location of neighborhood bins for recycling glass, plastic, and paper.

ELECTRICITY

To use electric-powered equipment purchased in the U.S. or Canada, **bring a converter and adapter.** The electrical current in Italy is 220 volts, 50 cycles alternating current (AC); wall outlets take Continental-type plugs, with two round prongs.

If your appliances are dual-voltage, you'll need only an adapter. Don't use 110-volt outlets marked FOR SHAVERS ONLY for high-wattage appliances such as blow-dryers. Most laptops operate equally well on 110 and 220 volts and so require only an adapter.

EMBASSIES AND CONSULATES

➤ AUSTRALIA: **Australian Embassy** (✉ Via Allesandria 215, Rome, ☎ 06/852721, FAX 06/85272300, WEB www.australia-embassy.it).

➤ CANADA: **Canadian Embassy** (✉ Via G.B. de Rossi 27, Rome, ☎ 06/445981).

➤ NEW ZEALAND: **New Zealand Embassy** (✉ Via Zara 28, Rome, ☎ 06/4417171, WEB www.nzemb.org).

➤ UNITED KINGDOM: **British Consulate** (✉ Via Lungarno Corsini 2, Florence, ☎ 055/219112). **British Embassy** (✉ Via XX Settembre 80A, Rome ☎ 06/4825441).

➤ UNITED STATES: **U.S. Consulate** (✉ Via Lungarno Vespucci 38, Florence, ☎ 055/2398276). **U.S. Embassy** (✉ Via Veneto 121, Rome, ☎ 06/46741, WEB www.usembassy.it).

EMERGENCIES

No matter where you are in Italy, **dial 113 for all emergencies,** or find somebody (your concierge, a passerby) who will call for you, as not all 113 operators speak English; the Italian word to use to draw people's attention in an emergency is *aiuto* (help; pronounced "ah-YOU-toh"). *Pronto soccorso* means first aid and when said to an operator will get you an *ambulanza* (ambulance). If you just need a doctor, you should ask for *un medico*; most hotels can refer you to a local doctor. Don't forget to ask the doctor for *una ricevuta* (an invoice) to show your insurance company in order to get a reimbursement. Other useful Italian words to use in an emergency are *al fuoco* (fire; pronounced "ahl fuh-WOE-co") and *al ladro* (follow the thief; pronounced "ahl LAH-droh").

Italy has a national police force (*carabinieri*) as well as local police (*polizia*). Both are armed and have the power to arrest and investigate crimes. Always report the loss of your passport to either the carabinieri or the police, as well as to your embassy. Local traffic officers are known as *vigili* (though their official name is *polizia municipale*)—they are responsible for, among other things, giving out parking tickets and clamping cars, so before you even consider parking the Italian way, make sure you are at least able to spot their white (in summer) or black uniforms (many are women). Should you find yourself involved in a minor car accident in town, you should contact the vigili. Many police stations have English-speaking staff to deal with travelers' problems. When reporting a crime, you'll be asked to fill out and sign a report form (*una denuncia*); keep a copy for your insurance company.

A country-wide toll-free number is used to call the carabinieri in case of emergency.

➤ CONTACTS: **Carabinieri** (☎ 112). **Emergencies** (☎ 113).

ENGLISH-LANGUAGE MEDIA

BOOKS

In Florence and Perugia, English-language books are easily found.

NEWSPAPERS AND MAGAZINES

The best source for news in English is the *International Herald Tribune,* which is sold at most news agents in the major cities and major tourist towns. *USA Today* and most of the London newspapers are also available. You can find the Sunday *New York Times* in some places, but be prepared to pay an exorbitant amount for it. Various national versions of *Vogue* are obtainable, as are *Time, Newsweek, Elle, The Economist, InStyle, The New Yorker, Vanity Fair, The Tatler,* and *People,* among others. But they don't come cheap: *Vanity Fair,* for example, costs more than €8.

RADIO AND TELEVISION

Radio broadcasts are almost completely in Italian. Near Lucca and Livorno, however, you may be able to pick up the radio station of the U.S. military depot at Camp Darby.

Unless you have satellite TV (with access to CNN or SkyNews), or unless you speak Italian, Italian television is inaccessible, as everything is either spoken in Italian or dubbed into it. MTV is sometimes broadcast in English with Italian subtitles, and from 1:30 AM–5:30 AM, the La7 TV station rebroadcasts Fox News.

ETIQUETTE AND BEHAVIOR

Italy is full of churches, and many of them contain significant works of art. Because they are places of worship, care should be taken with appropriate dress. Shorts, miniskirts, tank tops, spaghetti straps, and sleeveless garments are taboo in most churches; short shorts are inappropriate anywhere. When touring churches—especially in the summer when it's hot and no sleeves are desirable—carry a sweater or shawl to wrap around your shoulders before entering the church, and always remember to take off your hat. Do not enter a church with food, and don't drink from your water bottle while inside. If a service is in progress, don't go inside. And if you have a cellular phone, turn it off before entering.

Social behavior in Tuscany and Umbria tends to be more conservative and formal than in other parts of Italy. Upon meeting and leave-taking, both friends and strangers wish each other good day or good evening (*buon giorno, buona sera*); *ciao* isn't used between strangers. "Please" is *per favore,* "thank you" is *grazie,* and "you're welcome" is *prego.* When meeting, strangers will shake hands. Italians who are friends greet each other with a kiss, usually first on the right cheek, and then on the left. Very good friends might then kiss again on the right—but that's somewhat rare.

Table manners are formal; rarely do Italians share food from their plates. Flowers, chocolates, or a bottle of wine are appropriate hostess gifts when invited to dinner at the home of an Italian.

BUSINESS ETIQUETTE

Showing up on time for business appointments is the norm and expected in Italy. There are more business lunches than business dinners, and even business lunches aren't common, as Italians view mealtimes as periods of pleasure and relaxation. Business cards are used throughout Italy, and business suits are the norm for both men and women.

GAY AND LESBIAN TRAVEL

Same-sex couples should meet with no raised eyebrows from locals when traveling in Tuscany and Umbria. Nevertheless, overt displays of homosexual affection in public are rare. Florence, Perugia, Pisa, Viareggio, and Forte dei Marmi all have gay bars, and there are gay-friendly beaches at Torre del Lago, Parco dell'Uccellina, and Viareggio.

➤ GAY- AND LESBIAN-FRIENDLY TRAVEL AGENCIES: **Different Roads Travel** (✉ 8383 Wilshire Blvd., Suite 902, Beverly Hills, CA 90211, ☎ 323/651–5557 or 800/429–8747, FAX 323/651–3678, lgernert@tzell.com). **Kennedy Travel** (✉ 314 Jericho Turnpike, Floral Park, NY 11001, ☎ 516/352–4888 or 800/237–7433, FAX 516/354–8849, WEB www.kennedytravel.com). **Now,Voyager** (✉ 4406 18th St., San Francisco, CA 94114, ☎ 415/626–1169 or 800/255–6951, FAX 415/626–8626, WEB www.nowvoyager.com). **Skylink**

Travel and Tour (✉ 1006 Mendocino Ave., Santa Rosa, CA 95401, ☎ 707/546–9888 or 800/225–5759, FAX 707/546–9891, WEB www.skylinktravel.com), serving lesbian travelers.

➤ INFORMATION IN ITALY: **Azione Gay e Lesbica** (✉ c/o Andrea del Sarto, Via Manara 12, Florence, ☎ 055/671298, WEB www.azionegayelesbica.it). **Circolo di Cultura Omosessuale Mario Mieli** (✉ Via Corinto 5, Rome, ☎ 06/5960–4622, WEB www.mariomieli.org).

GUIDEBOOKS

Plan well and you won't be sorry. Guidebooks are excellent tools—and you can take them with you. *Exploring Tuscany* is full of color photos and thorough on culture and history; *Escape to Tuscany* highlights unique experiences; and pocket-size *Citypack Florence* includes supersize city maps. All are available at on-line retailers and bookstores everywhere.

HEALTH

The Centers for Disease Control and Prevention (CDC) in Atlanta caution that most of southern Europe is in the "intermediate" range for risk of contacting traveler's diarrhea. Part of this risk may be attributed to an increased consumption of olive oil and wine, which can have a laxative effect on stomachs used to a different diet. The CDC also advises all international travelers to swim only in chlorinated swimming pools, unless they are absolutely certain the local beaches and freshwater lakes are not contaminated.

As of this writing, there has been one reported case of mad-cow disease in a human in Italy. The Italian desire for beef hasn't abated, and *vitello* (veal), *vitellone* (young beef), and *manzo* (beef) are considered safe to eat by both the Italian government and the European Union (these are cuts that don't come in touch with spinal marrow). Nevertheless, many restaurants and butchers have been widening their repertoire of meat dishes.

Medical care in Tuscany and Umbria is excellent. English-speaking medical assistance is available in Florence, Pisa, Perugia, Siena, and Lucca.

OVER-THE-COUNTER REMEDIES

It's always best to travel with your own tried and true medicines. The regulations regarding what medicines require a prescription aren't likely to be the same in Italy as in your home country—all the more reason to bring what you need with you. You can buy aspirin (*aspirina*), ibuprofen (Cibalgina, Moment), antihistamines (*antistaminico*), and cough medicines (*sciroppo per la tosse*) at any pharmacy (*farmacia*). Tylenol and acetaminophen aren't available; a nonaspirin substitute called *paracetamolo,* also sold as Tachipirina or Efferalgan, is. In general, medications that require prescriptions outside of Italy require them in Italy, too.

➤ HEALTH WARNINGS: **National Centers for Disease Control and Prevention** (CDC; National Center for Infectious Diseases, Division of Quarantine, Traveler's Health Section, ✉ 1600 Clifton Rd. NE, M/S E-03, Atlanta, GA 30333, ☎ 888/232–3228 general information; 877/394–8747 travelers' health line, FAX 888/232–3299, WEB www.cdc.gov).

HOLIDAYS

National holidays include New Year's Day (January 1); Epiphany (January 6); Easter Sunday and Monday (April 20–21 in 2003; April 11–12 in 2004); Liberation Day (April 25); Labor Day or May Day (May 1); Assumption of Mary, also known as Ferragosto (August 15); All Saints' Day (November 1); Immaculate Conception (December 8); Christmas Day and Boxing Day (December 25 and 26).

The feast days of patron saints are observed locally. Many businesses and shops may be closed in Florence on June 24 (St. John the Baptist). (Also ☞ Festivals and Seasonal Events.)

INSURANCE

The most useful travel-insurance plan is a comprehensive policy that includes coverage for trip cancellation and interruption, default, trip delay, and medical expenses (with a waiver for preexisting conditions).

Without insurance you will lose all or most of your money if you cancel your trip, regardless of the reason.

Default insurance covers you if your tour operator, airline, or cruise line goes out of business. Trip-delay covers expenses that arise because of bad weather or mechanical delays. Study the fine print when comparing policies.

If you're traveling internationally, a key component of travel insurance is coverage for medical bills incurred if you get sick on the road. Such expenses are not generally covered by Medicare or private policies. U.K. residents can buy a travel-insurance policy valid for most vacations taken during the year in which it's purchased (but check preexisting-condition coverage).

Always **buy travel policies directly from the insurance company**; if you buy them from a cruise line, airline, or tour operator that goes out of business you probably will not be covered for the agency or operator's default, a major risk. Before making any purchase, **review your existing health and home-owner's policies** to find what they cover away from home.

➤ TRAVEL INSURERS: In the U.S.: **Access America** (✉ 6600 W. Broad St., Richmond, VA 23230, ☎ 800/284–8300, FAX 804/673–1491 or 800/346–9265, WEB www.etravelprotection.com). **Travel Guard International** (✉ 1145 Clark St., Stevens Point, WI 54481, ☎ 800/826–1300, 715/345–0505 international callers, FAX 800/955–8785, WEB www.travelguard.com).

➤ INSURANCE INFORMATION: In the U.K.: **Association of British Insurers** (✉ 51 Gresham St., London EC2V 7HQ, ☎ 020/7600–3333, FAX 020/7696–8999, WEB www.abi.org.uk). In Canada: **RBC Travel Insurance** (✉ 6880 Financial Dr., Mississauga, Ontario L5N 7Y5, ☎ 905/791–8700 or 800/668–4342, FAX 905/813–4704, WEB www.rbcinsurance.com). In Australia: **Insurance Council of Australia** (✉ Level 3, 56 Pitt St., Sydney, NSW 2000, ☎ 02/9253–5100, FAX 02/9253–5111, WEB www.ica.com.au). In New Zealand: **Insurance Council of New Zealand** (✉ Level 7, 111–115 Customhouse Quay, Box 474, Wellington, ☎ 04/472–5230, FAX 04/473–3011, WEB www.icnz.org.nz).

LANGUAGE

In the main tourist cities, such as
Florence, most hotels have English
speakers at their reception desks, and
you can always find someone who
speaks at least a little English otherwise. Remember that the Italian
language is pronounced exactly as it
is written. You may run into a language barrier in the countryside, but a
phrase book and the use of pan-
tomime and expressive gestures will
go a long way. Try to **master a few
phrases for daily use** and familiarize
yourself with the terms you'll need for
deciphering signs and museum labels.

LANGUAGES FOR TRAVELERS

A phrase book and language-tape set
can help get you started. *Fodor's
Italian for Travelers* (available at
bookstores everywhere) is excellent.

LODGING

The lodgings we list are the cream of
the crop in each price category. We
always list the facilities that are
available—but we don't specify
whether they cost extra: when pricing
accommodations, always ask what's
included and what costs extra. Properties are assigned price categories
based on the range from their least-
expensive standard double room at
high season (excluding holidays) to
the most expensive. Properties indicated by an ✕⌷ are lodging establishments whose restaurants warrant
a special trip.

Assume that hotels operate on the
European Plan (EP, with no meals)
unless we specify that they use the
Continental Plan (CP, with a Continental breakfast), **Breakfast Plan** (BP,
with a full breakfast), **Modified
American Plan** (MAP, with breakfast
and dinner), or the **Full American
Plan** (FAP, with all meals).

APARTMENT AND VILLA RENTALS

If you want a home base that's roomy
enough for a family and comes with
cooking facilities, **consider a furnished
rental.** These can save you money,
especially if you're traveling with a
group. Home-exchange directories
sometimes list rentals as well as
exchanges.

➤ INTERNATIONAL AGENTS: **At Home
Abroad** (✉ 405 E. 56th St., Suite 6H,
New York, NY 10022, ☎ 212/421–
9165, FAX 212/752–1591, WEB www.
athomeabroadinc.com). **Drawbridge
to Europe** (✉ 98 Granite St., Ashland,
OR 97520, ☎ 541/482–7778 or 888/
268–1148, FAX 541/482–7779, WEB
www.drawbridgetoeurope.com).
Hideaways International (✉ 767
Islington St., Portsmouth, NH 03801,
☎ 603/430–4433 or 800/843–4433,
FAX 603/430–4444, WEB www.
hideaways.com; membership $129).
Hometours International (✉ Box
11503, Knoxville, TN 37939, ☎ 865/
690–8484 or 800/367–4668, WEB
http://thor.he.net/~hometour/). **Inter-
home** (✉ 1990 N.E. 163rd St., Suite
110, N. Miami Beach, FL 33162,
☎ 305/940–2299 or 800/882–6864,
FAX 305/940–2911, WEB www.
interhome.com). **Vacation Home
Rentals Worldwide** (✉ 235 Kensing-
ton Ave., Norwood, NJ 07648,
☎ 201/767–9393 or 800/633–3284,
FAX 201/767–5510, WEB www.vhrww.
com). **Villanet** (✉ 11556 1st Ave.
NW, Seattle, WA 98177, ☎ 206/417–
3444 or 800/964–1891, FAX 206/417–
1832, WEB www.rentavilla.com).
Villas and Apartments Abroad
(✉ 1270 Ave. of the Americas, 15th
floor, New York, NY 10020, ☎ 212/
897–5045 or 800/433–3020, FAX 212/
897–5039, WEB www.ideal-villas.com).
Villas International (✉ 4340 Redwood
Hwy., Suite D309, San Rafael, CA
94903, ☎ 415/499–9490 or 800/221–
2260, FAX 415/499–9491, WEB www.
villasintl.com).

➤ ITALY AGENCIES: **Cuendet USA**
(✉ 165 Chestnut St., Allendale, NJ
07041, ☎ 201/327–2333). **Eurovillas**
(✉ 3212 Jefferson St., Suite 298,
Napa, CA 94558, ☎ 800/767–0275,
☎ FAX 707/648–2066). **Rentvillas.com**
(✉ 1742 Calle Corva, Camarillo, CA
93010, ☎ 805/987–5278 or 800/
726–6702, FAX 805/482–7976, WEB
www.rentvillas.com). **Vacanze in
Italia** (✉ 22 Railroad St., Great
Barrington, MA 01230, ☎ 413/528–
6610 or 800/533–5405).

➤ IN THE U.K.: **CV Travel** (✉ 43
Cadogan St., London SW3 2PR,
England, ☎ 020/7581–0851). **Magic
of Italy** (✉ 227 Shepherds Bush Rd.,
London W6 7AS, England, ☎ 020/
8748–7575).

CAMPING

Camping is particularly prevalent in beach towns and in the mountains. Campgrounds are generally crowded in summer (usually with Italians and Germans) and vary in amenities depending on the place: some have showers, toilets, sinks, bars, restaurants, and shade trees. These campgrounds, which tend to draw families that rent the same space year after year, can be noisy and full of children. Camping in the national parks and on the beaches is more rustic and private, but also more restrictive. (Sleeping on the beach is illegal in Italy, which is not to say that people don't do it.) You may be required to break camp every morning and clear your space.

FARM HOLIDAYS AND AGRITOURISM

Rural accommodations in the *agriturismo* (agritourism) category are increasingly popular with both Italians and visitors to Italy; you stay on a working farm or vineyard. Accommodations vary in size and range from luxury apartments, farmhouses, and villas to very basic facilities. Agriturist has compiled *Agriturism,* which is available only in Italian but includes more than 1,600 farms in Italy; pictures and the use of international symbols to describe facilities make the guide a good tool. Local APT tourist offices also have information.

➤ AGENCIES: **Agriturist** (✉ Corso Vittorio 101, 00186 Rome, ☎ 06/685–2342). **Essentially Tuscany** (✉ 30 York St., Nantucket, MA 02554, ☎ FAX 508/228–2514). **Italy Farm Holidays** (✉ 547 Martling Ave., Tarrytown, NY 10591, ☎ 914/631–7880, FAX 914/631–8831). **Terra Nostra** (✉ Via XXIV Maggio 43, 00187 Rome, ☎ 06/46821). **Turismo Verde** (✉ Via Flaminia 56, 00196 Rome, ☎ 06/361–1051).

HOME EXCHANGES

If you would like to exchange your home for someone else's, **join a home-exchange organization,** which will send you its updated listings of available exchanges for a year and will include your own listing in at least one of them. It's up to you to make specific arrangements.

➤ EXCHANGE CLUBS: **HomeLink International** (✉ Box 47747, Tampa, FL 33647, ☎ 813/975–9825 or 800/638–3841, FAX 813/910–8144, WEB www.homelink.org; $110 per year). **Intervac U.S.** (✉ 30 Corte San Fernando, Tiburon, CA 94920, ☎ 800/756–4663, FAX 415/435–7440, WEB www.intervacus.com; $90 yearly fee for a listing, on-line access, and a catalog; $50 without catalog).

HOSTELS

No matter what your age, you can **save on lodging costs by staying at hostels.** In some 4,500 locations in more than 70 countries around the world, Hostelling International (HI), the umbrella group for a number of national youth-hostel associations, offers single-sex, dorm-style beds and, at many hostels, rooms for couples and family accommodations. Membership in any HI national hostel association, open to travelers of all ages, allows you to stay in HI-affiliated hostels at member rates; one-year membership is about $25 for adults (C$35 for a two-year minimum membership in Canada, £13 in the U.K., A$52 in Australia, and NZ$40 in New Zealand); hostels run about $10–$25 per night. Members have priority if the hostel is full; they're also eligible for discounts around the world, even on rail and bus travel in some countries. For information about hostels in Italy, also check out www.ostellionline.org.

➤ ORGANIZATIONS: **Hostelling International—American Youth Hostels** (✉ 733 15th St. NW, Suite 840, Washington, DC 20005, ☎ 202/783–6161, FAX 202/783–6171, WEB www.hiayh.org). **Hostelling International—Canada** (✉ 400–205 Catherine St., Ottawa, Ontario K2P 1C3, ☎ 613/237–7884; 800/663–5777 in Canada, FAX 613/237–7868, WEB www.hihostels.ca). **Youth Hostel Association of England and Wales** (✉ Trevelyan House, 8 St. Stephen's Hill, St. Albans, Hertfordshire AL1 2DY, U.K., ☎ 0870/8708808, FAX 01727/844126, WEB www.yha.org.uk). **Youth Hostel Association Australia** (✉ 10 Mallett St., Camperdown, NSW 2050, ☎ 02/9565–1699, FAX 02/9565–1325, WEB www.yha.com.au). **Youth Hostels Association of New Zealand** (✉ Level

3, 193 Cashel St., Box 436, Christchurch, ☎ 03/379–9970, FAX 03/365–4476, WEB www.yha.org.nz).

HOTELS

Italian hotels are awarded stars (one to five) based on their facilities and services. Keep in mind, however, that these are general indications and that a charming three-star might make for a better stay than a more expensive four-star. In the major cities, room rates are on a par with other European capitals: deluxe and four-star rates can be downright extravagant. In those categories, **ask for one of the better rooms,** because the less-desirable rooms—and there usually are some—don't give you what you're paying for. Except in deluxe and some four-star hotels, rooms may be very small by U.S. standards, and bathrooms usually have showers rather than bathtubs. Hotels with three or more stars always have bathrooms in all rooms.

In all hotels, a rate card inside the door of your room or inside the closet door tells you exactly what you pay for that particular room (rates in the same hotel may vary according to the location and type of room). On this card, breakfast and any other options must be listed separately. Any discrepancy between the basic room rate and that charged on your bill is cause for complaint to the manager and to the police.

Although, by law, breakfast is supposed to be optional, most hotels quote room rates including breakfast. When you book a room, specifically **ask whether the rate includes breakfast** (*colazione*). You are under no obligation to take breakfast at your hotel, but in practice most hotels expect you to do so. The trick is to "offer" guests "complimentary" breakfast and have its cost built into the rate. However, it's encouraging to note that many of the hotels we recommend provide generous buffet breakfasts instead of simple, even skimpy "Continental breakfasts." Remember, if the latter is the case, you can eat for less at the nearest coffee bar.

Hotels in the $$ and $ categories may charge extra for optional air-conditioning. In older hotels the quality of the rooms may be very uneven; if you don't like the room you're given, request another. This applies to noise, too. Front rooms may be larger or have a view, but they also may have a lot of street noise. If you're a light sleeper, request a quiet room when making reservations. Rooms in lodgings listed in this guide have a shower and/or bath, unless noted otherwise. (All hotels listed have private bath unless otherwise noted.) Remember to specify whether you care to have a bath or shower—not all rooms have both. It's always a good idea to have your reservation, dates, and rate confirmed by fax or e-mail.

High season in Italy, when rooms are at a premium, generally runs from Easter through the beginning of November, and then for two weeks at Christmas time. During low season and whenever a hotel isn't full, it's often possible to negotiate a discounted rate. Major cities have no official off-season as far as hotel rates go, but some hotels do offer substantial discounts during the slower parts of the year and on weekends. Always **inquire about special rates.** Major cities have hotel-reservation service booths in train stations.

MAIL AND SHIPPING

The Italian mail system is notoriously slow. Allow up to 15 days for mail to and from the United States, Canada, Australia, and New Zealand. It takes about a week to and from the United Kingdom and within Italy. Posta Prioritaria (for Italy only) and Postacelere (for Italy and abroad) are special-delivery services from the post office that guarantee delivery within 24 hours in Italy and three to five days abroad.

OVERNIGHT SERVICES

Overnight mail is generally available in all major cities and at resort hotels. Pickups are daily, excluding weekends. Service is reliable. A Federal Express letter to the United States costs about €15, to the United Kingdom, €17, and to Australia and New Zealand €19. Overnight delivery usually means 24–36 hours.

In Florence and Perugia, many Internet cafés offer overnight mail services at reasonable rates using major overnight carriers; if your hotel can't help you out, try an Internet café.

➤ MAJOR SERVICES: **DHL** (☎ 199–199–345). **Federal Express** (☎ 800/123800). **SDA** (☎ 800/016027).

POSTAL RATES

Airmail letters and postcards (lightweight stationery) sent *ordinaria* to the United States and Canada cost 52 European cents for the first 20 grams, 77 European cents for 21 to 100 grams, and €1.55 for 101 to 349 grams. Always stick the blue airmail tag on your mail, or write "Airmail" in big, clear characters to the side of the address. Expect postcards and letters sent *ordinaria* to take at least two weeks to arrive, often longer. Postcards and letters sent *ordinaria* (for the first 20 grams) to the United Kingdom, as well as to any other EU country, including Italy, cost 41 European cents. Posta Prioritaria (stationery and small packages up to 2 kilograms) and the more expensive Postacelere (up to 20 kilograms) are special delivery services from the post office that guarantee delivery within 24 hours in Italy and three to five days abroad. Lightweight stationery sent as Posta Prioritaria to the United States and Canada costs 77 European cents (for the first 20 grams, double that for parcels up to 100 grams); to the United Kingdom, Italy, and all other EU countries it costs 62 European cents. Regular stamps aren't valid for this service, so be sure to buy the special golden Posta Prioritaria stamps. Postacelere rates to the United States and Canada are between €23.76 (€15.49 to the United Kingdom and Europe) for parcels up to 500 grams (a little over a pound) and €184.90 (€76.44 to the United Kingdom and Europe) for packages weighing 20 kilos.

You can buy stamps at tobacconists and post offices.

➤ POSTAL INFORMATION: **Informazioni Poste Italiane** (☎ 160, 31-European-cent information call in Italian about rates and local post offices' opening hours; 800/009966, toll-free Postacelere information, 𝖂𝖤𝖡 www.poste.it).

RECEIVING MAIL

Correspondence can be addressed to you in care of the Italian post office. Letters should be addressed to your name, "c/o Ufficio Postale Centrale," followed by "Fermo Posta" on the next line, and the name of the city (preceded by its postal code) on the next. You can **collect it at the central post office** by showing your passport or photo-bearing I.D. and paying a small fee. American Express also has a general-delivery service. There's no charge for cardholders, holders of American Express Traveler's checks, or anyone who booked a vacation with American Express.

SHIPPING PARCELS

You can ship parcels via air or surface. Air takes about two weeks, and surface anywhere up to three months. When purchasing antiques, ceramics, or other objects, ask whether the vendor will do the shipping for you; in most cases, this is a possibility.

MONEY MATTERS

As in most countries, prices vary from region to region and are a bit lower in the countryside than in cities. Umbria and the Marches offer good value for the money. Admission to the Galleria degli Uffizi is €9.30. A movie ticket is €7. A daily English-language newspaper is €1.80. A taxi ride (1½ km [1 mi]) costs €7.50.

Prices throughout this guide are given for adults, in euros. Substantially reduced fees are sometimes available for children, students, and senior citizens from the EU; citizens of non-EU countries rarely get discounts. For information on taxes, *see* Taxes.

ATMS

Fairly common in banks in large and small towns, as well as in airports and train stations, ATMs are the easiest way to get euros in Italy. You won't find an ATM (*bancomat* in Italian) in hotels or grocery stores, however. Before you leave home, **memorize your PIN in numbers,** not letters, because ATM keypads in Italy don't show letters. Check with your bank to confirm that you have an international PIN (*codice segreto*), to find out your maximum daily withdrawal allowance, and to learn what the bank fee is for withdrawing money.

CREDIT CARDS

In Italy, Visa and MasterCard are preferred to American Express, but in tourist areas American Express is usually accepted. While increasingly common, credit cards aren't accepted at all establishments, and some places require a minimum expenditure. If you want to pay with a card in a small hotel, store, or restaurant, it's a good idea to make your intentions known early on.

Throughout this guide, the following abbreviations are used: **AE**, American Express; **DC**, Diners Club; **MC**, MasterCard; and **V**, Visa.

Discover is rarely accepted in Italy.

➤ REPORTING LOST CARDS: **American Express** (☎ 336/668–5110 international collect, 06/72282 in Italy). **Diners Club** (☎ 702/797–5532 collect, 800/864064 in Italy). **MasterCard** (☎ 800/870866 in Italy). **Visa** (☎ 800/821001 in Italy).

CURRENCY

The euro is the main unit of currency in Italy, as well as in 11 other European countries. Under the euro system, there are eight coins: 1, 2, 5, 10, 20, and 50 *centesimi* (cents, at 100 centesimi to the euro), and 1 and 2 euros. There are seven notes: 5, 10, 20, 50, 100, 200, and 500 euros.

CURRENCY EXCHANGE

For the most favorable rates, **change money through banks.** Although ATM transaction fees may be higher abroad than at home, ATM rates are excellent because they are based on wholesale rates offered only by major banks. You won't do as well at exchange booths in airports or rail and bus stations, in hotels, in restaurants, or in stores. To avoid lines at airport exchange booths, **get a bit of local currency before you leave home.**

At this writing, the exchange rate is about €1 to US$1, 65 European cents to C$1, 57 European cents to A$1, 49 European cents to NZ$1, and €1.58 to the pound sterling.

➤ EXCHANGE SERVICES: **International Currency Express** (☎ 888/278–6628 orders, WEB www.foreignmoney.com). **Thomas Cook Currency Services** (☎ 800/287–7362 orders and retail locations, WEB www.us.thomascook. com).

TRAVELER'S CHECKS

Do you need traveler's checks? It depends on where you're headed. If you're going to rural areas and small towns, go with cash; traveler's checks are best used in cities. Lost or stolen checks can usually be replaced within 24 hours. To ensure a speedy refund, buy your own traveler's checks—don't let someone else pay for them: irregularities like this can cause delays. The person who bought the checks should make the call to request a refund.

PACKING

The weather is considerably milder, in the winter at least, in Italy than in the northern and central United States or Great Britain. In summer, stick with very light clothing, as things can get steamy in the height of summer; a sweater may be necessary for cool evenings, especially in the mountains and on islands even during the hot months. Sunglasses, a hat, and sunblock are essential. Brief summer afternoon thunderstorms are common in inland cities, so an umbrella will come in handy. In winter, bring a coat, gloves, hats, scarves, and boots. Even in mild areas, central heating may not be up to your standards, and interiors can be cold and damp; take wools or flannel rather than sheer fabrics. Bring sturdy shoes for winter and comfortable walking shoes in any season.

Italians dress exceptionally well. They do not usually wear shorts. Men aren't required to wear ties or jackets anywhere, except in some of the grander hotel dining rooms and top-level restaurants, but are expected to look reasonably sharp—and they do. Formal wear is the exception rather than the rule at the opera nowadays, though people in expensive seats usually do get dressed up.

A certain modesty of dress (no bare shoulders or knees) is expected in churches, and strictly enforced in many.

For sightseeing, **pack a pair of binoculars**; they will help you get a good look at painted ceilings and domes. If you stay in budget hotels, **take your own soap.** Many such hotels do not provide it or give guests only one tiny bar per room.

In your carry-on luggage, **pack an extra pair of eyeglasses or contact lenses and enough of any medication** you take to last the entire trip. You may also ask your doctor to write a spare prescription using the drug's generic name, since brand names may vary from country to country. In luggage to be checked, **never pack prescription drugs or valuables.** And don't forget to carry with you the addresses of offices that handle refunds of lost traveler's checks. Check *Fodor's How to Pack* (available in bookstores everywhere) for more tips.

To avoid customs and security delays, carry medications in their original packaging. Don't pack any sharp objects in your carry-on luggage, including knives of any size or material, scissors, manicure tools, and corkscrews, or anything else that might arouse suspicion.

CHECKING LUGGAGE

Airlines usually allow you to carry on one small to medium-size bag and one personal article, such as a purse or a laptop computer. Make sure that everything you carry aboard will fit under your seat or in the overhead bin. Get to the gate early, so you can board as soon as possible, before the overhead bins fill up.

If you are flying internationally, note that baggage allowances may be determined not by piece but by weight—generally 88 pounds (40 kilograms) in first class, 66 pounds (30 kilograms) in business class, and 44 pounds (20 kilograms) in economy.

Airline liability for baggage is limited to $2,500 per person on flights within the United States. On international flights it amounts to $9.07 per pound or $20 per kilogram for checked baggage (roughly $640 per 70-pound bag) and $400 per passenger for unchecked baggage. You can buy additional coverage at check-in for about $10 per $1,000 of coverage,

but it excludes a rather extensive list of items, shown on your airline ticket.

Before departure, **itemize your bags' contents** and their worth, and label the bags with your name, address, and phone number. (If you use your home address, cover it so potential thieves can't see it readily.) Inside each bag, **pack a copy of your itinerary.** At check-in, **make sure that each bag is correctly tagged** with the destination airport's three-letter code. If your bags arrive damaged or fail to arrive at all, file a written report with the airline before leaving the airport.

PASSPORTS AND VISAS

When traveling internationally, **carry your passport** even if you don't need one (it's always the best form of I.D.) and **make two photocopies of the data page** (one for someone at home and another for you, carried separately from your passport). If you lose your passport, promptly call the nearest embassy or consulate and the local police.

U.S. passport applications for children under age 14 require consent from both parents or legal guardians; both parents must appear together to sign the application. If only one parent appears, he or she must submit a written statement from the other parent authorizing passport issuance for the child. A parent with sole authority must present evidence of it when applying; acceptable documentation includes the child's certified birth certificate listing only the applying parent, a court order specifically permitting this parent's travel with the child, or a death certificate for the non-applying parent. Application forms and instructions are available on the Web site of the U.S. State Department's Bureau of Consular Affairs (www.travel.state.gov).

ENTERING ITALY

➤ AUSTRALIAN CITIZENS: You need only a valid passport to enter Italy for stays of up to 90 days.

➤ CANADIAN CITIZENS: You need only a valid passport to enter Italy for stays of up to 90 days.

➤ NEW ZEALAND CITIZENS: You need only a valid passport to enter Italy for stays of up to 90 days.

➤ U.S. CITIZENS: You need only a valid passport to enter Italy for stays of up to 90 days. Children are required to have a passport to enter and travel around Italy.

➤ U.K. CITIZENS: You need only a valid passport to enter Italy for an unlimited stay.

PASSPORT OFFICES

The best time to apply for a passport or to renew is in fall and winter. Before any trip, check your passport's expiration date, and, if necessary, renew it as soon as possible.

➤ AUSTRALIAN CITIZENS: **Australian State Passport Office** (☎ 131–232, WEB www.dfat.gov.au/passports).

➤ CANADIAN CITIZENS: **Passport Office** (☎ 819/994–3500; 800/567–6868 in Canada, WEB www.dfait-maeci.gc. ca/passport).

➤ NEW ZEALAND CITIZENS: **New Zealand Passport Office** (☎ 04/494–0700 or 04/474–8100 application procedures, WEB www.passports. govt.nz).

➤ U.K. CITIZENS: **London Passport Office** (☎ 0870/521–0410, WEB www. ukpa.gov.uk) for application procedures and emergency passports.

➤ U.S. CITIZENS: **National Passport Information Center** (☎ 900/225–5674; calls are 35¢ per minute for automated service, $1.05 per minute for operator service; WEB www.travel. state.gov).

REST ROOMS

Standards of cleanliness and comfort vary greatly in Tuscany and Umbria. The type of toilet might be small and low with no seat or even a porcelain hole in the floor with places for your feet. In cities, restaurants, hotel common areas, department stores, and McDonald's eateries tend to have the cleanest rest rooms. Pubs and bars rank among the worst. Gas stations also have facilities; again, the cleanliness varies greatly. Carry tissues with you wherever you go, in case there's no paper.

In Florence, all public eating and drinking establishments are required to provide toilet facilities to both customers and the general public alike. However, it is appropriate to pay for a little something—a few cents for a mineral water or coffee—before you use the facilities. Other private businesses can refuse to make their toilets available to the passing public.

Pay and attendant-supervised rest rooms are available in large towns and cities. (You can get a map of the pay toilets in Florence at city tourist-information offices.) Expect to pay or tip 50 European cents. There are bathrooms in most museums and all airports and train stations; in major train stations you'll also find well-kept pay toilets for 25 to 50 European cents. Churches, post offices, and public beaches don't have rest rooms.

SAFETY

The best way to protect yourself against purse snatchers and pickpockets is to wear a concealed money belt or a pouch on a string around your neck. Don't wear an exterior money belt or a waist pack, both of which peg you as a tourist. If you carry a bag or camera, be absolutely sure it has straps; you should sling it across your body bandolier-style and adjust the height to hip level or higher. Always be astutely aware of pickpockets, especially when in city buses, when making your way through train corridors, and in busy piazzas.

If you carry a purse or wallet, store only enough money there to cover casual spending. Distribute the rest of your cash and any valuables (including credit cards and your passport) between a deep front pocket, an inside jacket or vest pocket, and a hidden money pouch. Do not reach for the money pouch while in public.

LOCAL SCAMS

In Florence you may encounter "gypsies" who are adept pickpockets. One tactic the children use is to approach a tourist and proffer a piece of cardboard with writing on it. While you attempt to read the message *on* it, the children's hands are busy *under* it, trying to make off with purses or valuables. If you see such a group, avoid them—they are quick and know more tricks than you do. If traveling via rental car, it's not a bad idea when making stops along the highway to have someone remain near the car, as such cars are easily recognizable to professional thieves. Purse-snatching is not uncommon, and thieves operate on *motorini* (mopeds) as well as on foot.

WOMEN IN TUSCANY AND UMBRIA

Women traveling alone in Tuscany and Umbria encounter few special problems. Younger women have to put up with male attention, but it's rarely dangerous. Ignoring whistling and questions is a good way to get rid of unwanted attention; a firm *no, via, via* ("no, go away") usually works, too.

SENIOR-CITIZEN TRAVEL

To qualify for any age-related discounts, **mention your senior-citizen status up front** when booking hotel reservations (not when checking out) and, if you're an EU citizen over age 65, before buying museum tickets. Movie theaters also may offer discounts; look for signs at ticket counters that mention *65 anni* (65 years). When renting a car, ask about promotional car-rental discounts, which can be cheaper than senior-citizen rates.

➤ EDUCATIONAL PROGRAMS: **Elderhostel** (⊠ 11 Ave. de Lafayette, Boston, MA 02111, ☎ 877/426–8056, FAX 877/426–2166, WEB www.elderhostel. org). **Interhostel** (⊠ University of New Hampshire, 6 Garrison Ave., Durham, NH 03824, ☎ 603/862–1147 or 800/733–9753, FAX 603/862–1113, WEB www.learn.unh.edu).

SHOPPING

"Made in Italy" has become synonymous with style, quality, and craftsmanship. The best buys are leather goods of all kinds—from gloves to bags to jackets—silk goods, knitwear, gold jewelry, ceramics, and local handicrafts. The most important thing to keep in mind when shopping in Tuscany and Umbria is that every region has its specialties: Florence is known for leather, gold jewelry, paper goods, and antiques; Assisi produces wonderful embroidery; and Deruta and Gubbio have been ceramics centers for centuries.

The notice PREZZI FISSI (fixed prices) means just that—it's a waste of time to bargain unless you're buying a

sizable quantity of goods or a particularly costly object. Always try to bargain, however, at outdoor markets (except food markets) and with street vendors. For information on VAT refunds, *see* Taxes.

WATCH OUT

If you have purchased any work of art (painting, sculpture, miniature, cameo, etc.), make sure the piece is certified as being less than 50 years old. Any art deemed older than that must receive clearance from the Italian government to leave the country.

If you have purchased an antique, the dealer will provide you with a certificate attesting to the integrity of the piece and the price paid. Some dealers will ship the object for you; others leave it to you to arrange shipping.

SIGHTSEEING GUIDES

Every province in Italy has licensed tour guides who are allowed by Italian law to take groups and individuals to selected sites. Some of them are eminently qualified in relevant fields such as history and art history; others have simply managed to pass the test. Inquire at any tourist office for a licensed, English-speaking guide. When you speak to the guide, ask about his or her qualifications and specialties. Also check to make sure that the guide's English is understandable. The rates are fixed; find out what they are before hiring the guide. It's illegal for the guide to charge you more than the fixed fee. Tipping is appreciated but not obligatory.

Some places, such as the Duomo in Florence, offer free guided tours in English by a volunteer staff. Such guides may be longer on enthusiasm than knowledge.

STUDENTS IN ITALY

In major art cities, such as Florence, a popular student destination, lodging and sources of information geared to students' needs are plentiful. Students from EU member nations, if they possess valid I.D. cards, sometimes receive discounts at museums, galleries, exhibitions, and entertainment venues, and on some transportation. Students who aren't EU citizens generally pay the usual entrance fees.

TRAVEL AGENCIES

To save money, **look into deals available through student-oriented travel agencies.** To qualify you'll need a student ID card. Members of international student groups are also eligible.

➤ I.D.s AND SERVICES: **STA Travel** (☎ 212/627–3111 or 800/781–4040, FAX 212/627–3387, WEB www.sta.com). **Travel Cuts** (✉ 187 College St., Toronto, Ontario M5T 1P7, Canada, ☎ 416/979–2406 or 888/838–2887, FAX 416/979–8167, WEB www. travelcuts.com).

TAXES

HOTELS

The service charge and the 9% IVA, or VAT tax, are included in the rate except in five-star deluxe hotels, where the IVA (12% on luxury hotels) may be a separate item added to the bill upon departure.

RESTAURANTS

A service charge of approximately 15% is added to all restaurant bills; in some cases the menu may state that the service charge is already included in the menu prices.

VALUE-ADDED TAX

Value-added tax (IVA or VAT) is 20% on clothing, wine, and luxury goods. On consumer goods, it is already included in the amount shown on the price tag, whereas on services, it may not be.

Under Italy's IVA-refund system, a non-EU resident is entitled to a VAT refund. Shop with your passport and ask the store for an invoice itemizing the article(s), price(s), and the amount of tax.

When making a purchase of €151 or more, **ask for a V.A.T. refund form** and find out whether the merchant gives refunds—not all stores do, nor are they required to. Have the form stamped like any customs form by customs officials when you leave the country or, if you're visiting several European Union countries, when you leave the EU. Be ready to show customs officials what you've bought (pack purchases together, in your carry-on luggage); budget extra time for this. After you're through passport control, take the form to a refund-service counter for an on-the-spot refund, or mail it back to the store or a refund service after you arrive home.

A refund service can save you some hassle, for a fee. Global Refund is a Europe-wide service with 130,000 affiliated stores and more than 700 refund counters—located at every major airport and border crossing. Its refund form is called a Shopping Cheque. The service issues refunds in the form of cash, check, or credit-card adjustment, minus a processing fee. If you don't have time to wait at the refund counter, you can mail in the form instead.

➤ V.A.T. REFUNDS: **Global Refund** (✉ 99 Main St., Suite 307, Nyack, NY 10960, ☎ 800/566–9828, FAX 845/ 348–1549, WEB www.globalrefund. com).

TELEPHONES

Telephone service in Tuscany and Umbria is organized and efficient. Cell phones, however, are in wide use by Italians, resulting in a decrease in the number of public pay phones. Travelers who plan to stay in Italy and the surrounding EU countries should consider the practicality of buying or renting a cell phone. Although cell phones used in Italy cannot be used in the U.S., Australia and New Zealand, and vice versa, the cost of purchasing a basic phone runs between €80 and €125. The cost of renting a cell phone is about €20 a week plus the cost of a calling card or 10 to 25 cents a minute for calling time and no charge for the phone (a €100 to €125 refundable deposit is normal). Public pay phones usually require a phone card (*carta telefonica*) that can be purchased at newsstands, and some still take coins in addition to the cards. Hotel and rental apartment/house phones operate the same as phones in the U.S. and U.K., but each minute is measured and will be charged to you.

AREA AND COUNTRY CODES

The country code for Italy is 39. Area codes for major cities are as follows: Florence, 055; Perugia, 075; Pisa, 050; Siena, 0577. For example, a call from New York City to Florence would be dialed as 011 + 39 + 055 + phone number.

When dialing an Italian number from abroad, do not drop the initial 0 from the local area code. The country code is 1 for the United States and Canada, 61 for Australia, 64 for New Zealand, and 44 for the United Kingdom.

CELLULAR-PHONE RENTAL

Rental cell phones are available in cities and large towns. Many Internet cafés offer them, but shop around for the best deal.

➤ RENTAL AGENCIES: **Cells4Rent@ Internet Train** (✉ Via dell'Oriuolo 40r, Florence, ☎ 055/2638968, WEB www. cells4rent.com). **Platform 3000** (✉ Via Ghibellina 110, Florence, ☎ 055/ 471714, WEB www.platform3000.itb). **Webpuccino** (✉ Via dei Conti 22r, Florence, ☎ 055/2776469, WEB www. webpuccino.it).

DIRECTORY AND OPERATOR ASSISTANCE

For general information in English, dial 176. To place international telephone calls via operator-assisted service, dial 170 or long-distance access numbers (☞ International Calls).

INTERNATIONAL CALLS

Hotels tend to overcharge for long-distance and international calls; it's best to make such calls from public phones, using telephone cards.

You can **make collect calls from any phone by dialing 172–1011,** which will get you an English-speaking operator. Rates to the United States are lowest on Sunday around the clock and 10 PM–8 AM (Italian time) on weekdays and Saturday.

From major Italian cities, you can place a direct call to the United States by reversing the charges or using your phone calling-card number. You automatically reach an operator in the country of destination and thereby avoid all language difficulties.

LOCAL AND LONG-DISTANCE CALLS

For all calls within Italy—local and long distance—you must dial the regional area code (*prefisso*), which begins with a 0, such as 055 for Florence. If you are calling from a public phone you must deposit a coin or use a calling card to get a dial tone.

Rates vary during the day; it's less expensive to call within Italy during nonworking hours (before 9 AM and after 7 or 8 PM).

LONG-DISTANCE SERVICES

AT&T, MCI, and Sprint access codes make calling long distance relatively convenient, but you may find the local access number blocked in many hotel rooms. First ask the hotel operator to connect you. If the hotel operator balks, ask for an international operator, or dial the international operator yourself. One way to improve your odds of getting connected to your long-distance carrier is to travel with more than one company's calling card (a hotel may block Sprint, for example, but not MCI). If all else fails, call from a pay phone.

➤ ACCESS CODES: **AT&T Direct** (☎ 172–1011). **MCI WorldPhone** (☎ 172–1022). **Sprint International Access** (☎ 172–1877).

PHONE CARDS

Prepaid *carte telefoniche* (calling cards) are prevalent throughout Italy and more convenient than coins. You buy the card (values vary) at post offices, tobacconists, most news stalls, and bars. Tear off the corner of the card and insert it in the slot on a public pay phone. When you dial, its value appears in the window. After you hang up, the card is returned so you can use it until its value runs out. The phone card called Time Europa (€25) is a good value, allowing you to call Europe and the United States at only 28 European cents a minute during peak hours, although conventional phone cards remain cheaper when used from 10 PM to 8 AM and on Sunday. Shop around for long-distance cards; the prices have been going down.

PUBLIC PHONES

All large towns and most small ones have public pay phones (*telefono pubblico*). They usually can be found in bars and at gas stations or near the center piazza. These phones usually accept phone cards but some still take coins in addition to the cards.

TIME

Italy is six hours ahead of New York (so when it's 1 PM in New York it's

7 PM in Florence). Italy is one hour ahead of London, 10 hours behind Sydney, and 12 hours behind Auckland. Like the rest of Europe, Italy uses the 24-hour (or "military") clock, which means that after 12 noon you continue counting forward: 13:00 is 1 PM, 23:30 is 11:30 PM.

TIPPING

The following guidelines apply in major cities, but Italians tip smaller amounts in smaller cities and towns. In restaurants in Tuscany and Umbria a service charge of 10% to 15% sometimes appears on your check. It's not necessary to tip in addition to this amount. If service is not included, leave a tip of not more than 10%. At basic restaurants, if service is not included, leave €2 on the table. No one tips in bars in Florence.

Tip checkroom attendants 50 European cents per person and rest-room attendants 25 European cents (more in expensive hotels and restaurants). Italians rarely tip taxi drivers, which is not to say that you shouldn't do it. A tip of 10% or more, depending on the length of the journey, is appreciated—particularly if the driver helps with luggage. Railway and airport porters charge a fixed rate per bag. Tip an additional 25 European cents per person, and more if the porter is especially helpful. Give a barber €1–€1.55 and a hairdresser's assistant €1.50–€4.15 for a shampoo or cut, depending on the type of establishment.

On sightseeing tours, tip guides about €1 per person for a half-day group tour, more if they are very good. In museums and other sights where admission is free, a contribution (25–50 European cents) is expected. Service-station attendants are tipped only for special services, for example, 50 European cents for checking your tires.

In hotels, give the *portiere* (concierge) about 10% of his bill for services, or €2.50–€5 if he has been generally helpful. For two people in a double room, leave the chambermaid about 75 European cents per day, or about €5 a week, in a moderately priced hotel; tip a minimum of 50 European

cents for valet or room service. Double amounts in an expensive hotel. In very expensive hotels, tip doormen 50 European cents for calling a cab and €1 for carrying bags to the check-in desk, bellhops €1.50–€2.50 for carrying your bags to the room, and €1.50–2.50 for room service.

TOURS AND PACKAGES

Because everything is prearranged on a prepackaged tour or independent vacation, you spend less time planning—and often get it all at a good price.

BOOKING WITH AN AGENT

Travel agents are excellent resources. But it's a good idea to collect brochures from several agencies, as some agents' suggestions may be influenced by relationships with tour and package firms that reward them for volume sales. If you have a special interest, **find an agent with expertise in that area**; the American Society of Travel Agents (ASTA; ☞ Travel Agencies) has a database of specialists worldwide.

Make sure your travel agent knows the accommodations and other services of the place being recommended. Ask about the hotel's location, room size, beds, and whether it has a pool, room service, or programs for children, if you care about these. Has your agent been there in person or sent others whom you can contact?

Do some homework on your own, too: local tourism boards can provide information about lesser-known and small-niche operators, some of which may sell only direct.

BUYER BEWARE

Each year consumers are stranded or lose their money when tour operators—even large ones with excellent reputations—go out of business. So **check out the operator.** Ask several travel agents about its reputation, and try to **book with a company that has a consumer-protection program.** (Look for information in the company's brochure.) In the United States, members of the National Tour Association and the United States Tour Operators Association are required to set aside funds to cover your payments and travel arrangements in the event that the company defaults. It's also a good idea to choose a company that participates in the American Society of Travel Agents' Tour Operator Program (TOP); ASTA will act as mediator in any disputes between you and your tour operator.

Remember that the more your package or tour includes the better you can predict the ultimate cost of your vacation. Make sure you know exactly what is covered, and **beware of hidden costs.** Are taxes, tips, and transfers included? Entertainment and excursions? These can add up.

➤ TOUR-OPERATOR RECOMMENDATIONS: **American Society of Travel Agents** (☞ Travel Agencies). **National Tour Association** (NTA; ✉ 546 E. Main St., Lexington, KY 40508, ☎ 859/226–4444 or 800/682–8886, WEB www.ntaonline.com). **United States Tour Operators Association** (USTOA; ✉ 275 Madison Ave., Suite 2014, New York, NY 10016, ☎ 212/599–6599 or 800/468–7862, FAX 212/599–6744, WEB www.ustoa.com).

TRAIN TRAVEL

The fastest trains on the Ferrovie dello Stato (FS), the Italian State Railways, are the Eurostar trains, operating on several main lines, including Rome–Milan via Florence and Bologna. Supplement is included in the fare; seat reservations are mandatory at all times. All trains have smoking and nonsmoking cars. If smoke bothers you, ask for seats away from the smoking car, as the poorly designed partitions aren't smoke-proof. Some Eurostar trains (the ETR 460 trains) have little aisle and luggage space (though there is a space near the door where you can put large bags). To avoid having to squeeze through narrow aisles, board only at your car (look for the number on the reservation ticket). Car numbers are displayed on their exterior. The next-fastest trains are the Intercity (IC) trains, for which you pay a supplement and for which seat reservations may be required and are always advisable. *Interregionale* trains usually make more stops and are a little slower. *Regionale* and *locale* trains are the slowest; many serve commuters.

There is refreshment service on all long-distance trains, with mobile carts and a cafeteria or dining car. Tap water on trains is not drinkable.

Traveling by night can be inexpensive, but never leave your belongings unattended (even for a minute) and make sure the door of your compartment is locked.

Train service between Milan, Florence, Rome, and Naples is frequent throughout the day. For the most part, trains stick to the schedule, although delays may occur in the peak tourist season. Train strikes of various kinds are also frequent, so it's a good idea to make sure the train you want to take is in fact running.

➤ FROM THE U.K.: **British Rail** (☎ 020/7834–2345). **French Railways** (☎ 0891/515–477).

CLASSES

Many Italian trains have first and second classes, but regional trains frequently don't have first class. On interregional trains the higher first-class fare gets you little more than a clean doily on the headrest of your seat, but on long-distance trains you get wider seats, more legroom, and better ventilation and lighting. At peak travel times, first-class train travel is worth the difference. Remember always to **make seat reservations in advance,** for either class. One advantage of traveling first class is that the cars are almost always not crowded—or, at the very least, less crowded than the second-class compartments. A first-class ticket, in Italian, is *prima classe*; second is *seconda classe*.

CUTTING COSTS

To save money, **look into rail passes.** But be aware that if you don't plan to cover many miles you may come out ahead by buying individual tickets. If you're traveling only in Tuscany and Umbria, rail passes won't save you money.

If Italy is your only destination in Europe, **consider purchasing an Italian Flexi Rail Card Saver,** which allows a limited number of travel days within one month: for 4 days of travel ($239 first class, $191 second class); 8 days of travel ($334 first class, $268 second class); and 12 days of travel ($429 first class, $343 second class).

The Italian Kilometric Ticket (*biglietto chilometrico*) is valid for two months and can be used by as many as five people to travel a maximum of 20 journeys covering an overall distance of 3,000 km (1,800 mi). The price is €180.75 for first class and €110.50 for second class.

Once in Italy, inquire about the Carta Verde (Green Card) if you're under 26 (€23.25 for one year), which entitles the holder to a 20%–30% discount on first- and second-class travel. Those under 26 should also inquire about discount travel fares under the Billet International Jeune (BIJ) and Euro Domino Junior schemes. Also in Italy, you can purchase the Carta d'Argento (Silver Card) if you're over 60 (€23.25 for a year), which allows a 40% discount on first-class rail travel and a 20% discount on second-class travel. Travelers with disabilities who require assistance can acquire the Carta Blu (Dark-Blue Card; €5.15 for five years), which entitles their companions to free travel. For further information, check out the Ferrovie dello Stato (FS) Web site (www. trenitalia.it).

Don't assume that a rail pass guarantees a seat on the trains you wish to ride; you need to book seats ahead even if you use a rail pass. There's a nominal fee (usually €2.50) for the reservation.

➤ INFORMATION AND PASSES: **CIT Rail** (✉ 9501 W. Devon Ave., Suite 502, Rosemont, IL 60018, ☎ 800/248–7245). **DER Tours** (✉ Box 1606, Des Plaines, IL 60017, ☎ 800/782–2424, FAX 800/282–7474). **Rail Europe** (✉ 226-230 Westchester Ave., White Plains, NY 10604, ☎ 914/682–5172 or 800/438–7245, WEB www. raileurope.com; ✉ 2087 Dundas E., Suite 105, Mississauga, Ontario L4X 1M2, ☎ 416/602–4195).

➤ TRAIN INFORMATION: **Ferrovie dello Stato** (FS; ☎ 147/888–088 in Italy, WEB www.fs-on-line.com).

TICKETS, SCHEDULES, AND RESERVATIONS

Trains can be very crowded; it is always a good idea to make a reserva-

tion. In summer, it's fairly common to stand for a good part of the journey.

To avoid long lines at station windows, **buy tickets and make seat reservations up to two months in advance** at travel agencies displaying the FS emblem. Tickets can be purchased at the last minute, but seat reservations can be made at agencies (or the train station) up until about three hours before the train departs from its city of origin. For trains that require a reservation (all Eurostar and some Intercity), you may be able to get a seat assignment just before boarding the train; look for the conductor on the platform, but do this only as a last resort.

Tickets are good for two months after the date of issue, but right before departure you must **validate tickets in the yellow machines in the departure area.** Once stamped, tickets are valid for six hours on distances of less than 200 km (124 mi) or for 24 hours on longer distances. If you wish to stop along the way and your final destination is more than 200 km away, you can stamp the ticket a second time before it expires so as to extend its validity to a maximum of 48 hours from the time it was first stamped. If you forget to stamp your ticket in the machine, or you didn't make it to the station in time to buy the ticket, you must seek out a conductor and pay a €5.15 fine. Don't wait for the conductor to find out that you're without a valid ticket (unless the train is overcrowded and walking becomes impossible), as he might charge you a much heavier fine. However, you often can get out of paying the fine if you immediately write the time, date, name of the departure station on the back of the ticket and sign it—essentially "validating" it and making it unusable for another trip.

You can buy train tickets for nearby destinations (within a 200-km range) at tobacconists and at ticket machines in stations. You can pay for your train tickets in cash or with any major credit card such as American Express, Diner's Club, MasterCard, and Visa.

TRANSPORTATION

Driving is the best mode of transportation in the region, if not essential. Buses (☞ Bus Travel), which are usually more comfortable and more expensive than trains, offer more-frequent service to certain smaller cities and towns in Tuscany and Umbria, where train service is spotty. Ferries and hydrofoils (☞ Boat and Ferry Travel) travel between the islands and the mainland.

Tuscany and Umbria have an intricate network of autostrade routes, good highways, and secondary roads, making renting a car (☞ Car Rental) a better but expensive alternative (because of high gas prices and freeway tolls) to public transportation. A rental car can be a good investment for carefree countryside rambles, offering time to explore more-remote towns. Having a car in major cities, however, often leads to parking and traffic headaches, plus the additional expense of garage and parking fees.

TRAVEL AGENCIES

A good travel agent puts your needs first. Look for an agency that has been in business at least five years, emphasizes customer service, and has someone on staff who specializes in your destination. In addition, **make sure the agency belongs to a professional trade organization.** The American Society of Travel Agents (ASTA)—the largest and most influential in the field with more than 24,000 members in some 140 countries—maintains and enforces a strict code of ethics and will step in to help mediate any agent-client disputes involving ASTA members if necessary. ASTA (whose motto is "Without a travel agent, you're on your own") also maintains a Web site that includes a directory of agents. (If a travel agency is also acting as your tour operator, *see* Buyer Beware *in* Tours and Packages.)

➤ LOCAL AGENT REFERRALS: **American Society of Travel Agents** (ASTA; ✉ 1101 King St., Suite 200, Alexandria, VA 22314, ☎ 800/965–2782 24-hr hot line, ℻ 703/739–3268, WEB www.astanet.com). **Association of British Travel Agents** (✉ 68–71 Newman St., London W1T 3AH, ☎ 020/7637–

2444, ℻ 020/7637–0713, WEB www.abtanet.com). **Association of Canadian Travel Agents** (✉ 130 Albert St., Suite 1705, Ottawa, Ontario K1P 5G4, ☎ 613/237–3657, ℻ 613/237–7052, WEB www.acta.ca). **Australian Federation of Travel Agents** (✉ Level 3, 309 Pitt St., Sydney, NSW 2000, ☎ 02/9264–3299, ℻ 02/9264–1085, WEB www.afta.com.au). **Travel Agents' Association of New Zealand** (✉ Level 5, Tourism and Travel House, 79 Boulcott St., Box 1888, Wellington 6001, ☎ 04/499–0104, ℻ 04/499–0827, WEB www.taanz.org.nz).

VISITOR INFORMATION

➤ AT HOME: **Italian Government Tourist Board** (ENIT; ✉ 630 5th Ave., New York, NY 10111, ☎ 212/245–4822, ℻ 212/586–9249; ✉ 401 N. Michigan Ave., Chicago, IL 60611, ☎ 312/644–0990, ℻ 312/644–3019; ✉ 12400 Wilshire Blvd., Suite 550, Los Angeles, CA 90025, ☎ 310/820–0098, ℻ 310/820–6357; 1 Pl. Ville Marie, Suite 1914, Montréal, Québec H3B 3M9, ☎ 514/866–7667, ℻ 514/392–1429; 1 Princes St., London W1R 8AY, ☎ 020/7408–1254, ℻ 020/7493–6695; WEB www.italiantourism.com).

➤ TOURIST OFFICES IN TUSCANY AND UMBRIA: **Florence** (✉ Via Cavour 1/r, next to Palazzo Medici-Riccardi, 50129, ☎ 055/290832, WEB www.firenze.turismo.toscana.it). **Lucca** (✉ Piazza Guidiccioni 2, ☎ 0583/491205, WEB www.cribecu.sus.it/lucca). **Perugia** (✉ Piazza IV Novembre, ☎ 075/5723327, WEB www.perugiaonline.it).

➤ U.S. GOVERNMENT ADVISORIES: **U.S. Department of State** (✉ Overseas Citizens Services Office, Room 4811, 2201 C St. NW, Washington, DC 20520, ☎ 202/647–5225 interactive hot line or 888/407–4747, WEB www.travel.state.gov); enclose a self-addressed, stamped, business-size envelope.

WEB SITES

Do check out the World Wide Web when planning your trip. You'll find everything from weather forecasts to virtual tours of famous cities. Be sure to **visit Fodors.com** (www.fodors.com), a complete travel-planning site. You can research prices and book plane tickets, hotel rooms, rental cars, vacation packages, and more. In addition, you can post your pressing questions in the Travel Talk section. Other planning tools include a currency converter and weather reports, and there are loads of links to travel resources.

➤ SUGGESTED WEB SITES: For more information specifically on Italy, visit www.initaly.com and www.wel.it.

WHEN TO GO

The main tourist season runs from April to mid-October. For serious sightseers the best months are from fall to early spring. The so-called low season may be cooler and inevitably rainier, but it has its rewards: less time waiting in lines and closer-up, unhurried views of what you want to see.

Tourists crowd the major art cities at Easter, when Italians flock to resorts and to the countryside. From March through May, busloads of eager schoolchildren on excursions take cities of artistic and historical interest by storm. Italian beach vacations are best taken in June and September, to avoid the August crowds.

CLIMATE

Weatherwise, the best months for sightseeing are April, May, June, September, and October—generally pleasant and not too hot. The hottest months are July and August, when humidity can make things unpleasant and brief afternoon thunderstorms are common in inland areas. Winter is relatively mild in most places on the main tourist circuit but always includes some rainy spells.

If you can avoid it, don't travel at all in Italy in August, when much of the population is on the move, especially around Ferragosto, the August 15 national holiday; many cities are deserted during this time and many restaurants and shops are closed. (Of course, with residents away on vacation, this makes crowds less of a bother for tourists.) Except for a few year-round resorts, coastal resorts usually close up from October or November to April; they're at their best in June and September, when everything is open but uncrowded.

➤ FORECASTS: **Weather Channel Connection** (☎ 900/932–8437), 95¢ per minute from a Touch-Tone phone.

FLORENCE

Jan.	48F	9C	May	73F	23C	Sept.	79F	26C
	36	2		54	12		59	15
Feb.	52F	11C	June	81F	27C	Oct.	68F	20C
	37	3		59	15		52	11
Mar.	57F	14C	July	86F	30C	Nov.	57F	14C
	41	5		64	18		45	7
Apr.	66F	19C	Aug.	86F	30C	Dec.	52F	11C
	46	8		63	17		39	10

FESTIVALS AND SEASONAL EVENTS

Tuscany and Umbria's top seasonal events are listed below, and any one of them could provide the stuff of lasting memories. It's revealing that the Italian *festa* can be translated either as "festival" or "holiday" or "feast"—food is usually fundamental to Italian celebrations. Contact the Italian Government Tourist Board (☞ Visitor Information) for exact dates and further information.

➤ JAN. 6: Roman Catholic **Epiphany (Epifania) Celebrations** and decorations are evident throughout Italy.

➤ LATE FEB.–APR.: During **Carnevale in Viareggio**, masked pageants, fireworks, a flower show, and parades are among the festivities on the Tuscan Riviera. **Carnevale in San Gimignano** is smaller, with locals, dressed up in colorful costumes, marching through the streets. The biggest fete is, of course, held in Venice.

➤ LATE FEB.–APR.: The Easter Sunday **Scoppio del Carro,** or "Explosion of the Cart," in Florence is an eruption of fireworks; they shoot out of a highly ornate carriage after a mechanical dove swoops from the Duomo's high altar to set them off. **Settimana Santa** (Holy Week), the week after Easter, features parades and outdoor events at every major city and most small towns; the festivities in Florence are particularly notable.

➤ LATE APR.–EARLY JULY: The **Maggio Musicale Fiorentino** (Florence May Music Festival) is a series of internationally acclaimed concerts and recitals. It's the oldest and most prestigious Italian festival of the performing arts. Check www.maggiofiorentino.com for schedules and tickets.

➤ MID-MAY: During the **Festa dei Ceri** (Race of the Candles), a procession to the top of Mt. Ingino in Gubbio, young men in local costume carry huge wooden pillars.

➤ LATE MAY: The **Palio della Balestra** (Palio of the Archers) is a medieval crossbow contest in Gubbio that dates back to 1461 and is held the last Sunday in May.

➤ EARLY AND MID-JUNE: The **Battle of the Bridge,** in Pisa, is a medieval parade and contest. The **Luminaria** feast day on June 16 honors St. Ranieri, the patron saint of Pisa. Palaces along the Arno glow with white lights and fireworks. The **Regatta of the Great Maritime Republics** sees keen competition between the four former maritime republics—Amalfi, Genoa, Pisa, and Venice.

➤ JUNE 2: The **Feast of the Republic,** formerly the royal national holiday, is celebrated with a flurry of Italian flags.

➤ JUNE 24: **Calcio Storico,** soccer games in 16th-century costume representing Florence's six neighborhoods, are held in Florence on the feast day of St. John the Baptist, commemorating a match played in 1530. Festivities include fireworks displays.

➤ LATE JUNE–EARLY JULY: The **Festival dei Due Mondi** (Festival of Two Worlds), in Spoleto, is perhaps Italy's most famous performing-arts festival, bringing in a worldwide audience for concerts, operas, ballets, film screenings, and crafts fairs. Plan well in advance.

➤ JUNE–AUGUST: **Estate Fiesolana** is a festival of theater, music, dance, and film that takes place in the churches and the archaeological area of Fiesole.

➤ JULY: **Pistoia Blues** draws international blues artists who perform in the city's main square. **La Giostra dell'Orso** (Bear Joust), on July 25, celebrates St. James, patron saint of Pistoia. The **Umbria Jazz Festival,** in Perugia, brings in many of the biggest names in jazz each summer.

➤ JULY 2 AND AUGUST 16: The **Palio** horse race, in Siena, is a colorful bareback horse race with participants competing for the *palio* (banner).

➤ LATE JULY–EARLY AUGUST: Lucca's **Puccini Festival** in late July to early August celebrates the city's native son. **Estate Musicale Lucchese** runs throughout the summer in Lucca.

➤ LATE AUG.–EARLY SEPT.: The **Siena Music Week** features opera, concerts, and chamber music.

➤ EARLY SEPT.: The **Giostra del Saracino** (Joust of the Saracen) is a tilting contest with knights in 13th-century armor in Arezzo.

➤ MID-SEPT.: The **Giostra della Quintana** is a 17th-century-style joust and historical procession in Foligno.

➤ OCT. 4: The **Festa di San Francesco** (Feast of St. Francis) is celebrated in Assisi, his birthplace.

1 DESTINATION: FLORENCE, TUSCANY, AND UMBRIA

Introduction

What's Where

Pleasures and Pastimes

Fodor's Choice

INTRODUCTION

J UST AS TUSCANY AND UMBRIA straddle the boot, so their contribution to
the Italian jigsaw is massive and in-
escapable. Their influence pervades Italian culture and percolates far beyond, to
the extent that their impact has been felt
throughout European and even world history. Tuscany—and to a lesser extent Umbria—saw the birth of humanism, that
classically leaning, secular-tending current that blossomed in the Renaissance and
to which the West owes its cultural com-
plexion. In the graphic arts, architecture,
astronomy, sculpture, engineering, art history, poetry, political theory, biography . . . in every field of human
endeavor—the achievements of the people of these regions have loomed large. The
Italian language itself is Tuscan, due largely
to Dante's use of his local dialect to compose his *Divine Comedy*. When Italy became a modern state in 1865, Florence was
the natural choice for the national capital until Rome's entry six years later.

Although it's hard to think of any other
area that has seen such a dense concentration
of human achievement as Tuscany and
Umbria, it's equally difficult to find anywhere so riven by conflict and factions. The
strange thing is how neatly the periods of
maximum creativity and bellicosity coin-
cided. Was the restless, innovative impulse
a consequence of the social turmoil, or
the principal cause of it? It is surely no accident that Tuscany and Umbria in general
and Florence in particular contain the
most quarrelsome elements ever thrown together, as a cursory flip through some of
the names in the local annals can testify:
the Florentine Niccolò Machiavelli, who
became a very synonym for the Devil (Old
Nick); Savonarola, whose energetic career pitched church and state into headlong confrontation, igniting the famous
"bonfire of the vanities" in Florence's
main square, site of the Dominican friar's
own incineration not long afterward. Perugia was populated, according to the historian Sigismondo, by "the most warlike
people in Italy, who always preferred Mars
to the Muse"; and the very street names
of Florence and Siena recall the clash of

medieval factions. Outside the towns,
hardly a hill, stream, or mountain pass exists whose name doesn't evoke some siege,
battle, or act of treachery. The historic rivalry of Guelph and Ghibelline never
reached such intense acrimony as in these
seemingly tranquil hills, and nowhere was
allegiance worn so lightly, with communes
and families swapping sides whenever
their rivals changed theirs.

The sense of opposition is alive in Tuscany
and Umbria today. You can witness it on
every two-toned marble church front.
Blacks and whites imperial, feudal and
commercial, Renaissance and Gothic—
the antagonism is embedded in art history, revived in every discussion of the
background of every great work. It is a fixed
feature of the local scene: the Sienese are
still suspicious of the Florentines, the Florentines disdainful of the Sienese, while Siena
itself seems to live in a permanent state of
warfare within its own city walls, as any
spectator of the Palio and the months of
preparation that precede it can testify.
Outsiders contribute to the debate: for
Mary McCarthy, Florence was manly,
Siena feminine, and visitors take sides
whenever they lay down their reasons for
preferring Florence to Siena or vice versa.

Walking through the city streets of present-
day Florence, you can't fail to be struck
by the contrast between the austere and
unwelcoming external appearance of the
palaces and the sumptuous comforts
within, or by the 21st-century elegance and
modernity of the Florentines in the midst
of thoroughly medieval churches and piazzas. Florence is a modern industrial
city, and the Florentines themselves perennial modernists, their eyes fixed firmly in
front. This helps to explain both their
past inventiveness and the ambivalent attitude they hold toward that same past,
composed of roughly equal parts ennui and
fierce pride. To its inhabitants, that the city
of Florence stands on a par with Athens
and Rome is self-evident: To them tourism,
which feeds on the past, is reactionary, deca-
dent, and often intrusive, making a bur-
den of the historical heritage. It is tolerated
as a business, in a city that has a high re-

gard for business . . . but it is only one of many. In Italy, Florentines are reckoned the most impenetrable, cautious, and circumspect of Italians, a reputation they have held since the days of the Medicis. Nevertheless, Italians have coined a word—*fiorentinità*—to refer to the good taste and fine workmanship that are flaunted here, in a city renowned for its leather goods, handbags, shoes, jewelry, and a host of famous brand names. Pucci, Gucci, Ferragamo, Cellerini are just four of the high-profile craft-turned-fashion designers that exude fiorentinità. Neither are the region's cuisine and fine wines to be taken lightly. Talk to any Florentines about these present-day aspects of their civilization, and they will perk up and debate enthusiastically; mention their past glories and they will stifle a yawn.

O**THER TUSCAN CITIES** possess the same compelling mix of elements: What Tuscany's older centers share is an immaculate medieval setting, modern life taking place within the shell of the past; what divides them is a complex mental set. Needless to say, they all were rivals at one time or another, and each prevailed in distinct spheres. Pisa, for example, was one of Italy's four great maritime republics, its architectural style visible wherever its ships touched port. Once the most powerful force in the Tyrrhenian, it lost its hegemony on the sea to its trading rival, Genoa, and its dominance on land to Florence. Pisa owed its prestige to a university that bequeathed a scholarly, scientific, and legal tradition to the town, and to its location on the River Arno, though this position much later was responsible for its being one of the most devastated cities in World War II. Skillful rebuilding has ensured a relatively harmonious appearance, however, and the city would still hold plenty of interest if the Torre Pendente (Leaning Tower) had never been built.

Livorno, on the other hand, the main Tuscan port of today, is the Pisa that never was. By Tuscan standards it is a recent affair, developed as a sea outlet for Florence after Pisa's port had silted up. Livorno reveals a highly un-Tuscan cosmopolitan character, a result of 16th-century growth that brought immigration. Livorno's most famous son, the sculptor Amedeo Modigliani, for example, was brought up speaking French, Italian, English, and Hebrew, though in other ways this hard-drinking Bohemian didn't typify the soberly respectable citizens for whom Livorno is best known. Also heavily bombed in the war, the port wasn't restored as tastefully as Pisa, though it can at least boast a vigorous culinary tradition, with its range of fresh seafood.

South from Livorno stretches a riviera of varying degrees of summer saturation, including numerous select spots where sun- and sea-bathing can be enjoyed in relative peace. The island of Elba—scene of Napoléon's nine-month incarceration—is today more likely to be somewhere to escape *to* rather than *from,* and together with the islands of Giglio and Capraia offers everything from absurd overdevelopment to true isolation.

Lucca, the principal enemy of Pisa during the Middle Ages, has been called "the most enchanting walled town in the world." The city's formidable girdle of walls has resisted the intrusions of modern life better than any other Tuscan center and contains within a wealth of palaces and churches wildly out of proportion to the size of what is, after all, a small provincial town. Much of Lucca's present-day success is based on, of all things, the manufacture of lingerie.

A much weightier substance—gold—forms, together with antique furniture, the basis of the wealth of the less imposing town of Arezzo. Such worldly items again form a counterpoint to the fact that this town has produced more than its fair share of pioneers in literature (Petrarch, Pietro Aretino), art (Vasari), and music (Guido d'Arezzo, also called Guido Monaco, inventor of notation and the musical scale).

Arezzo shares a university with Siena, another Tuscan town preserved in the aspic of its medieval past. It is said that there are three subjects you should avoid if you're in a hurry while in Siena: wild pigs (a prized quarry for hunters), the Palio (an object of fanatical zeal), and the battle of Montaperti (Siena's moment of military glory—a perennial obsession). To the rest of Italy, Siena is best known for its banks and its mystics—a characteristically incompatible duo—while its foreign visitors are more enchanted by the city's artworks, its easy pace of life, and the pleasing hue of its rose-colored buildings.

Prato and Pistoia, a short roll up the autostrada from Florence, have traditionally fallen within the sphere of that city's influence. Prato combines some choice examples of Renaissance art and architecture with a strong industrial identity, mainly based on its wool exports; Pistoia, on the other hand, was renowned for its ironwork, and its citizens for their murderous propensities.

A CROSS THE REGIONAL boundary in Umbria, the hilltop town of Perugia is dominated by the cold Gothic stone of its major monuments, its secretive alleys and steps, yet its animating spirit is among the most progressive and trend-setting in Italy. Within its medieval walls the town hosts one of Europe's prime jazz festivals, a modern tradition that has taken its lead from the international Festival dei Due Mondi (Festival of Two Worlds) at nearby Spoleto. As in Tuscany, modernity lives alongside medievalism in Umbria, a case not so much of collision as coexistence. In the same spirit, the imposing monuments of its towns were built by a new wealthy mercantile class in the teeth of almost uninterrupted warfare throughout the Middle Ages. Spoleto, Gubbio, and Orvieto owed their influence not so much to their continual brawling as to their interchange of goods and ideas. A university was founded in Perugia as early as 1308, and it was the small Umbrian town of Foligno that published the first edition of Dante's *Divine Comedy*. The belligerence of the age paralleled an intense spiritual activity, championed by such towering religious figures as St. Francis, St. Clare, St. Benedict, and the locally venerated St. Rita (as well as the more worldly St. Valentine)—a legacy nowhere so apparent as in the town of Assisi.

Although many of the urban centers of Tuscany and Umbria have cleanly defined boundaries beyond which the countryside abruptly begins, the towns harmonize with the surrounding landscape more closely than anywhere else in Italy. Even if devoid of museums or souvenir shops, the hinterland holds as much of the region's quintessential character as the cities of Tuscany and Umbria, and such unsung treasures as Todi and Bevagna are as revealing as anything seen in the galleries. This is your chance to immerse yourself in the region's less tangible pleasures, to rest your eyes on the gentle ocher stone of villages artfully situated above vine-strung, neatly terraced slopes. From the wine-producing hills of Chianti to the Carrara mountains where Michelangelo quarried to the soft contours of the Vale di Spoleto, the tidy cypress-speared landscape displays a weird inertia like some illustration from a fable. It has a geometric precision that underlines the strict rural economy practiced by the Tuscan and Umbrian peasants, for whom every tree has its purpose. The Tuscans in particular have long been considered the most skilled and intelligent of Italian farmers, having created for themselves a region that is largely self-sufficient, producing a little of everything, and excelling in certain areas, not least in wine-production, for which the Tuscans have nurtured one of the most dynamic wine regions of Italy.

Like the great examples of urban architecture, the country in Tuscany and Umbria presents, for the most part, an ordered, rational, controlled appearance. It is the crust of civilization concealing the greatest paradox of all in this heartland of reason and classical elegance. For buried underneath lies a much older, earthier civilization of which most visitors to the region are oblivious. In every respect the ancient Etruscan civilization that flourished here was opposed to the values of the Renaissance, its vital, animistic spirit murky, dark, and mysterious to us, mainly known from subterranean tombs and wall-paintings. Almost erased from the face of the earth by the Romans, the Etruscan culture—its centers scattered throughout Tuscany and Umbria (Perugia, Orvieto, Chiusi, Roselle, Vetulonia, Volterra, Cortona, Arezzo, Fiesole were the main ones)—was central to the history of Tuscany and Umbria. Like the Hermes Trimegistus incongruously placed on the marble pavement of Siena's cathedral, the Etruscans are a mischievous element amid the harmony of Renaissance Tuscany and Umbria. Their precise influence is unclear, but it may well turn out to have been the contentious and destructive spirit ever-present in the golden age of these regions, harassing, hindering, entangling. Alternatively, it may have been the restless worm of invention, the defiant individuality that brought about the triumph of art in the face of adversity—which is, after all, the greatest achievement of Tuscany and Umbria.

— Robert Andrews

WHAT'S WHERE

Florence

Florence, the "Athens of Italy" and the key to the Renaissance, hugs the banks of the Arno River where it lies folded among the emerald cypress-studded hills of north-central Tuscany. Elegant and somewhat aloof, as if set apart by its past greatness, this historic center of European civilization still shares with Rome the honor of first place among Italian cities for the magnitude of its artistic works, among them Botticelli's goddess and Michelangelo's powerful *David*. Down every street and *vicolo* (alley) and in every piazza you'll make new discoveries of Romanesque, Gothic, or Renaissance architecture; sheltered within these churches, cloisters, and towers are masterful paintings and sculptures of the Quattrocento and Cinquecento periods. Equally as splendid are the magnificent chapels and palaces of the Medici—whose patronage rocketed Florence to the forefront of the Renaissance—which stand unabashed amid the city's vibrant modern pulse.

North of Florence

North and west of Florence are hills and mountains, snowcapped peaks, thermal waters, and miles of Mediterranean coast. The Apuan Alps split this area nearly in half, with the Lunigiana and the Garfagnana on either side: east of the Alps you're in Tuscany's Rockies; west of them the land flattens out to meet the Tyrrhenian Sea. Michelangelo, not to mention men 1,500 years his senior, quarried marble in Carrara. The Ligurian coast, encompassing the Cinque Terre and Forte dei Marmi, dazzles with its panoramic vistas.

Cities West of Florence

Nestled in valleys and fed along the Arno, the cities west of Florence were coveted by Florence: they provided access to the sea (Pisa) and were rich industrial centers (Prato). San Miniato al Monte, crowned

high on a hill, commands views of two valleys. Although the landscape isn't Tuscany's most majestic, the area is rich with superb Renaissance art and gurgling thermal waters, such as in Montecatini Terme.

Chianti

The vineyard-quilted lands spreading south from Florence to Siena—Greve, Radda, Castellina—make up the heart of Chianti. Ilex and cypress, castles and wineries, and sleepy hill towns dot the magical landscape, which has seduced many an expatriate who couldn't summon the will to return home. The market town Greve, just 20 minutes south of Florence, is the gateway to sublime Chianti wine and splendid views. Montepulciano and Montalcino, south of Siena, produce some of Italy's most esteemed wines.

Siena and the Hill Towns

The time traveler will be entranced by medieval Siena, "the Pompeii of the Middle Ages," as it was called by the philosopher Taine. Radiating from the Gothic bastion are ocher and emerald lands teeming with olive groves, vineyards, and rolling hills nurtured by the Elsa and the Arbia. Perched dramatically above a fertile valley, San Gimignano—with its skyline of medieval towers—may jettison you into a Who-turned-back-the-clock? sensation of Mark Twain's Connecticut Yankee when he arrived in King Arthur's court. With a glass of Vernaccia di San Gimignano in hand, you'll feel like lingering long. But the old Etruscan hill town of Volterra, with sweeping views of two valleys, is not to be overlooked.

Arezzo, Cortona, and Southern Tuscany

Heading south from Florence toward Rome to the heart of southern Tuscany, you'll find Arezzo, with its treasures by Piero della Francesca. Compact, perfect Pienza, a fusion of Renaissance and Gothic styles planned by Pope Pius II, overlooks a golden valley. In mystical Cortona, with sweeping views of Lago Trasimeno, you can take pleasure in the scattering of churches and medieval art, but street scenes revealing an old-fashioned way of life are just as essential. Mountainous Elba is rimmed with seductive beaches; Giglio, its sister island to the south, is tinier and rockier.

Perugia and Northern Umbria

Nestled east of Florence and stretching to the Adriatic, Perugia and Northern Umbria—including the eastern Marches region—boast dramatically rolling, checkerboarded hills in hues of green and gold, ablaze with sunflowers and poppies. The area encompasses the valley cradling the Tiber, which is exceptionally lush and rich. Undiscovered splendor awaits in the cities: Perugia, a magnet for visitors since the Middle Ages, has a magnificent piazza; Gubbio, to the northeast, is a tiny jewel built against a steep hill; and the beauty of the Renaissance court comes alive in Urbino.

Assisi, Spoleto, and Southern Umbria

There's magic in the air in this noble area just east of the Tiber. Assisi, birthplace of St. Francis, is surrounded by wheat fields and olive groves, and the tufa plateau of Orvieto—with its own magnificent Duomo—gives the hallowed town a warm, reddish glow. Hilltop Deruta has been making ceramics for more than 600 years, and Middle-Aged Todi seems nearly celestial behind its three sets of walls.

PLEASURES AND PASTIMES

The Art of Enjoying Art

Travel veterans will tell you that the endless series of masterpieces in Italy's churches, palaces, and museums can cause first-time visitors—eyes glazed over from a heavy downpour of images, dates, and names—to lean, Pisa-like, on their companions for support. After a surfeit of Botticellis and Bronzinos and the 14th Raphael, even the miracle of the High Renaissance may begin to pall. The secret, of course, is to act like a turtle—not a hare—and take your sweet time. Instead of trotting after briskly efficient tour guides, allow the splendors of the age to unfold—slowly. Get out and explore the actual settings—medieval chapels, Rococo palaces, and Romanesque town squares—for which these marvelous examples of Italy's art and sculpture were conceived centuries ago and where many of them may still be seen in situ.

Museums are only the most obvious places to view art; there are always the trompe l'oeil renderings of Assumptions that float across baroque church ceilings and piazza scenes that might be Renaissance paintings brought to life. Instead of studying a Gothic statue in Florence's Bargello, spend an hour in the medieval cloisters of the nearby convent of San Marco; by all means, take in Michelangelo's *David* in Florence's Accademia, but then meander down the 15th-century street, a short bus ride away, where he was born. You'll find that after three days of trotting through museums, a walk through a quiet neighborhood will act as a much-needed restorative of perspective.

Dining

Every region of Italy has a distinct, time-tested cuisine that's a source of pride equally felt in family kitchens, modest trattorias, and sophisticated restaurants. What Italians hold in common is a respect for the pleasures of the table. They take the utmost care in creating staples—bread, wine, cheese, and olive oil are just the beginning of the list—and build their cuisine from there. Another shared characteristic of Italian food is a tendency to revere the most humble ingredients; chefs will devote the same attention to day-old bread as to priceless truffles. There's often a hint of the exotic on the menu, but the more exotic an item seems to you, the more likely it is to be distinctly local in origin.

Il Caffè

The Italian day begins and ends with coffee, and more cups of coffee punctuate the time in between. To live like the Italians do, drink as they drink, standing at the counter or sitting at outdoor tables of the corner bar. (In Italy, the term always means coffee bar—establishments serving primarily alcoholic beverages are called pubs or American bars.) A primer: *Caffè* means coffee, and Italian standard issue is what Americans call espresso—short, strong, and usually taken very sweet. *Cappuccino* is a foamy half-and-half of espresso and steamed milk; cocoa powder (*cacao*) on top is acceptable, cinnamon not. If you're thinking of having a cappuccino for dèssert, think again—Italians drink only caffè or *caffè macchiato* (with a spot of steamed milk) after lunchtime. Confused? Homesick? Order *caffè americano* for a reasonable facsimile of good old filtered joe.

La Passeggiata

A favorite Italian pastime is the *passeggiata*, literally the promenade. In the late afternoon and early evening, especially on weekends, couples, families, and packs of teenagers stroll the main streets and piazzas of Italy's towns. It's a ritual of exchanged news and gossip, window-shopping, flirting, and gelato-eating that adds up to a uniquely Italian experience. To join in, simply hit the streets for a bit of wandering. You may feel more like an observer than a participant, until you realize that observing is what la passeggiata is all about.

Shopping

"Made in Italy" has become synonymous with style, quality, and craftsmanship, whether it refers to high fashion or Maserati automobiles. The best buys are leather goods of all kinds—from gloves to bags to jackets—silk goods, knitwear, gold jewelry, ceramics, and local handicrafts. The most important thing to keep in mind when shopping in Italy is that every region has its specialties. Florence is known for gold jewelry, antiques, paper products, and leather and straw goods; Assisi for embroidery; and Deruta and Gubbio for ceramics.

Thermal Baths

Thanks to its location in the Mediterranean region—one of the world's most active volcano belts—Italy is rich in thermo-mineral springs. Consequently, the Italians have developed a special attitude about what we call spas since the ancient Romans advanced the idea of *mens sana in corpore sano* (a sound mind in a healthy body). Taking the waters remains a unique part of Italian culture; it is state-supported and medically supervised. Never mind Greco-Roman worship of the body in templelike baths; choices now range from antiaging cures to U.S.-style exercise classes to fangotherapy (medicinal mud therapy). Today, more and more travelers are taking vacations from their vacations by visiting one of Italy's sybaritic spas. At these centers, drinking and bathing cures are based on naturally produced thermal mineral waters, with mornings devoted to sipping and strolling as well as occasional forays into espresso bars. Then come hot mud packs, massage, anticellulite treatments, and sinus-targeted steam inhalations. But forget the Roman origins and don't say spa (in Italian, s.p.a. denotes a business corporation): The term in Italy is *terme* (baths).

FODOR'S CHOICE

Even with so many special places in Tuscany and Umbria, Fodor's writers and editors have their favorites. Here are a few that stand out.

Dining

Cibrèo, Florence. Chef Fabrio Picci reinterprets regional classics, served in Tuscan surroundings gone upscale. Its location next to a marketplace promises the freshest of ingredients—and imagination. *$$$$*

Ristorante Arnolfo, Colle di Val d'Elsa. The sublime dishes here daringly straddle the line between innovation and tradition—almost always with spectacular results. *$$$$*

Beccofino, Florence. A savvy clientele comes here for creative Tuscan food and a view of the Arno and Palazzo Corsino across the way. *$$$–$$$$*

Da Delfina, Artimino (Prato). Nestled amid vineyards and olive trees, this haven of Tuscan cooking started as a refuge for hungry area hunters. Now it has four comfortably rustic dining rooms where the cooking highlights pure ingredients, seasonal vegetables, and savory meats accented with herbs. *$$–$$$*

Bucadisantonio, Lucca. The excellent service is just one reason to come to this restaurant, which has been around for more than 200 years. The menu, laden with expertly prepared regional classics, has something for everyone; hanging copper pots and a fireplace create a cozy setting. *$$*

Enoteca I Terzi, Siena. Whether you want to eat lunch and run or linger over an all-out dinner, this wine bar keeps pace with you. Or come for snacks and sample some of the many choices on the well-chosen wine list. *$$*

Lodging

Certosa di Maggiano, Siena. A former 14th-century monastery with a bucolic garden was converted into this exquisite country hotel. Trimmed with fine woods, leather, and traditional prints, rooms are a study in understated luxury and comfort. *$$$$*

Locanda dell'Amorosa, Sinalunga. The "inn" is a stunning high-end hotel in a 14th-century hamlet that includes a small stone church and is approached by a cypress-lined lane. The rooms are repositories for antiques; the bathrooms seem like little sitting rooms. *$$$$*

Relais Fattoria Vignale, Radda in Chianti. Vineyards and plum and olive trees surround this farmhouse lodging. White rooms with wood beams, terra-cotta floors, and classic furniture and rugs recall an English country manor. Dine on Tuscan specialties in the restaurant. *$$$$*

Beacci Tornabuoni, Florence. The definitive Florentine *pensione*, in a 14th-century palazzo, is in the city's swankiest shopping area. Don't miss the view from the terrace. *$$$*

Hotel San Luca, Spoleto. Built to old-world standards, the San Luca prides itself on attention to detail: rooms are spacious, bathrooms are elegant, and an ample breakfast buffet is served in a pretty room facing the central courtyard. *$$$*

Locanda della Posta, Perugia. This is the place, in the center of Perugia's historic district, to pamper yourself in the heart of Umbria. *$$$*

Calcione Country and Castle, Arezzo. You're on a centuries-old family homestead at this sophisticated yet rustic *agriturismo* convenient to Siena, San Gimignano, and Cortona. *$$*

Quintessential Tuscany and Umbria

Piazza del Campo, Siena. This shell-shaped central piazza symbolizes the grace and power of the proud medieval city whose prominence in the banking and wool trades spurred a bitter rivalry with Florence. Have a coffee on the Campo, then climb the Torre del Mangia for unparalleled views of Siena's red roofs and surrounding countryside.

San Gimignano. A guided walk in the nearby countryside is a precious opportunity to explore the Tuscan scenery so appreciated from the windows and ramparts of this medieval town. When you've had your fill, return to San Gimignano to taste the wines and to see its famous towers.

Torre Pendente, Pisa. Yes, the Leaning Tower is touristy, but it's touristy fun. Climb it if you have the energy.

Truffles in Umbria. After a long walk through the narrow, winding streets of an Umbrian town—the air rich with the smell of hearth fires and simmering pots—there's nothing like sitting down to a plate of homemade pasta dressed with the area's prized truffles.

Special Memories

Piazza del Duomo, Spoleto. Descending the stairs toward Spoleto's medieval cathedral, you see the broad piazza flanked by low medieval buildings. It fans out and spills down toward the pale stone sanctuary, which is studded with rose-color windows and mosaics and set against a verdant backdrop of Umbria's hills.

Ponte delle Torri, Spoleto. Spanning the gorge from Spoleto to Monteluco, the 14th-century bridge is an enchanting sight. Make a point of strolling out to its central lookout point and across to the paths along Monteluco, and then return at night to see it majestically lit from below.

San Gimignano. Stand on the steps of the Collegiata church at sunset as the swallows swoop in and out of the famous medieval towers, twittering softly as they coast on the air.

Where Art Comes First

Basilica di San Francesco, Arezzo. A portion of Piero della Francesca's frescoes of *The Legend of the True Cross,* executed on three walls of the choir of this 14th-century church, has been said to exhibit "the most perfect morning light in all Renaissance painting."

Basilica di San Francesco, Assisi. The Giotto fresco cycle illustrating the life of St. Francis is counted among the masterpieces of the Renaissance, and the soaring double basilica, still recovering from damage sustained in a 1997 earthquake, makes them a majestic home.

Cupola, Duomo, Florence. Brunelleschi's dome presides over the neo-Gothic cathedral—and Florence—with powerful dignity and grace. When Florentines are "homesick," they are afflicted with *nostalgia del cupolone* (homesickness for the dome).

Duomo, Orvieto. Few cathedrals can claim masterpieces inside and out, but here you'll find Italy's most perfect Gothic facade matched by the phenomenal intensity and variety of Luca Signorelli's frescoes—among the best in Umbria—in the Cappella di San Brizio.

Galleria degli Uffizi, Florence. One of the world's greatest art collections is housed in this Giorgio Vasari-designed palazzo. Botticelli, Caravaggio, Piero della Francesca, Rembrandt, Raphael—they're all here, along with a rare Michelangelo panel painting, Doni Tondo.

Palazzo Ducale, Urbino. If the Renaissance was, in ideal form, a celebration of the nobility of man and his works, of the light and purity of the soul, then in no other palace in Italy are these tenets better illustrated.

Santa Croce, Florence. The resting place of Michelangelo, Galileo, and Machiavelli also contains the most important art of any church in Florence.

2 FLORENCE

Florence, city of the lily, gave birth to the
Renaissance and changed the way we see
the world. For centuries its wondrous art has
captured the imagination of travelers, who
walk in the footsteps of native sons Dante,
Donatello, Botticelli, and Michelangelo;
a keystone of the Grand Tour in the
18th century, it continues to exert the same
fascination today.

Updated by
Patricia Rucidlo

YOU CANNOT IMAGINE ANY SITUATION more agreeable than Florence," wrote the peripatetic Mary Wortley Montagu in 1740. This agreeable situation called Florence has captured the hearts and minds of just about every visitor who has ever made his or her way here. Florence (Firenze in Italian) casts a spell in the way that few cities can—perhaps because of its sublime art; perhaps because of the views at sunset over the Arno; perhaps because somehow Florentine food and wine delight the palate. Maybe it's because the city hasn't changed all that much since the 16th century. Though Florence was briefly the capital of a newly united Italy (1865–71), its place in the sun rests squarely on its illustrious more-distant past.

Though Florence can lay claim to a modest antique importance, it didn't fully emerge into its own until the 11th century. In the early 1200s, Florence, like most of Italy, was rent by civic unrest. Two factions, the Guelphs and the Ghibellines, competed for power. The Guelphs supported the papacy, and the Ghibellines supported the Holy Roman Empire. Bloody battles—most notably the famous one at Montaperti in 1260—tore Florence and other Italian cities apart. Sometimes the Guelphs were in power and exiled the Ghibellines; at other times, the reverse was true. By the end of the 13th century the Guelphs ruled securely and Ghibellinism had been vanquished. This didn't end civic strife, however: the Guelphs split into the Whites and the Blacks for reasons still debated by historians. Dante, author of *The Divine Comedy,* was banished from Florence in 1301 because he was a White.

Local merchants had organized themselves into guilds by 1250 and in that year proclaimed themselves the *"primo popolo"* ("first people"). It was the first attempt at democratic, republican rule. Though the episode lasted only 10 years, it constituted a breakthrough in Western history. Such a daring stance by the merchant class can be attributed to its newfound power, as Florence was emerging as one of the economic powerhouses in 13th-century Europe. Florentines were papal bankers; they instituted the system of international letters of credit; and the gold florin became the international standard of currency. With this economic strength came a building boom. Public and private palaces, churches, and basilicas were built, enlarged, or restructured. Sculptors such as Donatello and Ghiberti were commissioned to decorate them; painters such as Giotto and Botticelli were commissioned to fresco their walls.

Though ostensibly a republic, Florence was blessed (or cursed, depending on point of view) with one very powerful family, the Medici, who came into power in the 1430s and became the de facto rulers of Florence for several hundred years. The Medici originally came from north of Florence, and it wasn't until the time of Cosimo Il Vecchio (1389–1464) that the family's foothold in Florence was securely established. Florence's golden age occurred during the reign of his grandson Lorenzo de' Medici (1449–92). Lorenzo was not only an astute politician, he was also a highly educated man and a great patron of the arts. Called "Il Magnifico" ("the Magnificent"), he gathered around him poets, artists, philosophers, architects, and musicians and organized all manner of cultural events, festivals, and tournaments.

Lorenzo's son, Piero (1471–1503), proved inept at handling the city's affairs. He was run out of town in 1494, and Florence briefly enjoyed its status as a republic while dominated by the demagogic Dominican friar Girolamo Savonarola (1452–98). Savonarola preached against perceived pagan abuses and convinced his followers to destroy their books, art, women's wigs, and jewelry in public "bonfires of the vanities." Eventually, he so annoyed the pope that he was declared a heretic and hanged.

After a decade of internal unrest, the republic fell and the Medici were recalled to power. But even with the return of the Medici, Florence never regained its former prestige. By the 1530s all the major artistic talent had left the city—Michelangelo, for one, had settled in Rome. The now ineffectual Medici, eventually attaining the title of grand dukes, remained nominally in power until the line died out in 1737, after which time Florence passed from the Austrians to the French and back again until the unification of Italy (1865–70), when it briefly became the capital under King Vittorio Emanuele II (1820–78).

Florence was "discovered" in the 18th century by upper-class northerners making the grand tour. It became a mecca for travelers, particularly the Romantics, who were inspired by the elegance of its *palazzi* and its artistic wealth. Today, millions of modern visitors follow in their footsteps. As the sun sets over the Arno and, as Mark Twain described it, "overwhelms Florence with tides of color that make all the sharp lines dim and faint and turn the solid city to a city of dreams," it's hard not to fall under the city's magic spell.

Pleasures and Pastimes

Dining

Florentines are justifiably proud of their robust food, claiming that it served as the basis for French cuisine when Catherine de' Medici took a battery of Florentine chefs with her after she reluctantly became queen of France in the 16th century. You can sample such specialties as creamy *fegatini* (a chicken-liver spread) and *ribollita* (minestrone thickened with bread and beans and swirled with extra-virgin olive oil) in bustling, convivial *trattorie,* where you share long wooden tables set with paper place mats. Like the Florentines, you can take a break at an *enoteca* (wineshop and/or wine bar) during the day and discover some little-known but excellent Chiantis and Super Tuscans. For general information, *see* Dining *in* Smart Travel Tips A to Z.

Lodging

No stranger to visitors, Florence is equipped with hotels for all budgets, and they are found throughout the city; for instance, you can find both budget and luxury hotels in the *centro storico* (historic center) and along the Arno. Whether you are in an ultraluxe hotel or a more modest establishment, you may have one of the greatest pleasures of all: a room with a view. Florence has so many famous landmarks that it's not hard to find lodging with a panoramic vista. And the equivalent of the genteel *pensioni* of yesteryear still exist, though they are now officially classified as hotels. Usually small and intimate, they often have a quaint appeal that fortunately doesn't preclude modern plumbing.

Shopping

Since the days of the medieval guilds, Florence has been synonymous with fine craftsmanship and good business. Such time-honored Florentine specialties as antiques (and reproductions), bookbinding, jewelry, lace, leather goods, silk, and straw attest to this. More recently, the Pitti fashion shows and the burgeoning textile industry in nearby Prato have added fine clothing to the long list of merchandise available in the shops of Florence. Another medieval feature is the distinct feel of the different shopping areas, a throwback to the days when each district supplied a different product.

EXPLORING FLORENCE

Sightseeing in Florence is easy: everything you want to see is concentrated in the relatively small historic center of the city. But the area packs in so much that you may find yourself slogging from one mind-boggling sight to another and feeling overwhelmed. If you are not an inveterate museum enthusiast, take it easy. Don't try to absorb every painting or fresco that comes into view. There is second-rate art even in the Galleria degli Uffizi and the Palazzo Pitti (*especially* the Pitti), so find some favorites and enjoy them at your leisure.

Walking through the streets and alleyways in Florence is a discovery in itself, but to save time and energy (especially on your third or so day in the city), make use of the efficient bus system. Buses also provide the least fatiguing way to reach Piazzale Michelangelo, San Miniato, and the Forte di Belvedere. It's easy to make excursions to, say, Fiesole or the Medici villas by city bus. Most churches are usually open from 8 or 9 until noon or 12:30 and from 3 or 4 until about 6. The Duomo, luckily, has continuous hours.

In between your blitzes into the Renaissance and beyond, stop to breathe in the city, the marvelous synergy between history and modern Florentine life. Firenze is a living, bustling metropolis that has managed to preserve its predominantly medieval street plan and mostly Renaissance infrastructure while successfully adapting to the insistent demands of 21st-century life. During the 12th and 13th centuries, Florence, like most other Italian towns, was a forest of towers—more than 200 of them, if including the smaller three- and four-story towers. Today only a handful survive, but if you look closely you'll find them as you explore the centro storico.

Numbers in the text correspond to numbers in the margin and on the Florence map.

Great Itineraries

You can see most of Florence's outstanding sights in three days. Plan your day around the opening hours of museums and churches; to gain an edge on the tour groups in high season, go very early in the morning or around closing time. If you can, allow a day to explore each neighborhood.

IF YOU HAVE 3 DAYS

Spend Day 1 exploring Florence's centro storico, which will give you an eyeful of such masterpieces as Ghiberti's bronze doors at the Battistero (these are copies; the originals are in the nearby Museo dell'Opera del Duomo), Giotto's Campanile (bell tower), Brunelleschi's cupola majestically poised atop the Duomo, and Botticelli's mystical *Primavera* and *Birth of Venus* at the Galleria degli Uffizi. On Day 2, wander north of the Duomo and take in the superb treasury of works ranging from Michelangelo's *David* at the Galleria dell'Accademia to the lavish frescoes at the Cappella dei Magi and the Museo di San Marco (don't miss San Lorenzo, Michelangelo's Biblioteca Medicea Laurenziana, and the Cappelle Medicee). On this afternoon (or on the afternoon of Day 3) head southeast to Santa Croce or west to Santa Maria Novella. On the third day, cross the Ponte Vecchio to the Arno's southern bank and explore the Oltrarno, being sure not to miss the Brunelleschi-designed church of Santo Spirito, the frescoes in the church of Santa Maria del Carmine, and the colorful and lively local atmosphere.

IF YOU HAVE 5 DAYS

Break down the tours in the above itinerary into shorter ones, adding a few sights such as Piazzale Michelangelo, halfway up a hill on the

14

Florence

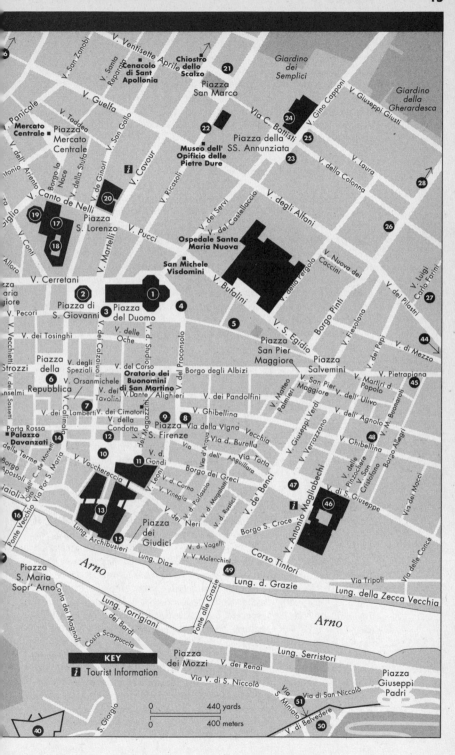

V. Ventisette Aprile
V. San Zanobi
V. Santa Reparata
Cenacolo di Sant Apollonia
Chiostro dello Scalzo
21
Giardino dei Semplici
Piazza San Marco
Giardino della Gherardesca

V. Guelfa
V. San Gallo
Via C. Battisti
V. Gino Capponi
V. Giuseppi Giusti

Mercato Centrale
Piazza Mercato Centrale
V. Taddeo
22
24
25
Piazza della SS. Annunziata
V. Laura
V. della Colonna
28

Museo dell' Opificio delle Pietre Dure
23
i
V. Cavour
V. Ricasoli
V. de Ginori
V. della Stufa

V. Canto de Nelli
20
Piazza S. Lorenzo
V. Pucci
V. dei Servi
V. del Castellaccio
V. degli Alfani
26

19 17
18
V. Martelli
Ospedale Santa Maria Nuova
V. Nuova dei Caccini
V. Luigi Carlo Farini
27
V. dei Pilastri

San Michele Visdomini
V. Cerretani
2
1
V. Bufalini
V. della Pergola
Borgo Pinti
V. Fiesolana

Piazza di S. Giovanni
3
Piazza del Duomo
4
V. delle Oche
V. dello Studio
5
V. S. Egidio
Piazza San Pier Maggiore
V. dei Pepi
V. di Mezzo
44

V. dei Tosinghi
V. dei Calzaioli
V. del Proconsolo
Piazza Salvemini
V. Pietrapiana
45

Piazza della Repubblica
6
V. degli Speziali
V. Orsanmichele
Oratorio dei Buonomini di San Martino
V. del Corso
Borgo degli Albizi
V. San Pier Maggiore
V. Matteo Palmieri
V. Martiri d. Popolo
V. dell' Ulivo

V. dei Tavolini
V.Dante Alighieri
V. dei Pandolfini
V. dell' Agnolo
48
V. M. Buonarroti

7
V. dei Cimatori
V. della Condotta
8
9
V. Ghibellina
V. Giuseppi Verdi
V. Verrazzano
V. Chibellina
Borgo Allegri

Palazzo Davanzati
14
V. dei Lamberti
12
Piazza S. Firenze
Via della Vigna Vecchia
V. delle Pinzochere
V. San Cristofano
Via dei Macci

Porta Rossa
delle Terme
10
11
V. Vacchereccia
V. Leoni
V. d. Gondi
Via d'Acqua
Via d. Burella
Via Torta
V. di S. Giuseppe
46

13
V. d. Corno
V. Vinegia
Borgo dei Greci
V. d. Anguillara
V. de' Benci
47
i
V. Antonio Magliabechi
Via delle Conce

15
Piazza dei Giudici
V. dei Neri
V. d. Magdalotti
V. d. Rustici
Borgo S. Croce
Lung. Archibusieri
V. d. Vagelli
V. V. Malenchini
Corso Tintori

Piazza S. Maria Sopr' Arno
Ponte Vecchio
Arno
Lung. Diaz
49
Lung. d. Grazie
Via Tripoli
Lung. della Zecca Vecchia

Lung. Torrigiani
V. dei Bardi
Costa dei Magnoli
Costa Scarpuccia
Ponte alle Grazie
Arno
Lung. Serristori

KEY
i Tourist Information

Piazza dei Mozzi
V. dei Renai
Via V. di S. Niccolò
Via V. di S. Niccolò
Via S. Miniato
Via di San Niccolò
Piazza Giuseppi Padri
51

0   440 yards
0   400 meters

40
V. di Belvedere
50

Arno's southern bank, and San Miniato—both with expansive views of the city. Climb Giotto's Campanile, which rewards you with sweeping views of the city and hills beyond. If you're feeling more adventurous, climb the narrow, twisting stairs to the top of the Duomo. Take Bus 7 from the station or Piazza del Duomo to enchanting Fiesole. Spend more time in the Galleria degli Uffizi and Bargello or at one of the smaller museums, such as the Museo dell'Opificio delle Pietre Dure, around the corner from the Galleria dell'Accademia. The little-visited but nevertheless wonderful Museo di Storia della Scienza is worth a trip, as is the Museo di Santa Maria Novella.

IF YOU HAVE 8 DAYS

Add an all-day excursion south to Siena or a couple of half-day trips to the Medici villas around Florence. Visit more of Florence's interesting smaller churches; there's a dazzling fresco by Perugino at Santa Maria Maddalena dei Pazzi and a brilliant Pontormo in the Oltrarno's Santa Felicita. On the trail of additional, lesser-known artistic gems, check out Andrea del Castagno's fresco of the *Last Supper* in the former refectory at Sant'Apollonia, northwest of the Museo di San Marco. It's worth the trip to see Andrea del Sarto's stunning grisaille frescoes in the Chiostro dello Scalzo, just north of the Museo di San Marco. The church of Santo Spirito, west of Piazza Pitti, is a fine example of 15th-century architectural rationalism. Take the bus and visit Pontormo's faded but splendid frescoes at the Certosa in Galluzzo, or visit the Museo Stibbert for an excellent window on what high-end collecting meant in the 19th century.

Centro Storico: From the Duomo to the Ponte Vecchio

Florence's centro storico, stretching from the Piazza del Duomo south to the Arno, is just possibly one of the most beautiful spots in the world. Indeed, this relatively small area is home to some powerful artistic treasures. This smorgasbord of churches, medieval towers, Renaissance palaces, and world-class museums and galleries is not only testimony to the artistic and architectural genius of the past millennium but also a shrine to some of the most outstanding aesthetic achievements of Western history.

A Good Walk

Start at the **Duomo** ① and **Battistero** ② and climb the **Campanile** ③ if you wish; then visit the **Museo dell'Opera del Duomo** ④, behind the Duomo. From there, take a quick walk down Via Oriuolo and duck in to the **Museo Firenze Com'era** ⑤. Teeming with maps, many from the 15th century, it gives you a good idea of what Florence looked like during the Renaissance. Exit and retrace your steps to Piazza del Duomo. Go directly south from the Duomo on Via dei Calzaiuoli, turning right on Via degli Speziali for a detour to **Piazza della Repubblica** ⑥ and take Via Orsanmichele to **Orsanmichele** ⑦, or instead go directly south from the Museo dell'Opera del Duomo along Via del Proconsolo to the **Bargello** ⑧, opposite the ancient **Badia Fiorentina** ⑨, restructured in 1285. Head west on Via della Condotta to Via Calzauioli, then south to discover the **Piazza della Signoria** ⑩, with its Loggia dei Lanzi and **Palazzo Vecchio** ⑪. Right on the square is the **Raccolta d'Arte Contemporanea Alberto della Ragione** ⑫. This collection of 20th-century art provides an interesting juxtaposition to the Renaissance. The **Galleria degli Uffizi** ⑬, perhaps Italy's most important art gallery, is at the south side of the piazza. If time permits, walk through the **Corridoio Vasariano.** Exit from the piazza's southwest corner along Via Vaccereccia. To the left, at the corner of Via Por Santa Maria, lined with stores, is the **Mercato Nuovo** ⑭. Follow Via Por

Santa Maria to the river; walk east along the north side of the Arno to Piazza dei Giudici to see the **Museo di Storia della Scienza** ⑮. Backtrack west along the Arno to the **Ponte Vecchio** ⑯.

TIMING

Though much of Florence's centro storico is closed to traffic, you still must dodge mopeds, cyclists, and masses of fellow visitors as you walk the narrow streets, especially in the area bounded by the Duomo, Piazza Signoria, Galleria degli Uffizi, and Ponte Vecchio. It takes about 90 minutes to walk the route, with 45 minutes to 1 hour each for the Museo dell'Opera del Duomo and the Palazzo della Signoria; 1 to 1½ hours for the Bargello; and a minimum of 2 hours for the Uffizi (reserve tickets in advance to avoid long lines). Allot another 45 minutes for the Corridoio Vasariano. The Museo Firenze Com'era can be visited in about half an hour; allow 45 minutes for the Raccolto d'Arte Contemporanea Alberto della Ragione.

Sights to See

⑨ **Badia Fiorentina.** Originally endowed by Willa, Marquess of Tuscany, in 978, this ancient church is an interesting mélange of 13th-century, Renaissance, baroque, and 18th-century architectural refurbishing. Its graceful bell tower, best seen from the interior courtyard, is beautiful for its unusual construction—a hexagonal tower built on a quadrangular base. The interior of the church (open Monday afternoons only) was halfheartedly remodeled in the baroque style during the 17th century. Three tombs by Mino da Fiesole (circa 1430–84) line the walls, including the *monumento funebre di Conte Ugo* (tomb sculpture of Count Ugo), widely regarded as Mino's masterpiece. Executed in 1469–81, it shows Mino at his most lyrical: the faces seem to be lit from within—no small feat in marble. The best-known work of art here is the delicate *Vision of St. Bernard,* by Filippino Lippi (circa 1457–1504), on the left as you enter. The painting—one of Lippi's finest—is in superb condition; note the Virgin Mary's hands, perhaps the most beautifully rendered in the city. On the right side of the church, above the cappella di San Mauro, is a monumental organ dating from 1558. Constructed by Onofrio Zeffirini da Cortona (1510–86), it's largely intact but is missing its 16th-century keyboard. ⊠ *Via Dante Alighieri 4, Bargello neighborhood,* ☎ *055/264402.* 🎫 *Free.* ☉ *Mon. 3–6.*

★ ⑧ **Bargello.** During the Renaissance, this building was headquarters for the *podestà*, or chief magistrate. It also was used as a prison, and the exterior served as a "most wanted" billboard: effigies of notorious criminals and Medici enemies were painted on its walls. Today, it houses the **Museo Nazionale,** home to what is probably the finest collection of Renaissance sculpture in Italy. The concentration of masterworks by Michelangelo (1475–1564), Donatello (circa 1386–1466), and Benvenuto Cellini (1500–71) is remarkable; the works are distributed among an eclectic array of arms, ceramics, and enamels. For Renaissance-art lovers, the Bargello is to sculpture what the Uffizi is to painting.

In 1401 Filippo Brunelleschi (1377–1446) and Lorenzo Ghiberti (circa 1378–1455) competed to earn the most prestigious commission of the day: the decoration of the north doors of the Baptistery in Piazza del Duomo. For the contest, each designed a bronze bas-relief panel depicting the sacrifice of Isaac; the panels are displayed together in the room devoted to the sculpture of Donatello, on the upper floor. The judges chose Ghiberti for the commission; see if you agree with their choice. ⊠ *Via del Proconsolo 4, Bargello neighborhood,* ☎ *055/ 2388606,* WEB *www.arca.net/db/musei/bargello.htm.* 🎫 *€4.10.* ☉ *Daily 8:15–1:50. Closed 2nd and 4th Mon. of month and 1st, 3rd, and 5th Sun. of month.*

★ ❷ **Battistero** (Baptistery). The octagonal Baptistery is one of the supreme monuments of the Italian Romanesque style and one of Florence's oldest structures. Local legend has it that it was once a Roman temple of Mars; modern excavations, however, suggest that its foundations date from the 4th to 5th and the 8th to 9th centuries AD, well after the collapse of the Roman Empire. The round-arched Romanesque decoration on the exterior probably dates from the 11th century. The interior dome mosaics from the beginning of the 14th century are justly renowned, but—glittering beauties though they are—they could never outshine the building's famed bronze Renaissance doors decorated with panels crafted by Lorenzo Ghiberti. The doors—or at least copies of them—on which Ghiberti worked most of his adult life (1403–52) are on the north and east sides of the Baptistery, and the Gothic panels on the south door were designed by Andrea Pisano (active circa 1290–1348) in 1330. The original Ghiberti doors were removed to protect them from the effects of pollution and acid rain and have been beautifully restored; the panels are now on display in the Museo dell'-Opera del Duomo.

Ghiberti's north doors depict scenes from the life of Christ; his later, east doors (dating from 1425–52), facing the Duomo facade, render scenes from the Old Testament. Both merit close examination, for they are very different in style and illustrate the artistic changes that marked the beginning of the Renaissance. Look at the far right panel of the middle row on the earlier (1403–24), north doors (*Jesus Calming the Waters*). Ghiberti here captured the chaos of a storm at sea with great skill and economy, but the artistic conventions he used are basically pre-Renaissance: Jesus is the most important figure, so he is the largest; the disciples are next in size, being next in importance; the ship on which they founder looks like a mere toy.

The exquisitely rendered panels on the east doors are larger, more expansive, more sweeping—and more convincing. The middle panel on the left-hand door tells the story of Jacob and Esau, and the various episodes of the story—the selling of the birthright, Isaac ordering Esau to go hunting, the blessing of Jacob, and so forth—have been merged into a single beautifully realized street scene. Ghiberti's use of perspective suggests depth: the background architecture looks far more credible than on the north-door panels, the figures in the foreground are grouped realistically, and the naturalism and grace of the poses (look at Esau's left leg and the dog next to him) have nothing to do with the sacred message being conveyed. Although the religious content remains, the figures and their place in the natural world are given new prominence and are portrayed with a realism not seen in art since the fall of the Roman Empire more than a thousand years before.

As a footnote to Ghiberti's panels, one small detail of the east doors is worth a special look. Just to the lower left of the Jacob and Esau panel, Ghiberti placed a tiny self-portrait bust. From either side, the portrait is extremely appealing—Ghiberti looks like everyone's favorite uncle—but the bust is carefully placed so that you can make direct eye contact with the tiny head from a single spot. When that contact is made, the impression of intelligent life—of *modern* intelligent life—is astonishing. It's no wonder that these doors received one of the most famous compliments in the history of art from an artist known to be notoriously stingy with praise: Michelangelo declared them so beautiful that they could serve as the Gates of Paradise. ✉ *Piazza del Duomo,* ☎ *055/2302885.* 🎫 *€2.60.* ⊙ *Mon.–Wed. and Fri. 10–7, Thurs. 10–3:20, Sat. 10–4:45 (until 3:30 1st Sat. of month), Sun. 1:30–4:45.*

❸ Campanile. The Gothic bell tower designed by Giotto (1266–1337) is a soaring structure of multicolor marble originally decorated with reliefs that are now in the Museo dell'Opera del Duomo. A climb of 414 steps rewards you with a close-up of Brunelleschi's cupola on the Duomo next door and a sweeping view of the city. ⊠ *Piazza del Duomo,* ☎ *055/2302885,* WEB *www.operaduomo.firenze.it.* 🖃 *€5.15.* ⊙ *Daily 8:30–7:30.*

★ ❶ Duomo (Cattedrale di Santa Maria del Fiore). In 1296 Arnolfo di Cambio (circa 1245–circa 1310) was commissioned to build "the loftiest, most sumptuous edifice human invention could devise" in the Romanesque style on the site of the old church of Santa Reparata. The immense Duomo wasn't completed until 1436, the year it was consecrated. The imposing facade dates only from the 19th century; it was added in the neo-Gothic style to complement Giotto's genuine Gothic 14th-century campanile. The real glory of the Duomo, however, is Filippo Brunelleschi's dome, presiding over the cathedral with a dignity and grace that few domes, even to this day, can match.

Brunelleschi's **cupola** was an ingenious engineering feat. The space to be enclosed by the dome was so large and so high above the ground that traditional methods of dome construction—wooden centering and scaffolding—were of no use. So Brunelleschi developed entirely new building methods, which he implemented with equipment of his own design (including a novel scaffolding method). Beginning work in 1420, he built not one dome but two, one inside the other, and connected them with common ribbing that stretched across the intervening empty space, thereby considerably lessening the crushing weight of the structure. He also employed a new method of bricklaying, based on an ancient Roman herringbone pattern, interlocking each new course of bricks with the course below in a way that made the growing structure self-supporting. The result was one of the great engineering breakthroughs of all time: most of Europe's later domes, including St. Peter's in Rome, were built employing Brunelleschi's methods, and today the Duomo has come to symbolize Florence in the same way that the Eiffel Tower symbolizes Paris. The Florentines are justly proud, and to this day the Florentine phrase for "homesick" is *nostalgia del cupolone* ("homesick for the dome").

The interior is a fine example of Florentine Gothic. Much of the cathedral's best-known art has been moved to the nearby Museo dell'Opera del Duomo. Notable among the works that remain are two towering equestrian frescoes honoring famous soldiers: *Niccolò da Tolentino,* painted in 1456 by Andrea del Castagno (circa 1419–57), and *Sir John Hawkwood,* painted 20 years earlier by Paolo Uccello (1397–1475); both are on the left-hand wall of the nave. A vast and crowded fresco of the *Last Judgment,* painted by Vasari and Zuccaro, covers the dome interior. Originally Brunelleschi wanted mosaics to cover the interior of the great ribbed cupola, but by the time the Florentines got around to commissioning the decoration, 150 years later, tastes had changed. Too bad: it's a fairly dreadful *Last Judgment,* and hardly worth the effort of craning your neck to see it.

You can explore the upper and lower reaches of the cathedral. The remains of a Roman wall and an 11th-century cemetery have been excavated beneath the nave; the way down is near the first pier on the right. The climb to the top of the dome (463 steps) is not for the faint of heart, but the view is superb. ⊠ *Piazza del Duomo,* ☎ *055/2302885,* WEB *www.operaduomo.firenze.it.* 🖃 *Duomo free, excavation €2.60, cupola €5.15.* ⊙ *Crypt: Mon.–Sat. 10–4:45 (1st Sat. of month 10–3:30),*

Sun. 1:30–5. Duomo: Mon.–Wed. and Fri. 10–5, Thurs. 10–5:30, Sat. 10–4:45, Sun. 1:30–4:45. Cupola: Weekdays 8:30–7, Sat. 8:30–4:45.

★ ⑬ **Galleria degli Uffizi.** The venerable Uffizi Gallery occupies the top floor of the U-shape **Palazzo degli Uffizi** (Uffizi Palace) fronting on the Arno, designed by Giorgio Vasari (1511–74) in 1560 to hold the *uffizi* (administrative offices) of the Medici Grand Duke Cosimo I (1519–74). Later, the Medici installed their art collections here, creating what was Europe's first modern museum, open to the public (at first only by request, of course) since 1591. If you're a hard-core museum aficionado, you might want to pick up a complete guide to the collections, sold in bookshops and on newsstands.

Among the collection's highlights are Paolo Uccello's *Battle of San Romano,* its brutal chaos of lances one of the finest visual metaphors for warfare ever captured in paint; the *Madonna and Child with Two Angels,* by Fra Filippo Lippi (1406–69), in which the impudent eye contact established by the foreground angel would have been unthinkable prior to the Renaissance; the *Birth of Venus* and *Primavera* by Sandro Botticelli (1445–1510), the goddess of the former seeming to float on air and the fairy-tale charm of the latter exhibiting the painter's idiosyncratic genius at its zenith; the portraits of the Renaissance duke Federico da Montefeltro and his wife, Battista Sforza, by Piero della Francesca (circa 1420–92); the *Madonna of the Goldfinch,* by Raphael (1483–1520), which, though darkened by time, captures an aching tenderness between mother and child; Michelangelo's *Doni Tondo* (the only panel painting that can be securely attributed to him); *Self-Portrait as an Old Man* by Rembrandt (1606–69); the *Venus of Urbino* by Titian (circa 1485–1576); and the splendid *Bacchus* by Caravaggio (circa 1571–1610). In the last two works, both great paintings, the approaches to myth and sexuality are diametrically opposed, to put it mildly. If panic sets in at the prospect of absorbing all this art at one go, visit in the late afternoon, when it's less crowded. The coffee bar inside has a terrace with a fine close-up view of the Palazzo Vecchio. Advance tickets can be purchased from Consorzio ITA. ⊠ *Piazzale degli Uffizi 6, Piazza della Signoria neighborhood,* ☏ *055/23885. Advance tickets: Consorzio ITA,* ⊠ *Piazza Pitti 1, 50121,* ☏ *055/294883,* WEB *www.uffizi.firenze. it.* ☞ *€7.75 (€1.55 reservation fee).* ⊙ *Tues.–Sun. 8:15–7.*

NEED A BREAK?   **GustaVino** (⊠ Via della Condotta 37/r, Piazza della Signoria neighborhood, ☏ 055/2399806) calls itself an "enoteca with cucina," which means that you can drink and eat. Its handy location (a minute or two from Piazza Signoria) makes it a perfect spot to recover after a trip to the Uffizi.

---

⑭ **Mercato Nuovo** (New Market). This open-air loggia was new in 1551. Beyond its slew of souvenir stands, its main attraction is a copy of Pietro Tacca's bronze *Porcellino* (which translates as "little pig" despite the fact the animal is, in fact, a wild boar) fountain on the south side, dating from around 1612 and copied from an earlier Roman work now in the Uffizi. The Porcellino is Florence's equivalent of the Trevi Fountain: put a coin in his mouth, and if it falls through the grate below (according to one interpretation), it means you'll return to Florence one day. ⊠ *Corner of Via Por Santa Maria and Via Porta Rossa, Piazza della Repubblica neighborhood.* ⊙ *Tues.–Sat. 8–7, Mon. 1–7.*

★ ❹ **Museo dell'Opera del Duomo** (Cathedral Museum). Ghiberti's original Baptistery door panels and the *cantorie* (choir loft) reliefs by Donatello and Luca della Robbia (1400–82) keep company with Donatello's *Mary Magdalen* and Michelangelo's *Pietà* (not to be confused with his more famous *Pietà* in St. Peter's in Rome). Renaissance sculpture is in part defined by its revolutionary realism, but in its palpable suffering, Donatello's *Magdalen* goes beyond realism. Michelangelo's heart-wrenching *Pietà* was unfinished at his death; the female figure supporting the body of Christ on the left was added by one Tiberio Calcagni (1532–65), and never has the difference between competence and genius been manifested so clearly. ✉ *Piazza del Duomo 9, Duomo neighborhood,* ☎ *055/2302885,* WEB *www.operaduomo.firenze.it.* ☑ *€5.15.* ⊙ *Mon.–Sat. 9–7:30, Sun. 9–1:40.*

⑮ **Museo di Storia della Scienza** (Museum of the History of Science). Although it tends to be obscured by the glamour of the neighboring Uffizi, this science museum has much to commend it: Galileo's own instruments, antique armillary spheres—some of them real works of art—and other reminders that the Renaissance made not only artistic but also scientific history. There's also a planetarium you can visit. ✉ *Piazza dei Giudici 1, Piazza della Signoria neighborhood,* ☎ *055/265311,* WEB *www.imss.fi.it.* ☑ *€6.20.* ⊙ *Oct.–May, Mon. and Wed.–Sat. 9:30–5, Tues. 9:30–1, 2nd Sun. of month 10–1; June–Sept., Mon. and Wed.–Fri. 9:30–5, Tues. and Sat. 9:30–1.*

⑤ **Museo Firenze Com'era.** The name of this museum translates as "Florence as it was"; it has prints, paintings, and other exhibits designed to show how Florence looked once upon a time. A diorama renders Roman Florence, of which little remains in the city today. Rooms dedicated to Florence during the Renaissance and later make up the rest of the museum. Of particular interest is any pre-19th century print or painting: check out the unfinished facade of the Duomo and the one of Santa Croce. Also note the sweeping size of various *piazze* and the wide streets—clearly, fantasies and wishful thinking on the part of the artists. ✉ *Via dell'Oriuolo 24, Duomo neighborhood,* ☎ *055/2616545.* ☑ *€2.58.* ⊙ *Fri.–Sat. and Mon.–Wed. 9–2, Sun. 8–1.*

Oratorio dei Buonomini di San Martino. Founded by Antoninus, Bishop of Florence, in 1441 to offer alms to the *poveri vergognosi* (the ashamed poor), this one-room oratory is decorated with 15th-century frescoes by the school of Ghirlandaio that vividly depict the activities of the confraternity. Still in existence today, the confraternity founded by Antoninus (the Compagnia dei Buonuomini, or Confraternity of the Good Men) links the Renaissance, and its notions of charity, very much to the 21st century. ✉ *Piazza San Martino, Bargello neighborhood,* ☎ *no phone.* ☑ *Free.* ⊙ *Mon.–Thurs. and Sat. 10–noon and 3–5, Fri. 10–noon.*

⑦ **Orsanmichele.** This multipurpose structure began as an 8th-century oratory and then in 1290 was turned into an open-air loggia for selling grain. Destroyed by fire in 1304, it was rebuilt as a loggia-market. Between 1367 and 1380 the arcades were closed and two stories added above; finally, at century's end it was turned into a church. Inside is a beautifully detailed 14th-century Gothic tabernacle by Andrea Orcagna (1308–68). The exterior niches contain sculptures dating from the early 1400s to the early 1600s by Donatello and Verrocchio (1435–88), among others, that were paid for by the guilds. Although it is a copy, Verrocchio's *Doubting Thomas* (circa 1470) is particularly deserving of attention. Here you see Christ, like the building's other figures, entirely framed within the niche, and St. Thomas standing on its bottom ledge, with his right foot outside the niche frame. This one detail, the positioning of a single foot, brings the whole composition to life. Most of the sculptures have since been replaced by copies; however, it's possible to see nearly all of them at the **Museo di Orsanmichele** (the museum entrance is on Via Arte della Lana). ✉ *Via dei Calzaiuoli,*

Piazza della Repubblica neighborhood, ☎ *055/284944.* 🎫 *Free.* ☉ *Daily 9–noon and 4–6. Closed 1st and last Mon. of month.*

Palazzo Davanzati. The prestigious Davanzati family owns this 14th-century palace, which has one of the few surviving fresco scenes (to be found in a private palazzo) from this early period of the Renaissance. Because of a long and agonizing restoration, at this writing only the palazzo lobby, with photographs of the restoration process, is open. ⊠ *Piazza Davanzati 13, Piazza della Repubblica neighborhood,* ☎ *055/2388610.* 🎫 *Free.* ☉ *Lobby Tues.–Sun. 9–2.*

⑪ Palazzo Vecchio (Old Palace). Florence's forbidding, fortresslike city hall was begun in 1299, presumably designed by Arnolfo di Cambio, and its massive bulk and towering campanile dominate the Piazza della Signoria. It was built as a meeting place for the heads of the seven major guilds that governed the city at the time; over the centuries it has served lesser purposes, but today it is once again City Hall. The interior courtyard is a good deal less severe, having been remodeled by Michelozzo (1396–1472) in 1453; the copy of Verrocchio's bronze *puttino* (little putto), topping the central fountain, softens the space.

The main attraction is on the second floor: two adjoining rooms that supply one of the most startling contrasts in Florence. The first is the vast **Sala dei Cinquecento** (Room of the Five Hundred), named for the 500-member Great Council, the people's assembly established by Savonarola, that met here. The sala was decorated by Giorgio Vasari, around 1563–65, with huge—almost grotesquely huge—frescoes celebrating Florentine history; depictions of battles with nearby cities predominate. Continuing the martial theme, the sala also contains Michelangelo's *Victory* group, intended for the never-completed tomb of Pope Julius II (1443–1513), plus other sculptures of decidedly lesser quality.

The second room is the little **Studiolo,** to the right of the sala's entrance. The study of Cosimo I's son, the melancholy Francesco I (1541–87), it was designed by Vasari and decorated by Vasari and Bronzino (1503–72). It is intimate, civilized, and filled with complex, questioning, allegorical art. It makes the Sala dei Cinquecento's vainglorious proclamations ring more than a little hollow. ⊠ *Piazza della Signoria,* ☎ *055/ 2768465.* 🎫 *€7.75.* ☉ *Mon.–Wed. and Fri.–Sat. 9–7, Thurs. and Sun. 9–2.*

⑥ Piazza della Repubblica. The square marks the site of the ancient forum that was the core of the original Roman settlement. The street plan in the area around the piazza still reflects the carefully plotted orthogonal grid of the Roman military encampment. The Mercato Vecchio (Old Market), which had been here since the Middle Ages, was demolished and the current piazza was constructed between 1885 and 1895 as a neoclassical showpiece. The piazza is lined with outdoor cafés affording an excellent opportunity for people-watching.

★ ⑩ Piazza della Signoria. This is by far the most striking square in Florence. It was here, in 1497, that the famous "bonfire of the vanities" took place, when the fanatical friar Savonarola induced his followers to hurl their worldly goods into the flames; it was also here, a year later, that he was hanged as a heretic and, ironically, burned. A bronze plaque in the piazza pavement marks the exact spot of his execution.

The statues in the square and in the 14th-century **Loggia dei Lanzi** on the south side vary in quality. Cellini's famous bronze *Perseus* holding the severed head of Medusa is certainly the most important sculpture in the loggia. Other works here include *The Rape of the Sabine* and *Hercules and the Centaur,* both late-16th-century works by Giambologna (1529–1608), and, in the back, a row of sober matrons dating from Roman times. (At this writing, *The Rape of the Sabine* is expected to be moved and replaced with a copy.)

In the square, the Neptune Fountain, from between 1550 and 1575, takes something of a booby prize. It was created by Bartolomeo Ammannati, who considered it a failure himself. The Florentines call it Il Biancone, which may be translated as "the big white man" or "the big white lump." Giambologna's equestrian statue, to the left of the fountain, pays tribute to Grand Duke Cosimo I. Occupying the steps of the Palazzo Vecchio are a copy of Donatello's proud heraldic lion of Florence, the *Marzocco* (the original is now in the Bargello); a copy of Donatello's *Judith and Holofernes* (the original is in the Palazzo Vecchio); a copy of Michelangelo's *David* (the original is in the Galleria dell'Accademia); and Baccio Bandinelli's *Hercules* (1534). The Marzocco, the Judith, and the David were symbols of Florentine civic pride—the latter two had stood up to their oppressors. They provided apt metaphors for the republic-loving Florentines, who often chafed at Medici hegemony.

★ ⑯ **Ponte Vecchio** (Old Bridge). This charmingly simple bridge is to Florence what the Tower Bridge is to London. It was built in 1345 to replace an earlier bridge that was swept away by flood, and its shops housed first butchers, then grocers, blacksmiths, and other merchants. But in 1593 the Medici Grand Duke Ferdinand I (1549–1609), whose private corridor linking the Medici palace (Palazzo Pitti) with the Medici offices (the Uffizi) crossed the bridge atop the shops, decided that all this plebeian commerce under his feet was unseemly. So he threw out the butchers and blacksmiths and installed 41 goldsmiths and eight jewelers. The bridge has been devoted solely to these two trades ever since.

The **Corridoio Vasariano** (✉ Piazzale degli Uffizi 6, Piazza della Signoria neighborhood, ☎ 055/23885 or 055/294883), the private Medici corridor, was built by Vasari in 1565. Though the ostensible reason for its construction was one of security, it was more likely designed so that the Medici wouldn't have to walk amid the commoners. It can be visited by prior special arrangement; morning tours are given Tuesday through Saturday, for €6.20 per person.

Take a moment to study the Ponte Santa Trinita, the next bridge downriver. It was designed by Bartolomeo Ammannati in 1567 (possibly from sketches by Michelangelo), blown up by the retreating Germans during World War II, and painstakingly reconstructed after the war. The view from the Ponte Santa Trinita is beautiful, which might explain why so many young lovers seem to hang out there.

⑫ **Raccolta d'Arte Contemporanea Alberto della Ragione.** If Renaissance-art fatigue has set in, consider this small museum for a change of pace. In 1970, the Genoese Alberto della Ragione donated his collection of contemporary Italian art to the city. There's a not-too-interesting De Chirico (*Les Bains Mysterieux*); a lovely Marini sculpture, *Cavallino* (*Little Horse*), from 1934; and some other lesser-known gems. Works by Felice Casorati, Gino Severini, and Renato Guttoso—preeminent 20th-century artists—are here, as are three lovely paintings by author Carlo Levi, who wrote the heartbreaking *Christ Stopped at Eboli*. ✉ *Piazza della Signoria 5,* ☎ *055/283078.* ▣ *€2.07.* ☉ *Wed.–Mon. 9–1:30.*

San Michele Visdomini. Afficionados of the 16th-century Mannerists should stop in this church, which has a *Sacra Conversazione* by Jacopo Pontormo (1494–1556). An early work, said by Vasari to have been executed on paper, it's in dire need of a cleaning. Its palette is somewhat bereft of the lively colors typically associated with Pontormo. ⊠ *Via dei Servi at Via Bufalini, Duomo neighborhood,* ☏ *055/292448.* ⌨ *Free.* ☉ *Daily 7–noon and 3–6.*

Ospedale Santa Maria Nuova. Folco Portinari, the father of Dante's Beatrice, founded this sprawling complex in 1288. It originally was a hostel for visiting pilgrims and travelers. During the Black Death of 1348, it served as a hospice for those afflicted. At another point, it served as an office where money could be exchanged and deposited and letters could be received; Michelangelo did his banking here. It had been lavishly decorated by the top Florentine artists of the day, but most of the works, such as the frescoes by Domenico Veneziano and Piero della Francesca, have disappeared or been moved to the Uffizi for safekeeping. Today it functions as a hospital in the modern sense of the word, but you can visit the single-nave church of **Sant'Egidio**, in the middle of the complex, where the frescoes would have stood. Imagine, too, Hugo van der Goes's (1435–82) magnificent *Portinari Altarpiece,* which once crowned the high altar; it's now in the Uffizi. Commissioned by Tommaso Portinari, a descendent of Folco, it arrived from Bruges in 1489 and created quite a stir. Bernardo Rossellino's immense marble tabernacle (1450), still in the church, is worth a look. ⊠ *Via Sant'Egidioand Piazza di Santa Maria Nuova, San Lorenzo neighborhood.*

Michelangelo Country: From San Lorenzo to the Accademia

Sculptor, painter, architect, and yes, even poet, native son Michelangelo was a consummate genius. Some of his finest work remains in his hometown. The Biblioteca Medicea Laurenziana is perhaps his most fanciful work of architecture. The key to understanding Michelangelo's genius is in the magnificent Cappelle Medicee, where his sculptural and architectural prowess can be clearly seen. Planned frescoes weren't completed, which is unfortunate because they would have shown in one space the artistic triple threat that he certainly was. The towering and beautiful *David,* his most famous work, resides in the Galleria dell'Accademia.

A Good Walk

Start at the church of **San Lorenzo** ⑰, visiting the **Biblioteca Medicea Laurenziana** ⑱ and its famous anteroom before circling the church to the northwest and making your way through the San Lorenzo outdoor market on Via del Canto de' Nelli to the entrance of the **Cappelle Medicee** ⑲. Retrace your steps through the market and take Via dei Gori east to Via Cavour and the **Palazzo Medici-Riccardi** ⑳, once the home of Florence's most important family throughout the Renaissance. Follow Via Cavour two blocks north to Piazza San Marco and the church of the same name, attached to which is the **Museo di San Marco** ㉑; it houses marvelous works by the pious and exceptionally talented painter–friar Fra Angelico. If you have time, go northwest from Piazza San Marco to see Castagno's *Last Supper* at Sant'Apollonia and then north to the Chiostro dello Scalzo. From Piazza San Marco, walk a half block south on Via Ricasoli (which runs back toward the Duomo) to the **Galleria dell'Accademia** ㉒. Return to the east side of Piazza San Marco and take Via Cesare Battisti east into Piazza della Santissima Annunziata, one of Florence's prettiest squares, site of the **Spedale degli Innocenti** ㉓ and, at the north end of the square, the church of **Santissima Annunziata** ㉔. The Pinacoteca at the Spedale degli Innocenti is worth a quick look: Domenico Ghirlandaio's 1488 *Adorazione dei Magi* is particularly lovely. One block southeast of the entrance to Santissima Annunziata, through the arch and on the left side of Via della Colonna, is the **Museo Archeologico** ㉕. Continue down Via della Colonna to **Santa Maria Maddalena dei Pazzi** ㉖, which harbors a superb fresco by Perugino. Return to Via della Colonna and continue heading southeast; take a right on Via Luigi Carlo Farini, where you'll find the **Sinagoga** ㉗ and its Museo Ebraico. Take a break and have a Mediterranean-kosher lunch at Ruth's or stop at a trattoria. Another option is a picnic lunch in Piazza d'Azeglio, a small but delightful park minutes from the Sinagoga. Retrace your steps on Via Luigi Carlo Farini. The park begins at the corner of Via Farini and Via della Colonna. After lunch, visit the **Cimitero dei Protestanti** ㉘, where you may pay your respects at the tomb of Elizabeth Barrett Browning.

TIMING

The walk alone takes about 1½ hours, plus 45 minutes for the Cappelle Medicee, 20 minutes for the Palazzo Medici-Riccardi, 40 minutes for the Museo di San Marco, 30 minutes for the Galleria dell'Accademia (*David*), and 40 minutes for the Museo Archeologico. Note that the Museo di San Marco closes at 1:50 on weekdays. The Cimitero dei Protestanti can be visited in under half an hour. After visiting San Lorenzo, resist the temptation to explore the market that surrounds the church before going to the Palazzo Medici-Riccardi; the market is open until 7 PM, so you can come back later, when the churches and museums have closed.

Sights to See

⑱ **Biblioteca Medicea Laurenziana** (Laurentian Library). Michelangelo the architect was every bit as original as Michelangelo the sculptor. Unlike Brunelleschi (the architect of San Lorenzo), however, he wasn't obsessed with proportion and perfect geometry. He was interested in experimentation and invention and in the expression of a personal vision at times highly idiosyncratic.

It was never more idiosyncratic than in the Laurentian Library, begun in 1524 and finished in 1568, and its famous **vestibolo.** This strangely shaped anteroom has had scholars scratching their heads for centuries. In a space more than two stories high, why did Michelangelo limit his use of columns and pilasters to the upper two-thirds of the wall? Why didn't he rest them on strong pedestals instead of on huge, decorative curlicue scrolls, which rob them of all visual support? Why did he recess them into the wall, which makes them look weaker still? The architectural elements here do not stand firm and strong and tall, as inside San Lorenzo, next door; instead, they seem to be pressed into the wall as if into putty, giving the room a soft, rubbery look that is one of the strangest effects ever achieved by classical architecture. It's almost as if Michelangelo purposely set out to defy his predecessors—intentionally flouting the conventions of the High Renaissance in order to see what kind of bizarre, mannered effect might result. His innovations were tremendously influential and produced a period of architectural experimentation, known as mannerism, that eventually evolved into the baroque. As his contemporary Giorgio Vasari put it, "Artisans have been infinitely and perpetually indebted to him because he broke the bonds and chains of a way of working that had become habitual by common usage."

The anteroom's staircase (best viewed head-on), which emerges from the library with the visual force of an unstoppable lava flow, has been exempted from the criticism, however. In its highly sculptural conception and execution, it is quite simply one of the most original and fluid staircases in the world. ✉ *Piazza San Lorenzo 9 (entrance to the left of*

San Lorenzo), San Lorenzo neighborhood, ☎ *055/213440.* ▣ *Free.*
🕑 *Mon.–Sat. 8:30–1.*

★ ⑲ **Cappelle Medicee** (Medici Chapels). This magnificent complex includes the **Cappella dei Principi,** the Medici chapel and mausoleum that
was begun in 1605 and kept marble workers busy for several hundred
years, and the **Sagrestia Nuova** (New Sacristy), designed by Michelangelo and so called to distinguish it from Brunelleschi's Sagrestia Vecchia (Old Sacristy) in San Lorenzo.

Michelangelo received the commission for the New Sacristy in 1520
from Cardinal Giulio de' Medici (1478–1534), who later became Pope
Clement VII and who wanted a new burial chapel for his cousins Giuliano (1478–1534) and Lorenzo (1492–1519). The result was a tour
de force of architecture and sculpture. Architecturally, Michelangelo
was as original and inventive here as ever, but it is, quite properly, the
powerful sculptural compositions of the side-wall tombs that dominate the room. The scheme is allegorical: on the wall tomb to the right
are figures representing Day and Night, and on the wall tomb to the
left are figures representing Dawn and Dusk; above them are idealized
sculptures of the two men, usually interpreted to represent the active
life and the contemplative life. But the allegorical meanings are secondary; what is most important is the intense presence of the sculptural figures, the force with which they hit the viewer. Michelangelo's
contemporaries were so awed by this force (in his sculpture here and
elsewhere) that they invented a word to describe the phenomenon: *ter-
ribilità* (dreadfulness). To this day it's used only when describing his
work, and it is in evidence here at the peak of its power. During his
stormy relations with the Medici, Michelangelo once hid out in a tiny
subterranean room that is accessed from the left of the altar. Ever the
artist, he drew charcoal sketches on the wall. If you want to see them,
tell the ticket vendor and reserve: admission is on the hour at 9, 10,
11, and noon and is limited to 12 people per hour. Your chance of getting in is better if you try for one of the earlier times. ✉ *Piazza di
Madonna degli Aldobrandini, San Lorenzo neighborhood,* ☎ *055/
2948832.* ▣ *€5.70.* 🕑 *Daily 8:15–5. Closed 1st, 3rd, and 5th Mon.
and 2nd and 4th Sun. of month.*

Cenacolo di Sant'Apollonia. The frescoes of the refectory of a former
Benedictine nunnery were painted in sinewy style by Andrea del
Castagno, a follower of Masaccio (1401–28). The *Last Supper* is a powerful version of this typical refectory theme. From the entrance, walk
around the corner to Via San Gallo 25 and take a peek at the lovely
15th-century cloister that belonged to the same monastery but is now
part of the University of Florence. ✉ *Via XXVII Aprile 1, San Marco
neighborhood,* ☎ *055/2388607.* 🕑 *Daily 8:30–1:50. Closed 1st, 3rd,
and 5th Sun. and 2nd and 4th Mon. of month.*

OFF THE
BEATEN PATH

CHIOSTRO DELLO SCALZO – Often overlooked, this small, peaceful 16th-
century cloister was frescoed in grisaille by Andrea del Sarto (1486–
1530), with scenes from the life of St. John the Baptist, Florence's patron
saint. ✉ *Via Cavour 69, San Marco neighborhood,* ☎ *055/2388604.*
🕑 *Mon., Thurs., and Sat. 8:15–1:50.*

㉘ **Cimitero dei Protestanti.** Formally known as the Cemetery of the Protestants but more familiarly known as the Cimitero degli Inglesi, or English Cemetery, this final resting place for some 1,400 souls was designed
in 1828 by Carlo Reishammer for the Swiss community in Florence.
Just outside Florence's 14th-century walls (no longer visible), the cemetery grew to accommodate other foreigners (read Protestants) living in

Florence. Its most famous resident is probably Elizabeth Barrett Browning (1809–61), who spent the last 15 years of her life in the city. Other expats, including Arthur Clough, Walter Savage Landor, Frances Trollope (mother of Anthony), and the American preacher Theodore Parker are buried in this cemetery, also referred to as the "Island of the Dead." (Swiss painter Arnold Böcklin [1827–1901] used the cemetery as inspiration for his haunting painting, *Island of the Dead*.) ⊠ *Piazzale Donatello 38, Santa Croce neighborhood,* ☎ *055/582608.* ⊡ *Free; donation requested from groups.* ☉ *Mon. 9–noon, Tues.–Fri. 3–6.*

★ ㉒ **Galleria dell'Accademia** (Accademia Gallery). The collection of Florentine paintings, dating from the 13th to the 18th centuries, is largely unremarkable, but the sculptures by Michelangelo are worth the price of admission. The unfinished *Slaves,* fighting their way out of their marble prisons, were meant for the tomb of Michelangelo's overly demanding patron Pope Julius II (1443–1513). But the focal point is the original *David,* moved here from Piazza della Signoria in 1873. *David* was commissioned in 1501 by the Opera del Duomo (Cathedral Works Committee), which gave the 26-year-old sculptor a leftover block of marble that had been ruined by another artist. Michelangelo's success with the block was so dramatic that the city showered him with honors, and the Opera del Duomo voted to build him a house and a studio in which to live and work.

Today *David* is beset not by Goliath but by tourists, and seeing the statue at all—much less really studying it—can be a trial. A Plexiglass barrier surrounds it, following a 1991 attack upon the sculpture by a hammer-wielding artist who, luckily, inflicted only a few minor nicks on the toes. The statue is not quite what it seems. It is so poised and graceful and alert—so miraculously alive—that it is often considered the definitive embodiment of the ideals of the High Renaissance in sculpture. But its true place in the history of art is a bit more complicated.

As Michelangelo well knew, the Renaissance painting and sculpture that preceded his work were deeply concerned with ideal form. Perfection of proportion was the ever-sought Holy Grail; during the Renaissance, ideal proportion was equated with ideal beauty, and ideal beauty was equated with spiritual perfection. But *David,* despite its supremely calm and dignified pose, departs from these ideals. Michelangelo didn't give the statue perfect proportions. The head is slightly too large for the body, the arms are too large for the torso, and the hands are dramatically large for the arms. The work was originally commissioned to adorn the facade of the Duomo and was intended to be seen from a distance and on high. Michelangelo knew exactly what he was doing, calculating that the perspective of the viewer would be such that, in order for the statue to appear proportioned, the upper body, head, and arms would have to be bigger as they are farther away from the viewer's line of vision. But he also did it to express and embody, as powerfully as possible in a single figure, an entire biblical story. David's hands *are* big, but so was Goliath, and these are the hands that slew him. Save yourself a long and tiresome wait in line by reserving tickets in advance. ⊠ *Via Ricasoli 60, San Marco neighborhood,* ☎ *055/294883 reservations; 055/2388609 gallery.* ⊡ *€7.75.* ☉ *Tues.–Sun. 8:15–6:50.*

Giardino dei Semplici. Created by Cosimo I in 1550, this delightful garden was designed by favorite Medici architect Niccolò Tribolo. Many of the plants here have been grown since the 16th century. Springtime, especially May, is a particularly beautiful time to visit, as multitudes of azaleas create a riot of color. ⊠ *Via Pier Micheli 3, San Marco neighborhood,* ☎ *055/2757402.* ⊡ *€3.* ☉ *Weekdays 9–1.*

Mercato Centrale. Some of the food at this huge, two-story market hall is remarkably exotic. The ground floor contains meat and cheese stalls, as well as some very good bars that offer nice *panini* (sandwiches), and the second floor teems with vegetable stands. If you're looking for an exotic ingredient in Florence, this is where you're most likely to find it. ⊠ *Piazza del Mercato Centrale, San Lorenzo neighborhood,* ☎ *no phone.* ⊘ *Daily 7–2.*

㉕ **Museo Archeologico** (Archaeological Museum). Of the Etruscan, Egyptian, and Greco-Roman antiquities here, the Etruscan collection is particularly notable—one of the largest in Italy. The famous bronze *Chimera* was discovered (without the tail, a reconstruction) in the 16th century. ⊠ *Via della Colonna 38, Santissima Annunziata neighborhood,* ☎ *055/23575.* ⊡ *€4.10.* ⊘ *Mon. 2–7, Tues. and Thurs. 8:30– 7, Wed. and Fri.–Sun. 8:30–2.*

Museo dell' Opificio delle Pietre Dure. Adjacent to this fascinating small museum is an Opificio, or workshop, that Ferdinand I established in 1588 to train craftsmen in the art of working with precious and semiprecious stones and marble (*pietre dure* is hard stone). Four hundred–plus years later, the workshop is renowned as a center for the restoration of mosaics and inlays in semiprecious stones. The museum is highly informative and includes some magnificent antique examples of this highly specialized and beautiful craft. ⊠ *Via degli Alfani 78, San Marco neighborhood,* ☎ *055/27511.* ⊡ *€2.10.* ⊘ *Mon. and Wed. and Fri.–Sat. 8:15–2, Thurs. 8:15–7.*

㉑ **Museo di San Marco.** A former Dominican convent adjacent to the church of San Marco now houses this museum, which contains many stunning works by Fra Angelico (circa 1400–55), the Dominican friar famous for his piety as well as for his painting. When the friars' cells were restructured between 1439 and 1444, he decorated many of them with frescoes meant to spur religious contemplation. His paintings are simple and direct and furnish a compelling contrast to those in the Palazzo Medici-Riccardi chapel. Whereas Gozzoli's frescoes celebrate the splendors of the Medici, Fra Angelico's exalt the simple beauties of the contemplative life. Fra Angelico's works are everywhere, from the friars' cells to the superb panel paintings on view in the museum. Don't miss the famous *Annunciation,* on the upper floor, and the works in the gallery just off the cloister as you enter. Here you can see his beautiful *Last Judgment*; as usual, the tortures of the damned are far more inventive and interesting than the pleasures of the redeemed. ⊠ *Piazza San Marco 1, San Marco neighborhood,* ☎ *055/2388608.* ⊡ *€4.10.* ⊘ *Weekdays 8:15–1:50, weekends 8:15–6:50. Closed 1st, 3rd, and 5th Sun. and 2nd, and 4th Mon. of month.*

★ ⑳ **Palazzo Medici-Riccardi.** The main attraction of this palace, begun in 1444 by Michelozzo for Cosimo de' Medici, is the interior chapel, the so-called **Cappella dei Magi** on the upper floor. Painted on its walls is Benozzo Gozzoli's famous *Procession of the Magi,* finished in 1460 and celebrating both the birth of Christ and the greatness of the Medici family. Like his contemporary Ghirlandaio, Gozzoli wasn't a revolutionary painter and today is considered not quite first rate, because of his technique, which was old-fashioned even for his day. Gozzoli's gift, however, was for entrancing the eye, not challenging the mind, and on those terms his success here is beyond question. The paintings are full of activity yet somehow frozen in time in a way that fails utterly as realism but succeeds triumphantly as soon as the demand for realism is set aside. Entering the chapel is like walking into the middle of a magnificently illustrated children's storybook, and this beauty makes it one of the most enjoyable rooms in the city. ⊠ *Via Cavour 1, San Lorenzo neighborhood,* ☎ *055/2760340.* ⊞ *€4.* ☉ *Thurs.–Tues. 9–7.*

⑰ San Lorenzo. The facade of this church was never finished. Filippo Brunelleschi designed the interior of San Lorenzo, like that of Santo Spirito on the other side of the Arno, in the early 15th century. The two interiors are similar in design and effect and proclaim with ringing clarity the beginning of the Renaissance in architecture. San Lorenzo, however, has a grid of dark, inlaid marble lines on the floor, which considerably heightens the dramatic effect. The grid makes the rigorous geometry of the interior immediately visible and is an illuminating lesson on the laws of perspective. If you stand in the middle of the nave at the church entrance, on the line that stretches to the high altar, every element in the church—the grid, the nave columns, the side aisles, the coffered nave ceiling—seems to march inexorably toward a hypothetical vanishing point beyond the high altar, exactly as in a single-point-perspective painting. Brunelleschi's **Sagrestia Vecchia** (Old Sacristy) has stucco decorations by Donatello; it's at the end of the left transept. ⊠ *Piazza San Lorenzo, San Lorenzo neighborhood,* ☎ *055/2728487.* ⊞ *€2.60.* ☉ *Mon.–Sat. 7–noon and 3:30–5:30, Sun. 3:30–5.*

㉖ Santa Maria Maddalena dei Pazzi. One of Florence's hidden treasures, a cool and composed *Crucifixion* by Perugino (circa 1445/50–1523), is in the chapter house of the monastery below this church. Here you can see the Virgin Mary and St. John the Evangelist with Mary Magdalen and Sts. Benedict and Bernard of Clairvaux posed against a simple but haunting landscape. The figure of Christ crucified occupies the center of this brilliantly hued fresco. Perugino's colors radiate—note the juxtaposition of the yellow-green cuff against the orange tones of the Magdalen's robe. ⊠ *Borgo Pinti 58, Santa Croce neighborhood,* ☎ *055/2478420.* ⊞ *Donation requested.* ☉ *Weekdays 9–noon, 5–5:20, 6:10–7; Sat. 5–6:20, Sun. 9–10:45 and 3–6:50.*

㉔ Santissima Annunziata. Dating from the mid-13th century, this church was restructured in 1447 by Michelozzo, who gave it an uncommon (and lovely) entrance cloister with frescoes by Andrea del Sarto (1486–1530), Pontormo (1494–1556), and Rosso Fiorentino (1494–1540). The interior is a rarity for Florence: a sumptuous example of the baroque. But it's not really a fair example, because it's merely 17th-century baroque decoration applied willy-nilly to an earlier structure—exactly the sort of violent remodeling exercise that has given the baroque a bad name. The **Cappella dell'Annunziata**, immediately inside the entrance to the left, illustrates the point. The lower half, with its stately Corinthian columns and carved frieze bearing the Medici arms, was commissioned by Piero de' Medici in 1447; the upper half, with its erupting curves and impish sculpted cherubs, was added 200 years later. Each is effective in its own way, but together they serve only to prove that dignity is rarely comfortable wearing a party hat. Fifteenth-century-fresco enthusiasts should also note the very fine Holy Trinity with St. Jerome in the second chapel on the left. Done by Andrea del Castagno (circa 1421–57), it shows a wiry and emaciated St. Jerome with Paula and Eustochium, two of his closest followers. ⊠ *Piazza di Santissima Annunziata,* ☎ *055/2398034.* ☉ *Daily 7–12:30 and 4–6:30.*

㉗ Sinagoga. Jews were well settled in Florence by 1396, when the first money-lending operations became officially sanctioned. Medici patronage helped Jewish banking houses to flourish, but by 1570 Jews were required to live within the large "ghetto," near today's Piazza della Repubblica, by the decree of Cosimo I, who had cut a deal with Pope Pius V (1504–72): in exchange for ghettoizing the Jews, he would receive the title of Grand Duke of Tuscany.

Construction of the modern Moorish-style synagogue, set in its lovely garden, began in 1874 as a bequest of David Levi, who wished to endow a synagogue "worthy of the city." Falcini, Micheli, and Treves designed the building on a domed Greek cross plan with galleries in the transept and a roofline bearing three distinctive copper cupolas visible from all over Florence. The exterior has alternating bands of tan travertine and pink granite, reflecting an Islamic style repeated in Giovanni Panti's ornate interior. Of particular interest are the cast-iron gates by Pasquale Franci, the eternal light by Francesco Morini, and the Murano glass mosaics by Giacomo dal Medico. The gilded doors of the Moorish ark, which fronts the pulpit and is flanked by extravagant candelabra, are decorated with symbols of the ancient Temple of Jerusalem and bear bayonet marks from vandals. The synagogue was used as a garage by the Nazis, who failed to inflict much damage in spite of an attempt to blow up the place with dynamite. Only the columns on the left side were destroyed, and, even then, the Women's Balcony above did not collapse. Note the Star of David in black and yellow marble inlaid in the floor. The original capitals can be seen in the garden.

Some of the oldest and most beautiful Jewish ritual artifacts in all of Europe are displayed in the small **Museo Ebraico,** upstairs. Exhibits document the Florentine Jewish community and the building of the synagogue. The donated objects all belonged to local families and date from as early as the late 16th century. Take special note of the exquisite needlework and silver items. A small but well-stocked gift shop is downstairs. ✉ *Via Farini 4, Santa Croce neighborhood,* ☎ *055/2346654.* ▣ *€3.10.* ☺ *Apr.–Oct., Sun.–Thurs. 10–5, Fri. 10–1; Nov.–Mar., Sun.–Thurs. 10–1 and 3–5, Fri. 10–1. English-guided tours 10:10, 11, noon, 1, 2.*

NEED A
BREAK?   **Ruth's** (✉ Via Farini 2/a, Santa Croce neighborhood, ☎ 055/ 2480888), adjacent to Florence's synagogue, is the only kosher–vegetarian restaurant in Tuscany. On the menu: inexpensive vegetarian and Mediterranean dishes and a large selection of kosher wines. It's closed for Friday dinner and Saturday lunch.

㉓ **Spedale degli Innocenti.** Built by Brunelleschi in 1419 to serve as a foundling hospital, it takes the historical prize as the very first Renaissance building. Brunelleschi designed its portico with his usual rigor, building it out of the two shapes he considered mathematically (and therefore philosophically and aesthetically) perfect: the square and the circle. Below the level of the arches, the portico encloses a row of perfect cubes; above the level of the arches, the portico encloses a row of intersecting hemispheres. The entire geometric scheme is articulated with Corinthian columns, capitals, and arches borrowed directly from antiquity. At the time he designed the portico, Brunelleschi was also designing the interior of San Lorenzo, using the same basic ideas. But because the portico was finished before San Lorenzo, the Spedale degli Innocenti can claim the honor of ushering in Renaissance architecture. The 10 ceramic medallions depicting swaddled infants that decorate the portico are by Andrea della Robbia (1435–1525/28), done in about 1487.

Within the Spedale degli Innocenti is the **Pinacoteca,** a small museum. Most of the objects are minor works by major artists, but well worth a look is Domenico Ghirlandaio's (1449–94) *Adorazione dei Magi (Adoration of the Magi)*, executed in 1488. His use of color, and his eye for flora and fauna, shows that art from north of the Alps made a great impression on him. The museum is open Thursday through Tuesday 8:30–2; admission is €2.60. ✉ *Piazza di Santissima Annunziata 1, Santissima Annunziata neighborhood,* ☎ *055/2491708 Pinacoteca.*

Santa Maria Novella to the Arno

Piazza Santa Maria Novella is near the train station, and like similar areas in many other European cities, it is marked by a degree of squalor, especially at night. Nevertheless, the streets in and around the piazza have their share of architectural treasures, including some of Florence's most tasteful palazzi.

A Good Tour

Start in the Piazza Santa Maria Novella, its north side dominated by the church of **Santa Maria Novella** ㉙; then take Via delle Belle Donne, which leads from the east side of the piazza to a minuscule square, at the center of which stands a curious shrine known as the Croce al Trebbio. Take Via del Trebbio east and turn right onto Via Tornabuoni, Florence's finest shopping street. At the intersection of Via Tornabuoni and Via Strozzi is the overwhelming **Palazzo Strozzi** ㉚. If you want a dose of contemporary art, head straight down Via della Spada to the **Museo Marino Marini** ㉛. One block west from Via Tornabuoni and Palazzo Strozzi, down Via della Vigna Nuova, is Leon Battista Alberti's ground-breaking **Palazzo Rucellai** ㉜. Follow the narrow street opposite the palazzo (Via del Purgatorio) east almost to its end; then zigzag right and left, turning east on Via Parione to reach Piazza di Santa Trinita, where, in the middle, stands the **Colonna della Giustizia** ㉝. Halfway down the block to the south (toward the Arno) is the church of **Santa Trinita** ㉞, home to Ghirlandaio's glowing frescoes. Then go east on Borgo Santi Apostoli, a typical medieval street flanked by tower houses, and take a right on Via Por Santa Maria to get to the Ponte Vecchio. Alternatively, walk from Piazza Santa Trinita to Ponte Santa Trinita, which leads into the Oltrarno neighborhood. If you want to detour to **Le Cascine** ㉟, head for the Ponte Vecchio but don't cross it; instead make a right and walk along the Arno to the entrance of the park. Another option is to head up Via Tornabuoni toward the station at Santa Maria Novella, making a left at Via Spada and a right onto Via delle Belle Donne. At the station, take Bus 4 to the **Museo Stibbert** ㊱.

TIMING

The walk takes about 30 minutes, plus 30 minutes for Santa Maria Novella and 15 minutes for Santa Trinita. A visit to the Santa Maria Novella museum and cloister takes about 30 minutes. If you decide to include a trip to the Cascine, add another hour for walking and picnicking. Allow about 2½ hours to get to Museo Stibbert and to visit its collection.

Sights to See

OFF THE BEATEN PATH

CENACOLO DI FOLIGNO – This delightful *Last Supper,* executed sometime in the 1470s, variously has been attributed to Perugino or to one of his followers. Its placement, at the end of a long room—the former refectory for a group of nuns—is simply breathtaking; because the white walls are otherwise unadorned, the fresco packs quite a visual punch. In the middle of the lunette in the upper center, Christ appears in the Garden of Gethsemane with the sleeping apostles. The delicate brush strokes of the leaves in the trees are exquisite. Judas, as is typical of so many representations of the Last Supper, is shown seated at the other side of the table quite apart from the other eleven apostles. Note how the artist has carefully labeled each apostle except for Judas. The tondi surrounding the fresco show portraits of prominent Franciscans such as St. Anthony of Padua, Francis of Assisi, St. Bernard of Siena, and St. Louis of Toulouse. ✉ *Via Faenza 42, Santa Maria Novella neighborhood,* ☎ *055/286982.* 🎟 *Free.* ◷ *Mon.–Tues. and Sat. 9–noon.*

③ **Colonna della Giustizia.** In the center of **Piazza Santa Trinita** is this column from Rome's Terme di Caracalla, given to the Medici Grand Duke Cosimo I by Pope Pius IV in 1560. Typical of Medici self-assurance, the name translates as the Column of Justice. The column was raised here by Cosimo in 1565 to mark the spot where he heard the news that Florentine ducal forces had prevailed over a ragtag army composed of Florentine republican exiles and their French allies at the 1554 battle of Marciano near Prato; the victory made his power in Florence all but absolute. ⊠ *Piazza Santa Trinita, Santa Maria Novella neighborhood.*

Croce al Trebbio. In 1338 the Dominican friars (the Dominican church of Santa Maria Novella is just down the street) erected this little granite column near Piazza Santa Maria Novella to commemorate a famous local victory: it was here in 1244 that they defeated their avowed enemies, the Patarene heretics, in a bloody street brawl. ⊠ *Via del Trebbio, Santa Maria Novella neighborhood.* .

③ **Le Cascine.** In the 16th century this vast park belonged to the Medici, who allegedly used it for hunting, one of their favorite pastimes. It was opened to the public in the 19th century. The park runs for nearly ·3 km (2 mi) along the Arno and has roughly 291 acres. It's ideal for strolling on nice days, and there are paths for jogging, allées perfect for biking, grassy fields for picnicking, and lots of space for rollerblading (as well as a place to rent skates). At the northern tip of the park is the **piazzaletto dell'Indiano,** an oddly moving monument dedicated to Rajaram Cuttraputti, Marajah of Kolepoor, who died in Florence in 1870. The park hosts sports enthusiasts, a weekly open-air market, and discotheques. But be warned: at night, there's a booming sex-for-sale trade. ⊠ *Main entrance: Piazza Vittorio Veneto, Viale Fratelli Roselli (at the Ponte della Vittoria).*

③ **Museo Marino Marini.** A 21-ft-tall bronze horse and rider, one of the major works by artist Marini (1901–80), dominates the space of the main gallery here. The museum itself is an eruption of contemporary space in a deconsecrated 9th-century church, designed with a series of open stairways, walkways, and balconies that allow you to peer at Marini's work from all angles. In addition to his Etruscanesque sculpture, the museum houses Marini's paintings, drawings, and engravings. ⊠ *Piazza San Pancrazio, Santa Maria Novella neighborhood,* ☎ *055/219432.* ☑ *€4.10.* ☼ *Oct.– May, Mon. and Wed.–Sat. 10–5, Sun. 10–1; June–Sept., Mon. and Wed.– Sat. 10–5, Thurs. 10–11:30, Sun. 10–1.*

Museo Salvatore Ferragamo. If a temple for footwear existed, it would be here. The shoes in this finely arranged collection were designed by Salvatore Ferragamo (1898–1960) beginning in the early 20th century; they are elegant and the presentation dramatic. Born in southern Italy, the late master jump-started his career in Hollywood by creating shoes for the likes of Mary Pickford and Rudolph Valentino. He then returned to Florence and set up shop here, in the 13th-century Palazzo Spini Ferroni. The collection includes about 10,000 shoes, and those exhibited are frequently rotated. ⊠ *Via dei Tornabuoni 2, Santa Maria Novella neighborhood,* ☎ *055/3360456.* ☑ *Free.* ☼ *Weekdays 9–1 and 2–6.*

③ **Museo Stibbert.** Federico Stibbert (1838–1906), born in Florence to an Italian mother and an English father, liked to collect things. Over a lifetime of doing so, he amassed some 50,000 objects. This museum, which also was his home, displays many of them. He had a fascination with medieval armor and also collected costumes, particularly Uzbek costumes, which are exhibited in a room called the Moresque Hall. These are mingled with an extensive array of swords, guns, and other devices whose sole function was to kill people. The paintings, most of which date to the 15th century, largely are second rate. The house itself is an interesting amalgam of neo-Gothic, Renaissance, and English eccentric. To get here, take Bus 4 from the station at Santa Maria Novella, get off at the stop marked FABBRONI 4 and follow signs to the museum. ⊠ *Via Federico Stibbert 26,* ☎ *055/47552086049.* ▣ *€5.* ⊘ *Mon.– Wed. 10–2; Fri.–Sun. 10–6. Tours every half hr.*

Ognissanti. The Umiliati owned this hodgepodge of a church before the Franciscans took it over in the mid-16th century. (They were ousted in 2001 and replaced by another order.) Beyond the fanciful baroque facade by Matteo Nigetti (1560–1649) are a couple of wonderful 15th-century gems. On the right nave is *Madonna della Misericordia* by Ghirlandaio; a little farther down is Botticelli's *St. Augustine in His Study.* A companion piece, directly across the way, is Ghirlandaio's *St. Jerome.* Pass through the rather dreadfully frescoed cloister to check out Ghirlandaio's superb *Last Supper*—which proves definitively that Leonardo da Vinci was not the only Tuscan painter who could do them well. ⊠ *Piazza Ognissanti, Santa Maria Novella neighborhood,* ☎ *055/ 2398700.* ▣ *Free.* ⊘ *Church daily 7–noon and 3–6; Last Supper Mon.–Tues. and Sat. 9–noon.*

㉜ Palazzo Rucellai. Architect Leon Battista Alberti (1404–72) designed perhaps the very first private residence inspired by antique models— which goes a step further than the Palazzo Strozzi. A comparison between the two is illuminating. Evident on the facade of the Palazzo Rucellai, dating between 1455 and 1470, is the ordered arrangement of windows and rusticated stonework seen on the Palazzo Strozzi, but Alberti's facade is far less forbidding. Alberti devoted a far larger proportion of his wall space to windows, which lighten the facade's appearance, and filled in the remainder with rigorously ordered classical elements borrowed from antiquity. The result, though still severe, is less fortresslike, and Alberti strove for this effect purposely (he is on record as saying that only tyrants need fortresses). Ironically, the Palazzo Rucellai was built some 30 years *before* the Palazzo Strozzi. Alberti's civilizing ideas here, it turned out, had little influence on the Florentine palazzi that followed. To Renaissance Florentines, power— in architecture, as in life—was just as impressive as beauty. While you are admiring the facade (the palazzo isn't open to the public), turn around and look at the Loggia dei Rucellai across the street. Built in 1463– 66, it was the private "terrace" of the Rucellai family, in-laws to the Medici. Its soaring heights and grand arches are a firm testament to the family's status and wealth. ⊠ *Via della Vigna Nuova, Santa Maria Novella neighborhood,* ☎ *no phone.*

㉚ Palazzo Strozzi. The Strozzi family built this imposing palazzo in an attempt to outshine the nearby Palazzo Medici. Based on a model by Giuliano da Sangallo (circa 1452–1516) dating from around 1489 and executed between 1489 and 1504 under Il Cronaca (1457–1508) and Benedetto da Maiaino (1442–97), it was inspired by Michelozzo's earlier Palazzo Medici-Riccardi. The palazzo's exterior is simple, severe, and massive: it's a testament to the wealth of a patrician, 15th-century Florentine family. The interior courtyard, entered from the rear of the palazzo, is another matter altogether. It is here that the classical vocabulary—columns, capitals, pilasters, arches, and cornices—is given uninhibited and powerful expression. Blockbuster art shows frequently occur here. ⊠ *Via Tornabuoni, Piazza della Repubblica neighborhood,* ☎ *055/2645155,* WEB *www.firenzemostre.com.* ⊘ *Daily 10–7.*

㉙ Santa Maria Novella. The facade of this church looks distinctly clumsy by later Renaissance standards, and with good reason: it is an architectural hybrid. The lower half was completed mostly in the 14th century; its pointed-arch niches and decorative marble patterns reflect the Gothic style of the day. About 100 years later (around 1456), architect Leon Battista Alberti was called in to complete the job. The marble decoration of his upper story clearly defers to the already existing work below, but the architectural motifs he added evince an entirely different style. The central doorway, the four ground-floor half-columns with Corinthian capitals, the triangular pediment atop the second story, the inscribed frieze immediately below the pediment—these are borrowings from antiquity, and they reflect the new Renaissance era in architecture, born some 35 years earlier at the Spedale degli Innocenti. Alberti's most important addition, however, the S-curve scrolls that surmount the decorative circles on either side of the upper story, had no precedent whatever in antiquity. The problem was to soften the abrupt transition between wide ground floor and narrow upper story. Alberti's solution turned out to be definitive. Once you start to look for them, you will find scrolls such as these (or sculptural variations of them) on churches all over Italy, and every one of them derives from Alberti's example here.

The architecture of the interior is, like that of the Duomo, a dignified but somber example of Florentine Gothic. Exploration is essential, however, because the church's store of art treasures is remarkable. Highlights include the 14th-century stained-glass rose window depicting the *Coronation of the Virgin* (above the central entrance); the Cappella Filippo Strozzi (to the right of the altar), containing late-15th-century frescoes and stained glass by Filippino Lippi; the *cappella maggiore* (the area around the high altar), displaying frescoes by Ghirlandaio; and the Cappella Gondi (to the left of the altar), containing Filippo Brunelleschi's famous wood crucifix, carved around 1410 and said to have so stunned the great Donatello when he first saw it that he dropped a basket of eggs.

Of special interest, for its great historical importance and beauty, is Masaccio's *Trinity,* on the left-hand wall, almost halfway down the nave. Painted around 1426–27 (at the same time he was working on his frescoes in Santa Maria del Carmine), it unequivocally announced the arrival of the Renaissance. The realism of the figure of Christ was revolutionary in itself, but what was probably even more startling to contemporary Florentines was the barrel vault in the background. The mathematical rules for employing perspective in painting had just been discovered (probably by Brunelleschi), and this was one of the first works of art to employ them with utterly convincing success.

In the cloisters of the **Museo di Santa Maria Novella** (✉ Piazza Santa Maria Novella, ☎ 055/282187), to the left of Santa Maria Novella, is a faded fresco cycle by Paolo Uccello depicting tales from Genesis, with a dramatic vision of the Deluge. Admission to the museum is an additional €2.60; it's open Wednesday through Monday 9–2. Earlier and better-preserved frescoes painted in 1348–55 by Andrea da Firenze are in the chapter house, or the **Cappellone degli Spagnoli** (Spanish Chapel), off the cloister. ✉ *Piazza Santa Maria Novella,* ☎ *055/210113.* ▣ *€2.60.* ⊙ *Mon.–Thurs. and Sat. 9:30–5, Fri. and Sun. 1–5.*

㉞ Santa Trinita. Started in the 11th century by Vallambrosian monks and originally Romanesque in style, the church underwent a Gothic remodeling during the 14th century. (Remains of the Romanesque construction are visible on the interior front wall.) Its major works are the cycle of frescoes and the altarpiece in the Cappella Sassetti, the second to the high altar's right, painted by Ghirlandaio from around 1480 to 1485. Ghirlandaio was a wildly popular but conservative painter for his day, and generally his paintings show little interest in the laws of perspective with which other Florentine painters had been experimenting for more than 50 years. But his work here possesses such graceful decorative appeal it hardly seems to matter. The wall frescoes illustrate the life of St. Francis, and the altarpiece, depicting the *Adoration of the Shepherds,* veritably glows. ✉ *Piazza Santa Trinita, Santa Maria Novella neighborhood,* ☎ *055/216912.* 🎫 *Free.* ⏲ *Daily 7–noon and 4–7.*

The Oltrarno: Palazzo Pitti, Giardino di Boboli, Santo Spirito

A walk through the Oltrarno takes in two very different aspects of Florence: the splendor of the Medici, manifest in the riches of the mammoth Palazzo Pitti and the gracious Giardino di Boboli; and the charm of the Oltrarno, literally "the other side of the Arno," a slightly gentrified but still fiercely proud working-class neighborhood with artisans' and antiques shops.

A Good Tour

Starting from Santa Trinita, walk toward the Arno on Via Tornabuoni, make a left onto the Lungarno degli Acciaiuoli, and cross the Arno over the Ponte Vecchio. If you want to take a Mannerist detour to see the Pontormo *Deposition* at **Santa Felicita** ㊲, head down Via Guicciardini and stop in the first piazza on your left. Head toward **Palazzo Pitti** ㊳, Florence's largest palace, by continuing on Via Guicciardini; it lies before you as you emerge onto Piazza Pitti. Behind the palace are the **Giardino di Boboli** ㊴; find time to walk through the splendid gardens. Then head for the Giardino del Cavaliere, which requires a gently demanding uphill climb. At the top, **Forte di Belvedere** ㊵ commands a wonderful view and sometimes has art exhibits. From here, it's an easy walk to Bus 37, which takes you to the **Certosa** ㊶. Return via bus and alight at the Santo Spirito stop to take in Piazza Santo Spirito, dominated at its north end by the unassuming facade of the church of **Santo Spirito** ㊷. Take Via Sant'Agostino, diagonally across the square from the church entrance, and follow it west to Via dei Serragli. Cross and follow Via Santa Monaca west through the heart of the Oltrarno to Piazza del Carmine and the church of **Santa Maria del Carmine** ㊸, where the famous fresco cycle by Masaccio, Masolino, and Filippino Lippi fills the Cappella Brancacci. Go to the far end of Piazza del Carmine and turn right onto Borgo San Frediano; then follow Via di Santo Spirito and Borgo Sant'Jacopo east to reach the Ponte Vecchio.

TIMING

The walk alone takes about 45 minutes; allow one hour to visit the Galleria Palatina in Palazzo Pitti and more if you visit the other galleries. Spend at least 30 minutes to an hour savoring the graceful elegance of the Giardino di Boboli. When you reach the crossroads of the Sdrucciolo dei Pitti and Via Michelozzi, you have a choice. If it's around noon, you may want to postpone the next stop temporarily to see the churches of Santo Spirito, Santa Felicita (if you didn't stop in before going to Palazzo Pitti), and Santa Maria del Carmine before they close for the afternoon. Otherwise, proceed to Palazzo Pitti. The churches can be visited in 15 minutes each. The trip to and tour of the Certosa takes about two hours total.

Sights to See

㊶ **Certosa.** The incredible Carthusian complex was largely funded in 1342 by the wealthy Florentine banker Niccolò Acciaolo, whose guilt at having amassed so much money must have been at least temporarily assuaged with the creation of such a structure to honor God. In the grand cloister are stunning frescoes of *Christ's Passion* by Pontormo. Though they suffer from much paint loss, their power is still unmistakable. Also of great interest are the monks' cells; apparently the monks could spend most of their lives tending their own private gardens without dealing with any other monks. To get here, you must take Bus 37 and get off at the stop marked Certosa or you need a car. ⊠ *From Florence, take Viale Petrarca to Via Senese and follow it for about 10 mins; the Certosa is on the right,* ☎ *055/2049226.* ☒ *Donations requested.* ☉ *Tues.–Sun. 9–11:30 and 3–5.*

⓵ **Forte di Belvedere** (Fort Belvedere). The impressive structure was built in 1590 to help defend the city against siege. But what was once a first-rate fortification is now a first-rate exhibition venue. Farther up the hill is Piazzale Michelangelo, but, as the natives know, the best views of Florence are right here. To the north, all the city's monuments are spread out in a breathtaking panorama. To the south, the nearby hills furnish a complementary rural view, in its way equally memorable. The fortress, occasionally a setting for art exhibitions, is adjacent to the top of the Giardino di Boboli. ⊠ *Porta San Giorgio.* ☒ *Varies with exhibit.*

⓷ **Giardino di Boboli** (Boboli Gardens). The main entrance to these landscaped gardens is from the right wing of ☞ **Palazzo Pitti.** The gardens began to take shape in 1549, when the Pitti family sold the palazzo to Eleanor of Toledo, wife of the Medici Grand Duke Cosimo I. The initial landscaping plans were laid out by Niccolò Tribolo (1500–50). After his death work was continued by Vasari, Ammannati, Giambologna, Bernardo Buontalenti (circa 1536–1608), and Giulio (1571–1635) and Alfonso Parigi (1606–56), among others, which produced the most spectacular backyard in Florence. The Italian gift for landscaping—less formal than the French but still full of sweeping drama—is displayed here at its best. A copy of the famous *Morgante,* Cosimo I's favorite dwarf astride a particularly unhappy tortoise, is near the exit. Sculpted by Valerio Cioli (circa 1529–99), the work seems to illustrate—very graphically, indeed—the perils of too much pasta. ⊠ *Enter through Palazzo Pitti, Piazza Pitti,* ☎ *055/294883,* ☒ *€2.05.* ☉ *Apr.–Oct., daily 8:15–5:30; Nov.–Mar., daily 8:15–4:30. Closed 1st and last Mon. of month.*

⓸ **Palazzo Pitti.** This enormous palace is one of Florence's largest—if not one of its best—architectural set pieces. The original palazzo, built for the Pitti family around 1460, comprised only the main entrance and the three windows on either side. In 1549 the property was sold to the Medici, and Bartolomeo Ammannati was called in to make substantial additions. Although he apparently operated on the principle that more is better, he succeeded only in producing proof that more is just that, more.

Today the palace houses several museums: The **Museo degli Argenti** displays a vast collection of Medici household treasures. The **Galleria del Costume** showcases fashions from the past 300 years. The **Galleria d'Arte Moderna** holds a collection of 19th- and 20th-century paintings, mostly Tuscan. Most famous of the Pitti galleries is the **Galleria Palatina,** which contains a broad collection of paintings from the 15th to 17th centuries. The rooms of the Galleria Palatina remain much as the Medici left them. Their floor-to-ceiling paintings are considered by some to be Italy's most egregious exercise in conspicuous consumption, aesthetic overkill, and trumpery. Still, the collection possesses high points, including a number of portraits by Titian and an unparalleled collection of paintings by Raphael, notably the double portraits of Angelo Doni and his wife, the sullen Maddalena Strozzi. The price of admission to the Galleria Palatina also allows you to explore the former **Appartamenti Reali** containing furnishings from a remodeling done in the 19th century. ⊠ *Piazza Pitti,* ☎ *055/210323.* ▦ *Museo degli Argenti €2.05, Galleria del Costume €4.10, Galleria d'Arte Moderna €4.10, Galleria Palatina €6.15.* ⊘ *Museo degli Argenti, Galleria del Costume, and Galleria d'Arte Moderna: Daily 8:15–1:50; closed 2nd and 4th Sun. and 1st, 3rd, and 5th Mon. of month. Galleria Palatina: Nov.–Mar., Tues.–Sun. 8:15–6:50; Apr.–Oct., Tues.–Sat. 8:15 AM–10 PM, Sun. 8:15–7.*

㊲ Santa Felicita. This late baroque church (its facade was remodeled 1736–39) contains the Mannerist Jacopo Pontormo's *Deposition,* the centerpiece of the Cappella Capponi (executed 1525–28) and a masterpiece of 16th-century Florentine art. The remote figures, which transcend the realm of Renaissance classical form, are portrayed in an array of tangled shapes and intense pastel colors (well preserved because of the low lights in the church), in a space and depth that defy reality. Note, too, the exquisitely frescoed *Annunciation,* also by Pontormo, at a right angle to the *Deposition.* The granite column in the piazza was erected in 1381 and marks a Christian cemetery. ⊠ *Piazza Santa Felicita, Via Guicciardini, Palazzo Pitti neighborhood.* ⊘ *Mon.–Sat. 9–noon and 3–6, Sun. 9–1.*

㊸ Santa Maria del Carmine. The **Cappella Brancacci,** at the end of the right transept of this church, houses a masterpiece of Renaissance painting: a fresco cycle that changed the course of Western art. Fire almost destroyed the church in the 18th century; miraculously, the Brancacci Chapel survived almost intact. The cycle is the work of three artists: Masaccio and Masolino (1383–circa 1447), who began it around 1424, and Filippino Lippi, who finished it some 50 years later, after a long interruption during which the sponsoring Brancacci family was exiled. It was Masaccio's work that opened a new frontier for painting, as he was among the first artists to employ single-point perspective; tragically, he died in 1428 at the age of 27, so he didn't live to experience the revolution his innovations caused.

Masaccio collaborated with Masolino on several of the paintings, but by himself he painted the *Tribute Money,* on the upper-left wall; *St. Peter Baptizing,* on the upper altar wall; the *Distribution of Goods,* on the lower altar wall; and, most famous, the *Expulsion of Adam and Eve,* on the chapel's upper-left entrance pier. If you look closely at the last painting and compare it with some of the chapel's other works, you should see a pronounced difference. The figures of Adam and Eve possess a startling presence primarily thanks to the dramatic way in which their bodies seem to reflect light. Masaccio here shaded his figures consistently, so as to suggest a single, strong source of light within the world of the painting but outside its frame. In so doing, he succeeded in imitating with paint the real-world effect of light on mass, and he thereby imparted to his figures a sculptural reality unprecedented in his day.

These matters have to do with technique, but with the *Expulsion of Adam and Eve* his skill went beyond mere technical innovation. In the faces of Adam and Eve, you see more than just finely modeled figures; you see terrible shame and suffering depicted with a humanity rarely achieved in art. ⊠ *Piazza del Carmine, Santo Spirito/San Frediano neighborhood,* ☎ *055/2382195.* ▦ *€3.10.* ⊘ *Mon. and Wed.–Sat. 10–5, Sun. 1–5.*

㊷ Santo Spirito. The plain, unfinished facade gives nothing away, but the interior, although it appears chilly (cold, even) compared with later

churches, is one of the most important examples of Renaissance architecture in Italy. The interior is one of a pair designed in Florence by
Filippo Brunelleschi in the early 15th century (the other is San Lorenzo).
It was here that Brunelleschi supplied definitive solutions to the two
main problems of interior Renaissance church design: how to build a
cross-shape interior using classical architectural elements borrowed from
antiquity and how to reflect in that interior the order and regularity
that Renaissance scientists (among them Brunelleschi himself) were at
the time discovering in the natural world around them.

Brunelleschi's solution to the first problem was brilliantly simple: turn
a Greek temple inside out. To see this clearly, look at one of the stately
arch-topped arcades that separate the side aisles from the central nave.
Whereas ancient Greek temples were walled buildings surrounded by
classical colonnades, Brunelleschi's churches were classical arcades
surrounded by walled buildings. This brilliant architectural idea over-
threw the previous era's religious taboo against pagan architecture once
and for all, triumphantly reclaiming that architecture for Christian use.

Brunelleschi's solution to the second problem—making the entire interior orderly and regular—was mathematically precise: he designed
the ground plan of the church so that all its parts were proportionally
related. The transepts and nave have exactly the same width; the side
aisles are precisely half as wide as the nave; the little chapels off the
side aisles are exactly half as deep as the side aisles; the chancel and
transepts are exactly one-eighth the depth of the nave; and so on, with
dizzying exactitude. For Brunelleschi, such a design technique would
have been a matter of passionate conviction. Like most theoreticians
of his day, he believed that mathematical regularity and aesthetic
beauty were flip sides of the same coin, that one was not possible without the other. In the **refectory** of Santo Spirito (⊠ Piazza Santo Spirito 29, ☎ 055/287043), adjacent to the church, you can see Andrea
Orcagna's fresco of the *Crucifixion*. It's open Tuesday through Sunday 9–2; admission is €2.05. ⊠ *Piazza Santo Spirito, Santo Spir-
ito/San Frediano neighborhood,* ☎ *055/210030.* ⌑ *Church free.* ☉
Thurs.–Tues. 8:30–noon and 4–6, Wed. 8:30–noon and 4–7.

<hr>

NEED A   **Cabiria** (⊠ Piazza Santo Spirito, Santo Spirito/San Frediano neighbor-
BREAK?   hood, ☎ 055/215732), just across the piazza from the church of
                Santo Spirito, draws funky locals and visitors in search of a cappuccino
                or quenching ade. When it's warm, sit outside on the terrace.

<hr>

From Santa Croce to San Miniato al Monte

The Santa Croce quarter, on the southeast fringe of the historic center, was built up in the Middle Ages just outside the second set of city
walls. The centerpiece of the neighborhood was the basilica of Santa
Croce, which could hold great numbers of worshipers; the vast piazza
could accommodate any overflow and also served as a fairground and
playing field for traditional, no-holds-barred soccer games. A center
of leather working since the Middle Ages, the neighborhood is still packed
with leather craftsmen and leather shops.

A Good Walk

Begin your walk at the church of **Sant'Ambrogio** ㊹. Exit the church
and proceed on Via Pietrapiana to the **Piazza dei Ciompi** ㊺. From here,
take Borgo Allegri until it meets Via San Guiseppe. Make a right here,
and follow it until you reach the church of **Santa Croce** ㊻; stop for a
moment to admire the beautiful **Piazza Santa Croce** ㊼. From here you
can take a quick jaunt up Via delle Pinzochere to **Casa Buonarroti** ㊽

to see works by Michelangelo. Return to Santa Croce, and at the southwest end of the piazza go south on Via de' Benci. Detour to the **Museo Horne** ㊾, former home of an assiduous 19th-century collector. Cross the Arno over Ponte alle Grazie. Turn left onto Lungarno Serristori and continue to Piazza Giuseppe Poggi; a series of ramps and stairs climbs to **Piazzale Michelangelo** ㊿, where the city lies before you in all its glory. From Piazzale Michelangelo, climb the stairs behind La Loggia restaurant to the church of San Salvatore al Monte, and go south on the lane leading to the stairs that climb to **San Miniato al Monte** (51), cutting through the fortifications hurriedly built by Michelangelo in 1529 when Florence was threatened by troops of the Holy Roman Emperor Charles V (1500–58). You can avoid the long walk by taking Bus 12 or 13 at the west end of Ponte alle Grazie and getting off at Piazzale Michelangelo or at the stop after for San Miniato al Monte; you still have to climb the monumental stairs to and from San Miniato, but you can then take the bus from Piazzale Michelangelo back to the center of town.

TIMING

The walk alone takes about 2½ hours one way, plus 15 to 30 minutes in Sant'Ambrogio, 30 minutes in Santa Croce, 30 minutes in the Museo di Santa Croce, and 30 minutes in San Miniato. Depending on the amount of time you have, you can limit your sightseeing to Santa Croce and Casa Buonarroti or continue on to Piazzale Michelangelo. The walk to Piazzale Michelangelo is a long uphill hike, with the prospect of another climb to San Miniato from there. If you decide to take a bus, remember to buy your ticket before you board. Also, because you go to Piazzale Michelangelo for the view, skip it if it's a hazy day. A visit to the Museo del Cenacolo takes two hours, including a round-trip on a city bus.

Sights to See

OFF THE BEATEN PATH

AMERICAN MILITARY CEMETERY – About 8 km (5 mi) south of Florence on the road to Siena is one of two American cemeteries in Italy (the other is in Nettuno). It contains 4,402 bodies of Americans who died in Italy during World War II. Spread across a gently rolling hill, the simple crosses and Stars of David bearing only name, date of death, and state seem to stretch endlessly. At the top of the hill is a place for reflection and large mosaic maps depicting the Allied assault in 1943. The two fronts—called the Gothic Line and the Gustav Line—are vividly rendered. ✉ *From Florence, take Via Cassia south to Località Scopeti,* ☎ *055/2020020.* 💴 *Free.* ⏲ *Weekdays 8–5, weekends 9–5.*

㊽ **Casa Buonarroti.** If you are really enjoying walking in the footsteps of the great genius, you may want to complete the picture by visiting the Buonarroti family home, even though Michelangelo never actually lived in the house. It was given to his nephew, and it was the nephew's son, also called Michelangelo, who turned it into a gallery dedicated to his great-uncle. The artist's descendents filled it with art treasures, some by Michelangelo himself—a marble bas-relief; the *Madonna of the Steps,* carved when Michelangelo was just a teenager; and his wooden model for the facade of San Lorenzo—and some by other artists that pay homage to him. ✉ *Via Ghibellina 70, Santa Croce neighborhood,* ☎ *055/241752.* 💴 *€6:15.* ⏲ *Wed.–Mon. 9:30–2.*

OFF THE BEATEN PATH

MUSEO DEL CENACOLO – This way-off-the-beaten-path museum (the name translates as the Museum of the Last Supper) has a stunning fresco by Andrea del Sarto. Begun sometime around 1511 and finished 1526–27, the fresco depicts the moment when Christ announced that one of

his apostles would betray him. Del Sarto has rendered the scene in subtle yet still brilliant colors. Also on display are a couple of lesser-known
works by Pontormo and copies of other 16th-century works. (Down the
street is the church of San Salvi, founded by John Gualbert and begun
in 1048. Though it suffered damage during the siege of 1529–30, the
interior has a modest but lovely *Madonna and Child* by Lorenzo di Bicci
as well as a 16th-century wood cross on the altar.) To get here, take Bus
6 from Piazza San Marco and get off at the Lungo L'Affrico stop—it's
the first stop after crossing the railroad tracks. ⊠ *Via San Salvi 16,* ☎
055/2388603. 🖻 *Free.* ☉ *Tues.–Sun. 8:15–1:50.*

㊾ Museo Horne. Englishman Herbert P. Horne (1864–1916), architect,
art historian, and collector, spent much of his life in his 15th-century
palazzo surrounded by carefully culled paintings, sculptures, and other
decorative arts mostly from the 14th to 16th centuries. His home has
since been turned into a museum, which aims to display the objects
much as they would have been displayed in his lifetime. Most of the
collection is decidedly B-list, but it's worth a visit just to see how a gen-
tleman lived in the 19th century. Many of the furnishings, such as the
15th-century *lettuccio* (divan), are exemplary. ⊠ *Via dei Benci 6, Santa
Croce neighborhood,* ☎ *055/244661.* 🖻 *€5.* ☉ *Mon.–Sat. 9–1.*

㊺ Piazza dei Ciompi. Now the site of a daily flea market, this piazza was
a working-class neighborhood of primarily wool- and silk-trade workers in the 14th century. The disenfranchised wool workers, forbidden
entry to the Arte della Lana (the Wool Guild, to which belonged the
wool merchants and managers), briefly seized control of the government. It was a short-lived exercise in rule by the nonrepresented and
was eventually overpowered by the ruling upper class. The loggia was
executed much later, in 1567, by Giorgio Vasari.

㊿ Piazzale Michelangelo. From this lookout, you have a marvelous view
of Florence and the hills around it, rivaling the vista from the Forte di
Belvedere. It has a copy of Michelangelo's *David* and outdoor cafés
packed with tourists during the day and with Florentines in the evening.
In May, the **Giardino dell'Iris** (Iris Garden) off the piazza is abloom
with more than 2,500 varieties of the flower. The **Giardino delle Rose**
(Rose Garden) on the terraces below the piazza is also in full bloom
in May and June.

㊼ Piazza Santa Croce. Originally just outside the city's set of 12th-
century walls, this piazza grew with the Franciscans, who used the large
square for public preaching. During the Renaissance, it was used for
giostre (jousts), including one sponsored by Lorenzo de' Medici. "Bonfires of the vanities" occurred here, as well as soccer matches in the
16th century. Lined with many palazzi dating to the 15th century, it
remains one of Florence's loveliest piazze and is a great place to sit and
people-watch.

51 San Miniato al Monte. This church, like the Baptistery, is a fine example of Romanesque architecture and one of the oldest churches in Florence, dating from the 11th century. The lively green-and-white marble
facade has a 12th-century mosaic topped by a gilt bronze eagle, emblem of San Miniato's sponsors, the Calimala (cloth merchants' guild).
Inside are a 13th-century inlaid-marble floor and apse mosaic. Artist
Spinello Aretino (1350–1410) covered the walls of the **Sagrestia** with
frescoes on the life of St. Benedict. The adjacent **Cappella del Cardi-
nale del Portogallo** (Chapel of the Portuguese Cardinal) is one of the
richest Renaissance works in Florence. Built to hold the tomb of a Portuguese cardinal, Prince James of Lusitania, who died young in Florence in 1459, it has a glorious ceiling by Luca della Robbia, a sculptured

tomb by Antonio Rossellino (1427–79), and inlaid pavement in multicolor marble. ⊠ *Viale Galileo Galilei, Piazzale Michelangelo, Lungarno Sud neighborhood,* ☎ *055/2342731.* ⊙ *Daily 8–6:30.*

★ ㊻ **Santa Croce.** Like the Duomo, this church is Gothic, but (also like the Duomo) its facade dates from only the 19th century. The interior is most famous for its art and its tombs. As a burial place, the church is a Florentine pantheon, probably containing more skeletons of Renaissance celebrities than any other church in Italy. Among others, the tomb of Michelangelo is immediately to the right as you enter; he is said to have chosen this spot so that the first thing he would see on Judgment Day, when the graves of the dead fly open, would be Brunelleschi's dome through Santa Croce's open doors. The tomb of Galileo Galilei (1564–1642), who produced evidence that Earth is not the center of the universe—and who was not granted a Christian burial until 100 years after his death because of it—is on the left wall, opposite Michelangelo's. The tomb of Niccolò Machiavelli (1469–1527), the Renaissance political theoretician whose brutally pragmatic philosophy so influenced the Medici, is halfway down the nave on the right. The grave of Lorenzo Ghiberti, creator of the Baptistery doors, is halfway down the nave on the left. Composer Gioacchino Rossini (1792–1868) is entombed at the end of the nave on the right. The monument to Dante Alighieri (1265–1321), the greatest Italian poet, is a memorial rather than a tomb (he is buried in Ravenna); it is on the right wall near the tomb of Michelangelo.

The collection of art within the church complex is by far the most important of any church in Florence. Historically, the most significant works are probably the Giotto frescoes in the two adjacent chapels immediately to the right of the high altar. They illustrate scenes from the lives of St. John the Evangelist and St. John the Baptist (in the right-hand chapel) as well as scenes from the life of St. Francis (in the left-hand chapel). Time has not been kind to them; over the centuries, wall tombs were introduced into the middle of them, whitewash and plaster covered them, and in the 19th century they were subjected to a clumsy restoration. But the reality that Giotto introduced into painting can still be seen. He didn't paint beautifully stylized religious icons, as the Byzantine style that preceded him prescribed; he instead painted drama—St. Francis surrounded by grieving friars at the very moment of his death. This was a radical shift in emphasis, and it changed the course of art. Before Giotto, the role of painting was to symbolize the attributes of God; after him, it was to imitate life. His work is indeed primitive, compared with later painting, but in the proto-Renaissance of the early 14th century it caused a sensation that was not equaled for another 100 years. He was, for his time, the equal of both Masaccio and Michelangelo.

Among the church's other highlights are Donatello's *Annunciation,* one of the most tender and eloquent expressions of surprise ever sculpted (on the right wall two-thirds of the way down the nave); 14th-century frescoes by Taddeo Gaddi (circa 1300–66) illustrating scenes from the life of the Virgin Mary, clearly showing the influence of Giotto (in the chapel at the end of the right transept); and Donatello's *Crucifix,* criticized by Brunelleschi for making Christ look like a peasant (in the chapel at the end of the left transept). Outside the church proper, in the **Museo dell'Opera di Santa Croce,** off the cloister, is the 13th-century *Triumphal Cross* by Cimabue (circa 1240–1302), badly damaged by the flood of 1966. A model of architectural geometry, the **Cappella Pazzi,** at the end of the cloister, is the work of Brunelleschi. ⊠ *Piazza Santa Croce 16,* ☎ *055/244619.* 🎟 *€2.58.* ⊙ *Church Mar.–Oct., Mon.–Sat. 9:30–*

5:30, Sun. 3–5:30; Nov.–Feb., Mon.–Sat. 9:30–noon and 3–5:30, Sun. 3–5:30. Cloister and museum Mar.–Oct., Thurs.–Tues. 10–7; Nov.–Feb., Thurs.–Tues. 10–12:30 and 3–6.

㊹ Sant'Ambrogio. Named for the Bishop of Milan, this 10th-century church once belonged to an order of Benedictine nuns. Just this side of austere, the church is one of the oldest in Florence. Though its facade is 19th-century, inside are 15th-century panel paintings and a lovely but rather damaged 1486 fresco by Cosimo Roselli, in the chapel to the left of the high altar. The tabernacle of the Blessed Sacrament was carved by Mino da Fiesole, who, like Verrocchio, Il Cronaca, and Francesco Granacci (1469/77–1543), is buried here. ✉ *Piazza Sant'Ambrogio, Santa Croce neighborhood,* ☎ *055/240104.* ⬚ *Free.* ☉ *Daily 8–noon and 3–6.*

DINING

A typical Tuscan repast starts with an antipasto of *crostini* (grilled bread spread with various savory toppings) or cured meats such as prosciutto *crudo* (cured ham thinly sliced) and *finocchiona* (salami seasoned with fennel). *Primi piatti* (first courses) can consist of local versions of pasta dishes available throughout Italy. Peculiar to Florence, however, are the vegetable-and-bread soups such as *pappa al pomodoro* (bread-and-tomato soup), ribollita, and, in the summer, a salad called *panzanella* (tomatoes, onions, vinegar, oil, basil, and bread). Before they are eaten, these are often christened with *un "C" d'olio,* a generous C-shape drizzle of the sumptuous local olive oil.

Unparalleled among the *secondi piatti* (main courses) is *bistecca alla fiorentina*—a thick slab of local Chianina beef, often seasoned with olive oil, salt, and pepper, grilled over charcoal, and served rare. *Trippa alla fiorentina* (tripe stewed with tomato sauce) and *arista* (roast loin of pork seasoned with rosemary) are also local specialties, as are many other roasted meats that pair especially well with Chianti. A *secondo* is usually served with a *contorno* (side dish) of white beans, sautéed greens, or artichokes in season, all of which can be drizzled with more of that fruity olive oil. Dining hours are earlier here than in Rome, starting at 1 for the midday meal and at 8 for dinner. Many of Florence's restaurants are small, so reservations are a must.

CATEGORY	COST.*
$$$$	over €18
$$$	€13–€18
$$	€8–€13
$	under €8

*Prices are for a second course (secondo piatto).

Centro Storico

$$–$$$$ ✕ La Posta. Only steps from Piazza della Repubblica, this restaurant has been around for more than 100 years. Ceilings reach high above the cloth-covered tables in the three dining rooms. Under the fine ministrations of owner Enzo Vocino, La Posta offers a large menu with typical Tuscan treats as well as less-common offerings such as *filetto alla tartara* (steak tartare) prepared tableside. The chef has a deft touch with fried vegetables, particularly the *fiori di zucca* (zucchini blossoms), which are so light that you forget they're cholesterol bombs. Reserve in warmer months for the lovely outdoor tables. ✉ *Via dei Lamberti 20, Piazza della Repubblica neighborhood,* ☎ *055/212701. AE, DC, MC, V. Closed Tues.*

$$–$$$$ ╳ **Osteria n. 1.** A good choice for a romantic dinner, this intimate restaurant is on the ground floor of an old palazzo in the historic center. The place is suffused with a rosy glow from the tablecloths and cream-color walls, lined with painted landscapes and the occasional coat of arms. The food is expertly handled—try *tagliatelle verdi ai broccoli e salsiccia* (flat noodles with sausage and broccoli) before moving on to any of the grilled meats. ✉ *Via del Moro 22, Santa Maria Novella neighborhood,* ☎ *055/284897. AE, DC, MC, V. Closed Sun. and 15 days in Aug. No lunch Mon.*

$$–$$$$ ╳ **Ottorino.** The waiters wear jackets and bow ties as they sashay through the brick-vaulted, high-ceiling rooms. The decor is simple—white walls, white tablecloths—but the menu is not. The chef's flights of fancy show up in the daily specials; the menu also includesTuscan standards. Primi such as *tortelli di carciofi con speck e pecorino* (large squares of pasta stuffed with artichokes and pecorino and sauced with cured ham and butter) do little for the waistline but much to lift the spirits. ✉ *Via delle Oche 12-16/r, Duomo neighborhood,* ☎ *055/281747 or 055/215151. AE, DC, MC, V. Closed Sun.*

$$–$$$ ╳ **Osteria del Porcellino.** Contemporary paintings line the candlelit room of this intimate restaurant serving perfectly inventive fare. *Pappa con melanzane e funghi porcini,* a bread-based soup with eggplant and porcini mushrooms, updates an often tired classic. *Pollo con harissa* (chicken with a peppered Moroccan sauce) is zesty and spicy—two adjectives not often associated with Tuscan food. Service is courteous and prompt and the wine list short but comprehensive. ✉ *Via Val di Lamona 7/r, Piazza della Repubblica neighborhood,* ☎ *055/264148. AE, DC, MC, V. No lunch weekdays.*

$$ ╳ **Birreria Centrale.** The feel here is more Munich beer hall than Florentine trattoria; indeed, although the menu lists plenty of Italian dishes, it also emphasizes sausages and goulash. The *würstel rossi con crauti, speck, e patate alla tedesca* (a large and quite plump hotdog with sauerkraut, cured beef, potatoes, and pickles), for instance, comes with a dollop of spicy mustard. Heavy wooden tables are set closely together, and copies of 19th-century paintings adorn the intensely yellow walls, along with two frescoed Michelangelesque nudes that cavort over a brick arch. There's outside seating in warm weather—a great place to enjoy a beer. ✉ *Piazza Cimatori 1/r, Duomo neighborhood,* ☎ *055/211915. AE, MC, V. Closed Sun.*

$$ ╳ **Il Latini.** Although it may well be the noisiest, most crowded trattoria in Florence, it's also one of the most fun precisely because it is so lively. Bottles of wine and prints line four big rooms, which somehow manage to feel cozy—perhaps because there are always a lot of happy Florentines and tourists tucking into their *salsicce e fagioli* (sausage and beans) or, in season, *agnello fritto* (fried lamb). Portions are big—you'll think you won't be able to eat it all, but you will. ✉ *Via dei Palchetti 6/r, Santa Maria Novella neighborhood,* ☎ *055/210916. AE, DC, MC, V. Closed Mon. and 15 days at Christmas.*

$$ ╳ **Osteria delle Belle Donne.** Down the street from the church of Santa Maria Novella, this gaily decorated spot, festooned with ropes of garlic and other vegetables, has an ever-changing menu and stellar service led by the irrepressible Giacinto. Even the checkered cloth napkins are cheery. The kitchen offers Tuscan standards, but shakes up the menu regularly with alternatives such as *sedani con bacon, verza, e uova* (thick noodles sauced with bacon, cabbage, and egg). If you want to eat outside, request a table when booking. ✉ *Via delle Belle Donne 16/r, Santa Maria Novella neighborhood,* ☎ *055/238 2609. AE, DC, MC, V.*

$–$$ ╳ **Le Mosacce.** Come to this tiny, cramped, and boisterous place for a quick bite to eat. The menu, written in three languages, includes hearty, stick-to-the-ribs Florentine food such as ribollita. Seating is commu-

44

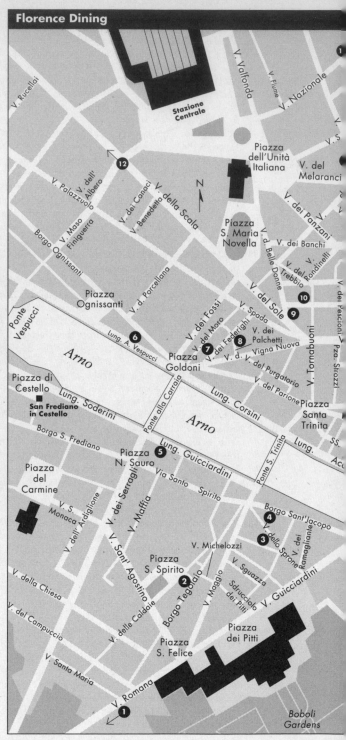

Florence Dining

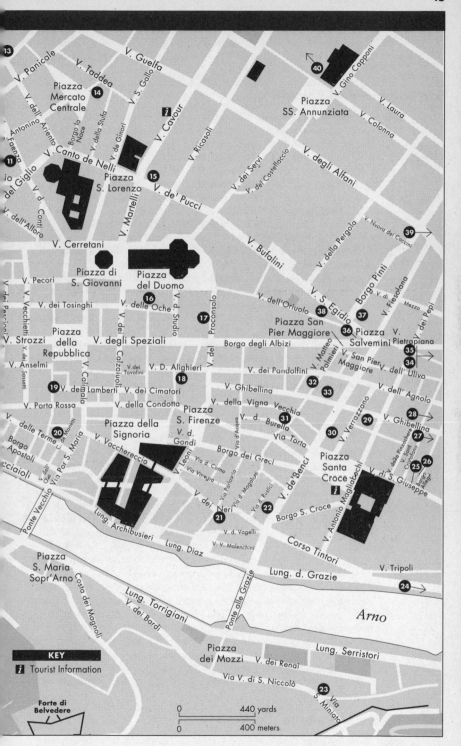

V. Panicale
V. Taddea
V. Guelfa

Piazza
Mercato
Centrale **14**

V. dell' Ariento
V. della Stufa
V. S. Gallo

V. de' Ginori

Borgo la Noce

40
V. Gino Capponi

Piazza
SS. Annunziata

V. Laura
V. Colonna

V. Cavour

V. Canto de Nelli

V. Ricasoli

V. degli Alfani

Piazza
S. Lorenzo **15**

V. de' Pucci

V. dei Servi
V. del Castellaccio

V. della Pergola

V. Nuova dei Caccini **39**

V. Martelli

V. Cerretani

V. Bufalini

Borgo Pinti

V. di Fiesolana
Mezzo

Piazza di
S. Giovanni

Piazza
del Duomo

V. S. Egidio

V. dei Pepi

V. Pecori

V. dei Tosinghi

V. delle Oche

V. dell'Oriuolo
38

37

V. Vecchietti

V. d. Studio

V. Proconsolo

16

17

Piazza San
Pier Maggiore **36**

Piazza
Salvemini

V. Pietrapiana

V. Strozzi
V. dei Pescioni

Piazza
della
Repubblica

V. degli Speziali

Borgo degli Albizi

V. Matteo Palmieri

V. San Pier
Maggiore

V. dell' Ulivo **34**

35

V. Anselmi
V. dei Sassetti

V. dei Calzaiuoli

V. D. Alighieri

V. dei Pandolfini

32

V. dell' Agnolo

V. dei Tavolini

18

19 V. dei Lamberti

V. dei Cimatori

V. Ghibellina

33

V. Porta Rossa

V. della Condotta

V. della Vigna Vecchia

28

Piazza
S. Firenze

V. d. Burella

31

Via Torta

30

V. Verrazzano

29

V. Ghibellina

27

V. delle Terme
20

Piazza della
Signoria

V. Vacchereccia

V. d.
Gondi

Via d'Acqua

V. della Pinzochere

V. Sant Cristofano

25 **26**

Borgo
Apostoli

V. C. de' Medici
Via Por S. Maria

V. Leoni

Via d. Corno

Borgo dei Greci

Via Vinegia

Via Palazzo

Via d. Magalotti

V. de' Benci

Piazza
Santa
Croce

V. di S. Giuseppe

Borgo Allegri

cciaioli

Ponte Vecchio

Lung. Archibusieri

Lung. Diaz

V. dei Neri
21

V. d. Rustici

22

Borgo S. Croce

V. Antonio Magliabechi

24

V. Vagelli

V. V. Malenchini

Corso Tintori

V. Tripoli

Piazza
S. Maria
Sopr'Arno

Costa dei Magnoli

Lung. Torrigiani

V. dei Bardi

Ponte alle Grazie

Lung. d. Grazie

Arno

Lung. Serristori

KEY

i Tourist Information

Piazza
dei Mozzi

V. dei Renai

Via V. di S. Niccolò

23 Via S. Miniata

Forte di
Belvedere

0   440 yards

0   400 meters

nal, so it's no surprise that fellow diners share the big, straw-covered flask of wine. Service is prompt and efficient; two nimble cooks with impeccable timing staff the small kitchen. ⊠ *Via del Proconsolo 55/r, Duomo neighborhood,* ☎ *055/294361. Reservations not accepted. AE, DC, MC, V. Closed weekends.*

San Lorenzo and Beyond

$$$$ ✕ **Taverna del Bronzino.** Want to have a sophisticated meal in a 16th-
★ century Renaissance artist's studio? There's nothing noteworthy about the decor in the former studio of Santi di Tito, a student of Bronzino's, save for its simple formality, with white tablecloths and place settings. Lots of classic, superb Tuscan food, however, graces the artful menu, and the presentation is often dramatic. A wine list of solid, affordable choices rounds out the menu. The service is outstanding. Reservations are advised, especially for eating at the wine cellar's only table. ⊠ *Via delle Ruote 27/r, San Lorenzo neighborhood,* ☎ *055/495220. AE, DC, MC, V. Closed Sun. and Aug.*

$$ ✕ **Antellesi.** Down the street from the Cappelle Medicee, this vaulted two-room trattoria has warm ocher walls, wood tables and chairs, and a polite but slightly absentminded staff. No matter: the *peposo alla fiorentina* (a peppery beef stew simmered in red wine and garlic) packs enough of a wallop that you won't care. This is honest Florentine cooking, which explains why locals love it. ⊠ *Via Faenza 9/r, San Lorenzo neighborhood,* ☎ *055/216990. AE, DC, MC, V. Closed Sun.*

$$ ✕ **Il Ritrovo.** Down a flight of stairs is this subterranean 15th-century room with candlelit tables. Highlights of the menu include *arrosto di vitello* (roast veal fragrantly spiked with rosemary). The light lunch special—a primo and secondo for €8—is a true bargain. ⊠ *Via de' Pucci 4/a, San Lorenzo neighborhood,* ☎ *055/281688. AE, DC, MC, V. Closed Mon.*

$$ ✕ **Le Fonticine.** The area around the train station isn't noted for its fine-
★ dining options, but this restaurant is a bright spot. It combines the best of two Italian cuisines: owner Silvano Bruci is from Tuscany and his wife, Gianna, is from Emilia-Romagna. Start with the mixed-vegetable antipasto plate or the delicate fried cauliflower balls and then move on to osso buco *alla fiorentina* (in a hearty tomato sauce) or any of the house-made pastas. The interior of the restaurant, filled with the Brucis' painting collection, provides a cheery setting for the soul-satisfying food. ⊠ *Via Nazionale 79/r, San Lorenzo neighborhood,* ☎ *055/ 282106. AE, DC, MC, V. Closed Sun.–Mon. and July 25–Aug. 25.*

$ ✕ **Mario.** Florentines flock to this narrow, unfussy, family-run trattoria to feast on lunches of Tuscan favorites savored at simple tables under a wood ceiling dating from 1536. A distinct cafeteria feel and genuine Florentine hospitality prevail: you're seated wherever there's room, which often means with strangers. Yes, there's a bit of extra oil in most dishes, which imparts taste as well as calories, but aren't you on vacation? Worth the splurge is *riso al ragù* (rice with ground beef and tomatoes). Come early to avoid a wait. ⊠ *Via Rosina 2/r, corner of Piazza del Mercato Centrale, San Lorenzo neighborhood,* ☎ *055/ 218550. Reservations not accepted. No credit cards. Closed Sun. and Aug. No dinner.*

Santa Maria Novella to the Arno

$$$$ ✕ **Harry's Bar.** You come to Harry's for the swank setting—it's cozy, with a tiny bar, pink tablecloths, and plenty of well-heeled customers captured in rosy lighting. Where else could you hope to see a gold-be-decked Florentine matron toting a Pekinese? Enjoy a Bellini (peach juice and Prosecco) or, better yet, Harry's absolutely superb martini, before tucking into the menu. The perfectly bilingual staff is more than affable. But don't expect any culinary punches: this is nursery food—often bland and unseasoned—for the privileged set, and you can eat better elsewhere in Florence. Reservations are advised. ⊠ *Lungarno Vespucci 22/r, Lungarno Nord neighborhood,* ☎ *055/2396700. AE, DC, MC, V. Closed Sun., 1 wk over Christmas, and 1 wk in Aug.*

$$–$$$$ ✕ **Cantinetta Antinori.** After a morning of shopping on Via Tornabuoni, stop for lunch in this 15th-century palazzo in the company of Florentine ladies (and men) who lunch and come to see and be seen. The panache of the food matches its clientele, but be prepared to pay dearly for such treats as *tramezzino con pane di campagna al tartufo* (country pâté with truffles served on bread) or *insalata di gamberoni e gamberetti con carciofi freschi* (crayfish and prawn salad with shaved raw artichokes). ⊠ *Piazza Antinori 3, Santa Maria Novella neighborhood,* ☎ *055/292234. AE, DC, MC, V. Closed weekends and Aug.*

The Oltrarno

$$$–$$$$ ✕ **Beccofino.** Written on the menu is "*esercizi di cucina italiana*" (Italian cooking exercises), which is a disarmingly modest way to alert the diner that something wonderfully different is going on here. A pale-wood serpentine bar separates the ocher-walled wine bar from the green-walled restaurant. Chef Francesco Berardinelli has paid some dues in the United States, and it shows in the inventiveness of his food (such as his pairing of scallops with bitter greens), which ends up tasting wholly and wonderfully Italian. The wine bar has a shorter and less expensive menu; in the summer, you can enjoy this food on a terrace facing the Arno. ⊠ *Piazza degli Scarlatti 1/r (Lungarno Guicciardini), Lungarno Sud neighborhood,* ☎ *055/290076. Reservations essential. AE, DC, MC, V. No lunch Mon.–Sat. Closed Mon. Nov.–Mar.*

$$–$$$ ✕ **Quattro Leoni.** The eclectic staff at this trattoria in a small piazza is an appropriate match for the eclectic menu. In winter, you can sample the wares in one of two rooms with high ceilings, and in the summer you can sit outside and admire the scenery. Tuscan favorites, such as *taglierini con porcini* (long, thin, flat pasta with porcini mushrooms), are offered, but so, too, are less typical dishes like the earthy cabbage salad with avocado, pine nuts, and drops of *olio di tartufo* (truffle oil). ⊠ *Piazza della Passera, Via dei Vellutini 1/r, Palazzo Pitti neighborhood,* ☎ *055/218562. AE, DC, MC, V. Closed Thurs.*

$$ ✕ **Cammillo.** You're likely to hear a lot of languages (English included) bantered about at this lively, multiroom trattoria crammed with tables. The restaurant has been in the capable hands of the Masiero family for three generations, and in this location since 1945. The family farm in the country supplies the olive oil and wines for the restaurant, which go nicely with the wide-ranging list of Tuscan specialties. Reservations are advised. ⊠ *Borgo Sant'Jacopo 57/r, Lungarno Sud neighborhood,* ☎ *055/212427. AE, DC, MC, V. Closed Wed., 15 days in Aug., and 15 days Dec.–Jan.*

$$ ✕ **Domani.** Chef Yukihiro Kojima was born in Japan and classically trained in French technique before moving to Italy and teaming up with chef Alberto Borborini to create this one-of-a-kind Japanese–Italian–French restaurant. It's a bit odd to see bouillabaisse on the same menu as spaghetti *alla carbonara* (with bacon, eggs, and Parmesan) and *maiale saltato con kimchi* (pork with pickled cabbage), but that's the beauty of this place. The Japanese food is particularly good, and well priced; Mr. Kojima says it's the food he grew up on. The restaurant's two large rooms are rather unremarkable, but it's all about the food here. ⊠ *Via Romana 80/r, Palazzo Pitti neighborhood,* ☎ *055/221166. AE, DC, MC, V. Closed Mon.*

$ ✗ **La Casalinga.** *Casalinga* means housewife, and this place has all the charm of a 1950s kitchen with Tuscan comfort food to match. Mediocre paintings clutter the semi-paneled walls, and tables are set close together. The place is usually jammed, and for good reason: the menu is extensive, portions are plentiful, and the service is prompt and friendly. If you eat ribollita anywhere in Florence, eat it here—it couldn't be more authentic. ✉ *Via Michelozzi 9/r, Santo Spirito/San Frediano neighborhood,* ☏ *055/218624. AE, DC, MC, V. Closed Sun., Christmas wk, and 3 wks in Aug. No lunch in July.*

$ ✗ **Osteria Antica Mescita San Niccolò.** It's always crowded, always good, and always cheap. The osteria is next to the church of San Niccolò, and if you sit in the lower part of the restaurant you will find yourself in what was once a chapel dating from the 11th century. The food is simple Tuscan style at its very best. The *pollo con limone* is tasty pieces of chicken in a lemon-scented broth. In the winter, try the *spezzatino di cinghiale con aromi* (wild boar stew with herbs). A plus: the kitchen's almost always open until 11:30 PM, and sometimes until midnight. ✉ *Via San Niccolò 60/r, San Niccolò neighborhood,* ☏ *055/2342836. No credit cards. Closed Sun.*

Santa Croce

$$$$ ✗ **Alle Murate.** Creative versions of classic Tuscan dishes—such as *zuppa di ceci e merluzzo* (pureed chickpeas with hints of cod)—are served at this sophisticated spot. The main dining room has a rich, uncluttered look, with warm wood floors and paneling and soft lights. In a smaller adjacent room called the *vineria,* you get the same, splendid service and substantially reduced prices. There's no middle ground with the wine list—only a smattering of inexpensive offerings before it soars to exalted heights. ✉ *Via Ghibellina 52/r, Santa Croce neighborhood,* ☏ *055/240618. AE, DC, MC, V. Closed Mon. No lunch.*

$$$$ ✗ **Cibrèo.** The food at this high-end trattoria is fantastic, from the creamy
★   crostini *di fegatini* (a savory chicken-liver spread) to the meltingly good desserts. If you thought you'd never try tripe—let alone like it— this is the place to lay any doubts to rest: the *trippa in insalata* (cold tripe salad) with parsley and garlic is an epiphany. Construe chef Fabio Picchi's unsolicited advice as a sign of his enthusiasm for his cooking; it's warranted, as the food is among the best and most creative in town. Around the corner is Cibreino, Cibrèo's budget version, with a shorter menu and a no-reservations policy. ✉ *Via A. del Verrocchio 8/r, Santa Croce neighborhood,* ☏ *055/2341100. Reservations essential. AE, DC, MC, V. Closed Sun.–Mon., July 25–Sept. 5, and Dec. 31–Jan. 7.*

$$$$ ✗ **Enoteca Pinchiorri.** A sumptuous Renaissance palace with high, frescoed ceilings and bouquets in silver vases provides the setting at this restaurant, one of the most expensive in Italy. Some consider it one of the best, and others consider it overpriced and overrated. The vast holdings of the wine cellar and the stellar service are definite pluses. Fish, game, and meat dishes are always on the menu, along with pasta combinations such as the *ignudi,* ricotta-cheese dumplings with a lobster and coxcomb fricassee. ✉ *Via Ghibellina 87, Santa Croce neighborhood,* ☏ *055/242777. Reservations essential. Jacket and tie. AE, MC, V. Closed Sun., Aug., and 1 wk in Dec. No lunch Mon. or Wed.*

$$$$ ✗ **La Giostra.** The clubby La Giostra, which means "carousel" in Ital-
★   ian, is owned and run by Prince Dimitri Kunz d'Asburgo Lorena, and his way with mushrooms is as remarkable as his charm. The unusually good pastas may require explanation from Dimitri or Soldano, the prince's good-looking twin sons. In perfect English they'll describe a favorite dish, *taglierini con tartufo bianco,* a decadently rich pasta with white truffles. Try the *spianata* (slices of thinly shaved beef baked

quickly and served with fresh rosemary and sage). Leave room for dessert: this might be the only place in town with a sublime tiramisu and a wonderfully gooey Sacher torte. ⊠ *Borgo Pinti 12/r, Santa Croce neighborhood,* ☎ *055/241341. AE, DC, MC, V.*

$$$ ✕ **Cantina Barbagianni.** *"Diverso dal solito"* (different from the usual) is the leitmotif here, and this attitude is reflected in the funky furnishings (lots of strategically placed drapery) and avante-garde paintings on the walls. Cristina, the proprietor, presides over it all with great ease. The regularly changing menu strays far from the typical Tuscan path: *l'anatra con mirtillo* (duck with blueberries) is a rare thing in these parts, and the chef is to be commended for his inventiveness. The *risotto al carciofi con scamorza* (artichoke risotto with smoked cheese) is heavenly. ⊠ *Via Sant'Egidio 13, Santa Croce neighborhood,* ☎ *055/ 2480508. AE, DC, MC, V. Closed Sun.*

$$$ ✕ **Simon Boccanegra.** Across the street from Teatro Verdi is this intimate restaurant, named after a famous Ghibelline *condottiere* (mercenary), that serves after midnight—a rarity in Florence. Ceilings are high, and candles on every table cast a romantically warm glow. The menu, although Tuscan, is hardly typical, as many dishes are spiced with ginger and saffron, and there's heavy emphasis on fish. The *gnudi di zucca giallo agli amaretti e grana* (pumpkin dumplings with crushed biscotti and cheese) is surprisingly savory, and a delight. ⊠ *Via Ghibellina 124/r, Santa Croce neighborhood,* ☎ *055/2001098. AE, DC, MC, V. No lunch. Closed Sun.*

$$–$$$ ✕ **Baldovino.** David and Catherine Gardner, expat Scots, have created this lively, brightly colored restaurant down the street from the church of Santa Croce. From its humble beginnings as a pizzeria, it has evolved into something more. It's a happy thing that pizza is still on the menu, but now it shares billing with sophisticated primi and secondi. The menu changes monthly and offers such treats as *filetto di manza alla Bernaise* (filet mignon with light béarnaise sauce). Baldovino also serves pasta dishes and grilled meat until the wee hours. ⊠ *Via San Giuseppe 22/r, Santa Croce neighborhood,* ☎ *055/241773. DC, MC, V. Closed Mon. and 2 wks in Aug.*

$$–$$$ ✕ **Danny Rock.** There's a bit of everything at this restaurant, which is always hopping with Italians eager to eat well-made cheeseburgers and fries or one of the many tasty crepes (served both sweet and savory). You can also find a basic plate of spaghetti as well as a respectable pizza here. Interior decor isn't high on the list: you dine at a green metal table with matching chairs. The young-at-heart feel might explain why the main dining room has a big screen showing Looney Tunes. ⊠ *Via Pandolfini 13/r, Santa Croce neighborhood,* ☎ *055/2340307. AE, DC, MC, V.*

$–$$$ ✕ **La Baraonda.** A Hollywood set of a Tuscan trattoria could take some cues from this charming place, with its tile floors that recall the 1930s and tables set with tiny fresh flowers and patterned plates—all signs that La Baraonda does things one notch better than most other places. The food is imaginative, from starters such as spaghetti *con quattro P* (literally, with four Ps: *pomodoro,* pecorino, *pepolino,* and *peperoncini,* or tomato, pecorino cheese, thyme, and chili peppers) to the *farinata* (a bread-based soup in this case). ⊠ *Via Ghibellina 67/r, Santa Croce neighborhood,* ☎ *055/2341171. AE, DC, MC, V. Closed Sun. and Aug. No lunch Mon.*

$–$$$ ✕ **Osteria de'Benci.** A few minutes from Santa Croce, this charming
★ osteria serves some of the most eclectic food in Florence, and at remarkably low prices. Try the spicy spaghetti *dell'ubriacone* (literally, "drunkard's spaghetti"), an amazing pasta cooked in red wine and unlike any plate of spaghetti you've ever had. The grilled meats are justifiably famous in these parts; the *carbonata* is a succulent piece of grilled beef served rare. When it's warm, you can dine outside with a view

of the 13th-century tower belonging to the prestigious Alberti family. The English-speaking staff shouldn't scare you off: Florentines *do* eat here. ☒ *Via de'Benci 11/13/r, Santa Croce neighborhood,* ☎ *055/ 2344923. AE, DC, MC, V. Closed Sun.*

$$ ✕ Acquacotta. With its closely spaced, red-checked tablecloths, you couldn't get any more "Italian" than this. You almost expect the chef to come out of the kitchen with an accordion and serenade you while you eat. Not to worry: service is offhand (sometimes dismissive), and the chef has better things to do than break into song. The highlight of the menu, with the usual list of grilled meats and pasta starters, is the *acquacotta,* literally cooked water—a regional favorite that seems to be disappearing from most menus. In this case it's a vegetable-based soup with mushrooms and onions that's topped with a poached egg. ☒ *Via dei Pilastri 51/r, Santa Croce neighborhood,* ☎ *055/242907. MC, V. Closed Sun. and Aug.*

$$ ✕ Cantinetta il Francescano. Plain wooden tables and nondescript walls provide the backdrop for some simply terrific Tuscan-with-a-twist food. Chef Katrin Rosenthal has clearly learned her way around a Tuscan kitchen and breathes new life into what are often tired standards. Her *peposo,* chunks of beef simmered in a tomato sauce with lots of black pepper, has bite and zest. The wine list is big and affordable, the staff friendly and attentive. Reservations are advised. ☒ *Largo Bargellini 16, Santa Croce neighborhood,* ☎ *055/241605. MC, V. Closed Tues.*

$$ ✕ La Maremma. The inexpensive paneled walls and simple tables say basic trattoria, but the food is better than basic. The menu offers Tuscan as well as other Italian treats (the version here of the Roman spaghetti alla carbonara is terrific); the *pollo al aceto* (chicken with balsamic vinegar) is luscious. Service is courteous and prompt. If you want to eat ostrich, here's the place to do it in Italy. ☒ *Via Verdi 16/r, Santa Croce neighborhood,* ☎ *055/244615. AE, DC, MC, V. Closed Wed.*

$$ ✕ Pallottino. With its tile floor, photograph-lined walls, and wooden tables, Pallottino is the quintessential Tuscan trattoria, serving hearty, heartwarming classics like pappa al pomodoro and *peposo alla toscana* (beef stew laced with black pepper). The menu changes frequently but always reflects what's seasonal; the staff is friendly, as are the other diners with whom you often share a table and, eventually, conversation. ☒ *Via Isola delle Stinche 1/r, Santa Croce neighborhood,* ☎ *055/ 289573. AE, DC, MC, V. Closed Mon. and 2–3 wks in Aug.*

$-$$ ✕ Antico Noe. If Florence had a dive restaurant, this would be it. The 30-seat place on one of the more unsavory half blocks in town (benign local addicts seem to congregate here, and the police patrol frequently) serves Tuscan classics with flare; Florentines are especially fond of it and rave about the *taglietelle ai porcini.* The mixed meat plate is fine, the *lardo di colonnata* (don't ask, just eat it) sublime. The wine list is short but includes great bargains. ☒ *Volta di San Piero 6/r, Santa Croce neighborhood,* ☎ *055/2340838. AE, DC, MC, V. Closed Sun.*

$-$$ ✕ Benvenuto. At this Florentine institution, beloved for decades by locals and Anglophone Renaissance scholars alike, the service is ebullient, the menu long (with often unwittingly humorous English typographical errors), and the food simple, Tuscan, and tasty. The list of primi and secondi is extensive, and there are daily specials as well. Don't miss the *scaloppine all Benvenuto* (veal cutlets with porcini). ☒ *Via della Mosca 16/r, at Via de' Neri, Santa Croce neighborhood,* ☎ *055/214833. AE, DC, MC, V. Closed Sun.*

$-$$ ✕ Sedano Allegro. You might be tempted to walk right by this place, which looks like a typical Florentine bar from the outside. But inside are two candlelit rooms (one for smoking), glowing service, and nary a meat dish on the menu. "Happy Celery," as the name translates into English, puts a tasty vegetarian spin on Italian classics. The *seitan alla* *normanna* (sautéed wheat gluten with porcini mushrooms), for one, maintains the integrity of the original meat-based dish. The menu doesn't include tofu dishes, however—the owner doesn't like it. There's a small terrace for use in warm weather. ⊠ *Borgo la Croce 20/r (near Piazza Beccaria), Santa Croce neighborhood,* ☎ *055/2345505. AE, DC, MC, V. Closed Mon.*

Beyond the City Center

$$–$$$$ ✕ **Caffè Concerto.** It looks and feels like California on the Arno at this sleek, airy restaurant a short ride from the city center. Owner–chef Gabriele Tarchiani has spent time in the United States, which shows in the plants that fill the interior as well as the creative touches on the menu, which changes monthly. It's a rare thing and a blessing in this part of Italy to find such imagination, as in the *composta di cozze cavolo cinese e carciofi,* a mound of artichokes and Chinese cabbage garnished with mussels. And the desserts are culinary works of art. No wonder Florentines come here to celebrate special occasions. ⊠ *Lungarno Colombo 7 (east of city center),* ☎ *055/677377. Reservations essential. AE, DC, MC, V. Closed Sun.*

$$$ ✕ **Zibibbo.** Benedetta Vitali, formerly of Florence's famed Cibrèo, has a restaurant of her very own. It's a welcome addition to the sometimes claustrophobic Florentine dining scene—particularly as you have to drive a few minutes out of town to get here. Off a quiet piazza, it has two intimate rooms with rustic, maroon-painted wood floors and a sloped ceiling. *Tagliatelle al sugo d'anatra* (wide pasta ribbons with duck sauce) are aromatic and flavorful, and *crocchette di fave con salsa di yogurt* (fava bean croquettes with a lively yogurt sauce) are innovative and tasty. *Via di Terzollina 3/r (northwest of city center),* ☎ *055/ 433383. AE, DC, MC, V. Closed Sun.*

Bars and Caffè

Caffè, or bars, in Italy serve not only coffee concoctions and pastries but also sweets, drinks, and panini, and some offer hot pasta and lunch dishes. They usually are open from early in the morning to late at night and are closed Sunday. **Bar Signorini Tosca** (⊠ Piazza Salvemini 14, Santa Croce neighborhood, ☎ 055/241016) is an innocuous-looking (and hard-to-find) place that prepares tasty sandwiches to order; it also serves a rather inexpensive and satisfying cheeseburger if you're in the mood for one. In the Oltrarno, **Caffè Ricchi** (⊠ Piazza Santo Spirito 9/r, Santo Spirito/San Frediano neighborhood, ☎ 055/ 215864) makes its own sandwiches and offers light fare as well. All bars in Italy ought to be like **Caffetteria Piansa** (⊠ Borgo Pinti 18/r, Santa Croce neighborhood, ☎ 055/2342362), great for breakfast, lunch, and drinks at night. The lunchtime salads, such as smoked salmon served with potatoes and a dollop of arugula mayonnaise, are terrific, and the panini are creative and delicious. At night **Capocaccia** (⊠ Lungarno Corsini 12/14r, Lungarno Nord neighborhood, ☎ 055/ 210751) can be a chaotic scene, but in the daytime it's significantly calmer. It offers light lunches and a lengthy list of panini, as well as a couple of outdoor tables with a view of the Arno. If you're craving Sunday brunch, Capocaccia has that, too. Down the street from the Galleria dell'Accademia, the **Gran Caffè** (⊠ Piazza San Marco 11/r, San Marco neighborhood, ☎ 055/215833) is a perfect place to rave about the majesty of Michelangelo's *David* over a marvelous panino or sweet.

Around the corner from the church of Santa Maria Novella, **i 5 Tavoli** (⊠ Via del Sole 26/r, Santa Maria Novella neighborhood, ☎ 055/ 294438) has only five tables (as its name implies), many fine sandwiches, hot pasta specials, and a very good (and inexpensive) cheese-burger. **La Ribotta** (⊠ Borgo Albizi 80/r, Santa Croce neighborhood, ☎ 055/2345668), which offers great panini and a fine selection of beers on tap (in addition to the ubiquitous wine), is a good place for a light lunch. **Nannini** (⊠ Borgo San Lorenzo 7/r, San Lorenzo neighborhood, ☎ 055/212680) offers light lunches and excellent coffee. Down the street from the church of Santissima Annunziata is **Oliandolo** (⊠ Via Ricasoli 38-40/r, Santissima Annunziata neighborhood, ☎ 055/211296), with an enticing list of panini and an affable barman who resembles a young Joe DiMaggio. **Polly Magu** (⊠ Via Panicale 27-29/r, San Lorenzo neighborhood, ☎ 055/2302259) is next to the Mercato Centrale. It opens early in the morning, closes late at night, and has daily pasta specials, panini, and drinks. **Procacci** (⊠ Via Tornabuoni 64/r, Santa Maria Novella neighborhood, ☎ 055/211656), closed Sunday and Monday, has been a classy Florentine institution since 1885; try one of the panini tartufati and swish it down with a glass of Prosecco. Stellar service, light snacks, and terrific aperitivi are the norm at **Rivoire** (⊠ Via Vacchereccia 4/r, Piazza della Signoria neighborhood, ☎ 055/214412), a top spot for people-watching. **Rose's** (⊠ Via del Parione 26/r, Santa Maria Novella neighborhood, ☎ 055/287090) draws businesspeople at lunch and people sporting multiple body piercings at night. An Italian menu is available at lunchtime, sushi in the evening. **Sant'Ambrogio Caffè** (⊠ Piazza Sant'Ambrogio 7–8/r, Santa Croce neighborhood, ☎ 055/241035) has outdoor summer seating with a view of an 11th-century church (Sant'Ambrogio) directly across the street.

Enoteche

Wine bars have been popping up all over Florence, and most of them offer light fare as well as lengthy wine lists—perfect places for lunch or dinner. Most are closed on Sunday. In the heart of the centro storico is **Cantinetta dei Verrazzano** (⊠ Via dei Tavolini 18/20/r, Piazza della Signoria neighborhood, ☎ 055/268590), where serious wines may be had as well as light lunches. It's hard to believe that **Coquinarius** (⊠ Via delle Oche 15/r, Duomo neighborhood, ☎ 055/2302153) is as close to the Duomo as it is; the place is serene, sophisticated, and perfect for resting one's soul. **Enoteca Baldovino** (⊠ Via San Giuseppe 18/r, Santa Croce neighborhood, ☎ 055/2347220) is a cozy little place with candlelit tile tables. Try the *piatti misti* (mixed plate of various specials of the day) while sipping a glass of wine. When it's warm, you can sit outside on a quiet, narrow side street. It's closed Monday.

Fuori Porta (⊠ Via Monte al Croce 10/r, San Niccolò neighborhood, ☎ 055/2342483), in the Oltrarno, is a stone's throw from Forte Belvedere. You can sit down (inside or out), have wine by the glass or by the bottle, and choose from a lengthy list of crostini and crostoni with various toppings. A hop, skip, and a jump from Orsanmichele in the centro storico is **I Fratellini** (⊠ Via dei Cimatori 38/r, Piazza della Signoria neighborhood, ☎ 055/2396096), in existence since 1875. It sells wines by the glass and has a list of 27 panini, including pecorino with sun-dried tomatoes and spicy wild-boar salami with goat cheese. There are no seats, so perch on the curb and make like a local. **Le Volpi e l'Uva** (⊠ Piazza de' Rossi 1, Palazzo Pitti neighborhood, ☎ 055/2398132), just off Piazza Santa Trinita, is an oenophile's dream: the waiters pour significant wines by the glass and serve equally impressive cheeses and little sandwiches to go with them. At **Pitti Gola** (⊠ Piazza Pitti 16, Palazzo Pitti neighborhood, ☎ 055/212704), you can order tasty tidbits to accompany your choices from the extensive and impressive wine list. The outdoor seats have a view of the Palazzo Pitti.

Foreign Foods

Eating ethnic in Florence is a hit-or-miss affair. Although numerous Asian restaurants have sprung up since the 1990s, most of them are nothing to write home about. Still, if you need a break from Italian, there are a few fairly decent options to consider.

Amon (⊠ Via Palazzuolo 26/28r, Santa Maria Novella neighborhood, ☎ 055/293146) is a standing-only spot that serves Egyptian and other Middle Eastern fare at rock-bottom prices. **Il Mandarino** (⊠ Via Condotta 17/r, Piazza della Signoria neighborhood, ☎ 055/2396130) has excellent hot-and-sour soup and more-than-passable dumplings. Enjoy them with white linen tablecloths and a bottle of Verdicchio. If you're craving doner kebab (thin, grilled slices of beef or lamb), look no further than **Mavi** (⊠ Via dei Benci 15/r, Santa Croce neighborhood, ☎ 055/2466760). Portions are copious, and the hot sauce is darn hot. Most dishes at **Mister Hang** (⊠ Via Ghibellina 134/r, Santa Croce neighborhood, ☎ 055/2344810) are Chinese, but the place also offers Thai options. **Saigon Restaurant** (⊠ Via del Ponte alle Mosse 2-8/r, ☎ 055/350541), just outside the centro storico on the other side of Porto al Prato, has a mixed Chinese and Vietnamese menu. Scotch bonnet peppers and sour cream are novelties in Florence (and, indeed, Italy), but they can be found at **Tacos** (⊠ Via dei Benci 47/r, Santa Croce neighborhood, ☎ 055/241970), popular with locals as well as foreign students.

Gelaterie and Pasticcerie

Head down colorful Borgo La Croce to **Dolci e Dolcezze** (⊠ Piazza C. Beccaria 8/r, Santa Croce neighborhood, ☎ 055/2345458), a somewhat off-the-beaten-path *pasticceria* (bakery), and you'll be rewarded with the prettiest and tastiest cakes, sweets, and tarts in town. But don't come Monday, because it's closed. **Gelaterie Carabe** (⊠ Via Ricasoli 60/r, San Marco neighborhood, ☎ 055/289476) specializes in things Sicilian (including cannoli). Its *granità* (granular flavored ices), made only in the summer, are tart and flavorful—perfect thirst-quenchers. Lemon is a good choice. Florentines with serious sweet tooths come to **I Dolci di Patrizio Corsi** (⊠ Borgo Albizi 15/r, Santa Croce neighborhood, ☎ 055/2480367), which offers a bewildering array of chocolate- and cream-filled sweets. It's closed on Sunday. The refined **Robiglio** (⊠ Via dei Servi 112/r, Santissima Annunziata neighborhood, ☎ 055/212784) offers biscotti, carefully crafted cakes and tarts, and all variations on coffee. Although **Vestri** (⊠ Borgo Albizi 11/4, Santa Croce neighborhood, ☎ 055/2340374) is devoted to chocolate in all its guises, it offers a small but sublime selection of chocolate-based gelati, including one with hot peppers.The *cioccolata con caffè* (chocolate ice cream heavily dosed with espresso) is one reason so many people think **Vivoli** (⊠ Via Isola delle Stinche 7, Santa Croce neighborhood, ☎ 055/292334) is one of the best gelaterie (ice-cream shops) in town.

Pizzerias

Pizzas in Florence can't compete with their counterparts in Rome or Naples, but you can sample a few good approximations. In the Oltrarno, **Borgo Antico** (⊠ Piazza Santo Spirito 6/r, Santo Spirito/San Frediano neighborhood, ☎ 055/210437), serves up pizza as well as other trattoria fare. The pizza at **Il Pizziauolo** (⊠ Via dei Macci 113/r, Santa Croce neighborhood, ☎ 055/241171) is probably as close as you're going to get in Florence to the Rome and Naples versions. It does a thick crust, Naples style. The pizza *con salsicce e friarielli* (with sausage and a bitter green that's native around Naples) deserves respect. The crust on the pizza at **Le Campane** (✉ Borgo La Croce 85/87/r, Santa Croce neighborhood, ☎ 055/2341101) falls between the typical Roman and Neapolitan versions in terms of thickness. The trattoria fare here emphasizes Sicilian specialties.

Rosticcerie and Tavole Calde

Rosticcerie and *tavole calde* are nice alternatives to the more-formal trattorie, osterie, and ristoranti dining options. Rosticcerie offer everything from soup to nuts in assembling lunch or dinner; sometimes they also offer seating. Tavole calde (literally, "hot tables") are sometimes synonymous with rosticcerie, but while a rosticceria almost always offers whole roast chickens, that's not always the case with a tavola calda. Both are significantly less expensive than full sit-down service—another part of their appeal.

At **Alfio e Beppe** (✉ Via Cavour 118-120/r, San Marco neighborhood, ☎ 055/214108), you can watch chickens roast over high flames as you decide which of the other delightful things you're going to eat with it. The daily specials at **Da Rocco** (✉ Piazza Ghiberti, off Via della Mattonaia, Santa Croce neighborhood, ☎ no phone), in the Mercato Sant'Ambrogio, can include *polpettine alla pizzaiuolo* (veal meatballs in tangy tomato-oregano sauce). Portions are generous. In summer, try the *panzanella,* a salad made with bread crumbs, tomatoes, and basil and doused with extra virgin olive oil. Near the Uffizi is **Guiliano Centro** (✉ Via de' Neri 74/r, Piazza della Signoria neighborhood, ☎ 055/2382723), with a lovely array of food including crisp *pollo fritto* (fried chicken). **La Ghiotta** (✉ Via Pietrapiana 7/r, Santa Croce neighborhood, ☎ 055/241237) sells whole and half chickens, grilled or roasted, among other things. The baked fennel is also a treat. Near Santa Maria Novella is **La Spada** (✉ Via del Moro 66/r, Santa Maria Novella neighborhood, ☎ 055/218757). Walk in and inhale the fragrant aromas of meats cooked in the wood-burning oven. La Spada also offers a complete line of take-out. **Ramraj** (✉ Via Ghibellina 61/r, Santa Croce neighborhood, ☎ 055/240999) offers Indian food to take away.

Salumerie

Salumerie, gourmet food shops strong on fine fresh ingredients such as meats and cheeses, are great for picking up a picnic lunch or assembling dinner. If you find yourself in the Oltrarno hungry for lunch or a snack, drop into **Azzarri Delicatesse** (✉ Borgo S. Jacopo 27/b–27/c, Santo Spirito/San Frediano neighborhood, ☎ 055/2381714), closed Sunday and Monday morning. You can get sandwiches made or get the fixings to go. Its list of cheeses, some of which come from France, is rather impressive. Looking for some cheddar cheese to pile in your panino? **Pegna** (✉ Via dello Studio 8, Duomo neighborhood, ☎ 055/282701), closed Sunday and Saturday afternoon, has been selling Italian and non-Italian food since 1860. In the Mercato Centrale, **Perini** (✉ enter at Via dell'Aretino, San Lorenzo neighborhood, ☎ 055/2398306), closed Sunday, sells everything from prosciutto and mixed meats to sauces for pasta and a wide assortment of antipasti. It's probably the most seductive little food shop in Florence—be prepared to drop a lot of money. At **Salumeria Verdi** (✉ Via Verdi 36/r, Santa Croce neighborhood, ☎ 055/244517), options include well-prepared sandwiches and everything to assemble a dinner. You can eat in or take out.

LODGING

Florence's importance not only as a tourist city but as a convention center and the site of the Pitti fashion collections guarantees a variety of accommodations. The high demand also means that, except in winter, reservations are a must. If you find yourself in Florence with no reservations, go to **Consorzio ITA** (⊠ Stazione Centrale, Santa Maria Novella neighborhood, ☎ 055/282893).

CATEGORY	COST*
$$$$	over €250
$$$	€175–€250
$$	€100–€175
$	under €100

Prices are for two people in a standard double room, including tax and service.

Centro Storico

$$$$ 🖫 **Brunelleschi.** Architects united a Byzantine tower, a medieval church,
★ and a later building into a stunning structure when creating this unique hotel. Medieval stone walls and brick arches contrast pleasantly with the plush, contemporary decor. The ample bathrooms are done in beige travertine marble. ⊠ *Piazza Sant'Elisabetta 3/r (off Via dei Calzaiuoli), Piazza della Signoria neighborhood, 50122, ☎ 055/27370, FAX 055/219653, WEB www.hotelbrunelleschi.it. 96 rooms, 7 suites. Restaurant, cable TV, bar, meeting room, parking (fee), some pets allowed. AE, DC, MC, V.*

$$$$ 🖫 **Grand Hotel Minerva.** Despite its size, this hotel, on a beautiful Renaissance square overlooking the church of Santa Maria Novella and minutes from the train station, is intimate. With their wicker furniture and bright fabrics, public rooms recall the 1960s. The doors to each room display full-size photographs of historic Florentine doors. Bathrooms are colorfully tiled and spacious. A sumptuous breakfast buffet is offered. ⊠ *Piazza Santa Maria Novella 16, Santa Maria Novella neighborhood, 50123, ☎ 055/27230, 055/2723182 reservations, FAX 055/268281, WEB www.grandhotelminerva.com. 83 rooms, 16 suites. Restaurant, in-room safes, in-room hot tubs (some), cable TV, in-room VCRs, minibars, pool, bicycles, bar, dry cleaning, laundry service, concierge, Internet, meeting rooms, parking (fee), some pets allowed, no-smoking rooms. AE, DC, MC, V. CP.*

$$$$ 🖫 **Hotel degli Orafi.** A key scene in *A Room with a View* was shot in this pensione, which today is adorned with chintz and marble. Many rooms have river views; a few have terraces. Breakfast is served in opulent surroundings—check out the crystal chandelier and the frescoed ceiling. ⊠ *Lungarno Archibusieri 4, Piazza della Signoria neighborhood, 50121, ☎ 055/26622, FAX 055/2662111, WEB www.hoteldegliorafi.it. 42 rooms. In-room safes, minibars, cable TV, bar, library, baby-sitting, laundry service, concierge, parking (fee). AE, DC, MC, V. BP.*

$$$$ 🖫 **Hotel Helvetia and Bristol.** Painstaking care has gone into making
★ this hotel one of the prettiest and most intimate in town. From the cozy yet sophisticated lobby with its pietra serena columns (made of a gray sandstone) to the guest rooms decorated with prints, you feel as if you're a guest in a well-appointed manor house. The restaurant serves sumptuous fare in a romantic setting. ⊠ *Via dei Pescioni 2, Piazza della Repubblica neighborhood, 50123, ☎ 055/26651, FAX 055/288353, WEB www.thecharminghotels.it/helvetia. 44 rooms, 23 suites. Restaurant, room service, in-room safes, in-room hot tubs (some), minibars, cable TV, in-room VCRs, bar, baby-sitting, dry cleaning, laun-*

56

Florence Lodging

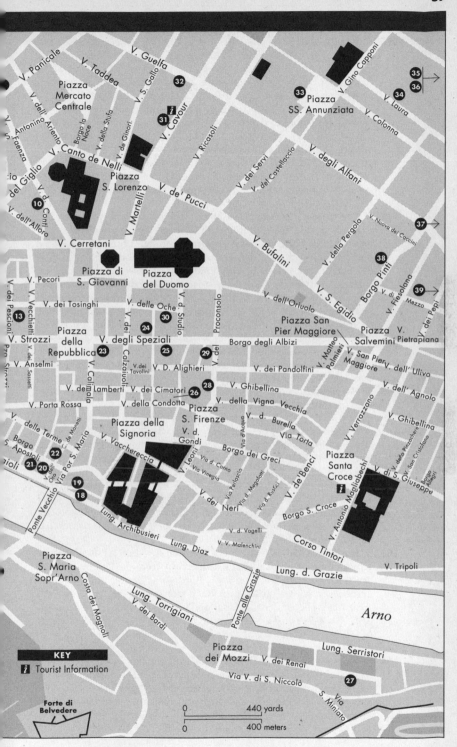

V. Panicale
V. Taddea
V. Guelfa
V. S. Gallo
32
V. Gino Capponi
35
36

Piazza Mercate Centrale
V. dell'Ariento
V. della Stufa
V. de' Ginori
31
i
V. Cavour

33 Piazza SS. Annunziata
V. Laura
34
V. Colonna

V. d'Antonino
V. Faenza
Borgo la Noce
V. Ricasoli
V. dei Servi
V. degli Alfani

V. Canto de Nelli
V. del Castellaccio

zio del Giglio
V. d. Conti
Piazza S. Lorenzo
V. de' Pucci

10
V. dell'Alloro
V. Martelli

V. Cerretani
V. Bufalini
V. della Pergola
V. Nuova dei Caccini
37

Piazza di S. Giovanni
Piazza del Duomo
V. S. Egidio
Borgo Pinti
38

V. Pecori
V. dei Vecchietti
V. dei Pescioni
V. dell'Oriuolo
V. d. Fiesolana
Mezzo
39

V. dei Tosinghi
V. delle Oche
30
V. d. Studio
Proconsolo
V. dei Pepi

13
V. Strozzi
Piazza della Repubblica
24
Piazza San Pier Maggiore
Piazza Salvemini
V. Pietrapiana

V. Anselmi
23
V. degli Speziali
25
Borgo degli Albizi
V. Matteo Palmieri
V. San Pier Maggiore
V. dell'Uliva

V. d. Sassetti
Pza Strozzi
V. Calimala
Calzaiuoli
V. dei Tavolini
V. D. Alighieri
29
V. dei Pandolfini
V. dell'Agnolo

V. dei Lamberti
V. dei Cimatori
26
28
V. Ghibellina
V. Verrazzano
V. Ghibellina

V. Porta Rossa
V. della Condotta
Piazza S. Firenze
V. della Vigna Vecchia
V. d. dalla Pinzochere
V. San Cristofano

V. delle Terme
C. dei Monaldi
Piazza della Signoria
V. d. Gondi
V. d. Acqua
V. d. Burella
Via Torta

Borgo S. Apostoli
22
V. Vacchereccia
V. Leoni
Via d. Corno
Borgo dei Greci
V. de' Benci
Piazza Santa Croce
Borgo degli Alberti
V. di S. Giuseppe

21 **20**
V. d. Opera
Via Por S. Maria
Via Vinegia
Via Perlaccio
Via d. Rustici

zioli
19
V. dei Neri
Via d. Megalotti
V. Antonio Magliabechi
i

18
Lung. Archibusieri
V. d. Vagelli
Borgo S. Croce

Ponte Vecchio
Lung. Diaz
V. V. Malenchini
Corso Tintori
V. Tripoli

Piazza S. Maria Sopr'Arno
Lung. d. Grazie

Costa dei Magnoli
Lung. Torrigiani
V. dei Bardi
Ponte alle Grazie
Arno
Lung. Serristori

Piazza dei Mozzi
V. dei Renai
V. dei Renai

Via V. di S. Niccolò
Via S. Miniato
27

KEY

i Tourist Information

Forte di Belvedere

0 — 440 yards
0 — 400 meters

dry service, concierge, Internet, meeting room, parking (fee). AE, DC, MC, V. CP, MAP.

$$$$ ⚟ **Hotel Savoy.** From the outside, the building looks very much like the turn-of-the-19th-century structure that it is. Inside, however, sleek minimalism prevails at this up-to-the-minute hotel in the heart of the centro storico. Sitting rooms have a funky edge, their cream-color walls dotted with contemporary prints. Muted colors dress the rooms, which have streamlined furniture and soaring ceilings; many have views of the Duomo's cupola or the Piazza della Repubblica. The deep marble tubs might be reason enough to stay here—but you'll also appreciate the efficient and courteous staff. *Piazza della Repubblica 7, 50123,* ☎ *055/27351,* 𝔽𝔸𝕏 *055/2735888,* 𝕎𝔼𝔹 *www.roccofortehotels.com. 98 rooms, 9 suites. Restaurant, in-room fax, in-room safes, minibars, cable TV, bar, concierge, Internet, meeting rooms, parking (fee). AE, DC, MC, V. EP.*

$$$ ⚟ **Grand Hotel Cavour.** The lobby of this hotel has high vaulted ceilings and marble floors dotted with Oriental rugs; a couple of strategically placed potted palms complete the scene. A building has stood on this site, in the heart of Dante's old neighborhood, since 978. Rooms are quietly cheerful with floral-print curtains and matching bedspreads; many of the walls have stenciled decorations. The breakfast room has contemporary stained-glass windows; the rooftop terrace offers a stunning view of the centro storico. The hotel is amazingly plush for the price. ✉ *Via del Proconsolo 3, Bargello neighborhood 50122,* ☎ *055/282461,* 𝔽𝔸𝕏 *055/218955,* 𝕎𝔼𝔹 *www.hotelcavour.com. 105 rooms. Cable TV, breakfast room, minibars, in-room safe, dry cleaning, laundry service, concierge, some pets allowed, no-smoking rooms, Internet. AE, DC, MC, V. CP.*

$$$ ⚟ **Hermitage.** A stone's throw from the Ponte Vecchio, this is a fine little hotel with an enviable location. All rooms are decorated differently with lively wallpaper; some have views of Palazzo Vecchio and others of the Arno. The rooftop terrace, where you can have breakfast or an aperitivo, is decked with flowers. The lobby feels like a friend's living room—its warm yellow walls are welcoming. Double glazing and air-conditioning help to keep street noise at bay. (The hotel has an elevator at the top of a short flight of stairs from the street.) *Vicolo Marzio 1 (Piazza del Pesce, Ponte Vecchio), Piazza della Signoria neighborhood, 50122,* ☎ *055/287216,* 𝔽𝔸𝕏 *055/212208,* 𝕎𝔼𝔹 *www.hermitagehotel. com. 27 rooms, 1 suite. Cable TV, baby-sitting, laundry service, parking (fee), some pets allowed. MC, V. BP.*

$$$ ⚟ **Hotel Benivieni.** It's hard to believe that this quiet, tranquil former 15th-century palace is just one block away from the Duomo. Rooms are spacious with high ceilings, hardwood floors, and sweeping draperies. A winter garden provides a wonderful place to while away some time. The affable Caldana family ably staffs the front desk. *Via delle Oche 5, Duomo neighborhood, 50122,* ☎ *055/2382133,* 𝔽𝔸𝕏 *055/2398248,* 𝕎𝔼𝔹 *www.hotelbenivieni.it. 15 rooms. In-room safes, cable TV, Internet, parking (fee), some pets allowed. AE, DC, MC, V. BP.*

$$ ⚟ **Alessandra.** The location, a block from the Ponte Vecchio, and the clean, ample rooms make this a good choice. The building, known as the Palazzo Roselli del Turco, was designed in 1507 by Baccio d'Agnolo, a student of Michelangelo's. Though little remains of the original design save for the high wood ceilings, there's still an aura of grandeur. Several of the rooms have views of the Arno, and the sole suite is spacious and a steal for this category. The English-speaking staff is friendly and helpful. *Borgo Santi Apostoli 17, Santa Maria Novella neighborhood, 50123,* ☎ *055/283438,* 𝔽𝔸𝕏 *055/210619,* 𝕎𝔼𝔹 *www.hotelalessandra.com. 26 rooms, 18 with bath; 1 suite. Cable TV with video games, Internet, parking (fee). AE, MC, V. Closed Dec. 10–26. BP.*

$$ ▦ **Torre Guelfa.** Enter this hidden hotel through an immense wooden door on a narrow street, and continue through an iron gate and up a few steps to an elevator that takes you to the third floor. A few more steps and you're in the 13th-century Florentine *torre* (tower). Some guest rooms have canopied beds, some have balconies. The Torre Guelfa once protected the fabulously wealthy Acciaiuoli family. Now it's one of the best-located small hotels in Florence, where you can have breakfast or drinks on a rooftop that provides unmatched Florentine panoramas. *Borgo Santi Apostoli 8, Santa Maria Novella neighborhood, 50123,* ☎ *055/2396338,* FAX *055/2398577. 18 rooms, 2 suites. Minibars, cable TV, bar, Internet, parking (fee), some pets allowed. AE, MC, V. CP.*

$ ▦ **Albergo Firenze.** A block from the Duomo, this hotel is in one of the oldest piazzas in Florence. Though the reception area and hallways have all the charm of a college dormitory, the similarity ends upon entering the spotlessly clean rooms. For the location, the place is a great bargain. *Piazza Donati 4, Duomo neighborhood, 50122,* ☎ *055/ 214203,* FAX *055/212370. 58 rooms. Cable TV, parking (fee); no air-conditioning. No credit cards. CP.*

$ ▦ **Cristina.** A friendly and enthusiastic staff runs this tiny hotel one block from the Uffizi and the Bargello. Rooms are large, clean, fresh, and well furnished, with desks and comfortable beds, but the prices are still low. A few rooms can accommodate up to four. ✉ *Via della Condotta 4, Duomo neighborhood, 50122,* ☎ FAX *055/214484. 9 rooms, 4 with bath. Parking (fee), some pets allowed; no air-conditioning, no room TVs. AE, DC, MC, V. CP.*

$ ▦ **Soggiorno Sani.** Intrepid budgeteers need look no further than this no-frills accommodation in the middle of the centro storico. Its six rooms feel like guest rooms in someone's house; each has a private shower and sink, but the bathroom is shared. The look is Spartan, which may explain why it attracts the occasional visiting academic. A few rooms have a tremendous view of Orsanmichele, while others look out over the Casa di Dante. There's no reception area or desk service, but if you're looking for a place to lay your head at exceptionally low prices, you've found your spot. ✉ *Piazza dei Giuochi 1, Duomo neighborhood, 50123,* ☎ *055/211235,* FAX *055/2654386. 6 rooms with 1 shared bath. Parking (fee); no air-conditioning, no room phones, no room TVs. No credit cards. CP.*

San Lorenzo and Beyond

$$$ ▦ **Porta Faenza.** A 12th-century medieval well discovered during renovations is a focal point in the lobby of this good-value hotel; rooms and bathrooms are spacious and decorated in Florentine style. Italian Antonio Lelli and his Canadian wife, Rose, go out of their way to make you feel at home. *Via Faenza 77, Santa Maria Novella neighborhood, 50123,* ☎ *055/284119,* FAX *055/210101,* WEB *www.hotelportafaenza. it. 25 rooms. In-room safes, cable TV, baby-sitting, parking (fee), some pets allowed, no-smoking floor. AE, DC, MC, V. BP.*

$$ ▦ **Bellettini.** You're in good hands at this small hotel on three floors
★ (the top floor has two nice rooms with a view). Sisters Marcia and Gina Naldini, along with their husbands, run the place and provide a relaxed atmosphere. Attractive public rooms have a smattering of antiques. The good-size rooms have Venetian or Tuscan provincial decor; bathrooms are bright and modern. The low room rates include an ample buffet breakfast and air-conditioning. ✉ *Via dei Conti 7, Santa Maria Novella neighborhood, 50123,* ☎ *055/213561,* FAX *055/283551,* WEB *www.hotelbellettini.com. 28 rooms. Cable TV, bar, parking (fee), some pets allowed. AE, DC, MC, V. CP.*

Near Piazza San Marco and Beyond

$$$ ⚇ **Il Guelfo Bianco.** The building, which dates from the 15th century, has been renovated but its Renaissance charm still shines. Rooms have high ceilings (some are coffered) and windows are triple-glazed. Price and location are selling points; the hotel couldn't be more central even though it feels somewhat off the beaten path. The young, English-speaking staff is helpful. ✉ *Via Cavour 29, San Marco neighborhood, 50129,* ☎ *055/288330,* FAX *055295203,* WEB *www.ilguelfobianco.it. 29 rooms. In-room safes, minibars, cable TV, dry cleaning, laundry service, business services, parking (fee), some pets allowed. AE, DC, MC, V. BP.*

$$$ ⚇ **Loggiata dei Serviti.** Although Brunelleschi didn't design the building this hotel occupies, he might as well have. A mirror image of the architect's famous Spedale degli Innocenti across the way, the Loggiato is tucked away on one of the city's loveliest squares. Occupying a 16th-century former monastery, the building was originally a refuge for traveling priests. Vaulted ceilings, tasteful furnishings (some antique), canopy beds, and rich fabrics make this a find if you want to get the feel of Florence in an attractively spare Renaissance building but also enjoy modern creature comforts. *Piazza Santissima Annunziata 3, Santissima Annunziata neighborhood, 50122,* ☎ *055/289592,* FAX *055/ 289595,* WEB *www.loggiatodeiservitihotel.it. 29 rooms. In-room safes, minibars, cable TV, bar, baby-sitting, laundry service, parking (fee), some pets allowed. AE, DC, MC, V. BP.*

$$ ⚇ **Hotel Casci.** In this refurbished 14th-century palace, the home of Giacchino Rossini in 1851–55, the friendly Lombardi family offers spotless rooms and a peaceful atmosphere. Rooms are functional, and many of them open out onto various terraces (a view doesn't necessarily follow, however). It's on a very busy thoroughfare, but triple-glazed windows allow for a sound night's sleep. Many rooms easily accommodate an extra bed or two, so this is a good option for people traveling with children. The hotel also offers cable TV and in-room hair dryers—a rarity for hotels at this price. ✉ *Via Cavour 13, San Marco neighborhood, 50129,* ☎ *055/211686,* FAX *055/2396461,* WEB *www.hotelcasci.com. 25 rooms. In-room safes, minibars, cable TV, dry cleaning, laundry service, Internet, parking (fee), some pets allowed. AE, DC, MC, V. CP.*

$$ ⚇ **Morandi alla Crocetta.** Near Piazza Santissima Annunziata, this is
★ a charming and distinguished residence in which you're made to feel like a privileged friend of the family. It's close to the sights but very quiet, in a former convent, and is furnished comfortably in the classic style of a gracious Florentine home. The Morandi is an exceptional hotel and a good value. It's small, so try to book well in advance. ✉ *Via Laura 50, Santissima Annunziata neighborhood, 50121,* ☎ *055/ 2344747,* FAX *055/2480954,* WEB *www.hotelmorandi.it. 10 rooms. In-room safes, minibars, room TVs, Internet, parking (fee), some pets allowed. AE, DC, MC, V. CP.*

Santa Maria Novella to the Arno

$$$$ ⚇ **Excelsior.** Florentine hotels don't get much more exquisite or expensive
★ than this, which explains why world leaders stay here when in Florence. Although furnished in the Empire style, the rooms still feel up-to-date. High ceilings, dramatic views overlooking the Arno, patterned rugs, tasteful prints—all these provide a sense of extravagant well-being. Public rooms have painted wooden ceilings, stained glass, and acres of Oriental carpets strewn over marble floors. ✉ *Piazza Ognissanti 3, Lungarno Nord neighborhood, 50123,* ☎ *055/264201,* FAX *055/210278,* WEB *www.westin.com. 168 rooms. Restaurant, minibars, room TVs with*

movies, baby-sitting, dry cleaning, laundry service, concierge, Internet, business services, meeting rooms, parking (fee), some pets allowed, no-smoking rooms. AE, DC, MC, V. CP.

$$$$ 🖭 **Gallery Art Hotel.** High design resides at this art showcase near the Ponte Vecchio. Rooms are sleek and uncluttered and dressed mostly in neutrals. Luxe touches, such as leather headboards and kimono robes, abound. But what else would you expect from property in the Salvatore Ferragamo group? ⊠ *Vicolo dell'Oro 5, Santa Maria Novella neighborhood, 50123,* ☎ *055/27263,* 🖾 *055/268557,* 🕸 *www. lungarnohotels.com. 65 rooms, 9 suites. Restaurant, room service, in-room fax, in-room safes, minibars, cable TV, bar, laundry service, concierge, Internet, business services, parking (fee), some pets allowed, no smoking rooms. AE, DC, MC, V. CP.*

$$$$ 🖭 **Grand.** Across the piazza from the Excelsior, this Florentine classic provides all the luxurious amenities of its slightly larger sister. Rooms are outfitted in either Renaissance or Empire style; the former scheme includes deep, richly hued damask brocades and canopy beds, and the latter a lovely profusion of crisp prints and patterned fabric offsetting white walls. The overall effect is sumptuous, as is the view either of the Arno or overlooking a small rectangular courtyard lined with potted orange trees. The sleek restaurant, with a cutting-edge menu, is a winner. *Piazza Ognissanti 1, Lungarno Nord neighborhood, 50123,* ☎ *055/288781,* 🖾 *055/217400,* 🕸 *www.grandhotelflorence. com. 107 rooms. Restaurant, minibars, room TVs with movies, piano bar, baby-sitting, dry cleaning, laundry service, concierge, Internet, business services, meeting rooms, parking (fee), no-smoking rooms. AE, DC, MC, V. CP.*

$$$ 🖭 **Beacci Tornabuoni.** Florentine pensioni don't come any more clas-
★ sic than this. In a 14th-century palazzo, it has old-fashioned style and just enough modern comfort to keep you happy. The sitting room has a large fireplace, the terrace has a tremendous view of some major Florentine monuments, and the wallpapered rooms are inviting. On Monday, Wednesday, and Friday nights, the dining room opens, serving Tuscan specialties. *Via Tornabuoni 3, Santa Maria Novella neighborhood, 50123,* ☎ *055/212645,* 🖾 *055/283594,* 🕸 *www.bthotel.it. 28 rooms. Restaurant, minibars, cable TV, bar, Internet, parking (fee), some pets allowed. AE, DC, MC, V. CP, MAP.*

$$–$$$ 🖭 **La Residenza.** On Florence's fanciest shopping street, on the upper floors of a restored 15th-century building, La Residenza has character and comfort. The roof garden and adjacent sitting room are added attractions. Paintings and etchings add interest to the rooms, which have soundproofing and satellite TV. Some rooms have private terraces (request when booking if you want one). ⊠ *Via Tornabuoni 8, Santa Maria Novella neighborhood, 50123,* ☎ *055/218684,* 🖾 *055/284197. 24 rooms, 20 with bath. Restaurant, room service, minibars, cable TV, bar, baby-sitting, dry cleaning, laundry service, concierge, parking (fee), some pets allowed. AE, DC, MC, V. CP, MAP.*

$$ 🖭 **Le Vigne.** Family-run and operated, this small hotel looks out over one of Florence's most beautiful and central squares. Despite soaring high ceilings, the feeling is comfortable and homey, with rooms furnished in 19th-century Florentine style. It's a good choice if you're on a budget. Nice touches include complimentary afternoon tea and homemade breakfast jams and cakes. There's also a children's play area. ⊠ *Piazza Santa Maria Novella 24, 50123,* ☎ *055/294449,* 🖾 *055/2302263. 25 rooms. Cable TV, Internet, parking (fee). AE, DC, MC, V. BP.*

$$ 🖭 **Nuova Italia.** Near the train station and within walking distance of major sights, this hotel is run by a genial English-speaking family. Its homey rooms are clean and simply furnished. Air-conditioning and triple-

glazed windows ensure restful nights. Some rooms can accommodate extra beds. Low bargain rates include breakfast. *Via Faenza 26, Santa Maria Novella neighborhood, 50123, ☎ 055/268430, FAX 055/210941. 20 rooms. Cable TV, parking (fee). AE, MC, V. CP.*

$$ ⊡ **Villa Azalee.** A five-minute walk from the train station and within spitting distance of the Fortezza da Basso (site of the Pitti fashion shows), this 19th-century villa deftly recalls its previous incarnation as a private residence. Quilted, floral-print slipcovers dress the furniture, and throw rugs cover the floors. Many rooms have views of the hotel's garden, and some have private terraces. *Viale Fratelli Rosselli 44, Santa Maria Novella neighborhood, 50018, ☎ 055/214242, FAX 055/268264, WEB www.villa-azalee.it. 25 rooms. Minibars, cable TV, bicycles, bar, parking (fee), some pets allowed. AE, DC, MC, V. CP.*

$ ⊡ **Pensione Ferretti.** Minutes from the Piazza Santa Maria Novella, this pensione has views onto a tiny piazza containing the Croce al Trebbio, as well as easy access to the historic center. English-speaking owner Luciano Michel and his South Africa–born wife, Sue, do just about anything to make you feel at home (including 24-hour free Internet access). Though housed in a 16th-century palazzo, accommodations are simple and no-frills. Ceiling fans are a help in warm months. *Via delle Belle Donne 17, Santa Maria Novella neighborhood, 50123, ☎ 055/2381328, FAX 055/219288. 16 rooms, 6 with bath. Fans, Internet, parking (fee), some pets allowed; no air-conditioning, no room TVs. AE, DC, MC, V. CP.*

The Oltrarno and Beyond

$$$$ ⊡ **Lungarno.** The location—directly across the river from the Palazzo Vecchio and the Duomo—couldn't be better. Rooms and suites have private terraces that jut out over the Arno. Four suites in a 13th-century tower preserve atmospheric details like exposed stone walls and old archways and look out onto a little square with another medieval tower covered in jasmine. The chic decor approximates a breezily elegant home, with lots of crisp white fabrics with blue trim. A wall of windows and a sea of white couches makes the lobby bar one of the nicest places in the city to stop for a drink. *Borgo San Jacopo 14, Lungarno Sud neighborhood, 50125, ☎ 055/27261, FAX 055/268437, WEB www.lungarnohotels.com. 60 rooms, 11 suites. Restaurant, cable TV with movies, bar, Internet, parking (fee), some pets allowed, no-smoking rooms. AE, DC, MC, V. BP.*

$$$$ ⊡ **Torre di Bellosguardo.** *Bellosguardo* means "beautiful view"; given the view of Florence you get here, the name is fitting. Perched atop a hill minutes from the *viale* (the outer limit defining the centro storico), the hotel is reached via a narrow road dotted with olive trees. Dante's friend Guido Calvacanti supposedly chose this serene spot for his country villa, but little remains from the early 14th century. The reception area, a former ballroom, has soaring ceilings with frescoes by Francavilla (1553–1615). Guest rooms, all with high ceilings, are simple and have heavy wooden furniture. *✉ Via Roti Michelozzi 2, 50124, ☎ 055/2298145, FAX 055/229008, WEB www.torrebellosguardo.com. 9 rooms, 7 suites. Pool, bar, free parking. AE, MC, V.*

$$$$ ⊡ **Villa La Massa.** You approach the tall and imposing villa, 15 min-
 ★   utes out of town, via a gravel drive lined with flowers. The public rooms are outfitted in Renaissance style, with a color scheme of deep green, gold, and crimson. Guest rooms have high ceilings, some with frescoes, plush carpeting, and deep bathtubs. A pool and beautiful views of the Arno are bonuses. The restaurant is superb and serves Tuscan classics as well as less-standard offerings; a pianist quietly plays old standards while you eat. A shuttle bus runs every hour to and from the center of

Florence. ⊠ *Via della Massa 24, Candeli, 50012,* ☎ *055/62611,* FAX *055/633102,* WEB *www.villalamassa.com. 19 rooms, 18 suites. Restaurant, minibars, room TVs with movies, pool, 15 tennis courts, bar, babysitting, dry cleaning, laundry service, concierge, business services, Internet, meeting rooms, parking (fee), some pets allowed, no-smoking rooms. AE, DC, MC, V. Closed Dec.–Mar. CP.*

$$ ⊡ **Albergeo La Scaletta.** For a tremendous view of the Boboli Gardens, look no farther than this exquisite pensione run by a mother-and-son team. Near the Ponte Vecchio and Palazzo Pitti, it has simply furnished yet rather large rooms and a sunny breakfast room. In warm weather two flower-bedecked terraces are open, one with a stunning 360-degree view of Florence. ⊠ *Via Guicciardini 13, Palazzo Pitti neighborhood, 50125,* ☎ *055/283028,* FAX *055/289562,* WEB *www.lascaletta.com. 11 rooms, 10 with bath. Bar, parking (fee), some pets allowed; no TV in some rooms. MC, V. CP.*

$$ ⊡ **Annalena.** The story goes that Annalena, a 15th-century maiden, married a Medici; another man, smitten with her and angry at her refusal to capitulate, murdered her husband and her young son. The devastated widow then turned her private home into a convent. Is it true? Well, it certainly is romantic, as is the former convent, now pensione, that bears her name. The Annalena, which was transformed from a convent into a school for young ladies before becoming a hotel, is down the street from the Palazzo Pitti. With its high ceilings and spacious rooms, it's a perfect place to unwind. Some rooms overlook a private garden, and one has a private terrace. ⊠ *Via Romana 34, Santo Spirito/San Frediano neighborhood, 50125,* ☎ *055/229600,* FAX *055/ 222403,* WEB *www.hotelannalena.it. 20 rooms. In-room safes, minibars, cable TV, baby-sitting, laundry service, parking (fee), some pets allowed; no air-conditioning in some rooms. AE, DC, MC, V. BP.*

$$ ⊡ **Hotel Silla.** The entrance to this slightly off-the-beaten-path hotel is through a 15th-century courtyard lined with potted plants and sculpture-filled niches. The hotel, formerly a palazzo dating from the 15th century, is up a flight of stairs and has two floors. Rooms are simply furnished and walls are papered; some have views of Via de' Renai and the Arno, while others overlook a less-traveled road. Breakfast may be taken in a room that preserves an Empire feel (including two chandeliers from the early 19th century); when it's warm, a large, sunny terrace offers the perfect place to read or to write that postcard. ⊠ *Via de' Renai 5, San Niccolò neighborhood, 50125,* ☎ *055/2342888,* FAX *055/2341437,* WEB *www.hotelsilla.it. 35 rooms. In-room safes, minibars, cable TV, bar, baby-sitting, dry cleaning, laundry service, concierge, parking (fee), some pets allowed. AE, DC, MC, V. CP.*

Santa Croce

$$$$ ⊡ **Hotel Regency.** The noise and crowds of Florence seem far from this stylish hotel in a residential district near the Sinagoga, though you're not more than 10 minutes from the Accademia and Michelangelo's *David.* Across the street is Piazza d'Azeglio, a small public park that somehow evokes 19th-century Middle Europe. Rooms dressed in richly colored fabrics and antique-style furniture remain faithful to the hotel's 19th-century origins as a private mansion. The restaurant here is equally sophisticated. *Piazza d'Azeglio 3, Santa Croce neighborhood, 50121* ☎ *055/245247,* FAX *055/2346735,* WEB *www.regency-hotel.com. 34 rooms. Restaurant, in-room safes, minibars, cable TV, bar, baby-sitting, concierge, Internet, parking (fee), some pets allowed, no-smoking rooms. AE, DC, MC, V. BP.*

$$$$ ⊡ **J&J.** Away from the crowds, on a quiet street within walking distance of the sights, this unusual hotel is a converted 16th-century

monastery. Its rooms are large and suitelike—ideal for honeymooners, families, and small groups. Some rooms are duplexes, and all are imaginatively arranged around a central courtyard and decorated with flair. The smaller rooms are more intimate, some opening onto a little shared courtyard. The gracious owners enjoy chatting in the light and airy lounge; breakfast is served in a glassed-in Renaissance loggia or in the central courtyard. *Via di Mezzo 20, Santa Croce neighborhood, 50121, ☎ 055/263121, FAX 055/240282, WEB www.jandjhotel.com. 20 rooms. Cable TV, bar, Internet, parking (fee) AE, DC, MC, V. BP.*

$$$$ ☷ **Monna Lisa.** Housed in a 15th-century palazzo, with parts of the build-
★   ing dating from the 13th century, this hotel retains some of its original wood-coffered ceilings from the 1500s, as well as its original marble staircase. Some rooms are small, but they're tastefully decorated, each with different floral wallpaper. The public rooms retain a 19th-century aura, and the intimate bar, with its red velveteen wallpaper, is a good place to unwind. *Borgo Pinti 27, Santa Croce neighborhood, 50121, ☎ 055/2479751, FAX 055/2479755, WEB www.monnalisa.it. 45 rooms. In-room safes, minibars, cable TV, bar, laundry service, parking (fee), some pets allowed, no-smoking rooms. AE, DC, MC, V. BP.*

$$ ☷ **Hotel Liana.** With this hotel, it's possible to experience palazzo life without breaking the bank. Steps from the *viale* (the outer limit defining the centro storico) but still very much within the bounds of the historic center, the Liana, originally a 19th-century villa, retains the feel of another era. The lobby has high ceilings and large windows; a sweeping staircase leads to the breakfast room, which has a period fresco on its ceiling. A small bar offers the makings of an aperitivo; sip it in the gazebo in the garden. ✉ *Via Alfieri 18, Santa Croce neighborhood, 50121, ☎ 055/245303 or 055/245304, FAX 055/2344596, WEB www.hotelliana.com. 24 rooms. In-room safes (some), minibars (some), bar, dry cleaning, parking (fee), some pets allowed; no air-conditioning in some rooms. AE, DC, MC, V. P.*

$ ☷ **Albergo Losanna.** Most major sights are within walking distance of this tiny pensione just within the viale. Despite its dated feel, the property is impeccably clean and the rooms have high ceilings. Try to get a room facing away from the street; you won't have a view but you will get a quiet night's sleep. ✉ *Via Alfieri 9, Santa Croce neighborhood, 50121, ☎ FAX 055/245840, WEB www.albergolosanna.com. 8 rooms, 3 with bath. Parking (fee), some pets allowed; no air-conditioning in some rooms, no room phones, no room TVs. MC, V. CP.*

NIGHTLIFE AND THE ARTS

The Arts

Festivals and Special Events

Teatro Tenda (✉ Lungarno Aldo Moro 3, ☎ 055/6503068), a large exhibition space, is the venue for many events throughout the year, including a large Christmas bazaar run by the Red Cross and rock concerts. Around St. Patrick's Day (March 17), Teatro Tenda hosts the week-long **Irlanda in Festa** (Ireland Festival), with "seminars" on Irish beer as well as lots of Irish music.

On **Holy Thursday** at the Duomo, a centuries-old ritual is reenacted with members of the Compagnia della Misericordia, a lay association that during the Renaissance comforted those condemned to death and provided dowries for poor girls as well as other services for its members. (Today the confraternity runs an efficient emergency-ambulance service.) A solemn procession of priests and confraternity members wends its way into the Duomo, and then the priests wash the feet of the confraternity members. It is a moving ritual, and a visual link to the Renaissance.

On Easter Sunday, Florentines and foreigners alike flock to the Piazza del Duomo to watch the **Scoppio del Carro** (the Explosion of the Cart): a monstrosity of a carriage, pulled by two huge oxen decorated for the occasion, makes its way through the city center and ends up in the piazza. Through an elaborate wiring system, an object representing a "dove" is sent from inside the church to the Baptistery just across the way. The dove sets off an explosion of fireworks that comes streaming from the carriage. You have to see it to believe it. If you don't like crowds, don't worry: video replays figure prominently on the nightly newscasts afterward.

On June 24, Florence grinds to a halt to celebrate the **Festa di San Giovanni** (Feast of St. John the Baptist) in honor of its patron saint. Many shops and bars close, and at night a fireworks display along the Arno attracts thousands.

The **Fortezza da Basso** (✉ Viale Strozzi 1, ☎ 055/49721), a vast space perfect for large events, hosts a remarkable festival of food and ethnic arts in early December, as well as other happenings throughout the year. The fashion world flocks to Florence several times a year for high-end designer shows that are held here. Visit the local tourist information center to see what's on while you're in town.

Film
La Nazione, the daily Florentine newspaper, has movie listings. Note that most American films are dubbed into Italian rather than subtitled. **Festival dei Popoli** (✉ Borgo Pinti 82/r, Santa Croce neighborhood, ☎ 055/244778) is a week-long documentary–and–feature film festival held in November or December, with screenings at various venues around town.

On Thursdays, the **Fulgor** (✉ Via Maso Finiguerra 22/r, Santa Maria Novella neighborhood, ☎ 055/2381881) shows first-run English-language films. The **Odeon** (✉ Piazza Strozzi, Piazza della Repubblica neighborhood, ☎ 055/214068) shows first-run English-language films on Monday and Tuesday at its magnificent Art Deco theater.

Music
The **Accademia Bartolomeo Cristofori** (✉ Via di Camaldoli 7/r, Santo Spirito/San Frediano neighborhood, ☎ 055/221646), also known as the Amici del Fortepiano (Friends of the Fortepiano), sponsors concerts on the noble instrument throughout the year. **Amici della Musica** organizes concerts at the Teatro della Pergola (✉ Via della Pergola 12/r, Santa Croce neighborhood, ☎ 055/2264333). The season runs from November through April and features everything from early modern music to solo performances by such greats as Yo-Yo Ma. The **Maggio Musicale Fiorentina,** a series of internationally acclaimed concerts, operas, ballets, and recitals, is held in the Teatro Comunale (box office: ✉ Via Alamanni 29 , ☎ FAX 055/210804) from mid-May through early July. You can book in Italy by dialing ☎ FAX 800112211, or from outside Italy by calling ☎ FAX 0577/223806. The **Orchestra da Camera Fiorentina** (✉ Via E. Poggi 6, Piazza della Signoria neighborhood, ☎ 055/783374) performs various concerts of classical music throughout the year. The venue is the Romanesque church of Santo Stefano a Ponte; this is a fine case of the setting being at least as interesting as the music. The concert season of the **Orchestra della Toscana** (✉ Via Ghibellina 99-101/r, Santa Croce neighborhood, ☎ 055/210804) runs from December to early June. You can hear organ music in the baroque church of **Santa Margherita in Maria de' Ricci** (✉ Via il Corso, Piazza della Sig-

noria neighborhood, ☎ 055/215044). Free concerts begin every night at 9:15, except Monday.

Opera

Operas are performed in the **Teatro Comunale** (✉ Corso Italia 16, Santa Maria Novella neighborhood, ☎ 055/211158) from September through December.

Theater

Theater lovers might want to try an evening at **Teatro della Pergola** (✉ Via della Pergola 12/r, Santa Croce neighborhood, ☎ 055/264333). The season runs from mid-October to mid-April. If the idea of hearing a play in Italian is too forbidding, just visit the lovely theater. Built in 1656 by Ferdinando Tacca, and once the private theater of the grand dukes, it was opened to the public in 1755. The theater has undergone several metamorphoses; its present incarnation dates to 1828, and the atrium was constructed nine years later. Call to arrange a guided visit.

Nightlife

Florentines are rather proud of their nightlife options. Most bars now have some sort of happy hour, which usually lasts for many hours and often offers snacks. Discos typically don't open until very late in the evening and don't get crowded until 1 or 2 in the morning. Though the cover charges might seem steep, finding free passes around town is fairly easy.

Bars

If you want to eat a light lunch, sip a sparkling aperitivo, or simply check your e-mail, stop in at the **Astor** (✉ Piazza del Duomo 20/r, Duomo neighborhood, ☎ 055/2399000), open from early in the morning till late at night. The bar at **Beccofino** (✉ Piazza degli Scarlatti 1/r (Lungarno Corsini), Lungarno Sud neighborhood, ☎ 055/290 076) serves one of the best martinis in town. **Capocaccia** (✉ Lungarno Corsini 12/14r, Lungarno Nord neighborhood, ☎ 055/210751) makes great Bloody Marys, and it's the place to be at cocktail time. At night, young Florentines crowd the doors and spill out into the street. **Danny Rock** (✉ Via Pandolfini 13/r, Santa Croce neighborhood, ☎ 055/2340307) bills itself as a "pub restaurant"; you can enjoy its divine cheeseburger (or have a plate of pasta) while watching Bugs Bunny cartoons on a big screen. For a swanky experience, lubricated with trademark bellinis and the best martinis in Florence, head to **Harry's Bar** (✉ Lungarno Vespucci 22/r, Lungarno Nord neighborhood, ☎ 055/2396700). **Il Caffe** (✉ Piazza Pitti 9, Palazzo Pitti neighborhood, ☎ 055/2396241) offers terrific cocktails, light lunches, and a view of Palazzo Pitti. The oh-so-cool vibe at **La Dolce Vita** (✉ Piazza del Carmine 6/r, San Spirito/San Frediano neighborhood, ☎ 055/284595) attracts Florentines and the occasional visiting American movie star. **Rex** (✉ Via Fiesolana 23–25/r, Santa Croce neighborhood, ☎ 055/2480331) attracts a trendy, artsy clientele. Although drinks aren't mixed with particular flare at **Slowly** (✉ Via Porta Rossa 63/r, Piazza della Repubblica neighborhood, ☎ 055/2645354), the twentysomethings (local and foreign) are too busy checking one another out to care. From mid-May through mid-September, **Via di Fuga** (✉ Via Ghibellina near Via dell'Agnolo, Santa Croce neighborhood, ☎ no phone) is one of the coolest spots to be; once the courtyard of Le Murate, a former Renaissance convent and 19th-century prison, it hosts big bands, performance art, movies, and more. **Zoe** (✉ Via dei Renai 13/r, San Niccolò neighborhood, ☎ 055/243111) calls itself a "caffetteria" and, while coffee may indeed be served, twentysomething Florentines flock here for the fine (and expensive) cocktails. Here's people-watching at its very best, done while listening to the latest CDs imported from England.

Nightclubs

BeBop (⊠ Via dei Servi 76/r, Santissima Annunziata neighborhood, ☎ no phone) has loud, live music and Beatles nights. **Central Park** (⊠ Via Fosso Macinante 2, ☎ 055/353505) is a great spot for those who want to put on their dancing shoes for some house and hip-hop music. **H2O2** (⊠ Via Ghibellina 47/r, Santa Croce neighborhood, ☎ 055/243239) was so trendy when it opened in 2000 that it was expected to meet a quick death. It didn't, and it's still trendy. Those craving a night out with less-raucous live music might want to check out **Jazz Club** (⊠ Via Nuova de' Caccini 3, corner of Borgo Pinti, Santa Croce neighborhood, ☎ 055/2479700), situated, smokily and appropriately enough, in a basement. When just about everything else has closed, go where the bartenders go when they get off work, **Loch Ness** (⊠ Via Verdi, Santa Croce neighborhood, ☎ no phone). It's on the right side of Via Verdi as you walk toward the river from Santa Croce. Live music, a well-stocked bar, and a cavernous underground space make for a rollicking good evening at **Loonees** (⊠ Via Porta Rossa 15, Piazza della Repubblica neighborhood, ☎ 055/212249).

Maracaná (⊠ Via Faenza 4, Santa Maria Novella neighborhood, ☎ 055/210298) is a restaurant and pizzeria featuring Brazilian specialties; at 11 PM it transforms itself into a cabaret floor show, and then into a disco until 4 AM. Book a table if you want to eat. Young up-to-the minute Florentines drink and dance 'til the wee hours at **Maramao** (⊠ Via dei Macci 79/r, Santa Croce neighborhood, ☎ 055/244341). This favorite opens at 11 PM and doesn't really get going until shortly before 2. **Meccanò** (⊠ Le Cascine, Viale degli Olmi 1, ☎ 055/331371) is a multimedia experience in a high-tech disco with a late-night restaurant. The two floors at **Montecarla** (⊠ Via de' Bardi 2, San Niccolò neighborhood, ☎ 055/2340259) are filled with people sipping cocktails, lots of exotic flowers, leopard-print chairs and chintz, and red walls and floors. Of all the hot spots in town, **Omi Club** (⊠ Via Tevere 100, ☎ no phone) is as hot as they get. **Space Electronic** (⊠ Via Palazzuolo 37, Santa Maria Novella neighborhood, ☎ 055/293082) has two floors, with karaoke downstairs and an enormous disco upstairs. It's full of Italian military types prowling for young foreign women. **Yab** (⊠ Via Sassetti 5/r, Piazza della Repubblica neighborhood, ☎ 055/215160) is one of the largest clubs, with a young clientele. It packs in foreigners and locals; Florentines especially favor Tuesday and Thursday nights.

OUTDOOR ACTIVITIES AND SPORTS

Participant Sports

Biking

Bikes are a great way to tour the centro storico, as the town center has no hills. Patience, however, must be maintained while dodging hordes of tourists and those pesky *motorini* (mopeds). The Cascine, a former Medici hunting ground turned into a large public park with paved pathways and lots of trees, admits no cars. The historic center can be circumnavigated via bike paths lining the Viali, a road that runs along the center's circumference. **Florence by Bike** (⊠ Via San Zanobi 120-122/r, San Lorenzo neighborhood, ☎ 055/488992) has designed some guided city bike tours that work quite well. They leave several times a day for one- to three-hour tours of major monuments or for tours with specific themes such as Renaissance Florence or 13th-century Florence. **I Bike Italy** (✉ Borgo degli Albizi 11, Santa Croce neighborhood, ☎ FAX 055/2342371) offers one-day tours of the countryside outside Florence. The **International Kitchen** (✉ 55 E. Monroe St., Suite 2840, Chicago, IL 60603, ☎ 800/945–8606) can arrange biking and walking tours of Florence and Tuscany that involve cooking and eating as well; tours should be arranged in advance through the U.S. office.

Golf

Circolo Golf dell'Ugolino (✉ Via Chiantigiana 3, Grassina, ☎ 055/2301009) is 10 km (6 mi) outside Florence. If you're a member of any other golf club in the world, you are welcome here. The 18-hole course is set amid the Chianti hills, replete with cypresses and pines and natural lakes. Local wildlife—pheasants, wild hares, geese, and squirrels—have been known to make their way onto the green. The restaurant here is open for lunch and dinner; the bar is open all day. There's also tennis and a swimming pool. **Tenuta di Castelfalfi** (✉ Tenuta di Castelfalfi, Montaione, ☎ 0571/698093) is about 50 km (31 mi) southwest of Florence. The course, set in rolling hills, is open to the public. Also on offer are a restaurant in an old castle, a pizzeria–trattoria, a tennis court, and a pool.

Health Clubs

Centro Sportivo Fiorentino Indoor Club (✉ Via del Caboto, ☎ 055/430275) has the usual gym amenities plus sauna (open to women Monday, Wednesday, and Friday, and to men Tuesday, Thursday, and Saturday) as well as two pools. The only drawback is that it's far from the center. Day use costs €15.45. **Palestra Ricciardi** (✉ Borgo Pinti 75, Santa Croce neighborhood, ☎ 055/2478444 or 055/2478462) has continuous stretching, aerobics, step aerobics, and bodybuilding classes daily; it also has free weights, stationary bikes, treadmills, and rowing machines. You pay €10.40 a day or €25.75 a week.

Running

Don't even think of running on the narrow city streets, where tour buses and triple-parked Alfa Romeos leave precious little space for pedestrians. Instead, head for **Le Cascine,** the park along the Arno at the western end of the city. You can run to Le Cascine along the Lungarno (stay on the sidewalk), or take Bus 17 from the Duomo. A cinder track lies on the hillside below **Piazzale Michelangelo,** across the Arno from the city center. The locker rooms are reserved for members, so come ready to run. A scenic, but not serene, run can be had along the Lungarno, those streets that frame both sides of the Arno.

Swimming

Piscina Bellarriva (✉ Lungarno Aldo Moro, Lungarno Nord neighborhood, ☎ 055/677521) has a 50-m pool and is open daily. **Poggetto** (✉ Via Michele Mercati 22, ☎ 055/677521) has a 25-m pool with 8 lanes and is open daily.

Tennis

Circolo Tennis alle Cascine (✉ Viale del Visarno 1, ☎ 055/332651) has been in existence since 1898 and is probably the most highfalutin tennis venue in town; however, the drawback is that you have to be staying at certain hotels (the Grand or the Excelsior among them), or have a member bring you in. There's also a bar and restaurant for unwinding after the match. At **Tennis Club Rifredi** (✉ Via Facibeni, ☎ 055/432552), four courts are available, with lighting for nighttime play. Changing rooms are provided, and there's a bar. Membership isn't a prerequisite to playing; this club's only inconvenience is that it's not in the center of town.

Spectator Sport

Soccer

Italians are passionate about *calcio* (soccer), and the Florentines are no exception; indeed, *tifosi* (fans) of the Florentia team are fervent supporters. The team plays its home games at the **Stadio Comunale** (Municipal Stadium; ✉ top of Viale Manfredo Fanti, northeast of the center) in Campo di Marte. Tickets used to be rather difficult to come by but, given a downturn in the team's success, are now easily obtainable. Try the ticket booth **Chiosco degli Sportivi** (✉ Via Anselmi, southwest side of Piazza della Repubblica, ☎ 055/292363). Games are usually played on Sunday afternoon, from about late August to May. A medieval version of soccer, **Calcio Storico,** is played around the Festa di San Giovanni on June 24 each year by teams dressed in costumes representing the six Florence neighborhoods. Games take place in Piazza Santa Croce, where they have allegedly been played since the middle of the 16th century.

SHOPPING

Window-shopping in Florence is like visiting an enormous contemporary-art gallery, for many of today's greatest Italian artists are fashion designers, and most keep shops in Florence. Discerning shoppers may find bargains in the street markets. Shops are generally open 9–1 and 3:30–7:30 and are closed Sunday and Monday morning most of the year. Summer (June–September) hours are usually 9–1 and 4–8, and some shops close Saturday afternoon instead of Monday morning. When looking for addresses of shops, you'll see two color-coded numbering systems on each street. The red numbers are commercial addresses and are indicated, for example, as 31/r. The blue or black numbers are residential addresses. Most shops take major credit cards and ship purchases, but because of possible delays it's wise to take your purchases with you.

Markets

Le Cascine's open-air market is held every Tuesday morning. The **Mercato Centrale** (✉ Piazza del Mercato Centrale, San Lorenzo neighborhood) is a huge indoor food market that has a staggering selection of things edible. The clothing and leather-goods stalls of the **Mercato di San Lorenzo** in the streets next to the church of San Lorenzo have bargains for shoppers on a budget. It's possible to strike gold at the **Mercato di Sant'Ambrogio** (✉ Piazza Ghiberti, off Via dei Macci, Santa Croce neighborhood), where clothing stalls abut the fruit and vegetables. If you're looking for cheery, inexpensive trinkets to take home, you might want to stop and roam through the stalls under the loggia of the **Mercato Nuovo** (✉ Via Por Santa Maria at Via Porta Rossa, Piazza della Repubblica neighborhood). You can find bargains at the **Piazza dei Ciompi flea market** (✉ Sant'Ambrogio, Santa Croce neighborhood) Monday through Saturday and on the last Sunday of the month. The second Sunday of every month brings the **Piazza Santo Spirito flea market.**

Shopping Districts

Florence's most fashionable shops are concentrated in the center of town. The fanciest designer shops are mainly on **Via Tornabuoni** and **Via della Vigna Nuova.** The city's largest concentrations of antiques shops can be found on **Borgo Ognissanti** and the Oltrarno's **Via Maggio.** The **Ponte Vecchio** houses reputable but very expensive jewelry shops, as it has since the 16th century. The area near **Santa Croce** is the heart of the leather merchants' district.

Specialty Stores

Antiques

Galleria Luigi Bellini (⊠ Lungarno Soderini 5, Palazzo Pitti neighborhood, ☎ 055/214031) claims to be Italy's oldest antiques dealer, which may be true, since father Mario Bellini was responsible for instituting Florence's international antiques biennial. **Giovanni Pratesi** (⊠ Via Maggio 13/r, Palazzo Pitti neighborhood, ☎ 055/2396568) specializes in Italian antiques, in this case furniture, with some fine paintings, sculpture, and decorative objects turning up from time to time. Vying with Galleria Luigi Bellini as one of Florence's oldest antiques dealers, **Guido Bartolozzi** (⊠ Via Maggio 18/r, Palazzo Pitti neighborhood, ☎ 055/215602) deals predominately in period Florentine pieces. At **Paolo Paoletti** (⊠ Via Maggio 30/r, Palazzo Pitti neighborhood, ☎ 055/214728), look for Florentine antiques with an emphasis on Medici-era objects from the 15th and 16th centuries. **Roberto Innocenti e C. S.N.C.** (⊠ Borgo Pinti 11-13/r and Via Matteo Palmieri 29/r, Santa Croce neighborhood, ☎ 055/2478668) specializes in things more recently antique such as art deco, art nouveau, and jugendstil.

Books and Paper

Alberto Cozzi (⊠ Via del Parione 35/r, Santa Maria Novella neighborhood, ☎ 055/294968) keeps an extensive line of Florentine papers and paper products. The artisans in the shop rebind and restore books and works on paper. **Alice's Masks Art Studio** (⊠ Via Faenza 72/r, Santa Maria Novella neighborhood, ☎ 055/287370) preserves the centuries-old technique of papier-mâché masks. On hand are masks typical of 18th-century Venice, as well as some more-whimsical ones: a mask of Vincent van Gogh is painted with brushstrokes reminiscent of his own inimitable style. **Centro Di** (⊠ Via dei Renai 20/r, San Niccolò neighborhood, ☎ 055/2342666) publishes art books and exhibition catalogs for some of the most important organizations in Europe. **FMR** (⊠ Via delle Belle Donne 41/r, Santa Maria Novella neighborhood, ☎ 055/283312), the shop of the world-famous art-book editor and tastemaker Franco Maria Ricci, offers exquisite art books, handmade papers, and small works on paper. One of Florence's oldest paper-goods stores, **Giulio Giannini e Figlio** (⊠ Piazza Pitti 37/r, Palazzo Pitti neighborhood, ☎ 055/212621) is *the* place to buy the marbleized stock, which comes in a variety of shapes and sizes, from flat sheets to boxes and even pencils. Photograph albums, frames, diaries, and other objects dressed in handmade paper can be purchased at **Il Torchio** (⊠ Via dei Bardi 17, San Niccolò neighborhood, ☎ 055/2342862). The stuff is high-quality, and the prices lower than usual. **La Tartaruga** (⊠ Borgo Albizi 60/r, Santa Croce neighborhood, ☎ 055/2340845) sells brightly colored, recycled paper in lots of guises (such as calendars and stationery), as well as toys for children. Long one of Florence's best art-book shops, **Libreria Salimbeni** (⊠ Via Matteo Palmieri 14–16/r, Santa Croce neighborhood, ☎ 055/2340905) has an outstanding selection. **Pineider** (⊠ Via Tornabuoni 76/r, Santa Maria Novella neighborhood, ☎ 055/211605; ⊠ Piazza della Signoria 13/r, Piazza della Signoria neighborhood, ☎ 055/284655) has shops throughout the world, but the business began in Florence and still does all its printing here. Personalized stationery and business cards are the mainstay, but the stores also sell fine leather desk accessories.

Clothing

The usual fashion suspects—Prada, Gucci, Versace, to name but a few—all have shops in Florence. The sleek, classic **Giorgio Armani** boutique (⊠ Via Tornabuoni 48/r, Santa Maria Novella neighborhood, ☎ 055/219041) is a centerpiece of the dazzling high-end shops clustered in this part of town. **Bernardo** (✉ Via Porta Rossa 87/r, Piazza della Repubblica neighborhood, ☎ 055/283333) specializes in men's trousers, cashmere sweaters, and shirts with details like mother-of-pearl buttons. **Cabó** (✉ Via Porta Rossa 77-79/r, Piazza della Repubblica neighborhood, ☎ 055/215774) carries that sinuous Missoni knitwear as well as some of the Fendi line. The outlandish designs of native son **Roberto Cavalli** (✉ Via Tornabuoni 83/r, Santa Maria Novella neighborhood, ☎ 055/2396226) appeal to Hollywood celebrities and to those who want a more-expensive Britney Spears look. **Emporio Armani** (✉ Piazza Strozzi 16/r, Santa Maria Novella neighborhood, ☎ 055/284315), sister store of the Giorgio Armani boutique, offers slightly more-affordable, funky, nightclub- and office-friendly garb. **Gianfranco Ferré** (✉ Via Tosinghi 52/r, Duomo neighborhood, ☎ 055/292003) captures beauty and luxury in various constructions and fabrics in his couture lines for women; he has also created a line of sleek jeans. **Prada** (✉ Via Tornabuoni 67/r, Santa Maria Novella neighborhood, ☎ 055/283439), known to mix schoolmarmish sensibility with sexy cuts and funky fabrics, appeals to an exclusive clientele. The aristocratic Marchese di Barsento, **Emilio Pucci** (✉ Via Tornabuoni 20-22/r, Santa Maria Novella neighborhood, ☎ 055/2658082), became an international name in the late 1950s when the stretch ski clothes he designed for himself caught on with the dolce vita crowd—his pseudopsychedelic prints and "palazzo pajamas" became all the rage. You can take home a custom-made suit or dress from **Giorgio Vannini** (✉ Via Borgo Santi Apostoli 43/r, Santa Maria Novella neighborhood, ☎ 055/293037), who has a showroom for his prêt-à-porter designs. The signature couture collection of **Gianni Versace** (✉ Via Tornabuoni 13–15/r, Santa Maria Novella neighborhood, ☎ 055/2396167) revolutionized the catwalk with rubber dresses and purple leather pants; sister Donatella continues the line of high-priced, over-the-top couture for rock stars and movie celebs. **Versus** (✉ Via Vigna Nuova 36–38/r, Santa Maria Novella neighborhood, ☎ 055/217619) is the more playful—and more affordable—Versace line.

The intrepid shopper might want to check out some other, lesser-known shops. Young Florentines have a soft spot in their hearts for the clingy, one-of-a-kind frocks designed by Angela Baldi at her tiny shop, **Babele** (✉ Borgo Pinti 34/r, Santa Croce neighborhood, ☎ 055/244729). For cutting-edge fashion, the fun and funky window displays at **Basic** (✉ Via Porta Rossa 109-115/r, Piazza della Repubblica neighborhood, ☎ 055/212995) merit a stop. The shop carries Alberta Ferretti's creations, as well as lesser-known Italian and English designers. **Blunata** (✉ Via del Proconsolo 69/r, Duomo neighborhood, ☎ 055/212460) sells casual, well-made clothes for men and women; it's the closest Italy comes to Gap-style clothes. Gals with a sense of daring-do and fashion flair should check out the stockings and tights at **Emilio Cavallini** (✉ Via della Vigna Nuova 52/r, Santa Maria Novella neighborhood, ☎ 055/2382789). They come in outrageous and stylish prints. **Geraldine Tayar** (✉ Sdrucciolo de Pitti 6/r, Palazzo Pitti neighborhood, ☎ 055/290405) makes clothing and accessories of her own design in eclectic fabric combinations. **Il Guardaroba/Stock House** (✉ Borgo Albizi 48/r, Santa Croce neighborhood, ☎ 055/2340271) is where savvy Florentines shop for designer clothes at affordable prices. If you're looking for something hot to wear to the clubs, check out **Liu-Jo** (✉ Via Calimala 14/r, Piazza della Repubblica neighborhood, ☎ 055/216164). The surreal window displays at **Luisa Via Roma** (✉ Via Roma 19–21/r, Duomo neighborhood, ☎ 055/217826) hint at the trendy yet tasteful clothing that can be found inside this fascinating, *alta moda* (high-style) boutique featuring the world's top designers as well

as Luisa's own line. **Maçel** (✉ Via Guicciardini 128/r, Palazzo Pitti neighborhood, ☎ 055/287355) has collections by lesser-known Italian designers, many of whom use the same factories as the A-list. The
women's clothing here is sophisticated and sexy. **Principe** (✉ Via del
Sole 2, Santa Maria Novella neighborhood, ☎ 055/292764) is a Florentine institution that offers casual clothes for men, women, and children at far-from-casual prices. It also has a great housewares department.

Gifts and Housewares

For housewares, nothing beats **Bartolini** (✉ Via dei Servi 30/r, Santissima Annunziata neighborhood, ☎ 055/211895) for well-designed
practical items. **Brandimarte** (✉ Via L. Bartolini 18/r, Santo Spir-
ito/San Frediano neighborhood, ☎ 055/2381557), a silversmith workshop, can be toured by prior arrangement; it makes everything from
salt and pepper shakers to gigantic serving trays, for sale in the attached
showroom. **La Scagliola** (✉ Piazza Pitti14/r, Palazzo Pitti neighborhood,
☎ 055/211523) practices the 17th-century art of scagliola, a less-ex-
pensive alternative to pietre dure; it's a composite that imitates marble, used here to form handsome tabletops, boxes, and picture frames.
Mandragora Art Store (✉ Piazza del Duomo 50/r, Duomo neighborhood, ☎ 055/292 559) is one of the first attempts in Florence to cash
in on the museum-store craze. The essence of a Florentine holiday is
captured in the sachets of the **Officina Profumo Farmaceutica di Santa
Maria Novella** (✉ Via della Scala 16/r, Santa Maria Novella neighborhood, ☎ 055/216276), an art nouveau emporium of herbal cos-
metics and soaps that are made following centuries-old recipes created
by friars. **Paolo Carandini** (✉ Via de' Macci 73/r, Santa Croce neighborhood, ☎ 055/245 397) works exclusively in leather, producing
exquisite objects such as picture frames, jewelry boxes, and desk accessories. **Pitti Mosaici** (✉ Piazza de' Pitti 23/r, Palazzo Pitti neighborhood, ☎ 055/282127) continues the pietre dure tradition that was all
the rage of 16th-century Florence. Stones are worked into exquisite tables, pictures, and jewelry. **Rampini Ceramiche** (✉ Borgo Ognissanti
32/34, Lungarno Nord neighborhood, ☎ 055/219720) sells exquisitely
crafted, and expensive, ceramics. **Sbigoli Terrecotte** (✉ Via Sant'Egidio
4/r, Santa Croce neighborhood, ☎ 055/2479713) carries traditional
Tuscan terra-cotta and ceramic vases, pots, and cups and saucers.
What to get that gal (or guy) who has everything? Drop into the
Shabby Shop (✉ Via del Parione 12/r, Santa Maria Novella neighborhood, ☎ 055/294286), which specializes in antique silver—mostly
English, dating from George I to George III (1698–1811), and jewelry
from the 1950s. For the record: there's nothing shabby about this shop.

Jewelry

Carlo Piccini (✉ Ponte Vecchio 31/r, ☎ 055/292030) has been around
for several generations, selling antique jewelry as well as making pieces
to order; you can also get old jewelry reset here. **Cassetti** (✉ Ponte Vecchio 52/r, ☎ 055/2396028) combines precious and semiprecious stones
and metals in contemporary settings. **Daniela Calzini** (✉ Via de' Neri
27/r, Santa Croce neighborhood, ☎ 055/2396899) sells works in silver, as well as jewelry inspired by the Etruscans. **Gatto Bianco** (✉
Borgo Santi Apostoli 12/r, Santa Maria Novella neighborhood, ☎
055/282989) has breathtakingly beautiful jewelry worked in semiprecious and precious stones; the feel is completely contemporary.
Gherardi (✉ Ponte Vecchio 5/r, ☎ 055/211809), Florence's king of coral,
has the city's largest selection of finely crafted pieces, as well as cul-
tured pearls, jade, and turquoise. **La Gazza Ladra** (✉ Piazza Salvemini 6, Santa Croce neighborhood, ☎ 055/2466008) is an
off-the-beaten-path and young-at-heart shop with affordable necklaces and rings, mostly in silver. The two women who run **Oreria**

(✉ Borgo Pinti, 87/a, Santa Croce neighborhood, ☎ 055/244708) create divine designs using silver and semiprecious stones. Send suitors to purchase significant gifts here. One of Florence's oldest jewelers, **Tiffany** (✉ Via Tornabuoni 25/r, Santa Maria Novella neighborhood, ☎ 055/215506) has supplied Italian (and other) royalty with finely crafted gems for centuries. Its selection of antique-looking classics has been updated with a selection of contemporary silver.

Linens and Fabrics

Antico Setificio Fiorentina (✉ Via L. Bartolini 4, Santo Spirito/San Frediano neighborhood, ☎ 055/213861) has been providing damasks and other fine fabrics for royalty and those who aspire to it since 1786. **Loretta Caponi** (✉ Piazza Antinori 4/r, Santa Maria Novella neighborhood, ☎ 055/213668) is synonymous with Florentine embroidery, and the luxury lace, linens, and lingerie have earned the eponymous signora worldwide renown. **Sant'Jacopo Show** (✉ Borgo Sant'Jacopo 66/r, Santo Spirito/San Frediano neighborhood, ☎ 055/2396912) is an offbeat shop specializing in mannequins, decorations, and shop fixtures. Sumptuous silks, beaded fabrics, lace, wool, and tweeds can be purchased at **Valli** (✉ Via Strozzi 4/r, Piazza della Repubblica neighborhood, ☎ 055/282485). It carries fabrics created by Armani, Valentino, and other high-end designers. **Valmar** (✉ Via Porta Rossa 53/r, Piazza della Repubblica neighborhood, ☎ 055/284493) is filled with tangled spools of cords, ribbons, and fringes, plus an array of buttons, tassels, sachets, and hand-embroidered cushions you can take home—or bring in your own fabric, choose the adornments, and you can have a cushion or table runner made.

Outlets

The Fendi Outlet (✉ Via Pian dell'Isola 66, Rignano sull'Arno, ☎ 055/834918) is about a ½-hr car or train ride from Florence. One-stop bargain shopping awaits at **The Mall** (✉ Via Europa, Leccio Reggello, ☎ 055/8657775), where the stores feature goods by such names as Bottega Veneta, Giorgio Armani, Loro Piana, Sergio Rossi, and the decidedly non-Italian Yves St. Laurent. Cognoscenti will drive or taxi about 45 minutes out of town to the **Prada Outlet** (✉ Levanella Spacceo, Estrada Statale 69, Montevarchi, ☎ 055/91911).

Shoes and Leather Accessories

The colorful, foot-friendly shoes at **Camper** (✉ Va Por Santa Maria 47/r, Piazza della Signoria neighborhood, ☎ 055/2670342) are made in Spain, but they cost a lot less here than they do in the United States. The ultimate fine leathers are crafted into classic shapes at **Casadei** (✉ Via Tornabuoni 33/r, Santa Maria Novella neighborhood, ☎ 055/287240), winding up as women's shoes and bags. The late Salvatore Ferragamo earned his fortune custom-making shoes for famous feet, especially Hollywood stars. The classy **Ferragamo** store (✉ Via Tornabuoni 2/r, Santa Maria Novella neighborhood, ☎ 055/292123), in a 13th-century Renaissance palazzo, displays designer clothing and accessories, but elegant footwear still underlies the Ferragamo success. **Lily of Florence** (✉ Via Guicciardini 2/r, Palazzo Pitti neighborhood, ☎ 055/294748) offers high-quality, classic shoe designs at reasonable prices and in American sizes. **Pollini** (✉ Via Calimala 12/r, Piazza della Repubblica neighborhood, ☎ 055/214738) has beautifully crafted shoes and leather accessories for those willing to pay that little bit extra. For sheer creativity in both color and design, check out the shoes at **Sergio Rossi** (✉ Via Roma 15/r, Duomo neighborhood, ☎ 055/294873) and fantasize about where you'd wear them.

Beltrami (✉ Via della Vigna Nuova 70/r, Santa Maria Novella neighborhood, ☎ 055/287779), which sells shoes and some apparel, has long been synonymous with style; classic looks are beautifully updated. **Cellerini** (✉ Via del Sole 37/r, Santa Maria Novella neighborhood, ☎ 055/282533) is an institution in a city where it seems that just about everybody wears an expensive leather jacket. **Coccinelle** (✉ Via Por Santa Maria 49/r, Piazza della Signoria neighborhood, ☎ 055/2398782) sells leather accessories in bold colors and funky designs. **Furla** (✉ Via Calzaiuoli 47/r, Piazza della Repubblica neighborhood, ☎ 055/2382883) makes beautiful leather bags and wallets in up-to-the-minute designs. **Giotti** (✉ Piazza Ognissanti 3–4/r, Lungarno Nord neighborhood, ☎ 055/294265) has a full line of leather goods, including clothing. At peak tourist times, status-conscious shoppers often stand in line outside **Gucci** (✉ Via Tornabuoni 73/r, Santa Maria Novella neighborhood, ☎ 055/264011), ready to buy anything with the famous initials. American Tom Ford infused freshness into its designs, which, not surprisingly, have a decidedly American flair. Beware, however, of shop assistants with severe attitude problems. **Il Bisonte** (✉ Via del Parione 31/r, off Via della Vigna Nuova, Santa Maria Novella neighborhood, ☎ 055/215722) is known for its natural-looking leather goods, all stamped with the store's bison symbol. **Leather Guild** (✉ Piazza Santa Croce 20/r, Santa Croce neighborhood, ☎ 055/241932) is one of many shops that produce inexpensive, antique-looking leather goods with mass appeal, but here you can see the craftspeople at work. **Madova** (✉ Via Guicciardini 1/r, Palazzo Pitti neighborhood, ☎ 055/2396526) has a rainbow array of high-quality leather gloves. Shoe styles at **Romano** (✉ Via Speziali 10/r, Piazza della Repubblica neighborhood, ☎ 055/216535) span the staid to the offbeat at appealing prices.

SIDE TRIPS FROM FLORENCE

Fiesole

A half-day excursion to Fiesole, set in the hills 8 km (5 mi) above Florence, gives you a pleasant respite from museums and a wonderful view of the city. From here, the view of the Duomo, with Brunelleschi's powerful cupola, will give you a new appreciation for what the Renaissance accomplished. Fiesole began life as an ancient Etruscan and later Roman village that held some power until it succumbed to barbarian invasions. Eventually it gave up its independence in exchange for Florence's protection. The medieval cathedral, ancient Roman amphitheater, and lovely old villas behind garden walls are clustered on a series of hilltops. A walk around Fiesole can take from one to two or three hours, depending on how far you stroll from the main piazza.

The trip from Florence by car or bus takes 20–30 minutes. Take Bus 7 from the Stazione Centrale di Santa Maria Novella, Piazza San Marco, or the Duomo. (You can also get on and off the bus at San Domenico.) There are several possible routes for the two-hour walk from central Florence to Fiesole. One route begins in a residential area of Florence called Salviatino (Via Barbacane, near Piazza Edison, on the Bus 7 route), and after a short time, offers peeks over garden walls of beautiful villas, as well as the view over your shoulder at the panorama of Florence in the valley.

The **Duomo** reveals a stark medieval interior. In the raised presbytery, the **Cappella Salutati** was frescoed by 15th-century artist Cosimo Rosselli, but it was his contemporary, sculptor Mino da Fiesole (1430–

84), who put the town on the artistic map. The Madonna on the altarpiece and the tomb of Bishop Salutati are fine examples of the artist's work. ⊠ *Piazza Mino da Fiesole,* ☎ *055/59400.* ⊙ *Apr.–Oct., daily 7:30–noon and 3–6; Nov.–Mar., daily 7:30–noon and 2–5.*

The beautifully preserved 2,000-seat **Anfiteatro Romano** (Roman Amphitheater), near the Duomo, dates from the 1st century BC and is still used for summer concerts. To the right of the amphitheater are the remains of the **Terme Romani** (Roman Baths), where you can see the gymnasium, hot and cold baths, and rectangular chamber where the water was heated. A beautifully designed **Museo Archeologico,** an intricate series of levels connected by elevators, is built amid the ruins and contains objects dating from as early as 2000 BC. The nearby **Museo Bandini** is a small collection with a lot of interesting paintings. It's filled with the private collection of Canon Angelo Maria Bandini (1726–1803); he fancied 13th- to 15th-century Florentine paintings, terra-cotta pieces, and wood sculpture, which he later bequeathed to the Diocese of Fiesole. ⊠ *Via San Francesco 3,* ☎ *055/59477.* ⊡ *€6 (includes amphitheater, ruins, and museums).* ⊙ *Apr.–Sept., daily 9–7; Oct.–Mar., Wed.–Mon. 9–4:30.*

The hilltop church of **San Francesco** has a good view of Florence and the plain below from its terrace and benches. Halfway up the hill, you'll see sloping steps to the right; they lead to a lovely wooded park with trails that loop out and back to the church.

If you really want to stretch your legs, walk 4 km (2½ mi) toward the center of Florence along Via Vecchia Fiesolana, a narrow lane in use since Etruscan times, to the church of **San Domenico.** Sheltered in the church is the *Madonna and Child with Saints* by Fra Angelico, who was a Dominican friar here. ⊠ *Piazza San Domenico, off Via Giuseppe Mantellini,* ☎ *055/59230.* ⊡ *Free.* ⊙ *Daily 8–noon.*

From the church of San Domenico, it's a five-minute walk northwest to the **Badia Fiesolana,** which was the original cathedral of Fiesole. Dating to the 11th century, it was first run by Camaldolese monks before going to the Benedictines and then the Augustinians. Thanks to Cosimo il Vecchio, the complex was substantially restructured. The facade, never completed due to the death of Cosimo, contains elements of its original Romanesque decoration. The attached convent once housed Cosimo's valued manuscripts; today it's the site of the European Institute, for pre- and postdoctoral candidates. Its mid-15th-century cloister is well worth a look. ⊠ *Via della Badia dei Roccettini,* ☎ *055/59155.* ⊡ *Free.* ⊙ *Weekdays 9–6, Sat. 9:30–12:30 (closed Sun.).*

Dining and Lodging

$$$ ✕ **I' Polpa.** A short distance up the street from Fiesole's main square, this family-owned and -run restaurant has great food and friendly service. Though it's laid out in two oddly shaped rooms, one of which has no windows, the creamy yellow walls and matching table linens impart a sunny feeling. Walls are lined with photos of famous visitors, including Luciano Pavarotti and Sting. The *coniglio in porchetta* (boned rabbit, stuffed and rolled with sausage) is alone worth the trip—has rabbit ever tasted this moist? ⊠ *Piazza Mino da Fiesole 21/22,* ☎ *055/59485. AE, DC, MC, V. Closed Wed.*

$–$$ ✕ **San Domenico.** Three-quarters of the way up the hill to Fiesole, this rather industrial-looking spot offers tasty *pizze* as well as pastas. If you're hiking in the nearby hills, or going to see the Fra Angelico at the church of San Domenico, this is a perfect place to break for lunch. There's outdoor seating in the summer that, unfortunately, looks directly on to a somewhat busy two-lane road. No matter: the air's still better here than in town and makes the pizza taste so much better. ✉ *Piazza San Domenico,* ☎ *055/59182. AE, DC, MC, V. No lunch Mon.*

$$$$ 🏠 **Villa San Michele.** The cypress-lined driveway is the elegant preamble to this incredibly gorgeous (and very expensive) hotel in the hills of Fiesole. The 16th-century building was originally a Franciscan convent designed by Santi di Tito. Not a single false note is struck in the reception area (formerly the chapel), the dining rooms (a covered cloister and former refectory), or the tasteful antiques and art that decorate the rooms. The open-air loggia, where lunch and dinner are served, provides one of the most stunning views of Florence—a good thing, too, as the food is overpriced and bland. ✉ *Via Doccia 4, 50014,* ☎ *055/59451,* 🗏 *055/598734. 41 rooms. Restaurant, in-room safes, minibars, cable TV, pool, gym, piano bar, dry cleaning, laundry service, concierge, Internet, some pets allowed. AE, DC, MC, V. Closed Dec.–mid-Mar. CP, MAP.*

$$$ 🏠 **Villa Aurora.** On the main piazza, this attractive hotel takes advantage of its hilltop spot, with beautiful views in many of the rooms, some of which are on two levels with beamed ceilings and balconies. The building, constructed as a theater in 1860, was transformed into a hotel in the late 19th century. It's fit for queens, and quite a few of them—Queen Victoria and Margherita di Savoia among others—have stayed here. Rooms are sophisticated but understated, as is the hotel. ✉ *Piazza Mino da Fiesole 39, 50014,* ☎ *055/59100,* 🗏 *055/59587,* 🌐 *www. aurorafiesole.com. 23 rooms, 2 suites. Restaurant, cable TV, bar, Internet, meeting room, some pets allowed. AE, DC, MC, V. BP.*

Nightlife and the Arts

From June through August, **Estate Fiesolana** (✉ Teatro Romano, ☎ 055/5978403) is a festival of theater, music, dance, and film that takes place in the churches and the archaeological park of Fiesole.

Settignano

A 20-minute car or bus trip east of Florence, this village is particularly appealing when Florence is overcrowded and hot—for most of the summer, that is. Its biggest claim to fame is that it was the birthplace of many noteworthy artists, including the sculptors Desiderio di Settignano (circa 1428–64), Antonio (1427–79) and Bernardo (1409–64) Rossellino, and Bartolomeo Ammannati (1511–92). Michelaneglo's wet nurse was the wife of a stonecutter in Settignano, and to her he attributed his later calling in life. Alas, though these artists' works cannot be found in their native town (Florence and other cities lay claim to them), Settignano is worth a visit simply to breathe its fresh air, walk its tiny streets, and sit in its small **piazza** with an aperitivo.

A 20-minute walk through scenic countryside from the piazza leads to the **Oratorio della Vannella** (✉ Località Corbignano). The exterior, dating from 1719–21, is unremarkable, but the fresco *Madonna and Child Enthroned* (circa 1470), attributed to a young Sandro Botticelli (1445–1510), is housed here. It's in sad shape but is said to work miracles and therefore was venerated by the local stonecutters and sculptors. To get here, take Via Desiderio di Settignano, walk around the very modern cemetery, turn left, and then follow the narrow path lined with olive trees. The oratory is open for 6 PM mass the last Sunday of each month; otherwise, you can ask Signor Miniati (☎ 055/604418) to open the doors.

To get to the village, take Bus 10 from Florence, from the station at Santa Maria Novella or at Piazza San Marco, and ride it all the way to the end of the line, the *capolinea*. It will put you in the middle of Settignano's small piazzetta.

Dining and Lodging

$$–$$$ ✕ **Il Rosellino.** Florentines like to get out of town, inhale the clean air, and imbibe at this little spot simply decorated with wood chairs and tables. The wine list is terrific, and the food pairs nicely with it. A favorite is tortelli *al sauternes* (with cream, Stilton, and Sauternes). Equally good is the *tagliatelle alle scorzetto* (thin flat noodles with cream, flavored with lemon and orange). Wines by the glass are matched with dishes such as *affetati misti* (mixed cured meats). ✉ *Via di San Romano 16,* ☎ *055/224192 MC, V. Closed Sun. and Aug.*

$–$$ ✕ **Osvaldo.** If you're making the trip to Settignano, this is a great dining option (get off Bus 10 at the stop called Ponte a Mensola). The small, unassuming family-run trattoria is situated along a street and a tiny stream; if you sit outside (there are no views, alas), you might hear the trickle of the stream. The food is terrific, and though it is described as *cucina casalinga* (home cooking), only the portions are homestyle. Service is prompt and courteous. Count yourself lucky if the menu includes *fritti di fiori di zucca* (fried zucchini flowers)—probably the lightest fried food you'll find anywhere. ✉ *Via G. D'Annunzio 51/r,* ☎ *055/ 603972. AE, DC, MC, V. Closed Wed. No lunch Tues.*

$$–$$$$ ⛺ **Fattoria di Maiano.** The farm, which produces an exquisite olive oil offers apartments housed in a variety of buildings. (Some accommodations are a few miles away.) These have wood floors and simple furniture but the kitchens are modern. ✉ *Via Benedetto da Maiano 11, Fiesole,* ☎ *055/599600,* FAX *055/599640,* WEB *www.fattoriadimaiano. com. 5 apartments, 2 houses. Kitchens, room TVs, no air-conditioning in some rooms. AE, MC, V. EP.*

Gracious Gardens Around Florence

Like any well-heeled Florentine, you, too, can get away from Florence's hustle and bustle by heading for the hills. Take a break from city sightseeing to enjoy the gardens and villas set like jewels in the hills around the city. Villa di Castello and Villa La Petraia, both just northwest of the center in Castello, can be explored in one trip. The Italian garden at Villa Gamberaia is a quick 8-km (5-mi) jaunt east of the center near Settignano. Plan for a full-day excursion, picnic lunch included, if visiting all three gardens. Spring and summer are the ideal times to visit, when flowers are in glorious bloom. For a prime taste of Medici living, venture farther afield to the family's Villa Medicea in Poggio a Caiano, just south of Prato (☞ Chapter 4).

Villa di Castello

A fortified residence in the Middle Ages, Villa di Castello was rebuilt in the 15th century by the Medici. The Accademia della Crusca, a 400-year-old institution that is the official arbiter of the Italian language, now occupies the palace, which isn't open to the public. The gardens are the main attraction. From the villa entrance, walk uphill through the 19th-century park laid out in Romantic style, set above part of the formal garden. You'll reach the terrace, which affords a good view of the geometric layout of the Italian garden below; stairs on either side descend to the parterre.

Though the original garden design has been altered somewhat over the centuries, the allegorical theme of animals devised by Tribolo in 1537 to the delight of the Medici is still evident. The artificial cave, Grotta degli Animali (Animal Grotto), displays an imaginative menagerie of sculpted animals by Giambologna and his assistants. An Ammannati sculpture, a figure of an old man representing the Appenines, is at the center of a pond on the terrace overlooking the garden. Two bronze sculptures by Ammannati, centerpieces of fountains studding the Italian garden, can now be seen indoors in Villa La Petraia. Allow about 45 minutes to visit the garden; you can easily visit Villa La Petraia from here, making for a four-hour trip in total.

To get to Villa di Castello by car, head northwest from Florence on Via Reginaldo Giuliani (also known as Via Sestese) to Castello, about 6 km (4 mi) northwest of the city center in the direction of Sesto Fiorentino; follow signs to Villa di Castello. Or take Bus 28 from the city center and tell the driver you want to get off at Villa di Castello; from the stop, walk north about ½ km (¼ mi) up the tree-lined allée from the main road. ⊠ *Via di Castello 47, Castello,* ☏ *055/454791.* ⌨ *€2.05 (includes entrance to Villa La Petraia).* ⊙ *Garden Nov.–Feb., daily 8:15–4:30, Mar.–Oct., daily 9–7. Closed 2nd and 3rd Mon. of month. Palace closed to public.*

Villa La Petraia

The splendidly planted gardens of Villa La Petraia sit high above the Arno plain with a sweeping view of Florence. The villa was built around a medieval tower and reconstructed after it was purchased by the Medici sometime after 1530. Virtually the only trace of the Medici having lived here is the 17th-century courtyard frescoes depicting glorious episodes from the clan's history. In the 1800s the villa served as a hunting lodge of King Vittorio Emanuele II (1820–78), who kept his mistress here while Florence was the temporary capital of the newly united country of Italy.

An Italian-speaking guide takes you through the 19th-century–style salons. The garden—also altered in the 1800s—and the vast park behind the palace suggest a splendid contrast between formal and natural landscapes. Allow 60 to 90 minutes to explore the park and gardens, plus 30 minutes for the guided tour of the so-called museum, the villa interior. This property is best visited after the Villa di Castello.

To get here by car, follow directions to Villa di Castello, but take the right off Via Reginaldo Giuliani, following the sign for Villa La Petraia. You can walk from Villa di Castello to Villa La Petraia in about 15 minutes; turn left beyond the gate of Villa di Castello and continue straight along Via di Castello and the imposing Villa Corsini; take Via della Petraia uphill to the entrance. ⊠ *Via della Petraia 40, Località Castello,* ☏ *050/454791.* ⌨ *€2.05 (includes entrance to Villa di Castello).* ⊙ *Oct.–Mar., garden daily 8:15–4:30, villa tours daily at 9:15, 10, 10:45, 11:30, 12:10, 1:30, 2:20, 3, and 3:40; Apr.–May and Sept., garden daily 9–5, villa tours daily at 9:15, 10, 10:45, 11:30, 12:10, 1:30, 2:20, 3, 3:40, and 4:45; June–Aug., garden daily 9–7, villa tours daily at 9:15, 10, 10:45, 11:30, 12:10, 1:30, 2:20, 3, 3:40, 4:45, 5:35, and 6:35. Closed 2nd and 3rd Mon. of month.*

Villa Gamberaia

Villa Gamberaia, near the village of Settignano on the eastern outskirts of Florence, was the rather modest 15th-century country home of Matteo di Domenico Gamberelli, the father of noted Renaissance sculptors Bernardo, Antonio, and Matteo Rossellino. In the early 1600s the villa eventually passed into the hands of the wealthy Capponi family. They spared no expense in rebuilding it and, more importantly, creating its garden, one of the finest near Florence. Studded with statues and fountains, the garden suffered damage during World War II but has been restored according to the original 17th-century design. This excursion takes about 1½ hours, allowing 45 minutes to visit the garden.

To get here by car, head east on Via Aretina, an extension of Via Gioberti, which is picked up at Piazza Beccaria; follow the sign to the turnoff to the north to Villa Gamberaia, about 8 km (5 mi) from the center. To go by bus, take Bus 10 to Settignano. From Settignano's main Piazza Tommaseo, walk east on Via di San Romano; the second lane on the right is Via del Rossellino, which leads southeast to the entrance of Villa Gamberaia. The walk from the piazza takes about 10 minutes. ✉ *Via del Rossellino 72, Settignano,* ☎ *055/697205.* ✇ *€8.* ◔ *Garden Mon.–Sat. 8–6, Sun. 8–noon. Parts of villa open by appointment.*

Villa Demidoff

Francesco I de' Medici commissioned the multitalented Bernardo Buontalenti in 1568 to build a villa and a grandiose park to accompany it. Its current name comes from Paolo Demidoff, who bought the villa in 1872 and attempted to bring back its former glory. The park, particularly the colossal and whimsical sculpture of the *Fontana dell'Appenino* (*Fountain of the Appenines*), executed by Giambologna in 1579–89, is worth the price of admission alone. It's a grotto that plays tricks on the eye; the Appenines are personified by a colossal figure that seems to rise with some amount of difficulty from the earth—well, the figure also is pressing upon the head of a monster. Besides providing a nice excursion from Florence, the villa offers an excellent spot to picnic.

To get here by car, head north from Florence on SS65 toward Pratolino and follow signs to the villa. Or take Bus 25 from Piazza San Marco and get off at Pratolino. ✉ *Località Pratolino, Vaglia,* ☎ *055/409427.* ✇ *€2.58.* ◔ *Mar. and Oct., Sun. 8:30–8; Apr.–Sept., Thurs.–Sun. 8:30–8.*

FLORENCE A TO Z

To research prices, get advice from other travelers, and book travel arrangements, visit www.fodors.com.

AIRPORTS AND TRANSFERS

Florence's Aeroporto A. Vespucci, called Peretola, services flights from Milan, Rome, London, and Paris. To get into the city from Peretola by car, take the autostrada A11. Pisa's Aeroporto Galileo Galilei is the closest landing point with significant international service. Take the S67 from Pisa airport; it leads directly to Florence. For flight information, call the Florence Air Terminal or Aeroporto Galileo Galilei.

A local bus service runs from Peretola into Florence. Buy a ticket at the second-floor bar. Take Bus 62, which goes directly from the airport to the train station at Santa Maria Novella; the bus shelter is beyond the parking lot. There's no direct bus service from Pisa's airport to Florence. Buses do go to and from Pisa, but then you have to change to a slow train service.

No train service exists between downtown Florence and Peretola. A scheduled service connects the station at Pisa's Aeroporto Galileo Galilei with Florence's Stazione Centrale di Santa Maria Novella, roughly a one-hour trip. Trains start running about 7 AM from the airport, 6 AM from Florence, and continue service every hour until about 11:30 PM from the airport, 8 PM from Florence. You can check in for departing flights at the air terminal office, which is just around the corner from train tracks 1 and 2.

➤ AIRPORT INFORMATION: **Aeroporto Galileo Galilei** (✉ 12 km [7 mi] south of Pisa and 80 km [50 mi] west of Florence, ☎ 050/500707, WEB www.pisa-airport.com). **Florence Air Terminal** (✉ Stazione Centrale di Santa Maria Novella, ☎ 055/216073). **Peretola** (✉ 10 km [6 mi] northwest of Florence, ☎ 055/373498, WEB www.safnet.it).

BIKE AND MOPED TRAVEL

Brave souls (cycling in Florence is difficult, at best) may rent bicycles at easy-to-spot locations at Fortezza da Basso, the Stazione Centrale di Santa Maria Novella, and Piazza Pitti. Otherwise try Alinari. If you want to go native and rent a noisy Vespa (Italian for "wasp") or other make of motorcycle or *motorino* (moped), you may do so at Maxirent. Massimo also rents mopeds. However unfashionable, helmets must be rented also, and by law are mandatory, much to the chagrin of many Italians.

If you have well-exercised legs and lungs, you can also take a guided half-day bicycle tour from Florence with tour groups I Bike Italy and Bike a Day in Tuscany.

➤ BIKE RENTALS: **Alinari** (✉ Via Guelfa 85/r, San Lorenzo neighborhood, ☎ 055/280500). **Bike a Day in Tuscany** (☎ 055/2645033, WEB www.bikeflorencetuscany.com). **I Bike Italy** (✉ Borgo degli Albizi 11, Santa Croce neighborhood, ☎ FAX 055/2342371). **Massimo** (✉ Via Cairoli 8, ☎ 055/573689). **Maxirent** (✉ Borgo Ognissanti 155/r, Santa Maria Novella neighborhood, ☎ 055/265420).

BUS TRAVEL TO AND FROM FLORENCE

Long-distance buses provide inexpensive if somewhat claustrophobic service between Florence and other cities in Italy and Europe. One operator is SITA; you can also try Lazzi Eurolines.

➤ BUS INFORMATION: **Lazzi Eurolines** (✉ Via Mercadante 2, Santa Maria Novella neighborhood, ☎ 055/363041, WEB www.lazzi.it). **SITA** (✉ Via Santa Caterina da Siena 17/r, Santa Maria Novella neighborhood, ☎ 055/214721).

BUS TRAVEL WITHIN FLORENCE

Maps and timetables are available for a small fee at the ATAF (Trasporti Area Fiorentina) booth next to the train station, or for free at visitor information offices. Tickets must be purchased in advance at tobacco stores, newsstands, from automatic ticket machines near main stops, or at ATAF booths. The ticket must be canceled in the small validation machine immediately upon boarding. Two types of tickets are available, both valid for one or more rides on all lines. One costs €1.03 and is valid for one hour from the time it is first canceled. A multiple ticket—four tickets, each valid for 60 minutes—costs €3.87. A 24-hour tourist ticket costs €3.10. Monthly passes are also available.

Small electric buses make the rounds of the centro storico and provide an easy alternative to footing it around town. Use the same ticket as for the regular bus.

➤ BUS INFORMATION: **ATAF** (✉ Piazza del Duomo 57/r, Duomo neighborhood, ☎ 800/019794 toll free).

CAR RENTAL

➤ LOCAL AGENCIES: **Avis** (✉ Via Borgo Ognissanti, 128/r, Santa Maria Novella neighborhood, ☎ 055/2398826). **Hertz Italiana** (✉ Via Finiguerra 33/r, Santa Maria Novella neighborhood, ☎ 055/317543). **Maggiore-Budget Autonoleggio** (✉ Via Termine 1, Santa Maria Novella neighborhood, ☎ 055/311256).

CAR TRAVEL

Abandon all hope of using a car in the city: most of the downtown area is accessible only to locals with properly marked vehicles. Florence is connected to the north and south of Italy by the Autostrada del Sole (A1). For assistance or information, call the ACI (Automobile Club Firenze).

➤ CONTACTS: **ACI** (Automobile Club Firenze; ☎ 055/2486246).

CONSULATES

➤ CONTACTS: **U.S. Consulate** (✉ Lungarno Vespucci 38, Lungarno Nord neighborhood, ☎ 055/2398276). **U.K. Consulate** (✉ Lungarno Corsini 2, Lungarno Nord neighborhood, ☎ 055/284133).

ENGLISH-LANGUAGE BOOKSTORES

Edison has three sprawling floors teeming with books (the English-language section is on the top floor) and a small café where you can grab a cappuccino and a sandwich.

➤ CONTACTS: **BM Bookshop** (✉ Borgo Ognissanti 4/r, Santa Maria Novella neighborhood, ☎ 055/294575). **Edison** (✉ Piazza della Repubblica 27/r, Piazza della Repubblica neighborhood, ☎ 055/213110). **Paperback Exchange** (✉ Via Fiesolana 31/r, Santa Croce neighborhood, ☎ 055/2478154).

EMERGENCIES

You can get a list of English-speaking doctors and dentists at the U.S. Consulate, or contact the Tourist Medical Service. If you need hospital treatment and an interpreter, you can call AVO, a group of volunteer interpreters; it's open Monday, Wednesday, and Friday 4–6 PM and Tuesday and Thursday 10–noon. Comunale No. 13, a local pharmacy, is open 24 hours a day, seven days a week. For a complete listing of other pharmacies that have late-night hours on a rotating basis, dial ☎ 192.

➤ CONTACTS: **AVO** (☎ 055/2344567). **Tourist Medical Service** (✉ Via Lorenzo il Magnifico, 59, ☎ 055/475411).

➤ EMERGENCY SERVICES: **Ambulance** (☎ 118). **Emergencies** (☎ 113). **Misericordia** (Red Cross; ✉ Piazza del Duomo 20, Duomo neighborhood, ☎ 055/212222). **Police** (✉ Via Zara 2, near Piazza della Libertà, San Lorenzo neighborhood, ☎ 055/49771).

➤ 24-HOUR PHARMACIES: **Comunale No. 13** (✉ Stazione Centrale di Santa Maria Novella, Santa Maria Novella, ☎ 055/289435).

LODGING

➤ VILLA-RENTAL AGENCIES: **The Best in Italy** (✉ Via Foscolo 72, Florence 50124, ☎ 055/223064, FAX 055/2298912). **Custom Travel and Special Events** (✉ Via dell'Ardiglione 19, Santo Spirito/San Frediano neighborhood, ☎ 055/2645526). **Florence and Abroad** (✉ Via San Zanobi 58, San Lorenzo neighborhood, 50129, ☎ 055/470603).

MAIL AND SHIPPING

➤ POST OFFICES: **Florence** (✉ Via Pellicceria 3, Piazza della Repubblica neighborhood, ☎ 055/211147; ✉ Via Pietrapiana 53/55, Santa Croce neighborhood, ☎ 055/214600).

➤ MAJOR OVERNIGHT SERVICES: **DHL** (✉ Via della Cupola 234/5, ☎ 800/123800 toll free). **Federal Express** (✉ Via Gioberti 3, ☎ 055/8974001, 800/123800 toll free).

➤ INTERNET CAFÉS: **Internet Train** (✉ Via dell'Oriuolo 40r, ☎ 055/2638968, WEB www.internettrain.it). **Platform 3000** (✉ Via Ghibellina 110, ☎ 055/471714). **Popcafé** (✉ Piazza Santo Spirito 18a/r, ☎ 055/211201). **Webpuccino** (✉ Via dei Conti 22r, ☎ 055/2776469, WEB www.webpuccino.it).

SAFETY

Florence is subject to the same types of petty thievery that are practiced in Italy's other large, heavily touristed cities. Pickpockets are known to frequent crowded places, particularly buses. Purse-snatchers sometimes operate on mopeds, making them quick and potentially dangerous. Groups of gypsy children have a number of ruses to part you from your property. Although the odds are against you falling prey to such crimes, it's always wise to keep your valuables well guarded, to be alert to your surroundings, and to err on the side of caution if you find yourself in suspicious circumstances.

TAXIS

Taxis usually wait at stands throughout the city (in front of the train station and in Piazza della Repubblica, for example), or you can call for one. The meter starts at €2.30, with a €3.60 minimum and extra charges at night, on Sunday, or for radio dispatch. A tip of at least 10% will be much appreciated.

➤ TAXI COMPANIES: **Taxis** (☎ 055/4390 or 055/4798).

TOURS

BUS TOURS

The major bus operators offer half-day itineraries, all of which use comfortable buses staffed with English-speaking guides. Morning tours begin at 9, when buses pick visitors up at the main hotels. Stops include the cathedral complex, the Galleria dell'Accademia, Piazzale Michelangelo, and the Palazzo Pitti (or, on Monday, the Museo dell'Opera del Duomo). Afternoon tours stop at the large hotels at 2 PM and take in Piazza della Signoria, the Galleria degli Uffizi (or the Palazzo Vecchio on Monday, when the Uffizi is closed), nearby Fiesole, and, on the return, the church of Santa Croce. A half-day tour costs about €24.75, including museum admissions.

➤ FEES AND SCHEDULES: **Lazzi Eurolines** (⊠ Via Mercadante 2, Santa Maria Novella neighborhood, ☎ 055/363041, WEB www.lazzi.it). **SITA** (⊠ Via Santa Caterina da Siena 17/r, Santa Maria Novella neighborhood, ☎ 055/214721).

TRAIN TRAVEL

Florence is on the principal Italian train route between most European capitals and Rome, and within Italy it is served frequently from Milan, Venice, and Rome by Intercity (IC) and nonstop Eurostar trains. Stazione Centrale di Santa Maria Novella, the main station, is in the center of town. Be sure to avoid trains that stop only at the Campo di Marte or Rifredi stations, which aren't convenient to the center.

➤ TRAIN INFORMATION: **Stazione Centrale di Santa Maria Novella** (☎ 8488/888088).

TRAVEL AGENCIES

➤ LOCAL AGENT REFERRALS: **American Express** (⊠ Via Dante Alighieri 22/r, Duomo neighborhood, ☎ 055/50981). **CIT Italia** (⊠ Piazza Stazione 51/r, Santa Maria Novella neighborhood, ☎ 055/284145 or 055/212606). **Micos Travel Box** (⊠ Via dell'Oriuolo 50–52/r, Santa Croce neighborhood, ☎ 055/2340228). **Thomas Cook** (⊠ Lungarno Acciaiuoli 7/r, Lungarno Nord neighborhood, ☎ 055/289781).

VISITOR INFORMATION

➤ TOURIST INFORMATION: **Fiesole** (⊠ Via Portigiani 3, 50014, ☎ 055/ 598720). **Florence** (Agenzia Promozione Turistica, or APT; ⊠ Via Cavour 1/r, next to Palazzo Medici-Riccardi, San Lorenzo neighborhood, 50100, ☎ 055/290832; ⊠ Stazione Centrale di Santa Maria Novella, Santa Maria Novella neighborhood, 50100, ☎ 055/212245; ⊠ Borgo Santa Croce 29/r, Santa Croce neighborhood, ☎ 055/ 2340444).

3 NORTH OF FLORENCE

The towns and countryside north of Florence might be Tuscany's last secret. The sheer wild beauty of the landscape is breathtaking: the sparsely populated forest valleys are bordered by craggy, often snowcapped, mountains where narrow roads wind up and down incredible heights. Even when it's hot elsewhere, it's cooler here—this is Tuscan mountain territory, which rolls down into pine-forested hills eventually to meet the wide sandy beaches of the Ligurian Sea.

By Patricia
Rucidlo

Updated by
Ann Reavis

CﾠﾠITIES AND TOWNS NORTH OF FLORENCE in the Mugello and in the Garfagnana and Lima valleys—aided by the natural barriers of high mountains and deep valleys—were often intimately involved with the defense of the great Tuscan cities Lucca and Florence, dominant powers during the Middle Ages and the Renaissance. The majestic Alpi Apuane (Apuane Alps) mountain chain cuts a swath between the Garfagnana and the Lunigiana, offering trails through the protected Parco Naturale delle Alpi Apuane with starkly beautiful landscapes. At the edge of the Alpi Apuane, quarries at Carrara and Pietrasanta have been sources of marble for builders and sculptors—Michelangelo among them—for 2,000 years. Seductively close to Tuscany's northwestern edge—north of the wide, sandy beaches of the resort towns of Viareggio and Forte dei Marmi—are the five seaside towns called the Cinque Terre, in the region of Liguria, where picturesque pastel houses cling to sheer cliffs and fishermen haul in their catches from a turquoise sea.

Pleasures and Pastimes

Dining

In the Mugello, sample the *tortelli del Mugello,* ravioli with potato stuffing, sauced in a variety of ways. Lardo di Colonnata, a deliciously obscene dish of herbed pork lard that has been cured for months in cool marble boxes and comes from near Carrara, should be sampled even by the skeptical. The Garfagnana Valley produces *farro* (emmer wheat or spelt), an ancient, pearly grain that resembles barley. It is used in local dishes and should definitely be tasted, either in *zuppa di farro* (farro and bean soup) or in *farro alla contadina,* a *primo piatto* (first course) in which the grain is cooked in water or broth and then tossed with extra-virgin olive oil and chopped fresh tomatoes. Restaurants in the Garfagnana stock Lucca's famed deep-green, fruity olive oil, which adds a distinctive flavor to every dish. The Garfagnana is also a huge chestnut-growing area; sample anything on the menu that has chestnuts, especially *polenta di castagne* (chestnut polenta). Specialties from the sea can be found in Forte dei Marmi and Viareggio and the many other resort towns dotting the coast.

Restaurants in the Lunigiana and the Mugello are generally less expensive than those in major Tuscan cities; however, prices frequently are higher in the resort towns of Forte dei Marmi and Viareggio.

CATEGORY	COST*
$$$$	over €18
$$$	€13–€18
$$	€8–€13
$	under €8

*Prices are for a second course (secondo piatto).

Lodging

Excluding the beach resort towns, lodging is generally less expensive here than in many other parts of Italy. Some real bargains can be found in the off-the-beaten-path towns. Consider staying at an *agriturismo,* a farm and/or vineyard that has opened its rooms or apartments—from rustic to stately—to guests. Many area hotels have restaurants that offer delicious fare.

CATEGORY	COST*
$$$$	over €175
$$$	€125–€175
$$	€75–€125
$	under €75

Prices are for two people in a standard double room, including tax and service.

Outdoor Activities and Sports

Serious hikers and trekkers come to this part of Tuscany for its network of trails and incredible views. The Apennine's Parco dell' Orecchiella in the Garfagnana has extensive forests with trails for hiking, biking, and horseback riding; in winter, this region is popular with Tuscan downhill and cross-country skiers. There is also some great terrain for mountain bikers in the Forte dei Marmi area. For race-car enthusiasts, the Formula 2 track near Scarperia is a prime destination. Along the Versilian and Ligurian coasts, sailing, windsurfing, and scuba diving are favorite pastimes.

Exploring North of Florence

Geographically, towns north of Florence are rather far apart. The best way to explore the region is by car, as part of the fun is driving on winding roads and stopping to take in the dramatic scenery. If you have to rely on public transportation, bus service to the region can get you around; train service, however, is extremely limited.

Numbers in the text correspond to numbers in the margin and on the Mugello and the Northwestern Tuscany and the Ligurian Coast maps.

Great Itineraries

You can get a good sense of this part of Tuscany in three days. The region is spread out and mountainous, and driving the narrow mountain roads takes considerable time. This is a geographically diverse area: you can be looking at soaring mountain vistas in the morning and lazing on the beach in the afternoon.

IF YOU HAVE 3 DAYS

For a period this short, to minimize the time spent getting from place to place, it's best to pick a specific area and explore it in depth. Drive either from Florence or Lucca to the Garfagnana and spend the first night in ⌖ **Castelnuovo di Garfagnana** ⑪. On Day 2, drive or hike in the nearby **Parco dell'Orecchiella** ⑩. Then head to the Lunigiana and stay the second night in ⌖ **Equi Terme** ⑭. On Day 3, drive to ⌖ **Forte dei Marmi** ⑲ or ⌖ **Viareggio** ⑰ via **Carrara** ㉑, where you can tour one or two of the marble caves before heading to the wide, sandy beaches on the Ligurian Sea.

IF YOU HAVE 5 DAYS

Though there's wonderful art to be seen and wonderful food to be eaten, the scenery takes precedence when you are touring this area. Drive north from Florence on S302 into the rolling hills of the Mugello. Visit the two Medici villas at **Trebbio** ③ and **Cafaggiolo** ② and stop at the **Bosco ai Frati** ⑤ monastery, having lunch along the way. Head south, back toward Florence; before reaching Florence, turn west, taking the A11 to Montecatini Terme. Then pick up the S633 and take it to the S12, which you'll follow north for a good 1½ hours to ⌖ **Abetone** ⑨, the mountain resort in the Garfagnana. Spend the night here after watching the sun set behind the peaks and dining on the northern Tuscan cuisine. From Abetone, drive south along winding roads to **Bagni di Lucca** ⑬, and then head north to **Barga** ⑫. Stop to see Barga's Duomo and admire the panorama from its little piazza before proceeding to

⊞ **Castelnuovo di Garfagnana** ⑪ to spend the second night. On Day 3, drive or hike in the nearby **Parco dell'Orecchiella** ⑩. Then head to the Lunigiana and stay in ⊞ **Equi Terme** ⑭. On Day 4, drive to ⊞ **Forte dei Marmi** ⑲ or ⊞ **Viareggio** ⑰ via **Carrara** ㉑ and the marble caves. Overnight in either Forte dei Marmi or Viareggio, doing nothing but sampling the fresh seafood and walking along the shore. On Day 5, relax on the beach in the morning (in the winter, bundle up and enjoy the empty beach and the crisp ocean air, or go shopping at the trendy stores along the boardwalk); in the afternoon, explore the art galleries and sculpture studios of **Pietrasanta** ⑱ before returning to Florence or going on to Lucca (☞ Chapter 4).

When to Tour North of Florence

Summer is the time to be in Forte dei Marmi and Viareggio: the towns are bustling with people and the beaches are crowded. To enjoy the beach—but not the crowds—come on the fringe of the tourist season in June or September, when the water is warm enough to take a swim. Another good time to visit Viareggio is during Carnevale, the period before Lent that culminates in a huge street party on Shrove Tuesday; it's said that Viareggio's celebrations are second only to those in Venice. If the torrid July and August temperatures in the major Tuscan cities become oppressive, head to the mountains of the Mugello or Garfagnana. Hiking, trekking, and mountain-biking vacations in the Alpi Apuane are spectacular in the summer months. To drive around and marvel at the gorgeous scenery, a trip any time from spring through autumn will be beautiful and rewarding.

THE MUGELLO

The lands of the Mugello—surrounding the upper reaches of the Sieve River and the vineyard-rich Val di Sieve—were distributed in the 1st century AD to those soldiers who fought for the Roman general Sulla (138–78 BC); they took over land previously inhabited by the Etruscans. The region's strategic defensive position and its rich agricultural resources attracted Florence, which conquered it in the 14th century. The area's native sons include the artists Giotto (1266–1337), Fra Angelico (1387–1455), and Andrea del Castagno (circa 1421–57). The small town of San Piero a Sieve gave birth to the Medici dynasty. Now the Mugello is quiet, its days of glory gone. Though parts of it are industrialized, flat, and uninteresting, other parts are extremely beautiful, with sharp hills and dramatic sunsets.

Barberino di Mugello

❶ *34 km (21 mi) north of Florence.*

Barberino di Mugello, the largest town on the western rim of the Mugello, has views of both the glorious Tuscan countryside and industrial complexes. It's not unusual to have each vista on either side of the road. Of note in the town center are the 15th-century **Palazzo Pretorio** (City Hall), emblazoned with colorful coats-of-arms, and the **Logge Medicee** (open-sided galleries), designed by Michelozzo (1396–1472).

In the center of town next to the parish church is the **Oratorio Dei Ss. Sebastiano e Rocco** (Oratory of Sts. Sebastian and Rocco), which dates from the 18th century. ⊠ *Corso Bartolomeo Corsini,* ☎ *no phone.* ▣ *Free.* ⊙ *Mon.–Sat. 4:30 PM–5:30 PM, Sun. 8 AM–9 AM.*

For a magnificent view of the Mugello region, drive 14 km (9 mi) north of town via SS65 to the top of **Passo della Futa,** with an altitude of 2,800 ft.

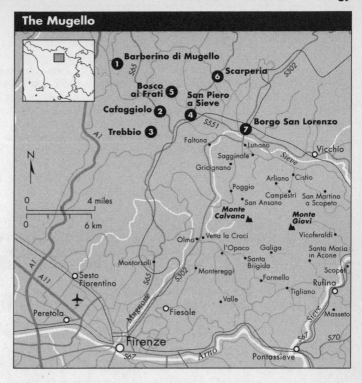

The Mugello

① Barberino di Mugello
⑥ Scarperia
Bosco ai Frati ⑤
San Piero a Sieve
Cafaggiolo ②
④
Trebbio ③
⑦ Borgo San Lorenzo

Faltona
Lutiano
Vicchio
Sagginale
Sieve
Gricignano
Arliano • Cistio
Poggio
Campestri   San Martino
San Ansano   a Scopeto
Monte Calvana ▲
Monte Giovi ▲
Olmo • • Vetta la Croci
Vicoferaldi
l'Opaco Galiga
Santa Maria in Acone
Montorsoli •
• Santa Brigida
Scopeti
• Montereggi
Formello
Rufina
○ Sesto Fiorentino
Tigliano
Peretola ○
○ Fiesole
• Valle
Masseto
Firenze ○
Pontassieve
Arno

N
0 — 4 miles
0 — 6 km

Dining and Lodging

$$ ✕ **Cosimo de' Medici.** The number of trucks parked in the lot is an indicator of a good cook and a great deal. The food is typically Tuscan, plentiful, and tasty. Grilled meats are a specialty, and the pastas are made in-house—try the pasta with a wild-hare meat sauce or *farfalle alla Cosimo,* bowtie pasta sauced with an herbed pesto. Also, don't miss the sausage of wild boar (*salsiccia di cinghiale*). ⊠ *Via del Lago 19,* ☎ *055/8420432. AE, DC, MC, V. Closed Mon. and 10–15 days in Aug.*

$–$$ ✕ **Marisa.** This restaurant serves up Tuscan fare in a light, airy space. Order the *lombatina di vitella al limone* (grilled veal chop with lemon); it's a great bargain, as are the pastas. *Panini* (sandwiches) are available to take away for a picnic lunch. Tuscan products are also for sale—local salami, cheeses, olive oil, and *biscottini* (small, hard cookies). ⊠ *Viale del Lago 21 (Exit 18 off the A1),* ☎ *055/8420045. No credit cards. Closed Tues.*

$$ ▥ **Poggio di Sotto.** Perched on a little hill (*poggio*), this agriturismo is a series of small, ocher-color buildings looking onto some pretty Mugellan countryside (with the inevitable view of industry from one side). The accommodations are simple and very well kept. Although there's no air-conditioning, this is not needed in the Mugello. You can borrow a mountain bike from the proprietor and explore the area if you wish; horseback riding is also nearby. A small restaurant features local specialties. This agriturismo generally operates on a no-meals basis, but does offer a half-pension (breakfast and dinner) option for €20 per person per night. ⊠ *Località Galliano, 50030,* ☎ *055/8428447 or 055/8428448,* ⓦⓔⓑ *www.wel.it/poggiodisotto. 9 rooms. Restaurant, some pets allowed (fee); no air-conditioning. AE, MC, V. Closed weekdays Nov.–Feb. MAP.*

Cafaggiolo

② *6 km (4 mi) south of Barberino di Mugello, 28 km (17 mi) north of Florence.*

Cafaggiolo is probably most famous for its **Villa Medicea di Cafaggiolo.** In 1454, Cosimo de' Medici (the Elder, 1389–1464) commissioned Michelozzo to convert this structure, originally a fortress, into a country hunting manor for the Medici. Lorenzo the Great spent part of his childhood here. The villa's castellated walls and massive tower decorated with a huge clock are impressive. The house and gardens are open daily for tours by prior arrangement, but only for groups of at least 20. Individual travelers can arrange to join scheduled groups. ⊠ *Via Nazionale, SS65 7½ km (4½ mi) southeast of Barberino di Mugello,* ☎ *055/841003 or 055/8417846.* ⊑ *€10.50.* ⊙ *Daily, by appointment.*

Dining

$–$$ ✕ **Girodibacco Osteria.** About 300 ft down the road from Villa Medicea di Cafaggiolo, this rustic *osteria* (tavern-style restaurant) serves such typical Tuscan dishes as *ribollita* (a thick soup of white beans, bread, cabbage, and onions), *pappa al pomodoro* (a bread and tomato soup), and grilled meats. There's also a bar in front that serves great espresso. ⊠ *Via Nazionale 8, Barberino di Mugello,* ☎ *055/8418173. AE, DC, MC, V. Closed Mon.*

Trebbio

③ *3 km (2 mi) south of Cafaggiolo, 25 km (16 mi) north of Florence.*

Trebbio is the site of the 14th-century **Castello del Trebbio,** which was transformed—on the orders of the Medici patriarch Cosimo the Elder—from a medieval fortress into an elegant villa with an imposing tower by Michelozzo in the 15th century. The narrow, serpentine road that leads to the villa is lined with cypresses and creates a sense of drama. The villa is privately owned and closed to tours, but a visit to the gardens, which are designed in the classical Italian style with a focus on terraces, trees, and sculpted hedges, can be arranged by previous appointment for groups of at least 20 (individual travelers can arrange to join scheduled groups). Don't bother coming without an appointment—nothing can be seen from the road. ⊠ *SS65, 8½ km/5 mi southeast of Barberino di Mugello, 7½ km/4½ mi west of Borgo San Lorenzo,* ☎ *055/8458793 or 055/848296.* ⊑ *€10.50.* ⊙ *Garden tours weekdays by appointment.*

San Piero a Sieve

④ *4 km (2½ mi) northeast of Trebbio, 26 km (16 mi) north of Florence.*

A grand Medici fort guards this little crossroads town. During the Renaissance, the fort belonged first to the Ubaldini before becoming a Florentine possession. The 11th-century parish church of **San Pietro** is worth a stop. It was greatly modified in the late 18th century, but retains the octagonal multicolor terra-cotta baptismal font from the early 16th century that is attributed to the school of Giovanni della Robbia (1469–circa 1529); there's also a panel painting, the *Madonna and Child,* that may have been executed by Lorenzo di Credi (circa 1456–1537). ⊠ *Via Provinciale,* ☎ *055/848751.* ⊑ *Free.* ⊙ *Daily 8–7.*

The **Fortezza di San Martino,** just southwest of San Piero a Sieve (turn left onto the dirt road 800 m/2,640 ft beyond the western village limits and follow signs), was built as a defensive fortification by Buontalenti on orders of Cosimo I (1519–74), the first Grand Duke of Tuscany, in the 1570s. The fort may be visited by appointment (☎ 055/848751 for information).

Dining and Lodging

$$ ✕🏨 **Hotel Ristorante Ebe.** Located conveniently along a two-lane highway, this charming family-run hotel was built in the 1960s and has a restaurant attached. The rooms are immaculate and given a great deal of care, with colorful throw pillows and wall decoration. The restaurant serves traditional Tuscan cuisine as well as a large selection of vegetarian dishes—six members of the delle Fabbriche family are devoted to vegetarianism. Want to eat *seitan* (made of wheat gluten), Italian style? Here's the place to do it. The family also runs the Villa Ebe, a couple of miles from the hotel. ✉ *Via Provinciale 1, 50027,* ☎ *055/848019,* 🖷 *055/848567. 24 rooms, 4 suites. Restaurant. DC, V.*

Bosco ai Frati

❺ *2 km (1 mi) northwest of San Piero a Sieve, 28 km (17 mi) north of Florence.*

At this Franciscan monastery set in the countryside, you get the feeling that not much has changed since St. Francis visited in 1212. It was here in 1273 that St. Bonaventure, biographer of St. Francis, was washing dishes when he heard the news that he had been made a cardinal. Cosimo de' Medici, a patron of the monastery, commissioned the young Michelozzo to redo the facade in 1420. The most important work of art remaining in the monastery is a wood sculpture of the Crucifixion by Donatello (circa 1386–1466) that dates from 1430. According to local legend, it was carved from a pear tree in the monastery's garden. ✉ *Off S65,* ☎ *055/848111.* 🎫 *Free.* ☉ *Daily 9–11:30 and 3–5.*

Scarperia

❻ *4 km (2½ mi) north of San Piero a Sieve, 30 km (19 mi) north of Florence.*

Florence created a strategic defensive post in the Mugello at Scarperia in the early 1300s. In the 16th and 17th centuries, the fast-growing township was the center of the cutlery-manufacturing trade for Tuscany—knives and scissors as well as daggers and swords. By the 20th century, the more than 40 businesses had been reduced to fewer than 10, but with the emerging popularity of the yearly market fair, an ever growing number of individual artisans have turned the town into a popular stop for collectors and aficionados of knifeware. The annual **Mostra Mercato dei Ferri Taglienti** (Market Exhibit of Knives and Swords)—displaying historic and modern cutlery, knives, swords, and daggers along with demonstrations of the skills of modern-day craftsmen—is held during the second half of May in the town center. ☎ *055/8468165,* 🖷 *055/8468862,* 🌐 *www.zoomedia.it/Scarperia/MostraFerriTaglienti.html.* 🎫 *Free or € 3.50 with admission to Museo dei Ferri Taglienti.*

The **Museo dei Ferri Taglienti** (Museum of Knives and Swords), in the Palazzo dei Vicari, provides a complete overview of not only 500 years of knife- and sword-making in northern Tuscany but also shows the techniques that modern artisans use to craft knives by hand. Guided tours are given every hour. ✉ *Palazzo dei Vicari, 50038 Scarperia* ☎ *055/8468027.* 🎫 *€3.50; €5 for guided tour.* ☉ *Sat. 3–7, Sun. 10–1 and 3–7.*

The **Oratorio della Madonna dei Terremoti** (Oratory of the Madonna of the Earthquakes) has a 15th-century fresco of the Madonna and Child that some believe is by Fra Filippo Lippi (1406–69). ✉ *Viale John F. Kennedy 18,* ☎ *no phone.* 🎫 *Free.* ☉ *Daily 9–7.*

The 14th-century facade and courtyard of the **Palazzo Pretorio** (City Hall; ☎ 055/8430671 or 055/8468165), in the town center, are adorned with stone and ceramic coats of arms. Frescoes, of a religious nature and of local coats of arms, decorate the interior. There's no fee to see the frescoes; the building isn't open Sunday.

The Augustinian church of **Ss. Jacopo e Filippo,** though dating from the 14th century, was restored in the 19th and early 20th centuries. Inside are frescoes attributed to Bicci di Lorenzo (circa 1373–1452). Note the marble tondo, *The Madonna and Child,* by Benedetto da Maiano (circa 1442–97) in the chapel to the left of the main altar. ✉ *Via San Martino 17,* ☎ *no phone.* 🎫 *Free.* ☉ *Daily 9–7.*

Lodging

$$$$ 🏨 **Sonesta Resort and Country Club.** This sophisticated resort and golf course, which comprises the lavish villa and dramatic grounds of a 16th-century noble family, is still being developed, with new facilities added each year. The luxurious rooms and common areas are decorated with fine fabrics in Tuscan hues and elegant antique furnishings. The restaurant serves traditional Tuscan cuisine with a nouvelle flair, and it presents an extensive wine list with many rare vintages. Packages are available that include cooking, art, history, and language classes. ✉ *Via S. Gavin,* ☎ *055/8468282,* FAX *055/8430439,* WEB *www.sonesta.com. 46 rooms, 2 suites. Restaurant, cable TV, driving range, 18-hole golf course, pool, health club, hot tub, bar, Internet, meeting rooms. DC, V. Closed Oct.–May.*

$$ 🏨 **Villa Ebe.** Amid rolling countryside but within minutes of Scarperia, Borgo San Lorenzo, San Piero a Sieve, and the Autodromo, this magnificently restored 15th-century villa is a perfect base for visiting the region. Each of its huge rooms is decorated in a different theme with many homey touches, including baskets of candy, swagged four-poster beds, and comfortable chintz-covered chairs. Some of the rooms have kitchenettes and there's a large garden landscaped in the traditional Tuscan manner. The villa is open June through September but can be rented in its entirety for large multiday house parties during the winter holidays. ✉ *Via di Ferracciano 20 (loc. Figliano), Borgo San Lorenzo,* ☎ *055/848019,* FAX *055/848567. 14 rooms. Restaurant, kitchenettes, room TVs, bar; no air-conditioning. DC, V. Closed Oct.–May.*

Outdoor Activities and Sports

About 1 km (½ mi) east of Scarperia, the **Autodromo Internazionale del Mugello** (International Autodrome of Mugello; ✉ 1 km/½ mi east of Scarperia, ☎ 055/8499111, WEB www.mugellocircuit.it) sports a 5-km (3-mi) racetrack built by the Florence Auto Club for Formula 2 race-car meets and world-championship motorcycle races. The track has a full schedule of events every weekend from mid-April through October.

The **Poggio dei Medici Golf and Country Club** (✉ Via S. Gavino 27, ☎ 055/8430436, WEB www.poggiodeimedici.com) provides the perfect Tuscan backdrop for its 18-hole, par 72, course designed to U.S.G.A. standards. The club welcomes day visitors. A driving range and putting green are available. A 1500s villa houses the club's restaurant. Greens fees are €60 on weekdays and €75 on weekends.

Borgo San Lorenzo

❼ *8 km (5 mi) southeast of Scarperia, 32 km (20 mi) north of Florence.*

Borgo San Lorenzo is the largest town in the Mugello, but its biggest claim to fame is that Giotto supposedly was born here—though some other places, including Vespignano, which claims to have the house that Giotto was born in, would dispute this. What is inarguable is that the town has Roman origins and that in the Middle Ages it was controlled by Florence. It saw some heavy fighting during World War II, and the plaque commemorating the heroism of its citizens, which can be seen on the wall of the Palazzo Pretorio, is moving in its strong and un-apologetic language. For those interested in the so-called minor decorative arts of the early 20th century, Borgo San Lorenzo has many Liberty-style buildings.

Documents refer to a church on the site of **San Lorenzo** as early as 941, and there is evidence to suggest that the foundation was built over a Roman temple dedicated to Bacchus. The 1263 bell tower, rebuilt from one dating to 1193, is a fine example of Roman-Byzantine architecture. Inside the church are works of art spanning the centuries, the most important of which is a Madonna attributed to Giotto. It is the only work of his still to be found in his native territory. ⊠ *Via San Francesco, off Piazza Garibaldi,* ☎ *no phone.* ⌨ *Free.* ⊙ *Daily 9–7.*

OFF THE BEATEN PATH **MUSEO DI CASA DI GIOTTO –** There's no evidence that the Museum of the House of Giotto in Vespignano (about 3 km/2 mi east of Borgo San Lorenzo) was once the artist's house, but inside are reproductions of his major works. There's also a tiny chapel, the **Cappellina della Bruna**, which has some 15th-century fresco fragments. You can get the key to the chapel at the museum. ⊠ *From Borgo San Lorenzo take SS551 east, turn left at the sign for the museum, and then continue on for 1 km (½ mi),* ☎ *055/8448251 for the Biblioteca Comunale which handles all requests.* ⌨ *€1.50.* ⊙ *Nov.–Mar., Tues. and Thurs. 4–7, weekends 10–noon and 4–7; Apr.–Oct., Tues. and Thurs. 3–6, weekends 10–noon and 4–6.*

Dining and Lodging

$–$$ ✕ **La Casa del Prosciutto.** This rustic, small osteria at the foot of a tiny 14th-century bridge in Vicchio—7 km (4½ mi) east of Borgo San Lorenzo—is a real find and worth the detour for lunch. Grilled and cured meats are the specialty, but all of the dishes are terrific, from an appetizer of *crostini alla Toscana* (toasted bread with various toppings) to luscious pastry and fruit desserts. Try the *tortelli del Mugello,* a regional specialty of pasta stuffed with potatoes, served with a sauce of porcini mushrooms, or duck, or a *ragù* (tomato sauce with meat). There is also an *alimentari* (deli) that will prepare *panini* (sandwiches) with delectable local prosciutto, cheeses, and Tuscan bread. Reservations are advised. ⊠ *Via Ponte a Vicchio 1,* ☎ *055/844031. AE, DC, MC, V. Closed Mon.–Tues. (deli remains open), most of Jan. and July. No dinner. Reservations essential.*

$$$ 🛏 **Park Hotel Ripaverde.** Although the hotel's glass-and-steel exterior might not be inviting, the interior is modern, clean, and comfortable and offers many amenities. Rooms are contemporary and well furnished. The restaurant serves regional and typical Italian specialties. The exercise room has a sauna and water massage. ⊠ *Viale Giovanni XXIII 36, 50032,* ☎ *055/8496003,* 𝖥𝖠𝖷 *055/8459379,* 𝖶𝖤𝖡 *www.berchielle.it. 51 rooms, 6 suites. Restaurant, cable TV, sauna, gym, bar, Internet, meeting rooms, some pets allowed. AE, DC, MC, V. CP, FAP, MAP.*

$-$$ ☎ **Casa Palmira.** About 11 km (7 mi) southwest of Borgo San Lorenzo and 20 km (12) mi north of Florence on SS302, this is a convenient base for touring both. This rural B&B has seven guest rooms decorated in a simple Tuscan style with hardwood floors, patchwork quilts, and country antiques. Cooking lessons are available in the Tuscan kitchen and courses in painting and photography can be arranged. Breakfast is included and dinner is available on request. ✉ *Località Feriolo, Via Faentina-Polcanto,* ☎ *055/8409749,* FAX *055/8409749. 7 rooms, 5 with bath. Room TVs, mountain bikes, Internet.* ☉ *Closed mid-Jan.– mid-Mar. No credit cards. CP.*

Outdoor Activities and Sports

BALLOONING AND PARAGLIDING

Arrange for hot-air ballooning or paragliding with **Aeroclub Volovelistico Mugello** (✉ Località Figliano, ☎ 055/8408665, WEB www.geoide. com/gliding/) and explore the Mugello from the air.

THE GARFAGNANA AND THE LIMA VALLEY

The heart of the Alpi Apuane is one of the most visually stunning in all of Tuscany. Roads marked by constant hairpin turns wind around precipitous, jagged peaks and through picturesque stone villages. Cool mountain air tempers even the sultriest summer. Most of the major cities and towns can be found along the Serchio, Italy's third-largest river, which runs north–south. The Val di Lima (Lima Valley), formed by the Lima River, has for centuries been known for its curative thermal waters and its lush chestnut groves.

San Marcello Pistoiese

❽ *20 km (12 mi) east of Bagni di Lucca, 50 km (31 mi) north of Lucca, 66 km (41 mi) northwest of Florence.*

This is a small vacation town, but it's the largest one in the surrounding mountains. It bustles especially in summer and winter, but calms down during spring and fall. Set amid spectacular scenery, its claim to fame is a dramatic suspension bridge across the Lima River. The **Museo Ferrucciano** has exhibits on the history of the area as well as on the 1530 battle, waged in the nearby village of Gavinana, in which the Republic of Florence resisted the troops of Charles V of Spain. ☎ 0573/621289. ☞ €1. ☉ July–Aug., daily 10–noon and 5–7; Sept.–June, Thurs. and Sat. 3–5.

The church of **San Marcello** dates from the 12th century. The interior was redone in the 18th century, and most of the art inside is from that period. ✉ *Piazza Arcangeli,* ☎ 0573/630179. ☞ *Free.* ☉ *Daily 9–1 and 3–6.*

Outdoor Activities and Sports

BIKING

You can rent mountain bikes from **Nonsolovolo** (✉ Via Marconi 22, ☎ 0573/6224089).

Abetone

❾ *20 km (12 mi) northwest of San Marcello Pistoiese, 65 km (40 mi) north of Lucca, 86 km (53 mi) northwest of Florence.*

Abetone is one of the most-visited vacation spots in the Apennines, where Tuscans, Emilia-Romagnans, and others go to ski. Set above two valleys, the resort town is on the edge of a lush and ancient forest of more than 9,000 acres. It's easily accessible from Florence and offers a number of trails, mostly for beginner and intermediate skiers (the entire area offers only two expert slopes). Summer is the time to trek or mountain bike in and around the beautiful hills and mountains.

OFF THE
BEATEN PATH

SAN PELLEGRINO IN ALPE – Between Abetone and Castelnuovo di Garfagnana, the monastery of San Pellegrino in Alpe is worth a stop to see its wooden cross and enjoy the staggering view. The story has it that a 9th-century Scot, Pellegrino by name, came to this spot to repent. Here you will also find the **Museo Etnografico** (Provincial Ethnographic Museum; ✉ €2.60), which is mostly devoted to farm objects. ⊠ *Via del Voltone 14,* ☎ *0573/649072.* ✉ *Monastery free.* ☉ *June–Sept., daily 9:30–1 and 2:30–7; Oct.–May, Tues.–Sun. 9–noon and 2–5.*

Dining and Lodging

$$ ✕ **La Capannina.** Fresh local ingredients—chestnuts, mushrooms, freshwater fish, cheeses, olive oil, and herbs—are the keys to the fabulous cooking of owners Luigi Ugolini and Romea Politi in this mountainside restaurant. The traditional rustic Tuscan soups and pastas are filling, but save room for dessert, especially anything made with the local chestnuts. There are also seven rooms for rent (€70 nightly). ⊠ *Via Brennero 256,* ☎ *0573/60562,* FAX *0573/607991,* WEB *www.abetonevacanze.it. AE, DC, MC. Closed Mon., 2 wks in May and Oct.*

$–$$ ✕ **La Locanda dello Yeti.** Stop at this restful osteria after a day on the slopes or a trek through the forest. The specialty of the house is mushrooms—on *crostini* (toasted bread), polenta, or pasta. Mushrooms also garnish the fine grilled meats. Try the refreshing local house wine. ⊠ *Via Brennero 324,* ☎ *0573/606974. Reservations essential. MC, V. Closed Tues.*

$$–$$$ 🏨 **Hotel Bellavista.** Originally a 19th-century villa that belonged to the Strozzi family—powerful bankers in Renaissance Florence—this is now a contemporary inn. Some of the public rooms have a quaint Victorian charm to them, but the guest rooms are of modern decor, with simple wooden furniture and no frills. In winter you can ski to the slopes; in summer the Bellavista is perfectly situated for trekking and mountain biking. ⊠ *Via Brennero 383, 51021,* ☎ *0573/60245,* FAX *0573/60028,* WEB *www.bellavista-abetone.it. 42 rooms. Restaurant, bar; no air-conditioning. AE, MC, V. Closed May and Oct.–Nov. CP, FAP, MAP.*

Outdoor Activities and Sports

SKIING

The area has 37 ski slopes, amounting to about 50 km (31 mi) of ski surface, all accessible through the purchase of a single Multipass. Contact **Consorzio Impianti** (⊠ Via Brennero 429, ☎ 0573/60557), which manages ski facilities, for information on the Multipass as well as maps, directions, and other information. **F. Ballantini** (⊠ Via Brennero 615, ☎ 0573/60482) rents skis.

Parco dell'Orecchiella

⑩ *Southeastern boundary is about 35 km (22 mi) northwest of Abetone.*

Parco dell'Orecchiella (Orecchiella Park), 52 square km (21 square mi), is protected parkland dedicated to preserving local flora and fauna, including eagles, mouflon, and deer. The southeastern boundary of the park is accessible via SS324, a pretty 30-minute drive on the winding two-lane road from Abetone. There is a botanical garden and, for avid hikers, many trails marked with the length of time necessary to complete them—anywhere from 2½ to 5 hours. ☎ *0583/619098 visitors center and information office; 0583/955525 National Forest Admin-*

istration. ✉ *Free.* ☉ *Apr.–May., Sun. 9* AM*–twilight; June, weekends 9–7; July–Aug., daily 9–7; Sept., daily 9* AM*–twilight; Oct.–Nov., weekends 9* AM*–twilight.*

Dining

$–$$ ✕ **Bar Ristorante Orecchiella.** This little place is quite rustic, set in the woods in San Romano in Garfagnana, near the main parking lot at Parco dell'Orecchiella. The Signora Ilda presides in the kitchen, serving up meals or snacks, all of which are Tuscan specialties. Grilled meats—*cinghiale* (wild boar) is often on the menu—and rich pasta dishes are house specialties. ✉ *Parco dell'Orecchiella, San Romano in Garfagnana,* ☎ *0583/619010. No credit cards. Closed Mon.–Sat. Nov.–Mar. and Fri. mid-Sept.–Oct. and Apr.–mid-June*

Castelnuovo di Garfagnana

⓫ *57 km (35 mi) west of Abetone, 47 km (29 mi) north of Lucca, 121 km (75 mi) northwest of Florence.*

Castelnuovo di Garfagnana might be the best base for exploring the Garfagnana, as it is centrally located with respect to the other towns. During the Renaissance, the town's fortunes were frequently tied to those of the powerful d'Este family of Ferrara.

La Rocca (The Fortress), in Piazza Umberto I, dates from the 13th century and has a plaque commemorating writer Ludovico Ariosto's brief tenure here as commissar general for the d'Este. Ariosto (1474–1533) wrote the epic poem *Orlando Furioso* (1516), among other works. The **Duomo** (✉ Piazza del Duomo, ☎ 0583/62170), a cathedral dedicated to St. Peter, was begun in the 11th century and was reconstructed in the early 1500s. Inside is a crucifix dating from the 14th to 15th century. There's also an early 16th-century terra-cotta attributed to the school of Della Robbia. Entry to the Duomo, open daily 9–7, is free.

OFF THE   **PARCO NATURALE DELLE ALPI APUANE** – Preserved ancient forests and
BEATEN PATH   barren rocky peaks create the dramatic scenery in the Natural Park of the Apuan Alps, a national park area that encompasses several towns. Its highest peak, Monte Pisanino, rises more than 6,000 ft and towers over an artificial lake, Lago di Vagli, which covers the submerged village of Fabbricca. The tiny stone villages of Vagli di Sotto and Vagli di Sopra sit alongside the lake. A two-lane winding road through the park connects Castelnuovo di Garfagnana to the sea coast. ☎ *0583/ 644354.* ✉ *Free.*

Dining and Lodging

$$ ✕ **Osteria Vecchio Mulino.** An antique marble serving counter, wooden tables, and rush-seated chairs create a warm ambience at this tiny eatery. The mixed antipasto plate is a satisfying starter, with various vegetables *sott'olio* (under oil), beans, and marinated anchovies. Traditional local dishes of farro, polenta, pecorino cheese, and salami round out the menu. ✉ *Via Vittorio Emanuele 12,* ☎ *0583/62192. AE, DC, MC, V. Closed Mon. and Sept.*

$–$$ ✕🏠 **La Lanterna.** A few minutes' drive from the center of town—up a long, winding road—this contemporary inn has beautiful mountain views. The rooms are modern, with white walls and wall-to-wall carpeting. The hotel restaurant ($$–$$$; closed Tues.) serves bountiful regional specialties; the food, featuring farro in several guises, is fantastic and inexpensive. The chef also has a gift for sauces—try the pork in a radicchio sauce. ✉ *Località alle Monache, Piano Pieve 55032,* ☎ FAX *0583/62272,* WEB *www.hotellalaterna.com. 42 rooms. Restaurant, cable TV, meeting rooms, some pets allowed. AE, DC, MC, V. CP, FAP, MAP.*

Outdoor Activities and Sports

HIKING AND CLIMBING

For detailed maps and information about trekking in the mountains around Castelnuovo di Garfagnana and particularly for the Parco Naturale delle Alpi Apuane, stop in at **CAI** (Club Alpino Italiano; Italian Alpine Club; ⊠ Via Vittrio Emanuele, ☎ 0583/65577) or **Centri Accoglienza Parco** (⊠ Piazza Erbe 1, ☎ 0583/65169).

Barga

⑫ *13½ km (8 mi) southeast of Castelnuovo di Garfagnana, 37 km (23 mi) north of Lucca, 111 km (69 mi) northwest of Florence.*

Barga is a lovely little hill town with a finely preserved medieval core. It produced textiles—particularly silk—during the Renaissance and wool in the 18th century. Here, the black American squadrons, known as the Buffalo Soldiers, are remembered for their bravery defending this mountainous area during World War II. The **Duomo,** dedicated to St. Christopher, is an elegant limestone Romanesque cathedral that saw four separate building campaigns; the first began in the 9th century. Inside, there's an intricately carved high pulpit supported by pillars. Two pillars sit on the backs of stone lions, one with a dragon and the other being stabbed by a man; a third rests on a dwarf. The Duomo offers a beautiful panorama of the surrounding countryside. ⊠ *Via del Duomo,* ☎ *no phone.* 🎫 *Free.* ☉ *Daily 9–7.*

OFF THE
BEATEN PATH

GROTTA DEL VENTO – About 14 km (9 mi) southwest of Barga, following a winding road flanked by both sheer cliffs and fabulous views, you will come to Tuscany's windy cave, in Fornovolasco. As the result of a steady internal temperature of 10.7°C (about 51°F), the "wind" is sucked into the cave in the winter and blown out in the summer. It has a long cavern with stalactites, stalagmites, "bottomless" pits, and subterranean streams. One-, two-, and three-hour guided tours of the cave are given. (In winter only the one-hour tour is offered.) ☎ *0583/722024.* 🎫 *€6.50 for 1 hr, €10 for 2 hrs, €15 for 3 hrs.* ☉ *Daily 10–6.*

Lodging

$$$$ 🏨 **Il Ciocco.** North of Barga 7 km (4½ mi), this huge resort and convention hotel has every amenity, including its own soccer stadium, basketball court, and full equestrian facilities and riding trails. The rooms are modern but tastefully decorated, and most have balcony views of the surrounding pine-forested hills and the distant Alpi Apuane. Apartments and chalets are also available for rental by the week. ⊠ *Castelvecchio Pascoli, 55020,* ☎ *0583/7191 or 0583/719204,* 📠 *0583/723197,* WEB *www.ilciocco.it. 220 rooms, 15 suites, 56 apartments, 12 chalets. Restaurant, pizzeria, cable TV, 8 tennis courts, pool, health club, bicycles, cinema, dance club, Internet, some pets allowed. AE, DC, MC, V. BP, FAP, MAP.*

Nightlife and the Arts

From mid-July to mid-August, the stony streets of Barga come alive with the participants and spectators of the **Opera Barga** (⊠ Piazza Angelio 4, WEB www.barganews.com/operabarga), a highly regarded opera festival held in the **Teatro dell' Accademia dei Differenti** (Theater of the Academy of the Different). The Opera Barga was started in 1967 when a workshop was offered to young singers and musicians. The Opera Barga puts on smaller, lesser known operas of the baroque period together with more modern and even contemporary compositions. The Barga visitor center has additional information.

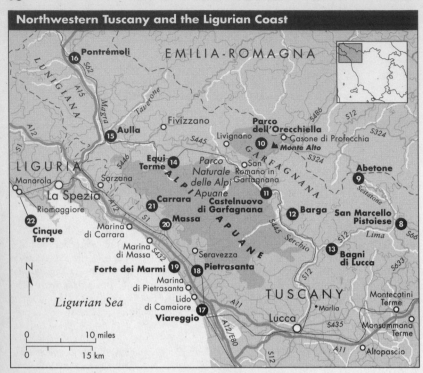

Northwestern Tuscany and the Ligurian Coast

Bagni di Lucca

13 *18 km (11 mi) southeast of Barga, 27 km (17 mi) north of Lucca, 101 km (63 mi) northwest of Florence.*

Pretty Bagni di Lucca was a fashionable spa town in the early 19th century—in part because of its thermal waters. The Romantic poet Percy Bysshe Shelley (1792–1822) installed his family here during the summer of 1818. He wrote to a friend in July of that year that the waters here were "exceedingly refreshing": "My custom is to undress and sit on the rocks, reading Herodotus, until perspiration has subsided, and then to leap from the edge of the rock into this fountain." In 1853, Robert and Elizabeth Browning spent the summer in a house on the main square. Its heyday behind it, the town is now a quiet, charming place where elegant thermal spas still enliven the temperate summer days.

Dining

$$–$$$ ✕ **La Ruota.** About 3 km (2 mi) west of Bagno di Lucca in the tiny village of Fornoli, La Ruota is known for dishes that are traditional in the region along the Serchio river, such as smoked trout, tortelli with duck sauce, steak with porcini mushrooms, and fried frog legs. ✉ *Via Giovanni XXIII 29, Fornoli,* ☎ *0583/805627. Reservations essential. Closed July and Tues. No dinner Mon. AE, DC, MC, V.*

THE LUNIGIANA

The Lunigiana (Land of the Moon) was of strategic importance in pre-Roman times as a commercial center for trading between the Celts and the Ligurians. It maintained its economic strength during the early Middle Ages, serving as a junction between cities north of the Alps and those south. It also was a stopping point for pilgrims en route to Rome.

The area was hotly contested territory between the Milanese, the Genoese, and the Florentines during the Renaissance. This is the place where medieval fantasies run wild: the hills are steep, the mountains are plentiful, and there are lots of castles—more than 100 of them, still whole or in ruins—that provide testimony to the Lunigiana's tumultuous past. Built in the 13th and 14th centuries, the castles and defensive towers set amid the rocky, forested landscape create a powerful effect.

Equi Terme

⑭ *63 km (39 mi) northeast of Bagni di Lucca, 30 km (19 mi) southeast of Aulla, 45 km (28 mi) east of La Spezia.*

This pretty little spa town nestled in the mountains is a great place for an affordable spa experience. Though the Romans first discovered these waters (a warm 27°C [81°F]), it wasn't until the end of the 19th century that the thermal springs became a draw. At the **Stabilimento Termale di Equi Terme,** there's a large pool with warm thermal waters for a lengthy soak under the clear blue mountain sky, and many spa services—sauna, massage, water therapy, and water massage, among others—offered within. ⊠ *Via Umberto I 20,* ☎ *0585/949300.* 🎫 *Treatments €8.5–€25.* ⊙ *June–Oct., daily 9–1 and 2–6.*

Dining and Lodging

$ ✕🎫 **La Posta.** This is a slightly ramshackle but totally fun place to stay
★ and eat, directly across a little stream from the Hotel Terme. The seven rooms are basic, with baths and high ceilings, but the restaurant ($$$–$$$$; closed Tues.) is a real treat and worth a trip. The *ravioli alle ortiche* (spinach ravioli stuffed with nettles and lightly dressed with a creamy nut sauce) is a good choice; the house special, *lasagne la spagnola,* made—as the proprietor says—with "top-secret" ingredients, definitely includes five cheeses and tastes as light as a feather. ⊠ *Via Provinciale 26, 54022,* ☎ *0585/97937. 7 rooms. Restaurant; no air-conditioning. AE, DC, MC, V. Closed Jan. and Feb. CP, FAP, MAP.*

$ 🎫 **Hotel Terme.** More than a century old, this cool and comfortable hotel is a great place to unwind; next door is a spa that offers all sorts of soothing things for body and soul. A small river runs near it, which might be the only noise you'll hear. The restaurant offers local specialties, and the menu changes frequently. ⊠ *Via Noce Verde 51, Equi Terme 54022,* ☎ *0585/97830,* ☎ FAX *0585/97831,* WEB *www.termediequi.it. 20 rooms. Restaurant, pool, bar, Internet, meeting room; no air-conditioning. AE, DC, MC, V. FAP, MAP.*

Aulla

⑮ *30 km (19 mi) northwest of Equi Terme, 23 km (14 mi) northeast of La Spezia, 152 km (94 mi) northwest of Florence.*

Aulla is a sleepy little town just off the autostrada. It was heavily bombed by the United States during World War II, so much of what you see is postwar reconstruction. However, on the outskirts of town is a park with an old castle that affords some superb views.

The castle **La Brunella** dates from the 16th century, and you can see remnants of a 9th-century abbey dedicated to St. Caprasio. The English couple Aubrey Waterfield and Linda Duff-Gordon bought it in the early 1900s and turned it into a country home; they also created its garden. D. H. Lawrence (1885–1930), among others, was a visitor. Inside the complex is the **Museo di Storia Naturale della Lunigiana** (Museum of Natural History of the Lunigiana; 🎫 €3.50). ⊠ *Castle la Brunella,* ☎ *0187/400252 or 0187/409077.* 🎫 *Park free.* ⊙ *Castle*

*and museum: summer, Tues.–Sun. 9–noon and 4–7; winter, 9–noon and
3–6. Park: summer, daily 8:30–7:30; winter, daily 8:30–6:30.*

Pontrémoli

16 *17½ km (11 mi) north of Aulla, 40 km (25 mi) northeast of La Spezia,
164 km (102 mi) northwest of Florence.*

In a beautiful setting where the Magra and Verde rivers meet, Pontrémoli has a historic center developed according to a medieval matrix.
During the Middle Ages, the city was a point of contact between north
and south, which helped it to flourish economically. Here originated
the *libri ambulanti* (traveling book fair), and a prestigious literary
prize, the Premio Bancarella, is still awarded. The town is especially
bursting with activity on Wednesday and Saturday, when an open-air
market with fruits, vegetables, and clothing takes over the Piazza del
Duomo and the adjoining Piazza Repubblica.

The 17th-century **Duomo** is an exercise in baroque excess—the lime-
green walls, accentuated with pale pink on the pilasters, and the white
molding throughout make it look like a gaudy wedding cake. ⊠ *Piazza del Duomo,* ☎ *no phone.* ⊡ *Free.* ☉ *Daily 9–noon and 3–6:30.*

The **Chiesa di Nostra Donna** (Church of Our Lady), which was finished in the 1730s, has a pretty rococo facade that's worth a look. It's
on the Via Mazzini, on the other side of the Magra River from the Piazza del Duomo. The lovely **Parco della Torre** (Park of the Towers)
along the Magra is great for a picnic; it's at the end of Via Mazzini, at
the Chiesa di Nostra Donna.

Castello di Piagnaro was built in the 9th and 10th centuries—though
not much remains from that period—with alterations made between
the 15th and 16th centuries. What does remain is a fully formed castle with stupefying views; it's home to the **Museo delle Statue Stele Lu-
nigianesi** (Museum of Lunigian Stele Statues), which contains a collection
of stele found in the area. Many of the large, prehistoric, carved stone
slabs depict stylized warriors, and others are of women. ⊠ *Via Garibaldi,*
☎ *0187/831439.* ⊡ *€2.6, including museum.* ☉ *Oct.–Mar., Tues.–
Sun. 9–noon and 2–5; Apr.–Sept., Tues.–Sun. 9–noon and 3–6.*

A very tiny chapel built between 1883 and 1893, **La Chiesetta di Sant'
Ilario** (The Chapel of St. Ilario) is without artistic or historic merit, but
it is so cute that it's worth a visit. The exterior, with its orange and
yellow paint, is almost Disneyesque in style; inside are ceiling decorations that were executed after World War II by the members of the Tri-
ani family, Pontrémoli natives. (Ask at the Duomo for chapel access.)
It's just a few minutes' walk from the Castello di Piagnaro. ⊠ *Via Piagnaro 13,* ☎ *no phone.* ⊡ *Free.* ☉ *Daily 9–noon.*

Dining

$$ ✕ **Da Busse'.** Just around the corner from the Duomo, this family eatery
serves up solid local fare in a casual, understated way. The interior is
brightly lighted, the tables are close together, and there's a hum from
the kitchen and chatting diners. *Zuppa con ragu e parmigiano* (soup
with meat sauce and parmesan) has been pleasing crowds for the past
20 years. Other kitchen favorites include vegetable tarts, lasagna made
with chestnut flour, and stuffed veal. ⊠ *Piazza Duomo 31,* ☎ *0187/
831371. Reservations essential weekends. No credit cards. Closed Fri.
and July. No dinner Sun.–Thurs. except on holidays.*

THE VERSILIAN COAST AND THE ALPI APUANE

In full view of the Alpi Apuane, the colorful resort towns of the Versilian Coast bustle in July and August with vacationing Italians drawn by the sea breezes and fine, wide sandy beaches. From the coast, roads climb over the rolling hills blanketed with pine forests and into the mountains where marble quarries have been operating since before Michelangelo (1475–1564) came to pick his own blocks of Carrara marble. North of Versilia, the coast changes to rocky cliffs on which cling the picturesque villages of the Cinque Terre.

Viareggio

⑰ *20 km (13 mi) northwest of Pisa, 97 km (60 mi) northwest of Florence.*

Tobias Smollett (1721–71), an English novelist, wrote in the 1760s that Viareggio was "a kind of sea-port on the Mediterranean . . . The roads are indifferent and the accommodation is execrable." Much has changed here since Smollett's time. For one, this beach town becomes very crowded during summer, so accommodations are plentiful. But Viareggio can be loud and brassy, so if you're looking for peace and quiet, come in the autumn and early spring.

Viareggio has numerous buildings decorated in the Liberty style and a wide promenade parallel to the sea where tourists and locals alike come out to stroll. Lining the promenade are bars, cafés, and some very fine restaurants. If you can't make it to Venice for **Carnevale** (Carnival), come here, which in some ways is more fun than Venice. The city is packed with revelers from all over Tuscany who come to join in the riot of colorful parades with giant floats and other festivities. Try to book lodging far in advance, but beware: lots of people want to be here to celebrate Carnival, and hotels acknowledge this fact by charging high-season prices.

Dining and Lodging

$$$–$$$$ ✕ **Romano.** This fine restaurant, run by Romano Franceschini and his
★ family, is sophisticated dining at its best, with superb service. An excellent host, Romano is ebullient and proud of his food, and for good reason. Fresh local fish and shellfish are prepared according to simple Tuscan recipes but are presented in fine style on large white platters. The mixed seafood grill and lightly fried *calamaretti* (tiny squid) are delights. The chef's special dessert is a coconut mousse with apple dumplings. ☒ *Via Mazzini 122,* ☎ *0584/31382. Reservations essential. AE, DC, MC, V. Closed Mon. (and Tues. in August) and Jan.*

$$$$ ⛳ **Grand Hotel Royal.** A hotel since 1899, the Grand Hotel Royal looks majestic from the outside, and sweepingly high ceilings maintain the feeling inside. The *salone,* which doubled as a ballroom in the past, is very romantic, with high ceilings and pink tablecloths; dinner is served here in cooler months. There's also a yellow breakfast room flooded with sunlight. Individual rooms have tile floors, and some have balconies overlooking the sea (additional charge). In high season, a three-day minimum stay is required. The restaurant changes its menu daily. ☒ *Viale Carducci 44, 55049,* ☎ *0584/45151,* ℻ *0584/31438,* 🕸 *www.bestwestern.it/royal_lu. 102 rooms, 2 suites. Restaurant, minibars, cable TV, pool, Ping-Pong, bicycles, Internet, meeting room, some no-smoking rooms. AE, DC, MC, V. Closed Nov. FAP, MAP.*

$$$$ ⛳ **Hotel President.** A quiet elegance exudes here. The rooms have slightly formal decor, high ceilings, and pastel walls; some look directly out at the sea, across the promenade. Two of the suites have hot tubs. The hotel restaurant, Ristorante Gaudi, has panoramic views and is

open to the public (hours vary so call ahead) The hotel bar has an outdoor terrace and furniture from the early 1900s. ⊠ *Viale Carducci 5, 55049,* ☎ *0584/962712,* ℻ *0584/963658,* ☒ *www.hotelpresident. it. 31 rooms, 6 suites. Restaurant, in-room safe, minibars, bar, Internet, meeting room, some pets allowed. AE, DC, MC, V. FAP, MAP.*

Outdoor Activities and Sports

SAILING

Club Nautico Versilia (Nautical Club of Versilia; ⊠ Piazza Artiglio, ☎ 0584/31444) can assist sailors who wish to tour the coastal waters.

Pietrasanta

⑱ *8 km (5 mi) north of Viareggio, 104 km (65 mi) northwest of Florence.*

Historically Pietrasanta has been the major town in Versilia for two reasons: at first because of its military importance to the Romans, and later as an artistic center, thanks in part to the availability of marble in the area. Donatello and, later, Michelangelo used marble quarried nearby.

The buildings of the Renaissance **Piazza del Duomo** give you a feel for how grandly 15th-century architects conceived of urban planning. On the piazza near Via Barsanti is a plaque commemorating a contract signed on that spot by Michelangelo in 1518 for marble to build the facade of San Lorenzo in Florence (a project that ultimately wasn't built).

The **Duomo** is dedicated to St. Martin and was begun in the mid-13th century. Most of the art inside dates from the 16th and 17th centuries. ⊠ *Piazza del Duomo,* ☎ *058/790177.* ☒ *Free.* ☉ *8–noon and 3-7.*

The church of **Sant'Antonio Abate** (also known as the church of San Biagio) dates from the 14th century and is dedicated to St. Biagio. Inside are two wood polychrome sculptures of St. Biagio and St. Anthony Abate that date from the 16th century. Frescoes by Colombian artist Fernando Botero (born 1932)—*La Porta del Paradiso* (*The Gates of Heaven*) and *La Porta dell'Inferno* (*The Gates of Hell*), dating from the 1990s—are worth the visit on their own. ⊠ *Via G. Mazzini 103,* ☎ *0584/70055.* ☒ *Free.* ☉ *Daily 8–noon and 3–7:30.*

The church of **Sant'Agostino** was built in the 14th century by the Augustinians. The building no longer functions as a church but is used for special exhibitions. Some 15th-century frescoes and paintings from the 17th and 18th centuries are contained within. ⊠ *Via Sant'Agostino,* ☎ *no phone.* ☒ *Free.* ☉ *Daily 9:30–12:30 and 5–7.*

The **Museo dei Bozzetti** contains a collection of sculptural sketches and models made by contemporary Italian and foreign artists, including the most important sculptors of the 20th century in the Versilian workshops. ⊠ *Via Sant'Agostino 1,* ☎ *0584/795500 or 0584/795588.* ☒ *Free.* ☉ *Tues.–Fri. 9–1 and 2–7, Sat. 2–7.*

The **Civico Museo Archeologico** has objects from the 3rd millennium BC as well as pottery dating from the Renaissance. The collection is housed in the 15th-century **Palazzo Moroni.** ⊠ *Palazzo Moroni, Piazza del Duomo,* ☎ *0584/795500. The museum was closed for restoration through 2002; call for information.*

Forte dei Marmi

⑲ *5 km (3 mi) north of Pietrasanta, 14 km (9 mi) north of Viareggio, 104 km (65 mi) northwest of Florence.*

Forte dei Marmi is a playground for wealthy Italians and equally well-heeled tourists. Its wide, sandy beaches—strands are 6 km (4 mi) long—have the Alpi Apuane as a dramatic backdrop. The town was, from Roman times, the port from which marble quarried in Carrara was transported. In the 1920s, it became the fashionable seaside resort it is today. During the winter, the town's population is about 10,000; in the summer, it swells seven to eight times that.

Dining and Lodging

$$$–$$$$ ✕ **Bistrot.** For beach-side dining, this seafood restaurant can't be beat. Standouts here include the delicious *carpaccio di branzino* (thin slices of raw sea bass), which are quickly seared and then served with fragrant local olive oil, basil, and tomatoes. The pastas are homemade and the *sauté di frutti di mare,* a cross between a soup and stew, features *vongole* (clams), tomatoes, and garlic, in a heavenly broth. For starters, try the *assaggini* ("little tastes"), which can change daily depending on what's fresh from the sea that day. ✉ *Viale Franceschi 14,* ☎ *0584/89879. AE, DC, MC, V. Closed Tues. Oct.–May.*

$$$–$$$$ ✕ **Lorenzo.** Owned for more than 20 years by the affable Lorenzo Viani,
★ this restaurant is crowded even in the dead of winter. The focus here is on seafood. Start with the chilled raw oysters before moving on to seafood pasta, sea bass with chopped tomatoes, or a fish tartare. This is one of the best restaurants in Versilia for fish, and the desserts are exceptional, too. ✉ *Via Carducci 61,* ☎ *0584/84030. Reservations essential. AE, DC, MC, V. Closed mid-Dec.–Jan. and Mon. No lunch July–Aug.*

$$$$ 🏨 **Byron.** The pale yellow exterior only hints at the elegance inside this
★ hotel, which was created by joining two Liberty villas that date from 1899 and 1902. The beach is directly across the street, and there's a pool on property. This fine hotel also includes the restaurant La Magnolia, which serves regional cuisine pool-side during the summer. ✉ *Viale Arthur-Jules Morin 46, 55042,* ☎ *0584/787052,* 𝖥𝖠𝖷 *0584/ 787152,* 🖳 *www.hotelbyron.net. 24 rooms, 6 suites. Restaurant, pool, billiards, meeting rooms. AE, DC, MC, V. FAP, MAP.*

$$$–$$$$ 🏨 **The Ritz.** This hotel built in the 1930s occupies what was once a majestic villa. Designed in the Beaux Arts style, it has a warm, inviting ambience; classic yet without the stuffiness associated with some other upscale hotels. The late contemporary artist Henry Moore found inspiration for a few of his classic sculptures while residing at the Ritz. The hotel is just one block from the area's beach clubs, and it's a short walk to the center of town. ✉ *Via Flavio Gioia 2, 55042,* ☎ *0584/ 787531,* 𝖥𝖠𝖷 *0584/787522,* 🖳 *www.ritzfortedeimarmi.com. 32 rooms, 1 suite. Restaurant, cable TV, pool, bar, Internet, meeting room. AE, DC, MC, V. CP, FAP, MAP.*

$$$ 🏨 **Goya.** This hotel in the center of town is built in the Liberty style and evokes old-world charm. The rooms have high ceilings, and some have their own little balconies with a view to the sea. There's also an outdoor hot tub. ✉ *Via Carducci 69, 55042,* ☎ *0584/787221,* 𝖥𝖠𝖷 *0584/ 787269,* 🖳 *www.hotelgoya.it. 47 rooms, 1 suite. Restaurant, cable TV, hot tub. AE, DC, MC, V. FAP, MAP.*

Nightlife and the Arts

After a day at the beach, the place to meet and greet the rich and famous is **Alma Rosa Art Music and Bar** (✉ Viale Morin 89/a, ☎ 0584/ 82503). The clientele during high season frequently includes Italian national soccer players and other young, good-looking celebs and politicos. Leonardo, the owner-bartender, is charming and speaks English.

Outdoor Activities and Sports

BIKING

Claudio Maggi Cicli (✉ Viale Morin 85, ☎ 0584/89529, 𝖥𝖠𝖷 0584/81669, 🖳 www.ciclimaggi.it), which is near the beach, has just about everything for the biker. From May through September, it's open daily 8–1 and 3–8; from October through April, it's closed Wednesday and Sunday. **Maggi-Coppa** (⊠ Via A. Franceschi 4d, ☎ 0584/83528), which rents bicycles, is right on the beach and keeps late hours: 8 AM–midnight daily from May through August, 8–8 daily the rest of the year.

The **Forte dei Marmi Club Alpino Italiano** (Forte dei Marmi Italian Alpine Club; ⊠ Via Michelangelo 49, ☎ 0584/89808) can provide information on hiking and rock climbing and about guided tours.

For information about the best places to scuba dive on the Versilian and Ligurian coasts, call the **Associazione Subacquei Versilia** (Versilia Scuba Association; ⊠ Via S. Allende 38, ☎ 0584/82070 or 329/9413130).

Massa

㉠ *8½ km (5 mi) north of Forte dei Marmi, 22 km (14 mi) north of Viareggio, 115 km (74 mi) northwest of Florence.*

The best reasons to visit this modern town are the large fountains, marble sculptures, and **La Rocca** (☎ 0585/490526), which was built between the 14th and 16th centuries. The hours can vary; you're most likely to get in Friday 9:30–12:30 and 3–6 and Sunday 9–6, however it's best to call ahead (admission is free). The exterior alone is impressive, but be warned that getting to La Rocca requires a steep climb. Things are livelier in **Marina di Massa,** Massa's port (5 km [3 mi] south), where there's a busy beach and many eateries.

Dining and Lodging

$$–$$$ ✕ **Circolo della Vela.** Despite its setting at the local yacht club, this restau-
★ rant is quite affordable. The specialties of the house are octopus with olives, pasta with scallops or shrimp, and the grilled fresh catch of the day. ⊠ *Viale Vespucci 84, ☎ 0585/244544. Closed Mon. Mar.–July and Tues. Mar.–June. No lunch Mar.–June. No credit cards.*

$$$–$$$$ 🛏 **Hotel Excelsior.** The spacious rooms in this modern hotel have either panoramic views of the sea or of the Alpi Apuane; three are wheelchair-accessible. The marble quarries are only 5 km (3 mi) away, and there's an 18-hole golf course only 8 km (5 mi) from here. The hotel restaurant (closed Dec.–Mar.), Il Sestante, specializes in local and international dishes. ⊠ *Lungomare Vespucci, Via Cesare Battisti I, 54037, ☎ 0585/8601, FAX 0585/869795, WEB www.hotelexcelsior.it. 71 rooms, 7 suites. Restaurant, room service, in-room safes, minibars, cable TV, pool, laundry service, Internet, meeting room, some pets allowed (fee). AE, DC, MC, V. FAP, MAP.*

$–$$ 🛏 **Hotel Tirreno e Milano.** This once private Liberty villa about 100 ft from the sea was converted into two hotels in the 1950s; they are run by the same management and share facilities, including the reception desk. The rooms are decorated in cool pastel colors and have high ceilings that contribute to a grand sense of space. Those in the Tirreno ($$) are larger and fancier than those in the Milano ($). Full pension is required in August. The restaurant is open only from April through October. ⊠ *Piazza Betti, Marina di Massa, 54037, ☎ 0585/246173, FAX 0585/240827, WEB www.hoteltirrenomarinadimassa.com. 27 rooms, 5 suites in the Tirreno; 55 rooms in the Milano. Restaurant, cable TV, meeting room, some pets allowed. DC, MC, V. Closed Nov.–Mar. FAP, MAP.*

Carrara

㉑ *26 km (16 mi) north of Viareggio, 7 km (4½ mi) north of Massa, 126 km (79 mi) northwest of Florence.*

Carrara, from which the famous white marble takes its name, lies in a beautiful valley midway up a spectacular mountain in the Apenines. The surrounding peaks are bare of foliage and white as snow, even in summer, because they are full of marble stone. Marble has been quarried in the area for the past 2,000 years. The art historian Giorgio Vasari (1511–74) recorded that Michelangelo came to Carrara with two apprentices to quarry the marble for the never-completed tomb of Julius II (1443–1513).

According to Vasari, Michelangelo spent eight months among the rocks conceiving fantastical ideas for future works. Carrara has a lot of still-active quarries—well over 100 at last count. Most of them are not open to the public for safety reasons. However, it is possible to tour specific caves. The Carrara visitor information center (☞ Visitor Information *in* North of Florence A to Z) has details about which areas are open to visitors.

Carrara's history as a marble-producing center is well documented in the **Museo del Marmo** (Museum of Marble), beginning with early works from the AD 2nd century. Exhibits detail the production of marble, from quarrying and transporting it to sculpting it. ⊠ *Viale XX Settembre,* ☎ *0585/845746.* ☞ *€3.50.* ☉ *June–Sept., Mon.–Sat. 10–8; Oct. and May, Mon.–Sat. 10–5; Nov.–Apr., Mon.–Sat. 8:30–7:30.*

Work began on the **Duomo** in the 11th century and continued into the 14th. The cathedral is dedicated to St. Andrew and is the first church of the Middle Ages constructed entirely of marble. Most of the marble comes from Carrara (the white, light-blue gray, black, and red). The tremendous facade is a fascinating blend of Pisan Romanesque architecture and Gothic. Note the human figures and animals on Corinthian capitals. ⊠ *Piazza del Duomo,* ☎ *no phone.* ☞ *Free.* ☉ *Daily 9–7.*

The lovely baroque church of **San Francesco** is worth a look simply because of its understated elegance. It dates from the 1620s to 1660s, and even though it was built during the peak years of the baroque, the only excess can be found in the twisting marble columns that embellish the altars. ⊠ *Piazza XXVII Aprile,* ☎ *no phone.* ☞ *Free.* ☉ *Daily 9–7.*

During the 19th and 20th centuries, Carrara became a hotbed for anarchism, and during World War II, it put up fierce resistance to the Nazis. The town is still lively thanks to its art institute. The **Accademia di Belle Arti,** founded by Maria Teresa Cybo Malaspina d'Este in 1769, draws studio art students from all over Italy. Their presence explains the funky atmosphere that's found in some of the piazzas.

Lodging

$$ ⌂ **Hotel Mediterraneo.** As the hotel options in Carrara are somewhat grim, this hotel in Marina di Carrara (a 10-minute drive south) is a nice alternative. The Mediterraneo is just 150 ft from the sea, although you'll have to walk a little farther to get to a beach. Many of the rooms have balconies, and breakfast is served on a terrace with both sea and mountain views. The restaurant, where the menu changes daily, derives inspiration from the sea, but there are meat options as well. ⊠ *Via Genova 2/h, Marina di Carrara 54036,* ☎ FAX *0585/785222,* WEB *www.hotelmediterraneo.com. 42 rooms, 1 suite. Restaurant, cable TV, bar, meeting room. AE, DC, MC, V. FAP, MAP.*

$–$$ ⌂ **Hotel Carrara.** Though this quiet hotel isn't actually in Carrara, it's right down the street from the Avenza-Carrara train station (4 km

[2½ mi] southeast of Carrara). The rooms are simple, with tile floors, and there's an extensive breakfast buffet. ⊠ *Via Petacchi 21, 54031 Avenza,* ☎ *0585/52371,* FAX *0585/50344,* WEB *www.hotelcarra.it. 32 rooms. Breakfast room, cable TV, Internet, some pets allowed. AE, DC, MC, V.*

Cinque Terre

㉒ *Riomaggiore is about 158 km (98 mi) northwest of Florence and 45 km (28 mi) north of Carrara.*

The aura of isolation that has surrounded the five Ligurian coastal villages known as the Cinque Terre (Five Lands), together with their dramatic coastal scenery, has made them one of the Italian Riviera's premier attractions. Clinging haphazardly to steep cliffs, they are linked by footpaths, by train, and by a narrow, unpaved, serpentine road with one-lane tunnels and no parking opportunities.

The popular, well-established hiking trails that connect the Cinque Terre traverse protected park land, showcase breathtaking ocean views, and provide access to rugged, secluded beaches and grottoes. For much of the villages' history, the trails were the only way to get from one town to the next on land. These days, the local train on the Genoa–La Spezia line stops at each of the Cinque Terre, from Monterosso, the northernmost village, to Riomaggiore, at the east end. (A 24-hour Cinque Terre Tourist train ticket, which allows unlimited travel between the five towns, is available at the five train stations.)

The largest of the five fishing towns is **Monterosso al Mare** (population 1,730), its village center and bustling markets high on a hillside. Below is the port, connected by stone steps, where there are boats for hire. The parish church is built in the 12th-century Ligurian Gothic style, and the town has a lively nightlife and three small beaches. Be sure to try some Sciacchetrá, the sweet, local wine.

To the east of Monterosso is **Vernazza,** founded by the Romans on a rocky spit of land. It is a charming colorful village of narrow streets, and small squares and arcades, with the remains of two towers that date from the Middle Ages.

The buildings, narrow lanes, and stairways of **Corniglia**—the middle of the Cinque Terre—are strung together amid vineyards high on the cliffs; on a clear day, the views of the entire coastal strip are excellent. Lacking the beach and harbor activity of the others, Corniglia is the most peaceful of the five towns. If you take the train, a challenging climb up 365 steps from the station to the village awaits.

The enchanting pastel houses of **Manarola,** which is built on an enormous black rock, are nestled into a steep hill overlooking a spectacular turquoise swimming cove and a bustling harbor.

At the eastern end of the Cinque Terre is **Riomaggiore,** the most accessible of the villages (via car or train from La Spezia). It is curved around a tiny harbor that's ringed with lively cafés and dotted with fishing boats.

Dining and Lodging

$$$ ✕ **Miki.** Specialties at this popular eatery include anything having to do with seafood. The *insalata di mare* (cold squid and fish salad) is more than tasty; so are the grilled fish and the *linguini al mare* (seafood pasta). Pizza is available, too; try the one topped with shrimp. Miki has a beautiful little garden in back, perfect for lunch on a sunny day. ⊠ *Via Fegina 104, Monterosso al Mare,* ☎ *0187/817608. AE, DC, MC, V. Closed Nov.–Feb. and Tues.*

$$–$$$ ✕ **A Cantina de Mananan.** This minuscule osteria with marble tables lists its daily changing menu of traditional Ligurian fare on a blackboard. Good bets, when available, include the anchovy starter, followed by spaghetti with either clams, crab, or pesto sauce. Another favorite is the rabbit fried in local olive oil. For a simple dessert, do as the locals do and order the milk custard drizzled with honey. ⌧ *Via Fiechi 117, Corniglia,* ☎ *0187/821166. No credit cards. Closed Tues. in summer. Call for hrs. in winter. No lunch in summer.*

$$–$$$ ✕ **Il Pirata.** High-quality Ligurian seafood sets this port-side trattoria apart. Preferred seating is at the long porch table outside, and weekend reservations are essential. Try the starters with anchovy or tiny squid. Soups and pastas with seafood are also highly recommended. Chef/owner Roberto has developed a tasting menu that offers the best the sea has to offer each day. This intimate space is less appropriate for children than others in the region. ⌧ *Via Molinelli 6/8, Monterosso al Mare,* ☎ *0187/817536, AE, DC, MC, V. Closed Nov. and Jan. No lunch weekdays.*

$$–$$$ ✕ **Ripa del Sole.** In summer, meals at this notable seafood eatery can be enjoyed on the terrace. Try some of the great local wine with the chef's signature dish, *scampi con tartufo bianco* (shrimp with white truffles), or with one of the other house specialties: *calamari con farro* (squid with barley), *gamberi con fagioli e rucola* (shrimp with beans and greens), or the *trofie fatte a mano con pesto* (handmade curly pasta in a pesto sauce). ⌧ *Via De Gasperi 282, Riomaggiore,* ☎ *0187/ 920143,* 𝔽𝔸𝕏 *0187/920143. Reservations essential. No credit cards. Closed Nov.–Dec. and Mon. May–Sept. No lunch.*

$$–$$$ ✕ **Trattoria Gianni Franzi.** This is the place to order pesto on *fagiolini* (green beans), a Ligurian specialty that somehow tastes better when you're here eating outside in a beautiful Ligurian *piazzetta* (small square) with a view of the port. Many of the other dishes here focus on seafood. An adjoining hotel has 23 rooms. ⌧ *Piazza Marconi 1, Vernazza,* ☎ *0187/812228,* 𝔽𝔸𝕏 *0187/812228. Reservations essential. AE, DC, MC, V. Closed Jan.–Mar. and Wed.*

$$$$ ▦ **Porto Roca.** In a panoramic position above the sea, Porto Roca is
★ slightly, and blessedly, removed from the crowds that visit the Cinque Terre. It has the look of a well-kept villa; interiors contain authentic antique pieces, and there are ample terraces. All rooms have sea views. Porto Roca is on a network of not-too-demanding hill walks and has a faithful American clientele. ⌧ *Via Corone 1, Monterosso al Mare 19016,* ☎ *0187/817502,* 𝔽𝔸𝕏 *0187/817692,* 𝕎𝔼𝔹 *www.portaroca.it. 42 rooms. Restaurant, cable TV, bar, some pets allowed (fee). AE, DC, MC, V. Closed Nov. 4–Mar. 23. MAP.*

$$ ▦ **Degli Amici.** The location of this tidy hotel in the old part of Monterosso—only 165 yards from the beach—is the main reason to stay here. The decor is simple and the rooms small, but everything is neat and clean. ⌧ *Via Buranco 36, Monterosso al Mare 19016,* ☎ *0187/ 817574,* 𝔽𝔸𝕏 *0187/817424,* 𝕎𝔼𝔹 *www.hotelamici.it. 43 rooms. Restaurant, cable TV. DC, MC, V. Closed Nov.–Jan. MAP.*

$$ ▦ **Villa Argentina.** This small hotel affords fabulous views of the turquoise water. The rooms are clean, bright, and airy, if simple. A bountiful Continental breakfast is included, which provides fuel for any guest planning to hike the Cinque Terre trails. ⌧ *Via de Gasperi 170, Riomaggiore 19017,* ☎ 𝔽𝔸𝕏 *0187/920213. 15 rooms. Restaurant, cable TV, some pets allowed. AE, DC, MC, V. CP.*

$ ▦ **Cá d'Andrean.** For a stay in one of the less-crowded Cinque Terre villages, this tiny, very simple hotel is an excellent option. In summer, breakfast is served in a flower garden. ⌧ *Via Discovolo 101, Man-*

arola 19010, ☎ *0187/920040,* FAX *0187/920452. 10 rooms. Breakfast room, cable TV, some pets allowed. No credit cards. Closed Nov.*

Outdoor Activities and Sports

HIKING

The best-known and easiest hiking trail is the **Via dell'Amore** (Lover's Lane), which—going east to west—links Riomaggiore with Manarola (2 km [1 mi], 30 mins) with a flat path cut into the cliff side. The same trail continues to Corniglia (3 km [2 mi], 45 mins), then becomes more difficult between Corniglia and Vernazza (3 km [2 mi], 2 hrs) and more challenging still from Vernazza to Monterosso (2 km [1 mi], 90 mins). Additionally, trails lead from Monterosso up the mountainside and back down to Vernazza, and into the mountains from Corniglia, Manarola, and Riomaggiore, with historic churches and great views along the way. Trail maps are available at the Monterosso tourist office. Be sure to wear sturdy shoes and a hat, and bring a water bottle, as there is little shade. If you start your Cinque Terre hike in Monterosso, the **Proloco** tourist office there (⊠ Via del Molo, below the train station, ☎ 0187/817204, WEB www.cinqueterre.it) has trail maps and boat schedules.

NORTH OF FLORENCE A TO Z

To research prices, get advice from other travelers, and book travel arrangements, visit www.fodors.com.

AIR TRAVEL

Most visitors to the area fly in to Pisa's Aeroporto Galileo Galilei and Florence's Aeroporto Peretola. For the Mugello, Bologna's Aeroporto Guglielmo Marconi is a logical option.

➤ AIRPORTS: **Aeroporto A. Vespucci** (known as Peretola; ☎ 055/3061700, WEB www.safnet.it). **Aeroporto Galileo Galilei** (☎ 050/500707, WEB www.pisa-airport.com). **Aeroporto Guglielmo Marconi** (☎ 051/6479615).

BUS TRAVEL

Most bus service to areas North of Florence originates in Florence or Pisa, depending on which is closest to the area you plan to tour. The Mugello's small towns rely on bus service from Copit, SITA, and Lazzi with erratic connections to Florence; Lazzi has the most extensive service within the area north of Florence. Buses can get you around the Garfagnana and are more practical than trains. Bus service to and in the Lunigiana and along the coast is limited. It's also possible to take a bus from Pistoia or Florence to get to Abetone. A car is necessary to see Massa and Carrara because bus service is sporadic.

➤ BUS INFORMATION: **Copit** (⊠ Largo Alinari 11, Florence, ☎ 055/214637). **Lazzi** (⊠ Piazza Stazione 3r–4, Florence, ☎ 055/351061). **SITA** (⊠ Via Santa Caterina da Siena 15r, Florence, ☎ 055/214721 or 800/373760).

CAR RENTAL

➤ AGENCIES: **Avis** (⊠ Piazza della Repubblica 1/a, ☎ 0575/354232, WEB www.avis.com).

CAR TRAVEL

Aside from the isolated Cinque Terre, which is impractical for car travel, driving is the best way to get around this area. The east–west A11 autostrada connects Viareggio, Lucca, Montecatini Terme, Pistoia, Prato, and Florence. The A1 runs north–south from Milan through Bologna, Florence, and down to Rome and Naples. And the A12 will take you up the coast. Most of these towns are approached by lesser highways and two-lane roads.

EMERGENCIES
In an emergency, dial 113 for paramedics, police, or the fire department.

TRAIN TRAVEL
With the exception of Viareggio and Borgo San Lorenzo, which are on a main FS train line, the towns and cities in this region are difficult to get to by train. In the Garfagnana, train connections are extremely limited. Trains make their way to some parts of the Lunigiana, but it, too, is best explored by car. To explore Massa and Carrara, the two marble towns, properly, a car is necessary because service is spotty and the train station in Carrara is not near the center of town. Viareggio, because it is on a major train line, is easily reachable from Florence and Rome. To get to the Cinque Terre, take a train to La Spezia and then take a local train to any of the five towns. The central station in Florence, Firenze Santa Maria Novella, is well served by Intercity (IC) and Eurostar trains.

➤ TRAIN INFORMATION: **Firenze Santa Maria Novella** (✉ Piazza Santa Maria Novella, ☎ 055/288785, WEB www.fs-on-line.it).

VISITOR INFORMATION
➤ TOURIST INFORMATION: **Abetone** (✉ Via Pescinone 15, ☎ 0573/607811). **Barga** (☎ no phone, WEB www.barganews.com). **Borgo San Lorenzo** (✉ Via Togliatti 45, ☎ 055/845271). **Carrara** (✉ Lungomare A. Vespucci 24, Marina di Massa, ☎ 0585/240063). **Castelnuovo di Garfagnana** (✉ Rocco Loggiato Porto 10, Via Cavaliere de Vittorio Veneto, ☎ 0583/644354). **Cinque Terre** (WEB www.cinqueterre.it). **Forte dei Marmi** (✉ Via A. Franceschi 8b, ☎ 0584/80091). **Marina di Massa** (✉ Lungomare A. Vespucci 24, ☎ 0585/240063). **Monterosso al Mare** (✉ Via Fegina 38, ☎ 0187/17506; ✉ Via del Molo, below the train station, ☎ 0187/817204). **Pietrasanta** (✉ Piazza del Duomo, ☎ 0584/20331). **San Marcello Pistoiese** (✉ Via Pietro Leopoldo10/24, ☎ 0573/62121). **Viareggio** (✉ Vialle Carducci 10, ☎ 0584/962233).

4 CITIES WEST OF FLORENCE

The cities strung along the autostrada west of Florence—Prato, Pistoia, Montecatini Terme, and Lucca—all have well-preserved medieval and Renaissance centers. As you head west, the landscape becomes progressively more dramatic, with the craggy Alpi Apuane in the distance. Toward Pisa the land flattens out as it nears the sea.

D URING THE MIDDLE AGES and the Renaissance, Prato, Pistoia, Lucca, and Pisa were the bane of Florence, which waged many wars in her struggle to become the dominant force in Tuscany. Eventually these cities—with the exception of Lucca—came under Florentine influence. It's best when traveling to the region to resist the pull of Florence that persists today: the fine churches and museums in these cities are fewer but no less rich. Lucca's charm lies in the medieval walls that surround the historic center, and the beauty of Pisa's Duomo, Battistero, and Torre Pendente (Leaning Tower) complex is unsurpassable. Prato has many works by Fra Filippo Lippi, a native son, and Pistoia, with its Duomo and Battistero, preserves its medieval aura.

Updated by
Patricia Rucidlo

Pleasures and Pastimes

Architecture

The Middle Ages left their mark on these cities. Many of their churches bear the green-and-white marble striping typical of churches built during the period, and historic centers have palaces adorned with coats of arms from various prominent families. If your taste leans toward the art nouveau, look for buildings in the Liberty style, popular in the late-19th and early-20th centuries. It's most evident in Lucca, where the main thoroughfare, the Fillungo, is dotted with examples.

Dining

Most restaurants in the region serve dishes that will be familiar to you if you've eaten in Florence—*bistecca alla fiorentina* (grilled local Chianina beef) and *ribollita* (a vegetable soup thickened with stale Tuscan bread and cannellini beans), for instance. Pistoia and environs are famous for their *maccheroni all'anatra* (pasta in a sauce made of duck). Prato is home of the famous *biscotti di Prato,* an exquisite hard cookie made for dunking into steaming cappuccino or *vin santo,* a sweet dessert wine. Pisa can lay claim to *ceccina,* a pancake made of chickpea flour that can be eaten alone or rolled with various toppings. Montecatini has its *cialda,* a thin, sweet wafer usually topped with gelato. Lucca is famous for its *farro,* an early type of wheat also known as emmer in English. It's been cultivated for several thousand years and is unique to the region. You can eat it in soup or cooked in the manner of risotto (some wags refer to it as *farrotto*), or as a cold grain salad. And then there's the region's olive oil, which adds depth and soul to any dish it garnishes; to many palates it's the best in the world.

CATEGORY	COST*
$$$$	over €18
$$$	€13–€18
$$	€8–€13
$	under €8

Prices are for a main course (secondo piatto)

Lodging

For a taste of the country, you can stay outside Florence—particularly in the warmer months, when Florence is at its hottest and most crowded—and avail yourself of the excellent train service for day trips into the city. Another option might be to stay in an *agriturismo,* or farm, and experience a different kind of Tuscany, one based more in the 19th and early-20th centuries. More-lavish accommodations can be found in Montecatini, where it's perfectly permissible to pamper yourself with spa treatments—people have been doing it there since the 19th century.

CATEGORY	COST*
$$$$	over €175
$$$	€125–€175
$$	€75–€125
$	under €75

All prices are for two people in a standard double room, including tax and service.

Exploring Cities West of Florence

The best way to see this part of Tuscany is by car, as some of the smaller cities are otherwise difficult to get to. However, cities such as Lucca, Pisa, Prato, Pistoia, Empoli, and Montecatini have regular train and bus service, which makes getting around easy. Five days is ample time to tour the area, as most of the towns are close to one another and— with the exception of Lucca and Pisa, which demand more time—can be toured relatively quickly.

Numbers in the text correspond to numbers in the margin and on the Cities West of Florence; Lucca; and Pisa maps.

Great Itineraries

Lucca and Pisa are the most-visited Tuscan cities west of Florence, and with good reason. Lucca's charm is preserved within the medieval walls surrounding the historic center, and Pisa has perhaps the most famous tower in the world. Less visited but eminently worthwhile are Pistoia and Prato, smaller cities with fine Romanesque churches, good restaurants, and fewer tourists. A different taste of Tuscany can be had by heading west to Empoli, San Miniato, and other small cities. Part of the pleasure of visiting these places comes from being slightly off the well-trod path, and a greater part comes from discovering the smaller treasures these places offer.

IF YOU HAVE 3 DAYS

From Florence, travel to **Prato** ① and spend the morning in the Duomo, the Museo del Tessuto, and the Museo di Pittura Murale before heading off to **Pistoia** ② for the afternoon. In Pistoia, see the lovely Cattedrale di San Zeno, with its magnificent silver altar, and the Spedale del Ceppo, which has a multicolor terra-cotta frieze. Spend the night in ⊞ **Montecatini Terme** ③, and take in the sights from the lively and bustling Piazza del Popolo. On Day 2, travel to **Lucca** ⑥–⑯ in the morning. Tour the Duomo and see the early-15th-century tomb of Ilaria del Caretto. Be sure to take time to walk the walls; in the afternoon, go to ⊞ **Pisa** ⑰–㉖ and see the Torre Pendente, Duomo, and Battistero, but also go beyond the tourist spots to visit the Piazza dei Cavalieri and stroll along the Arno. Spend the night in Pisa. In the morning, travel to the area around **Empoli** ㉗. You can enjoy the view from the Torre di Federico II in **San Miniato** ㉚ and purchase hand-crafted goods in the area around **Vinci** ㉙ and **Montelupo** ㉘, or visit the small, exquisite Collegiata di Sant'Andrea back in Empoli. Head back to Florence in the afternoon.

IF YOU HAVE 5 DAYS

Using Florence as a starting point, travel to ⊞ **San Miniato** ㉚ and book a hotel. Explore the little town and see the Medici villa in Cerreto Guidi in the morning before heading south to **Certaldo** ㉜ to pay homage to the birthplace (and final resting spot) of Giovanni Boccaccio, Certaldo's most famous son. The next morning, explore **Empoli** ㉗ and its Collegiata; then go to **Pisa** ⑰–㉖ to spend the afternoon. Stay in Pisa or at a local agriturismo. On Day 3 go to ⊞ **Lucca** ⑥–⑯ and spend most of the day seeing the Duomo, Palazzo Pfanner, and the churches of San Fredi-

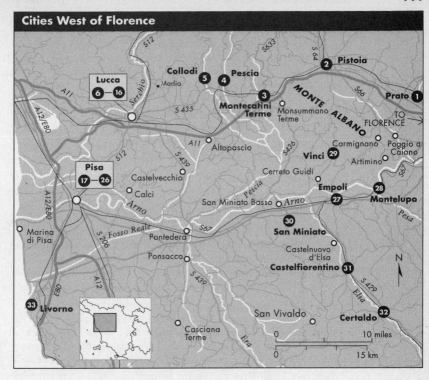

Cities West of Florence

ano and San Michele. Pop into the Museo Nazionale di Palazzo Mansi and spend some time in the room with portraits of various Medici. Stay over in Lucca on the third night, leaving time for walking the town center's walls. Drive to ☒ **Montecatini Terme** ③ the next morning and spend the day taking the waters, or simply walking through the thermal parkland, and take the funicular up to Montecatini Alto. Stay overnight in Montecatini Terme, and return to Florence in the morning.

When to Tour Cities West of Florence

The best time to visit these cities—particularly in the cases of Lucca and Pisa—is any time but July and August, when the tourist season is in full swing and the sun is at its hottest. If you visit during the summer months, plan to do early-morning or late-afternoon touring, when the crowds and the heat are somewhat less oppressive. Stay in one of the hill towns—such as San Miniato—to avoid crowds and heat. Or discover the joys of Pistoia, Prato, and Empoli, three wonderful but rarely visited cities that each hold treasures of Renaissance art.

If you're in Pisa in June, try to see its Luminaria, held June 16. Blues lovers might want to check out Pistoia Blues in July. Also in July is Pistoia's La Giostra dell'Orso (Bear Joust). Lucca's famous annual Puccini Festival is held at the end of July and in early August. The traveling gourmand might want to sample the various black-truffle celebrations that take place in and around San Miniato in October. And if you love ceramics, the two-week International Ceramics Festival in Montelupo in June includes art shows, demonstrations, and plenty of beautiful items—for buying as well as looking.

FROM FLORENCE TO COLLODI

The journey from Florence to Collodi takes you north and west of Florence via industrial Prato. Pistoia is a short distance away. After Pistoia, the countryside becomes a little hillier and much prettier. At Montecatini, wander north along the Pescia River to Pescia, a flower-market town with worthwhile art, and to Collodi, where there's an amusement park devoted to Pinocchio.

Prato

❶ *19 km (12 mi) northwest of Florence, 81 km (50 mi) east of Pisa.*

The wool industry in this city, one of the world's largest producers of cloth, was known throughout Europe as early as the 13th century. Business was further stimulated in the 14th century by a local cloth merchant, Francesco di Marco Datini, who built his business, according to one of his surviving ledgers, "in the name of God and of profit." One thing that distinguishes Prato from other Italian towns of its size is the presence of modern public art—most notably Henry Moore's mammoth, marble *Square Form with Cut* in the Piazza San Marco. But Prato also holds the fine, earlier artworks expected of a Tuscan city of this size.

Prato's Romanesque **Duomo,** reconstructed from 1211, is famous for its **Pergamo del Sacro Cingolo** (Chapel of the Holy Girdle), to the left of the entrance, which enshrines the sash of the Virgin Mary. It is said that the girdle was given to the apostle Thomas by the Virgin Mary when she miraculously appeared after her Assumption into heaven. The Duomo also contains 15th-century frescoes by Prato's most famous son, Fra Filippo Lippi (1406–69). His scenes from the life of St. Stephen are on the left wall of the **Cappella Maggiore** (Main Chapel); those from the life of John the Baptist are on the right. Restoration begun on the frescoes in 2001 is expected to take some time: with a reservation, you can peer at the frescoes from the scaffolding. ⊠ *Piazza del Duomo,* ☎ *0574/26234, 0574/24112 reservations.* ⊙ *Oct.–June, Mon.–Sat. 7–12:30 and 3–6:30, Sun. 7–12:30 and 3–8; July–Sept., daily 7:30–12:30 and 4–7:30.*

| NEED A BREAK? | Prato's biscotti (literally "twice cooked") have an extra-dense texture, lending themselves to submersion in your caffè or vin santo. The best biscotti in town are at **Antonio Mattei** (⊠ Via Ricasoli 20/22). |

A sculpture by Donatello (circa 1386–1466) that originally adorned the Duomo's exterior pulpit is now on display in the **Museo dell'Opera del Duomo.** The museum also includes such 15th-century gems as Fra Filippo Lippi's *Madonna and Child,* Giovanni Bellini's (circa 1432–1516) *Christ on the Cross,* and Caravaggio's (1571–1610) *Christ Crowned with Thorns.* ⊠ *Piazza del Duomo 49,* ☎ *0574/29339.* ▨ *€5.15 (includes Museo di Pittura Murale).* ⊙ *Mon. and Wed.–Sat. 9:30–12:30 and 3–6:30, Sun. 9:30–12:30.*

The permanent collection in the **Museo di Pittura Murale** (Museum of Mural Painting) contains frescoes removed from sites in and around Prato. ⊠ *Piazza San Domenico 8,* ☎ *0574/440501.* ▨ *€5.15 (includes Museo dell'Opera del Duomo).* ⊙ *Mon. and Wed.–Sat. 10–6, Sun. 10–1.*

Prato's **Centro per l'Arte Contemporanea L. Pecci** (L. Pecci Center of Contemporary Art) has a burgeoning collection of works by Italian and other artists. ⊠ *Viale della Repubblica 277,* ☎ *0574/5317,* WEB *www.comune.prato.it/pecci.* ▨ *€6.20.* ⊙ *Mon. and Wed.–Sun. 10–7.*

Preserved in the **Museo del Tessuto** (Textile Museum) is what made this city a Renaissance economic powerhouse. The collection includes clothing, fragments of fabric, samples, and the machines used to make them from the 14th to the 20th centuries. Check out the 15th-century fabrics with pomegranate prints, a virtuoso display of Renaissance textile wizardry. ⊠ *Piazza del Commune,* ☎ *0574/611503.* ▣ *€2.58.* ☉ *Mon. and Wed.–Fri. 10:30–12:30, Sat. 10:30–2:30; Sun. 11–7. Tours by appointment.*

The church of **Santa Maria delle Carceri** was built by Giuliano Sangallo in the 1490s and is a landmark of Renaissance architecture. ⊠ *Piazza Santa Maria delle Carceri, off Via Cairoli and southeast of the cathedral,* ☎ *0574/27933.* ▣ *Free.* ☉ *Daily 7–noon and 4–7:30.*

Though in ruins, the formidable **Castello** (Castle), adjacent to Santa Maria delle Carceri, is an impressive sight. Built for Frederick II Hohenstaufen (1194–1250), it's the only castle of its type outside southern Italy. ⊠ *Piazza Santa Maria delle Carceri,* ☎ *0574/38207.* ▣ *Free.* ☉ *Nov.–Feb., Mon. and Wed.–Fri. 10–1, Sat. 9–1 and 3–5; Mar.–Oct., Wed.–Mon. 10–7.*

OFF THE
BEATEN PATH

POGGIO A CAIANO – For a look at gracious country living Renaissance style, take a detour to the Medici Villa in Poggio a Caiano. Lorenzo "il Magnifico" (1449–92) commissioned Giuliano da Sangallo (circa 1445–1516) to redo the villa, which was lavished with frescoes by important Renaissance painters such as Andrea del Sarto (1486–1530) and Pontormo (1494–1557). You can walk around the austerely ornamented grounds while waiting for entry. ⊠ *7 km (4½ mi) south of Prato (follow signs),* ☎ *055/877012.* ▣ *€2.05.* ☉ *Garden: Mar., April, Sept.–Oct., Mon.–Sat. 9–5:30; Nov.–Feb., 9–4:30; May–Aug., 9–6:30, Sun. 9–12:30. Villa: Mon.–Sat. 9–1:30, Sun. 9–noon. Guided visits only, hourly on the ½ hr (from 9:30 to 1 hr before closing). Closed 2nd and 3rd Mon. of month.*

CARMIGNANO – *The Visitation* by Pontormo is in this small village, a short car ride from Poggio a Caiano. The Franciscan church of San Michele, which was dedicated in 1211, houses the work. The painting dates from 1528–29 and it may well be Pontormo's masterpiece. The colors are luminous, the drapery is flowing, and the steady gaze shared between the Virgin and St. Elizabeth is breathtaking. The church's small cloister, shaded by olive trees, is always open and offers a quiet place to sit. ⊠ *15 km (9 mi) south of Prato, through Poggio a Caiano, up Mt. Albano,* ☎ *055/8712046.* ▣ *Free.* ☉ *Oct.–Apr., daily 7–5; May–Sept., daily 7–6.*

ARTIMINO – In this small town next door to Carmignano is the Villa Medicea La Ferdinanda di Artimino. Built by Ferdinando I de' Medici (1549–1609) in the 1590s, it was used as a hunting lodge. You can visit it only by appointment. ⊠ *15 km (9 mi) south of Prato (head east from Carmignano or south from Poggio a Caiano, up Mt. Albano),* ☎ *055/8718081.* ▣ *Free.* ☉ *Weekdays by appointment.*

Dining and Lodging

$$–$$$ ✗ **Baghino.** In the heart of the historic center, Baghino's menu includes typical Tuscan fare as well as such less common regional dishes as spaghetti *all'amatriciana* (with bacon in a spicy tomato sauce) and penne *con vongole e curry* (with clams and curry). You can dine on the charming outdoor terrace in summer. ⊠ *Via dell'Accademia 9,* ☎ *0574/27920. AE, DC, MC, V. No dinner Sun., no lunch Mon.*

$$–$$$ ✕ **Biagio Pignatta.** A lovely restaurant, this is a great stop after touring Artimino. If you come here in summer, you can dine outdoors in a loggia with a beautiful view of Tuscan hills behind you. The food is Tuscan with some unexpected twists—including pasta with shellfish and a sublime carpaccio. The fried vegetables are as delectable as potato chips, and it's hard to stop eating them. Try the delightful, crisp rosé that's made in the neighborhood. Reservations are a good idea, especially if you want an outside table. ⊠ *Viale Papa Giovanni XXIII 1, Artimino,* ☎ *055/8718086 or 055/8718086. AE, DC, MC, V. No lunch Tue. or Thurs.*

$$–$$$ ✕ **Da Delfina.** Delfina began cooking many years ago for hungry
★   hunters, and now she has four comfortably rustic dining rooms in her namesake restaurant, which is set amid vineyards and olive trees. The dishes use pure ingredients, seasonal vegetables, and savory meats accented with herbs. The *secondi* (second courses) such as *coniglio con olive e pignoli* (rabbit sautéed with olives and pine nuts) are a real treat. ⊠ *Via della Chiesa 1, Artimino,* ☎ *055/8718074. Reservations essential. No credit cards. Closed Mon. and 1 wk in Dec.–Jan.*

$$–$$$ ✕ **La Veranda.** A large antipasto buffet greets you as you enter this restaurant near the 13th-century Castello. The interior, which has Venetian chandeliers, is as elegant as it is friendly. Tuscan specialties include *agnello alla cacciatora* (lamb with a tangy wine-vinegar sauce). ⊠ *Via dell'Arco 10,* ☎ *0574/38235. AE, DC, MC, V. Closed weekends.*

$$–$$$ ✕ **Piraña.** Named for the cannibalistic fish swimming in an aquarium that's in full view of the diners, this sophisticated restaurant, done in shades of blue with steely accents, is a local favorite. Seafood, the specialty, may take the form of ravioli *di branzino in crema di scampi* (stuffed with sea bass and in a creamy shrimp sauce) and *rombo al forno* (baked turbot). It's a bit out of the way for sightseers but handy if you have a car, as it's near the Prato Est autostrada exit. ⊠ *Via G. Valentini 110,* ☎ *0574/25746. AE, DC, MC, V. Closed Sun. and Aug. No lunch Sat.*

$ ✕ **La Vecchia Cucina di Soldano.** Pratesi specialties, including the odd but tasty *sedani ripieni* (stuffed celery), are served here in a completely unpretentious setting. It feels as if you're sitting in your Italian grandmother's kitchen; tablecloths have red and white checks, and the service is friendly and casual. The place teems with locals enjoying the superb *tagliolini sui fagioli* (thin noodles with beans); clearly those who live here like the rock-bottom prices too. ⊠ *Via Pomeria 23,* ☎ *0574/ 34665. No credit cards. Closed Sun.*

$$$ ▥ **Hotel President.** Despite the 1970s exterior, the interior of this hotel, a five-minute walk from the historic center, is calm, cool, and well furnished. The rooms are spacious, and each of the four floors has a different color scheme. Pale green and pink leather couches give one of the two bars a slight art deco feel. ⊠ *Via Simintendi 20 (at Via Baldinucci), 59100,* ☎ *0574/30251,* ℻ *0574/36064,* 𝚆𝙴𝙱 *www.hotel_ president.net. 78 rooms. Restaurant, in-room safes, minibars, cable TV, 2 bars, concierge, business services, meeting rooms, free parking, some pets allowed. AE, DC, MC, V. CP.*

Pistoia

②   *18 km (11 mi) northwest of Prato, 61 km (38 mi) east of Pisa, 37 km (23 mi) northwest of Florence.*

Founded in the 2nd century BC as a support post for Roman troops, Pistoia had grown into an important trading center, but then it was caught up in the brutal Guelph-Ghibelline conflict of the Middle Ages. Reconstructed after heavy bombing during World War II, it has preserved some fine Romanesque architecture. Modern-day Pistoia's major industries include the manufacture of rail vehicles (including the cars for Washington, D.C.'s metro) and tree and plant nurseries, which flourish in the alluvial plain around the city.

The Romanesque **Duomo,** the Cattedrale di San Zeno dates from as early as the 5th century. It houses the *Dossale di San Jacopo,* a magnificent silver altar. The two half-figures on its left side are by Filippo Brunelleschi (1377–1446), better known as the first Renaissance architect (and designer of Florence's magnificent Duomo cupola). The octagonal **Battistero,** with green and white marble panels, dates from the middle of the 14th century. Three of its eight sides have doorways; the main door facing the piazza is crowned with a rose window. Note the lovely little lantern that crowns the top of the building. ⊠ *Piazza del Duomo,* ☎ *0573/25095.* ▣ *Free; illumination of altarpiece €2.60.* ☉ *Church daily 9–noon and 4–7; altar daily 10–noon and 4–5:45.*

The Palazzo del Comune, begun around 1295, houses the **Museo Civico,** which contains works by local artists from the 14th to 20th centuries. ⊠ *Piazza del Duomo 1,* ☎ *0573/371296.* ▣ *€2.60; free Sat. 3–7.* ☉ *Tues.–Sat. 10–7, Sun. 9–12:30.*

On its ground level, the **Antico Palazzo dei Vescovi** (Old Bishop's Palace) contains the spectacular treasures of the cathedral—including ornate pieces in gold, rings with jewels the size of small eggs, and solemn, powerful statuary. Below, however, are Roman, medieval, and even Etruscan archaeological sites uncovered in a 1970s renovation. The warren of corridors and caves below and the plain, spare rooms above both show off their treasures with simple, effective elegance. ⊠ *Piazza del Duomo,* ☎ *0573/369277.* ▣ *€3.60.* ☉ *Tues. and Thurs.–Fri. 10–1 and 3–5.*

Founded in the 13th century and still a functioning hospital, the **Spedale del Ceppo** reveals a superb early-16th-century exterior terracotta frieze. Begun by Giovanni della Robbia (1469–1529), the frieze was completed by the workshop of Santi and Benedetto Buglioni between 1526 and 1528. ⊠ *Piazza Ospedale, down Via Pacini from Piazza del Duomo.*

In the church of **Sant'Andrea,** the fine pulpit by Giovanni Pisano (circa 1250–1314) depicts scenes from the life of Christ. ⊠ *Via Pappe to Via Sant'Andrea,* ☎ *0573/21912.* ▣ *Free.* ☉ *Nov.–Mar., daily 8–1 and 4–6:30; Apr.–Oct., daily 8–12:30 and 3:30–7.*

The 16th-century mannerist-style **Palazzo Rospigliosi** houses the **Museo Rospigliosi** and the **Museo Diocesano,** with a collection of mostly 17th-century works. The Museo Rospigliosi contains a room referred to as Pope Clement IX's (1600–69) apartment, although there's no evidence that the Pistoian native, born Giulio Rospigliosi, actually stayed in these rooms. The Museo Diocesano has liturgical objects and furnishings from the diocese of Pistoia. Many of them date from the 13th, 14th, and 15th centuries. ⊠ *Ripa del Sale 3,* ☎ *0573/28740.* ▣ *Museo Rospigliosi €3.10, Museo Diocesano €3.10, €6.20 combination ticket (both museums and Centro di Documentazione e la Fondazione Marino Marini).* ☉ *Tues.–Sat. 10–1 and 4–7.*

Lest you think that Tuscany produced artists only in centuries long gone, the **Centro di Documentazione e la Fondazione Marino Marini** presents many works from this modern native Pistoian (1901–80). Sculpture, etchings, painting, engraving, and mixed media have all been installed in the elegantly renovated, 14th-century Convento del Tao. ⊠ *Corso Silvano Fedi 30,* ☎ *0573/30285,* 𝖥𝖠𝖷 *0573/31332.* ▣ *[eur:3.10, €6.20 combination ticket (includes Museo Rospigliosi and Museo Diocesano).* ☉ *Tues.–Sat. 9–1 and 3–7, Sun. 9–12:30.*

An architectural gem revealed in green-and-white marble, the medieval church of **San Giovanni Fuorcivitas** holds a *Visitation* by Luca della Robbia (1400–82), a painting attributed to Taddeo Gaddi, and a holy-water font that may have been made by Fra Guglielmo around 1270. ⊠ *Via Cavour,* ☎ *0573/24784.* ☉ *Daily 8–noon and 4–6:30.*

A 20-minute drive out of town brings you to the **Giardino Zoologico,** a small zoo especially laid out to accommodate the wiles of both animals and children. Take Bus 29 from the train station. ⊠ *Via Pieve a Celle 160/a,* ☎ *0573/911219.* 🎫 *€8.30.* ☉ *Apr.–Sept., daily 9–7; Oct.–Mar., daily 9–5.*

Dining and Lodging

$$–$$$$ ✕ **Corradossi.** A short walk from the Piazza del Duomo, this lovely pan-Italian restaurant makes an excellent place to break for lunch or dinner. The food is simply prepared, the service quick and attentive, and the prices more than reasonable. Start with the *trofie e gamberi,* corkscrew-shape pasta in a sauce of perfectly cooked shrimp and sliced baby zucchini; follow with the crispy *frittura di mare* (fried fish and shellfish). ⊠ *Via Frosini 112,* ☎ *0573/25683. AE, DC, MC, V. Closed Sun.*

$$–$$$$ ✕ **S. Jacopo.** This charming restaurant minutes from the Piazza del ★ Duomo has white walls, tile floors, and a gracious host, who is fluent in English. Tasteful prints and photographs on the walls contrast nicely with the rustic blue table linens. The menu has mostly regional favorites, such as the *maccheroni S. Jacopo,* wide ribbons of house-made pasta in a duck sauce, but the restaurant can turn out perfectly grilled squid as well. Save room for dessert, especially the apple strudel. ⊠ *Via Crispi 15,* ☎ *0573/27786. AE, DC, MC, V. Closed Mon. No lunch Tues.*

$–$$ ✕ **La BotteGaia.** Just off Piazza del Duomo, this popular wine bar has rustic tables set in a couple of rooms with exposed brick and stone walls. Jazz plays softly in the background. Typical wine-bar fare such as *salami e formaggi* (cured ham and cheeses) shares the menu with surprisingly sophisticated daily specials that can include *insalatina con foie gras condita con vinaigrette* (foie gras with dressed greens). You can dine alfresco with a view of Piazza del Duomo in the warmer months. ⊠ *Via del Lastrone 4,* ☎ *0573/365602. Reservations essential. AE, DC, MC, V. Closed Mon. and 15 days in Aug. No lunch Sun.*

$ ✕ **Trattoria dell'Abbondanza.** Entering from a quiet side street, you walk into a small place with clean, cream-color walls that's busy but not noisy, its staff friendly but never pushy. Traditional dishes include, for first courses, *minestra di farro* (a hearty soup made with farro) and *maccheroni sull'anatra* (in a duck sauce). For seconds, there's *baccalà alla Livornese* (salt cod in a tomato sauce), roast rabbit, and tripe. *Torta rustica,* a cake of cornmeal and cream, makes a fine dessert. ⊠ *Via dell'Abbondanza 10 (off Via degli Orafi),* ☎ *0573/368037. No credit cards. Closed Wed. No lunch Thurs.*

$$ 🏨 **Hotel Leon Bianco.** Most everything you want to see in Pistoia is only a few minutes' walk from this small, family-run hotel. Here you'll find a lobby decorated in chintz, a small bar at which to enjoy an *aperitivo* (aperitif), and lively innkeepers who speak perfect English. Florence is 45 minutes away by train, which makes this a good base for the budget-conscious traveler. ⊠ *Via Panciatichi 2, 51100,* ☎ *0573/26675 or 0573/26676,* 📠 *0573/26704,* 🌐 *www.hotelleonbianco.it. 30 rooms. Bar, baby-sitting, dry cleaning, laundry service, Internet, some pets allowed; no air-conditioning in some rooms, no-smoking rooms. AE, DC, MC, V. CP.*

Nightlife and the Arts

In mid-July, **Pistoia Blues** brings international blues artists to town for performances in the main square. Contact Associazione "Blues in"

(☎ 0573/358195, WEB www.pistoiablues.com) for more information. **La Giostra dell'Orso** (Bear Joust), on July 25, celebrates St. James, Pistoia's patron saint. During the staged event, three knights from each section of the city fight a "bear." The visitor information center has more information on the event.

Montecatini Terme

③ *15 km (9 mi) west of Pistoia, 49 km (30 mi) west of Florence, 49 km (30 mi) northeast of Pisa.*

Immortalized in Fellini's *8½*, Montecatini Terme is the home of Italy's premier *terme* (spas). Reputed for their curative powers—and, at least once upon a time, for their great popularity among the wealthy—the mineral springs flow from five sources and are taken for liver and skin disorders. Those "taking the cure" report each morning to one of the town's *stabilimenti termali* (information: ⊠ Viale Verdi 41, ☎ 0572/778451), or thermal establishments, to drink their prescribed cupful of water.

The town's wealth of art nouveau buildings went up during its most active period of development, at the beginning of the 20th century. Like most other well-heeled resort towns, Montecatini attracts the leisured traveler, and it's trimmed with a measure of neon and glitz; aside from taking the waters and people-watching in Piazza del Popolo, there's not a whole lot to do here. There are, however, plenty of places to stay, making the town a good base from which to explore the region. The most attractive art nouveau structure in town, **Terme Tettuccio** (⊠ Viale Verdi 71, ☎ 0572/778501) has lovely colonnades. Here fountains set up on marble counters dispense mineral water, bucolic scenes painted on tiles decorate walls, and an orchestra plays under a frescoed dome.

Piazza del Popolo, the main square in town, teems with caffès and bars. It's an excellent spot for people-watching; in the evenings and on weekends it seems like everyone is out walking, seeing, and being seen. The Piazza del Popolo offers a view of the basilica of **Santa Maria Assunta** (⊠ Piazza del Popolo, ☎ no phone). The church and bell tower were completed in 1962. The bold geometric lines are a little incongruous among its more ornate neighbors. Admission to the church, which is open daily 8–noon and 3–5:30, is free.

NEED A
BREAK?
Cialde, a local specialty said to have been invented by St. Brigitte, are circular wafers made with flour, sugar, and eggs. Whether this industrious saint had time to do so isn't all that important—what is important is trying the cialda topped with several scoops of the local gelato. Try this favorite at **Bargilli** (⊠ Viale Grocco 2, ☎ 0572/79459), probably the best gelateria in town.

The older town, **Montecatini Alto,** sits atop a hill nearby and is reached by a funicular from Viale Diaz. Though there isn't much to do once you get up there, the medieval square is lined with restaurants and bars, the air is crisp, and the views of the Nievole, the valley below, are gorgeous.

Lodging

$$$–$$$$ ▥ **Croce di Malta.** Taste and sophistication have been the calling cards of this hotel since 1911. It's a short walk on tree-lined streets from the center of town; it's even closer to the thermal baths. Rooms are spacious, with high ceilings; many have deep bathtubs with water jets. You

can enjoy an aperitivo in the majestic lobby before dining at the restaurant ($$–$$$). The menu changes daily and offers Tuscan specialties as well as other options; the food is as elegant as the hotel. ☒ *Viale IV Novembre 18, 51016,* ☏ *0572/9201,* ⅢⅩ *0572/767516,* ⅦⅢ *www. crocedimalta.com. 122 rooms, 22 suites. Restaurant, room service, minibars, cable TV, pool, gym, massage, baby-sitting, dry cleaning, laundry service, concierge, business services, meeting rooms, parking (fee), some pets allowed, no-smoking rooms. AE, DC, MC, V. CP.*

Pescia

❹ *8 km (5 mi) west of Montecatini Terme, 19 km (12 mi) northeast of Lucca, 61 km (38 mi) northwest of Florence.*

This sleepy little town has a large flower market and some lesser-known but rather interesting Renaissance art. During the early Middle Ages, it was dominated by Lucca, but by 1339 it had come under Florence's influence, under which it remained throughout the Renaissance.

The **Santuario della Madonna di Pie di Piazza,** a little chapel built in 1447 and designed by Andrea Cavalcanti, the adopted son of Filippo Brunelleschi, is the only example of Brunelleschi's style outside of Florence. Inside is a 15th-century *Madonna and Child* on a wood panel that was transported to the church in a solemn procession in 1605. ☒ *Piazza Mazzini,* ☏ *no phone.* 🎟 *Free.* ⊙ *Daily 8–7:30.*

The church of **Santi Stefano e Niccolò** is an odd combination of Romanesque and baroque. It dates from as early as the 11th century and had alterations as late as the 18th century. A *Madonna and Child with Angels,* by the school of Orcagna (active 1343/44–1368), and a panel painting of the *Madonna and Child with Sts. Niccolo and John the Baptist* (circa 1400) are among the more interesting works in the church, but given their presence on side walls in the presbytery, they are difficult to see. ☒ *Piazza Stefano,* ☏ *no phone.* 🎟 *Free.* ⊙ *Daily 10–12:30 and 4–6.*

The **Palazzo del Podestà** presents a lovely 13th-century facade; inside, however, are banal early-20th-century sculpted works by local artist Libero Andreotti (1875–1933). ☒ *Piazza del Palagio,* ☏ *0572/490057.* 🎟 *Free.* ⊙ *Nov.–Mar., Wed.–Sat. 3–6; Apr.–Oct., Wed.–Sat. 10–1 and 4–7, Sun. 4–7.*

The **Museo Civico** contains Tuscan paintings, a Lorenzo Monaco triptych, Etruscan objects, and works attributed to the school of Fra Angelico and Fra Bartolommeo. At this writing, the museum is closed for restoration. Contact the Tourist Information office for further information. ☒ *Piazza Santo Stefano,* ☏ *0572/490057.* 🎟 *Free.* ⊙ *Nov.–Mar., Wed. and Fri.–Sat. 10–1 and 3–6; Apr.–Oct., Wed. and Fri.–Sat. 10–1 and 4–7.*

Sant'Antonio Abate, a tiny oratory, has an amazing wood sculpture of the *Deposition.* In seven pieces, it dates from the second half of the 12th century. Early 14th-century frescoes depict scenes from the life of St. Anthony the Abbot. If the door is locked, nearby businesses may know where to get the key. ☒ *Via Battisti,* ☏ *no phone.* 🎟 *Free.* ⊙ *Daily 8–7:30.*

The church of **San Francesco** has a wood-panel painting by Bonaventura Berlinghieri (active 1228–43) that dates from 1235; it depicts the life of St. Francis. ☒ *Piazza San Francesco,* ☏ *no phone.* 🎟 *Free.* ⊙ *Daily 8–noon and 2–7:30.*

Unless you're a great fan of the late baroque, the **Duomo** is a disappointment compared to Pescia's other churches. ⊠ *Piazza del Duomo,* ☎ *no phone.* 🎫 *Free.* ⊙ *Daily 8–7:30.*

OFF THE
BEATEN PATH

CENTRO DI DOCUMENTAZIONE SULLA LAVORAZIONE DELLA CARTA (Center for the Documentation of Paper-Making) – Handmade Italian paper is becoming rarer and rarer, although only two generations ago more than 15 small factories for the hand-making of paper operated on the banks of the Pescia River. Raw materials—old paper and cloth—were broken up in great stone basins, the soggy masses poured onto forms, and the water drained out. The sheets were then stacked, hung to dry, pressed, and pressed again. This small museum in Pietrabuona, with two informative videos (albeit narrated in Italian), a room of old paper-making machinery, and the nearby remains of an old factory, attempts to preserve the knowledge even if it cannot forestall the decline of the industry. ⊠ *Piazza la Croce, Pietrabuona (3 km [2 mi] north of Pescia),* ☎ *0572/ 476252.* 🎫 *Free.* ⊙ *By appointment only.*

Collodi

❺ *4 km (2½ mi) west of Pescia, 17 km (11 mi) northeast of Lucca, 63 km (39 mi) northwest of Florence.*

"Collodi" was the pen name of Carlo Lorenzini (1826–90), author of *Pinocchio.* His mother was born in the little village, and he spent summers here as a child. **Parco di Pinocchio,** a theme park devoted to the former marionnette, has sculptures illustrating various characters and scenes from the story. It's a fine place to bring children and to have a picnic. The park makes more sense if the story is fresh in your mind—so you might want to reread it or watch the 1940 Disney film beforehand. ⊠ *Via San Gennaro 2,* ☎ *0572/429342.* 🎫 *€7.* ⊙ *Daily 8:30–sunset.*

LUCCA

In this picturesque fortress town, Caesar, Pompey, and Crassus agreed to rule Rome as a triumvirate in 56 BC; it was later the first Tuscan town to accept Christianity. Lucca still has a mind of its own, and when most of Tuscany was voting communist as a matter of course, Lucca's citizens rarely followed suit. Within the city's ramparts (built in the 16th to 17th centuries), the famous composer Giacomo Puccini (1858–1924) was born; he is celebrated, along with his peers, during the summer **Opera Theater of Lucca Festival.** The ramparts themselves, which circle the center city, are the perfect place to take a stroll, ride a bicycle, kick a ball, or just stand and look down onto Lucca both within and without.

Exploring Lucca

Traffic (including motorbikes) is restricted in the walled historic center of Lucca. Walking is the best, most enjoyable way to get around. Otherwise, you can rent a bicycle; getting around on bike is easy, as the center is quite flat.

A Good Walk

Begin your walk with an overview of the *centro storico* (historical center) on the **Ramparts** ⑥. Climb the stairs to them, at Piazza Vittorio Emanuele. If you want to walk the entire Ramparts, it takes about 45 minutes; if not, descend and start your tour at the **Museo Nazionale di Palazzo Mansi** ⑦ on Via Galli Tassi, just within the walls. Walk down

Via del Toro to Piazza del Palazzo Dipinto, and follow Via di Poggio to **San Michele in Foro** ⑧. From Piazza San Michele, walk down Via Beccheria through Piazza Napoleone, and make a left through the smaller Piazza San Giovanni, which leads directly to the **Duomo** ⑨. Check out the lively facade before going into the church and looking at the Volto Santo and the *Tomb of Ilaria del Caretto*. The **Museo della Cattedrale** ⑩ is to the north of the Cathedral itself. If you have time, duck into the church of **Ss. Giovanni e Reparata** ⑪ and check out the fragments of Early Christian architecture mingling with the baroque. Walk down Via dell'Arcivescovado, which is behind the Duomo and turns into Via Guinigi, toward the other side of the old city. You can climb the Torre Guinigi for an admirable view. The **Museo Nazionale di Villa Guinigi** ⑫ is a 10- to 15-minute walk east through Piazza San Francesco and on Via della Quarquonia. Backtrack to the Torre Guinigi; take Via Sant'Andrea to Via Fillungo to see the many Liberty-style buildings. Head a bit south on Via Fillungo to see the **Torre delle Ore** ⑬, whose view is especially worth a visit if you are traveling with children. Take Via Fillungo northward; at Via Fontana, make a left and follow it a short distance to Via Cesare Battisti, onto which you make a right. Head toward the church of **San Frediano** ⑭, which holds the mummified remains of St. Zita, the patron saint of domestic workers. Before returning to the Fillungo, walk behind the church and take the narrow via Cesare Battisti to **Palazzo Pfanner** ⑮. Retrace your steps to San Frediano, and head to Via Fillungo. Make a right and then a left, and head into the **Piazza dell Anfiteatro Romano** ⑯, where the Anfiteatro Romano once stood. Relax and have an aperitivo at one of the many sidewalk cafés.

TIMING

The walk takes about three hours, perhaps a little longer if you linger in the museums.

Sights to See

Casa Natale di Giacomo Puccini. Lucca's most famous musical son was born in this house. It includes the piano on which Puccini composed *Turandot*, musical scores of important early compositions, letters, costumes and costume sketches, and family portraits. ✉ *Corte San Lorenzo 9 (on Via di Poggio)*, ☎ *0583/584028.* 🎫 *€3.* ☉ *Tues.–Sun. 10–1 and 3–6.*

★ ⑨ **Duomo.** The round-arched facade of the cathedral is a fine example of the rigorously ordered Pisan Romanesque style, in this case happily enlivened by an extremely varied collection of small carved columns. Take a closer look at the decoration of the facade and that of the portico below; they make this one of the most entertaining church exteriors in Tuscany. The Gothic interior contains a moving Byzantine crucifix—called the Volto Santo, or Holy Face—brought here, according to legend, in the 8th century (though it probably dates from between the 11th and early-13th centuries). The masterpiece of the Sienese sculptor Jacopo della Quercia (circa 1371–1438) is the marble *Tomb of Ilaria del Caretto* (1406). ✉ *Piazza del Duomo*, ☎ *0583/490530.* 🎫 *Tomb €2; €5.50 combination ticket (includes Museo della Cattedrale and San Giovanni's baptistery and archaeological works).* ☉ *Duomo weekdays 7–6; Sat. 9:30–6:45; Sun. 9–9:50, 11:30–11:50, and 1–5. Tomb Nov.–Mar., weekdays 9:30–4:45, Sat. 9:30–6:45, Sun. 11:30–noon and 1–1:45; Apr.–Oct., weekdays 9:30–5:45, Sat. 9–6:45, Sun. 9–10 and 11:30–noon and 1–5:45.*

⑩ **Museo della Cattedrale.** The cathedral museum exhibits many items too precious to be in the church, most notably the finely worked golden decorations of the Volto Santo, the Byzantine crucifix that re-

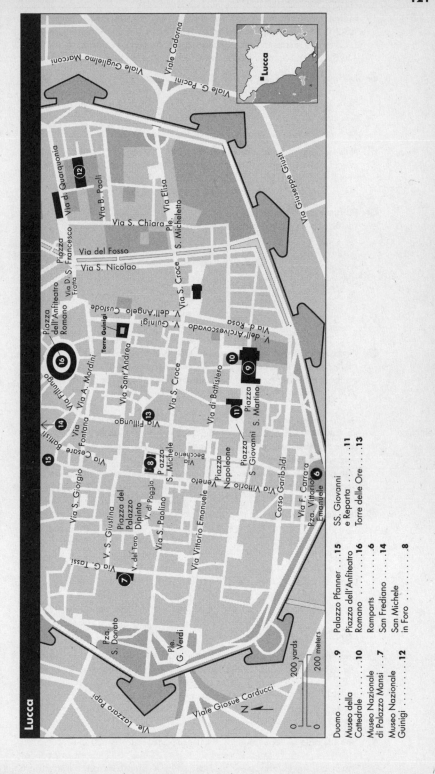

Lucca

Via Guglielmo Marconi
Viale G. Pacini
Via Cadorna
Via Giuseppe Giusti
Lucca

Via di Quaraquonia
Via B. Paoli
Via Elisa
Ple. Via S. Micheletto
Via S. Chiara
Piazza S. Francesco
Via del Fosso
Via S. Nicolao
Via D. S. Fratta
Piazza dell'Anfiteatro Romano
Via S. Croce
V. dell'Angelo Custode
V. Guinigi
V. dell'Arcivescovado
Via d. Rosa
Torre Guinigi
Via A. Mordini
Via Sant'Andrea
Via S. Croce
Via di Battistero
Piazza S. Martino
Via Fillungo
Via Cesare Battisti
Via Fontana
Via Fillungo
Via S. Croce
P.zza S. Michele
Via Beccheria
Piazza Napoleone
Piazza S. Giovanni
Via Vittorio Veneto
Via S. Giorgio
Piazza del Palazzo Dipinto
V. di Poggio
P.zza S. Michele
Via S. Paolino
Via Vittorio Emanuele
Via Giustina
Via G. Tassi
V. S. Giustina
V. del Toro
Via F. Carrara
Pza. Vittorio Emanuele
Corso Garibaldi
Via Vittorio Emanuele
Pza. S. Donato
Ple. G. Verdi
Via Lazzaro Papi
Viale Giosuè Carducci

0   200 yards
0   200 meters
N

mains in the Duomo. ✉ *Piazza Antiminelli*, ☎ *0583/490530.* 🖼
*€3.15; €5.50 combination ticket (includes tomb in Duomo and San
Giovanni's baptistery and archaeological works). ⊙ Nov.–Mar., daily
10–2; Apr.–Oct., daily 10–6.*

❼ Museo Nazionale di Palazzo Mansi. Highlights here include the lovely
Portrait of a Youth by Pontormo as well as portraits of the Medici painted
by Bronzino (1503–72) and others. ✉ *Palazzo Mansi, Via Galli Tassi
43 (near west walls of old city)*, ☎ *0583/55570.* 🖼 *€5.* ⊙ *Tues.–Sat.
9–7, Sun. 9–2.*

⑫ Museo Nazionale di Villa Guinigi. On the eastern end of the historic
center, this museum houses an extensive collection of local Romanesque
and Renaissance art. ✉ *Villa Guinigi, Via della Quarquonia,* ☎ *0583/
496033.* 🖼 *€4.10.* ⊙ *Tues.–Sat. 8:30–6:30, Sun. 8:30–1.*

⑮ Palazzo Pfanner. Here you can rest your feet and let time pass, surrounded by a harmonious arrangement of sun, shade, blooming plants,
water, and mysterious statuary. The palazzo's well-kept formal garden,
which abuts the walls of Lucca, centers on a large fountain and pool.
Allegorical statues pose along pebbled paths that radiate outward. The
palazzo, built in the 17th century, was purchased in the 19th century
by the Pfanners, a family of Swiss brewers. The family, which eventually gave the town a mayor, still lives here. ✉ *Via degli Asili 33,* ☎
0583/919931. 🖼 *Garden €2.50; palazzo €2.50; garden and palazzo
€4.* ⊙ *Mar.–mid-Nov., daily 10–6; mid-Nov.–Feb., by appointment only.*

⑯ Piazza dell'Anfiteatro Romano. On this site the **Anfiteatro Romano,**
or Roman Amphitheater, once stood; some of the medieval buildings
built over the amphitheater retain its original oval shape and brick arches.
✉ *Off Via Fillungo near north side of the old town.*

....

NEED A
BREAK?
Guido Cimino Ray Bar (✉ Anfiteatro 37–40, ☎ no phone), within the
Roman Amphitheater, offers good drinks and light lunches (including
some novel salad combinations and startlingly good house-made ter-
rines). You can also sit outside when it's warm. An airy upstairs gallery
with a second bar and seating on small sofas and plush armchairs is the
perfect spot for romance.

....

★ ❻ The Ramparts. Any time of day when the weather is clement, you can
find the citizens of Lucca's historic district cycling, jogging, strolling,
or playing ball in this green, beautiful, and very large park—neither
inside nor outside the city but rather right on the ring of ramparts that
defines Lucca. Sunlight streams through two rows of tall plane trees
to dapple the *passeggiata delle mura* (walk on the walls), almost 5 km
(3 mi) in total length. Ten bulwarks are topped with lawns, many with
picnic tables, some with play equipment for children. Be aware at all
times of where the edge is—there are no railings and the drop to the
ground outside the city is a precipitous 40 ft.

⑭ San Frediano. The church of San Frediano, just inside the middle of
the north town wall, contains works mainly by Jacopo della Quercia
(circa 1371–1438) as well as the lace-clad mummy of St. Zita (circa
1218–72), the patron saint of household servants. ✉ *Piazza San Frediano,* ☎ *no phone.* 🖼 *Free.* ⊙ *Mon.–Sat. 8:30–noon and 3–5, Sun.
10:30–5.*

❽ San Michele in Foro. Slightly west of town center is this church with a
facade even more fanciful than that of the Duomo. The upper levels of
the facade have nothing but air behind them (after the front of the church
was built, there were no funds to raise the nave), and the winged
Archangel Michael, who stands at the very top, seems precariously poised

for flight. The facade was heavily restored in the 19th century and so, thanks to the times, displays busts of 19th-century Italian patriots such as Garibaldi and Cavour in addition to the earlier work. Check out the superb Filippino Lippi (1457/58–1504) panel painting of Sts. Girolamo, Sebastian, Rocco, and Helen in the right transept. ⊠ *Piazza San Michele,* ☏ *no phone.* 🎟 *Free.* 🕐 *Daily 7:40–noon and 3–6.*

⓫ **Ss. Giovanni e Reparata.** The baptistery of this church, one piazza over from the Duomo, is lovely enough, but the unusual element here is an archaeological site, discovered in 1969, where five layers of Luccan history have been uncovered. As you walk the paths and catwalks suspended above the delicate sites in the caves under the church, you move from era to era—from the 2nd-century BC site of a Roman temple through the 5th, 8th, 9th, and 11th centuries. When seen after coming up the stairs from underground, the 12th-century church feels almost modern. ⊠ *Piazza San Giovanni,* ☏ *0583/490530.* 🎟 *Baptistery €1.03, baptistery and archaeological site €2.07, €5.50 combination ticket (includes tomb in Duomo and Museo della Cattedrale).* 🕐 *Mid-Mar.–Oct., daily 10–6; Nov.–mid-Mar., weekends 10–6.*

🄯 ⓭ **Torre delle Ore** (Tower of the Hours). The highest spot in Lucca is at the top of this tower, first purchased by the city in 1490 as its "civic tower." The tower has held several clocks over the centuries; the current timepiece was installed in 1754. The reward for the climb to the top is a panoramic view. ⊠ *Via Fillungo at Via D. Arancio,* ☏ *no phone.* 🎟 *€3.10.* 🕐 *Daily 10–7.*

Torre Guinigi. The tower of the medieval Palazzo Guinigi contains one of the city's most curious sights: a grove of ilex trees has grown at the top of the tower and their roots have pushed their way into the room below. From the top, you have a magnificent view of the city and the surrounding countryside. (Only the tower is open to the public, not the palazzo.) ⊠ *Palazzo Guinigi, Via Sant'Andrea,* ☏ *0583/496033.* 🎟 *€2.60.* 🕐 *Tues.–Sat. 9–7, Sun. 9–2.*

OFF THE BEATEN PATH

VILLA REALE – Eight kilometers (5 mi) north of Lucca in Marlia, this villa was once the home of Napoléon's sister, Princess Elisa. Restored by the Counts Pecci-Blunt, the estate is celebrated for its spectacular gardens, laid out in the 16th century and redone in the middle of the 17th. Gardening buffs adore the legendary *teatro di verdura,* a theater carved out of hedges and topiaries; concerts are occasionally held here. One of Tuscany's most popular summer events, the **Festival di Marlia** is held in Marlia in July and August; contact the Lucca tourist office for details. ⊠ *Marlia (north of Lucca along the river Serchio, in the direction of Barga and Bagni di Lucca),* ☏ *0583/30108.* 🎟 *€6.* 🕐 *Mar.–Nov., guided visits Tues.–Sun. at 10, 11, noon, 3, 4, 5, and 6; Dec.–Feb. by appointment only.*

Dining and Lodging

$$$ ✕ **La Mora.** Detour to this former stagecoach station, now a gracious, ★ rustic country inn 9 km (5½ mi) north of Lucca, for local specialties— from minestra di farro to homemade *tacconi* (a thin, short, wide pasta) with rabbit sauce and lamb from the nearby Garfagnana hills. You might be tempted by the varied *crostini* (toasted bread) and delicious desserts. ⊠ *Via Sesto 1748, Ponte a Moriano,* ☏ *0583/406402. AE, DC, MC, V. Closed Wed. and 3 wks in Jan.*

$$ ✕ **Bucadisantonio.** It's easy to see why this restaurant has been around ★ since the 1800s. The white-walled interior adorned with copper pots, the expertly prepared food, and an able staff make dining here a real treat. The menu includes simple but blissful dishes like *tortelli lucchesi al sugo* (meat-stuffed pasta with tomato–meat sauce) to more-daring entrées such as roast *capretto* (kid) with herbs. ✉ *Via della Cervia 3,* ☎ *0583/55881. AE, DC, MC, V. Closed Mon., 2 wks in Jan., and 2 wks in July. No dinner Sun.*

$$ ✕ **Il Giglio.** Just off Piazza Napoleone, this restaurant has quiet, late-19th-century charm and classic cuisine. It's a place for all seasons, with a big fireplace for chilly weather and an outdoor terrace in summer. Among the local specialties are farro *garfagnino* (a thick soup with grain and beans) and *coniglio con olive* (rabbit stew with olives). ✉ *Piazza del Giglio 2,* ☎ *0583/494508. AE, DC, MC, V. Closed Wed. and 15 days in Aug. No dinner Tues.*

$$ ✕ **Osteria del Neni.** Tucked away on a side street a block from San Michele, this delightful little place offers up tasty treats in a cozy space with paper place mats, wooden tables, and walls sponged in two hues of orange. All the pasta is made in house, and if you're lucky enough to find ravioli *spinaci e anatra in salsa di noci* (stuffed with duck and spinach, in creamy but light walnut sauce), order it. The menu changes regularly; in the summer, you can eat alfresco. ✉ *Via Pescheria 3,* ☎ *0583/492681. Reservations essential. MC, V. Closed Mon.*

$–$$ ✕ **Trattoria da Leo.** A few short turns away from the facade of San Michele, this noisy, informal, traditional trattoria delivers *cucina alla casalinga*—home cooking—in the best sense. Try the typical minestra di farro to start or just go straight to *secondi piatti* (entrées); in addition to the usual roast meats, there's excellent chicken with olives and a good cold dish of boiled meats served with a sauce of parsley and pine nuts. Save some room for dessert, which includes a rich, sweet fig-and-walnut torte as well as a lemon sorbet brilliantly dotted with bits of sage, which taste almost like mint. ✉ *Via Tegrimi 1, at corner of Via degli Asili,* ☎ *0583/492236. No credit cards. Closed Sun.*

$ ✕ **Da Giulio in Pelleria.** If Lucchesi businesspeople had a lunchtime cafeteria, it would be here. This loud, cavernous trattoria serves tasty, traditional Tuscan favorites, as well as such local specialties as *farinata* (vegetable soup thickened to a stewlike consistency by the addition of cornmeal), to hordes of diners, both local and from out of town. Don't be surprised to see an affable waiter expertly balancing in one hand five plates brimming with food. ✉ *Via delle Conce 47,* ☎ *0583/ 555948. AE, DC, MC, V. Closed Mon. and 1st, 2nd, and 4th Sun. of every month.*

$$$$ ✕🏠 **Locanda l'Elisa.** When Napoléon's sister, Elisa Baciocchi, arrived in Lucca to preside over it as a princess, she came with an entourage. One member built this delightful indigo villa 3 km (2 mi) south of Lucca. Surrounded by rosemary, lavender, and azaleas, the hotel preserves the intimacy of a well-furnished home; it's decorated in Empire style, with 19th-century furniture, prints, and fabrics. The attached restaurant elevates Lucchesi specialties such as *tordelli lucchese con sfoglia di farina di farro integrale al ragù d'anatra* (tortelli made with farro and served in a duck sauce) to new heights. ✉ *Massa Pisana 55050,* ☎ *0583/379737,* FAX *0583/379019,* WEB *www.lunet.it/aziende/locandaelisa. 3 rooms, 8 suites. Restaurant, cable TV, in-room safes, minibars, pool, bar, baby-sitting, dry cleaning, laundry service, Internet, some pets allowed. AE, DC, MC, V. Closed early Jan.–early Feb. EP.*

$$$$ 🏠 **Hotel Ilaria.** This beautifully appointed hotel faces the wide Via del Fosso. A terra-cotta terrace wraps around the side and back of the building and overlooks the garden of the neighboring Villa Botini, which has magnificent old, tall trees. Three rooms open directly onto the back terrace; two rooms are accessible to people who use wheelchairs. ✉ *Via del Fosso 26, 55100,* ☎ *0583/469200,* FAX *0583/991961,* WEB *www. hotelilaria.com. 30 rooms, 3 suites. In-room safes, minibars, bicycles,* *bar, baby-sitting, dry cleaning, laundry service, concierge, meeting rooms, free parking, some pets allowed (fee), no-smoking rooms. AE, DC, MC, V. CP.*

$$$$ 🖫 **Villa La Principessa.** Some rooms in this exquisitely decorated 19th-century country mansion 3 km (2 mi) outside Lucca have handsome beamed ceilings, and doors are individually decorated. Antique furniture and portraits impart an aura of gracious living. The grounds are well manicured, the pool large and inviting. A stay here evokes the time of Napoléon's court, when many of his retinue built their summer pleasure palaces outside the city. The restaurant is open for dinner only (but closed Tuesday). ⊠ *Via Nuova per Pisa 1616, Massa Pisana 55050,* ☎ *0583/370037,* FAX *0583/379136,* WEB *www.hotelprincipessa.com. 34 rooms, 7 suites. Restaurant, room service, minibars, cable TV, pool, bar, baby-sitting, dry cleaning, laundry service, concierge, Internet, meeting rooms, some pets allowed. AE, DC, MC, V. Closed Nov.–Mar. EP.*

$$$ 🖫 **Palazzo Alexander.** This small, elegantly appointed boutique hotel
★ is on a quiet side street a stone's throw from San Michele in Foro. The building, dating from the 12th century, has been restructured to create the ease common to Lucchesi nobility: timbered ceilings, warm yellow walls, and brocaded chairs adorn the public rooms, and the motif continues into the guest rooms, all of which have high ceilings and that same glorious damask. Top-floor suites have sweeping views of the town. ⊠ *Via S. Giustina 48, San Michele, 55100,* ☎ *0583/583571,* FAX *0583/ 583610,* WEB *www.palazzo-alexander.it. 9 rooms, 3 suites, 1 apartment. In-room safes, minibars, bicycles, wine bar, baby-sitting, dry cleaning, laundry service, concierge, Internet, meeting rooms, no-smoking rooms, parking (fee). AE, DC, MC, V. EP.*

$$ 🖫 **Albergo San Martino.** Down a narrow street facing a quiet, sun-sprinkled *piazzale* (small square) stands this small hotel. The brocade bedspreads are fresh and crisp, the proprietor friendly. Although around the corner from the Duomo, the busy Corso Garibaldi, and the great walls of Lucca, the Albergo, tucked away as it is, feels private—a place to retreat to when you have seen all the church facades you can stand. Two of the eight rooms are wheelchair-accessible. ⊠ *Via della Dogana 9, 55100,* ☎ *0583/469181,* FAX *0583/991940,* WEB *www. albergosanmartino.it. 8 rooms, 2 suites. Minibars, bicycles. AE, DC, MC, V. CP.*

$$ 🖫 **Fattoria di Fubbiano.** Lucca is famous for producing some of the world's finest olive oil, and it could be argued that the best of all is produced here at this agriturismo 10 minutes outside Lucca's *centro storico.* In addition to olive oil, the firm also makes wine and has lodging available. There's a villa that sleeps up to 14; a small house reached by a narrow road often dotted with horses grazing at the side; and an apartment. The apartment has a kitchenette; the house and villa both have kitchens. During high season, a one-week stay is mandatory; during low season, the minimum is two nights. ⊠ *San Gennaro, 55010,* ☎ *0583/ 978011,* FAX *0583/978344,* WEB *www.fubbianof.fattoriadifubbiano.it. 1 apartment, 1 farmhouse, 1 villa. Refrigerators, 3 pools, laundry facilities; no air-conditioning. MC, V. EP.*

$$ 🖫 **La Luna.** On a quiet, airy courtyard close to the Piazza del Mercato, this family-run hotel occupies two renovated wings of an old building. The bathrooms are modern, but some rooms still have the flavor of Old Lucca. ⊠ *Corte Compagni 12, at Via Fillungo, 55100,* ☎ *0583/493634,* FAX *0583/490021. 30 rooms. Parking (fee). AE, DC, MC, V. Closed for 4 wks Jan.–Feb. EP.*

$$ 🖫 **Piccolo Hotel Puccini.** Steps from the busy square and church of San Michele, this little hotel is quiet, calm, and handsomely decorated. It also offers parking (which must be reserved in advance) at a reasonable fee—a great advantage. ⊠ *Via di Poggio 9, 55100,* ☎ *0583/55421,*

FAX *0583/53487,* WEB *www.hotelpuccini.com. 14 rooms. In-room safes, bar, Internet, parking (fee); no air-conditioning. AE, DC, MC, V. EP.*

Nightlife and the Arts

The **Estate Musicale Lucchese,** one of many Tuscan music festivals, runs throughout the summer in Lucca. Contact the Lucca tourist office for details. The **Opera Theater of Lucca Festival,** sponsored by the Opera Theater of Lucca and the music college of the University of Cincinnati, runs from mid-June to mid-July; performances are staged in open-air venues. Call the Lucca tourist office, the Opera Theater of Lucca (☎ 0583/46531), or the University of Cincinnati, College-Conservatory of Music (☎ 513/566–5662) for information.

Outdoor Activities and Sports

One of the best ways to get around this lovely medieval town is on a bike. You can rent bikes at **Barbetti Cicli** (⊠ Via Anfiteatro 23, ☎ 0583/954444) or at **Poli Antonio Biciclette** (⊠ Piazza Santa Maria 42, ☎ 0583/493787).

Shopping

Chocolate
Chocolate lovers will be pleased with the selection at **Caniparoli** (⊠ Via San Paolino 96, ☎ 0583/53456). The store is closed in July and August.

Food
Lucca's olive oil, available in food shops all over the city, is exported throughout the world. Look for extra-virgin oil whose label clearly indicates that it is entirely from Italy or, better, entirely from Tuscany, or better yet, the product of a local *fattoria,* or farm. *Olio nuovo,* or new oil, is available from November, when the olive-picking season begins, until about February. This new oil is full-tasting and peppery— great for drizzling on soup, pasta, and bread—and it's nearly impossible to find in North America.

In addition, Lucca is famous for its farro, an ancient barleylike grain that has found its way into regional specialties such as *zuppa* (or *minestra*) *di farro* (farro soup). Buy some at **Marsili Costantino** (⊠ Piazza San Michele 38, ☎ 0583/491751) to take home, as it's hard to find elsewhere. The store also has locations at Via del Moro 18/22 and at Via dei Borghi 103.

Markets
On the second Sunday of the month, there's a **flea market** in Piazza San Martino.

Looking for old prints? Old postcards? Old comic books? Just behind the church of S. Guisto (off Via Becchieria, which runs for about two blocks between Piazza Napoleone and Piazza San Michele) are **bookstalls** that open their cupboard doors on clement days, from about 10– 6. You may uncover anything from hand-tinted prints of orchids to back issues of *Uomo Ragno* (Spider-Man looks and acts just the same even when he is speaking Italian).

Pasticceria
A particularly delicious version of buccellato—the sweet, anise-flavor bread with raisins that is a specialty of Lucca—is baked at **Pasticceria Taddeucci** (⊠ Piazza San Michele 34, ☎ 0583/494933).

PISA

If you can get beyond the kitsch that's around the Torre Pendente, the Leaning Tower, you'll find that Pisa has much to offer. Its treasures are more subtle than Florence's, to which it is inevitably compared; Pisa's cathedral-baptistery-tower complex on Piazza del Duomo is among the most dramatic in Italy.

Pisa may have been inhabited as early as the Bronze Age. It was certainly populated by the Etruscans and, in turn, became part of the Roman Empire. In the early Middle Ages, it flourished as an economic powerhouse—along with Amalfi, Genoa, and Venice, it was one of the maritime republics. But the city's economic and political power ebbed in the early 15th century as it fell under Florence's domination, though it enjoyed a brief resurgence under Cosimo I in the mid-16th century. Though Pisa sustained heavy damage during World War II, the Duomo and Tower were spared, along with some other grand Romanesque structures.

Exploring Pisa

Pisa, like many other Italian cities, is best seen on foot, and most of what you'll want to see is within walking distance. The views along the Arno are particularly grand and shouldn't be missed—there's a feeling of spaciousness that doesn't exist along the same river in Florence.

As you set out, keep in mind the various combination-ticket options for sights on the Piazza del Duomo. The tickets are all sold at the sights themselves.

A Good Walk

Start in the Campo dei Miracoli (Field of Miracles), exploring the piazza complex containing the **Torre Pendente** ⑰, **Duomo** ⑱, **Battistero** ⑲, **Camposanto** ⑳, **Museo dell'Opera del Duomo** ㉑, and the **Museo delle Sinopie** ㉒. Walk down Via Santa Maria—the Campanile will be behind you. Somewhere along the way, to recover from the crowds at the Campo, stop to have a coffee or a gelato. Once on these streets, you are surrounded by students, professors, and the buildings housing the faculties of the University of Pisa, for centuries one of the finest Italian institutions of higher education. At Piazza Felice Cavalloti, go left on to Via dei Mille. On the right is the Romanesque church of **Santo Sisto** ㉓. Continue straight on Via dei Mille to **Piazza dei Cavalieri** ㉔, a study in Renaissance symmetry. Go straight through the piazza to Via Dini, and make a right on to Borgo Stretto, a major thoroughfare lined with cafés. On the left, before the river, is the church of San Michele in Borgo, whose early-14th-century Pisan Romanesque facade resembles a wedding cake. Walk up to Piazza Garibaldi and turn left along the Lungarno Mediceo. Practically at the Ponte della Fortezza, on the left, is the **Museo Nazionale di San Matteo** ㉕. Cross over the bridge and turn right on to Lungarno Galileo Galilei. Take a left on the little side street Vicolo Lanfranchi, which is at the corner of Palazzo Lanfranchi. At the end of the street is the church of San Martino. Make a right on to Via San Martino and walk until you reach Piazza XX Settembre, where the large, freestanding Logge di Banchi (loggias) stand on the right. Go left on to Corso Italia, another major shopping thoroughfare. Or, if you wish to continue the walk, take a right on Corso Italia instead and walk until you reach the Arno. Make a left, and follow the curve of the sidewalk until you come upon **Santa Maria della Spina** ㉖, a Gothic gem.

TIMING

The walk takes a little more than 1½ hours without stops—but there's lots to see along the way; it could take a few hours, depending upon how long you stay in the Museo Nazionale di San Matteo.

Sights to See

⑲ **Battistero.** This lovely Gothic baptistery, which stands across from the Duomo's facade, is best known for the pulpit carved by Nicola Pisano (circa 1220–84; father of Giovanni Pisano) in 1260. Ask one of the ticket takers if he'll sing for you inside; the acoustics are remarkable (a tip of €3 is appropriate). ☒ *Piazza del Duomo,* ☏ *050/561820,* [WEB] *www.duomo.pisa.it.* ☒ *€4.65 (including 1 other Campo dei Miracoli site).* ☉ *Late June–late Sept., daily 8–7:40; late Sept.–late Dec. and late Mar.–late June, daily 9–5:40; late Dec.–late Mar., daily 9–4:40.*

⑳ **Camposanto.** According to legend, the cemetery—a walled structure on the western side of the Campo dei Miracoli—is filled with earth that returning Crusaders brought back from the Holy Land. Contained within are numerous frescoes, notably *The Drunkenness of Noah,* by Renaissance artist Benozzo Gozzoli (1422–97), and the disturbing *Triumph of Death* (14th century; authorship uncertain), whose subject matter shows what was on people's minds in a century that saw the ravages of the Black Death. ☒ *Campo dei Miracoli,* ☏ *050/561820,* [WEB] *www.duomo.pisa.it.* ☒ *€4.65 (including 1 other Campo dei Miracoli site).* ☉ *Late June–late Sept., daily 8–7:40; late Sept.–late Dec. and late Mar.–late June, daily 9–5:40; late Dec.–late Mar., daily 9–4:40.*

OFF THE
BEATEN PATH

LA CERTOSA DI PISA – A certosa (charterhouse) is a monastery whose monks belong to the strict Carthusian order. This vast and sprawling complex, begun in 1366, was suppressed by Napoléon, and then again in 1866. Most of the art and architecture you see date from the 17th and 18th centuries. The Carthusians returned here, only to leave it permanently in 1969. Also within it is the **Museo di Storia Naturale e del Territorio.** This museum of natural history contains fossils, 24 whale skeletons that serve to trace the mammal's development over the millennia, and some exhibits of local minerals. ☒ *10 km (6 mi) east of Pisa via road north of Arno, through Mezzana and then toward Calci and Montemagno,* ☏ *050/937751.* ☒ *€3.10.* ☉ *Tues.–Sat. 4–8, Sun. 10–11 and 4–8.*

⑱ **Duomo.** Pisa's cathedral was the first building to use the horizontal marble stripe motif (borrowed from Moorish architecture) that became common to Tuscan cathedrals. It is famous for the Romanesque panels on the transept door facing the tower that depict the life of Christ. The beautifully carved 14th-century pulpit is by Giovanni Pisano (son of Nicola). ☒ *Piazza del Duomo,* ☏ *050/561820,* [WEB] *www.duomo.pisa.it.* ☒ *€1.55, free Oct.–Mar.* ☉ *Late June–late Sept., Mon.–Sat. 10–7:40, Sun. 1–7:40; late Sept.–late Dec. and late Mar.–late June, Mon.–Sat., 10–7:40, Sun. 1–7:40; late Dec.–late Mar., Mon.–Sat. 10–12:45, Sun. 3–4:45.*

㉒ **Museo delle Sinopie.** The well-arranged museum on the south side of the Piazza del Duomo holds the *sinopie,* or preparatory drawings, for the Camposanto frescoes. ☒ *Piazza del Duomo,* ☏ *050/560547,* [WEB] *www.duomo.pisa.it.* ☒ *€4.65 (including 1 other Campo dei Miracoli site).* ☉ *Late June–late Sept., daily 8–7:40; late Sept.–late Dec. and late Mar.–late June, daily 9–5:40; late Dec.–late Mar., daily 9–4:40.*

㉑ **Museo dell'Opera del Duomo.** At the southeast corner of the sprawling Campo dei Miracoli, this museum holds a wealth of medieval sculptures and the ancient Roman sarcophagi that inspired Nicola Pisano's figures. ☒ *Via Arcivescovado,* ☏ *050/560547,* [WEB] *www.*

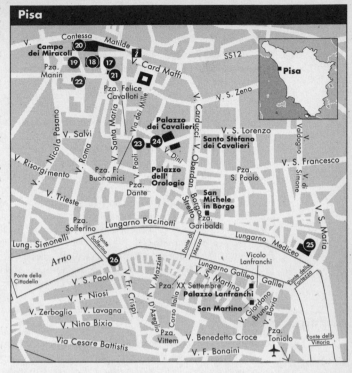

duomo.pisa.it. ⊠ *€4.65 (including 1 other Campo dei Miracoli site).* ☉ *Late June–late Sept., daily 8–7:40; late Sept.–late Dec. and late Mar.– late June, daily 9–5:40; late Dec.–late Mar., daily 9–4:40.*

㉕ Museo Nazionale di San Matteo. Along the northern side of the Arno, this museum contains some incisive examples of local Romanesque and Gothic art. ⊠ *Lungarno Mediceo,* ☎ *050/541865.* ⊠ *€4.10.* ☉ *Tues.– Sat. 9–7, Sun. 9–2.*

㉔ Piazza dei Cavalieri. The piazza, which holds the fine Renaissance **Palazzo dei Cavalieri, Palazzo dell'Orologio,** and **Santo Stefano dei Cavalieri,** was laid out by Giorgio Vasari in about 1560. The square was the seat of the Ordine dei Cavalieri di San Stefano (Order of the Knights of St. Stephen), a military and religious institution that was meant to defend the coast from possible invasion by the Turks. Also in this square is the prestigious **Scuola Normale Superiore,** founded by Napoléon in 1810 on the French model. Here graduate students pursue doctorates in literature, philosophy, mathematics, and science. In front of the school is an oversize statue of Ferdinando I de' Medici dating from 1596. On the extreme left is the tower where the hapless Ugolino della Gherardesca (died 1289) was imprisoned with his two sons and two grandsons; legend holds that he ate them. Dante immortalized him in Canto XXXIII of *The Inferno.* Duck into the **Church of Santo Stefano** and check out Bronzino's *Nativity of Christ* (1564–65).

㉖ Santa Maria della Spina. Originally an oratory dating from the 13th century, this gem of a church has been restored several times, most recently in 1996–98, due to flood damage. It's a delicate, tiny church, and a fine example of Tuscan Gothic. ⊠ *Lungarno Gambacorti,* ☎ *no phone.* ⊠ *Free.* ☎ *050/910365.* ☉ *Jun.–Aug., Tue.–Fri. 11–1:30 and 2:30–6, Sat. 11–1:30 and 2:30–8; Apr., May, Sept., Tues.–Fri. 10–2 and 2:30–5, weekends 10–1:30 and 2:30-7; Oct.–Mar., Tues.–Sun. 10–2.*

㉓ **Santo Sisto.** Dating from the 11th century, this church reveals a simple yet elegant arcaded colonnade and stone interior. ⊠ *Piazza Francesco Buonamici,* ☏ *no phone.* ⊡ *Free.* ⊙ *Daily 8–7:30.*

⑰ **Torre Pendente** (Leaning Tower). Legend holds that Galileo conducted an experiment on the nature of gravity by dropping metal balls from the top of the 187-ft-high Leaning Tower of Pisa. Historians, however, say this legend has no basis in fact—which isn't quite to say that it is false. Work on this tower, built as a campanile (bell tower) for the Duomo, started in 1173: the lopsided settling began when construction reached the third story. The tower's architects attempted to compensate through such methods as making the remaining floors slightly taller on the leaning side, but the extra weight only made the problem worse. The settling continued, and by the late 20th century it had accelerated to a point that led many to fear the tower would simply topple over, despite all efforts to prop it up. The structure since has been firmly anchored to the earth. The final phase to restore the tower to its original tilt of 300 years ago was launched in early 2000 and finished two years later. The last phase removed some 100 tons of earth from beneath the foundation. Reservations, which are essential, can be made via the Web or by calling the Museo dell'Opera del Duomo. ⊠ *Campo dei Miracol,* ☏ *050/560547 Museo dell'Opera del Duomo,* ▯ *www.duomo. pisa.it.* ⊡ *€15.*

Dining and Lodging

$$$ ✕ **Al Ristoro dei Vecchi Macelli.** The "Inn by the Old Slaughterhouse" retains its name even though the slaughterhouse is no longer in use. Head here for sophisticated, special food. You can order a fixed-price seafood or meat menu or choose dishes à la carte. The menu changes regularly to reflect the season; in the cooler months, look for *ravioli salsicce cavolfiore con i broccoli saltato* (ravioli stuffed with sausage and cauliflower and in a broccoli sauce). The room has low, subdued lighting; an old wooden ceiling; terra-cotta floors; and walls lined with stylish black-and-white photographs. ⊠ *Via Volturno 49,* ☏ *050/20424. AE, DC, MC, V. Closed Wed. and 2 wks in mid-Aug. No lunch Sun.*

$$–$$$ ✕ **La Mescita.** This cheerful trattoria has high, vaulted brick ceilings and stenciled walls lined with colorful contemporary prints. It's a great place to eat some of the tasty and inventive food on offer: the *tagliolini con salsiccia e porri sopra salsa di cabernet sauvignon* (housemade thin noodles with sausage and leeks in wine sauce) is extraordinary. The wine list has been carefully compiled, and service is friendly and efficient. ⊠ *Via Cavalca 2,* ☏ *050/544294. AE, DC, MC, V. Closed last 3 wks in Aug. and 3 wks in Jan. No lunch Mon.–Thur.*

$–$$$ ✕ **Beny.** Apricot walls hung with etchings of Pisa make this small, single-room restaurant warmly romantic. Beny specializes in fish: its *ripieno di polpa di pesce a pan grattato con salsa di seppie e pomodoro* (fish-stuffed ravioli with tomato–octopus sauce) is a delight. Another flavorful dish is the *sformato di verdura* (a flan with Jerusalem artichokes), which comes embellished with sweet *gamberoni* (shrimp). ⊠ *Piazza Gambacorti 22,* ☏ *050/25067. AE, DC, MC, V. No lunch weekends.*

$–$$$ ✕ **Osteria dei Cavalieri.** This charming white-walled restaurant, a few
★   steps from Piazza dei Cavalieri, is reason enough to come to Pisa. They can do it all here—serve up exquisitely grilled fish dishes, please vegetarians, and prepare *tagliata* (thin slivers of rare beef) for meat lovers. Three set menus, from the sea, garden, and earth, are available, or you can order à la carte—which can be agonizing because everything sounds so good. And it is. Finish your meal with a lemon sorbet bathed in Pros-

ecco (a dry sparkling wine), and walk away feeling like you've eaten like a king at plebeian prices. ⊠ *Via San Frediano 16,* ☏ *050/580858. AE, DC, MC, V. Closed Sun. and late July–late Aug. No lunch Sat.*

$$ ✕ **Il Re di Puglia.** The name means "the King of Puglia," and it's somewhat hard to account for its presence in the countryside about 15 minutes outside of Pisa. In winter, you can enjoy Tuscan favorites in a large room with a fireplace; in summer, however, it's even better, as you sit outside on a covered terrace. On the very large grill, beef, sausage, vegetables, and bruschetta are prepared: they're all done well. Paired with the formidable wine list and friendly service, it makes for a memorable meal. ⊠ *Via Aurelia Sud 7,* ☏ *050/960157. Reservations essential. No credit cards. No lunch. Closed Mon.–Tues.*

$–$$ ✕ **La Pergoletta.** On an old-town street named for its "beautiful towers," this small, simple restaurant is in one itself. There's also a shady garden for outdoor dining. Signora Forte, the proprietor–chef, cooks such traditional Tuscan classics as *minestra di farro* (grain soup) and choice interpretations of *grigliata* (grilled beef, veal, or lamb). Her sense of whimsy accounts for some of the non-Italian ingredients that pepper her dishes. ⊠ *Via delle Belle Torri 36,* ☏ *050/542458. MC, V. Closed Mon. and 1 wk in Aug.*

$$ ⊞ **Hotel Verdi.** Down the street from Teatro Verdi, this small hotel often provides lodging for actors and musicians who are drawn by the hotel's quiet location, simple rooms with high ceilings, and intimate feel. The small bar is well stocked, and the lounge area is pleasant. ⊠ *Piazza Repubblica 5/6, 56100,* ☏ *050/598947,* FAX *050/598944. 32 rooms. Bar, lounge, Internet, free parking. AE, DC, MC, V. Closed 2 wks. in Aug. CP.*

$$ ⊞ **Royal Victoria.** In a pleasant palazzo facing the Arno, a 10-minute walk from the Campo dei Miracoli, this comfortably furnished hotel has been in the same family since 1837. Such continuity may help to explain why such notables as Charles Dickens and Charles Lindbergh have enjoyed staying here. Antiques and reproductions are in the lobby and in some rooms, whose style ranges from the 1800s, complete with frescoes, to the 1920s. ⊠ *Lungarno Pacinotti 12, 56126,* ☏ *050/ 940111,* FAX *050/940180,* WEB *www.royalvictoria.it. 48 rooms, 40 with bath. Bar, Internet, parking (fee), some pets allowed; no air-conditioning in some rooms. AE, DC, MC, V. CP.*

$ ⊞ **Fattoria di Migliarino.** Martino Salviati and his wife Giovanna have
★ turned their working *fattoria,* or farm, on which they raise soybeans, corn, and sugar beets, into an inn. The ten charming, spacious apartments accommodate anywhere from two to eight people and are rustically furnished, many of them with fireplaces. There's even a farmhouse that sleeps 27. The pool is framed by fields, and the only sound you're likely to hear is the clucking of the hens they keep for eggs. The surrounding woods can be explored on horseback or with a mountain bike. During high season, there is a one-week minimum stay. ⊠ *Viale dei Pini 289, Migliarino (10 km [6 mi] northwest of Pisa) 56010,* ☏ *050/ 803046,* FAX *050/803170. 10 apartments, 1 house. Kitchenettes, pool, Internet; no room TVs. MC, V. EP.*

Nightlife and the Arts

The **Luminaria** feast day, on June 16, is Pisa at its best. The day honors St. Ranieri, the patron saint of the city. Palaces along the Arno are lit with white lights, and there are plenty of fireworks.

EMPOLI AND CENTRAL HILL TOWNS

Off the beaten track in Empoli, San Miniato, and the neighboring hill towns are fine examples of art—especially in Empoli and Castelfiorentino—and stirring views. The terrific restaurants in this area are less expensive than in the cities to the north. This is also a good place to find local handmade products—ceramics in Montelupo, glass and leather in the Empoli-Vinci area, as well as local wine and oil, both in Certaldo and in Vinci.

Empoli

㉗ *50 km (31 mi) east of Pisa, 33 km (21 mi) west of Florence.*

Set along the Arno roughly halfway between Florence and Pisa, Empoli is a bustling town with a long history. References to the city first appear in documents from the 800s. By 1182, it was completely aligned with Florence. In 1260, after the Battle of Montaperti, the leader of the proimperial faction called the Ghibellines, Farinata degli Uberti, made the decision while in Empoli not to burn Florence to the ground, a decision that Dante wrote about in Canto X of *The Inferno*.

Now Empoli is a sleepy little town only a half hour's train ride from Florence. If you're traveling in the summer, you might want to consider staying here and hopping on the train for day trips into Florence. But don't forget to see the sights in Empoli—they're worth it.

★ A woman who works at the **Collegiata di Sant'Andrea** describes it as a "little jewel," and she's completely right. In this museum, with its cloister filled with terra-cotta sculptures from the della Robbia school, including one by Andrea della Robbia, is a magnificent 15th-century fresco by Masolino (circa 1383–1440) of the *Pietà*; there's also a small Fra Filippo Lippi and a wonderful tabernacle attributed to Francesco Bottincini (circa 1446–97) and Antonio Rossellino (1427–79). ✉ *Just off Piazza Farinata degli Uberti,* ☎ *0571/76284.* 🎟 *€2.58; €6 combination ticket (includes Museo Leonardiano in Vinci and Museo Archeologico e della Ceramica in Montelupo).* 🕐 *Tues.–Sun. 9–noon and 4–7.*

Originally founded by the Augustines in the 11th century, **Santo Stefano** can be seen only by asking for a tour in the Collegiata di Sant'Andrea. It's worth the walk around the corner and down the street, as there are sinopie (preparatory drawings) by Masolino depicting scenes from the *Legend of the True Cross*. He left without actually frescoing them; it may be that the Augustinian friars were late in making payment. ✉ *Via de' Neri,* ☎ *0571/76284.* 🎟 *Free.* 🕐 *Tues.–Fri. 9–noon.*

NEED A BREAK?	**Vinegar** (✉ Piazza della Vittoria 36–37, ☎ 0571/74630) is a nice bar near the train station that sells many sorts of panini as well as coffees and aperitifs.

A short but not very scenic walk from the center of town brings you to the little **San Michele in Pontorme,** chiefly notable for the gorgeous *St. John the Evangelist* and *Michael the Archangel,* two works dating from about 1519 by Jacopo Carrucci (1494–1556), better known as Pontormo. ✉ *Piazza San Michele,* ☎ *no phone.* 🎟 *Free.* 🕐 *Ring for sacristan.*

OFF THE BEATEN PATH	**VILLA MEDICEA –** On the night of July 15, 1576, Isabella de' Medici, daughter of the all-powerful Cosimo I, was murdered by her husband in the Villa Medicea in the town of Cerreto Guidi for "reasons of honor"—

that is, she was suspected of adultery. These days, although the villa's formal garden is in somewhat imperfect condition, the vast halls and chambers within remain majestic. Copies of portraits of various Medici, including Isabella, cover the walls. Cosimo chose to build this villa on the ruins of a castle that originally belonged to the Guidi counts, and the choice speaks volumes about what he believed himself to be. The Medici buildings sit atop the highest point in Cerreto Guidi, encircled by two narrow streets where the daily business of the town goes on. As you stand on the wide, flat front lawn, high above the streets of the town, with the villa behind you and terraced hillsides of olive groves and vineyards stretching into the distance, you can imagine what it was like to be a Medici. To see the villa, ring the bell for the custodian. ⊠ *Cerreto Guidi (8 km [5 mi] west of Empoli)*, ☎ *0571/55707.* ▣ *€2.07.* ☉ *Daily 8:15–6:30.*

Dining and Lodging

$$–$$$$ ✕ **Il Galeone.** This relaxed and friendly place is known for its fish, but
★ the meat dishes are as delicious. Pale-pink walls and pink tablecloths play off the gray-and-white tile floors. You may have trouble deciding what to order, but give the *moscardini con fagioli e rucola* (baby squid gently heated with cannellini beans, diced tomatoes, and olive oil and served on a bed of arugula) a try; the *spiedini di seppioline e gamberoni* (kebabs of squid with shrimp) is terrific, too. Pizza is also served here. ⊠ *Via Curtatone e Montanara 67,* ☎ *0571/72826. AE, DC, MC, V. Closed Sun. and Aug.*

$–$$ ▣ **Hotel Il Sole.** Across the street from the railway station, Il Sole has been in the hands of the Sabatini family since 1905. Each of the 12 rooms is an eclectic, unique interpretation of the Victorian style. If you are on a budget, this is a good alternative to staying in Florence, which is about a half-hour train ride away. ⊠ *Piazza Don Minzoni 18, 50053,* ☎ *0571/73779, FAX 0571/79871. 11 rooms, 10 with bath; 1 suite. Bar, some pets allowed; no air-conditioning in some rooms. AE, DC, MC, V. CP.*

Shopping

Large or small, formal or sporty—women are likely to find something to fit the bill at the high-quality **Modyva outlet** (☎ 0571/9501, FAX 0571/83314, WEB www.modyva.it). The store is outside Empoli, hidden away near Modyva's factory with no sign outside: retail shops had complained that the outlet was too visible from the FI-PI-LI superstrada. The prices and selection are excellent; all four of the fashion house's lines are sold here at reduced prices, with those for irregulars (meticulously marked) lowered further. The sales staff is friendly and professional. Like many other Italian businesses, Modyva is family-run, with the third generation being groomed to take on increasing leadership. To get to the outlet, take either of the Empoli Ovest exits from the FI-PI-LI autostrada and turn left at the bottom of the ramp; at the traffic light go straight across the road and into the Terrafino industrial park. Modyva's *spazio aziendale* (selling space) is in the first building on your left. It's open Monday through Saturday 9–1 and 3:30–7.

Montelupo

㉘ *6 km (4 mi) east of Empoli, 30 km (19 mi) southwest of Florence.*

This small town, which straddles the Arno, and surrounding villages have been producing ceramics for centuries. Many of the shops in Montelupo's centro storico (historical center) are devoted to selling these ceramics, especially tableware and pots.

The **Museo archeologico e della ceramica** (Museum of Archaeology and Ceramics) has some 3,000 objects devoted to majolica, a glazed pottery that has been made in this region since the early-14th century. The museum includes a good section on archaeology and pre-historic finds, clear explanations of the technology and history of making ceramics from the earliest days to the present, and a beautifully mounted and arranged collection of local work that dates from the early-14th century to the late 18th. Most fascinating are the coats of arms sporting important Renaissance names such as Medici and Strozzi. ⊠ *Via Bartolomeo Sinibaldi 45,* ☎ *0571/51087.* ⌷ *€2.58; €6 combination ticket (includes Museo Leonardiano in Vinci and Collegiata di Sant'Andrea in Empoli).* ⊙ *Tues.–Sun. 10–6.*

Nightlife and the Arts

FESTIVAL

Every June, Montelupo is host to the weeklong **Festa della Ceramica,** a ceramics festival that includes exhibitions of local and international contemporary artists, demonstrations of techniques new and ancient, street theater and music—and, of course, sales of ceramics from around the world. Additional information about the ceramics festival is available from the Montelupo Fiorentino tourist office (☎ 0571/518993).

Shopping

CERAMICS

Montelupo's ceramics museum proudly displays the work of the past, but the finest tribute to centuries of craft is the fact that top-quality ceramics are still being produced by hand in the region. Much work is in traditional styles, but there are also some artists who bring modern inspiration to their wheels. Not all of the stores will ship for you, although many will wrap the objects for you to carry home.

Bartoloni: La Ceramics Tradizionale di Montelupo (⊠ Corso Garibaldi 34, ☎ 0571/51242 or 0571/913569) is down the road from the Museo Archeologico e Della Ceramica. The articles produced are done in many kinds of styles. The small shop is open daily 10–1 and 4–8.

Ceramica ND Dolfi (⊠ Via Toscoromagnola 1, Località Antinoro, ☎ 0571/51264) has been a family business for three generations. The compound, including a sun-drenched spazio aziendale (selling floor), the factory workshop, the family residence, and a yard where terra-cotta planters are displayed, is 3 km (2 mi) from Montelupo on the east road toward Florence. The ceramics, all priced reasonably for such high-quality handcrafted work, include big floor vases, plates suitable for wall display, and bright serving pieces for the table. The shop is open daily from 8–8.

Le Ceramiche del Borgo (⊠ Via G. Marconi 2/4, ☎ 0571/518856) sells the work of Eugenio Taccini, which includes bowls, platters, tiles, and plates. The large shop, which is open daily, is next to a bridge in Montelupo's historical center; the store's proprietor, Lea Taccini, speaks good English.

Some serious ceramics lovers think **Maioliche Dolfi Otello** (⊠ Via Toscoromagnola Nord 8/b, Località Camaioni, ☎ 0571/910105, WEB www.otellodolfi.it) is the best. The shop, in the same building as the factory, is a couple of miles outside Montelupo, down SS67 in the direction of Florence, and well worth the ride. In addition to fine platters, vases, pitchers, and the like, the shop produces devotional ceramics by hand, in the style of the della Robbia studio. Maioliche Dolfi Otello is open weekdays 8–noon and 2–6:30, weekends 4–7. You can often watch the artisans at work.

Vinci

㉙ *10 km (6 mi) north of Empoli, 45 km (28 mi) west of Florence.*

The small hill town from which Leonardo da Vinci derived his name is a short bus ride north of Empoli. At the church of Santa Croce, near the town square, you can see the baptismal font in which Leonardo was baptized. But if you want to see the house where he was born, you'll have to travel to Anchiano, 3 km (2 mi) north of Vinci. In any case, it's worth a trip to Vinci for the views alone.

Museo Ideale Leonardo da Vinci. A small museum houses an idiosyncratic hodgepodge of items related to Leonardo, including mechanical objects from the time of Leonardo and copies of his sketches, including one of this region. ⊠ *Via Montalbano 2,* ☎ *0571/56296.* ⊠ *€4.13.* ☉ *Daily 10–1 and 3–7.*

Museo Leonardiano. If you are interested in Leonardo or the history of science, this museum, atop the castle belonging to the Guidi family in the historical center of Vinci, has replicas of many of Leonardo's machines and gadgets. The typically Tuscan views are not at all bad. ⊠ *Via della Torre 2,* ☎ *0571/56055.* ⊠ *€5; €6 combination ticket (includes Collegiata di Sant'Andrea in Empoli and Museo Archeologico e della Ceramica in Montelupo).* ☉ *Daily 9:30–6.*

Lodging

$$ ⊞ **Il Fondaccio.** This moderately priced agriturismo overlooks the hills near Vinci. Five apartments are available for groups of two to six people. One apartment is entirely accessible for people who use wheelchairs. If you're traveling with children, il Fondaccio is a perfect spot to tour the sights (Pisa, Lucca, San Gimignano, and beaches are all nearby); the pool provides a fine option for non-sightseeing days. ⊠ *Via del Fondaccio 19, 50059,* ☎ *0571/558862, 0339/7038497 for language assistance in English,* ⅎ⅄ *0571/959703,* ₩ℇℬ *www.netty.it/fondaccio. 5 apartments. Air-conditioning, kitchenettes, pool, bicycles, playground, kennel. No credit cards. Closed Nov.–Mar. EP.*

Shopping

GLASS

In the small factory at **Fornace di Vinci** (⊠ Via Provinciale di Mercatale 10, ☎ 0571/501860, 0571/922414 factory visits), men lift slugs of molten glass out of furnaces using long, hollow iron poles and then roll, slam, and blow the glass into shape—into a vase, a goblet, a bowl, a candlestick. The modest showroom has works for sale at good prices; it's open weekdays 9–noon and 3–5:30 and Saturday 9–noon. Visits to the factory are by appointment only.

LEATHER

As you drive around this part of Tuscany, you see advertisements for *venditta diretta* (direct sales) at the small local factories that work in leather and furs. Of course, not every factory is set up for doing this or carries high-quality goods, and the stock is extremely limited. In the spazio aziendale, **ESSEBI** (⊠ Via del Torrino 33, behind the Cantine Leonardo da Vinci, ☎ 0571/902172) has a small but excellent selection of leather jackets, pants, shirts, skirts, and coats. It also has silky-soft suede. The stock, including colors and sizes, varies depending on the season (more windbreakers in the colder months). Prices here are not low, but the cost is reasonable for what you are getting. The retail space is open Tuesday–Saturday 8:30–12:30 and 2:30–6:30. If you need to call, be sure to ask "for the space," *per lo spazio.*

OLIVE OIL

L'Oleificio Cooperativo Montalbano (✉ Via Beneventi 2/c, ☎ 0571/56247), a cooperative *frantoio* (olive mill)—where many local farmers bring their olives to be pressed at late autumn's harvest—sells oil made only from fruit on these hills. Other locally made goods, including wine and vinegar and herb-flavored oils, are sold here, too. Look for oil pressed as recently as possible; if kept out of the sunlight, it should keep for two years. The cooperative is open weekdays 8–noon and 2–6, Saturday 8–noon.

WINE

As you walk in **Cantine Leonardo da Vinci** (✉ Bivio di Streda, ☎ 0571/902444), you will see three huge vats with large nozzles, resembling those used to pump gasoline, and a choice of white and two types of red wine. It's all good, straightforward table wine (the minimum purchase is 6 liters—the equivalent of 8 bottles). This *cantina* (wine shop), open Monday–Saturday 8:30–12:30 and 2:30–6:30, also sells a range of Italian wines; look for those produced and bottled in Vinci.

San Miniato

③⓪ *20 km (12 mi) southeast of Vinci, 43 km (27 mi) west of Florence.*

Dating from Etruscan and Roman times, this town was named San Miniato after the saint (also known as St. Mineas) to whom the Lombards dedicated a church in the 8th century. The Holy Roman Empire had very strong ties to San Miniato; in fact, its castle was built in 962 under the aegis of Otto I (912–973). Matilde of Tuscany was born here in the mid-11th century. Eventually the town, with its Ghibelline (proimperial and anticlerical) sympathies, passed into the hands of the Florentines. Today the pristine, tiny hill town's narrow, cobbled streets are lined with austere 13th- to 17th-century facades, some of them built over buildings that were already centuries old. San Miniato's artistic treasures are somewhat limited in comparison with Florence's, but the town prettiness makes a trip well worth it.

St. Francis founded the 1211 **Convento e Chiesa di San Francesco** (Convent and Church of St. Francis), containing two cloisters and an ornate wooden choir. For a dose of monastic living, you can stay overnight. ✉ *Piazza San Francesco,* ☎ *0571/43051.* 🖬 *Free.* ⊙ *Daily 9–noon and 3–7 (or ring bell).*

The **Convento e Chiesa di Santi Jacopo e Filippo** (Convent and Church of Sts. Jacob and Philip) is also known as the church of San Domenico, which refers to the fact that the Dominicans took over the church in the 14th century. Most of the interior suffers from too much baroque, but there is a lovely sculpted tomb by Bernardo Rossellino of Giovanni Chellini, a doctor who died in 1461. ✉ *Piazza del Popolo,* ☎ *0571/418739.* 🖬 *Free.* ⊙ *Daily 9–noon and 3–7.*

NEED A
BREAK?

Bar Cantini (✉ Via Conti 1, ☎ 0571/43030) might be the meeting place for all San Miniatans; its panini are wonderful, in part because it bakes its own bread. Try any *cazzotto* ("little punch"), a tiny, round sandwich stuffed with fillings. There's also pizza by the slice and homemade ice cream in the summer.

The only thing remarkable about the **Duomo,** set in a pretty piazza, is its 13th-century facade, which has been restored. The interior is largely uninteresting; a moment of poignancy occurs when you view the plaque commemorating the 55 citizens who were killed in this church in July 1944 by German occupying forces (the Taviani brothers' 1982 movie, *The Night of San Lorenzo*, was about these events). ⊠ *Piazza del Castello,* ☎ *no phone.* ☐ *Free.* ⊙ *Daily 9–noon and 3–7.*

Although the **Museo Diocesano** is small, the modest collection incorporates a number of subtle and pleasant local works of art. Note the rather odd Crucifixion by Fra Filippo Lippi, Verrocchio's (1435–88) *Il Redentore,* and the small but exquisite *Education of the Virgin* by Tiepolo (1696–1770). ⊠ *Piazza del Castello,* ☎ *0571/418071.* ☐ €1. ⊙ *Nov.–Mar., Sat. and Sun. 9–noon and 2:30–5; Apr.–Oct., Tues.– Sun. 9–noon and 2:30–5.*

The **Torre di Federico II,** dating from around the time of Frederick II (1194–1250), was destroyed during World War II. A point of civic pride for the San Miniatans and visible for miles and miles around, the tower was rebuilt and reopened in 1958. The hapless, ill-fated Pier della Vigna, chancellor and minister to Frederick II, was imprisoned here; Dante writes about him in Canto XIII of *The Inferno.* The hill on which the tower sits—a surprisingly large, flat oval of green grass—is one of the loveliest places in the area to munch a panino, enjoy the 360-degree view, or join local children in a pickup game of *calcio* (Italian soccer). Just don't let the ball go over the edge, because you'll never see it again. ⊠ *Piazza del Popolo,* ☎ *0571/42745.* ☐ €5. ⊙ *Tues.–Sun., 9:30–1 and 3–7.*

Dining and Lodging

$$–$$$ ✕ **L'Antro di Bacco.** You'd never know it was here even though it's in the center of town, as you first have to enter a *salumeria* (delicatessen) and then descend. It's worth seeking out: the food is superb, and the chef has a deft touch with slightly atypical combinations. The Roman-inspired, but completely Tuscan *involtini con pecorino tartufo* (flattened bits of stuffed rolled beef with truffles and pecorino) is delicious. ⊠ *Via Quattro Novembre 13,* ☎ *0571/43319. MC, V. Closed Sun. and 1 wk. in Aug. No dinner Wed.*

$$ ✕ **Il Convio-Maiano.** The stenciled walls, brightly colored tablecloths,
★   and absolute calm make this charming restaurant homey. Start with the *crostone al lardo e tartufato,* a big piece of grilled Tuscan bread served with an amalgam of four cheeses, and speckled with truffles and lard. The *contorni* (vegetables) are also worth investigating; the *cavolfiore in umido* (cauliflower cooked with tomatoes) proves that this vegetable doesn't have to be boring. Il Convio-Maiano is 2 km (1 mi) from the historic center, in San Miniato Basso. ⊠ *Via San Maiano 2, San Miniato Basso,* ☎ *0571/408114. MC, V. Closed Wed. and 15 days in mid-Jan.*

$ ▥ **Convento San Francesco.** For a complete change of pace, you can stay in this 13th-century monastery in the company of five Franciscan friars. Rooms are simple, bordering on spartan, but quiet. You are given keys, so you're not expected back by a certain time. You can partake in some spiritual activities, or skip them altogether. All rooms have baths, and there are five rooms that groups can rent. It's a 10-minute walk from the city center. ⊠ *Piazza San Francesco, 56020,* ☎ *0571/43051,* ℻ *0571/43398. 27 rooms. No air-conditioning, no room phones, no room TVs, no kids under 12. No credit cards.*

Castelfiorentino

③   *12 km (7 mi) south of San Miniato, 50 km (31 mi) southwest of Florence.*

Like San Miniato, Castelfiorentino can claim Roman origins. During the Middle Ages, it was of strategic importance in the struggles between the Holy Roman Empire and the Papacy. Now it is a sleepy little town.

Admirers of Renaissance artist Benozzo Gozzoli (1420–97) have much to see at the **Biblioteca Comunale,** where the detached frescoes and sinopie from two tabernacles executed by him are on display. The Tabernacolo della Visitazione shows scenes from the life of the Virgin Mary; another tabernacle, *Madonna della Tosse* (literally, "Madonna of the Coughs"), from 1484, has exquisite renderings of major events in the life of the Virgin Mary, including the Assumption. ✉ *Via Tilli 41,* ☎ *0571/64019.* ☞ *€1.55.* ☉ *Weekdays 2:30–7:30, Sun. 10–noon and 4–7 (or ring doorbell for custodian).*

Certaldo

③② *9 km (6 mi) south of Castelfiorentino, 56 km (35 mi) west of Florence.*

Certaldo is probably most famous for having produced Giovanni Boccaccio (1313–75), the witty and irreverent author of *The Decameron* (circa 1351). It seems as if practically every shop in town has managed to incorporate his name into its title. The town was greatly damaged during World War II, and much of what you see of its brick buildings is postwar reconstruction. The centro storico, Certaldo Alto, is high above the rest of town and has magnificent views into Chianti.

The dimly lit church of **Santissimi Jacopo e Filippo,** begun in the 12th century, is where Boccaccio is buried. A tomb slab bearing his likeness is found in the center aisle, and a Latin epitaph written by Florentine chancellor Coluccio Salutati is near it on the left wall. Also of interest are two terra-cotta tabernacles dated 1499 and 1502 from the school of the della Robbia. On the right wall is a stupendous, multicolor terra-cotta altarpiece, attributed to one of the della Robbia, depicting the *Madonna of the Snow.* ✉ *Piazza Ss. Jacopo e Filippo,* ☎ *no phone.* ☞ *Free.* ☉ *Daily 8–noon and 4–8.*

Begun in the late-12th century, the **Palazzo Pretorio,** speckled with terra-cotta coats of arms on its facade, served as the city's town hall and also provided space for a women's prison. Now it houses a gallery for art exhibitions, a permanent display of Etruscan pottery, and fragments of 14th-century murals. All of its spaces are open to visitors; you can crawl under the low sills of the doorways leading into the prison cells (where lines are scored on the walls, presumably by inmates keeping track of the dismal days), or you can walk outside, across a wide walled-in lawn to narrow brick stairs that ascend the back garden wall to a balcony that runs the length of the palazzo, looking straight up into Chianti. Also in this complex is the church of **San Tommaso e Prospero,** which contains a Benozzo Gozzoli tabernacle (1466–67) depicting scenes from the life of Christ. You can view the sinopie that he executed for the tabernacle. too. ✉ *Piazzetta del Vicariato,* ☎ *0571/ 661219.* ☞ *€3.* ☉ *Nov.–Mar., Tues.–Sun. 10:30–12:30 and 2:30–5:30; Apr.–Oct., daily 8–7.*

At the **Casa di Boccaccio,** they say that the room in which Boccaccio died is the only part of the house to have survived a World War II bombing. ✉ *Via Boccaccio 25,* ☎ *0571/664208.* ☞ *€3.10.* ☉ *Apr.–Sept., daily 10–7; Oct.–Mar., Wed.–Mon. 10:30–4:30.*

NEED A BREAK?   **La Saletta di Dolci Follie** (✉ Via Roma 3, in Certaldo Basso, ☎ 0571/ 668188), closed Tuesday, serves tasty light lunches and delectable sweets.

Dining and Lodging

$$–$$$ ✕🏠 **Osteria del Vicario.** In the historic center, this is a full-service stop for the weary traveler. Here you can have a coffee or a glass of wine,

stay for dinner, or even spend the night; next to the Palazzo Pretorio complex, what was once a monastery is now an upscale bar, restaurant, and inn. Five of the rooms are former monks' cells, decorated in a well-appointed (and most un-monkish) fashion; ten additional rooms are in a building nearby. Traditional and innovative Tuscan cooking is served elegantly along with a wide selection of wines in the restaurant ($$$$; closed Wednesday). In warm weather you can dine in the open-air cloister and enjoy a view of the countryside. ✉ *Via Rivellino 2, 50052,* ☎ *0571/668228,* FAX *0571/668676,* WEB *www.osteriadelvicario. it. 15 rooms. Restaurant, baby-sitting, Internet, no-smoking rooms; no air-conditioning. AE, DC, MC, V. Closed Jan.–Feb. EP.*

Shopping

WINE

Cantina Sociale Certaldo (✉ Via Agnoletti 97, just north of Certaldo city limits, ☎ 0571/667403), a typical wine cooperative, sells the local wine in bulk amounts (bring a container of at least 6 liters) as well as bottled wine from the region, which stretches over to Montalbano, up to Pontassieve, and down to Poggibonsi near Siena. This local wine, because it is intended to be consumed in a fairly short time, is a good table wine. Bulk wine is offered in red, white, and often rosé; local olive oil is also available. The cooperative is open Monday through Saturday 8:30–noon.

Livorno

③③ *50 km (31 mi) northwest of Certaldo, 187 km (116 mi) west of Florence.*

The ferry hub of Livorno is a gritty city with a long and interesting history. In the early Middle Ages, it alternately belonged to Pisa and then to Genova (Genoa). In 1421, Florence, seeking access to the sea, bought it. Cosimo I (1519–74) started construction of the harbor in 1571, putting Livorno on the map. After Ferdinando I de' Medici (1549–1609) proclaimed Livorno a free city, it became a haven for people suffering from religious persecution; Roman Catholics from England and Jews and Moors from Spain and Portugal, among others, settled here. The *Quattro Mori* (Four Moors), also known as the Monument to Ferdinando I, commemorates this. (The statue of Ferdinand I dates from 1595, the bronze Moors by Pietro Tacca from the 1620s.)

In the following centuries, and particularly in the 18th, Livorno boomed as a port. In the 19th century, the town drew a host of famous Britons, passing through on their Grand Tours. Livorno's prominence continued up to World War II, when it was heavily bombed. Much of Livorno's architecture therefore now postdates the war, and it's somewhat difficult to imagine what it might have looked liked. Livorno has recovered from the war, however, as her influence in shipping—particularly container shipping—continues.

Most of Livorno's artistic treasures date from the 17th century and aren't all that interesting unless you dote on obscure baroque artists. (However, Livorno's most famous native artist, Amedeo Modigliani (1884–1920), was of much more recent vintage.

There may not be much in the way of art, but it's still worth strolling around the city—the **Mercato Nuovo,** which has been around since 1894, sells all sorts of fruits, vegetables, grains, meat, and fish. Outdoor markets nearby are also chock-full of local color. The presence of Camp Darby, an American military base just outside of town, accounts for the availability of many American products.

If you have time, Livorno is at least worth a stop for lunch or dinner.

Dining

$–$$ ✕ **Cantina Nardi.** It's only open for lunch, and it's well off the beaten
path even if it is very much in the center of Livorno's shopping district. But getting here is worth the trouble: this tiny place, lined with
bottles of wine, has a small menu that changes daily, a superb wine
list, and gregarious staff. Their *baccalà alla livornese* (deep-fried salt
cod served with chickpeas) is succulently crisp; their soups, such as ribollita, are very soothing. ✉ *Via Cambini 6/8,* ☎ *0586/808006. MC,
V. Closed Sun. No dinner.*

CITIES WEST OF FLORENCE A TO Z

*To research prices, get advice from other travelers, and book travel ar-
rangements, visit www.fodors.com.*

AIRPORTS

The largest airports in the region are Pisa's Aeroporto Galileo Galilei
and Florence's Peretola (officially Aeroporto A. Vespucci).
➤ AIRPORT INFORMATION: **Aeroporto A. Vespucci** (known as Peretola;
☎ 055/3061700). **Aeroporto Galileo Galilei** (☎ 050/500707, WEB
www.pisa-airport.com).

BUS TRAVEL

Most of the cities covered here do have bus stations, but service is often
sporadic or complicated; it's easier to take the train to Pisa, Prato, Pistoia, Lucca, Montecatini Terme, Livorno, and Empoli, where service
is regular and trains run frequently. Pescia is an easy bus ride from the
train station at Montecatini Terme; you can purchase bus tickets at the
station at the news vendor. San Miniato and environs are best reached
by car, as service is limited.

CAR RENTALS

➤ AGENCIES: **Avis** (✉ Sant'Anna, Via Luporini 1411/a, Lucca, ☎ 0583/
513614). **Hertz** (✉ Via Montegrappa 208, Prato, ☎ 0574/527774; ✉
Aeroporto Galileo Galilei, Pisa, ☎ 050/49187; ✉ c/o Garage Olimpia,
Via Manin 8, Montecatini Terme, ☎ 0572/72946).

CAR TRAVEL

The A1 connects Florence to Prato; for Pistoia, Montecatini, and
Lucca, follow signs for Firenze Nord, which connects to the A11. For
Empoli, Pisa, and hill towns west, take the FI-PI-LI superstrada from
Scandicci (just outside Florence).

Renting a car is the best way to see the cities west of Florence, as many
of them are not on train lines or are served by buses that run sporad-
ically. Prato, Pistoia, Montecatini Terme, Lucca, and Pisa are especially
easy to travel between because they are all off the A1. The other cities
are along secondary two-lane roads.

EMERGENCIES

Many of the smaller towns post the name and address of late-night
pharmacies, which are open on a rotating basis, in the windows of the
tourist information centers as well as at individual pharmacies. Pharmacies that hang the big green cross above their doorways—most
do—light up the sign when the pharmacy is open.
➤ EMERGENCY SERVICES: **Ambulance** (☎ 118). **Carabinieri** (federal
military police; ☎ 112). **Emergencies** (☎ 113). **Fire** (☎ 115).

MAIL AND SHIPPING

➤ POST OFFICE: **Lucca** (✉ Via Vallisneri 2).

➤ INTERNET CAFÉS: **Internet Train** (WEB www.internettrain.it; IT.Empoli, ✉ Via Cavour 5/9, Empoli, ☎ no phone; IT.Prato.BarCiardi, ✉ Piazza Ciardi 16, Prato, ☎ 0574/22238; IT.Prato.Garibaldi, ✉ Via Garibaldi 102, Prato, ☎ 0574/31912; IT.Prato.Repubblica, ✉ Viale della Repubblica 284, Prato, ☎ 0574/596764).

TRAIN TRAVEL

Trains from Rome and Milan run regularly to Florence, which serves as the hub for many connections, such as those going to Prato, Pistoia, Montecatini, Lucca, Empoli, Pisa, and Livorno. Empoli is easily reached via train, but the surrounding towns—Certaldo, Castlefiorentino, San Miniato—are not.

Trains from the main station at Santa Maria Novella in Florence run regularly to Prato, Pistoia, Montecatini, and Lucca, which are all on the same line. Trains from Florence to Empoli and Pisa, on the same line, run frequently as well.

➤ TRAIN LINES: **FS Information** (☎ 147/888088 toll-free within Italy, WEB www.fs-on-line.com or www.trenitalia.it).

TRAVEL AGENCIES

➤ AGENCIES: **Azienda Promozione Turistica Montecatini/Vadlinievole** (✉ Viale Verdi 66/68, Montecatini Terme, ☎ 0572/772244).

VISITOR INFORMATION

➤ TOURIST INFORMATION: **Castelfiorentino** (✉ Via Costituente, ☎ 0571/64602). **Certaldo** (☎ 0571/661211 or 0571/661241). **Empoli** (✉ Piazza Farinata degli Uberti 9, ☎ 0571/76115). **Lucca** (✉ Piazzale Verdi, ☎ 0583/419689, WEB www.lucca.turismo.toscana.it). **Montecatini Terme** (✉ Viale Verdi 66–68, ☎ 0572/772244). **Montelupo** (☎ 0571/518993). **Pescia** (✉ Località Pietrabuona Castello 118, ☎ 0572/408292). **Pisa** (✉ Via Cammeo 2, ☎ 050/560464). **Pistoia** (✉ Palazzo dei Vescovi, ☎ 0573/21622). **Prato** (✉ Piazza delle Carceri 15, ☎ 0574/24112). **San Miniato** (✉ Piazza del Popolo 3, ☎ 0571/42745). **Vinci** (✉ Via delle Torre 11, ☎ FAX 0571/567930).

5   CHIANTI

Blessedly compact, Chianti has hardly a hillside without something enriching—culturally, aesthetically, or gastronomically. Snuggled into the hills between Florence and Siena, Chianti is dotted with delightful villages and medieval castles. And graced as it is with its particular combination of sun, soil, and slopes, Chianti has produced some of Italy's best red wine and olive oil for thousands of years.

Updated by
Patricia Rucidlo

IN CHIANTI, TWO SHAPES on the landscape come into focus immediately. Country roads wind around hilltops that often appear to catch and hold on to the clouds. And straight lines in the planted vineyards, fields, and orchards turn those curving hills into a patchwork of colors and textures that has inspired artists and delighted travelers for centuries. It's an enticing landscape, one that invites you to follow those roads to see where they go. Perhaps you'll come to a farmhouse selling splendid olive oil or the region's Chianti Classico wine; or perhaps you'll visit a medieval country church (*pieve*), an art-filled abbey (*badia* or *abbazia*), a fortress (*castello*), or a restaurant where a flower-bedecked terrace offers respite from the summer heat as well as a spectacular panorama.

It's hard to imagine that this gentle area was once the battleground of warring Sienese and Florentine armies, but until Florence finally defeated Siena in 1550, these enchanting walled cities were strategic defensive outposts in a series of seemingly never-ending wars. Since the 1960s, many British and northern Europeans have relocated here: they've been drawn to the unhurried life, balmy climate, and picturesque villages. They've bought and restored farmhouses, many given up by the young heirs who decided not to continue life on the farm and instead found work in cities. There are so many Britons, in fact, that the area has been nicknamed Chiantishire. But don't let this be a deterrent to a visit: there's lots of Chianti to go around, and it remains strongly Tuscan in character.

Pleasures and Pastimes

Biking

In the spring, summer, and fall, bicyclists are as much a part of the landscape as the cypress trees. A drive on any steep Chianti road takes you past groups of bikers peddling up and down endless hills. Many are on weeklong organized tours, but it's also possible to rent bikes for jaunts in the countryside or to join afternoon or day minitours. Most Tuscan roads are in excellent condition, though often narrow, winding, and steep. That said, be cautious—especially as some of the drivers on these narrow, twisting roads may have just stopped at a vineyard for a tasting.

Dining

Chianti restaurants serve seasonal Tuscan dishes typical to the entire region, but they also include some local specialties such as *pici*—a long, thick noodle. In most cases, however, menus are similar to those found in Florence. The pecorino (sheep's-milk cheese) produced in these parts is particularly good and should be sampled at every opportunity. (Don't confuse the cheese here with its better known and coarser cousin, pecorino romano.) As for the wine: well, some of Italy's greatest wines are produced in Chianti. They pair marvelously with the area's ubiquitous grilled meats.

Most restaurants in the countryside have terraces for dining in good weather and large picture windows for captivating views. Though many restaurants take credit cards, quite often village *trattorie* (trattorias) and roadside *osterie* (basic, down-to-earth taverns) don't. Lunch is usually served from 12:30 to 2:30, and many bars and trattorie now offer a quick plate of pasta and salad for lunch. If you decide to go all out and order a *primo* (first course), *secondo* (second course), and a *dolce* (dessert or sweet), you might want to operate on local siesta time, especially if you've tested a Chianti. Dinner can start as early as 7:30, but most Italians consider dining before 9 PM uncivilized. During the high season, advanced booking is *always* recommended.

CATEGORY	COST*
$$$$	over €18
$$$	€13–€18
$$	€8–€13
$	under €8

Prices are for a second course (secondo piatto).

Lodging

Agriturismo (agritourism) may be a good choice for those who want a more rustic holiday. In the Chianti countryside, such accommodations range from a farmhouse turned into an inn to entire medieval villages or grand villas that have been purchased by developers and turned into resorts with tennis courts, swimming pools, and fancy restaurants. A stay on a working farm offers a quick immersion in simple country life, while villas and village developments offer the joys of gentrified country living.

Small hotels and *pensioni* (pensions) abound in Chianti towns teeming with small shops, street markets, and lively *piazze* (squares). But be prepared in your rambles, for many lodgings in Chianti are booked far in advance, especially in the height of summer—when you'll also discover that air-conditioning is a rarity.

CATEGORY	COST*
$$$$	over €175
$$$	€125–€175
$$	€75–€125
$	under €75

All prices are for two people in a standard double room, including tax and service.

Vineyards

Those picturesque vineyards on the Chianti hillsides are not cinematic backdrops; they are working farms, and when fall comes and their grapes are harvested and processed, they produce that world-famous *vino rosso* (red wine) that has been complementing Tuscan food for ages. Chianti's heritage dates back thousands of years, but the borders that define Chianti Classico weren't officially drawn until 1932. The Chianti region is actually surprisingly large, stretching from Pistoia, north of Florence, to Montalcino, south of Siena. (It includes all the areas where various types of Chianti grapes are grown.)

Chianti Classico is at the heart of the Chianti region. Its *gallo nero* (black rooster) logo dates from the 12th century, when the rooster was the symbol of the Chianti League, a military alliance that defended the Florentine border against Siena. Now that rooster signifies some of the highest-quality wines in the entire Chianti region.

Wine tasting lures travelers who want to give their eyes a rest after looking at all those halos in the churches and museums of Florence and Siena. Most of the vineyards have figured this out and offer direct sales and samplings of their products. Some have roadside stands, and others have elaborate sampling rooms in which snacks are served. Tourist-information offices in most Chianti towns have maps to guide you through an itinerary of vineyard hopping.

Exploring Chianti

By far the best way to discover Chianti is by car, as its beauty often reveals itself along the road less traveled. But Chianti is not as spontaneous a place for exploration as it used to be. Even though area farmers are subdividing their barns and calling them *agriturismi*, rooms are still at a premium, particularly during high season, which now runs from the end of March to mid-November.

Chianti overflows with people who also have come to take in the fresh air, inviting *enoteche* (wine bars), and fragrant trattorie. You certainly can rent a bicycle, stop the car at an interesting fork in the road, or go for a stroll. But don't count on taking off by bicycle, car, or foot in the morning and then being able to find a romantic hideaway to spend the night—reserve well in advance.

Numbers in the text correspond to numbers in the margin and on the Chianti map.

Great Itineraries

An itinerary can give you the big picture, but it's also important to look for the little picture and to know that if you see something that looks interesting, it's often a good idea to turn the wheel, head down the road, and check it out. Beautiful cypress-lined paths for walking, curving roads for biking, friendly residents for asking directions, and an abundance of fresh air and country smells await you.

IF YOU HAVE 3 DAYS

Leaving from Florence on Day 1, explore **San Donato in Poggio** ⑧ and surroundings, including **Passignano** ⑦ (even if its abbey is closed, as the town is set in stunning countryside) or ▦ **Barberino Val d'Elsa** ⑤, and conclude with a ramble to Sant'Appiano and a miniature reproduction of a a famous Florentine cupola. Spend Day 2 exploring the hamlets and vineyards in the hills off the Strada Chiantigiana (S222): **Greve in Chianti** ⑨, an attractive market town with a piazza lined with wine bars, cafés, and boutiques; tiny **Panzano** ⑩; **Castellina in Chianti** ⑪, an equally charming town with a lively main street full of enoteche; ▦ **Radda in Chianti** ⑫, a small wine town and just as enchanting; and **Volpaia,** a lost-in-time hilltop castle.

On Day 3, go south to **Montalcino** ⑮, for some wine tasting and a walk through the streets, and **Montepulciano** ⑯, another architectural gem. Head back north to **Castelnuovo Berardenga** ⑭ and enjoy an *aperitivo* (aperitif) in the charming main piazza.

When to Tour Chianti

In summer, the peak season, hotels and restaurants fill up and foreign license plates and rental cars cram the roads. There's a reason for the crush: summer is a glorious time to be driving in the hills and sitting on terraces.

Summer is not, however, the best time for biking. Temperatures, particularly in July and August, can soar to unbearable highs. It's better to plan bike tours for the spring or fall, when the heat is not so intense and the likelihood of cool breezes becomes a distinct possibility. Spring can be especially spectacular, with blooming poppy fields, bursts of yellow *ginestra* (broom), and wild irises growing by the side of the road. Fall is somewhat more soothing, when all those colors typically associated with Tuscany—burnt siena, warm ochers, mossy forest greens—predominate.

In winter, you might wonder who invented the term "sunny Italy"; the panoramas, however, are still beautiful, even with overcast skies, chill-

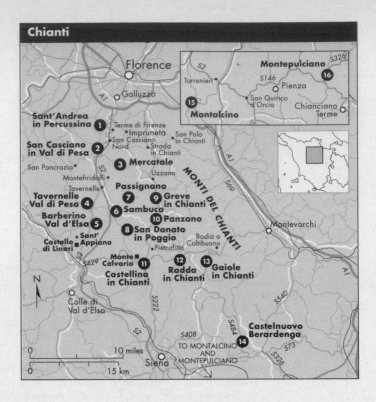

Chianti

ing winds, and, sometimes, depending upon where you are, a sprinkling of snow. Many hotels, agriturismi, wine estates, and restaurants close November through March.

WESTERN CHIANTI

Just beyond Florence's reach are magnificently preserved country churches, abbeys, and little-visited towns that make for perfect jaunts and offer relief from taking in too much art. But there's art to be had as well, such as at Badia a Passignano, which shelters the 15th-century *Last Supper* by Domenico and Davide Ghirlandaio.

Western Chianti also offers affordable, relaxed country lodging with easy access to Florence. The Certosa interchange provides entrance to the area with a choice of two roads—the Florence–Siena superstrada (no number), which is a four-lane, divided road with exits that allow you to weave in and out of the countryside, and the S2, the ancient Roman Via Cassia, a paved road since 154 BC. The superstrada is more direct, but it often has a lot of traffic, especially on Sunday evening, when Italians return from weekends in the countryside or at the beach. Keep in mind that roads often lack shoulders in these parts and that gas stations are rarely open on Sunday.

Sant'Andrea in Percussina

❶ *15 km (9 mi) south of Florence.*

Niccolò Machiavelli (1469–1527) lived in this tiny village when he was exiled from Florence in 1513 by the Medici. An unassuming building called **L'Albergaccio** (loosely, "the nasty hotel") because of its humble origins is where Machiavelli wrote *The Prince* and *Discourses*. A small, rarely open **Museo Machiavelli** shows his actual studio, kitchen, and bedroom just as they looked when he lived here. You might be able to gain entry by heading to the Taverna Machiavelli, across the road, where he went when in need of friendship and food. ⊠ *Via dei Scopeti,* ☎ *no phone.* ☞ *Free.*

The small Romanesque church of **Sant'Andrea,** perched on a hillside near L'Albergaccio, is rarely open but is worth a closer look. ⊠ *Via dei Scopeti,* ☎ *no phone.* ☞ *Free.*

OFF THE BEATEN PATH

AMERICAN MILITARY CEMETERY – About 8 km (5 mi) south of Florence on the road to Siena is one of two American cemeteries in Italy (the other is in Nettuno). It contains 4,402 bodies of Americans who died in Italy during World War II. On a gentle hill, the sea of simple crosses and Stars of David bearing only name, date of death, and state seems to stretch endlessly. At the top of the hill are a place for reflection and large mosaic maps depicting the Allied assault in 1943. The two fronts—called the Gothic Line and the Gustav Line—are vividly rendered. ⊠ *From Florence, take Via Cassia (S2) south to Località Scopeti,* ☎ *055/2020020.* ☞ *Free.* ⊙ *Weekdays 8–5, weekends 9–5.*

En Route If you continue on Via Cassia toward San Casciano in Val di Pesa, you will find the tiny hamlet of Spedaletto and the church of **Santa Maria di Casavecchia,** where there's a terra-cotta *Assumption* by Benedetto Buglioni (1461–1521).

Dining

$–$$$ ✕ **Taverna Machiavelli.** Across the road from Machiavelli's residence, L'Albergaccio, this place was the old neighborhood tavern. Five centuries later, it's a fine restaurant with a typical Tuscan menu and an extensive wine list. You can have a *merenda* (afternoon snack) of *bruschetta* (grilled bread rubbed with garlic, brushed with olive oil, and topped with fresh tomatoes) and a glass of wine (their own Chianti, of course). Proprietors of the restaurant will take patrons across the street to see the Museo Machiavelli. ⊠ *Via dei Scopeti,* ☎ *055/828471. MC, V. Closed Mon.–Tues.*

San Casciano in Val di Pesa

❷ *4 km (2½ mi) south of Sant'Andrea in Percussina, 18 km (13 mi) south of Florence (take San Casciano exit, first exit south of Florence on Florence–Siena superstrada).*

Parts of the original mid-14th-century walls and gates of San Casciano in Val di Pesa—one of the larger towns in Chianti—are still standing. They serve to weave the old and new parts of the town together. A large wooded city park with parking is near the city center.

The oratory of **Santa Maria sul Prato,** next to the remains of one of the city gates, dates from 1335. The church contains a restored crucifix by Sienese artist Simone Martini (1280/85–1344). A carved marble pulpit depicting the Annunciation was made by Giovanni di Balduccio da Pisa, a student of Andrea Pisano (1290/1295–1349). For entrance, ring the bell at the Misericordia, which is next door to the oratory. ⊠ *Via Morrocchesi 19,* ☎ *055/820023.* ☞ *Free.*

The **Museo d'Arte Sacra** in the church of **Santa Maria del Gesù** contains many works originally in small country churches in the area. The pieces, including a Sienese wood crucifix and four bronze crosses (circa 14th–15th centuries) and the carved pedestal of a marble baptismal font dating from the early 12th century, were brought here to protect them from thieves and the elements. ⊠ *Via Roma 31,* ☎ *055/8229444.* ⊡ *Free.* ⊙ *Oct.–Apr., Sat. 4:30–7, Sun. 10–12:30 and 4–7; May–Sept., Sat. 5–7:30, Sun. 10–12:30 and 4–7.*

En Route   If you're traveling from San Casciano in Val di Pesa to Mercatale and feel the need for some art, stop off about 5 km (3 mi) along the Via Cassia and visit the **Chiesa dei Cappuccini**; the church has a terra-cotta *Adoration of the Child* by Andrea della Robbia (1435–1525/28), and it's worth a detour. Continue southeast toward Calcinaia and visit the **capela dello Strozzo** (Chapel of the Strozzi). Inside is a fresco of the Pietà, much restored, attributed to Agnolo Bronzino (1503–72).

Dining and Lodging

$$$$ ╳ **La Tenda Rossa.** What began as a simple pizzeria some years ago has turned into one of Italy's finest restaurants. The menu changes frequently but offers such treats as *minestra di cappelletti di baccalà* (a delicate soup with tiny pillows of pasta stuffed with dried cod). The sophisticated wine list is comprehensive and pairs beautifully with the food. ⊠ *Cerbaia Val di Pesa, 5 km (3 mi) west of San Casciano in Val di Pesa,* ☎ *055/826132. Reservations essential. AE, DC, MC, V. Closed Sun. No lunch Mon.*

$–$$$ ╳ **Cantinetta del Nonno.** Walk through the front-room *salumeria* (delicatessen), where you can buy prosciutto and other cured meats, then past an open kitchen, and then into the back dining room. If it's warm, you can sit outside under the tented terrace lined with impatiens. The menu offers typical Tuscan treats as well as slightly less typical dishes such as *fusilli con pesto di arugula* (fusilli with an arugula pesto). Service is gracious and prompt. ⊠ *Via 4 Novembre,* ☎ *055/820570. MC, V. Closed Wed. and Nov.*

$$ ╳▥ **Antica Posta.** It was once an old post house where travelers stopped to exchange their horses as they traveled the old Roman road between Florence and Siena. Since then, this 400-year-old building has been a hotel as well as a restaurant ($$–$$$) for more than 150 years. The rooms are basic and comfortable. Because the current owner's father is a butcher, you can count on the *bistecca alla fiorentina* (grilled local Chianina beef). ⊠ *Piazza Zannoni 1–3,* ☎ *055/822313,* ℻ *055/822278. 10 rooms. Restaurant, fans, cable TV, dry cleaning, laundry service, some pets allowed; no air-conditioning. AE, MC, V. Closed Tues. CP.*

$$ ╳▥ **Castello Il Corno.** A remodeled 13th-century castle and Renaissance-style villa now feel like a luxury hotel in the middle of a farm. There are two rooms in the castles itself; the 17 apartments are in cottages with 19th-century furnishings. More than 10,000 olive trees dot the property, which also produces wine, including a high-quality *vin santo* (sweet dessert wine). The restaurant's dishes, based on family recipes, are composed of fresh ingredients from the farm's garden. During high season (July through September), a minimum stay of one week is required. ⊠ *Via di Malafrasca 64, 50026,* ☎ *055/8248009,* ℻ *055/ 8248035. 2 rooms, 17 apartments. Restaurant, cable TV, 2 pools, baby-sitting, meeting rooms, some pets allowed; no air-conditioning. AE, MC, V. Closed early Jan.–Feb.*

$–$$ ▥ **La Ginestra.** This *agriturismo* 10 km (6 mi) south of San Casciano makes and sells organic pasta, salami, prosciutto, honey, wine, and olive oil. You can stay in small houses on the grounds. The villa il Mandorlo has its own garden and can sleep 12 people. All apartments have white walls and heavy, rustic wooden furniture. A large barn can serve as a conference room or a large-scale party space. Horseback riding and tennis are available nearby. Even during high season, you are welcome to stay as little as one night if you want. ⊠ *Via Pergolata 3, Località Santa Cristina, San Pancrazio 50020,* ☎ ℻ *055/8248196. 6 apartments, 1 villa, for 2–12 people. Restaurant,* kitchens, refrigerators, pool, baby-sitting, laundry service, meeting rooms, free parking, some pets allowed; no air-conditioning, no room phones, no room TVs. MC, V.

Mercatale

❸ 6 km (4 mi) southeast of San Casciano in Val di Pesa, 25 km (16 mi) south of Florence.

As its name implies, Mercatale began in 1237 when the mayor of a neighboring town ordered the construction of a public square to serve as a marketplace for his court. The city center doesn't have much to offer in the way of important art, but its villa-lined roads make for pleasant country strolls.

Lodging

$–$$ 🔲 **Salvadonica.** This friendly place in Mercatale has owners who will take those staying here on tours of area vineyards and olive groves. Each well-cared-for apartment has a small kitchen. A communal room surrounded by glass functions as the lobby. If you're interested in the real country Italian experience, there's even a boccie ball court. Another bonus: the pool has hydromassage. ✉ Via Grevigiana 82, 50024, ☎ 055/8218039, 𝔽𝔸𝕏 055/8218043, 𝕎𝔼𝔹 www.salvadonica.com. 5 rooms, 11 apartments. Fans, kitchenettes, refrigerators, tennis court, pool, billiards, boccie, playground, free parking, some pets allowed; no air-conditioning, no room TVs. AE, DC, MC, V. Closed Nov.–Mar. CP.

Tavarnelle Val di Pesa

❹ 13 km (8 mi) southwest of Mercatale, 28 km (15 mi) south of Florence, 12 km (7½ mi) south of San Casciano in Val di Pesa.

The name Tavarnelle comes from *tabernulae*, which were the stopover villages between Florence and Siena for travelers on their way to Rome. Its location kept it out of the fierce battles between Florence and Siena, which explains the absence of towers and fortifications. Today Tavarnelle is a busy center—it's a good place to shop and is centrally located for side trips.

San Pietro in Bossolo, one of the most beautiful country churches in the area, is just outside the city center. Dating from the 10th century, it has a 14th-century marble sanctuary and a 16th-century portico. The bell tower dates from the mid-1800s. Inside the small attached museum is *Virgin Mary with Child and Saints,* by Coppo di Marcovaldo (active 1260–80), an early and important example of the Florentine school. ✉ Via della Pieve 19, ☎ 055/8077255. 🎫 Free. ☉ Nov.–Mar., weekends 3:30–6; Apr.–Oct. weekends 4:30–7.

At the same spot where you see the sign for Sambuca near the superstrada you will also see an unimposing monastery on the south side of the road. This church of **Santa Maria del Carmine,** was built in 1466 and is near the tiny hamlet of Morrocco. Inside is a terra-cotta Annunciation from the school of Andrea della Robbia, but the main attraction is the group of industrious Carmelite nuns from Australia. When they came here in 1982, they rescued the old monastery, which had fallen into 200 years' worth of disrepair. It's worth making sure you arrive at 5 any afternoon, when the nuns sing their vespers service with pure, beautiful voices. The pews are filled for Sunday and holiday masses with appreciative Italians and an English-speaking community who come from a wide area. The nuns also make and sell products such as perfumed candles, creams, and lotions using traditional formulas. ✉ Via di Morrocco 35, ☎ 055/8076067. 🎫 Free. ☉ Daily 9–7.

Dining and Lodging

$$$$ ✕ **Borgo Antico.** Some restaurants have wine tastings; this one offers olive-oil tastings during the olive harvest season (usually in October and November). The owner keeps several bottles of locally produced extra-virgin olive oil for you to sample. All the pasta is made in-house—the ravioli *con melone* (sauced with creamy cantaloupe) is one of the prize choices—and the desserts will probably stay in your memory for quite a while, especially the tart lavished with figs and hazelnuts. ⊠ *Via Roma 55,* ☎ *055/8076180. AE, DC, MC, V. Closed Wed.*

$$ ✕ **Osteria della Gramola.** With its delicately stenciled walls and rustic tables and chairs, you might feel as if you've entered someone's well-appointed cottage in the woods. This family-run eatery serves up Tuscan food and does it admirably well. The *farinata con verdure* (a type of cornmeal mush served with vegetables) is a real treat, as is the *frittatina con cavolfiore* (an omeletlike dish with cauliflower). Order anything with truffles on it, marvel at the extensive wine list, and save room for dessert; the *torta cioccolata* (chocolate torte) is extraordinary, as is the *torta con formaggio* (cheesecake). ⊠ *Via delle Fonti 1,* ☎ ꜰᴀx *055/8050321. MC, V. No lunch Tues.*

$$$ ▥ **Fattoria Querceto.** Each of the large, two-floor apartments here has a fireplace and a living room. They also come with games for children. The kitchens are modern, and some of the apartments have separate dining rooms; all have private outside areas and antique furniture. You can taste and buy the wine, olive oil, honey, jellies, and eggs that are produced here. Television is available for a fee of €8/day. The message on the phone is in Italian only; press 2 to get directions to the Fattoria. ⊠ *Il Querceto, 53011,* ☎ *055/8070135,* ꜰᴀx *055/8070171. 6 apartments. Kitchens, pool, mountain bikes, library, laundry service, some pets allowed. AE, MC, V.*

$$ ▥ **Park Hotel Chianti.** Don't let the fact that it's close to the highway turn you off. This is a great place to stop if you've been in the car all day and want new-world amenities instead of old-world charm. The hotel, at the Tavernelle exit of the Florence–Siena superstrada, has uninspired motel furniture, but it's impeccable and the rooms have sound-proof windows; it also has a beautiful pool and gardens. ⊠ *Località Pontenuovo, 50028,* ☎ *055/8070106,* ꜰᴀx *055/8070121,* ᴡᴇʙ *www. parkhotelchianti.com. 43 rooms. In-room safes, minibars, cable TV, pool, Internet. AE, MC, V. Closed early Dec.–early Jan. CP.*

$$ ▥ **Sovigliano.** The affable Bicego family runs this 12th-century farmhouse in Tavarnelle. They've kept the agriturismo aspect of the operation to a minimum, maintaining the natural gardens filled with herbs, wildflowers, and pines. The firm beds and contemporary bathrooms are a happy anachronism. The pool, surrounded by fragrant rosemary bushes, offers a perfect place to relax. ⊠ *Via Strada Magliano 9, 50028,* ☎ *055/8076217,* ꜰᴀx *055/8050770,* ᴡᴇʙ *www.sovigliana.com. 4 rooms, 4 apartments. Refrigerators, pool, bicycles, Internet; no air-conditioning in some rooms. MC, V. CP.*

$ ▥ **Albergo Vittoria.** Though it's on a busy street, quadruple-pane soundproof windows covered with heavy drapes help you forget that fact. Rooms are large, the furniture is modern, and the bathrooms are new. Katia Torresi, the hands-on owner, works to make sure you are happy. She provides all kinds of tips for travelers and even shares her computer if you need to send or receive e-mail. ⊠ *Via Roma 57, 50028,* ☎ ꜰᴀx *055/8076180. 7 rooms. Fans, cable TV, baby-sitting, parking (fee), some pets allowed, no-smoking rooms; no air-conditioning. AE, DC, MC, V. CP.*

$ ▥ **La Villa.** You ring the bell at the front door, walk directly into a garden, and find the hotel in a restored 16th-century convent on the other side of a field. There's a rustic, country style to the six simply furnished apartments, which are situated around an enclosed courtyard filled with fruit trees. The young owners are enthusiastic about their work and are happy to act as guides for you. There's a minimum stay of a week during high season and a minimum of three days the rest of the year. ⊠ *Strada Romita 42, 50028,* ☎ FAX *055/8070105. 6 apartments. Pool, some pets allowed; no air-conditioning, no room phones. No credit cards.*

Barberino Val d'Elsa

⑤ *2½ km (1½ mi) southwest of Tavarnelle Val di Pesa, 28 km (17 mi) south of Florence.*

The medieval wall surrounding this town has two gates—one faces Florence and the other Siena. Via Francesco da Barberino connects the two and is the main street of this town, which offers glorious views of the surrounding hills and is a perfect jumping-off point for countryside explorations. The town dates from the 11th century, the walls from the 14th. The 13th-century Renaissance **Palazzo Pretorio,** in Piazza Barberini, is decorated with the coats of arms of the *podestà* (judges) who adjudicated over civil and criminal cases during the Middle Ages and Renaissance. ⊠ *Piazza Barberini.*

A tiered walkway from Piazza Barberini leads to Via Vittorio Veneto, site of the church of **San Bartolomeo.** It's worth a visit to admire its 14th-century frescoes. ⊠ *Via Vittorio Veneto,* ☎ *no phone.* 🎫 *Free.* ☉ *Sun. 9–1.*

OFF THE
BEATEN PATH

SANT'APPIANO – Signs on the Via Cassia (S2) south of Barberino Val d'Elsa lead to this lovely Romanesque church, parts of which date to the 11th century. The interior contains some fragments of a fresco of the Madonna and Child by an anonymous master that date to the middle of the 15th century. There are also 14th- and 15th-century fresco fragments from the schools of Giotto and Ghirlandaio; a tomb dating to 1331 in the right nave holds the remains of Gherarduccio Gheradini, one of the church's patrons. There's also a two-room museum that's open weekends 4–8. The road here actually takes you to the back of the church—the front faces an intriguing set of ancient stone stairs that descends to the village of Petrognano below. Rising in the grass field between the road and the stairs are four mysterious sandstone pillars—the remains from a 5th-century baptistery that was destroyed by an earthquake in the early 19th century. ⊠ *Via Sant'Appiano 1 (8 km [5 mi] south of Barberino Val d'Elsa; follow signs on Via Cassia [S2]),* ☎ *055/8075519.* 🎫 *Donations accepted.* ☉ *Daily by appointment.*

CASTELLO DI LINARI – This nearly abandoned village has a commanding position atop a hill. On a wall beyond the Gothic entrance, across the street from Via Santa Maria 11, is an Etruscan advertisement inviting travelers and shepherds to stop at Linari for food and shelter. Today the ruins of the castle make for an interesting stop along the road during a walk. ⊠ *1 km (½ mi) south of Sant'Appiano (follow signs).*

En Route Northward from Castello di Linari in the direction of Barberino Val d'Elsa, a sign for Semifonte Petrognano leads to the **Cappella di San Michele Arcangelo** (Chapel of St. Michael the Archangel), one of the biggest surprises in Tuscany. Just 2 km (1 mi) past Semifonte Petrognano you will see ahead of you what appears to be the Duomo of Florence. Here in the Chianti countryside is a 1:8 scale model of Brunelleschi's dome built in 1597 and designed by Santi di Tito (1536–1603). The "cupola" is in disrepair, but still a glorious sight, surrounded by cypress trees. The castle and village of Semifonte Petrognano were totally destroyed by the Florentines in 1202 and orders were given not to build any new buildings. Nearly 400 years passed before this small chapel, celebrating Florence, was built. ⊠ *2 km (1 mi) west of Semifonte Petrognano,* ☎ *no phone.* ✆ *Free.* ☉ *Contact Florence tourist office for hrs.*

Sambuca

❻ *6 km (4 mi) east of Tavarnelle Val di Pesa, 25 km (15 mi) south of Florence, 1 km (½ mi) west of the San Donato exit off the Florence–Siena superstrada.*

Next to the Pesa River, Sambuca itself is an unattractive industrial town, but its graceful arched bridge and riverside park make the 10-minute detour worth it. The **Ponte Romano** was built in 1069 as part of the Via Francigena that brought pilgrims from northern Europe to Rome. The bridge was partially destroyed during World War II and rebuilt later. Documents indicate that Leonardo da Vinci himself once walked across this bridge.

Lodging

$ ⊡ **Hotel Torricelle Zucchi.** This hotel is in a commercial area of Sambuca and has no eye appeal, but you're in central Chianti. It's a terrific place to use as a base, as Florence, Siena, San Gimignano, and even Pisa are within easy reach. The rooms and bathrooms are large, the price is low, and without too much begging you might convince owner Andrew McCauley to play a bit of Chopin on his baby grand piano in the lobby. ⊠ *Via B. Cellini 32, 50020,* ☎ *055/8071780,* ⅁⅃ *055/8071102. 13 rooms. Refrigerator, bar, laundry service; no air-conditioning in some rooms. MC, V. Closed last wk in Dec.–3rd wk in Jan. CP.*

Passignano

❼ *4 km (2½ mi) east of Sambuca, 29 km (18 mi) south of Florence.*

One of the finest and best-preserved works of art in Italy is in the refectory (dining hall) of the towering 11th-century **Badia a Passignano**: a stunningly massive, 21-ft-wide *Last Supper* (1476) by Domenico and Davide Ghirlandaio. The monastery's church of **San Michele Arcangelo**, also called San Piaggio, has a 13th-century sculpture of St. Michael slaying the dragon. All visits are conducted via 20-minute tours by the resident monks. At this writing the Badia is closed for restoration, but even if you can't get in to see the Last Supper, it's worth the drive to see its fairy-tale surroundings and to walk on the beautiful hillside. ⊠ *Passignano (about 7 km [4 mi] from Tavarnelle-Passignano exit off A1),* ☎ *055/8071622.* ✆ *Free; donations are encouraged.* ☉ *Monastery and church Sun. 3–5:30 PM.*

Dining

$–$$$ ✕ **La Scuderia.** Across the street from the Badia a Passignano, this traditional Tuscan restaurant specializes in country cooking, especially roast chicken and duck and stewed rabbit. And when you ask for house wine, that's literally what you're getting: the owners make their own. If you want to eat here on a Sunday, you must reserve. ⊠ *Passignano (about 7 km [4 mi] from Tavarnelle-Passignano exit off A1),* ☎ *055/8071623. No credit cards. Closed Thurs.*

San Donato in Poggio

❽ *5 km (3 mi) south of Passignano.*

Great care has been taken by the residents of San Donato in Poggio to ensure that this gem of a medieval city maintains its ancient qualities.

Cars aren't permitted in this perfectly preserved walled village, which is also free of neon signs and advertising posters. A village has existed on this site since 1033, when a fortified castle was built high on the hill between San Casciano in Val di Pesa and Colle di Val d'Elsa.

The original castle was destroyed during a conflict in 1289. A new wall was constructed immediately after the fighting ended, and it still stands, enclosing the city with two gates—one facing Siena and one facing Florence. The only remains of the original castle walls can be seen in the base of the present-day municipal bell tower. The main square, **Piazza Malaspina,** contains the Renaissance palazzo belonging to the Malaspina family as well as the 15th-century church of **Santa Maria delle Neve.**

The **Pieve di San Donato in Poggio,** just outside the town's walls, dates from 989, although the existing building is probably from the early 12th century. In the baptistery of this parish church is a baptismal font by Giovanni della Robbia that illustrates scenes from the life of St. John the Baptist. ⊠ *Via della Pieve 25,* ☎ *055/8072934.* ☜ *Free.* ⊘ *Hours vary; call ahead.*

Dining and Lodging

$$$–$$$$ ✕ **Il Paese dei Campanelli.** An old *cantina* (wine-storage building) surrounded by glorious gardens where summer meals are served houses one of Chianti's top restaurants. Typical Tuscan recipes fill the menu, but there are also some creative variations using exquisite ingredients, especially seasonal mushrooms. The duck comes rare, and the salads are works of art, but all the dishes are presented with artistry. Make reservations well in advance. ⊠ *Località Petrognano, 4 km (2½ mi) south of Barberino Val d'Elsa,* ☎ *055/8075318. Reservations essential. V. Closed Sun. No lunch.*

$–$$ ✕ **L'Archibugio.** Within the walls of Barberino Val d'Elsa, this place is great for a thin-crust pizza or a plate of inexpensively priced spaghetti. In summer you can dine on the covered terrace and enjoy a respite from the heat; in winter, you can eat inside, next to a comforting fireplace. Residents from surrounding towns eat here year-round. ⊠ *Via Vittorio Veneto 48,* ☎ *055/8075209. No credit cards. Closed Wed.*

$$$ ⊞ **Fattoria Casa Sola.** Near Barberino Val d'Elsa, this romantic agriturismo has views from each of its six eclectically furnished apartments. Each apartment has its own garden or terrace. The owners are ready to supply information about local cultural events and, with a group of six or more, also offer courses in painting, cooking, or photography. There is a one-week minimum for all stays. ⊠ *Località Le Cortine, Barberino Val d'Elsa 50021,* ☎ *055/8075028,* ℻ *055/8059194. 6 apartments. Pool, baby-sitting, laundry service, Internet, some pets allowed, free parking; no air-conditioning, no room phones, no room TVs. MC, V.*

$$$ ⊞ **La Spinosa.** The owners have organized a group of 17th-century farmhouses into an agriturismo and have dedicated their lives to helping produce perfect vacations. The buildings have been renovated, but they maintain their original character through a mix of Italian farmhouse furniture and antiques. The public spaces include a game room, library, and small bar. There is a two-night minimum stay. ⊠ *Via Le Masse 8, 50021,* ☎ *055/8075413,* ℻ *055/8066214,* ⅏ *www.laspinosa.it. 5 rooms, 4 suites. Pool, archery, volleyball, bar, library, recreation room, Internet, some pets allowed; no air-conditioning, no room phones. MC, V. Closed mid-Nov.–mid-Mar. MAP.*

$$ ⊞ **Il Paretaio.** This peaceful, extremely private retreat attracts the horsey set and offers riding lessons as well as trails. A chef comes daily with fresh coffee cakes for breakfast and prepares excellent dinners for the guests, who either eat in the farmhouse dining room or in the gar-

den. The six guest rooms are in the farmhouse. A one-week minimum stay is required. ⊠ *Località San Filippo, Barberino Val d'Elsa 50021,* ☎ *055/8059218,* ℻ *055/8059231,* 🌐 *www.ilparetaio.it. 6 rooms, 2 apartments. Restaurant, pool, horseback riding, Internet; no air-conditioning, no room phones. No credit cards. MAP.*

$$ 🍴 **Le Filigare.** This was one of Chianti's pioneer agriturismo operations, set in the middle of a beautiful vineyard in San Donato in Poggio. It's actually an entire medieval *borghetto* (village) that's been converted into a mellow, extremely private inn and filled with a combination of antique and modern furnishings. Le Filigare is known throughout the area for its excellent wine, oil, grappa, and vin santo, all of which can be tasted and purchased from its cellars. The minimum stay is one week. ⊠ *Località Le Filigare, 50020,* ☎ *055/8072796,* ℻ *055/755766. 7 apartments. Cable TV, tennis court, pool, sauna, mountain bikes, fishing, horseback riding, Ping-Pong, baby-sitting, playground, laundry facilities. AE, DC, MC, V.*

STRADA CHIANTIGIANA FROM FLORENCE

The Strada Chiantigiana (Chianti Road, S222) cuts through the center of Chianti; it's a much more winding drive than the more straightforward S2 and the superstrada. Here you are in the heartland, where both sides of the road are embraced by glorious panoramic views of vineyards, olive groves, castle towers, and even an occasional flock of sheep waiting (or sometimes not waiting) to cross the road. It gets crowded during the high season, but no one is in a hurry, and the slow pace gives you time to soak up the beautiful scenery.

Greve in Chianti

❾ *28 km (17½ mi) south of Florence.*

If there is a capital of Chianti, it is Greve, a friendly market town with no shortage of cafés, enoteche, and crafts shops along its pedestrian street. The sloping, asymmetrical **Piazza Matteotti** is an attractive arcade whose center holds a statue of the discoverer of New York harbor, Giovanni da Verrazano (circa 1480–1527). At the small end of the Piazza Matteotti is the church of **Santa Croce** (☎ no phone, 🎫 free). It has a triptych by Bicci di Lorenzo (1373–1452) and an *Annunciation* by an anonymous Florentine master that dates to the 14th century. The church is open daily 9–1 and 3–7.

A mile west of Greve in Chianti is the tiny hilltop hamlet of **Montefioralle**; it's the ancestral home of Amerigo Vespucci (1454–1512), the mapmaker, navigator, and explorer who named America. (His niece Simonetta may have been the model for Sandro Botticelli's *Birth of Venus*, painted sometime in the 1480s.)

OFF THE
BEATEN PATH

LAMOLE – This tiny village contains the **Chiesa di San Donato a Lamole,** a Romanesque church that was greatly modified in 1860; the only remnant of its earlier incarnation can be found in its simple facade. Inside is a 14th-century altarpiece of saints and the Madonna and Child, as well as a curious side chapel on the right that is decorated with rather garish 20th-century religious works.

Practically right next door to the Chiesa di San Donato is **Ristoro di Lamole** ($$;☎ 055/8547050), a bar–restaurant with superb panini and more-substantial fare. The *primi*, particularly any featuring game, are excellent. The desserts are made in-house and are some of the best in the area. The terrace, with its sweeping views of valleys and a glimpse of Panzano in the distance, makes the drive, via a maddeningly twisting road, worth it. ✉ *From Greve in Chianti, drive south on SS222 for about 1 km (½ mi); take a left and follow signs for Lamole.*

Dining and Lodging

$–$$ ✕ **Il Camineto.** Tuscan fare is served at this small, cozy country restaurant. The pasta is all homemade, and the *gnocchi ripieno ai funghi porcini* (potato dumplings stuffed with porcini mushrooms) are a real treat. There's a terrace for summer dining under the shade of lime trees. ✉ *Via della Montagnola 52,* ☎ *055/8588909. MC, V. Closed Tues. No lunch Mon.–Sat.*

$–$$ ✕ **Locanda il Gallo.** Terrific thin-crust pizzas come out of the wood-burning oven at this informal country restaurant about 4 km (2½ mi) north of Greve. The large dining rooms have stone walls and wood-beamed ceilings, and there's a veranda for dining outside in summer. ✉ *Via Lando Conti 16, Chiocchio,* ☎ *055/8572266. AE, DC, MC, V. Closed Tues.*

$$ ✕🏰 **Castello Vicchiomaggio.** Formerly a fortified castle, this building, now a prestigious wine estate with a tasting facility you can visit, dates from 956 (it was rebuilt during the Renaissance). Throughout the nine apartments and two farmhouses is wonderful heavy wooden furniture, in keeping with the estate's history. The restaurant ($$$) serves homemade pastas and specialties such as *stracotto*, beef cooked in the farm's own prize-winning Chianti Classico. ✉ *Via Vicchiomaggio 4, 50022,* ☎ *055/854079,* FAX *055/853911,* WEB *www.vicchiomaggio.it. 8 apartments, 2 farmhouses. Restaurant, in-room safes, kitchenettes, refrigerators, cable TV, pool; no air-conditioning. MC, V.*

$$$–$$$$ 🏰 **Villa Vignamaggio.** A historic estate contains a villa with guest rooms and apartments, as well as two small houses and a cottage. The villa, surrounded by manicured classical Italian gardens, dates from the 14th century but was restored in the 16th. It's reputedly the birthplace of Monna Lisa, the woman later made famous by Leonardo da Vinci. The staff can often prove unhelpful, but the place is so pretty, you might not notice. ✉ *Via Petriolo 5, Greve in Chianti, 50022,* ☎ *055/854661,* FAX *055/8544468,* WEB *www.vignamaggio.com. 2 rooms, 15 apartments, 1 cottage, 2 houses. Minibars, tennis court, 2 pools, playground, some pets allowed, no-smoking rooms. DC, MC, V. Closed late Dec.–early Jan.*

$$ 🏰 **Albergo del Chianti.** At a corner of the main piazza, this hotel has modernized rooms with contemporary, functional furniture and views over the piazza or out over neighborhood terraces and rooftops toward surrounding hills. The swimming pool and terrace, behind the hotel, are a nice surprise. ✉ *Piazza Matteotti 86, 50022,* ☎ *055/853 764,* FAX *055/853 763,* WEB *www.albergodelchianti.it. 16 rooms. Restaurant, minibars, cable TV, pool, bar. No credit cards. Closed late Dec.–early Jan. CP.*

$ 🏰 **Il Caseno.** Trees surround the farm of Patrizia Falciani, 1 km (½ mi) from Greve in Chianti. Apartments are comfortable and well furnished in typical country Tuscan style. Signora Falciani speaks no English but still manages to communicate with those who don't speak Italian. Washing machines, a barbecue, and a small but delightful pool are all available for guest use. Olive oil and wine are also sold here. ✉ *Via di Melazzano 5, 50022,* ☎ FAX *055/8544505,* FAX *055/2301003,* WEB *www.patriziafalciani.it. 7 apartments. Fans, kitchens, refrigerators, pool, babysitting, laundry facilities, Internet, free parking, some pets allowed; no air-conditioning. No credit cards.*

BACCHUS IN TUSCANY

USCANY IS ITALY'S CLASSIC WINE country. In addition to the world-famous Chianti, one of Italy's top wine exports, Tuscan winemakers produce other renowned wines. Many of these are recognizable by the DOCG (Denominazione di Origine Controllata e Garantita) or DOC (Denominazione di Origine Controllata) on their labels, notations that identify the wine within not only as coming from the officially delineated wine regions but also as adhering to rigorous standards of production. Don't be afraid to sample something that doesn't bear this label, however; Tuscans have been making wine for 25 centuries, and DOC or not, most of the winemakers here seem to know what they're doing.

Vino Nobile di Montepulciano, the "Noble Wine," lays claim to its aristocratic title by virtue of royal patronage and ancient history: the Etruscans were making wine here before Rome had even been founded. Much later, in 1669, England's William III sent a delegation to Montepulciano in order to procure this splendid wine. It was an appropriate choice: according to poet Francesco Redi, "*Montepulciano d'ogni vino è il re*" ("of all wine, Montepulciano is the king"). The less noble but no less popular **Rosso di Montepulciano,** a light, fruity DOC red, is also produced in the area.

With its velvety black berries and structured tannins, **Brunello di Montalcino** is no less sophisticated than Vino Nobile. The strain of the Sangiovese grape variety used to make it was developed in 1870 by a local winemaker in need of vines that would be better able to cope with windy weather. The wine became popular quickly and remained so—it had such success that in 1988 Italy's then-president Francesco Cossiga presided over the centennial or its first vintage. Brunello has a younger sibling, the DOC **Rosso di Montalcino.**

Not all of Tuscany's great wines are reds; in fact, many give the region's highest honors to a white wine, **Vernaccia di San Gimignano.** This golden wine is made from grapes native to Liguria, and it's thought that its name is a corruption of Vernazza, a village that's part of the Ligurian coast's Cinque Terre. Pope Martin IV (1281–85) used to like his with eel; you might try it with rabbit, sausage, or prosciutto and other cured meats.

To the foreigner, **Chianti** evokes Tuscany as readily as gondolas evoke Venice, but if you think Chianti is about straw-covered jugs and deadly headaches, think again. This firm, full-bodied, and powerful wine pressed from mostly Sangiovese grapes is the region's most popular, and it's easy to taste why. More difficult to understand is the difference between the many kinds of Chianti: this DOCG region has seven sub-regions, including Chianti Classico, the oldest wine-growing area of the region, whose wines can be identified by a *gallo nero* (black rooster) on the label. Each of these (Chianti Classico, Colli Fiorentini, Colli Senesi, Colli Aretini, Colline Pisane, Montalbano, and Rufina) has its own particularities, but the most noticeable—and costly—difference to keep in mind is that between regular Chianti and the *riserva* (reserve) stock, aged for at least four years.

Some Italian winemakers, chafing at the strict limitations imposed upon them when making Chianti, sought to break free of the chains by mixing wines the way they wanted, paying little heed to the well-defined recipe. Thus was born the so-called Super Tuscan, a largely fanciful title dreamed up by North American journalists. But there's nothing fanciful (or inexpensive) about these French oak–aged wines, which are the toast of Tuscany—and most of the rest of Italy.

$ ⚄ **La Camporena.** The farmhouse of La Camporena, 3 km (2 mi) south of Greve, dates from the 1200s. The rooms are rustic, with typical farm furnishings. Here you can discover the joys of farm life, take walks in the countryside, and dine with the hosts. ⊠ *Via Convertoie 27, 50022,* ☎ *055/853184,* ℻ *055/8544784. 17 rooms. Restaurant, bar, Internet, some pets allowed, no-smoking rooms; no air-conditioning. AE, DC, MC, V.*

Shopping
Guarding the door of the area's most famous butcher shops, **Antica Macelleria Falorni** (⊠ Piazza Matteotti 69–71, ☎ 055/853029) is a stuffed wild boar. Try to make a stop here for tastes of traditional salami, cured meats, and other Tuscan specialties.

Panzano

🔟 *7 km (4½ mi) south of Greve, 40 km (25 mi) south of Florence.*

The magnificent views easily make Panzano one of the prettiest stops in Chianti. At the town centerpiece, the church of **Santa Maria Assunta,** you can see an Annunciation attributed to Michele di Ridolfo del Ghirlandaio (1503–77). ⊠ *Panzano Alto,* ☎ *no phone.* 🎟 *Free.* ☉ *Daily 7–noon and 4–6.*

An ancient church even by Chianti standards, **San Leolino** probably dates from the 10th century, but it was completely rebuilt in the Romanesque style sometime in the 13th century. The 3-km (2-mi) trip south of Panzano is well worth it for this hilltop church's exterior simplicity and 14th-century cloister. The 16th-century terra-cotta tabernacles are attributed to Giovanni della Robbia, and there's also a remarkable triptych (attributed to the Master of Panzano) that was executed sometime in the mid-14th century. Check with the tourist office in Greve in Chianti for open days and hours. ⊠ *SS222, Località San Leolino,* ☎ *no phone.* 🎟 *Free.*

Dining and Lodging

$$$-$$$$ ✕ **Vescovino.** The terrace, festooned with wisteria, acacia, jasmine, and bay, is the best thing about this place. The view of the valley below is also magnificent, and the interior, with its high ceilings and Arts and Crafts chairs, is as pretty as the view from outside. The menu is limited, and the food and service are a hit-or-miss affair. But the *fritti funghi* (fried porcini mushrooms) are standouts, and the wine list is fairly comprehensive. ⊠ *Via Ciampolo da Panzano 9,* ☎ *055/852464. AE, DC, MC, V. Closed Tues.*

$$-$$$ ✕ **Oltre il Giardino.** This ancient stone house has a tasteful dining area with a large terrace and spectacular views of the valley. Try to book a table in time to watch the sunset. The menu captures a little more fantasy than typical Tuscan cuisine. Try the *tagliatelle all'anatra* (a flat noodle tossed with a savory duck sauce) or the *peposo* (beef stew laced with black pepper). On weekends, reservations are a must. ⊠ *Piazza G. Bucciarelli 42,* ☎ *055/852828. DC, MC, V. Closed Mon.*

$-$$ ✕ **Il Vinaio.** It almost feels as if you've walked into someone's living room at this intimate "enoteca pub." Locals linger over coffee, watch TV, and catch up on the latest gossip. The simple menu offers some nice, whimsical treats, including various *panini corretti* ("corrected" sandwiches, a play on *caffe corretto,* espresso "corrected" by the addition of grappa) such as the *finocchiona e pecorino stagionati con grappa* (salami laced with fennel, topped with aged pecorino, and then splashed with grappa). You can eat in the modest garden in back, where there's an absolutely stunning view. ⊠ *Via S. Maria 22,* ☎ *055/852603. AE, MC, V. Closed Thurs. from Nov.–Mar.*

$$$$ ⊞ **Villa La Barone.** Once the home of the Viviani della Robbia family,
★   this 16th-century villa still feels like a private home. The honor bar allows you to either enjoy an aperitivo in the tiled barroom or on the
terrace while admiring the view. And there are views here in spades,
from the pool to the rose garden to the back of the villa. Guest rooms
have tile floors, white walls, and timbered ceilings. The meal plan is
mandatory. ⊠ *Pieve di Panzano 50020,* ☎ *055/852621,* FAX *055/
852277. 30 rooms. Dining room, tennis court, pool, baby-sitting,
laundry service, concierge; no air-conditioning in some rooms. AE, MC,
V. Closed Nov.–Easter. FAP.*

$$ ⊞ **Villa Sangiovese.** In the town square, this simple, shipshape hotel
has terra-cotta tile floors and an enclosed courtyard for summer din-
ing. Country-style rooms are furnished with antiques; half of them look
out over the hillside and the other half face the piazza. The restaurant,
which makes regional dishes, feels more like a hotel dining room than
a restaurant, but the locals don't seem to care: they come here in
droves. A minimum stay of three nights is required. ⊠ *Piazza G. Buc-
ciarelli 5, 50020,* ☎ *055/852461,* FAX *055/852463. 17 rooms, 2 suites.
Restaurant, pool; no air-conditioning, no room TVs. MC, V. Closed
mid-Dec.–mid-Mar. Restaurant closed Wed. CP.*

Shopping

BUTCHER

One of the highlights in Panzano is a visit to **Antica Macelleria Cec-
chini** (⊠ Via XX Luglio 11, ☎ 055/852020), which may be the world's
most dramatic butcher shop, and probably the only one for which reser-
vations are suggested. Here, amid classical music and lively conversa-
tion, owner Dario Cecchini holds court; while quoting Dante, he'll offer
samples of his very fine *sushi di Chianina* (raw slices of Chianina beef
gently salted and peppered). He has researched recipes from the 15th
century and offers pâtés and herb concoctions found nowhere else. Se-
rious gourmands should not miss the place.

SHOES

Carlo Fagiani (⊠ Via G. da Verrazzano 17, ☎ 055/852239) makes
beautiful handmade shoes for men and women. He works in vari-
ous leathers, specializes in elegant flats for women (though he's
happy to add heels, too), and will make shoes to order. The sandals
and other shoes cost from €80–€140. He also sells leather jackets
and belts.

Castellina in Chianti

⑪   *20 km (12 mi) south of Greve, 59 km (35 mi) south of Florence.*

Castellina in Chianti, or simply Castellina, is on a ridge above the Val
di Pesa, Val d'Arbia, and Val d'Elsa. No matter what direction you gaze
in, the panorama is bucolic. The strong 15th-century medieval walls
and fortified town gate give a hint of the history of this village, which
was an outpost during the continuing wars between Florence and
Siena. In the main square, there's a 15th-century palace and **La Rocca,**
a 15th-century fort constructed around a 13th-century tower. It now
serves as the town hall.

NEED A
BREAK?   For a respite from the various enoteche and wine shops, you can treat
yourself to one of the terrifically fragrant ice creams at **L'Antica Delizia**
(⊠ Via Fiorentina 4, ☎ 0577/741337). The fruit flavors—*fragola*
(strawberry), *melone* (cantaloupe), *limone* (lemon)—are particularly
good.

Dining and Lodging

$$$–$$$$ ✕ **Osteria alla Piazza.** In the middle of a vineyard 15 km (8 mi) north of Castellina, with one of Chianti's most spectacular views, sits this restaurant. It's worth the drive into the countryside to relax on the terrace, enjoy the sophisticated menu and, certainly, the delicious desserts. Try the *girasole ai quattro sapori,* a giant vegetable-filled ravioli flavored with fresh tomato sauce and a few drops of cream; it arrives at the table looking much like a *girasole* (sunflower). ⊠ *Località La Piazza,* ☎ *0577/733580. Reservations essential weekends. MC, V. Closed Mon. and Jan.–Feb.; closed weekdays Mar. and Nov.–Dec.*

$$$ ✕ **Albergaccio.** The fact that it can only seat 35 diners at a time is one of the nicest things about eating at this small restaurant. The ever-changing menu mixes traditional and creative cuisine and is accompanied by an excellent wine list. There are some real seasonal treats here, including *zuppa di funghi e castagne* (a mushroom and chestnut soup). You can dine alfresco on the terrace when it's warm. ⊠ *Via Fiorentina 25,* ☎ *0577/741042. Reservations essential. No credit cards. Closed Sun. No lunch Wed.–Thur.*

$$–$$$ ✕ **Osteria di Fonterutoli.** Though there's nothing memorable about this 30-seat trattoria's interior, it doesn't really matter because it sits in the middle of vineyards that belong to the Fonterutoli wine estate, and the views on the drive here and the wine are both lovely. Pair your choices from the menu with the estate's especially fine Chianti. The *crostini misti,* a selection of toasted breads with various toppings, include an unusual spread with pureed olives and pine nuts. The *tagliata al vino rosso* (rare slices of beef in a red-wine sauce) is a delight, as is the *carpaccio al tartufo* (rare slices of beef with slivers of black truffle). ⊠ *Località Fonterutoli,* ☎ *0577/740212. AE, DC, MC, V. Closed Tues.*

$$–$$$ ✕ **Ristorante Le Tre Porte.** The specialty of the house is *bistecca alla fiorentina,* a thick slab of steak usually served very rare. Paired with grilled fresh porcini mushrooms when in season (in spring and fall), it's a rather heady combination. The dish can be enjoyed in an intimate dining room with linen napkins and tablecloths. Reservations are essential in summer. ⊠ *Via Trento e Trieste 4,* ☎ *0577/741163. AE, DC, MC, V. Closed Tues.*

$$$$ 🏠 **Vescine.** A former Etruscan settlement has been transformed into
★ this secluded complex of low-slung medieval stone buildings, connected by cobbled paths and punctuated by cypress trees. Unfussy white rooms have terra-cotta tile floors, attractive woodwork, and comfortable furnishings typical of Tuscany. ⊠ *5 km (3 mi) west of Radda in Chianti, 53017,* ☎ *0577/741144,* 🖷 *0577/740263. 20 rooms, 5 suites. Minibars, cable TV, tennis court, pool, library, free parking, some pets allowed. AE, MC, V. Closed Nov.–Mar. (except over Christmas).*

$$$–$$$$ 🏠 **Locanda Le Piazze.** What was once an old farmhouse has been carefully and lovingly turned into a marvelous and intimate hotel tucked in among vineyards. The three common rooms are cozy but elegant; the breakfast room looks out on a sweeping panorama. Rooms have timbered ceilings, white walls, and terra-cotta floors. The grounds are awash in flowers, and chirping birds are just about the only noise you'll hear. ⊠ *Locanda Le Piazze, 53011,* ☎ *0577/743190,* 🖷 *0577/743191,* 🌐 *www.chiantinet.it/lepiazze. 20 rooms. Restaurant, fans, cable TV (some), pool, bar, laundry service, free parking; no air-conditioning. AE, DC, MC, V. Closed Nov.–Apr. CP.*

$$$–$$$$ 🏠 **Villa Casalecchi.** This beautiful villa is filled with antique furniture. All guest rooms are in the elegant main house, while the three apartments, in a nearby farmhouse, are more rustic. The villa's wood-paneled restaurant is cozy. There's also a pool, which overlooks vineyards. ⊠ *Località Casalecchi in Chianti 53011,* ☎ *0577/740240,* 🖷 *0577/*

741111. 16 rooms, 3 apartments. Restaurant, in-room fax, in-room safes, tennis court, pool, boccie, bar, baby-sitting, dry cleaning, laundry service, Internet, business services, meeting rooms, free parking, some pets allowed; no air-conditioning in some rooms. AE, DC, MC, V. CP.

$$–$$$ ⊞ **Collelungo.** One of the loveliest *agriturismi* in the area, Collelungo consists of a series of abandoned farmhouses that have been carefully remodeled by Briton Tony Rocca and his Italian wife, Mira. Set amid a notable vineyard (it produces internationally recognized Chianti Classico), the apartments—all with cooking facilities and dining areas—have exposed stone walls and that typical Tuscan tile floor. The *salone* (lounge), which possibly dates to the 14th century, has a satellite-dish TV; adjacent to it is an honor bar. In high season, a weeklong stay is required. ⊠ *Podere Collungo 53011,* ☎ FAX *0577/740489,* WEB *www. collelungo.it. 12 apartments. Pool, bar, lounge, laundry service; no air-conditioning, no kids under 8. AE, DC, MC, V. Closed Nov.–Mar.*

$$–$$$ ⊞ **Hotel Belvedere di San Leonino.** There are wonderful gardens for strolling around this restored country complex, which dates from the 14th century. The guest rooms are in two houses that look out upon vineyards to the north and Siena to the south. The homey rooms have antique furniture and exposed beams. The dining room, open to guests only, has a fixed menu. In the summer you can eat dinner by the pool in the garden. ⊠ *Località San Leonino, 53011,* ☎ *0577/740887,* FAX *0577/740924. 28 rooms. Dining rooms, pool, baby-sitting, Internet; no air-conditioning. Closed mid-Nov.–mid-Mar. AE, MC, V. BP.*

$$ ⊞ **Hotel Salivolpi.** The owners of this family-run farmhouse took special care not to alter the feeling of the house when they converted it to accommodate guest rooms. Each room is furnished with antiques, and there is a large pool reserved for guests. ⊠ *Via Fiorentina 89, 53011,* ☎ *0577/740484,* FAX *0577/740998,* WEB *www.hotelsalivolpi. 19 rooms. Fans (some), cable TV, pool, Internet, free parking; no air-conditioning. AE, MC, V. CP.*

$$ ⊞ **Palazzo Squarcialupi.** A refurbished 15th-century palace on the
★   main street in town offers a pleasant, restful place to stay. Rooms have high ceilings, white walls, and tile floors; bathrooms are tiled in local stone. Many of the rooms have a view of the valley below. Common areas are elegant but comfortable, and the breakfast buffet is ample. The multilingual staff is courteous and goes out of its way to be helpful. Though there is no restaurant, the hotel will arrange for a light lunch during the warmer months. ⊠ *Via Ferruccio 26, 53011,* ☎ *0577/741186,* FAX *0577/740386,* WEB *www.chiantiandrelax.com. 9 rooms, 8 suites. Pool, bar, Internet, some pets allowed. AE, DC, MC, V. Closed Nov.–Mar.*

Shopping

Antiquario Mario Cappelletti (⊠ Via Ferruccio 34, ☎ 0577/740980) carries interesting prints, cards, and reproductions of well-known Renaissance artworks. **Cappelletti** (⊠ Via Ferruccio 39–43, ☎ 0577/740420) has been producing quality leather goods at more-than-reasonable prices since 1893. The briefcases here are especially nice. **La Giravolta** (⊠ Via delle Volte 32, ☎ 0577/742004) sells nothing but *i prodotti biologici,* organic products. The merchandise includes wines, candles, and spaghetti sauces. **Le Volte Enoteca** (⊠ Via Ferruccio 12, ☎ 0577/741314) has an ample and well-chosen supply of local favorites such as Chianti produced from small estates and the latest in Super Tuscans.

Radda in Chianti

⑫ *22 km (13 mi) east of Castellina in Chianti, 55 km (34 mi) south of Florence.*

Radda in Chianti sits on a hill stretching between the Val di Pesa and Val d'Arbia. It's another one of those tiny Chianti villages with steep streets for strolling; follow the signs that point you toward the *camminamento*, a covered 14th-century walkway that circles part of the city inside the walls. In Piazza Ferrucci, you'll find the **Palazzo del Podestà**, or Palazzo Comunale, the city hall that has served the people of Radda for more than four centuries and has 51 coats of arms imbedded in the facade. Ice cream lovers and those with an interest in how ice was made in the 16th century might want to check out **La Ghiacciaia del Granducato** (the Grandduke's Ice House), just outside the town walls. Built partially underground in a pyramid shape, it supplied the ice for the main Medici ice house in the Cascine in Florence.

NEED A BREAK?	Join the many locals and travelers at **Bar Dante Alighieri** (✉ Piazza D. Alighieri, ☎ 0577/738815), where you can sip a glass of Brunello while sitting at an outdoor table.
OFF THE BEATEN PATH	**VOLPAIA** – This hamlet, perched on a hill 10 km (6 mi) north of Radda, was a military outpost from the 10th–16th centuries and once offered lodging to those on the pilgrimage trail to Rome and Jerusalem. Today it makes a significant wine (Castello di Volpaia) that can be purchased directly or sampled in a bar in the town's tiny piazza. Every July, for the Festa di San Lorenzo, people come to Volpaia to watch for falling stars and enjoy a traditional fireworks display put on by the family that owns the Castello di Volpaia (✉ Piazza della Cisterna 1, 53017, ☎ 0577/738066), a wine estate and agriturismo lodging.

Dining and Lodging

$–$$ ✕ **La Bottega di Carla.** In the central piazza of Volpaia, 10 km (6 mi) north of Radda, this place looks like a sandwich shop, but there's a seemingly hidden upstairs dining room. When it's warm, opt for an outside seat on a terrace teeming with flowers; you'll get a nice view of Radda, too. Skip the limp crostini and head directly to the sublime primi; leave room for the secondi: Carla has a deft touch with such Tuscan specialties as *cinghiale* (wild boar) and rabbit. ✉ *Piazza della Torre 2, Volpaia,* ☎ *0577/738001. MC, V. Closed Tues. and Feb. No dinner.*

$$$$ ⌂ **Relais Fattoria Vignale.** On the outside, it's an unadorned farmhouse
★ with an annex across the street. Inside, it's as comfortable as an English country house, with terra-cotta floors, sitting rooms, and nice stone- and woodwork. White rooms with exposed wood beams and brick contain simple wooden bed frames and furniture, charming rugs and prints, and modern white-tile bathrooms. The grounds, lined with vineyards and plum and olive trees, are equally inviting. The rustic Ristorante Vignale, which offers two- and three-course meals, serves excellent wines and Tuscan specialties such as *il petto d'anatra all'aceto e miele* (duck breast with vinegar and honey). ✉ *Via Pianigiani 9, 53017,* ☎ *0577/738300 or 0577/738094,* ℻ *0577/738592,* 🌐 *www.vignale. it. 34 rooms, 5 suites. Restaurant, in-room safes, pool, bar, wine shop, library, meeting room, Internet, no-smoking rooms. AE, DC, MC, V. Closed early Dec.–late Mar.*

$$$ ⌂ **Podere Terreno.** One wing of this 16th-century farmhouse, about 5 km (3 mi) north of Radda in Chianti on the road to Volpaia, has been converted into seven double rooms, each with a bath and furnished with traditional furniture. People come from all over the world to enjoy the quiet country life here. Dinners, which are included in rates along with breakfast, are inventive. The friendly owners, who speak English, enjoy cooking for their guests, serving the wine they made themselves

and helping to spark friendly conversation at the dinner table. ⊠ *Via della Volpaia, 53017,* ☎ *0577/738312,* FAX *0577/738400. 7 rooms. Restaurant, some pets allowed, no-smoking rooms; no air-conditioning. AE, MC, V. Closed Dec. 23–Dec. 28. MAP.*

$ ⊡ **La Bottega di Giovannino.** The name is actually that of the *alimentari* (grocery store) run by Giovannino Bernardoni, who also rents rooms in his house just next door. This is a fantastic place for the budget-conscious traveler, as rooms are immaculate and beds comfortable. Most of the rooms have a view of the stunning landscape just outside. All rooms have their own bath, though most of them necessitate taking a short trip outside one's room. ⊠ *Via Roma 6–8, 53017,* ☎ FAX *0577/ 738056. 10 rooms. Bar; no air-conditioning, no room phones, no room TVs. No credit cards.*

Shopping
BUTCHER
If you're lucky enough to be here on the right day, the butcher at **Porciatti Alimentari** (⊠ Piazza IV Novembre 1, ☎ 0577/738055) offers samples and will even walk you across the street to show you his spotless *laboratorio,* where his handmade salamis and sausages are aging.

CERAMICS
Like its sister shop in Florence, **Ceramiche Rampini** (⊠ Casa Beretone, ☎ 0577/738043, WEB www.rampiniceramics.com), just outside Radda in Chianti, produces exquisite (and expensive) hand-painted ceramic objects, including plates, bowls, and candlesticks. The firm ships anywhere in the world and keeps its customers' information on file. If you break a plate or want more, they'll know exactly what your pattern is.

LINENS
La Bottega delle Fantasie (⊠ Via Roma 30, ☎ 0577/738978) has colorful pillows and carefully crafted linens in sun-drenched Tuscan hues. The items will remind you of your trip long after you've returned home.

Gaiole in Chianti

⑬ *9 km (5½ mi) southeast of Radda in Chianti, 69 km (43 mi) south of Florence, 28 km (17 mi) northeast of Siena.*

Gaiole, undistinguished except for the stream that runs through its center and the flowers that adorn many of its houses, has been a market town since 1200 and now is a central destination for touring southern Chianti. The area around it is dotted with castles; perched on hilltops (the better to see the approaching enemy), they were of great strategic importance during the Renaissance. Today it just means that the views are always dazzling. One good loop for castle-seeing is from Gaiole to San Polo in Rose, to Montelucco, Ama, and Brolio.

A turnoff from S408 leads to **Badia a Coltibuono**—4 km (2½ mi) north of Gaiole in Chianti—which has been owned by Lorenza de' Medici's family for more than a century and a half (the family isn't closely related to the Renaissance-era Medici). Ever since it was founded by Vallombrosan monks in the 11th century, the "Abbey of the Good Harvest" produced wine. Today the family continues the tradition, making Chianti Classico and other wines, along with high-quality cold-pressed olive oil and various flavored vinegars and floral honeys. A small Romanesque church with campanile is surrounded by 2,000 acres of oak, fir, and chestnut woods threaded with walking paths—open to all—and dotted with two small lakes. Though the abbey itself, built between the 11th and 18th centuries, is the family's home, parts are open for tours spring through fall (in English, German, or Italian). Visits include the jasmine-draped main courtyard, the inner cloister with its antique well, the musty old aging cellars, and the Renaissance-style garden redolent of lavender, lemons, and roses. Groups of 10 or more may arrange tours and wine tastings by appointment. The shop, L'Osteria (☎ FAX 0577/749479), sells Coltibuono's wine and other products, including beeswax hand-lotion cakes in little ceramic dishes that make great gifts. ✉ *Badia a Coltibuono,* ☎ *0577/749498,* FAX *0577/749235,* WEB *www. coltibuono.com.* 🎫 *Abbey €3.* ⏱ *Tours May–July and Sept.–Oct. (except public holidays), weekdays 2:30, 3, 3:30, 4.*

OFF THE BEATEN PATH

CASTELLO DI BROLIO – This stunning castle, about 2 km (1 mi) southeast of Gaiole, is one of the most impressive in the area. Its winery is justifiably world famous, so this is the castle to visit if you only have time for one. At the end of the 12th century, when Florence conquered southern Chianti, Brolio became Florence's southernmost outpost, and it was often said, "When Brolio growls, all Siena trembles." Today there's a sign at the Brolio gate that translates as "ring bell and be patient." You pull a rope and the bell above the ramparts peals, and in a short time, the caretaker arrives to let you in. Although the grand, mostly 19th-century manor house is not open to the public (the current baron is very much in residence), the grounds are worth visiting. Brolio was built about AD 1000 and owned by the monks of the Badia Fiorentina; the "new" owners, the Ricasoli family, have owned it since 1141. Bettino Ricasoli (1809–80), the so-called Iron Baron, was one of the founders of modern Italy and is also said to have invented the present-day formula for Chianti wine. Brolio is one of Chianti's best-known labels, and the cellars may be visited by appointment. There are also two apartments here available for rent by the week. ✉ *Località Brolio, Gaiole in Chianti 53013,* ☎ *0577/730.* 🎫 *€3.* ⏱ *June–Sept., daily 9–noon and 2– 6:30; Oct.–May, Sat.–Thurs. 9–noon and 2–6:30.*

CASTELLO DI MELETO – It's a pretty drive up winding and curving roads to this castle from the 13th century. Attached to it is an 18th-century villa; more importantly, there's a wine shop that offers tastes of the locally produced wine as well as honeys and jams. It's worth touring the castle if you want to get a sense of how 18th-century aristocrats lived; if that doesn't interest you, proceed directly to the enoteca for a tasting. Six apartments clustered near the castle are available for rent. ✉ *Gaiole in Chianti 53010,* ☎ *0577/749496 castle and cantina; 0577/ 749129 enoteca,* WEB *www.castellomeleto.it.* 🎫 *Tour and tasting, €8.* ⏱ *Guided tours Mon. 3 and 4:30; Tues.–Sat. 11:30, 3, and 4:30; Sun. 11:30, 4, and 5*

Dining and Lodging

$$$$ ✕ **Badia a Coltibuono.** Just outside the walls of Badia a Coltibuono itself is the abbey's pleasant restaurant, with seating outside or in soft-yellow rooms divided by ancient brick arches. The *crema di peperoni e patate* (a creamless red pepper and potato soup) arrives at the table garnished with the home-grown olive oil; the *lasagnette agli asparagi al forno* (lasagna with asparagus and pecorino) is fragrant. It all pairs marvelously with the Badia's own wines. Between 2:30 and 7:30, a bistro menu with sandwiches, salads, appetizers, and desserts is available. ✉ *Badia a Coltibuono, 4 km (2½ mi) north of Gaiole in Chianti,* ☎ *0577/ 749031. MC, V. Closed Mon.*

$$$–$$$$ ✕ **Osteria del Castello.** Nestled within the woods a stone's throw from the Castello di Brolio, this is a lovely place to sample fine fare. South African–born chef Seamus de Pentheny O'Kelly trained extensively in Paris and uses sophisticated techniques for his up-to-the-minute takes on Italian food. His *insalata di prosciutto con aceto balsamico* (mixed

greens with blanched prosciutto drizzled with aged balsamic vinegar) is a delight, as is just about everything else on the menu. The wine list derives its inspiration from Brolio's best offerings. ⊠ *Località Castello di Brolio,* ☎ FAX *0577/747277. Reservations essential. AE, DC, MC, V. Closed Tues.*

$$–$$$ ✕ **La Grotta della Rana.** A perfect stop for lunch while you're exploring Chianti's wineries, this trattoria's *cucina casalinga* (home cooking) can be eaten on a lovely outdoor patio (there's also seating indoors). Outstanding primi include *maccheroni alla nonna,* macaroni with asparagus in a light cream sauce dotted with truffle oil. The *misto alla griglia* (mixed grilled meats) includes succulent pork. Also notable is the *filetto al pepe verde* (Chianina beef in a creamy green-peppercorn sauce). If you time dinner right, you might get to watch a memorable sunset while you're eating. ⊠ *Località San Sano, off SS408,* ☎ *0577/ 746020. AE, MC, V. Closed Wed. and Feb.–mid-Mar.*

$$$$ ✕🏠 **Castello di Spaltenna.** If you're after rustic elegance, look no
★   more. This former convent dates from the 1300s; the Romanesque church next to it is even older. The complex has been transformed into a romantic country hotel and first-class restaurant ($$$$). The hotel's minisuites have fireplaces and massage tubs. Some rooms have canopied beds; most have gorgeous views of hills, woods, and vineyards. Dinners by candlelight employ dishes that are sophisticated versions of Tuscan classics—they are served in a flower-filled cloister during the summer. The pool is tucked into a beautiful terrace. ⊠ *Pieve di Spaltenna, 53013,* ☎ *0577/749483,* FAX *0577/749269. 37 rooms. Restaurant, room service, fans, minibar, cable TV, tennis court, 1 pool, 1 indoor pool, wading pool, sauna, billiards, bar, baby-sitting, dry cleaning, laundry service, Internet, business services, meeting rooms, free parking. AE, DC, MC, V. Closed early Jan.–early Mar. CP.*

$$$ 🏠 **Borgo Argenina.** Elena Nappa, a former interior designer, is now the consummate hostess at this centuries-old villa that she has completely renovated. Rooms are lovingly decorated with antique quilts and furniture, but there is a nod to modern times with in-room telephones and minibars (gratis). Bianca, the resident dog, greets you at the steep drive upon your arrival, and might even hang out with you all day. Elena is an authority on the surrounding Chianti area and happily draws maps and suggests wine-tasting and -touring routes for guests. ⊠ *MM 15 on S408 (follow signs for San Marcellino Monti) 53013,* ☎ *0577/747117,* FAX *0577/747228,* WEB *www.borgoargenina.it. 5 rooms, 2 suites, 2 cottages, 1 villa. Minibars, laundry service, no-smoking rooms; no air-conditioning. AE, DC, MC, V. CP.*

$$$ 🏠 **Castello di Tornano.** If you'd like a bit of whimsy on your holiday, this agriturismo may be the place for you. There's an 11th-century tower, a swimming pool that is roughly where the moat was, and a prison and chapel that have been converted into rooms. It's remarkably private, so if you're looking for peace and quiet, this may be the perfect choice. ⊠ *Località Tornano, 53013,* ☎ FAX *0577/746067,* WEB *www.castladitornano.it. 7 apartments, 1 house. Restaurant, tennis court, pool, fishing, Ping-Pong, playground, some pets allowed. AE, DC, MC, V. CP.*

$$$ 🏠 **Hotel Residence San Sano.** Housed in a renovated 13th-century fortress 10 km (6 mi) from Chianti in Gaiole, this small hotel has retained the charm of the original structure, with an open hearth fireplace and hand-hewn stone porticoes. The slew of modern amenities that have been added include a beautiful outdoor pool. Rooms are bright and spacious, and the gardens are strewn with lavender and rosemary. ⊠ *Località San Sano, Lecchi in Chianti, 53010,* ☎ *0577/746130,* FAX *0577/746156,* WEB *www.hotelsansano.it. 14 rooms. Restaurant, in-*

room safes, minibars, cable TVs (some rooms), pool, laundry facilities, free parking, some pets allowed. AE, DC, MC, V. Closed Nov.–Mar. CP.

SOUTHEASTERN REACHES

Reaching southeast from Chianti proper are the fortified hilltop villages of Montalcino and Montepulciano, where you can continue your wine exploration with tastings of the heady Brunello di Montalcino and Vino Nobile di Montepulciano. Heading south of Siena and Chianti, you'll notice a change in the landscape: Chianti's verdant, cypress-punctuated hills give way to le Crete, the area around Asciano marked by rich red earth and rolling vineyards.

Castelnuovo Berardenga

(14) *20 km (12 mi) southeast of Gaiole in Chianti, 23 km (14 mi) east of Siena, 90 km (56 mi) southeast of Florence.*

This is the southernmost village in Chianti territory. Its compact center, with its hilly, curving streets and plethora of piazzas, invites wandering. Peek at the gardens of **Villa Chigi**, a 19th-century villa built on the site of a 14th-century castle (actually the "new castle" from which Castelnuovo got its name). It is closed to the public, but its manicured gardens are open for visiting on Sunday and holidays. ⊠ *Strada la Ragnaia,* ☎ *no phone.* ☑ *Free.* ⊙ *Sun. and holidays Apr.–Sept., 10–8 and Oct.–Mar., 10–5.*

The neoclassical church of **San Giusto e San Clemente,** built in the 1840s on a Greek-cross plan, contains a Madonna and Child with angels by an anonymous 15th-century master. Also inside it is the *Holy Family with St. Catherine of Siena,* attributed to Arcangelo Salimbeni (1530/40–79). ⊠ *Piazza Matteotti 4,* ☎ *0577/355133.* ☑ *Free.* ⊙ *Daily 7:30–7.*

OFF THE BEATEN PATH

SAN GUSMÈ – Jauntily atop a hilltop is the oldest and most interesting of the medieval villages that surround Castelnuovo Berardenga. San Gusmè retains its original early 1400s layout, with arched passageways, gates topped with coats of arms, narrow squares, and steep streets. You can walk through the entire village in 20 minutes, but in those 20 minutes you will feel as if you have stepped back in time some 600 years. ⊠ *Take the Strada Chiantigiana (SS222) 5 km (3 mi) north from Castelnuovo Berardenga and follow signs for San Gusmè.*

Lodging

$$$$ 🏨 **Borgo San Felice.** For a sophisticated but rustic experience in the hills outside Siena, look no further. This elegant hotel, spread across five buildings, used to be a small medieval town. Now it's given over to luxury, which is immediately apparent upon entering the reception area and public rooms: white walls, high vaulted ceilings, and furniture covered in exquisite country chintz mingle with tasteful etchings and watercolors. Rooms have tile floors, spacious bathrooms, and windows that open out onto peace and tranquillity. The restaurant, Poggio Antico, serves sophisticated versions of Tuscan classics. ⊠ *Località San Felice, 53019,* ☎ *0577/3964,* ℻ *0577/359089,* ᴡᴇʙ *www.borgosanfelice.com. 43 rooms, 15 suites. Restaurant, room service, in-room safes, minibars, cable TV, 2 tennis courts, pool, gym, hair salon, massage, bicycles, billiards, boccie, bar, wine shop, baby-sitting, dry cleaning, laundry service, concierge, Internet, business services, meeting rooms, free parking, some pets allowed. AE, DC, MC, V. Closed Nov.–Mar. CP.*

Montalcino

🅯 *40 km (25 mi) south of Castelnuovo Berardenga, 41 km (25½ mi) south of Siena, 109 km (68 mi) south of Florence.*

Tiny Montalcino, with its commanding view high on a hill, can claim an Etruscan past. It saw a fair number of travelers as it was directly on the road from Siena to Rome. During the early Middle Ages, it enjoyed a brief period of autonomy before falling under the orbit of Siena in 1201. Now Montalcino's greatest claim to fame is that it produces Brunello di Montalcino, one of Italy's most esteemed reds. You can sample it in wine cellars in town or visit a nearby winery, such as Fattoria dei Barbi, for a guided tour and tasting; you must call ahead for reservations.

Driving up to Montalcino, you pass through the Brunello vineyards and arrive at the 14th-century Sienese **La Fortezza,** which has an enoteca for tasting wines. From the fortress, you can wander down into the town, where you'll have no problem finding a place to taste or buy the excellent but expensive red stuff. ⊠ *Piazzale La Fortezza,* ☎ *0577/849211.* 🎫 *€2.05.* ⊙ *Nov.–Mar., Tues.–Sun. 9–6; Apr.–Oct., daily 9–8.*

Though the sacred art here, compiled from area churches, can be labeled "B-list," the **Museo Civico e Diocesano d'Arte Sacra** itself and its holdings' presentation make the museum a must-see when in Montalcino. The building for the City and Diocesan Museum of Sacred Art once belonged to the Augustinians—the ticket booth is in the glorious refurbished cloister—and the collection can be found in two floors of former living quarters. The very fine altarpiece by Bartolo di Fredi (circa 1330–1410) of the Madonna and Child with saints makes dazzling use of gold. Also on hand are many wood sculptures, a typical medium in these parts during the Renaissance. ⊠ *Via Ricasoli 21,* ☎ *0577/846014.* 🎫 *€4.50.* ⊙ *Jan.–Mar., Tues.–Sun. 10–1 and 2–5; Apr.–Oct., Tues.–Sun. 10–6; Nov.–Dec., Tues.–Sun. 10–1 and 2–6.*

Dining and Lodging

$$$$ ✕ **Poggio Antico.** The renowned chef Roberto Minnetti abandoned his highly successful restaurant in Rome and moved to the country just outside Montalcino. Now he and his wife, Patrizia, serve Tuscan cuisine masterfully interpreted. The seasonal menu offers *pappardelle al ragù di agnello* (flat, wide noodles in a lamb sauce) and venison in a sweet-and-sour sauce. The dining room is relaxed but regal, with arches and beamed ceilings. ⊠ *Località I Poggi, 4 km (2½ mi) outside Montalcino on road to Grosseto,* ☎ *0577/849200. MC, V. Closed Mon. and 20 days in Jan. No dinner Sun.*

$–$$ ✕ **Enoteca Osteria Osticcio.** If you want to sample the local wine, this is one of the prettiest places in Montalcino in which to do so. Tullio and Francesca Scrivano have beautifully remodeled this wine shop–enoteca. Upon entering, you descend a curving staircase into a tasting room complete with rustic wood tables; adjacent is a small dining area with a splendid view of the hills far below, and just outside is a lovely little terrace perfect for sampling Brunello di Montalcino when the weather is warm. The menu is light and pairs nicely with the wines, which are the main draw. The *acciughe sotto pesto* (anchovies with pesto) are a particularly fine treat. ⊠ *Via Matteotti 23,* ☎ *0577/848271. AE, DC, MC, V. Closed Sun. No dinner.*

$–$$ ✕ **Il Grappolo Blu.** The interior, with its white walls and odd collection of cheap prints, doesn't leave much of an impression, but this is as fine a place as any to have *piatti tipici* (typical plates). *Pici all' aglione* (thick, long noodles served with sautéed cherry tomatoes and many cloves of garlic), a local specialty, is done particularly well here. The chef has a deft touch with vegetables; if there's fennel on the menu (written in many languages), order it. Reservations are strongly advised. ✉ *Scale di via Moglio 1,* ☎ *0577/847150,* FAX *0577/8464000. AE, DC, MC, V. Closed Fri.*

$$ ✕⚏ **Fattoria dei Barbi e del Casato.** The rustic taverna ($$) of this family-owned wine estate, which produces excellent Brunello and Rosso di Montalcino, is set among vineyards and has a large stone fireplace. The estate farm produces many of the ingredients used in such traditional specialties as *stracotto nel brunello* (braised beef cooked with beans in Brunello wine). Six comfortable, traditionally furnished agri-tourist apartments are next to the cantina—a one-week minimum stay is required. Reservations for a meal or a stay are essential. ✉ *Località Podernuovi, 53024,* ☎ *0577/841200 taverna; 0577/841111 fattoria,* FAX *0577/841112. 6 apartments. Some pets allowed; no air-conditioning. AE, DC, MC, V. Taverna closed Wed. and mid-Jan.–mid-Feb. No dinner Tues. Nov.–Mar.*

$$ ⚏ **La Crociona.** A quiet and serene family-owned farm, La Crociona is in the middle of a small vineyard with glorious views. The rooms have such comforts as antique iron beds and 17th-century wardrobes. There's a big terrace and you are invited to hang out around the pool and use the family barbecue, as well as to sample the owner's own wine supply. ✉ *Località La Croce, Montalcino, 53024,* ☎ FAX *0577/848007,* WEB *www.lacrociona.com. 6 apartments. Cable TV, pool, baby-sitting, dry cleaning, laundry facilities, Internet; no air-conditioning, no room phones. MC, V.*

Montepulciano

⑯ *40 km (25 mi) east of Montalcino, 65 km (40 mi) southeast of Siena, 12 km (7 mi) east of Pienza, 13 km (8 mi) west of the A1, 65 km (40 mi) south of Florence.*

Perched on a hilltop, Montepulciano is made up of a pyramid of red-brick buildings set within a circle of cypress trees. At an altitude of almost 2,000 ft, it is cool in summer and chilled in winter by biting winds sweeping down its spiraling streets. The town has an unusually harmonious look, the result of the work of three architects: Antonio Sangallo "il Vecchio" (circa 1455–1534), Vignola (1507–73), and Michelozzo (1396–1472). The group endowed it with fine palaces and churches in an attempt to impose Renaissance architectural ideals on an ancient Tuscan hill town.

★ Montepulciano's pièce de résistance is the beautiful **Piazza Grande,** filled with handsome buildings. On the Piazza Grande is the **Duomo,** whose unfinished facade doesn't measure up to the external beauty of the neighboring palaces. On the inside, however, its Renaissance roots shine through. You can see fragments of the tomb of Bartolomeo Aragazzi, secretary to Pope Martin V (who reigned from 1417–31); it was created by Michelozzo between 1427–36, and parts of it have been dispersed to museums in other parts of the world. ✉ *Piazza Grande,* ☎ *0578/757761.* ⚏ *Free.* ☉ *Daily 9–12:30.* Though parts of the **Palazzo Comunale** may date to the late 13th century, it was restructured in the 1300s and again in the mid-15th century. Michelozzo oversaw this last phase. From the tower, a commanding view of Siena, Mt. Amiata (the highest point in Tuscany), and Lake Trasimeno (the largest lake on the Italian peninsula) can be seen on a clear day. ✉ *Piazza Grande,* ☎ *no phone.* ⚏ *Free.* ☉ *Daily 8–1.*

In the Piazza Michelozzo is the church of **Sant'Agostino,** which was founded in 1285 and renovated in the early 1400s. Michelozzo had a hand in the beautiful travertine facade. He also carved the terra-cotta

relief of the Madonna and Child above the door. ⊠ *Piazza Michelozzo,*
☎ *0578/757761.* 🎫 *Free.* ◯ *Daily 9–12:30 and 3:30–7:30.*

On the hillside below the town walls is the **Tempio di San Biagio,** designed by Antonio Sangallo il Vecchio. A paragon of Renaissance architectural perfection, it's considered by many to be his masterpiece.
Inside the church is a painting of a Madonna. According to legend,
the picture was the only thing remaining in an abandoned church that
two young girls entered on April 23, 1518. The two girls saw the eyes
of the Madonna moving, and that same afternoon so did a farmer and
a cow, who knelt down in front of the painting. In 1963 the image was
proclaimed the Madonna del Buon Viaggio (Madonna of the Good Journey), the protector of tourists in Italy. ⊠ *Via di San Biagio,* ☎ *0578/
7577761.* 🎫 *Free.* ◯ *Daily 9–12:30 and 3:30–7:30.*

Dining and Lodging

$$$ ✕ **La Grotta.** Just across the street from the Tempio di San Biagio, this
★ place has an innocuous entrance that might lead you to pass right by.
Don't—the food is fantastic. The *tagliolini con carciofi e rigatino* (thin
noodles with artichokes and bacon) and the *tagliatelle di grano sara-
ceno con asparagi e zucchine* (flat noodles with asparagus and zucchini)
are both wonderful. Follow with any of the wonderful *secondi,* and
wash it down with the local wine, which just happens to be one of Italy's
finest—Vino Nobile di Montepulciano. ⊠ *Località San Biagio,* ☎
0578/757479. AE, MC, V. Closed Wed.

$$ 🏨 **Il Marzocco.** A 16th-century building within the town walls, this hotel
evokes the 19th century, complete with old-fashioned parlors and a bil-
liard room. Furnished in heavy late-19th-century style or in spindly white
wood, many bedrooms have large terraces overlooking the countryside and are big enough to accommodate extra beds. ⊠ *Piazza
Savonarola 18, 53045,* ☎ *0578/757262,* FAX *0578/757530. 16 rooms,
15 with bath. Restaurant, billiards, Internet; no air conditioning. AE,
DC, MC, V. Closed late Jan.–early Feb.*

$$ 🏨 **La Bandita.** Great charm abounds throughout this attractive old
farmhouse, which has terra-cotta floors and lace curtains. Antiques
adorn the bedrooms, and a fireplace and 19th-century Tuscan provin-
cial furniture fill the large, brick-vaulted living room. Some rooms can
accommodate an extra bed. A garden is available to guests. The
restaurant is closed Tuesday. ⊠ *Via Bandita 72, Bettolle, 53040, 1
km (½ mi) from Valdichiana exit off A1 autostrada,* ☎ FAX *0577/
624649,* WEB *www.locandalabandita.it. 9 rooms. Restaurant, some pets
allowed; no air-conditioning, no room phones, no room TVs. AE, DC,
MC, V.*

Nightlife and the Arts

The **Cantiere Internazionale d'Arte,** which begins at the end of June
and runs through July, is a multifaceted festival of figurative art, music,
and theater, ending with a major theatrical production in the Piazza
Grande. For details, contact the Montepulciano tourist office.

CHIANTI A TO Z

*To research prices, get advice from other travelers, and book travel ar-
rangements, visit www.fodors.com.*

AIRPORTS

The closest major airports are Rome's Fiumicino (officially Aeroporto
Leonardo da Vinci), Pisa's Galileo Galilei, and Florence's Peretola (of-
ficially Aeroporto A. Vespucci).

➤ AIRPORT INFORMATION: **Aeroporto A. Vespucci** (known as Peretola; ☎ 055/3061700). **Aeroporto Galileo Galilei** (☎ 050/500707, WEB www.pisa-airport.com). **Aeroporto Leonardo da Vinci** (known as Fiumicino; ☎ 06/6594420, WEB www.adr.it).

BIKE TRAVEL
➤ BIKE RENTALS: **Lorenzo Minocci** (✉ Montalcino, ☎ 0577/848282 or 0577/847029).

BUS TRAVEL
The best way to explore the region is by car. That said, several buses do run daily between Rome and Siena (2½ hours), and there is frequent service between Florence and Siena (one hour), with connections to Greve, Radda, Gaiole in Chianti, and Montepulciano. Service between Florence and Greve is frequent. Radda, however, is difficult to reach by bus from Florence; although there's twice-daily service, the only return bus is very early in the morning, which makes a simple day trip quite difficult. Radda is more easily reached by bus from Siena, which has several buses daily.

Tra-In goes to Sant'Andrea in Percussina, San Casciano in Val di Pesa, Tavarnelle Val di Pesa, Barberino Val d'Elsa, Gaiole in Chianti, Castelnuovo Berardenga, Montalcino, and Montepulciano. SITA goes to Sant'Andrea in Percussina, San Casciano in Val di Pesa, Tavarnelle Val di Pesa, Barberino Val d'Elsa, Gaiole in Chianti, Mercatale, Sambuca, Badia a Passignano, San Donato in Poggio, Greve in Chianti, Panzano, Castellina, and Radda in Chianti. Alessi goes to Montepulciano.
➤ BUS LINES: **Alessi** (☎ 055/215155 in Florence). **SITA** (✉ Via Santa Caterina da Siena 15/r, Florence, ☎ 0577/204270 in Siena, 055/47821 in Florence, WEB www.sita-on-line.it). **Tra-In** (☎ 0577/204111 in Siena, WEB www.trainspa.it).

CAR RENTALS
➤ AGENCIES: **Avis** (WEB www.avis.com; ✉ Piazza della Repubblica 1/a, Arezzo, ☎ 0575/354232; ✉ Via Simone Martini 36, Siena, ☎ 0577/ 270305). **Hertz** (WEB www.hertz.com; ✉ Aeroporto Galileo Galilei, Pisa, ☎ 050/49187; ✉ Viale Sardegna 37, Siena, ☎ 0577/45085).

CAR TRAVEL
The area is easily reached by car via the A1 autostrada (Autostrada del Sole), which runs between Rome and Florence (exit on S326 for Siena). The Strada Chiantigiana (SS222) is the slower, scenic route, winding its way from Florence to Siena through Chianti's vineyards. The Via Cassia (SS2) also connects Rome and Siena. Greve is only 28 km (17½ mi) south of Florence, and the northernmost reaches of Chianti, including Greve, can be reached in about 30 minutes, depending upon traffic. The prettiest way is via the S222. From Greve, you can easily reach Castellina, Radda, and Gaiole.

Getting to southern Chianti from Florence is considerably more involved, and unless you're up for a long day trip with about 2½ hours of driving on either end, plan to stay overnight. At a distance of 260 km (161 mi), Greve is a haul from Rome; however, towns such as Montalcino, at a distance of 213 km (132 mi), are more easily approached. Take the A1 from Rome, and expect a car ride of about 3½ hours.

Local roads plus sensational vistas make driving a joy in the region. The towns and landmarks are well signed, but you should arm yourself with a good map and nerves of steel to contend with speedy local drivers.

EMERGENCIES

In an emergency, dial 113 for paramedics, police, or the fire department.

All pharmacies post the addresses of the nearest late-night pharmacies outside their doors.

LODGING

APARTMENT AND VILLA RENTALS

Best in Italy acts as a broker for properties throughout Tuscany. Chianti e Terre in Toscana rents villas and country houses, most of them in vineyard estates.

➤ LOCAL AGENTS: **Best in Italy** (✉ Via Foscolo 72, Florence 50124, ☎ 055/223064, ℻ 055/2298912). **Chianti e Terre in Toscana** (✉ Casella Postale 8, Montefiridolfi 50020, ☎ 0577/8244211, ℻ 0577/8244382).

BED-AND-BREAKFASTS

Contact any of the tourism information offices if you're looking to rent a room either in a private apartment or in a hotel.

TAXIS

There is a taxi stand next to the Chiusi train station. The area has few taxi companies as such, but several of Chianti's towns have firms from which cars and drivers can be hired.

➤ IN GREVE: **Giovanni Gemini** (☎ 0349/4588440). **Pistolesi** (☎ 055/8544953). **Sandra** (☎ 0328/5458585).

➤ IN MONTALCINO: **Mulinari** (☎ 0348/5175154). **Pierangeli** (☎ 0577/848656 or 0577/849113).

➤ IN MONTEPULCIANO: **Paolo Cencini** (☎ 0330/7322723). **Stefano Bernardini** (☎ 0578/716081 or 0348/2868790).

TOURS

I Bike Italy offers one-day tours of the countryside.

➤ BIKING TOURS: **I Bike Italy** (✉ Borgo degli Albizi 11, Florence, ☎ ℻ 055/2342371).

TRAIN TRAVEL

Train service from Siena is limited to Montepulciano, Radda, and Gaiole, but the stations themselves aren't anywhere near the center of town. It's best to rent a car or rely on buses if you must take public transportation.

Train service from Florence to Montepulciano, Radda, and Gaiole is virtually nonexistent. Local trains run from Siena to Montepulciano as well as to Chiusi, but the connecting bus service to the center of town is infrequent. It is better to take a bus from Siena or Chiusi.

Information is available from the state railway, Ferrovie dello Stato.

➤ TRAIN LINES: **Ferrovie dello Stato** (FS; ☎ 147/888088 toll-free within Italy, WEB www.fs-on-line.com or www.trenitalia.it).

TRAVEL AGENCIES

➤ AGENCIES: **Machiavelli Viaggi** (✉ Via Machiavelli 49, San Casciano in Val di Pesa 50026, ☎ 055/822324). **Vinea Viaggi** (✉ Via Roma 41, Greve in Chianti 50022, ☎ 055/854352). **Xtramondo Viaggi** (✉ Via Roma 238, Tavarnelle Val di Pesa 50028, ☎ 055/805023).

VISITOR INFORMATION

The tourist office in Tavarnelle Val di Pesa also handles Barberino Val d'Elsa inquiries.

➤ TOURIST INFORMATION: **Castellina in Chianti** (✉ Piazza del Comune 1, ☎ 0577/740620). **Castelnuovo Berardenga** (✉ Via Roma 8, ☎ 0577/

355500). **Greve in Chianti** (⊠ Viale Giovanna da Verrazzano 33, ☎ 055/8346287). **Montalcino** (⊠ Costa del Municipio 8, ☎ 0577/849331, WEB www.prolocomontalcino.it). **Montepulciano** (⊠ Via di Gracciano nel Corso 59/r, ☎ 0578/757341, WEB www.prolocomontepulciano.it). **Radda in Chianti** (⊠ Piazza Ferrucci 1, ☎ 0577/738494). **Tavarnelle Val di Pesa** (⊠ Piazza Matteotti 39, ☎ 055/805 081).

6 SIENA AND THE HILL TOWNS

Once Florence's most fearsome rival,
Siena remains the perfect medieval city
to the south, rich with Gothic palaces
and magnificent art. Proud of its past,
Siena celebrates the Palio with energy
and emotion unchanged over the centuries.
Siena is the perfect introduction to the
celebrated hill towns, with the towers of
San Gimignano and the Etruscan shadows
of Volterra close at hand.

ITALY'S MOST ENCHANTING MEDIEVAL CITY, Siena is the one stop you should make in Tuscany if you make no other. Once there, you'll undoubtedly be drawn to Italy's most famous hill town, San Gimignano, known as the "medieval Manhattan" because of its enormous towers, built by rival families, that still stand today. Like Siena, it benefited from commerce and trade along the pilgrimage routes, as the wonderful art in its churches and museums attests. Equally intriguing is a visit to Volterra, an Etruscan town famous for its alabaster. Southern Tuscany is perhaps less familiar than the Chianti region to the north, but prestigious wines are made south of Siena, too, and the scenery is classically Tuscan. On your way down, don't miss a stop at the Abbazzia di Monte Oliveto Maggiore to see its sublime Renaissance frescoes.

Updated by
Patricia Rucidlo

Pleasures and Pastimes

Dining

If you've already been eating in Tuscany, chances are you'll recognize much of what's on the menu in these towns. Perhaps, too, you'll note the subtle flair of extra herbs and garlic that the Sienese often add to their rendition of traditional Tuscan fare. In Siena and the surrounding region, *antipasti* (usually made of the simplest ingredients) are extremely satisfying. A typical starter might be *fettunta,* a slice of good, toasted bread drizzled with olive oil and rubbed with fresh garlic, and a variety of excellent locally cured meats. As you pass on to the first course, specialties include *pici* (a thick, hand-rolled spaghetti often tossed in a meat ragù or sprinkled with bread crumbs that have been dressed in oil) and *tagliatelle* or *pappardelle* pastas served with a savory ragù of *cinghiale* (wild boar) or *lepre* (hare). The Sienese also have many hearty soups as first courses; these are often made with lentils or beans and sometimes thickened with bread. *Panzanella,* a salad of tomato, basil, and onion, is a common first course found on summer menus. Second courses are traditionally game meats. Not surprisingly, local wines tend to be robust in order to hold up to the local cuisine. Many prestigious wines come from the Siena area and are labeled Chianti Colli Senesi. White-wine drinkers can try Vernaccia di San Gimignano, which is a common white wine of the region and sold in every *enoteca,* or wine bar. After your meal, try some delicious amber-colored Vin Santo, the perfect accompaniment to Sienese sweets such as *ricciarelli,* a succulent almond-flavored cookie.

CATEGORY	COST*
$$$$	over €18
$$$	€13–€18
$$	€8–€13
$	under €8

Prices are for a second course (secondo piatto).

Lodging

Siena, San Gimignano, and Volterra are among the most visited towns in Tuscany, so there's no lack of choice for hotels across the price range. The best accommodations, however, are often a couple of miles outside town. Every year there seem to be more old villas and monasteries converted into charming, first-rate hotels, as well as simpler *agriturismo* (agritourist) farmhouses, usually available for weekly rentals. Their location makes a car necessary, but the splendor of the surroundings usually outweighs any problems getting in and out of town.

CATEGORY	COST*
$$$$	over €175
$$$	€125–€175
$$	€75–€125
$	under €75

All prices are for two people in a standard double room, including tax and service.

Exploring Siena and the Hill Towns

As the smaller towns are a bit too far from one another to make for easy coming and going, Siena makes the most sensible base from which to explore central Tuscany.

Numbers in the text correspond to numbers in the margin and on the Siena and the Hill Towns; Siena; and Volterra maps.

Great Itineraries

IF YOU HAVE 3 OR 4 DAYS

Spend a couple of days getting to know 🖭 **Siena** ①–⑨, exploring its medieval streets and neighborhoods as well as major sites like the Campo, Palazzo Pubblico, Duomo, and surrounding museums. Then make a day or overnight trip to see 🖭 **San Gimignano** ⑫ and its medieval towers or 🖭 **Volterra** ⑬–⑲ and its marvelous Museo Etrusco Guarnacci. Returning to Siena, take an excursion south through the countryside to the **Abbazia di Monte Oliveto Maggiore** ㉑, with its remarkable frescoes and stunning scenery.

IF YOU HAVE 5 OR 6 DAYS

The itinerary above can be easily expanded to include an extra day in 🖭 **Siena** ①–⑨ and visits to **San Gimignano** ⑫, **Volterra** ⑬–⑲, and **Colle di Val d'Elsa** ⑪; the drive south from Siena can be extended to take in the town of **Asciano** ⑳ and/or the thermal baths at Rapolano Terme on the way down to the **Abbazia di Monte Oliveto Maggiore** ㉑.

When to Tour Siena and the Hill Towns

The region enjoys particularly sparkling weather in spring and fall. In summer, the same sun that makes the grapes grow can turn the packed streets unpleasantly hot. In this case, consider that it's always easier to work with the local schedule rather than against it. If you get an early start, you can enjoy the sites in the cooler morning hours and return to have an afternoon siesta while the sun is at its highest. Make a point of catching the *passeggiata* (evening stroll), when the locals throng the Via di Città, the city's main street. Siena fills to the brim in the weeks surrounding the running of the Palio on July 2 and August 16, when prices, crowds, and commotion are at their highest. In the winter months you'll probably have the towns mostly to yourself, although the choices for hotels and restaurants can be a bit more limited than when the season is in full swing. Siena may be quite cold in winter, but it can be a treat to have the streets and museums practically deserted. From November through February it's fairly difficult to find an open hotel in San Gimignano and Volterra: plan accordingly.

SIENA

The she-wolf and suckling twins on the city's emblem show Siena's claim to share common ancestry with Rome; the town's legendary founder, Senius, was a son of Remus, the twin brother of Rome's founder, Romulus. Archaeological evidence suggests there were prehistoric as well as Etruscan settlements here first, which undoubtedly made way for Saena Julia, the Roman town established by Augustus in the 1st century BC.

Siena and the Hill Towns

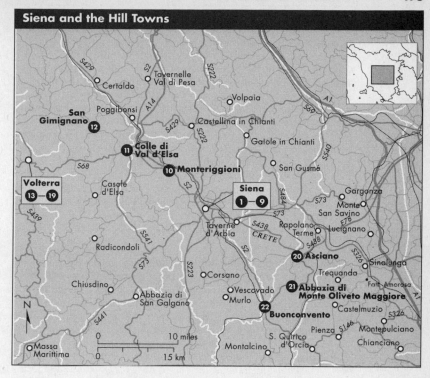

Siena rose to prominence as an essential stop on that most important of medieval roads, the Via Francigena (or Via Romea), prospering from the yearly flow of thousands of Christian pilgrims coming south to Rome from northern Europe. Siena developed a banking system (the first bank, Monte dei Paschi, is still very much in business) and dominated the wool trade, thereby establishing itself as a rival to Florence. The two towns became regional powers and bitter enemies, each town taking a different side in the struggle that divided the peninsula between the Guelphs (loyal to the Pope) and Ghibellines (loyal to the Holy Roman Emperor). Siena took the side of the latter.

Victory over Florence in 1260 at Montaperti marked the beginning of Siena's golden age. Even though the Florentines avenged the loss nine years later, Siena continued to prosper. Over the following decades, Siena erected its greatest buildings, including the Duomo and Palazzo Pubblico; established a model city government presided over by the Council of Nine; and became a great center of art. All of these achievements came together in the decoration of the Sala della Pace in the Palazzo Pubblico.

That Siena was for centuries the great rival in art, trade, textiles, and banking to Florence makes us wonder what greatness the city might have gone on to achieve had its fortunes been different. But the plague of 1348 decimated the population, brought an end to the Council of Nine, and left Siena economically weak and vulnerable to outside domination. After four centuries of conflict, Siena succumbed to Florentine rule in the mid-16th century, when a year-long siege virtually eliminated the native population. Ironically, it was precisely this decline that, along with the steadfast pride of the Sienese, prevented further development, to which we owe the city's marvelous condition.

With its narrow streets and steep alleyways, stunning Gothic Duomo, bounty of early Renaissance art, and the glorious Palazzo Pubblico overlooking its magnificent Campo, Siena is often described as Italy's best-preserved medieval city. But while much looks as it did in the early 14th century, Siena is no museum. Walk through the streets and you can witness a charming anachronism: The medieval *contrade*, the 17 neighborhoods into which the city has been historically divided, are vibrant and very much alive. Look up from just about any street and you will know the *contrada*—Tartuca (turtle), Oca (goose), Istrice (porcupine), Torre (tower)—you are walking in, as its symbol will likely be emblazoned on a banner or engraved in the street. The Sienese still strongly identify themselves by the contrada into which they were born and raised; loyalty and rivalry run deep. At no time is this more visible than during the centuries-old Palio, a twice-yearly horse race through the main square, but you need not visit during the wild festival to come to know the rich culture and enchanting pleasures of Siena.

Exploring Siena

If you come by car, you're better off leaving it in one of the parking lots around the perimeter of town, as car access is always difficult or just plain prohibited in certain parts of the city center. Practically unchanged since medieval times, Siena is laid out in a "Y" over the slopes of several hills, dividing the city into *terzi* (thirds). Although the most interesting sites are in a fairly compact area around the Campo at the center of town, be sure to leave some time to wander into the narrow streets that rise and fall steeply from the main thoroughfares. If your feet have had enough, head for one of the cabs usually found at the bottom of the Campo or take one of the orange electric minibuses that ply their way through the crowds and between the major sites. Also, keep a few €1 coins at hand; several sights still use coin-operated illuminations.

A Good Walk

Try to avoid passing through Siena in less than a day, missing the opportunity to really explore the town, which is more than the sum of its most notable sites. Begin with a coffee on the **Piazza del Campo** ①, the focal point of the city and considered by many to be the finest public square in Italy. Visit the **Palazzo Pubblico** ②, with its Museo Civico and adjacent tower, the Torre del Mangia. Cross the piazza and exit via the stairs to the left of the Fonte Gaia to Via di Città. Just to the left is the 15th-century Loggia della Mercanzia, where merchants and money traders once did business. Commerce is still pretty active along Via di Città, Siena's main shopping street, which climbs to the left. Up ahead on Via di Città is the enchanting Palazzo Chigi-Saracini, where concerts are often held. Step in to admire the especially well-preserved courtyard. Continue up the hill on Via di Città and take the second street on the right, Via del Capitano, which leads to the Piazza del Duomo. The **Duomo** ③ is a must-see, along with the frescoes inside in the Biblioteca Piccolomini. Off to the side are the **Museo dell'Opera Metropolitana** ④ and the **Battistero** ⑤ (around the other side of the Duomo), and across from the Duomo are the **Spedale di Santa Maria della Scala** ⑥ and its Museo Archeologico. Chief among Siena's other gems is the **Pinacoteca Nazionale** ⑦, several blocks straight back down Via del Capitano (which becomes Via San Pietro). The church of **San Domenico** ⑧ lies in the other direction (you could take Via della Galluzza to Via della Sapienza), and nearby is the **Casa di Santa Caterina** ⑨, where one of Italy's patron saints was born.

DUST NEVER SETTLES ON THE PALIO

JUST THREE LAPS AROUND A MAKESHIFT track in Piazza del Campo, and it's all over in less than two minutes, but the spirit of Siena's Palio—which takes place every July 2 and August 16—lives all year long.

The first recorded race was run on August 16, 1310, and another Palio on July 2 was added in 1649. Rules established soon after moved the event to the Campo (it had previously been run through the streets of the town) and set up the current system whereby 10 of Siena's 17 contrade are chosen at random to run in the July Palio. The August Palio is run with 3 of those 10 and the 7 contrade left out the first time. Although the races are officially of equal importance, any Sienese will tell you that it is better to win the second Palio and have bragging rights for the rest of the year.

At first it might not seem like much of a race: there is barely room for the 10 horses along the course, so falls and collisions are inevitable. The competing contrade root emphatically for nameless horses (chosen at random three days before the race) and jockeys from other towns hired by each contrada. At stake is the respect or scorn of the neighboring and rival contrade, and the event is so important to the Sienese that almost nothing is too underhanded. Bribery, secret plotting, and betrayal are commonplace (so much so that the word for"jockey" in Italian, fantino, has come to mean "untrustworthy" in Siena). There have been incidents of drugging (the horses) and kidnapping (the jockeys); only sabotaging a horse's reins remains taboo.

Official festivities kick off three days prior to the Palio, with the selection and blessing of the horses, trial runs, ceremonial banquets, betting, speculation, and late-night celebrations. Residents don scarves with their contrada's colors and march through the streets in medieval costumes. The Campo is transformed into a race-course lined with a thick layer of yellow sand. In the early afternoon, each horse is brought to the church of the contrada for which it will run, where it is blessed and told "Go little horse and return a winner." The piazza begins to fill in the mid-afternoon, and spectators crowd into every available space until bells ring and the piazza is sealed off. Processions of flag wavers in traditional dress march to the beat of tambourines and drums and the roar of the crowds. The palio itself, a banner dedicated to the Virgin Mary, makes an appearance, followed by the competitors and their jockeys.

The race is set off by one horse chosen to ride up from behind, but there are always a number of false starts, adding to the already frenzied mood. Finally the horses are off, and the race is over almost before the dust settles. The winning rider is carried away on the shoulders of his jubilant supporters, back to the streets of the winning contrada, where in the past tradition dictated that the victory entitled him to the local girl of his choice. But the celebration is far from over. TV replays, winners, and losers go over the race from every possible angle—but only one contrada will celebrate long into the night, with long tables piled high with food and drink, the champion horse the guest of honor.

At a time when so many festivals in Europe are staged in a soulless attempt to impose charm on a town, the Palio is by and for the Sienese. Visitors are welcome, but keep in mind that the reserved seating in the stands is sold out months in advance. The entire area in the center is free, but you'll need to show up early in order to secure a prime spot against the barriers. For ticket information, see Outdoor Activities and Sports in Siena.

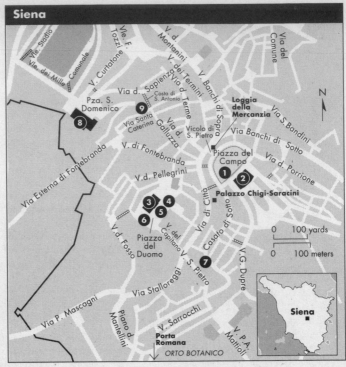

TIMING

It's a joy to walk in Siena—hills notwithstanding—as it's a rare opportunity to stroll through a medieval city rather than just a town. (There is quite a lot to explore, unlike in tiny hill towns that can be crossed in minutes.) The walk can be done in as little as a day, but plan on two days to enjoy the various sites fully. If you only have one day in Siena, don't miss the Duomo, its museum, the Palazzo Pubblico, and the view from the top of the Torre del Mangia. Several of the sites have reduced hours on Sunday afternoon and Monday.

Sights to See

⑤ Battistero. The Duomo's 14th-century Gothic Baptistery was built to prop up one side of the Duomo. There are frescoes throughout, but the highlight is a large bronze 15th-century baptismal font designed by Jacopo della Quercia (1374–1438) and adorned with bas-reliefs by various artists, including two by Renaissance masters: the *Baptism of Christ* by Lorenzo Ghiberti (1378–1455) and the *Feast of Herod* by Donatello. ⊠ *Piazza San Giovanni,* ☎ *no phone,* WEB *www.operaduomo. it.* ⊡ *€1.50; combined ticket with Museo del'Opera del Duomo and Biblioteca Piccolomini €7.50.* ☉ *Mid-Mar.–Sept., daily 9–7:30; Oct., daily 9–6; Nov.–mid-Mar., daily 10–1 and 2:30–5.*

⑨ Casa di Santa Caterina. Caterina Benincasa was born here in 1347, and although she took the veil of the Domenican Tertiary order at age eight, she lived in a cell here, devoting her life to the sick and poor in the aftermath of the devastating plague of 1348. She had divine visions and received the stigmata but is most famous for her writings and her argumentative skills (though she was unable to write—her letters, many of which are preserved in the Biblioteca Comunale, were dictated). She is credited with single-handedly convincing the Pope (the Frenchman Gregory XI, 1329–78) to return the papacy to Rome after 70 years in Avignon and French domination, partially ending the Great Schism that divided the Church. Caterina died in Rome in 1380 and was canonized in 1461. A few years later she was made patron saint of Siena, and the city purchased the family house and turned it into a shrine, one of the first examples of its kind in Italy. The rooms of the house, including her cell and the kitchen, were converted into a series of chapels and oratories and decorated by noteworthy artists over the following centuries with scenes from Caterina's life. In 1939, she was made patron saint of Italy, along with St. Francis of Assisi. In 1970, she was elevated to Doctor of the Church, the highest possible honor in Christendom. ⊠ *Entrance on Costa di San Antonio, off Via della Sapienza,* ☎ *0577/280801.* 🎫 *Free.* ⊙ *Daily 9–1 and 3–5:30.*

★ ❸ **Duomo.** Several blocks west of Piazza del Campo, Siena's Duomo is beyond question one of the finest Gothic cathedrals in Italy. The facade, with its multicolored marbles and painted decoration, is typical of the Italian approach to Gothic architecture, lighter and much less austere than the French. The cathedral as it now stands was completed in the 14th century, just as Siena reached its peak of power and prestige. But the Sienese had even bigger plans. They wanted to enlarge the building by using the existing church as a transept for a new church, with a new nave running toward the southeast, to make what would be the largest church in the world. But only the side wall and part of the new facade were completed when the Black Death struck in 1348, decimating Siena's population. The city fell into decline, funds dried up, and the plans were never carried out. (The dream of building the biggest church was actually doomed to failure from the start—subsequent attempts to get the project going revealed that the foundation was insufficient to bear the weight of the proposed structure.) The beginnings of the new nave, extending from the right side of the Duomo, were left unfinished, perhaps as a testament to unfulfilled dreams, and ultimately enclosed to house the Museo dell'Opera Metropolitana.

The amazingly detailed facade has few rivals in the region, although it is quite similar to the Duomo in Orvieto. It was completed in two brief phases at the end of the 13th and 14th centuries. The statues and decorative work were designed by the Pisano family, although most of what we see today are copies, the originals having been removed to the adjacent Museo dell'Opera Metropolitana for protection. The gold mosaics are 18th-century restorations. The Campanile (no entry) is among central Italy's finest, with the number of windows increasing with each level.

The Duomo's interior, with its black-and-white striping throughout and finely coffered and gilded dome, is simply striking. Step in and look back up at Duccio's (circa 1255–1319) panels of stained glass that fill the circular facade window. Finished in 1288, it is the oldest example of stained glass in Italy. The Duomo is most famous for its unique and magnificent inlaid marble floors, which took almost 200 years to complete (beginning around 1370); more than 40 artists contributed to the work, made up of 56 separate compositions depicting biblical scenes, allegories, religious symbols, and civic emblems. The floors are covered for most of the year for conservation purposes but are unveiled every September for the entire month. The Duomo's carousel pulpit, also much appreciated, was carved by Nicola Pisano (circa 1220–84) around 1265; the *Life of Christ* is depicted on the rostrum frieze. In striking contrast to all the Gothic decoration in the nave are the magnificent Renaissance frescoes in the **Biblioteca Piccolomini,** off the left aisle. Painted by Pinturicchio (circa 1454–1513) and completed in 1509, they depict events from the life of native son Aeneas Sylvius Piccolomini (1405–64), who became Pope Pius II in 1458. The frescoes are in excellent condition and have a freshness rarely seen in work so old. ⊠ *Piazza del Duomo,* ☎ *0577/283048,* WEB *www.operaduomo.it.* 🖾 *Duomo free; Biblioteca Piccolomini €1.50; combined ticket with Battistero and Museo del'-Opera del Duomo €7.50.* ☉ *Duomo Nov.–mid-Mar., daily 7:30–4:30; mid-Mar.–Oct., daily 9–7:30. Biblioteca Nov.–mid-Mar., daily 10–12:45 and 2–4:45; mid-Mar.–Oct., daily 9–7:30.*

NEED A
BREAK?

Not far from the Duomo and the Pinacoteca, Siena's **Orto Botanico** (Botanical Gardens; ⊠ V. Pier Andrea Mattioli 4, ☎ 0577/232874) is a great place to relax and enjoy views onto the countryside below. It's open weekdays 8–12:30 and 2:30–5, Saturday 8–noon.

---

❹ **Museo dell'Opera Metropolitana.** Built into part of the unfinished nave of what was to have been the new cathedral, the museum contains the Duomo's treasury and some of the original decoration from its facade and interior. The first room on the ground floor displays weather-beaten 13th-century sculptures by Giovanni Pisano (circa 1250–1314) that were brought inside for protection and replaced by copies, as was a tondo of the *Madonna and Child* (now attributed to Donatello) that once hung on the door to the south transept. The masterpiece is unquestionably Duccio's *Maestà,* one side with 26 panels depicting episodes from the Passion, the other side with a *Madonna and Child Enthroned.* Painted between 1308 and 1311 as the altarpiece for the Duomo (where it remained until 1505), its realistic elements, such as the lively depiction of the infant Jesus and the treatment of interior space, proved an enormous influence on later painters. The second floor is divided between the treasury, with a crucifix by Giovanni Pisano and several statues and busts of biblical characters and classical philosophers, and La Sala della Madonna degli Occhi Grossi (the Room of the Madonna with the Big Eyes), named after the namesake painting it displays by the Maestro di Tressa, who painted in the early 13th century. The work originally decorated the Duomo's high altar before being displaced by Duccio's *Maestà.* There is a fine view from the tower inside the museum. ⊠ *Piazza del Duomo, next to the Duomo,* ☎ *0577/283048.* 🖾 *€5.50; combined ticket with Battistero and Biblioteca Piccolomini €7.50.* ☉ *Nov.–mid-Mar., daily 9–1:30; mid-Mar.–Sept., daily 9–7:30; Oct., daily 9–6.*

★ ❷ **Palazzo Pubblico.** Considered Italy's finest Gothic town hall, Palazzo Pubblico has been the symbol of the city and the seat of its government for almost 700 years. Several of the rooms are decorated with some of Italy's finest early Renaissance frescoes. The main doorway opens onto the Cortile del Podestà (Courtyard of the Podestà), at the left of which is the entrance to the Torre del Mangia. The Magazzini del Sale (salt warehouses), where salt—once a precious commodity—was kept safe, are now used for temporary exhibits.

To the right of the Cortile del Podestà is the entrance to the **Museo Civico.** The first room is the Sala del Risorgimento, with 19th-century panels telling the story of Italian Unification. Cut through to the main hall, the Sala del Mappamondo, named for a circular frescoed map of the Sienese state by Ambrogio Lorenzetti (1319–48), now lost. The room features Simone Martini's (circa 1284–1344) early 14th-century *Maestà* and *Portrait of Guidoriccio da Fogliano..*

The next room in the museum, the Sala della Pace (Hall of Peace), is decorated by the largest secular pictorial cycle of the Middle Ages and one of Italy's greatest fresco cycles, the *Allegories of Good and Bad*

Government, painted by Ambrogio Lorenzetti in 1337–39. The Council of Nine commissioned him to decorate the room in which they met, perhaps to be ever reminded of the right thing to do. On the entrance wall is a city scene that depicts the effects of good government—easily identified as a utopian view of 14th-century Siena, of course. The painting is full of bright, vibrant colors; well-maintained buildings; happy, productive people; and a rich fertile landscape outside the town. Running across the foreground is the lifeblood of the city, the pilgrims of every sort who came through Siena on the Via Francigena (or Via Romea) on their way to or from Rome.

On the front wall is the personification of Good Government, the wise old man dressed in the colors of the *comune,* representing the town council. At his feet are the twin sons of Remus, one of whom, according to legend, founded Siena. Hovering above his head are the three theological virtues: Faith, Charity, and Hope. To his sides are the virtues of good government (left to right, Peace, Force, Prudence, Magnanimity, Temperance, and Justice), each holding corresponding symbols. To the left is the figure of Justice, looking up at Wisdom while balancing her scales. The left side represents commutative justice (the distribution of wealth and power) and the right, distributive justice (the absolution of the innocent and punishment of the guilty). In the foreground are the town's 24 magistrates, who hold cords connecting them to the scales. Also included in the scene are those who execute the orders of the government (the soldiers) and those who oppose it (the prisoners).

If good government served as an ideal, the allegory of Bad Government on the opposite wall was a corresponding injunction against tyranny, the figure who takes the place of the wise old man in the adjacent wall. He is surrounded by a nasty bunch of negative attributes: Avarice, Pride, and Vanity hang in the air, while Cruelty, Deceit, Fraud, Fury, Discord, and War sit on either side, fondling strange animals. Interestingly, the Bad Government fresco is severely damaged, while the Good Government fresco is in terrific condition. You can barely make out the figure of Justice (all tied up), her scales lying on the ground, but the conditions in the town leave little doubt as to the results of bad government: buildings in ruin, brutal soldiers everywhere, the landscape barren. Note that this was the view that visitors had on entering the room, only then turning to see the Council of Nine and the effects of their good government.

The next rooms in the museum feature more frescoes by Sienese artists from the 13th to 15th century, including frescoes attributed to Ambrogio Lorenzetti (*San Michele Arcangelo*) and Neroccio di Bartolomeo (1447–1500; *Predica di San Bernardino*). Off the Sala del Mappamondo is the Antechapel, with frescoes by Taddeo di Bartolo (circa 1362–1422), and the adjacent chapel with marvelous inlaid-wood choir stalls.

Built to reach the height of the Duomo's Campanile, thereby asserting the power of temporal rule, the **Torre del Mangia** soars to a height of 330 ft, making it the second tallest in Italy. Its curious name comes from one of the tower's first bell ringers, Giovanni di Duccio (called Mangiaguadagni, or earnings eater). The climb up to the top is long and steep, but the superb view makes it worth every step. ⊠ *Piazza del Campo,* ☎ *0577/292226.* 🎫 *Torre di Mangia €5.50; Museo Civico €6.50.* ⊙ *Torre di Mangia Nov.–mid-Mar., daily 10–6; mid-Mar.–Oct., daily 10–7. Museo Civico late Nov.–mid-Feb., daily 10–5:30; mid-Feb.–mid-Mar., daily 10–6:30, mid-Mar.–Oct., daily 10–7.*

★ ❶ **Piazza del Campo.** Built in the 14th century on a market area that was originally the site of the Roman Forum, this fan-shape piazza is known simply as Il Campo (the Field). Unclaimed by any contrada, it was neutral ground and thus the logical place to set up the town government. Strips in gray stone divide the brick pavement into nine sections—one for each of the medieval Council of Nine, which fan out from the Palazzo Pubblico. Now most associated with the running of the Palio (it's hard to walk very far in Siena without seeing a poster or calendar of the yearly event), the Campo remains the heart of Sienese life all year long and is a pleasant place to take a rest and enjoy one of the greatest examples of medieval city planning. The surrounding buildings were restored in the 19th century with neo-Gothic facades to bring back the original appearance of the Campo, although the daily market was relocated. Several openings lead out to the main streets of the three wings of the city. At the top of the Campo is the **Fonte Gaia**, decorated in the early 15th century by Siena's greatest sculptor, Jacopo della Quercia, with 13 reliefs of biblical events and virtues. The reliefs that now line the rectangular fountain are 19th-century copies; the originals are in the Spedale di Santa Maria della Scala.

❼ **Pinacoteca Nazionale.** The superb collection of five centuries of local painting in Siena's national picture gallery will easily convince you that the Renaissance was by no means just a Florentine thing—Siena was arguably just as important a center of art and innovation as its rival to the north, especially at the beginning of the period. Accordingly, the most interesting section of the collection, chronologically arranged, is the initial part, which features several important "firsts." Room 1 contains a painting of the *Stories of the True Cross* (1215) by the so-called Master of Tressa, the earliest identified work by a painter of the Sienese school, and is followed in Room 2 by late-13th-century artist Guido da Siena's *Stories from the Life of Christ,* one of the first paintings ever made on canvas (earlier painters used wood panels). Rooms 3 and 4 are dedicated to Duccio, a student of Cimabue (circa 1240–1302) and considered to be the last of the proto-Renaissance painters. Ambrogio Lorenzetti's landscapes in Room 8 are the first truly secular paintings in Western art. Among later works in the rooms on the floor above, keep an eye out for the preparatory sketches used by Domenico Beccafumi (circa 1486–1551) for the 35 etched marble panels he made for the floor of the Duomo. ⊠ *Via San Pietro 29,* ☎ *0577/ 281161.* 🎫 *€4.10.* ☉ *Mon. 8:30–1:30, Tues.–Sat. 9–7, Sun. 8–1.*

❽ **San Domenico.** While the Duomo is celebrated as a triumph of 13th-century Gothic architecture, this church, built at about the same time, turned out as an oversize, hulking brick box that never merited a finishing coat in marble, let alone a graceful facade. Although named for the founder of the Domenican order, the church is now more closely associated with St. Catherine of Siena. Just to the right of the entrance is the chapel in which she received the stigmata. On the wall is the only known contemporary portrait of the saint, made in the late 14th century by Andrea Vanni (circa 1332–1414). Farther down is the famous **Cappella di Santa Caterina,** the church's official shrine to Catherine, although only her head and finger are here (kept in a reliquary on the altar). Revered throughout the country long before she was officially named patron saint of Italy in 1939, Catherine, or bits and pieces of her, was literally spread all over the country—a foot is in Venice, the rest of her body in Rome. On either side of the chapel are well-known frescoes by Il Sodoma (a.k.a. Giovanni Bazzi, 1477–1549) of *St. Catherine in Ecstasy.* Don't miss the view from the apse-side terrace onto the Duomo and town center. ⊠ *Piazza San Domenico,* ☎ *0577/280893.* 🎫 *Free.* ☉ *Daily 9–12:30 and 3:30–6.*

NEED A
BREAK? Not far from the church of San Domenico, the **Enoteca Italiana** (⊠ Fortezza Medicea, Viale Maccari, ☎ 0577/288497) is a fantastically stocked wine cellar in the bastions of the Fortezza Medici. The enoteca offers wines by the glass and snacks, but if you love wine or are simply curious, take some time to peruse the labels that are on the shelves (the wines of more than 400 wineries are in stock here). It's open daily from noon to 1 AM. On Friday evenings in winter, there's also a piano bar.

Sinagoga. Down a small street around the corner from Il Campo, this synagogue is worth a visit simply to view the two sobering plaques that adorn its facade. One commemorates June 28, 1799, when 13 Jews were taken from their homes in the ghetto by a fanatic mob and burned in Il Campo. The other memorializes the Sienese Jews who were deported, and never returned, during World War II. ⊠ *Vicolo delle Scotte 14,* ☎ *0577/284647.*

6 **Spedale di Santa Maria della Scala.** For more than a thousand years, this complex across from the Duomo was home to Siena's hospital, but now it serves as a museum to display some terrific frescoes and other Sienese Renaissance treasures. Restored 15th-century frescoes in the Sala del Pellegrinaio (once the emergency room) tell the history of the hospital, which was created to give refuge to passing pilgrims and those in need and to distribute charity to the poor. Incorporated into the complex is the church of the Santissima Annunziata, with a celebrated *Risen Christ* by Vecchietta (also known as Lorenzo di Pietro, circa 1412–80). The curious will want to head down into the dark Cappella di Santa Caterina della Notte, where St. Catherine went to pray at night. A portion of the building is occupied by Siena's **Museo Archeologico,** right on the piazza, with an underrated collection. Assembled from various private collections and a few relics found locally, the displays—including the *bucchero* (dark, reddish clay) ceramics, Roman coins, and tomb furnishings—are clearly marked and can serve as a good introduction to the history of regional excavations. Don't miss della Quercia's original sculpted reliefs from the Fonte Gaia. Although the fountain has been faithfully copied for the Campo, there's something incomparably beautiful about the real thing. ⊠ *Piazza del Duomo, opposite the front of the Duomo,* ☎ *0577/224811.* 🎟 *€5.20.* ☉ *Nov.–Mar., daily 10–4:30; Apr.–Oct., daily 10:30–6.*

Dining and Lodging

$$$$ ✕ **Antica Trattoria Botteganova.** Just outside the city walls, along the
★ road that leads north to Chianti, the Botteganova is arguably the best restaurant in Siena. Chef Michele Sorrentino's cooking is all about clean flavors, balanced combinations, and inviting presentation. Look for inspiring dishes such as spaghetti *alla chitarra in salsa di astice piccante* (spaghetti with a spicy lobster sauce). The interior, with high vaulting, is relaxed yet classy, and the service is first rate. There's a small room for nonsmokers. ⊠ *Strada per Montevarchi (SS408) 29, 2 km (1 mi) north of Siena,* ☎ *0577/284230. AE, DC, MC, V. Closed Mon.*

$$$ ✕ **Le Logge.** Near Piazza del Campo, this classic Sienese trattoria has rustic dining rooms on two levels and outside seating from June to October. Tuscan fare is on the menu, with dishes like *malfatti all'osteria* (ricotta and spinach dumplings in a cream sauce) and *anatra al finocchio* (roast duck with fennel). ⊠ *Via del Porrione 33,* ☎ *0577/48013. Reservations essential. AE, DC, MC, V. Closed Sun. and 2 wks in Nov.*

$$–$$$ ✕ **Al Marsili.** Under the broad, brick-vaulted ceilings of this 900-year-old wine cellar, you'll choose from marvelous Tuscan and Italian specialties, among them homemade pastas such as *tortelloni burro e salvia* (large cheese-filled ravioli with a butter and sage sauce). The wine list

includes stars from the nearby Chianti country. ✉ *Via del Castoro 3, between Piazza del Campo and the cathedral,* ☎ *0577/47154. AE, DC, MC, V. Closed Mon.*

$$–$$$ ✕ **Hosteria il Carroccio.** For an intimate meal, angle for one of the few seats here to try dishes both creative and deliciously simple. The *palline di pecorino con lardo e salsa di pere* (pecorino cheese balls wrapped with luscious pork fat and briefly grilled), for instance, is sublime. In summer, you can sit outdoors. ✉ *Via Casato di Sotto 32,* ☎ *0577/41165. MC, V. Closed Wed.*

$$–$$$ ✕ **La Taverna di San Giuseppe.** Though it's close to the Campo, this long, cavernous dining room is decidedly untouristy, as it's on a residential street. The menu teems with Tuscan favorites with Sienese twists, such as prosciutto *di cinta senese* (prosciutto made from local, once nearly extinct, pigs). Here they make an aromatic, flavorful version of *fegatini*, a chicken-liver spread, with spleen. ✉ *Via G. Duprè 132,* ☎ *0577/42286. AE, DC, MC, V. Closed Sun.*

$$ ✕ **Enoteca I Terzi.** Owner Michele Incarnato happily calls his place "an-
★ archic" because it offers a little bit of everything—leisurely or quick business lunches for the locals, lavish dinners, and significant snacks in between. This wine bar, on the ground floor of a 12th-century tower, is hard to beat for a good glass of wine from a lengthy and carefully chosen list. The pasta specials change daily, and you'll be blessed if *pici all'anatra e funghi* (thick spaghetti with a duck and mushroom sauce) is on the menu. ✉ *Via dei Termini 7,* ☎ *0577/44329. AE, DC, MC, V. Closed Sun.*

$$ ✕ **Osteria Castelvecchio.** In a stall in the oldest part of town, this little restaurant with high ribbed vaults mixes classics and unconventional combinations on its daily menu. You're likely to find such Sienese standards as spaghetti *saporiti con gli aromi* (with tomatoes and herbs) as well as offbeat selections such as *sformatino del pastore con soia e cardi al vino* (a ricotta and greens concoction with cardoons and tofu). Owners Mauro Lombardini and Simone Romi are committed to *piatti di verdura* (vegetarian dishes), and they've got a great wine list. ✉ *Via Castelvecchio 65,* ☎ *0577/49586. AE, MC, V. Closed Tues.*

$$$$ 🏨 **Certosa di Maggiano.** A former 14th-century monastery converted
★ into an exquisite country hotel, this haven of gracious living is about 1½ km (1 mi) from the center of Siena. Classic prints and bold colors like daffodil yellow warm the guest rooms. Common rooms are luxurious, with fine woods and leather. In warm weather, breakfast is served on the patio next to a garden ablaze with flowers. Half-board is required in high season. ✉ *Via Certosa 82 (take the Siena Sud exit off superstrada), 53100,* ☎ *0577/288180,* ℻ *0577/288189,* 🌐 *www.certosadimaggiano. it. 6 rooms, 11 suites. Restaurant, minibars, tennis court, pool, exercise equipment, dry cleaning, laundry service, helipad; no kids under 12, no-smoking rooms. AE, MC, V. BP.*

$$$$ 🏨 **Grand Hotel Continental.** Pope Alexander VII of the famed Sienese Chigi family gave this palace to his niece for a wedding present in 1600; through the centuries it has been a private family home as well as a grand hotel. Now completely refurbished, it exudes elegance, from the pillared entrance to the linen sheets. Some guest rooms take in panoramic views, while others have 18th-century frescos and massive chandeliers. A shuttle makes constant runs to the nearby Park Hotel, which shares its golf and pool facilities with the Grand. ✉ *Banchi di Sopra 85, 53100,* ☎ *0577/56011,* ℻ *0577/5601555,* 🌐 *www.grandhotelcontinentalsiena. it. 40 rooms, 11 suites. Restaurant, room service, in-room fax (on request), in-room safes, minibars, cable TV, wine bar, baby-sitting, dry cleaning, laundry services, concierge, Internet, meeting room, parking (fee); no-smoking rooms. AE, DC, MC, V. EP.*

$$$$ ⊞ **Palazzo Ravizza.** There might not be a more romantic place in the
★ center of Siena than this quietly charming pensione just outside Porta
San Marco. Rooms have high ceilings, antique furniture, big windows,
and bathrooms decorated with hand-painted tiles. Try and book a room
overlooking the garden; its fountain makes for lovely water music while
falling asleep. Half-board is mandatory during the high season. The cost
is toward the low end of this price category. ⊠ *Pian dei Mantellini, 34,
53100,* ☎ *0577/280462,* ℻ *0577/221597,* ⓦⓔⓑ *www.palazzoravizza.it.
31 rooms, 9 suites. Restaurant, in-room safes, bar, laundry service, concierge, free parking, some pets allowed. AE, DC, MC, V. EP.*

$$$$ ⊞ **Park.** This hotel's refined roots as a 16th-century home for the prosperous Gori family are still in evidence, from the highly polished terra-
cotta floors and comfortable couches in the public areas to the plush
carpeting and large bathrooms of the guest rooms. Many rooms face a
courtyard, complete with a well, and have stunning views of olive trees
and Siena beyond. The staff is extraordinarily helpful and polite. ⊠ *Via
Marciano 18, 53100,* ☎ *0577/44803,* ℻ *0577/49020,* ⓦⓔⓑ *www.
parkhotelsiena.it. 63 rooms, 6 suites. Restaurant, room service, in-room
fax, minibars, 6-hole golf course, tennis court, pool, bar, baby-sitting,
dry cleaning, laundry service, concierge, business services, meeting rooms,
some pets allowed. AE, DC, MC, V. BP.*

$$$ ⊞ **Duomo.** Occupying the top floor of a 17th-century building near
Piazza del Campo, this quiet hotel is furnished in a neat contemporary
style, with traces of the past showing in the artfully exposed brickwork
in the breakfast room. Many bedrooms have views of the city's tow-
ers and the hilly countryside. Two rooms have balconies, and there's
a rooftop terrace, often with blooming flowers, that offers another splen-
did view. Free parking is available a short distance from the hotel. ⊠
Via Stalloreggi 38, 53100, ☎ *0577/289088,* ℻ *0577/43043,* ⓦⓔⓑ *www.
hotelduomo.it. 23 rooms. Laundry service, free parking, some pets al-
lowed. AE, DC, MC, V. BP.*

$$$ ⊞ **Santa Caterina.** Just outside Porta Romana—a 10-minute walk to
★ the Campo—the Santa Caterina is an extremely pleasant, well-run hotel.
The owners are about as welcoming, hospitable, and enthusiastic
about the town as you could ever imagine, and their attention to detail makes this one of Siena's little gems. Rooms are all nicely appointed
with simple Tuscan furniture and firm beds; rooms in the back look
out onto the garden or the countryside in the distance. Breakfast is served
in a sunny enclosed patio or out in the garden. ⊠ *Via Piccolomini 7,
53100,* ☎ *0577/221105,* ℻ *0577/271087,* ⓦⓔⓑ *www.hscsiena.it. 22
rooms. Minibars, baby-sitting, dry cleaning, laundry service, concierge,
some pets allowed, no-smoking rooms. AE, DC, MC, V. BP.*

$$ ⊞ **Antica Torre.** A restored 16th-century tower within the town walls
in the southeast corner of Siena, Antica Torre is a 10-minute walk from
Piazza del Campo. The cordial owners create the atmosphere of a pri-
vate home, with only eight simply but tastefully furnished guest rooms.
The old stone staircase, wooden beams, and original brick vaults here
and there are reminders of the building's great age. ⊠ *Via Fieravec-
chia 7, 53100,* ☎ ℻ *0577/222255. 8 rooms. Minibars, Internet; no
air-conditioning, no TV in some rooms. AE, DC, MC, V. EP.*

$$ ⊞ **Chiusarelli.** Caryatids stud the grounds of this well-kept neoclassic villa.
Its guest rooms are functional, airy, and reasonably quiet, but the handy
location is the big plus: near the long-distance bus terminal and parking area and only a 10-minute walk from the main sights. The small garden invites reading; a downstairs restaurant caters to tour groups. ⊠ *Viale
Curtatone 15, 53100,* ☎ *0577/280562,* ℻ *0577/271177,* ⓦⓔⓑ *www.
chiusarelli.com. 49 rooms. Restaurant, in-room safes, cable TV, bar, concierge, meeting room, free parking, some pets allowed. AE, MC, V. EP.*

Nightlife and the Arts

The Arts

MUSIC

In late July and August, Siena hosts the **Settimane Musicali Senesi,** a series of classical music concerts held in churches and courtyards with performances of local and other music. For information, contact the Siena tourist office (☎ 0577/280551) or the event organizers (☎ 0577/22091). From late June through July, the **Fondazione Musicale Chigiana** (☎ 0577/22091, WEB www.chigiana.it) presents a series of classical concerts all over town in historic settings such as Santa Maria della Scala and the church of Sant'Agostino.

Nightlife

Join the locals for *aperitivi* at **Caffè del Corso** (⊠ Banchi di Sopra 22, ☎ no phone). **Enoteca I Terzi** (⊠ Via dei Termini 7, ☎ 0577/44329) is lively and open late. **L'Officina** (⊠ Piazza del Sale 3, ☎ 0577/286301) is a happening local hangout, with live music on Thursday; the other nights, DJs spin different sounds, from Latin-inspired rhythms to dance and rock. The popular tea room **Porta Giustizia 11** (⊠ Via Porta Giustizia 11, ☎ 0577/222753) is open late.

Outdoor Activities and Sports

Siena's thrilling Palio horse race takes place every year on July 2 and August 16. Three laps around the track in Piazza del Campo earn participants of the Palio the respect or scorn of the other 16 contrade. Tickets usually sell out months in advance of the events, but some hotels reserve a number of tickets for guests; call the **tourist office** (⊠ Piazza del Campo 56, ☎ 0577/280551). It is possible you might luck out and get an unclaimed seat or two; of course, the center of the piazza is free to all on a first-come, first-served basis, until just moments before the start.

Shopping

Arts and Crafts

For centuries, Siena has been famous for its embroidered work, and that tradition lives on at **Siena Ricama** (⊠ Via di Città 61, ☎ 0577/288339), which carries embroidered items for the home. **Antiche Dimore** (⊠ Via di Città 115, ☎ 0577/45337) has embroidered linens and other housewares.

Fioretta Bacci (⊠ Via San Pietro 7, ☎ 0577/282200) weaves beautiful scarves, sweaters, and other accessories on her loom, which stands in the center of her tiny shop.

If you've always wanted a 14th- or 15th-century Sienese painting to hang on your walls but bemoaned the high costs of acquiring one, consider purchasing one of the superb copies made by Chiara Perinetti Casoni at **Bottega dell'Arte** (⊠ Via Stalloreggi 47, ☎ 0577/40755). Her work in tempera on panel and gold leaf is of the highest quality.

Sweets and Wines

In addition to its distinctive crafts, Siena is known for its delectable variety of cakes and cookies with recipes dating back to medieval times. Some Sienese sweets are *cavallucci* (sweet spice biscuits), *panforte* (a traditional Christmas delicacy with honey, hazelnuts, almonds, and spices), *ricciarelli* (almond-paste cookies), and *castagnaccio* (a baked Tuscan treat made in the fall and winter from a batter of chestnut flour, topped with pine nuts and rosemary). The best place in town to find delicious Sienese desserts, as well as to grab a cappuccino, is **Nannini** (⊠ Banchi di Sopra 24, ☎ 0577/239009). A good place to have a slice of castagnaccio is **Pizza al Volo** (⊠ Via Pellegrini 19, ☎ 0577/280095).

Siena's excellent food and wine shops sell a good selection of local products. For the finest pecorino cheeses, try **La Antica Fattoria** (⊠ Via di Città 51, ☎ 0577/4225). Besides offering the usual cured meats and cheeses, **La Bottega dei Sapori Antichi** (⊠ Via delle Terme 41, ☎ 0577/ 285501) stocks an impressive array of *verdure sott'olio* (vegetables marinated in extra-virgin olive oil). The city also has some serious wine shops. Italy's only state-sponsored enoteca, **Enoteca Italiana** (⊠ Fortezza Medicea, ☎ 0577/288497), sells wines from all over Italy. At **Enoteca I Terzi** (⊠ Via dei Termini 7, ☎ 0577/44329), the selection of wines is small but comprehensive. **Enoteca San Domenico** (⊠ Via del Paradiso 56, ☎ 0577/271181) has, in addition to a rich selection of red wines from all over Tuscany, baskets full of locally made panforte in various sizes, wrappings, and degrees of spiciness.

HILL TOWNS WEST OF SIENA
Toward Volterra

From Siena, the road northwest to Florence (SS2) leads up to two pretty towns, Monteriggioni and Colle di Val d'Elsa, both good places to take a break. From there it's a short climb to San Gimignano, known for its wine and medieval towers, or a longer ride west to Volterra, city of the Etruscans. Although these two famous hill towns make easy day trips from Siena, each is interesting enough in its own right to be worthy of an overnight stay.

Monteriggioni

❿ *20 km (12 mi) southeast of San Gimignano, 93 km (58 mi) southeast of Pisa, 55 km (34 mi) south of Florence.*

Tiny Monteriggioni makes a nice stop for a quiet walk on the way north to Colle di Val d'Elsa, San Gimignano, or Volterra. It's hard to imagine that this little town surrounded by open countryside and poppy fields was ever anything but sleepy. But in the 13th century, Monteriggioni served as Siena's northernmost defense against impending Florentine invasion, so it's likely that the residents of the town spent many a sleepless night. The town's formidable walls are in good condition, although the 14 square towers are not as tall as in Dante's (1265–1321) time, when the poet likened them to the four giants who guarded the horrifying central pit of hell.

Dining and Lodging

$$$ ✕ **Il Pozzo.** Dig into hearty Tuscan country cooking at this rustic tavern on the village square. The specialties are homemade fresh pasta, main courses of *filetto alla boscaiola* (fillet of Chianina beef with porcini mushrooms), *piccione ripieno* (stuffed squab), and homey desserts. ⊠ *Piazza Roma 2,* ☎ *0577/304127. AE, DC, MC, V. Closed Mon., Jan. 7–Feb. 7, and Aug. 1–7. No dinner Sun.*

$$$$ ▥ **Borgo San Luigi.** The San Luigi occupies a 17th-century villa just outside Monteriggioni, lined with lavender bushes and cypress trees. The furnishings in the villa and the workers' quarters—converted into 10 apartments—are rustic, but you'll enjoy all the comforts of a four-star establishment. A poolside restaurant is open in summer. ⊠ *Via della Cerretta 38, Località San Luigi Strove, 53035, 4 km (2½ mi) from Monteriggioni on local road to Colle di Val d'Elsa,* ☎ *0577/301055,* FAX *0577/301167,* WEB *www.borgosanluigi.it. 54 rooms, 10 apartments. Restaurant, in-room fax, in-room safes, cable TV, in-room VCRs,*

kitchenette, minibars, pool, 2 tennis courts, gym, exercise equipment, health club, bar, baby-sitting, concierge, business services, meeting rooms, some pets allowed, free parking. AE, DC, MC, V. CP.

Colle di Val d'Elsa

⑪ *12 km (7 mi) west of Monteriggioni, 25 km (16 mi) northwest of Siena.*

Most people pass right through on their way to and from popular tourist destinations Volterra and San Gimignano—a shame, since Colle di Val d'Elsa has a lot to offer. Another town on the Via Francigena that benefited from trade along the pilgrimage route to Rome, Colle got an extra boost in the late 16th century when it was given a bishopric, probably related to an increase in trade when nearby San Gimignano was cut off from the well-traveled road. From the 12th century onward, the flat lower portion of town was given over to a flourishing paper-making industry; today the area is mostly modern, and efforts have shifted toward the production of fine glass and crystal. Buses arrive at Piazza Arnolfo, named after the town's favorite son, Arnolfo di Cambio (1245–1302), the early-Renaissance architect who designed Florence's Duomo and Palazzo Vecchio (but sadly nothing here). There is a convenient parking lot off S68, with stairs leading up the hill.

Make your way to the better-preserved upper part of town, arranged on two levels. The best views of the valley are to be had from Viale della Rimembranza, the road that loops around the west end of town, past the church of San Francesco. The early 16th-century Porta Nuova was inserted into the preexisting medieval walls, just as several handsome Renaissance-style *palazzi* were placed into the medieval neighborhood to create what is now called the Borgo. Halfway down Via Campana, the main street, is the **Chiesa di Santa Caterina,** with a life-size terra-cotta depiction of the *Lamentation*. The road passes through the facade of the surreal Palazzo Campana, an otherwise unfinished building that serves as a door connecting the two parts of the upper town. Via delle Volte, named for the arches that cover it, leads straight through to Piazza del Duomo.

Several restructurings have left little of the once-Romanesque **Duomo** to admire. Inside is the Cappella del Santo Chiodo (Chapel of the Holy Nail), built in the 15th century to hold a nail allegedly from the cross upon which Jesus was crucified. (Perhaps it inspired the locals to go into the nail-making business, which became another of the town's flourishing industries.) ⊠ *Piazza del Duomo,* ☎ *no phone.* ☞ *Free.* ۞ *Daily 8–noon and 4–6.*

A pair of museums on Via del Castello is well worth looking into. **Museo d'Arte Sacra** displays religious relics as well as triptychs from the Sienese and Florentine schools dating to the 14th and 15th centuries. The **Museo Civico** features the town's tribute to Arnolfo di Cambio, with photos of the buildings he designed for other towns and some models of the town. Down Via del Castello, at No. 63, is the house-tower where Arnolfo was born in 1245. (It's not open to the public.) ⊠ *Via del Castello 33,* ☎ *0577/923888.* ☞ *€5 combined admission.* ۞ *Nov.–Mar., weekends 10–noon and 3:30–6:30; Apr.–Oct., Tues.–Sun. 10–noon and 4–7.*

Dining and Lodging

$$$$ ✕ **Ristorante Arnolfo.** Food lovers should not miss Arnolfo, possibly
★   one of Tuscany's finest restaurants. From its tranquil spot in the center of town, it sets high standards of creativity. Chef Gaetano Trovato's balance between innovation and tradition results in dishes such as a pasta-less ravioli with a tarragon pesto. The menu changes frequently

and features two fixed-price options, but you're sure to find fish in summer. ⊠ *Piazza XX Settembre 52,* ☎ FAX *0577/920549. AE, DC, MC, V. Reservations essential. Closed Tues., mid-Jan.–mid-Feb., and 2 wks in Aug.*

$$$–$$$$ ✕ **L'Antica Trattoria.** The homemade ravioli stuffed with leeks and ricotta cheese is worth the trip here, not to mention the refined decor and beautiful terrace where the meals are served in the summer. The *ribollita,* a long-cooked Tuscan soup made with bread, along with *cavolo nero* (Tuscan cabbage), is a good choice on cold days. ⊠ *Piazza Arnolfo di Cambio 23, Colle Basso,* ☎ *0577/923747. Reservations essential. AE, DC, MC, V. Closed Tues.*

$$–$$$ ✕ **Il Frantoio.** Once the olive-oil pressing room of a Renaissance palace, this is now the place to come for culinary experimentation. The candlelit room is cavernous yet intimate, the daily menu's fresh pastas and meat savory. Everything that's put on the table is made in-house. If they manage to augment that somewhat limited wine list, the place would be flawless. ⊠ *Via del Castello 38,* ☎ *0577/923652. MC, V. Closed Mon..*

$$–$$$ ✕ **Molino il Moro.** This early-12th-century grain mill, now a romantic, top-notch restaurant, still perches over a rushing river. The chef concocts sophisticated spins on traditional Tuscan dishes, such as the divine *filetto di coniglio in crosta con purèe di pruge e vinaigrette di lamponi* (rabbit loin with a prune purée). The wine list is short but sweet, the service note-perfect. ⊠ *Via della Ruota 2,* ☎ *0577/920862. MC, V. Closed Mon.*

$$ ✕ **Osteria di Sapia.** A short and simple à la carte seasonal menu that changes frequently is one of the advantages of eating here. Diners can choose between four *antipasti* (appetizers), four *primi* (first courses), four *secondi* (second courses), and four *dolci* (desserts). All of this can be enjoyed in the warmer months on a terrace offering a sweeping view. ⊠ *Via del Castello 4, Colle Alta,* ☎ *0577/921453. DC, MC, V. Closed Mon. May–Sept. and Mon.–Wed. Oct.–Apr.*

$$ ✕🏨 **Vecchia Cartiera Restaurant/Hotel.** The Vecchia Cartiera, an early-13th-century paper factory, has been beautifully renovated to preserve the feeling of the old building while providing comfortable rooms for guests. The restaurant serves local cuisine on dishes made by ceramicists from the area, as well as a satisfying buffet breakfast, complete with marmalade-filled tarts, home-cured meats, and local cheeses. ⊠ *Via Oberdan 5–9, 53034,* ☎ *0577/921107,* FAX *0577/923688. 38 rooms. Restaurant, minibars, cable TV, bar, baby-sitting, concierge, meeting rooms, parking (fee). AE, DC, MC, V. Restaurant closed Sun. No dinner Mon.*

$$$$ 🏨 **La Suvera.** Pope Julius II once owned this luxurious estate; he'd likely
★ still be satisfied with the magnificent papal villa and adjacent building. Stenciled walls and canopied beds warm the the antiques and vaulted ceilings in the guest rooms. First-rate facilities, including drawing rooms, a garden, a park, and the Oliviera restaurant (serving estate wines), make it hard to tear yourself away. Thanks to a somewhat isolated location, there won't be any outside distractions to break your reverie. ⊠ *Pievescola (Casola d'Elsa), off SS541, 53030,* ☎ *0577/ 960300,* FAX *0577/960220,* WEB *www.lasuvera.it. 15 rooms, 16 suites. Restaurant, tennis court, pool, exercise room, massage, Turkish bath, library, mountain bikes, bar, meeting room, Internet; no kids under 12. AE, DC, MC, V. Closed Nov.–Easter.*

$$$ 🏨 **Villa Belvedere.** In addition to the pleasure of staying in a 17th-century villa that overlooks a formal Italian garden, here you can enjoy exquisite views of San Gimignano. The villa feels like a private home, with several common areas and guest rooms filled with period furniture. The pastas and desserts served in the restaurant are all made in-

house. Guests also have access to three tennis courts, about 2 km (1 mi) away. ⊠ *Località Belvedere, Colle di Val d'Elsa 53034,* ☎ *0577/ 920966,* 🖷 *0577/92412,* 🕮 *www.villabelvedere.com. 15 rooms. Restaurant, cable TV, pool, tennis court, bar. AE, DC, MC, V. CP.*

$ 🖭 **Arnolfo Hotel.** The excellent location and key amenities should be enough to convince you to stay here if you want to stay in town. It's on the main street of Colle Alta, and there are views from the windows that face the valley (Val d'Elsa). Though the rooms are simply furnished, they're not bare-bones; all in all it's a great deal. ⊠ *Via F. Campana 8, Colle Alta 53034,* ☎ *0577/922020,* 🖷 *0577/922324. 32 rooms. Fans, minibars, cable TV, Internet, some pets allowed; no air-conditioning. AE, DC, MC, V. CP.*

San Gimignano

★ ⑫ *14 km (9 mi) northwest of Colle di Val d'Elsa, 27 km (17 mi) east of Volterra, 38 km (24 mi) northwest of Siena, 54 km (34 mi) southwest of Florence.*

When you're high on a hill surrounded by crumbling towers in silhouette against the blue sky, it's difficult not to fall under the medieval spell of San Gimignano. Its tall walls and narrow streets are typical of Tuscan hill towns, but it's the medieval "skyscrapers" that set the town apart from its neighbors and give it a uniquely photogenic skyline. Today 14 towers remain, but at the height of the Guelph-Ghibelline conflict there was a forest of more than 70, and it was possible to cross the town by rooftop rather than road. The towers were built partly for defensive purposes—they were a safe refuge and useful for pouring boiling oil on attacking enemies—and partly for bolstering the egos of their owners, who competed with deadly seriousness to build the highest tower in town.

The relative proximity of San Gimignano, arguably Tuscany's best-preserved medieval hill town, to Siena and Florence also makes it one of Italy's most visited. But the traffic is hardly a new thing; the Etruscans were here, and later the Romans made it an outpost at the intersection of the two main roads in the region—the Via Pisana, which went west to the coast, and the Via Francigena, which crossed the Alps. With the yearly flow of pilgrims to and from Rome in the Middle Ages, the town— then known as Castel di Selva—became a prosperous market center. When locals prayed to a martyred bishop from Modena for relief from invading barbarians, relief they got, and in gratitude they rechristened the town in his honor as San Gimignano. Devastated by the Plague of 1348, the town subsequently fell under Florentine control. Things got going again in the Renaissance, with some of the best and brightest painters in the area—Ghirlandaio (1449–94), Gozzoli (1420–97), and Pinturicchio (1454–1513)—coming to decorate, but soon after, the main road moved, cutting San Gimignano off and sending it into decline.

Today, San Gimignano isn't much more than a gentrified walled city, touristy but still very much worth exploring because, despite its remarkable profusion of chintzy souvenir shops lining the main drag, there's some serious Renaissance art to be seen here. Unfortunately, tour groups arrive early and clog the wine-tasting rooms—San Gimignano is famous for its light white Vernaccia—and art galleries for much of the day, but most sights are open through late afternoon during summer. In the morning, you can enjoy San Gimignano's exceptionally fine countryside and return to explore the town in the afternoon and evening, when things quiet down and the long shadows cast by the imposing towers take on fascinating shapes. A combination ticket (€7.50) for all the local sites except the private Museo di Criminologia Medioevale is available, but it's a good deal only if you plan on visiting all of them.

Porta San Giovanni, an opening in San Gimignano's medieval walls, is the main entrance into town. Via San Giovanni leads the short way to the center of town, tracing the Roman Via Francigena. Souvenir shops lining the way leave no doubt about the lifeblood of the town, but better things lie ahead. Pass under **Arco dei Becci,** a leftover from the city's Etruscan walls, to Piazza della Cisterna, named for the cistern at its center and once the main piazza in town. To the right is an unusual museum. It's not hard to guess that the **Museo di Criminologia Medioevale** is a private museum—no state museum would be so bold as to scrutinize medieval criminology. Just to let you know that the Middle Ages were about more than walled towns, praying monks, mosaics, and illuminated manuscripts, the museum presents what was once the cutting edge in torture technology. Though some scholars dispute the historical accuracy of many of the instruments displayed, the final, very contemporary object—an electric chair imported from the United States—does give pause. ⊠ *Via del Castello 1-3,* ☎ *0577/942243.* 🖾 *€7.75.* ☉ *Mar.–mid-July, daily 10–7; mid-July–mid-Sept., daily 10–midnight; mid-Sept.–Oct., daily 10–8; Nov.–Feb., weekdays 10–6 and weekends 10–7.*

Beyond the twin towers built by the Ardinghelli family is the Piazza del Duomo, lined with San Gimignano's main civic and religious buildings. Behind the simple facade of the Romanesque **Collegiata,** the town's main church (not officially a *duomo* because San Gimignano has no bishop), lies a treasure trove of fine frescoes, covering nearly every part of the interior. Bartolo di Fredi's 14th-century fresco cycle of Old Testament scenes extend along one wall. Their distinctly medieval feel, with misshapen bodies, buckets of spurting blood, and lack of perspective, contrasts with the much more reserved scenes from the *Life of Christ* (attributed to 14th-century artist Lippo Memmi), painted on the opposite wall just 14 years later. Taddeo di Bartolo's otherworldly *Last Judgment* (late 14th century), with its distorted and suffering nudes, reveals the great influence of Dante's horrifying imagery in *The Inferno* and was surely an inspiration for later painters. Proof that the town had more than one protector, Benozzo Gozzoli's arrow-riddled *St. Sebastian* was commissioned in gratitude after the locals prayed to the saint for relief from plague. The Renaissance **Cappella di Santa Fina** is decorated with a fresco cycle by Domenico Ghirlandaio illustrating the life of St. Fina. A small girl who suffered from a terminal disease, Fina repented for her sins—among them having accepted an orange from a boy—and in penance lived out the rest of her short life on a wooden board, tormented by mice. The scenes depict the arrival of St. Gregory, who appeared to assure her that death was near; the flowers that miraculously grew from the wooden plank; and the miracles that accompanied her funeral, including the healing of her nurse's paralyzed hand and the restoration of a blind choir boy's vision. ⊠ *Piazza del Duomo,* ☎ *0577/940316.* 🖾 *Free; Cappella di Santa Fina €3.50.* ☉ *Apr.–Oct., Mon.–Sat. 9:30–7:30, Sun. 1–7:30; Nov.–Mar., Mon.–Sat. 9:30–5, Sun. 1–5. Closed Jan. 20–Feb. 28 and for funerals and weddings.*

Even with all the decoration in the Collegiata, the fine collection of various religious articles at the **Museo d'Arte Sacra,** through the pretty courtyard, is still worth a look. The highlight is a *Madonna and Child* by Bartolo di Fredi. Other pieces include several busts, wooden statues of Christ and the Virgin Mary and the angel Gabriel, and several illuminated songbooks. ⊠ *Piazza Pecori,* ☎ *0577/942226.* 🖾 *€3.*

⊙ *Apr.–Oct., weekdays 9:30–7:30, Sat. 9–5, Sun. 1–7; Nov.–Jan. 20 and Feb. 28–Mar., Mon.–Sat. 9:30–5, Sun. 1–5.*

Across the piazza from the Museo d'Arte Sacra is the **Palazzo Vecchio,** appropriately named as it is the "old" town hall (1239). Its tower was built by the municipality in 1255 to settle the raging "my-tower-is-bigger-than-your-tower" contest—as you can see, a solution that just didn't last.

★ The impressive **Museo Civico** occupies what was the "new" Palazzo del Popolo; the Torre Grossa is adjacent. Dante visited San Gimignano for only one day as a Guelph ambassador from Florence to ask the locals to join the Florentines in supporting the pope—just long enough to get the main council chamber named after him, which now holds a large *Maestà* (14th century) by Lippo Memmi. Off the stairway is a small room containing the racy frescoes by Memmo di Filippuccio (active 1288–1324) depicting the courtship, shared bath, and wedding of a young, androgynous-looking couple. That the space could have been a private room for the commune's chief magistrate may have something to do with the work's highly charged eroticism.

Upstairs, famous paintings by Renaissance stars Pinturicchio (*Madonna Enthroned*) and Gozzoli (*Madonna and Child*) and *Annunciation* tondoes by Filippino Lippi (circa 1457–1504) attest to the importance and wealth of San Gimignano. Also worth seeking out are Taddeo di Bartolo's *Life of San Gimignano*, with the saint holding a model of the town as it once appeared, and Lorenzo di Niccolò's gruesome martyrdom scene in the *Life of St. Bartholomew* (1401) and scenes from the *Life of St. Fina* (☞ Collegiata) on a tabernacle that was designed to hold her head. The admission price to Torre Grossa is steeper than the climb, but on a clear day the views are spectacular. ⊠ *Piazza del Duomo,* ☎ *0577/940008.* 🎫 *Museum €5, tower €5, combination ticket €7.50.* ⊙ *Mar.–Oct., daily 9:30–7:30; Nov.–Feb., daily 10–5:50.*

If you want more of that quintessential Tuscan landscape, walk up to the **Rocca,** open daily sunrise to sunset. Built after the Florentine conquest to keep an eye on the town, and dismantled a few centuries later, it is now a public garden. From the Rocca, bird lovers will want to take the steps down to the **Museo Ornitologico,** set in an ex-church at the base of the former fortress. ⊠ *Via Quercecchio,* ☎ *0577/941388.* 🎫 *€7.50 combination ticket.* ⊙ *Mar.–Oct., daily 11–6; Nov.–Feb., Sat.–Thurs. 9:30–1 and 2:30–5.*

Via San Matteo is San Gimignano's most handsome street, framed by stout medieval buildings in excellent condition, with flowers here and there lightening up the heavy stone facades. The road ends at Porta San Matteo. Just before the end of Via San Matteo, cut right into Piazza Sant'Agostino and make a beeline for Benozzo Gozzoli's superlative frescoes inside the church of **Sant'Agostino.** This Romanesque–Gothic church contains Benozzo Gozzoli's stunning 15th-century fresco cycle depicting the life of St. Augustine. Augustine's work was essential to the early development of church doctrine. As thoroughly discussed in his autobiographical *Confessions* (an acute dialogue with God), Augustine, like many saints, sinned considerably in his youth before finding God. But unlike the lives of other saints, where the story continues through a litany of miracles, deprivations, penitence, and often martyrdom, Augustine's life and work focused on philosophy and the reconciliation between faith and thought. Gozzoli's 17 scenes on the choir wall depict Augustine as a man who traveled and taught extensively in the 4th–5th centuries. The 15th-century altarpiece by Piero del Pollaiolo (1443–96) depicts *The Coronation of the Virgin* and the various protectors of the city. On your way out of Sant'Agostino, stop in at the **Cappella di San Bartolo,** with a sumptuously elaborate tomb by Benedetto da Maiano (1442–97). ✉ *Piazza Sant'Agostino,* ☎ *0577/907012.* ☞ *Free.* ☉ *Daily 7–noon and 3–7.*

NEED A
BREAK?
There's no shortage of places to try Vernaccia di San Gimignano, the justifiably famous white wine with which San Gimignano would be singularly associated—if it weren't for all those towers. At **Enoteca Gustavo** (✉ Via San Matteo 29, ☎ 0577/940057), you can get a bottle of Vernaccia di San Gimignano to accompany a picnic or sit down and nibble cheese and salami. On your way back into town, mosey on down to **Bar-Pasticceria Maria e Lucia** (✉ Via San Matteo 55, ☎ 0577/940379) for some homemade gelato or desserts. **Antica Latteria di Maurizio e Tiziana** (✉ Via San Matteo 19, ☎ 0577/941952), closed Sunday, serves up salads and *panini* (sandwiches) any way you want them, priced by weight.

Dining and Lodging

The **Cooperativa Hotels Promotion** (✉ Via di San Giovanni 125, ☎ 0577/940809) offers commission-free booking services in local hotels and farmhouses.

$$–$$$$ ✕ **Le Terrazze.** Seasonal Tuscan classics are prepared and served at this inn in the heart of San Gimignano. A charming view of the countryside and specialties like handmade pasta, a variety of grilled mushrooms, and grilled meats are in store. ✉ *Piazza della Cisterna 23,* ☎ *0577/940328. AE, DC, MC, V. Closed Tues. and Nov.–Mar. 9. No lunch Wed.*

$$–$$$ ✕ **La Mangiatoia.** Gaily colored gingham tablecloths contrast with austere 13th-century rib-vaulted ceilings in this cozy spot. The lighthearted feminine touch might be explained by chef Susi Cuomo, who has been presiding over her kitchen for more than 20 years. The menu is seasonal—in the autumn, don't miss her *filetto d'anatra con tartufo* (truffled duck breast). In summer, try for a table on the intimate, flower-bedecked terrace in the back. ✉ *Via Mainardi 5, off Via San Matteo,* ☎ *0577/941528. MC, V. Closed Tues., 3 wks in Nov., and 1 wk in Jan.*

$$ ✕ **Osteria delle Catene.** This popular restaurant shares its look and philosophy with many other Tuscan *trattorie* opened in the '90s by young food lovers. Expect to find the most traditional dishes—some of them almost a rarity these days—served in a stylish room with a vault. Standouts include *nana col cavolo nero* (duck with Tuscan kale) and *maiale con i gobbi* (pork loin with cardoons). A glass of *vin santo* is a better end to the meal than the less-than-exciting desserts. ✉ *Via Mainardi 18,* ☎ *0577/941966. AE, DC, MC, V. Closed Wed. and Jan.*

$ ✕ **Enoteca Gustavo.** One look inside this enoteca on Via San Matteo and you'll know the owners mean business. Lined up behind a solid wooden counter is a complete hit parade of Tuscany's greatest wines, both red and white. Take a seat in the back room for an informal sampling of typical enoteca fare: *affettati e formaggi* (locally produced cured meats and cheeses), homemade pickles, and *bruschetta* (grilled Tuscan bread drizzled with olive oil, rubbed with garlic, and topped with tomatoes or liver pâté). ✉ *Via San Matteo 29,* ☎ *0577/940057. AE, DC, MC, V. Closed Fri. and for family vacation 1 month (always different) per year.*

$$ ✕🔲 **Bel Soggiorno.** If you're searching for a memorable place within
★ the town walls, look no further. This establishment, run by one family for over 100 years, unites high quality with simplicity. For instance, the restaurant's focal point is a glass wall, with a sweeping view of the hillsides. The room might be considered plain; the food, however, is not. Dishes such as *timballo di riso basmati con asparagi e zafferano*

su crema fredda di pomodorini (a timbale of asparagus and saffron in a cherry tomato sauce) are a real treat. The attached hotel has crisp, airy rooms with high ceilings and white walls, many with a stunning view. ⊠ *Via San Giovanni 91, 53037,* ☎ *0577/940375,* 𝙵𝙰𝚇 *0577/ 940375,* 𝚆𝙴𝙱 *www.hotelbelsoggiorno.it. 17 rooms, 4 suites. Restaurant, parking (fee). AE, DC, MC, V. Closed Wed. and Jan. 6–Feb.*

$$$$ ⊞ **La Collegiata.** After serving as a Franciscan convent and then residence of the noble Strozzi family, the Collegiata, about 1 km (½ mi) north of San Gimignano, has become one of the region's finest hotels, with no expense spared in the effort. Surrounded by a park, all the rooms (some with private balconies) are furnished with antiques and precious tapestries; bathrooms have whirlpool baths. A summer restaurant occupies the ex-church, with tables set out on the entrance. ⊠ *Località Strada 27, 53037,* ☎ *0577/943201,* 𝙵𝙰𝚇 *0577/940566,* 𝚆𝙴𝙱 *www.lacollegiata.it. 19 rooms, 1 suite. Restaurant, in-room safes, cable TV, pool, bar, wine bar, Internet, meeting room, free parking, some pets allowed. AE, DC, MC, V. Closed Jan. CP.*

$$$$ ⊞ **Relais Santa Chiara.** Layered with balconies and terraces, this low contemporary building sits on a hillside just outside San Gimignano's walls. Most of the rooms have balconies, though only about half of them have full views of the hills and the hotel gardens below. The hotel has no restaurant but serves an ample buffet breakfast, plus light snacks in summer. ⊠ *Via Matteotti 15, 53037,* ☎ *0577/940701,* 𝙵𝙰𝚇 *0577/942096,* 𝚆𝙴𝙱 *www.rsc.it. 39 rooms, 2 suites. Minibars, in-room safes, cable TV, pool, baby-sitting, dry cleaning, laundry service, business services, meeting room. AE, DC, MC, V. Closed early Dec.–early Mar. CP.*

$$ ⊞ **Pescille.** Restrained contemporary and classic motifs blend smoothly in this rambling, handsome hotel, formerly a farmhouse. It's 4 km (2½ mi) outside San Gimignano, placed to get a splendid view of the town's bristling towers. ⊠ *Località Pescille, Strada Castel San Gimignano, 53037,* ☎ *0577/940186,* 𝙵𝙰𝚇 *0577/943165,* 𝚆𝙴𝙱 *www.pescille.it. 38 rooms, 12 suites. Minibars in some rooms, tennis court, pool, gym, concierge, Internet; no air-conditioning in some rooms. AE, DC, MC, V. Closed Nov.–Mar.*

Nightlife and the Arts

San Gimignano is one of the few small towns in the area that make a big deal out of **Carnevale** festivities, with locals dressing up in colorful costumes and marching through the streets on the four Sundays preceding Shrove Tuesday from 3:30 to 6:30. If you visit in summer, check with the tourist office (⊠ Piazza del Duomo 1, ☎ 0577/940008) about concerts and performances related to the **Estate San Gimignanese,** one of Tuscany's oldest summer arts festivals (mid-June to August).

Outdoor Activities and Sports

The pristine olive groves and vineyards outside the walls are easily accessible on foot, without unreasonably steep grades or ugly peripheries to pass through. The tourist office leads guided walks in high season (☞ Tours *in* Siena and the Hill Towns A to Z).

Shopping

The lovely countryside is so close and good ingredients so near at hand, it's hard to resist a picnic on a nice day in San Gimignano. The **grocery store** (⊠ Piazza Cisterna, ☎ no phone) stays open through the afternoon but is closed on Sunday. As everywhere else, the town brightens up on **open-air market** mornings, every Thursday and Saturday in Piazza del Duomo. It's the place to pick up fresh fruits and other snacks—then head for Via San Matteo to fill up your basket.

VOLTERRA

As you make the dramatic climb up to Volterra through bleak, rugged terrain, you'll see that not all Tuscan hill towns rise above rolling fields of green, and also just how beautiful a change of scenery can be. The town began as the northernmost city of the 12 that made up the Etruscan league, and excavations in the 18th century revealed a bounty of relics now on exhibit at the impressive Museo Etrusco Guarnacci. Volterra's fortress, walls, and gates still stand mightily over *Le Balze,* a stunning series of gullied hills and valleys formed by erosion that has slowly eaten away at the foundation of the town, now considerably smaller than it was during its Etruscan glory days 25 centuries ago. The Romans and later the Florentines laid siege to the town to secure its supply of minerals and stones, particularly alabaster, which is still worked into handicrafts on sale in many of the shops around town.

Exploring Volterra

A combination admission ticket (€6.20) allows entrance to all three of Volterra's museums (Museo d'Arte Sacra, Pinacoteca, and Museo Etrusco Guarnacci). Volterra has several parking lots around the perimeter of the city walls; the most convenient one is the underground parking lot at Piazza Martiri della Libertà.

A Good Walk

Begin in Piazza Martiri della Libertà and take Via Marchesi to Piazza dei Priori, lined with an impressive collection of medieval buildings, including the imposing **Palazzo dei Priori** ⑬, the seat of city government for more than seven centuries. Across the piazza is the Palazzo Pretorio topped by the Torre del Porcellino, named after the sculpted little boar mounted at the upper window. Walk down Via Turazza along the side of the **Duomo** ⑭ to the triangular Piazza San Giovanni, and head out the left corner of the piazza to steal a look at the ancient **Porta all'Arco Etrusco** ⑮. Return to the piazza and step inside the Duomo and its baptistry. Next to the Duomo is Palazzo Vescovile with the **Museo Diocesano d'Arte Sacra** ⑯ (entrance around the corner), the first of Volterra's three worthwhile museums. From there proceed straight up Via Roma to the **Pinacoteca** ⑰. Via dei Sarti leads to Piazza San Michele, with the eponymous church decked out in black and white marble stripes. Via Guarnacci goes left to Porta Fiorentina and the ruins just outside the walls of the 1st-century BC **Teatro Romano** ⑱. Retrace your steps to Piazza San Michele and continue across town on Via di Sotto, through Piazza XX Settembre to Via Don Minzoni and the **Museo Etrusco Guarnacci** ⑲. Farther along the street is the edge of the Rocca (fortress), one of the few still in use in the country, which serves as the town jail. Via del Castello leads back down the hill, along the Parco Archeologico, a pleasant public park with a few Etruscan stones here and there.

TIMING

The town can easily be seen in a day, although its distance from everything else makes it a good stopover as well. Allow at least three hours for the tour. Off-season, it's best to make an early start in order to have time in the museums.

Sights to See

⑭ **Duomo.** Behind the textbook 13th-century Pisan Romanesque facade is proof that Volterra counted for something during the Renaissance, when many important Tuscan artists came to decorate the church. Stucco portraits of local saints stick out from Francesco Capriani's gold, red, and blue ceiling (1580), including St. Linus, the successor to St. Peter

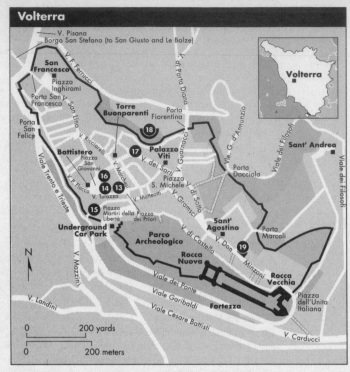

as pope and claimed by the Volterrans to have been born here. The church is dedicated to Santa Maria Assunta, but local or patron saints are also venerated. Reliquary busts of St. Linus, St. Giusto, and St. Clement are locked away in the sacristy; out front a chapel contains the remains of St. Octavian (his empty head-shaped reliquary was moved to the Museo d'Arte Sacra), who became a patron saint of the town after prayers to him ended a plague in the early 16th century. The highlight of the Duomo is the brightly painted 13th-century wooden life-size *Deposition* in the chapel of the same name. The unusual Cappella dell'Addolorata (Chapel of the Grieved) has two terracotta Nativity scenes; the depiction of the arrival of the Magi has a background fresco by Benozzo Gozzoli. The 16th-century pulpit in the middle of the nave is lined with fine 14th-century sculpted panels, attributed to a member of the Pisano family. Across from the Duomo in the center of the piazza is the **Battistero,** with stripes that match the Duomo. Evidently this baptistry got a lot of use, as the small marble baptismal font carved by Andrea Sansovino in 1502 was moved to the wall to the right of the entrance in the mid-18th century to make room for a larger font. ✉ *Piazza San Giovanni,* ☎ *0588/86192.* ✇ *Free.* ☼ *Duomo and Battistero daily 7–7.*

OFF THE
BEATEN PATH

LE BALZE – From Piazza San Giovanni, take Via Franceschini (which becomes Via San Lino) to the church of San Francesco, well worth a look inside for the celebrated early 15th-century frescoes of the *Stories of the True Cross* by a local artist. It traces the history of the wood used to make the cross upon which Jesus was crucified. Continue along the road, through Porta San Franceso, and out Borgo Santo Stefano. This area was originally part of the Etruscan town (called Vlathri; as usual the current name is closer to the Roman name, Volaterrrae) as evidenced by walls that extend another half mile toward the old Porta Menseri.

Toward the end of the road, on the right, is the church of San Giusto (with terra-cotta statues of the town's patron saints). The church was built to replace an earlier church that disappeared into Le Balze—a desolate, undulating landscape of yellow earth drawn into crags and gullies, as if worn down by a desert torrent long past. Instead the haunting phenomenon is thought to have been created when rainwater collected and wore down the soil substructure. The bus for Borgo San Giusto, leaving from Piazza Martiri, goes through Le Balze (about 10 runs per day).

⑯ Museo Diocesano d'Arte Sacra. Appropriately housed in the Bishop's Palace, this museum made up of religious art collected from local churches includes an unusual reliquary with the head of St. Octavian in silver resting on four golden lions by Antonio Pollaiolo and a fine terra-cotta bust of St. Linus by Andrea della Robbia (1435–1525/28). Two paintings are also noteworthy: Rosso Fiorentino's (1495–1540) *Madonna di Villamagna* and Daniele da Volterra's (1509–1566) *Madonna di Ulignano,* named for the village churches (now abandoned) in which they were originally placed. ⊠ *Palazzo Vescovile, Via Roma 1,* ☎ *0588/86290.* ⊞ *Combination ticket for Museo Etrusco Guarnacci, the Pinacoteca and the Museo d'Arte Sacra €7.* ⊙ *Late June–late Sept., Tues.–Sun. 9–1 and 3–6; late Sept.–late June, Tues.–Sun. 9–1.*

⑲ Museo Etrusco Guarnacci. Although Etruscan sites are spread throughout Tuscany and northern Lazio, the major relics have been assembled in state museums and the Musei Vaticani in Rome, leaving precious little for the towns closest to the excavations. Fortunately in the case of Volterra, an extraordinarily large and unique collection of relics remains close to home, made all the more interesting by clear explanations in English. You will find the usual display of Attic vases, bucchero ceramics, jewelry, and household items, but the bulk of the collection is made up of roughly 700 carved funerary urns. The oldest, dating to the 7th century, were made from tufa (volcanic rock); a handful are of terra-cotta. The vast majority—from the 3rd to 1st century BC—are from alabaster. The urns are grouped by subject and taken together form a fascinating testimony about Etruscan life and death. Some illustrate domestic scenes, others the funeral procession of the deceased. Greek gods and mythology, by then adopted by the Etruscans, also figure prominently. The sculpted figures on many of the covers are thought to have been made in the image of the deceased, reclining and often holding the cup of life overturned. Particularly well known is *Gli Sposi* (*Husband and Wife*), a haunting portrait in terra-cotta. ⊠ *Via Don Minzoni 15,* ☎ *0588/86347.* ⊞ *Combination ticket for Museo d'Arte Sacra, the Pinacoteca and Museo Etrusco Guarnacci €7.* ⊙ *Mid-Mar.– Oct., daily 9–7; Nov.–mid-Mar., daily 9–2.*

⑬ Palazzo dei Priori. Tuscany's first town hall was built between 1208 and 1254, with a no-nonsense facade, fortresslike crenellations, and a five-sided tower. Such fortifications were necessary and commonplace at the time; these served as a model for other similar structures throughout the region, including Florence's Palazzo Vecchio. The Florentine medallions that adorn the facade here were added after the Florentines conquered Volterra. The town leaders still meet on the first floor in the Sala del Consiglio; the room is open to the public and has a mid-14th century fresco of the *Annunciation.* ⊠ *Piazza dei Priori,* ☎ *0588/ 87257.* ⊞ *€1.* ⊙ *Mar.–Oct., weekdays 10–1 and 2–5, weekends 9–1 and 3–6; Nov.–Feb., Mon., Wed., Fri. 9–1, Tues., Thurs., and weekends 9–1 and 3–6.*

⑰ Pinacoteca. Arranged in chronological order on two floors in one of Volterra's best-looking buildings, the Pinacoteca has an impressive collection of Tuscan paintings. Head straight for Room 12, where you will find Luca Signorelli's (circa 1445–1523) *Madonna and Child with Saints* and Rosso Fiorentino's *Deposition*. Both are masterpieces, and though painted just 30 years apart, they serve to illustrate the shift in style in the early 16th century from late-Renaissance painting to all-out mannerist style: the balance of Signorelli's composition becomes purposefully skewed in Fiorentino's painting, where the colors go from vivid but realistic to emotive and garish. Other important paintings in the small museum include Ghirlandaio's *Apotheosis of Christ with Saints* and a polyptych of the *Madonna and Saints* by Taddeo di Bartolo, which once hung in the Palazzo dei Priori. ⊠ *Via dei Sarti 1,* ☎ *0588/87580,* WEB *www.comune.volterra.pi.it/museiit/pinac.html.* 🎟 *Combination ticket for Museo d'Arte Sacra, Museo Etrusco Guarnacci and Pinacoteca €7.* ⊙ *Mid-Mar.–Oct., daily 9–7; Nov.–mid-Mar., daily 9–2.*

⑮ Porta all'Arco Etrusco. Even if a good portion of the arch was rebuilt by the Romans, the three dark, weather-beaten, 3rd-century BC heads carved in basaltic rock (thought to represent Etruscan gods) still face outward, greeting those who enter. A plaque recalls the efforts of the locals who saved the arch from destruction by filling it with stones during the German withdrawal at the end of World War II.

⑱ Teatro Romano. Just outside the walls past Porta Fiorentina are the ruins of the 1st-century BC Roman theater, one of the best preserved in Italy, with adjacent remains of the Roman *terme* (baths). ⊠ *Viale Francesco Ferrucci.* 🎟 *Free.* ⊙ *May–Oct., daily 11–4; closed when raining.*

Dining and Lodging

$$ ✗ Da Badò. This is the place in town to eat traditional food elbow-to-elbow with the locals. Da Badò is a typical family-run place (open only at lunch), and the chef's efforts concentrate on just a few dishes, so it won't take long to decide between the standards, all prepared with a sure hand: *zuppa alla volterrana* (a Tuscan soup made with vegetables and bread), *pappardelle alla lepre* (wide fettuccine in a hare sauce), and a stew of either rabbit or wild boar. A slice of homemade almond tart is a must. ⊠ *Borgo San Lazzaro 9,* ☎ *0588/86477. AE, DC, MC, V. Closed Wed. No dinner.*

$–$$ ✗ Il Sacco Fiorentino. The understated tone of this small, two-room restaurant gives nothing away. You'd never guess from the unremarkable decor how good the food can be, from the antipasti of sautéed chicken liver, porcini mushrooms, and polenta drizzled with balsamic vinegar to the *tagliatelle del Sacco Fiorentino*, a riot of curried spaghetti with chicken and roasted red peppers. ⊠ *Piazza XX Settembre 18,* ☎ *0588/88537. AE, DC, MC, V. Closed Wed.*

$$ 🏨 San Lino. This hotel, once a convent, pairs classic elements like wood beams and terra-cotta floors with modern-day amenities. It's within the town walls, a 10-minute walk from the main piazza. The restaurant, open only for guests and groups of 20 or more, serves regional specialties, including *zuppa alla volteranna,* a very thick vegetable soup. ⊠ *Via San Lino 26, 56048,* ☎ *0588/85250,* FAX *0588/80620,* WEB *www.hotelsanlino.com. 43 rooms. Restaurant, minibars, pool, concierge, Internet, parking (fee); no air-conditioning in some rooms. AE, DC, MC, V. Closed Nov.–Jan.*

Nightlife and the Arts

On the first Sunday in September is the **Astiludio,** a festival with flag throwing and processions. Volterra's **Jazz Festival** lasts for three weeks between July and August. Contact the town's visitor information center for more information.

Shopping

Volterra's market is held on Saturday morning in Piazza dei Priori from November to April and on Viale Ferrucci (just outside the city walls) from May through October.

Shopping

Volterra has a number of shops that sell boxes, jewelry, and other objects made of alabaster. The **Cooperativa Artieri Alabastro** (✉ Piazza dei Priori 5, ☎ 0588/87590) has two large showrooms in a medieval building with an array of alabaster objects. In a former medieval monastery, the **Gallerie Agostiniane** showrooms (✉ Piazza XX Settembre 3, ☎ 0588/86868) craft alabaster objects of all kinds. You can see a video about how the mineral is quarried and carved. At **Rossi Camillo** (✉ Via Lungo Mura del Mandorlo 2, ☎ 0588/86133), you can actually see the craftspeople at work; there are objects for all tastes and budgets.

THROUGH LE CRETE
Southeast of Siena

Van Gogh never saw the area south of Siena known as le Crete (*creta* means "clay" in Italian), but in the bare clay hills around Asciano—the rolling wheat fields, the warm light, the dramatic gullies and ravines cut by centuries of erosion—he would have perhaps found worthy subjects, as these landscapes seem carved into the earth much in the way that the furrows of paint layer his canvases.

Take the S73 southeast out of Siena toward Taverne d'Arbia, where the S438 branches off and goes 21 km (13 mi) to Asciano. About halfway you will notice a distinct change in landscape from the farming valleys surrounding Siena to the much hillier Asciano. The road to the north goes to Rapolano Terme, one of several towns in the area known for its thermal baths. The road south passes through even more dramatic Crete countryside. At the Abbazia di Monte Oliveto Maggiore, the road turns and leads down to Buonconvento and the Via Cassia, the Roman consular road that runs south to Rome. A fun excursion can also be made to the east, passing through little-visited towns such as Trequanda, Sinalunga, and Montefollonico.

Asciano

⍛ *25 km (16 mi) southeast from Siena, 124 km (77 mi) southeast of Florence.*

Founded by the Etruscans around the 5th century BC, Asciano's now a sleepy little town still retaining its 13th-century walls. It's only of passing interest, except for the surprisingly rich collection of Sienese painting from the 14th and 15th centuries in its **Museo d'Arte Sacra.** Unfortunately, only a portion of the collection, which includes works by lesser-known Sienese artists, is on display. ✉ *Next to the Collegiata Sant'Agata,* ☎ *0577/718207.* ⌨ *Free.* ☉ *By appointment only.*

If you do stroll through town, a few other museums are close at hand. Via Mameli leads left from the 13th-century Romanesque-Gothic Collegiata di Sant'Agata to the **Museo Cassioli,** with portraits and drawings by the 19th-century artist Amos Cassioli (1832–91). ✉ *Via Mameli*

36, ☏ no phone. ⊠ €1.55. ⊙ May–Sept., Tues.–Sun. 10–12:30 and 4:30–6:30; Oct.–Apr., Tues.–Sun. 10–12:30.

The **Museo Civico Archeologico** in the former church of San Bernardino has relics from the nearby Etruscan necropolis. It will be closed for part of 2003. ⊠ *Corso Matteotti 46, ☏ no phone. ⊠ €4.50, including admission to Galleria Cassioli. ⊙ May–Sept., Tues.–Sun. 10–12:30 and 4:30–6:30; Oct.–Apr., Tues.–Sun. 10–12:30.*

The local **Farmacia De Munari** holds the town's most important Roman artifact, a polychrome Roman mosaic that dates from the 1st–2nd centuries AD, in the basement. ⊠ *Corso Matteotti 82, ☏ 0577/718124. ⊠ Free. ⊙ Weekdays 9–1 and 4–8, Sat. 9–1.*

Abbazia di Monte Oliveto Maggiore

㉑ *9 km (5½ mi) south of Asciano, 36 km (22 mi) southeast of Siena.*

Monte Oliveto Maggiore, Tuscany's most-visited abbey, sits in an oasis of olive and cypress trees amid the harsh landscape of le Crete. It was founded in 1313 by Giovanni Tolomei, a rich Sienese lawyer who, after miraculously regaining his lost sight, changed his name to Bernardo in homage to the saint and created an order dedicated to the restoration of the founding principles of Benedictine monasticism. The order is named the White Benedictines, after a vision that Bernardo had in which Jesus, Mary, and his own mother were all clad in white, and also as the Olivetans, after the hill where the monastery was built. Famous for maintaining extreme poverty—their feast-day meal consisted of two eggs—they slept on straw mats and kept a vow of silence. Although the monks look like they are eating a little better these days and are not afraid to strike up a conversation, the monastery still operates, and most of the area is off limits to visitors. One of Italy's most important book restoration centers is located here, and the monks still produce a wide variety of traditional liqueurs (distilled from herbs that grow on the premises), which are available in the gift shop along with enough food products to fill a pantry, all produced by monks in various parts of Italy.

From the entrance gate, a tree-lined lane leads down to the main group of buildings, with paths leading off to several shrines and chapels dedicated to important saints of the order. The church itself is not particularly memorable, but the exquisite choir stalls (1503) by Fra Giovanni of Bologna are among the finest examples of wood inlay in Italy. Forty-eight of the 125 stalls have inlaid decoration, each set up as a window or arched doorway that opens onto a space (a town, a landscape) or an object (a musical instrument, a bird), rendered in marvelous perspective. Check at the entrance for the schedule of masses, as the monks often chant the liturgy.

In the abbey's main cloister, frescoes by Luca Signorelli and Il Sodoma depict scenes from the life of St. Benedict. Signorelli began the cycle by painting scenes from the saint's adult life as narrated by St. Gregory the Great, and although his nine scenes are badly worn, the individual expressions are fittingly austere and pensive, full of serenity and religious spirit, and as individualized as those he painted in the San Brizio chapel in Orvieto's Duomo. Later Sodoma filled in the story with scenes from the saint's youth and the last years of his life. The results are also impressive, but here for the use of color and earthier depiction. Note the detailed landscapes; the rich costumes; the animals that Sodoma was known to keep as pets; and the scantily clad boys he apparently preferred (for this he was called "the Sodomist" and described by Vasari as "a merry and licentious man . . . of scant

chastity"). ✉ *S451 south from Asciano,* ☎ *0577/707611.* 🎫 *Free.* ☉
Daily 9:15–noon and 3:15–5:45.

Dining and Lodging

$–$$ ✕ **La Torre.** Lodged in the massive tower at the abbey's entrance, this
pleasant restaurant and café serves straightforward Tuscan fare in a
cozy dining room or, when it's warm, on an attractive terrace. The *pici
ai funghi* (thick, short spaghetti with mushroom sauce) or *zuppa di funghi*
(mushroom soup) can take the sting out of a crisp winter day, and any
of the grilled meats are a good bet at any time of year. There's also a
remarkably good wine list. ✉ *Abbazia di Monte Oliveto Maggiore,*
☎ *0577/707022. AE, DC, MC, V. Closed Tues.*

$$$$ ✕🏨 **La Chiusa.** Worthy of reverie, this beautifully restored farmhouse
in nearby Montefollonico emphasizes total relaxation. It's lovingly run
by an Italian couple and a top-notch staff. The rosemary and lavender in the large garden can make a walk here almost aromatherapy.
Guest rooms have simple antique furniture and throw rugs; many of
them open out to marvelous views. A charming medieval hamlet is on
hand should you feel the urge to explore, but the joy here is to eat and
rest well. The 14 impeccable rooms are all a bit different, with prices
varying accordingly. ✉ *Via della Madonnina 88, Montefollonico (25
km [15 mi] east of the Abbazia di Monte Oliveto Maggiore), 53040,*
☎ *0577/669668,* 🖷 *0577/669593,* 🕸 *www.ristorantelachiusa.it. 14
rooms. Restaurant, fans, in-room safes in some rooms, minibars, cable
TV, baby-sitting, dry cleaning, laundry service, concierge, Internet, free
parking, some pets allowed; no air-conditioning. AE, DC, MC, V.
Closed mid-Jan.–Mar. CP.*

$$$$ ✕🏨 **Locanda dell'Amorosa.** This "inn" occupies the 14th-century
★ stone-and-brick hamlet of Amorosa, in the hills just south of Sinalunga.
The stunning setting is matched by the gorgeous, perfectly restored buildings. A cypress-lined lane brings you to the village gateway. The bedrooms are handsomely decorated with antiques, and the bathrooms
are large. The restaurant ($$$), located in the old stables, serves both
traditional and contemporary seasonal dishes. ✉ *Località Amorosa,
Sinalunga, 10 km (6 mi) from the Valdichiana exit off A1, 53048,* ☎
0577/677211, 🖷 *0577/632001,* 🕸 *www.amorosa.it. 14 rooms, 6 suites.
Restaurant, in-room safes, mountain bikes (fee), wine bar, baby-sitting,
dry cleaning, laundry service, concierge, Internet; no-smoking rooms.
AE, DC, MC, V. Closed Jan.–Feb. EP.*

$–$$ 🏨 **Fattoria del Colle.** Set amid rolling vineyards and olive trees in Trequanda, 12 km (7 mi) east of Monte Oliveto Maggiore abbey and 8
km (5 mi) west of Sinalunga, is the agriturismo Il Colle, a *fattoria* (farmhouse) that produces fine Chianti and olive oil. The main stone farmhouse, surrounded by six apartments sleeping from 2 to 14 and a
separate house sleeping 22, retains its enormous stone fireplace and a
16th-century family chapel next door. The simple, comfortable apartments have traditional Tuscan wood furniture, some antique, and full
kitchens and linens; some have fireplaces. ✉ *15 km (9 mi) west of the
A1, Trequanda 53020,* ☎ *0577/662108,* 🖷 *0577/849356. 2 doubles,
19 apartments. Restaurant, 3 pools, tennis court, hiking, mountain bikes,
laundry service. EP.*

Buonconvento

㉒ *9 km (5½ mi) southwest of Abbazia di Monte Oliveto Maggiore, 27
km (17 mi) southeast of Siena.*

Buonconvento reached the height of its importance when it served as
a major outpost along the Roman Via Cassia, although it is also remembered by the history books as the place where Holy Roman Em-

peror Henry VII was poisoned by a Eucharist wafer. Today quiet Buon-convento is worth a stop for a look at its tiny **Museo d'Arte Sacra,** a two-room picture gallery with more than its fair share of works by Tus-can artists such as Duccio and Andrea di Bartolo. The highlight is a trip-tych with the *Madonna and Saints Bernardino and Catherine* by Sano di Pietro. ✉ *Via Soccini 17,* ☎ *0577/807181.* ☜ *€3.10.* ◷ *Nov.–Feb. weekends 10–1 and 3–5; Mar.–Oct. Tues.–Sun. 10–1 and 3–7.*

While there, have a look at the well-preserved **Porta Senese,** extra for-tified to make up for the town's lack of natural defenses, when it served as the southern gate to Siena. Also worth visiting is the hand-some, fortified **Castello di Bibbiano**; it was completed in the 14th cen-tury, but some parts date back to the mid-9th century. The building, now in private hands, offers an incredible vision of a medieval castle. It's 6 km (4 mi) to the west; call the tourist office in Siena for opening hours.

OFF THE
BEATEN PATH

MURLO – If you're heading northwest to Siena, stray 9 km (5½ mi) west of the main road (Via Cassia or SS2) to Vescovado and follow the signs from there 2 km (1 mi) south to Murlo, a tiny fortified medieval *borgo* (village) that has been completely restored. It consists of a cluster of houses and an imposing bishop's palace that holds the **Antiquarium Poggio Civitate** named after the nearby site from which most of the Etruscan relics were excavated. Although there are many more beautiful pieces on display, the almost entirely complete roof and pediment from a 5th-century BC Etruscan house are especially rare. ✉ *Piazza della Cat-tedrale 4,* ☎ *0577/814099.* ☜ *€3.10.* ◷ *Apr., June, and Sept., daily 9:30–12:30 and 3–7; July and Aug., daily 9:30–12:30, 3–7, and 9–11; Mar. and Oct., Tues.–Sun. 9:30–12:30 and 3–5:30; Nov.–Feb., Tues.–Sun. 10–12:30, weekends 10–12:30 and 2:30–5.*

SIENA AND THE HILL TOWNS A TO Z

To research prices, get advice from other travelers, and book travel ar-rangements, visit www.fodors.com.

AIR TRAVEL
If you're coming from the U.S. and are set on flying nonstop, you will have to travel to Rome. The airports of Pisa and Florence are signifi-cantly closer to this region, but flights stop elsewhere before continu-ing to either city. Otherwise, Florence is the most convenient transfer point, as you can take the autostrada to Siena.

AIRPORTS
The airports nearest to the region are Rome's Fiumicino (officially Aero-porto Leonardo da Vinci), Pisa's Galileo Galilei, and Florence's Pere-tola (officially Aeroporto A. Vespucci).
➤ AIRPORT INFORMATION: **Aeroporto A. Vespucci** (known as Peretola; ☎ 055/3061700). **Aeroporto Galileo Galilei** (☎ 050/500707, WEB www.pisa-airport.com). **Aeroporto Leonardo da Vinci** (known as Fi-umicino; ☎ 06/6594420, WEB www.adr.it).

BIKE TRAVEL
Hills pose a greater difficulty than distance, but all the towns are con-nected by roads that make for good cycling and rewarding panoramas. The Siena tourist office can recommend places for bike rental.

BUS TRAVEL
Tra-In buses run several times a day between Rome and Siena (2½ hrs). There is frequent SITA service between Florence and Siena (1 hr),

stopping in Poggibonsi. From Poggibonsi, Tra-In buses shuttle to San Gimignano, Volterra, and Colle di Val d'Elsa.

Buses are a reliable, but time-consuming, means of getting around the region. Many of the routes, so-called "milk runs," stop in every town and hamlet. In some cases, you'll need to have a strong stomach as the roads are twisting and winding.

Tra-In buses also run frequently around Siena, including through the historic center. Tickets cost 80 European cents and can be bought at tobacconists or newsstands. Routes are marked with signposts.
➤ Bus Lines: **SITA** (☎ 0577/204270 in Siena, 055/214721 in Florence, WEB www.sita-on-line.it). **Tra-In** (☎ 0577/204111, WEB www.trainspa.it).

CAR RENTALS
Siena has a handful of car-rental agencies, open weekdays and just a half-day on Saturday.
➤ Agencies: **Avis** (✉ Via Simone Martini 36, ☎ 0577/270305, WEB www. avis.com). **Hertz** (✉ Viale Sardegna 37, ☎ 0577/45085, WEB www.hertz. com).

CAR TRAVEL
The area is easily reached by car on the A1 Motorway (Autostrada del Sole), which runs between Rome and Florence; exit on SS326 for Siena. From Florence, the fastest way to Siena and the hill towns is via the autostrada, which takes roughly an hour. Alternatively, the Strada Chiantigiana (SS222) is the scenic route through Tuscany's famous wine country. The SS2 also connects Siena to Rome and Florence, but it's much faster to go north to Florence via the A1, the Siena–Florence autostrada or down to Rome by taking the SS73 east and the SS326 toward Sinalunga to pick up the A1.

A dense network of roads can get you into all kinds of local corners. A few towns in this area, including Monteriggioni, Buonconvento, and Asciano, can only be reached by driving. Nonresidents are generally forbidden to drive in the historic centers of most towns, including Siena. Traffic in and out of Siena slows during rush hour (as much as Italians can rush), usually between 8 and 9:30 or 10 AM and 5:30 and 7:30 PM. Both the SS2 and the A14 go through Monteriggioni and pass just east of Colle; the SS68 runs from Colle to Volterra.

EMERGENCIES
In an emergency, dial **113** for paramedics, police, or the fire department.

Pharmacies take turns staying open late or on Sunday; for the latest information, consult the list posted outside each pharmacy, or ask at the local tourist office.

TOURS
From Florence, American Express operates one-day bus excursions to Siena and San Gimignano. CIT has a three-day Carosello bus tour from Rome to Florence, Siena, and San Gimignano. Both have English-speaking guides.

Another option is the Florence-based, American-owned and operated Custom Travel and Special Events, which runs customized day trips into Chianti wine country and other selected spots in Tuscany.

The San Gimignano tourist office organizes three-hour walks in the countryside around town with English-speaking guides from March through October, Wednesday, Friday, and Saturday afternoon, Sunday morning, or by appointment, for €10.30 per person.

➤ CONTACTS: **American Express** (⊠ Via Dante Alighieri 22/r, Florence, ☎ 055/50981). **CIT** (⊠ Piazza Stazione 51/r, Santa Maria Novella, Florence, ☎ 055/284145 or 055/212606). **Custom Travel and Special Events** (⊠ Via dell'Ardiglione 19, Florence, ☎ 055/264 5526). **San Gimignano visitor bureau** (⊠ Piazza del Duomo 1, ☎ 0577/ 940008, WEB www.sangimignano.com).

TRAIN TRAVEL

Getting between Siena and Florence by train is relatively quick and convenient; trains make the 80-minute trip between the two cities several times a day. Train service also runs between Siena and Chiusi–Chianciano Terme, where you can make Rome–Florence connections. Siena's train station is outside the *centro storico,* but cabs and city buses are readily available.

Train service within this region is limited and in many cases, bus trips are quicker. For instance, the nearest train station to Volterra is at Saline di Volterra (11 km [6 mi] west) with very slow connections to Cecina and the Rome–Pisa rail line along the coast. To and from Siena, trains run north to Poggibonsi and southeast to Sinalunga. Trains run from Chiusi–Chianciano Terme to Siena (1 hr) with stops to Montepulciano, Sinalunga, and Asciano. There are no direct train connections to San Gimignano or Monteriggioni.

You can contact the state railway, FS, for information, or stop in any travel agent, as many book and print train tickets and are more likely to speak English.
➤ CONTACT: **FS Information** (☎ 147/888088 toll-free, WEB www.fs-on-line.com or www.trenitalia.it).

TRAVEL AGENCIES

➤ SIENA: **Cotus** (⊠ Via Camollia 3, ☎ 0577/282011, WEB www.vacanzesenesi.it). **Palio Viaggi** (⊠ Piazza Gramsci 7, ☎ 0577/280828).
➤ SAN GIMIGNANO: **Mundi Travel** (⊠ Via San Matteo 74, ☎ 0577/ 940827, WEB www.munditravel.com).
➤ VOLTERRA: **Pro-Volterra** (⊠ Piazza Priori, ☎ 0588/86150, WEB www.provolterra.it). **Volterra Viaggi** (⊠ Piazza Martiri della Libertà, ☎ 0588/ 86333).

VILLA RENTALS

➤ CONTACTS: **The Best in Italy** (⊠ Via Ugo Foscolo 72, 50124 Florence, ☎ 055/223064, FAX 055/2298912). **Custom Travel and Special Events** (⊠ Via dell'Ardiglione 19, Santo Spirito, San Frediano 50124 Florence, ☎ 055/2645526). **Florence and Abroad** (⊠ Via San Zanobi 58, 50129 Florence, ☎ 055/470603, WEB www.florenceandabroad.com).

VISITOR INFORMATION

Tourist bureaus in larger towns typically open from 8:30 to1 and 3:30 to 6 or 7; bureaus in villages are usually seasonal.

In addition to the local Web sites included below, www.turismo.toscana.it and www.comune.siena.it/ can be helpful resources.
➤ TOURIST INFORMATION: **Asciano** (⊠ Corso Matteotti 18, ☎ 0577/ 719510, WEB www.cretesenesi.com). **Buonconvento** (⊠ Via Soccini 41, ☎ 0577/807181). **Colle di Val d'Elsa** (⊠ Via Campana 43, ☎ 0577/ 922791). **Monteriggioni** (⊠ Largo Fontebranda 5, ☎ 0577/304810). **San Gimignano** (⊠ Piazza del Duomo 1, ☎ 0577/940008, WEB www.sangimignano.com). **Siena** (⊠ Piazza del Campo 56, ☎ 0577/280551, WEB www.siena.turismo.toscana.it). **Sinalunga** (⊠ Piazza Giuseppe Garibaldi 43, ☎ 0577/630364). **Volterra** (⊠ Piazza dei Priori 19, ☎ 0588/86150, WEB www.comune.volterra.pi.it).

7 AREZZO, CORTONA, AND SOUTHERN TUSCANY

Antique architecture and artisan trades come together in a setting that's charming and off the beaten path. After touring perfect Pienza and the Val d'Orcia, lose yourself in the steep backstreets of Cortona, where local women hang out the wash, or peruse the monthly antiques fair in frescoed Arezzo. Rugged terrain marks the romantic, rough shores of Elba and Giglio and the crags of Monte Amiata.

S OUTHERN TUSCANY IS AS DIVERSE AS ITALY ITSELF, ranging from the cool mountain enclaves of Monte Amiata to the sandy beaches at Punta Ala. It contains the wildest parts of Tuscany—
the Maremma, once a malaria-ridden swampland where *butteri,* Italy's cowboys, rounded up their cattle, now a peaceful woodland fringed with beaches; Monte Amiata, a scruffy mountain landscape where goats gnaw at clumps of brown grass among scattered rocks; and the still-wild islands of the Tuscan archipelago. Some of Tuscany's best-kept secrets lie here in the south, among them the Abbazia di San Galgano, open to the sky, and the town of Pienza, built in just three years as Pope Pius II's ideal town. This is Etruscan country, where the necropolis near Sovana hints at a rich and somewhat mysterious pre-Roman civilization.

Updated by
Patricia Rucidlo

The lovely hill towns of Arezzo and Cortona carry on age-old local traditions—each September Arezzo's beautiful Franciscan, Gothic, and Romanesque churches are enlivened by the Giostra del Saracino, a costumed medieval joust. Since ancient times, Arezzo has been home to important artists: from the Etruscan potters who produced those fiery-red vessels to the poet Petrarch and Giorgio Vasari, writer, architect, and painter. Fine examples of the work of native son Luca Signorelli are preserved in Cortona.

The road between San Quirico d'Orcia and Pienza, above the Val d'Orcia, lies along views of quintessential Tuscany: round, green knolls topped by a single stone house and a cluster of cypresses. In the region's deep south, near Saturnia and Sorano, the earth is pocked with gurgling hot springs, odoriferous thermal sulfur baths, and natural geysers. The poppy and sunflower seasons in late spring and summer blanket the lands in vibrant colors, deepened by a backdrop of blue skies, earthy ocher hills, and emerald valleys.

Pleasures and Pastimes

Beaches

Though most Tuscan beaches are crowded in July and August, they are much less so in June and also in September, when the days are shorter but the water is still quite warm.

Dining

Tuscan specialties and wines can be savored everywhere in this region. Traditional dishes are based around porcini mushrooms and game such as hare, rabbit, and *cinghiale* (wild boar). The Val d'Orcia has its own special pasta called *pici* (short, thick spaghetti), sometimes served with a tomato sauce and other times thickened with wild boar. On the coast and islands, you can feast on a bounty of delectably fresh seafood.

CATEGORY	COST*
$$$$	over €18
$$$	€13–€18
$$	€8–€13
$	under €8

Prices are for a second course (secondo piatto).

Lodging

Southern Tuscany is a great place to enjoy the *agriturismo* lifestyle, but here you will also find hotels: modern affairs in cities, surfside beach resorts, and stately, time-worn villas. For budget travelers, there are nice, upscale campgrounds in the Punta Ala area. If you have a week to stay in a farmhouse, pick someplace central, such as Pienza, and explore the region from that base. It may be so relaxing and the food so good that you'll have trouble wandering away.

CATEGORY	COST*
$$$$	over €175
$$$	€125–€175
$$	€75–€125
$	under €75

All prices are for two people in a standard double room, including tax and service.

Thermal Baths

Southern Tuscany is shadowed with smoky clouds of steam billowing from natural geysers in the earth. There are also several outdoor naturally heated pools that smell of sulfur but are reputed to be therapeutic. Saturnia is the most famous; others are Venturina, near Piombino; Galleraie, near Montieri; Bagno Vignoni, near San Quirico d'Orcia; and Chianciano Terme, near Chiusi and not far from Lago Trasimeno in neighboring Umbria. But be aware that the baths can be crowded in summer.

Exploring Arezzo, Cortona, and Southern Tuscany

You can visit the whole region in about five days. This vast area can also be explored in bits and pieces, combined with visits to Chianti, the hill towns, and Umbria. Keep in mind that southern Tuscany isn't well served by trains, so if you aren't renting a car you'll have to plan around sometimes difficult bus schedules, and the going will be slow.

Great Itineraries

Numbers in the text correspond to numbers in the margin and on the Arezzo, Cortona, and Southern Tuscany; Arezzo; and Cortona maps.

IF YOU HAVE 3 DAYS

Visit **Arezzo** ①–⑦ and 🎦 **Cortona** ⑨–⑰ the first day, and overnight in Cortona. In the morning, head down to **Chiusi** ⑱, and wend your way along the Val d'Orcia to **Chianciano and Chianciano Terme** ⑲; 🎦 **Pienza** ⑳, stopping for lunch; **San Quirico d'Orcia** ㉑; and the **Abbazia di Sant'Antimo** ㉒. On your way, you can drop in on Montepulciano and Montalcino if you haven't already (☞ Chapter 4). Stay overnight in the Pienza or Montalcino (☞ Chapter 4) area. The next day, head south to **Pitigliano** ㉕ or **Saturnia** ㉔, being sure to visit **Sovana** ㉖ and **Sorano** ㉗, too.

Alternatively, from Siena head southwest to the **Abbazia di San Galgano** ㉘. Then make your way over to **Massa Marittima** ㉙ and spend the night there. The next day, visit the island of 🎦 **Elba** ㉝, taking the ferry from Piombino. On your third day, head south for **Monte Argentario** ㉜, seeing Porto Ercole and Porto Santo Stefano, where you can take a ferry to the island of **Giglio** ㉟.

IF YOU HAVE 5 DAYS

Start your trip visiting **Arezzo** ①–⑦ and 🎦 **Cortona** ⑨–⑰, overnighting in Cortona. On the second day, drive either north of Arezzo to the sunflower-blanketed Casentino or south to 🎦 **Pienza** ⑳, **San Quirico d'Orcia** ㉑, and the other towns in the Val d'Orcia. On Day 3, wander up **Monte Amiata** ㉓ and down to 🎦 **Pitigliano** ㉕, where you can spend the night. On Day 4, head west to **Monte Argentario** ㉜ and visit the island of 🎦 **Giglio** ㉟. Head back toward Siena on Day 5, taking time out to visit the **Abbazia di San Galgano** ㉘ and the hill towns around it.

When to Tour Arezzo, Cortona, and Southern Tuscany

Be prepared for steamy heat in the region in July and August. Coastal areas get crowded during this time, when Italians move en masse to their

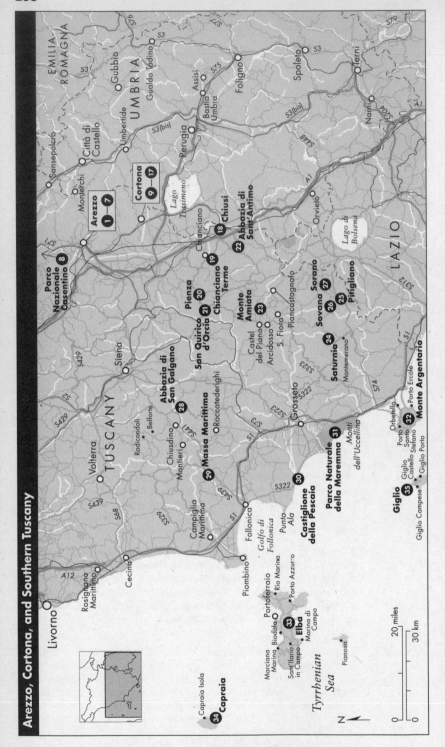

208

Arezzo, Cortona, and Southern Tuscany

beach homes, especially in August. On the other hand, if you visit southern Tuscany in July you'll see a spectacular explosion of sunflowers, creating an effect of blue sky over bright yellow fields. Spring and fall are the nicest seasons for southern sojourns, with relatively few tourists and pleasant temperatures, but beware of possible rainy seasons, especially in November and April. Winter can be fairly cold—warm boots, mittens, scarves, and heavy coats can sometimes be a necessity—and in the hilly areas near Umbria and especially Monte Amiata, it's freezing.

AREZZO

The birthplace of the poet Petrarch (1304–74), the Renaissance artist and art historian Giorgio Vasari, and of Guido d'Arezzo, the inventor of musical notation, Arezzo is today best known for the magnificent Piero della Francesca frescoes in the church of San Francesco. Arezzo dates from pre-Etruscan times, when around 1000 BC the first settlers—who continue to puzzle scholars today—erected a cluster of huts. Arezzo thrived as an Etruscan capital from the 7th to the 4th centuries BC and was one of the most important cities in the Etruscans' anti-Roman 12-city Dodecapolis federation, resisting Rome's rule to the last. The city eventually fell and in turn flourished under Roman rule. In 1248, Guglielmino degli Ubertini, a member of the powerful Ghibelline family, was elected bishop of Arezzo. This sent the city headlong into the enduring conflict between the Ghibellines (pro-emperor) and the Guelphs (pro-pope). In 1289, Florentine Guelphs defeated Arezzo in a famous battle at Campaldino. Among the Florentine soldiers was Dante Alighieri (1265–1321), who often referred to Arezzo in his *La Divina Commedia* (*The Divine Comedy*). Guelph-Ghibelline wars continued to plague Arezzo until the end of the 14th century, when Arezzo lost its independence to Florence.

Exploring Arezzo

Central Arezzo is pretty small, and you'll be able to explore it in a few hours, adding time to linger for some window-shopping at Arezzo's many antiques shops. It's best to look for parking at the top of the town, near the Duomo; otherwise, you'll have to park fairly far from the historic center.

A Good Walk

Start at the top of Arezzo with a visit to the **Duomo** ①. From here you can walk up Via San Domenico to **San Domenico** ② and the **Casa di Giorgio Vasari** ③. Retracing your steps to the Duomo, walk down Via dell'Orto off Piazza della Libertà, past the Casa del Petrarca (House of Petrarch). Turn right on Via dei Pileati (note the old library covered with Renaissance family crests), then left under the Vasari loggia and into **Piazza Grande** ④. Lovely antiques shops line this spacious square, which is also the center of a monthly antiques fair and an annual jousting event. Leave the square, taking Via Seteria, and visit **Santa Maria della Pieve** ⑤ on your right. Then turn left on Corso Italia, right on Via Cavour, and walk past Piazza San Francesco, visiting the **Basilica di San Francesco** ⑥. For a look at Arezzo's ancient past, head to the lower part of town to the **Museo Archeologico** ⑦. Take Via Guido Monaco all the way down and turn left onto Via Spinello, which becomes Via Niccolo'Aretino; the museum is at the corner of Via Margaritone.

TIMING
The walk itself takes about a half hour, but allow a half day to see the sights and the city at a leisurely pace and to squeeze in some shopping.

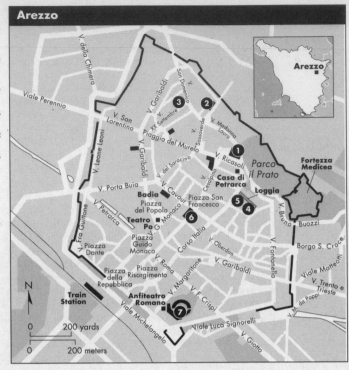

Sights to See

★ ❻ **Basilica di San Francesco.** The famous Piero della Francesca frescoes depicting *The Legend of the True Cross* (1452–66) were executed on three walls of the choir of this 14th-century church. What Sir Kenneth Clark called "the most perfect morning light in all Renaissance painting" may be seen in the lowest section of the right wall, where the troops of the Emperor Maxentius flee before the sign of the cross. The restored frescoes can be seen by reservation only, so call ahead or consult the Web site. ⊠ *Piazza San Francesco,* ☎ *0575/900404,* WEB *www. pierodellafrancesca.it.* ⊠ *€5.15.* ☉ *Nov.–Mar., weekdays 9–5:30, Sat. 9–5, Sun. 1–5; Apr.–Oct., weekdays 9–7, Sat. 9–6:15, Sun. 1–6:15. Admission limited to 25 people every ½ hr. Reservations required.*

❸ **Casa di Giorgio Vasari** (Giorgio Vasari House). Giorgio Vasari (1511–74), the region's leading Mannerist artist, architect, and art historian, designed and decorated the house after he bought it in 1540. He ended up not spending much time there, since he and his wife moved to Florence in 1554. Today the building houses archives on Vasari, and underwhelming works by the artist and his peers are on view. In the first room, which Vasari called the "Triumph of Virtue Room," a richly ornamented wooden ceiling shows Virtue combatting Envy and Fortune in a central octagon. Frescoes on the walls depict, among other things, Extravagance, Charity, the Fire of Troy, and a panorama of a Rome cow field. ⊠ *Via XX Settembre 55,* ☎ *0575/409040.* ⊠ *Free.* ☉ *Mon. and Wed.–Sat. 9–6:30, Sun. 9–1.*

❶ **Duomo.** Arezzo's medieval cathedral at the top of the hill contains an eye-level fresco of a tender *Magdalen* by Piero della Francesca (1420–92); look for it in the north aisle next to the large marble tomb near the organ. Construction of the Duomo began in 1278 but twice came to a halt, and the church wasn't completed until 1510. The facade, designed by Arezzo's Dante Viviani, was added as late as 1901–14. ⊠ *Piazza del Duomo,* ☎ *0575/23991.* ☜ *Free.* ⊙ *Daily 7–12:30 and 3–7.*

⑦ **Museo Archeologico.** The Archaeological Museum, on the south side of Arezzo in the **Convento di San Bernardo,** just outside the Roman amphitheater, exhibits a fine collection of Etruscan bronzes. ⊠ *Via Margaritone 10,* ☎ *0575/20882.* ☜ *€4.* ⊙ *Daily 8:30–7.*

<table>
<tr><td>NEED A
BREAK?</td><td>The old-fashioned-looking **Pasticceria Carraturo** (⊠ Corso Italia 61, ☎ 0575/355757) has scrumptious pastries and *cappuccini,* plus a tiny restaurant in the back.</td></tr>
</table>

④ **Piazza Grande.** With its irregular shape and sloping brick pavement, framed by buildings of assorted centuries, Arezzo's central piazza echoes Siena's Piazza del Campo. Though not quite so magnificent, it is lively enough during the outdoor antiques fair the first Sunday of the month and when the **Giostra del Saracino** (Saracen Joust), featuring medieval costumes and competition, is held here on the first Sunday of September.

② **San Domenico.** Just inside the northern city walls, this church was begun by Dominican friars in 1275 and completed in the 14th century. The walls were once completely frescoed and decorated with niches and chapels. Very little remains of the original works: a famous 13th-century crucifix by Cimabue (circa 1240–1302), frescoes by Spinello Aretino (1350–1410), and some 14th- and 15th-century paintings. ⊠ *Piazza San Domenico,* ☎ *0575/22906.* ☜ *Free.* ⊙ *Daily 7–1 and 3:30–6.*

⑤ **Santa Maria della Pieve** (church of Saint Mary of the Parish). The curving, tiered apse on Piazza Grande belongs to one of Tuscany's finest Romanesque churches. Santa Maria della Pieve was originally a Paleo-Christian church built on the remains of an old Roman temple. It was redone in Romanesque style in the 12th century. The facade is original, dating back from the early 13th century, but includes granite columns from the Roman period. Inside, frescoes by Piero della Francesca, Lorenzo Ghiberti (1378–1455), and Pietro Lorenzetti (circa 1290–1348) were sadly lost in the 16th, 17th, and 18th centuries. To the left of the altar, there is a 16th-century Episcopal throne by Vasari. ⊠ *Via dei Pileati, end of Corso Italia,* ☎ *0575/377678.* ☜ *Free.* ⊙ *Daily 8–12:30 and 3:30–6.*

Dining and Lodging

$$–$$$ ✕ **Buca di San Francesco.** A frescoed cellar restaurant in a centuries-old building next to the church of San Francesco, this *buca* (literally "hole," figuratively "cellar") doesn't seem to have changed much from the Middle Ages. You can choose from several straightforward local specialties, including *ribollita* (minestrone thickened with beans and bread). The lean Chianina beef and the *saporita di Bonconte* (a selection of several meats) are succulent treats. ⊠ *Via San Francesco 1,* ☎ FAX *0575/23271. AE, DC, MC, V. Closed Tues. and 2 wks in July. No dinner Mon.*

$$ ✕ **Osteria del Borro.** Getting here from Arezzo takes about 40 minutes by car, but the terrific food and stunning scenery make the trip worth it. The trattoria is on one side of a dramatically high, centuries-old stone bridge; on the other side is Il Borro, a little burg high on a hill. In warm weather you can eat outside, enjoying the splendid views while savoring Tuscan classics such as *pici con coniglio* (rounded, spaghetti-type noodles with a headily fragrant rabbit sauce). The interior is also pleasant, with high, stenciled ceilings. The wine list is par-

ticularly strong on Chiantis, and service is prompt. ⊠ *Località il Borro 52, San Giustino Valdarno,* ☎ *055/977026. MC, V. Closed Wed.*

$$ ✕ **Tastevin.** Here you'll find creative cooking that respects tradition— try risotto *alla Tastevin* (with a creamy truffle sauce) or one of the seafood dishes. Two of the dining rooms are furnished in a warm Tuscan provincial style, one in more sophisticated bistro style. At the small bar the talented owner plays and sings Sinatra and show tunes. ⊠ *Via dei Cenci 9, close to San Francesco and the central Piazza Guido Monaco,* ☎ *0575/28304. AE, DC, MC, V. Closed Sun. (except 1st Sun. of month) and 1 wk in Aug.*

$$ ▦ **Calcione Country and Castle.** The elegant Marchesa Olivella Lot-
★ teringhi della Stufa has turned her centuries-old family homestead into a top-notch agriturismo. Think sophisticated rustic—many of the apartments have fireplaces, the houses each have a private pool (the rest of the units share the estate pool), and there are private lakes for fishing and windsurfing. Calcione is convenient to Siena, San Gimignano, and the delights of Umbria. During high season, a one-week stay is mandatory. ⊠ *Lucignano, 52046,* ☎ *0575/837100,* ☒ *0575/837153,* 🖳 *www.calcione.com. 2 houses, 1 cottage, 6 apartments. 3 pools, 3 lakes, baby-sitting, Internet, some pets allowed; no air-conditioning, no phones in some rooms, no room TVs. No credit cards. Closed Nov.–Mar.*

$$ ▦ **Castello di Gargonza.** Enchantment reigns at this tiny 13th-century hamlet in the countryside near Monte San Savino, part of the fiefdom of the aristocratic Florentine Guicciardini; it was restored by the mod- ern Count Roberto Guicciardini, who rescued the dying village by turn- ing it into a hotel. A castle, church, and cobbled streets set the stage; medieval buildings house guest rooms, which are simply but carefully furnished. In high season, there's a one-week minimum stay; at other times it's a three-night minimum. La Torre restaurant (closed Tues.) adds flare to traditional Tuscan fare such as *chianina con rosmarino* (rare beef in rosemary sauce). ⊠ *Monte San Savino, 52048,* ☎ *0575/ 847021,* ☒ *0575/847054,* 🖳 *www.gargonza.it. 6 rooms, 11 apart- ments, 1 suite. Restaurant, pool; no air-conditioning, no room TVs. AE, DC, MC, V. Closed 3 wks in Jan., 3 wks in Nov.*

Outdoor Activities and Sports

Horseback Riding

A well-reputed outfit is **Etruria Ippo Trekking** (⊠ Via Michelangelo da Caravaggio 34–36, just behind Piazza Giotto, ☎ 0575/300417).

Shopping

The first Sunday of each month, a colorful flea market selling antiques and not-so-antiques takes place in the **Piazza Grande.**

Antiques

Alma Bardi Antichità (⊠ Corso Italia 97, ☎ 0575/20640) specializes in antique silver and jewelry. **Grace Gallery** (⊠ Via Cavour 30, ☎ 0575/ 354963) deals in antique furniture and paintings. **La Belle Epoque** (⊠ Piazza San Francesco 18, ☎ 0575/355495) collects antique lace and embroidered linens. For fine antique furniture and jewelry, peruse the objects at **La Nuova Chimera** (⊠ Via San Francesco 18, ☎ 0575/ 350155).

Gold

Gold production here is on an industrial scale. **Uno-A-Erre** is the biggest of several factories. Big-time baubles can be purchased on a small scale in the town center. For gold jewelry set with precious or semiprecious stones, try **Aurea Monilia** (⊠ Piazza San Francesco 15,

☎ 0575/355525). **Borghini** (✉ Corso Italia 126, ☎ 0575/24678) has beautiful bracelets and matching necklaces, among other lovely pieces. **Il Diamante** (✉ Via Guido Monaco 69, ☎ 0575/353450) carries sparkling, well-priced objects. **Prosperi** (✉ Corso Italia 76, ☎ 0575/20746) contains the full range of ornaments; the earrings are particularly stunning.

Knitwear

A cottage knitwear industry is burgeoning in Arezzo. For wool, cotton, and silk sweaters, try **Maglierie Mely's** (✉ Piazza Grande, ☎ 0575/324719).

THE CASENTINO

East of Florence and north of Arezzo is The Casentino, a virtually unknown area of Tuscany that holds hidden treasures. In 1289 Dante fought here in the battle that ended the centuries-long struggle between the Guelphs and the Ghibellines (the site of the battle—Campaldino—is marked today by a column outside Poppi at the crossing of the S70 and the road to Stia). Later, exiled from Florence, he returned, traveling from castle to castle, and recorded his love of the countryside in throughout *La Divina Commedia*.

The sparsely populated region—defined as the upper valley of the Arno, which originates here as a spring on Mt. Falterona—contains enough castles and Romanesque parish churches and unspoiled villages to keep you happily exploring for days. But the jewels in its crown are contained within the Parco Nazionale Casentino, an 89,000-acre preserve of great beauty. The heart of the park, on an Apennine ridge between the Arno and the Tiber, straddling Tuscany and Emilia-Romagna, is the antique forest tended as a religious duty for eight centuries by the monks of the Abbazia Camaldoli, designers of the world's first forestry code. The result of their intelligent and diligent husbandry, which included planting 4,000–5,000 saplings every year, are the large tracts of early-growth forest. While they began by maintaining the mix of silver firs and beeches, eventually they planted only firs, creating vast, majestic stands of the deep green trees whose 150-ft-tall, straight black trunks were once floated down the Arno to be used for the tallest masts of warships.

Parco Nazionale Casentino

★ ⑧ *Pratovecchio: 55 km (34 mi) north of Arezzo.*

A drive through the park, especially on the very winding 34-km (21-mi) road between the Monastero di Camaldoli and Santuario della Verna, passing through the lovely abbey town of Badia Prataglia, reveals one satisfying vista after another, from walls of firs to velvety pillows of pastureland where sheep or white cattle may be spied picturesquely grazing. In autumn, the beeches add a mass of red-brown to the palette, and in spring, torrents of bright golden broom pour off the hillsides with an unforgettable profusion and fragrance. Walking the forests—which also include sycamore, lime, maple, ash, elm, oak, hornbeam, and chestnut trees and are laced with abundant brooks and impressive waterfalls—is the best way to see some of the wilder creatures, from deer and mouflon (wild sheep imported from Sardinia in 1872 and later) to eagles and many other birds, as well as 1,000 species of flora, including many rare and endangered plants and an orchid found nowhere else. *Headquarters: ✉ Via Brocchi 7, Pratovecchio 52015, ☎ 0575/50301, FAX 0575/504497, WEB www.parks.it/parco.nazionale.for.casentinesi.*

Outdoor Activities and Sports

HIKING

The **Great Apennine Excursion** (Grande Escursione Apennine, or GEA) hiking route runs along the winding ridge, and the park organizes theme walks in summer and provides English-speaking guides anytime with advance notice.

Monastero di Camaldoli

20 km (12 mi) east of Pratovecchio, 55 km (34 mi) north of Arezzo.

In 1012, St. Romualdo, scion of a noble Ravenna family, came upon the forests of the Casentino and found their remoteness, their beauty, and their silence conducive to religious contemplation. He stayed, and founded a hermitage, Monastero Camaldoli (named for Count Maldoli, who donated the land), which became the seat of a new, reformed Benedictine order. Four centuries after its founding by St. Benedict, Romualdo felt it had become too permissive. An important requirement of the order was preserving its ascetic atmosphere: "If the hermits are to be true devotees of solitude, they must take the greatest care of the woods." When the flow of pilgrims began to threaten that solitude, Romualdo had a monastery and hospital built 1 km (2 mi) down the mountain to create some distance. Today the hermitage, **Sacro Eremo di** —where the monks live in complete silence in 20 separate little cottages, each with its own walled garden—can be seen through gates, and the church and original cell of Romualdo, the model for all the others, can be visited. The church, rebuilt in the 13th century and transformed in the 18th to its present appearance, strikes an odd note in connection with such an austere order and the simplicity of the hermits' cells, because it is done up in gaudy baroque style, complete with gilt cherubs and frescoed vault. Its most appealing artwork is the glazed terra-cotta relief *Madonna and Child with Saints* (including a large figure of Romualdo and a medallion depicting his fight with the devil) by Andrea della Robbia.

Within the monastery are the church (repeatedly restructured) containing 14th-century frescoes by Spinello Aretino, seven 16th-century panel paintings by Giorgio Vasari, and a quietly lovely monastic choir with 18th-century walnut stalls, more Vasari paintings, and a serene fresco (by Santi Pacini) of St. Romualdo instructing his white-robed disciples. In a hospital built for sick villagers in 1046 is the 1543 **Antica Farmacia** (Old Pharmacy), with original carved walnut cabinets. Here you can buy herbal teas and infusions, liqueurs, honey products, and toiletries made by the monks from centuries-old recipes as part of their daily routine balancing prayer, work, and study (the monastery is entirely self-supporting). In the back room is an exhibit of the early pharmacy's alembics, mortars, and other equipment with which the monks made herbs into medicines. ⊠ *Camaldoli 52010 (take S71 to Serravalle, then follow signs),* ☎ *0575/556021 Monastero; 0575/556013 Foresteria Monastero,* FAX *0575/556001,* WEB *www.camaldoli.it.* ☜ *Free.* ☉ *Daily 9–1 and 3:30–6.*

Santuario della Verna

34 km (21 mi) southeast of Monastero di Camaldoli, 65 km (40 mi) north of Arezzo.

A hill or two away from the Monastero di Camaldoli, dramatically perched on a sheer-walled rock surrounded by firs and beeches, is La Verna. St. Francis of Assisi founded it in 1214; the land was given to him by a count who heard him speak and was moved by his holiness.

Ten years later, after a 40-day fast, St. Francis—who had dedicated his life to following as closely as possible in Christ's footsteps—had a vision of Christ crucified, and when it it was over, Francis had received the stigmata. As Dante rendered it: "On the crag between Tiber and Arno then, in tears of love and joy, he took Christ's final seal, the holy wounds." A stone in the floor of the 1263 Chapel of the Stigmata marks the spot, and the Chapel of the Relics in the basilica contains a cloth stained with the blood that issued from his wounds. A covered corridor through which the monks pass chanting in a solemn procession each afternoon at 3 PM on the way to mass is lined with simple frescoes of the *Life of St. Francis* by a late 17th-century Franciscan artist. The true artistic treasures of the place, though, are 15 della Robbia glazed terra-cottas, including some of the finest works of Andrea. Some were commissioned, like the huge Crucifixion in the Chapel of the Stigmata; others have been donated throughout the centuries by the faithful. Most, like a heartbreakingly beautiful Annunciation, are in the 14th- to 15th-century basilica, whose 5,000-pipe organ sings out joyously at masses.

Several chapels, each with their own story, can be visited, and some natural and spiritual wonders can also be seen. A walkway along the 230-ft-high cliff leads to an indentation where the rock is said to have miraculously melted away to protect St. Francis when the devil tried to push him off the edge. Most touching is the enormous Sasso Spicco (Projecting Rock), detached on three sides and surrounded with mossy rocks and trees, where St. Francis meditated. You can also view the Letto di San Francesco (St. Francis's Bed), a slab of rock in a cold, damp cave with an iron grate on which he prayed, did penance, and sometimes slept. A 40-minute walk through the woods to the top of Mt. Penna passes some religious sites and ends in panoramic views of the Arno Valley, but those from the wide, cliff-edge terrace are equally impressive, including the tower of the castle in Poppi, the Prato Magno (great meadow), the olive groves and vineyards on the lower slopes, and a changing skyscape that seems to echo the mystical feel of the monastery and the woods that surround it. Santuario della Verna's *foresteria* (pilgrims' hostel) also offers travelers simple but comfortable rooms with or without bath. A restaurant ($) with basic fare is open to the public, and a shop sells souvenirs and the handiworks of the monks. ☒ *S208 east from Bibbiena, Santuario della Verna, 52010,* ☎ *0575/5341 or 0575/534211,* ☒ *0575/599320.* ☒ *Free.* ☉ *Daily 7:30–7.*

As you leave La Verna, be glad you needn't do it as Edith Wharton (1862–1937) did on a 1912 visit during a drive across the Casentino. As she wrote, her car "had to be let down on ropes to a point about ¾ mi below the monastery, Cook steering down the vertical descent, and twenty men hanging on to a funa that, thank the Lord, didn't break."

Lodging

$–$$ ☷ **Fattoria di Celli.** For less austere lodgings than those the monasteries provide, this former *fattoria*—a dormitory housing farm workers—is a great choice. Set on a gentle rise in the countryside outside the castle town of Poppi, it's a tranquil place whose lawns are punctuated with flowers and modern sculptures, play areas for children, and picnic tables placed to appreciate mountains views. Apartments have working fireplaces, some have original stone walls. In July and August, rentals require a one-week minimum stay. ☒ *Località Celli, Poppi 52013,* ☎ *0575/500294,* ☒ *0575/500191,* ☒ *www.tuscany.net/celli. 10 apartments, 3 villas. Restaurant, 2 pools, tennis court, basketball, laundry facilities; no air-conditioning, no room TVs. No credit cards.*

CORTONA

Magnificently situated, with olive groves and vineyards creeping up to its walls, one of Tuscany's prettiest towns commands sweeping views over Lago Trasimeno and the plain of the Valdichiana. Its two fine galleries and scattering of churches are worth a visit; its delightful medieval streets are a pleasure to wander for their own sake.

Cortona may be one of Italy's oldest towns—"Mother of Troy and Grandmother of Rome" in popular speech. Tradition claims that it was founded by Dardanus, the founder of Troy (after whom the Dardanelles are named). He was fighting a local tribe, so the story goes, when he lost his helmet (*corythos* in Greek) on Cortona's hill. In time a town grew up that took its name (Corito) from the missing headgear. By the 4th century BC the Etruscans had built the first set of town walls, whose cyclopean traces can still be seen in the 3-km (2-mi) sweep of the present fortifications. As a member of the Etruscans' 12-city Dodecapolis, Cortona became one of the federation's leading northern cities. An important consular road, the Via Cassia, which passed the foot of its hill, maintained the town's importance under the Romans. Medieval fortunes waned, however, as the plain below reverted to marsh. After holding out against such neighbors as Perugia, Arezzo, and Siena, the *comune* was captured by King Ladislas of Naples in 1409 and sold to the Florentines two years later.

Exploring Cortona

Cortona is very steep, and it's easy to get winded. Take it slowly and stop frequently to visit sights or just to enjoy a gelato.

A Good Tour

Start in Piazza della Repubblica, the heart of Cortona, where the Palazzo Comunale (City Hall) stands. Move on to the adjacent Piazza Signorelli, and stroll into the courtyard of the picturesque **Palazzo Pretorio** ⑨, which houses the Museo dell'Accademia Etrusca and its important collection of Etruscan bronzes. Across Via Casali is the Teatro Signorelli; walk north on Via Casali toward the Piazza del Duomo and the 15th-century **Duomo** ⑩, and the **Museo Diocesano** ⑪, opposite. Then walk past the **Chiesa del Gesù** ⑫ down Via Jannelli and turn left on Via Roma to head back to Piazza della Repubblica. From Piazza della Repubblica, if you're in shape for another climb and have the time, head behind the Palazzo del Capitano del Popolo up into Via Santucci to the 13th-century church of **San Francesco** ⑬ (at this writing, closed for restoration) and the 1441 Ospedale di Santa Maria della Misericordia. From Piazza San Francesco climb up the steep Via Berrettini, turn right on Via San Marco, and walk until you get to the church of **San Niccolò** ⑭. From here, it's just a little farther along Via Santissima Trinità to Via Santa Margherita, the road on the edge of town that leads all the way to the church of **Santa Margherita** ⑮ and the Fortezza Medicea behind it. On your way back, complete the circle by taking Via Santa Croce to the church of **San Cristoforo** ⑯, and pass by the convent of Santa Chiara on your way back down Via Berrettini. The 3-km (2-mi) drive downhill along Via Guelfa to the fine Renaissance **Santa Maria del Calcinaio** ⑰, a church dedicated to medieval tanners, could well be your most rewarding stop in Cortona. You could also see the church on your way in or out of the city.

TIMING

It takes about an hour to complete the tour as far as San Niccolò, which does not include the detours to Santa Margherita and Santa Maria delle Grazie al Calcinaio. The whole tour, adding time to see the sights, takes the good part of a day.

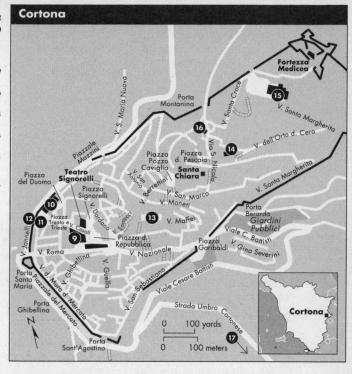

Cortona

Sights to See

⑩ Duomo. Cortona's cathedral stands on an edge of the city, next to what's left of the Etruscan and medieval walls running from Porta Santa Maria to Porta Colonia. It was built on the site of an old Romanesque church, but the present Renaissance church was begun in 1480 and finished in 1507. An arcade along the outside wall was erected in the 16th century. Inside, the Duomo is a mixture of Renaissance and Baroque styles featuring an exquisite 1664 baroque tabernacle on the high altar by Francesco Mazzuoli. ✉ *Piazza del Duomo,* ☎ *no phone.* 🎫 *Free.* ☉ *Daily 8–noon and 3–6:30.*

⑪ Museo Diocesano (Diocesan Museum). The museum houses an impressive number of large and splendid paintings by native son Luca Signorelli (1445–1523), as well as a beautiful *Annunciation* by Fra Angelico (1387/1400–1455), a delightful surprise in this small town. Below the Museo Diocesano is the former oratory of the Compagnia del Gesù, reachable by descending the 1633 staircase opposite the Duomo. The church was built between 1498 and 1505 and restructured by Giorgio Vasari in 1543. Frescoes depicting sacrifices from the Old Testament by Doceno (1508–56), based on designs by Vasari, line the walls. ✉ *Piazza del Duomo 1,* ☎ *0575/62830.* 🎫 *€5.* ☉ *Oct., Tues.–Sun. 10–1 and 3:30–6; Nov.–Mar., Tues.–Sun. 10–1 and 3–5; Apr.–Sept., Tues.–Sun. 9:30–1 and 3:30–7.*

⑨ Palazzo Pretorio. Wander into the courtyard of the picturesque *palazzo,* which also is called Palazzo Casali after the family that had it built and lived in it until 1409. The side of this building that faces Via Casali maintains its 13th-century style, and the front, facing the piazza, was redone in 1608. Today the building houses the Accademia Etrusca, which has an extensive library, **La Biblioteca comunale,** and the **Museo del'Accademia Etrusca.** Beyond the museum's centuries-old stone staircase is an eclectic mix of Egyptian objects, Etruscan and Roman bronzes and statuettes, and Renaissance paintings by artists such as Luca Signorelli and Pinturcchio (circa 1454–1513). From May through September, guided tours are available in English with prior arrangement. ⊠ *Piazza Signorelli 9,* ☎ *0575/630415.* 🎫 *€4.20.* ☉ *Oct.–Mar., Tues.–Sun. 10–5; Apr.–Sept., Tues.–Sun. 10–7.*

NEED A
BREAK? **Caffè degli Artisti** (⊠ Via Nazionale 18, ☎ 0575/601237) is a pleasant place to stop for a cappuccino or snack.

⑯ **San Cristoforo.** In the 12th-century church of St. Christopher is a 14th-century fresco by unknown artists of the Umbrian Sienese school depicting the Crucifixion, the Annunciation, and the Ascension. ⊠ *Piazza San Cristoforo,* ☎ *0575/630352.* 🎫 *Free.* ☉ *Open only for mass.*

⑬ **San Francesco.** In the mid-13th century, this Gothic-style church was built on the site of Etruscan and Roman baths. It contains frescoes dating from 1382, a big crucifix by Giuseppe Piamontini of Florence, and the *Relic of Santa Croce,* a vestige from the True Cross given to Brother Elia when he served as an envoy for Federico II in Constantinople. The church had a beautiful organ, built in 1466, that was almost completely destroyed during World War II. ⊠ *Piazza San Francesco,* ☎ *0575/ 630352.* 🎫 *Free. Closed for restoration.*

⑭ **San Niccolò.** On the main altar of this delightful, 15th-century Romanesque church is a fresco by Luca Signorelli, the *Deposition of Jesus,* painted around 1510. On the left wall is another fresco by Signorelli of the Madonna and Child, which was plastered over in 1768 and rediscovered in 1847. ⊠ *Via Santissima Trinità,* ☎ *0575/604591.* 🎫 *Free.* ☉ *Daily 9–noon and 3–7.*

⑮ **Santa Margherita.** Not as charming as Cortona's other churches from the outside, this large 19th-century basilica was completed as recently as 1897, over the foundation of a 13th-century church dedicated to the same saint. What makes the 10-minute uphill walk worthwhile, however, is the richly decorated interior. The body of the 13th-century saint Margherita—clothed but with skull and bare feet clearly visible—is displayed in a case on the main altar. ⊠ *Piazzale Santa Margherita,* ☎ *0575/603116.* 🎫 *Free.* ☉ *Daily 8:30–noon and 3–7.*

★ ⑰ **Santa Maria del Calcinaio.** Down the hill, about 3 km (2 mi) from town center, is a Renaissance sanctuary most likely designed by Sienese architect Francesco di Giorgio (1439–1502) and built between 1485 and 1513. Legend has it that the image of the Madonna appeared on a wall of a medieval *calcinaio* (lime pit), the site on which the church was then built. The linear gray-and-white interior recalls Florence's Duomo. It's a terrific example of Renaissance architectural principles outside Florence. ⊠ *Località Calcinaia 227,* ☎ *0575/62537.* 🎫 *Free.* ☉ *Daily 4:30–7.*

Dining and Lodging

$–$$ ✕ **La Loggetta.** Above Cortona's main medieval square, this attractive restaurant is housed in a 16th-century wine cellar. In good weather you can eat outdoors, overlooking the 13th-century town hall and dining on regional dishes and specialties such as *ravioli gnudi* ("naked ravioli," made with spinach and ricotta but without pasta) and *tagliata* (thin slivers of rare beef). The owners pride themselves on their selection of Tuscan wines. ⊠ *Piazza Pescheria 3,* ☎ *0575/630575. AE, DC, MC, V. Closed Wed. and two weeks in Nov.*

$–$$ ✕ **Osteria del Teatro.** Just up the street from Teatro Signorelli, this small osteria is lined with photographs from theatrical productions spanning many years. The food is deliciously simple—try the *filetto in crema di tartufo* (beef in a creamy truffle sauce); service is warm and friendly. ✉ *Via Maffei 5,* ☎ *0575/630556. AE, DC, MC, V. Closed Wed. and 2 wks in Nov. and Jan.*

$$$$
★ ✕▥ **Il Falconiere.** This might be as close as you can come to dying and going to heaven in Italy. Run by the husband-wife team of Riccardo and Silvia Baracchi, the hotel, just minutes outside Cortona, consists of rooms in an 18th-century villa and suites in the *chiesetta* (little church) once belonging to an obscure 19th-century Italian poet and hunter. Rooms are spacious, and many have sweeping views of the plain below. The restaurant's marvelous, inventive menu is complemented by the wine list, the product of Silvia's extensive sommelier training. ✉ *Località San Martino 370, 52044,* ☎ *0575/612679,* ℻ *0575/ 612927,* ⓦⓔⓑ *www.ilfalconiere.com. 13 rooms, 6 suites. Restaurant, room service, in-room safes, minibars, 2 pools, bar, laundry service, dry cleaning, Internet, some pets allowed. AE, DC, MC, V.*

Shopping

For nice ceramics, with many pieces depicting the brilliant sunflowers that blanket local fields, check out **Il Cocciaio** (✉ Via Nazionale 54, ☎ 0575/604405).

PIENZA AND THE VAL D'ORCIA

The Val d'Orcia (Orcia Valley) is a sumptuous, green valley with breathtaking views of the Orcia River. The area's long-standing agricultural tradition has left it utterly undeveloped, and so the vistas here are classic Tuscany—rolling hills, wide plains, swaths of blooming color punctuated by vineyards and olive groves. Picture-perfect Pienza and medieval San Quirico d'Orcia are great photo-op stops, and amateur archaeologists will enjoy pondering Chiusi's painted Etruscan tombs. Chianciano's thermal baths are a sybaritic treat, the intricate carvings of the Abbazia di Sant'Antimo a more mystical one.

Chiusi

⓲ *2½ km (1½ mi) east of the A1, 67 km (42 mi) south of Arezzo, 84 km (50 mi) southeast of Siena, 126 km (78 mi) southeast of Florence.*

Chiusi was once one of the most powerful of the ancient cities of the Dodecapolis Etruscan federation, and it's now a valuable source of information on the archaic civilization; 5th-century BC tombs unearthed in 1928 have provided archaeologists with a wealth of artifacts, and, more unusually, several frescoes in the Tomba della Scimmia (Monkey Tomb) depict scenes from ordinary life 2,500 years ago. Most of the artifacts found in the excavations have been taken from the tombs for safekeeping and placed in the **Museo Nazionale Etrusco** (✉ Via Porsenna 93/r, ☎ 0578/20177, ⊠ tomb €2), which, at this writing, was closed for a lengthy restoration; you can still view the tombs, however, by prior arrangement. These underground caverns are still evocative of ancient life, particularly in the Tomba della Pellegrina (Pilgrim Tomb), left virtually intact since the time of excavation. Reservations are required to visit the tombs (book through the museum). Chiusi is on the A1 autostrada and the main train line between Florence and Rome, making it an easy day trip from either city.

Chianciano and Chianciano Terme

⓳ *11 km (7 mi) northwest of Chiusi, 73 km (44 mi) southeast of Siena, 132 km (79 mi) southeast of Florence.*

The walled medieval town of Chianciano is best known by its proximity to the much-more visited Chianciano Terme, a renowned spa center drawing visitors and cure takers from around the world. Nevertheless, Chianciano's quaint, well-preserved historic center is appealing. The **Museo Civico Archeologico** (City Archaeological Museum; ⊠ Via Dante, ☎ 0578/30471) contains a good collection of Etruscan and Roman sculpture and pottery excavated around Chianciano. The museum is open April–October, daily 9:30–1 and 4–7:30, weekends 10–1 and 3–7 the rest of the year. Admission is €4.10.

The area's innumerable mineral-water springs are reputed to restore and maintain the health of the liver and skin, among other things. This is nothing new; as early as the 5th century BC, Chianciano was the site of a temple to Apollo the Healer. It's no secret, either—Terme di Chianciano alone claims to draw 120,000 visitors a year, and Italian state health insurance covers visits to the baths and springs for qualified patients. But you can test the waters yourself at a number of springs. **Terme di Chianciano** offers a choice of **Acqua Santa** (⊠ Piazza Martiri Perugini, Chianciano Terme, ☎ 9578/68411), known for curing liver and digestive ailments, €7.75; **Acqua Fucoli** (⊠ Viale G. Bacelli, Chianciano Terme, ☎ 0578/68430), for intestinal irritations, €4.65; and steamy-hot **Acqua Sillene** (⊠ Piazza Marconi, Chianciano Terme, ☎ 0578/68551), used for mineral and mud baths, €11.35 and €9.80, respectively; as well as nonaquatic activities including massage, tennis, boccie, and miniature golf (all for additional fees). Morning visitors can use Acqua Santa tickets to get into Acqua Fucoli. ☉ *Mid-Apr.–mid-Nov., Mon.–Sat. 8–noon and 4–6, Sun. 8 AM–11 PM; mid-Nov.–mid-Apr., Mon.–Sat. 8–noon.*

At **Terme Sant'Elena** (⊠ Viale dell Libertà 112, Chianciano Terme, ☎ 0578/31141), the waters are said to help with kidney and urinary-tract ailments and all manner of digestive disorders; there are boccie courts and a pretty park to stroll in while you drink. On summer afternoons, you can dance to live orchestra music in the park. The terme is open mid-April–mid-November; admission is €5.95.

Pienza

★ ⓴ *22 km (14 mi) west of Chianciano, 52 km (31 mi) southeast of Siena, 120 km (72 mi) southeast of Florence.*

Pienza owes its appearance to Pope Pius II (1405–64), who had grand plans to transform his home village of Corsignano—the town's former name—into a compact model Renaissance town. The man entrusted with the transformation was Bernardo Rossellino (1409–64), a protégé of the great Renaissance architectural theorist Leon Battista Alberti (1404–72). His mandate was to create a cathedral, a papal palace, and a town hall (plus miscellaneous buildings) that adhered to the vainglorious Pope's principles. Gothic and Renaissance styles were fused, and the buildings were decorated with Sienese paintings. The net result was a project that expressed Renaissance ideals of art, architecture, and civilized good living in a single scheme: it stands as an exquisite example of the architectural canons that Alberti formulated in the early Renaissance and which were utilized by later architects, including Michelangelo, in designing many of Italy's finest buildings and piazzas. Today the cool nobility of Pienza's center seems almost surreal in this otherwise unpretentious village, known locally for *pienzino*, a smooth sheep's-milk pecorino cheese. Pius II commissioned Rossellino in 1459 to design the perfect palazzo for his papal court. The architect took Florence's Palazzo Rucellai by Alberti as a model and designed the **Palazzo Piccolomini** with exactly 100 rooms. Three sides of the building fit perfectly into the urban plan around it, while the fourth, looking over the valley, has a lovely loggia uniting it with the gardens in back. You can visit the papal apartments, including a beautiful library, the Sala delle Armi—with an impressive weapons collection—and the music room, with its extravagant wooden ceiling forming four letter P's, for Pope, Pius, Piccolomini, and Pienza. ⊠ *Piazza Pio II,* ☎ *0578/748503.* ▨ *€3.* ☉ *Oct.–July, Tues.–Sun. 10–12:30 and 3–6; Aug.–Sept., Tues.–Sun. 10–12:30 and 4–7.*

The 15th-century **Duomo** was also built by Rossellino under the influence of Alberti. The facade is divided in three parts with Renaissance arches under the Pope's coat of arms encircled by a wreath of fruit. Inside, the cathedral is simple but richly decorated with Sienese paintings. The Duomo's perfection didn't last long—the first cracks appeared immediately after the building was completed, and its foundations have shifted slightly ever since as rain erodes the hillside behind. You can see this effect if you look closely at the base of the first column as you enter the church and compare it with the last. ⊠ *Piazza Pio II.* ▨ *Free.* ☉ *Tues.–Sun. 10–1 and 3–7.*

The **Museo Diocesano** is at the left of the Duomo. It is small but has a few interesting papal treasures and rich Flemish tapestries. The most precious piece is a rare mantle woven in gold with pearls and embroidered religious scenes that belonged to Pope Pius II. ⊠ *Piazza Pio II,* ☎ *0578/ 749905.* ☉ *Wed.–Mon. 8–1 and 3–7.*

Part of the acclaimed 1996 film *The English Patient* was filmed at **Sant'Anna in Camprena,** an abandoned Benedictine monastery in the open country 7 km (4½ mi) north of Pienza. You can view frescoes by Sodoma (1477–1549) in the refectory (dining hall) and in the room where the eponymous patient lay in bed. It is best reached by car or bicycle (public transportation isn't available). The Pienza tourist office (☞ Visitor Information *in* Arezzo, Cortona, and Southern Tuscany A to Z) also has information on Sant'Anna in Camprena. ⊠ *From Pienza take road to San Quirico for 1 km (½ mi) and turn right, following signs for monastery; continue 6 km (4 mi) and turn left; follow tree-lined dirt road to church.* ☎ *0578/748303.* ▨ *Free.* ☉ *Easter–mid-Oct., Thurs.–Sun. 5 PM–7 PM, or by appointment.*

Dining and Lodging

$–$$ ✕ **La Chiocciola.** A no-frills trattoria a few minutes' walk from the historic center, this place offers typical fare from Pienza, including homemade local pici with hare or wild-boar sauce. Their take on *formaggio in forno* (baked cheese) with such assorted accompaniments as fresh porcini mushrooms is reason enough to eat here. ⊠ *Via dell'Acero 2,* ☎ *0578/748063. MC, V. Closed Wed. and 10 days in Feb.*

$ ✕ **Osteria Sette di Vino.** Tasty dishes based on the local cheeses are the specialty at this simple and inexpensive osteria, set on a quiet and pleasant square in the center of Pienza. Try various versions of pici or the starter of radicchio baked quickly to brown at the edges. The local specialty pecorino appears often on the menu—the *pecorino grigliata con pancetta* (grilled cheese with unsmoked, cured bacon) is divine, as is the pecorino tasting menu. ⊠ *Piazza di Spagna 1,* ☎ *0578/749092. No credit cards. Closed Wed., July 1–15, and Nov.*

$$ ▣ **Hotel Corsignano.** This modern, comfortable property lies just outside the old city walls. Two light-beige buildings, the older one right on the road, are connected by a hallway. The rooms in the newer half of the hotel in the back are quieter and larger and have newer furniture; all have carpeting except for a few in the older front rooms, which have tile floors. The furniture is plain and made of wood. ⊠ *Via della Madonnina 11, 53026,* ☎ *0578/748501,* ℻ *0578/748166,* ⓦⒺⒷ *www.*

*corsignano.it. 40 rooms. In-room safes, minibars, cable TV, dry clean-
ing, laundry service, Internet, free parking, some pets allowed. AE, DC,
MC, V. CP.*

$ 🏨 **Camere di Pienza.** A Renaissance building on Pienza's main street
houses this tiny hotel with only four rooms. They make up for their
small number in quality, with pretty, if simple, decoration and particularly nice ceilings—three with wood beams and one with a fresco. ⊠
*Corso Il Rossellino 23, 53026, ☎ 0578/748500. 4 rooms. No air-con-
ditioning. No credit cards. EP.*

San Quirico d'Orcia

㉑ *9½ km (5½ mi) southwest of Pienza, 43 km (26 mi) southeast of Siena,
111 km (67 mi) southeast of Florence.*

San Quirico d'Orcia, on the Via Cassia (S2) south from Siena toward
Rome, has almost-intact 15th-century walls topped with 14 turrets. The
pleasantly crumbling appearance of the town recalls days of yore, and
it's well suited for a stop to enjoy a gelato in a local bar or a meal and
to see its 13th-century Romanesque **Collegiata** church with its three majestic portals, one possibly the work of Giovanni Pisano (circa 1245/
48–1318). Against the walls of San Quirico d'Orcia is the **Horti Leonini,**
a public park with Italian-style gardens that retain merely a shimmer
of their past opulence. Near Horti Leonini stands **Palazzo Chigi,** named
after the family to whom the Medici gave San Quirico in 1667. Just outside the town are the thermal baths of **Bagno Vignoni** and the **Castello
di Vignoni** (Castle of Vignoni), which offers nice views of the valley.

Dining and Lodging

$–$$ ✕ **Trattoria Al Vecchio Forno.** A meal here is truly delicious. Special-
ties include dishes accented with porcini mushrooms, such as the excellent mushroom soup, pici with tomato or boar sauce, and roast boar
and game, all rounded out by the good wine selection. There's a nice
garden out back. ⊠ *Via Piazzola 8, ☎ 0577/897380. No credit cards.
Closed Wed. and for about 10 days in mid-Nov. and 2 wks in mid-
Jan.*

$$$ 🏨 **Hotel Residence Casanova.** Just 1,000 ft from the city walls, this
lovely old villa has been converted into an upscale inn. Views of the
Val d'Orcia are stunning, and the rooms are nicely decorated with prac-
tical Tuscan furniture. Some suites have kitchen facilities, a bonus for
families or longer stays. The restaurant, La Taverna del Barbarossa ($$;
closed Mon.), is set inside a classic Tuscan country house that dates to
the 13th century. Its name commemorates a meeting held here in medieval times between papal messengers and Frederick I (circa 1123–
90), called Il Barbarossa. ⊠ *S146 Località Casanova, 53027, ☎ 0577/
898177, FAX 0577/898190. 44 rooms, 26 suites. Restaurant, some
kitchens, cable TV, tennis court, sauna, spa, steam room, pool, gym,
mountain bikes, billiards, Ping-Pong, bar, recreation room, baby-
sitting, playground, Internet, some pets allowed (fee). AE, DC, MC,
V. CP, MAP.*

Abbazia di Sant'Antimo

㉒ *20 km (13 mi) southwest of San Quirico d'Orcia, 10 km (6 mi) south
of Montalcino, 31 km (19 mi) south of Siena, 100 km (60 mi) south
of Florence.*

It's well worth your while to visit this 12th-century Romanesque abbey,
as it's a gem of pale stone set in the silvery green of an olive grove. The
exterior and interior sculpture is outstanding, particularly the nave capitals, a combination of French, Lombard, and even Spanish influences.

The **sacristy** (rarely open) forms part of the primitive Carolingian church (founded in AD 781), its entrance flanked by 9th-century pilasters. The small **vaulted crypt** dates from the same period. Above the nave runs a *matroneum* (women's gallery), an unusual feature once used to separate the congregation. Equally unusual is the ambulatory, of which the three radiating chapels (rare in Italian churches) were probably copied from the French model. Stay for mass to hear the ceremony performed in Gregorian chant. ⊠ *Castelnuovo dell'Abate*, ☎ *0577/835659*. ⊠ *Free*. ☉ *Apr.–Sept., daily 9–noon and 2–7; Oct.–Mar., daily 10–noon and 2–4; mass Mon.–Sat. 9* AM *and 7* PM, *Sun. 11* AM *and 6:30* PM.

THE MAREMMAN INLAND

The wildest part of Tuscany is here in its southern heart. And it's here that you get a sense of what the region looked like before Tuscany became a must-see on the Grand Tour. The landscape alternates between rolling hills and tufa cliffs; hill towns abound, linked by narrow, winding roads. Saturnia—with its superior hotels, restaurants, and one-of-a-kind hot springs—makes a good base to explore and sample the best of what the South has to offer: ancient Etruscan tombs and caverns at Sovana and Sorano, the famous white wine of Pitigliano, and wild mushrooms and chestnut honey from the rugged slopes of Mount Amiata, which presides over Tuscany with views from Arezzo to the sea.

Monte Amiata

㉓ *86½ km (52 mi) southeast of Siena, 156½ km (94 mi) southeast of Florence.*

At 5,702 ft, this benign volcano is one of Tuscany's few ski slopes, but it's no Mont Blanc. Come in warmer months to take advantage of its greatest appeal: panoramic views of all of Tuscany on the winding road up to the summit. Along the way, you'll pass through a succession of tiny medieval towns, including Castel del Piano, Arcidosso, Santa Flora, and Piancastagnaio, where you can pick up picnic supplies and sample the chestnuts and game for which the mountain is famous. The thousand year old village of **Abbadia San Salvatore** is worth a stop—skip the nondescript new town and head straight to the *centro storico* (historic center) to explore winding stone streets with tiny churches around every corner. The abbey for which the town was named was founded in 743; its current appearance reflects an 11th-century renovation, but the original crypt remains intact.

There's no reason to stay on the road, though. Stray off the asphalt and you'll find an abundance of hiking trails that cross wide meadows full of wildflowers and slice through groves of evergreens on their way up the mountainside. Trail maps are available at the Monte Amiata tourist office in Abbadia di San Salvatore (☞ Visitor Information *in* Arezzo, Cortona, and Southern Tuscany A to Z).

Saturnia

㉔ *47 km (30 mi) south of Monte Amiata, 129 km (77 mi) south of Siena, 199 km (119 mi) south of Florence.*

Saturnia was settled even before the Etruscans, but nowadays it's best known not for what lies buried beneath the ground but for what comes up from it: hot, sulfurous water that supplies the town's world-famous spa. According to an oft-repeated local legend, the 3,000-year-old thermal baths were created when Saturn, restless with earth's bickering mortals, threw down a thunderbolt and created a hot spring whose miraculously calming waters created peace among them. Today, these magnesium-rich waters bubble forth from the clay, drawing Italians and non-Italians alike seeking relief for skin and muscular ailments as well as a bit (well, a lot) of relaxation. Unlike better-known spa centers such as Montecatini Terme, nature still has her place here; just outside town, on the road to Montemerano, the hot, sulfurous waters cascade over natural limestone shelves at the **Cascate del Gorello** (Gorello Falls), affording bathers a sweeping view of the open countryside. Also outside town and free to visit, the pre-Etruscan tombs at the **Necropoli del Puntone,** on the road from Saturnia to Poggio Murello, aren't kept up well, but they're interesting simply for their age, as they're even older than Saturnia's legendary baths.

Dining and Lodging

$$$$ ✕ **Da Caino.** At this excellent restaurant in the nearby town of Montemerano (on the road to Scansano), specialties include tomatoes and peppers on crisp phyllo dough, lasagna with pumpkin, and such hearty dishes as *cinghiale lardolato con olive* (wild boar larded with olives). ✉ *Via della Chiesa 4, Montemerano, 7 km (4½ mi) south of Saturnia,* ☎ *0564/602817. Reservations essential. AE, DC, MC, V. Closed Jan.– Feb. and Wed. No dinner Thurs.*

$$–$$$$ ✕ **I Due Cippi–Da Michele.** Owner Michele Aniello has a terrific restau-
★ rant with a lengthy and creative menu; the emphasis is on Maremman cuisine, such as wild boar and duck—though there are other treats as well; try the *tortelli di castagne al seme di finocchio* (chestnut-stuffed tortelli with butter sauce and fennel seeds). In good weather you can enjoy your meal on a terrace overlooking the town's main square. ✉ *Piazza Veneto 26/a,* ☎ *0564/601074. Reservations essential. AE, DC, MC, V. Closed Tues. in Oct.–June, Dec. 20–26, and Jan. 10–25.*

$$$$ ▦ **Terme di Saturnia.** Cure takers looking for a most refined approach
★ can don their bathrobes here at the region's premier resort. The hotel, an elegant stone building, wraps around three tufa-rock pools built over the hot springs' source. Every imaginable type of health and beauty treatment is available, supplemented by decidedly unspalike meals in the restaurant. Half-board rates are a good deal. ✉ *Saturnia, 58050,* ☎ *0564/601061,* FAX *0564/601266,* WEB *www.termedisaturnia.it. 80 rooms, 10 suites. Restaurant, snack bar, in-room safes, minibars, in-room VCRs, driving range, 2 tennis courts, 4 pools, hair salon, health club, sauna, spa, steam room, bar, piano bar, shops, dry cleaning, laundry facilities, concierge, Internet, helipad, some pets allowed. AE, DC, MC, V.*

$$ ▦ **Albergo La Stellata.** Sitting prettily on a hilltop with views of neighboring fields, this rustic stone farmhouse is a low-key base for a visit to Saturnia's baths and the Maremman countryside. The natural hot waterfall is less than 2 km (1 mi) away, as is the Terme di Saturnia complex, where La Stellata guests can use the facilities for €13.40 a day. ✉ *Località Pian del Bagno, 58050,* ☎ *0564/602978,* FAX *0564/602934,* WEB *www.termedisaturnia.it. 13 rooms. Cable TV, bar, baby-sitting, concierge, free parking, some pets allowed; no air-conditioning in some rooms. AE, DC, MC, V. CP, MAP.*

$$ ▦ **Villa Acquaviva.** Perched on top of a hill off the main road 1 km (½ mi) from Montemerano, this elegant villa painted antique rose appears at the end of a tree-lined driveway. It has expansive views and quintessential Tuscan charm. Tastefully decorated rooms are in both the main villa and in a guest house. The farm that fans out around it produces both wine and olive oil. ✉ *Strada Scansanese, Montemerano, 58050,* ☎ *0564/602890,* FAX *0564/602895,* WEB *www. laltramaremma.it/acquaviva. 24 rooms, 2 suites. Restaurant, tennis court, pool, bar, playground, some pets allowed. AE, DC, MC, V.*

TERME: WRATH OF THE GODS

I N A COUNTRY KNOWN FOR MILLEN- NIA as a hotbed of seismic activity, Tuscany seems to have gotten a lucky break. While Campania and Sicily are famous for active volcanoes, and Umbria and the Marches stand on notoriously shaky ground, Tuscany's underground activity makes itself known in the form of steamy and sulfurous hot springs that have earned the region a name as a spa goer's paradise.

Tuscany is dotted throughout with small *terme,* or thermal baths, whose hot waters flow from natural springs deep under the earth's surface. Since the time of the Etruscans, Tuscany's first rulers, these hot springs have been valued for their curative properties; the Romans, in their turn, attributed the springs' origins to divine thunderbolts that split the earth open and let flow the miraculous waters. Although the findings of modern geology rob the springs of some of their mystery, their appeal endures, as the presence of thousands of people taking the waters in the Maremma attests.

For the thermal-spring connoisseur, each of the terme has different curative properties, attributable to the various concentrations of minerals and gases that individual water flows pick up on their way to the earth's surface. Carbon dioxide, for example, is said to promote drainage and strengthen the immune system, while sulphur, its characteristic rottenegg smell notwithstanding, is said to relieve pain and aid in relaxation. Although customs and conventions vary between spa establishments, visitors generally pay an admission fee to swim in baths that range from hot natural lakes and waterfalls (with all the accompanying mud) to giant limestone swimming pools distinguish-

able from the garden variety only by their cloudy, bright blue, and steaming water. Larger establishments then offer a wide variety of treatments based on the springs, which can range from mineral mud baths to doctor-supervised steam inhalations, all with much-touted curative effects. Believers swear that Tuscany's hot springs have a positive effect on everything from skin disorders to back pain to liver function to stress, and spa personnel will gladly offer up case histories and scientific studies to prove their point. Whatever your opinion, a good soak in a Tuscan spring is a relaxing way to take a break, and as far as geological phenomena go, it beats an earthquake or a volcanic eruption any day.

A few of the region's spas, notably the world-famous Montecatini Terme (☞ Chapter 3), are well known outside of Tuscany. For the most part, however, the local establishments that run the springs are not well publicized; this can mean a more local flavor, lower prices, and fewer crowds than you'll find at the big spas. Places such as the **Terme di Bagni di Lucca** (✉ Bagni di Lucca, ☎ 0583/87221), near Lucca (☞ Chapter 5) ; **Terme di Chianciano** (✉ Chianciano Terme, ☎ 0578/ 68111), near Grosseto ; and **Terme di Saturnia** (✉ Saturnia, ☎ 0564/601061), like many other smaller spa establishments, offer the experience of a visit to the waters without the accompanying overkill of a famous spa town. Local tourist offices have the most up-to-date information on many of these smaller springs, many of which are only open for part of the year; contact an APT or Pro Loco in the area you plan to visit for recommendations on where to go for a nice, hot bath.

$$ ▣ **Villa Clodia.** The best hotel in Saturnia's hilltop town center, this
★ former private villa has splendid views over the neighboring hills and
the steamy clouds coming from the terme. Inside it's just as nice, with
hand-painted decoration in spacious rooms and a cozy library with a
marble fireplace. Breakfast is served in a country-style room with ging-
ham tablecloths, but early risers may be able to stake a claim on one
of the terrace tables overlooking the valley. ⊠ *Via Italia 43, 58050,*
☎ *0564/601212,* FAX *0564/601305,* WEB *www.laltramaremma.it. 8
rooms, 2 suites. In-room safes, minibars, pool, free parking. AE, DC,
MC, V. Closed Dec. CP.*

$$ ▣ **Villa Garden.** All the rooms at this small place, charmingly furnished
with comfortable beds, flowered curtains and bedspreads, and tiled bath-
rooms floors, are named for flowers. A few minutes by car from the
center of town, it's a perfect place to stay if you want to take the waters without breaking the bank. The buffet breakfast is good and filling, the staff courteous and efficient. ⊠ *Via Sterpeti 56, 58014,* ☎ *0564/
601182,* FAX *0564/601207,* WEB *www.laltramaremma.it/villa_garden.
10 rooms. Cable TV, minibars, bar, Internet, some pets allowed, free
parking. AE, DC, MC, V. CP.*

Pitigliano

㉕ *33 km (21 mi) east of Saturnia, 147 km (92 mi) southeast of Siena,
217 km (136 mi) southeast of Florence.*

From a distance the medieval stone houses of Pitigliano look as if they
melt into the cliffs of soft tufa rock they are perched on. Etruscan tombs,
which locals use to store wine, are connected by a network of caves
and tunnels. At the beginning of the 14th century, the Orsini family
moved their base from Sovana to the naturally better-fortified Pitigliano. They built up the town's defenses and fortified their home,
Palazzo Orsini. Later, starting in 1543, Antonio da Sangallo the Younger
added to the town's fortress aspect, building bastions and towers
throughout the town and adding the 16th-century **aqueduct** as well.

Wander down the narrow streets of the old **Jewish Ghetto,** where Jews
took refuge from 16th-century Catholic persecution. Savory local specialties include the famous Pitigliano white wine, olive oil, cold cuts,
and cheeses; local restaurants serve up good food at modest prices. Pitigliano is becoming a trendy locale for Italian summer rentals, making the town center livelier in summertime than in the past.

The 18th-century Baroque **Duomo** has a single nave with chapels and
various paintings on the sides. There are two altarpieces by local artist
Francesco Zuccarelli (1702–88), a rococo landscape artist and a founder
of the British Royal Academy who was a favorite of George III. ⊠ *Piazza S. Gregorio,* ☎ *0564/616090.* ▣ *Free.* ☽ *Daily 9–7.*

Inside the **Palazzo Orsini** is the **Museo Zuccarelli,** featuring paintings
by Zuccarelli as well as a Madonna by Jacopo della Quercia (1371/
1374–1438), a 14th-century crucifix, and other works of interest. ⊠
Piazza della Repubblica, ☎ *0564/616074.* ▣ *€2.60.* ☽ *Mid-Oct.–mid-
Apr., Tues.–Fri. 10–1 and 3–5, weekends 3–6; mid-Apr.–July and Sept.
mid-Oct., Tues.–Sun. 10–1 and 3–7; Aug., Mon.–Sun. 10–1 and 3–8.*

Lodging

$ ▣ **Hotel Guastini.** Centrally located, this plain beige three-story build-
ing is actually the only show in town. It's comfortable enough, with
brick floors and wooden furniture dating to the 1960s. Rooms have
nice views of the town center; two of them have small terraces. It's a
reliable budget option. ⊠ *Piazza Petruccioli 4, 58017,* ☎ *0564/616065,*

FAX *0564/716652. 27 rooms. Restaurant, cable TV, Internet, parking (fee), some pets allowed; no air-conditioning. AE, DC, MC, V. CP, EP.*

Sovana

㉖ *5 km (3 mi) north of Pitigliano, 155 km (97 mi) southeast of Siena, 225 km (141 mi) southeast of Florence.*

This town of Etruscan origin was once the capital of the area in southern Tuscany ruled by the Aldobrandeschi family, whose reign was at its height in the 11th and first half of the 12th centuries. One member of the family, Hildebrand, was the 11th-century Catholic reformer Pope Gregory VII (circa 1020–85). The 13th- to 14th-century Romanesque fortress known as the **Rocca Aldobrandesca** is now in ruins. The town extends from the fortress on one end to the imposing **Duomo** on the other, almost outside the town. **Via di Mezzo,** its stones arranged in a fishtail pattern, is the main street running the length of the town. It leads to the central **Piazza del Pretorio,** with the 13th-century **Palazzo Pretorio,** whose facade is adorned with crests of Sovana's captains of justice, and the Renaissance **Palazzo Bourbon dal Monte.** A bit farther along is the little 14th-century church of **Santa Maria Maggiore,** which has frescoes from the late-15th-century Sienese Umbrian school. About 2 km (1 mi) from Sovana is an **Etruscan necropolis,** with rock tombs dating from the 2nd–3rd centuries BC.

Dining

$$–$$$ ✕ **Scilla.** Uncomplicated Tuscan fare is served at this restaurant in a medieval palazzo close to Sovana's central square. Try the *zuppa di ricotta,* a thick vegetable soup with ricotta cheese, or the *pici all'aglione* (a thick pasta with even thicker slices of sautéed garlic). The house specialty, a succulent *coniglio in crosta* (baked rabbit), is a perfect dish to savor when it's cold outside. The outdoor terrace provides plenty of fresh air. ✉ *Via Rodolfo Silviero 1-3,* ☎ *0564/616531. AE, DC, MC, V. Closed Tues. and Feb.*

Sorano

㉗ *10 km (6 mi) east of Sovana, 138 km (86 mi) southeast of Siena, 208 km (130 mi) southeast of Florence.*

Sorano's history follows the pattern of most settlements in the area: it was an ancient Etruscan citadel, built up in the 15th century and fortified by one of the many warring families of Tuscany (in this case, the Orsini). It's the execution that sets it apart. With its tiny, twisted streets and stone houses connected by wood stairways and ramps, Sorano looks like it was carved from the tufa beneath it—and that's because it was. Underneath the town, visible as you approach, is a vast network of *colombari,* Etruscan-era rooms lined with hundreds of niches carved into stone walls, dating from the 1st century BC. The colombari aren't yet open to the public, but Sorano is worth a visit regardless, if only to walk its medieval alleyways and to watch old-style artisans at work. Views of the densely forested hills around town will have you reaching for your camera.

THE MAREMMAN COAST

Tuscany's coast is blessed with the best of both worlds: steep hills flanked by evergreen forests and classic Tuscan views back-to-back with an enviable stretch of sandy beaches and sparkling sea. The ruined, fairytale Abbazia di San Galgano is a must-see, and the chain of hill towns around it are as classically pretty as anything Chianti has to offer. But this part of the Maremma is best known for its beaches and coastal towns, less developed than those to the north but even more popular among summer-vacationing cognoscenti.

Abbazia di San Galgano

㉘ *33 km (20 mi) southwest of Siena, 101 km (63 mi) southwest of Florence.*

Time has had its way with this Gothic cathedral without a rooftop, a hauntingly beautiful sight well worth a detour. The church was built in the 13th century by Cistercian monks, who designed it after churches built by their order in France. But starting in the 15th century it fell into ruin, declining gradually over centuries. Grass has grown through the floor, and the roof and windows are gone. What's left of its facade and walls makes a grandiose and desolate picture. Behind it, a short climb up a hill brings you to the charming little **Chiesetta di Monte Siepi**, with frescoes by painter Ambrogio Lorenzetti (documented 1319–48), and a sword in stone. Legend has it that Galgano, a medieval warrior and bon vivant, was struck by a revelation on this spot in which an angel told him to give up his fighting and frivolous ways forever. He replied that this would be as likely as spearing a stone with his sword, but as he demonstrated, the sword miraculously pierced the stone, in which it remains to this day.

Dining and Lodging

$–$$ ✕ **Il Granaio.** Run by the uncommon culinary combination of a Tuscan and his Sardinian wife, this old stone granary at the entrance to Radicondoli has a menu reflecting the influence of both. Tuscan specialties include penne *alla boscaiola*, with porcini mushrooms, and *bistecca* or *tagliata*, thin slices of top-quality local Chianina beef. To eat Sardinian-style, try *gulugiones*, elongated pasta stuffed with cheese, potato, and spices (something like long ravioli). ⊠ *Via G. di Vittorio 1, Radicondoli,* ☎ *0577/790611. AE, DC, MC, V. Closed Wed. and Jan. 15–Feb. 15.*

$$ ⌂ **Fattoria Solaio.** This elegant farm near Radicondoli has sculpted gardens and a swimming pool. The rooms are plain, with baked-clay floors and simple furniture. The owners are friendly and the scenery is breathtaking, making this perfect for a quiet country *agriturismo* vacation. In high season, a minimum two-night stay is mandatory. ⊠ *Località Solaio, Frazione Anqua, Radicondoli 53030,* ☎ *0577/719029,* FAX *0577/791015,* WEB *www.fattoriasolaio.it. 9 rooms, 3 apartments. Restaurant, pool, free parking; no room phones. No credit cards. Closed Nov.–Mar. EP.*

$$ ⌂ **Rifugio Prategiano.** Equestrians take note: horseback tours through Tuscany's cowboy country are an integral part of the country living at Rifugio Prategiano, just outside the town of Montieri, beyond Chiusdino. The hosts can organize picnics accessible via horseback and also suggest great routes for trekking with equines. But nonriders don't have to mope at the bar—this *agriturismo* also has a pool and idyllic views. ⊠ *Via dei Platani 3/b, Località Prategiano, Montieri 58026,* ☎ *0566/997703,* FAX *0566/997891,* WEB *www.prategiano. 24 rooms. Restaurant, pool, horseback riding, free parking, some pets allowed; no air-conditioning. MC, V. CP, EP.*

Massa Marittima

㉙ *32 km (20 mi) southwest of Abbazia di San Galgano, 62 km (39 mi) southwest of Siena, 132 km (82 mi) southwest of Florence.*

Massa Marittima is a charming medieval hill town with a rich mining and industrial heritage—pyrite, iron, and copper were found in these parts. After a centuries'-long slump (most of the minerals having been depleted), the town is now popular simply for its historic streets. The central Piazza Garibaldi, dating from the 13th to early 14th centuries, contains the Romanesque **Duomo,** with sculptures of the life of patron saint Cerbone above the door. ✉ *Piazza Garibaldi,* ☎ *0566/902237.* 🎫 *Free.* ☉ *Daily 8–noon and 3–6.*

The 13th-century **Palazzo Pretorio,** on the Piazza Garibaldi, is home to the **Museo Archeologico,** with plenty of Etruscan artifacts. The most famous painting in the **Pinacoteca** (painting gallery), also housed in the palace, is Ambrogio Lorenzetti's *Maestà.* ✉ *Piazza Garibaldi,* ☎ *0566/902289.* 🎫 *€3 (includes both museums).* ☉ *Nov–Mar., Tues.– Sun. 10–12:30 and 3–5; Apr.–Oct., Tues.–Sun. 10–12:30 and 3:30–7.*

The **Museo Arte e Storia della Miniera** (Museum of the Art and History of Mining), in the upper part of town, shows how dependent Massa Marittima was, since Etruscan times, on copper, lead, and silver mining. Exhibits trace the history of the local mining industry. ✉ *Palazzetto delle Armi, Corso Diaz,* ☎ *0566/902289.* 🎫 *€2.60.* ☉ *Tues.–Sun. 10– 11 and 5–6:30.*

You can see an old olive-oil press, called the **Antico Frantoio,** in a small stone farm building next to the Palazzo delle Armi. Mules harnessed to the heavy stone wheel pulled it around, and as it rolled, the olives on the flat surface were crushed by its weight, extracting the precious oil—the same technique is used today (minus the mules). ✉ *Corso Diaz, next to Palazzetto delle Armi,* ☎ *0566/902289.* 🎫 *€1.50.* ☉ *Apr.– Oct., Tues.–Sun. 11:30–1 and 5–6:30; Nov.–Mar. by appointment.*

Nightlife and the Arts
On the first Sunday after May 22, and again on the first Sunday in August, Massa Marittima's three traditional neighborhood groups dress in medieval costumes, parade through the town, and compete in the **Balestro del Girifalco** (Falcon Crossbow Contest), where contestants try to shoot down a toy falcon.

Castiglione della Pescaia

➌⓪ *44 km (27 mi) south of Massa Marittima, 94 km (59 mi) southwest of Siena, 162 km (101 mi) southwest of Florence.*

The medieval town built around a hilltop fortress here is as inviting as many others in Tuscany, but Castiglione's real appeal is found below on its white sandy beaches bordered by pine forest. It's become a seaside playground of Italy's smart set by virtue of its vicinity to Florence and the north. The lovely marina has a good fresh-fish market. Punta Ala, known for alabaster, is just down the road and has a pretty beach and a port with chic shops and waterfront pubs. There are some very nice campgrounds in the area, but if you prefer sleeping in a bed, book hotels early—both Castiglione and Punta Ala fill up quickly from June to October.

Lodging
$$$$ 🏨 **Hotel Roccamare.** On a private sandy beach 5 km (3 mi) west of Castiglione della Pescaia, this expensive, exclusive modern hotel is a summer resort first and foremost. Windsurfing equipment and beach chairs and umbrellas are provided, and a beautiful pool and tennis court are an alternative to seaside diversions. When you tire of the sun, retire to airy rooms in the main building or in one of the several cottages that surround it. Rooms have whitewashed walls and tile floors and look out either on a pine grove or onto the beach. ✉ *Strada Provinciale, Rocchette, 58043,* ☎ *0564/941124,* FAX *0564/941133,* WEB *www.*

roccamare.it. 51 rooms, 101 cottages. Restaurant, cable TV, minibar, tennis court, pool, beach, windsurfing, basketball, bicycles, free parking. AE, DC, MC, V. Closed Nov.–Easter. CP, EP.

$$ ⊞ **Hotel Miramare.** In the new part of town, this hotel is the best choice for those who want to stay close to the center of the action. Although one side of the hotel is on the main street going into town, the other side is on a private beach—a must in August. Rooms are fairly lackluster but they are modern and clean. ⊠ *Via Vittorio Veneto 35, Castiglione della Pescaia 58043,* ☎ *0564/933524,* FAX *0564/933695,* WEB *www.hotelmiramare.it. 25 rooms. Restaurant, cable TV, beach, bar, baby-sitting, dry cleaning, laundry service, concierge, Internet, parking (fee). AE, DC, MC, V. Closed Nov.–Mar. CP, EP.*

Outdoor Activities and Sports

Castiglione is prime sailing and windsurfing territory. Rent boats, boards, and kayaks at the many vendors along the beach. You may want to charter one of the Castiglione-based boats owned by **Agua** (⊠ Via San Gervasio 21/c, Florence 50131, ☎ 055/588958).

Parco Naturale della Maremma

③ *23 km (14 mi) southeast of Castiglione della Pescaia, 88 km (55 mi) southwest of Siena, 156 km (97 mi) south of Florence.*

The well-kept nature preserve at **Monti dell'Uccellina** is an oasis of green hills sloping down to small, secluded beaches on protected coastline. Wild goats and rabbits, foxes and wild boars make their home among miles of sea pines, rosemary, and juniper bush; the park also has scattered Etruscan and Roman ruins and a medieval abbey, the **Abbazia di San Rabano.** Enter from the south at Talamone (turn right 1 km [12 mi] before town) or from Alberese, both reachable from the SS 1 (Via Aurelia). Daily limits restrict the number of visitors, so it's best to reserve in summertime; contact the visitors' office for bookings, nighttime visits, and English-language guides. ⊠ *Via del Fante, Alberese,* ☎ *0564/407098.* 🎫 *€3–€8 depending on itinerary.* ☉ *Daily 9–1 hr before sunset.*

Monte Argentario

③ *30½ km (19 mi) south of Parco Naturale della Maremma, 118½ km (74 mi) southwest of Siena, 186½ km (116 mi) southwest of Florence.*

Connected to the mainland only by three thin strips of land, Monte Argentario feels like an island. The north and south isthmuses, La Giannella and La Feniglia, have long sandy beaches popular with families, but otherwise the terrain is rough and wild. The mountain itself rises 2,096 ft above the sea, and it's ringed with rocky beaches and sheer cliffs that afford breathtaking views of the coast. On the north side, busy and colorful **Porto Santo Stefano**—one of the two port towns here—is Monte Argentario's main center, with markets, hotels, and restaurants, and ferry service to Giglio and Giannutri (☞ Tuscan Islands). On the south, picturesque **Porto Ercole** is the haunt of the rich and famous, with top-notch hotels and restaurants perched on the cliffs. The rest of Monte Argentario is rugged, dotted with luxurious vacation houses (including Sophia Loren's) and wildflowers. There are beautiful views from the panoramic mountain road encircling the promontory, and a drive here is a romantic sunset excursion.

Dining and Lodging

$$$ ✕ **Armando.** This may not be the place for a romantic candlelit meal, but the food makes up for the lack of ambience. The nautical-style family-run restaurant is known for spaghetti *alle briciole* (literally, "with

crumbs"), and the kitchen here conjures up a richly inventive version, dressed with garlic, olive oil, hot peppers, and anchovies. The *moscardini con fagioli* (similar to cuttlefish, served with beans) is tastily aromatic. ✉ *Via Marconi 1/3, Porto Santo Stefano,* ☎ *0564/812568. AE, DC, MC, V. Closed Wed. and Nov.–Mar.*

$$$ ✕ **Gambero Rosso.** Right on the port, this excellent restaurant is a seaside Italian classic. The menu is just what you'd expect: simple preparations of fresh fish drawn from local waters. Try the house specialty, antipasto *sorpresa del Gambero* (surprise), an ever-changing array of six, sometimes seven, different fish dishes prepared in a variety of ways (fried, chilled, and baked, for example). The chef lets his imagination run wild, and it's only to the benefit of the happy diners. It's even better if you enjoy it on the terrace with a view. ✉ *Lungomare Andrea Doria, Porto Ercole,* ☎ *0564/832650. AE, DC, MC, V. Closed Wed. and mid-Nov.–mid-Jan.*

$$ ✕ **La Fontanina di San Pietro.** The scene here is romantic, with grape vines climbing on a trellis and cherry trees in a country setting overlooking the port. Dine on scampi with zucchini and spaghetti *allo scoglio,* with fresh clams and mussels in a light tomato sauce, while enjoying a fruity white from the well-chosen wine list. The catch of the day can be prepared a number of ways and is priced by weight; the *pescespada* (swordfish) is terrific. ✉ *Via del Campone (on road outside San Pietro),* ☎ *0564/825261. AE, DC, MC, V. Closed Wed. and Jan.*

$$$ ⊞ **Hotel Don Pedro.** The private beach more than makes up for the lack of a swimming pool at this mid-size, modern hotel in Porto Ercole. Rooms are spacious, with tile floors and functional wooden furniture. There's a good restaurant and a bar on the beach, and the hotel provides beach chairs and umbrellas to its guests. ✉ *Via Panoramica 7, Porto Ercole 58018,* ☎ *0564/833914,* ℻ *0564/833129,* 🅆🅔🅑 *www. hoteldonpedro.it. 44 rooms. Restaurant, beach, bar, baby-sitting, dry cleaning, laundry service. AE, MC, V. Closed Nov.–Easter. CP, EP.*

$$ ⊞ **Hotel Vittoria.** A steep walk up the hill from the center of Porto Santo Stefano, this 1970s hotel has a gorgeous view of the port. Several rooms have terraces with sea views, and the 10 suites have spacious sitting areas. Decoration is simple, with tile floors and wood furniture. ✉ *Strada del Sole 65, Porto Santo Stefano 58019,* ☎ *0564/818580,* ℻ *0564/818055,* 🅆🅔🅑 *www.hvittoria.com. 18 rooms, 10 suites. Restaurant, pool, tennis court, baby-sitting, concierge, free parking; no air-conditioning. AE, DC, MC, V. Closed Nov.–Mar. CP, EP.*

TUSCAN ISLANDS

The six main islands in the waters between the Tuscan coast and the French island of Corsica make up the **Parco Nazionale dell'Arcipelago Toscano** (Tuscan Archipelago National Park), an emerald swath of clean, deep water and small rocky islets that contains the largest protected marine area in Europe. Long, sandy beaches and tranquil coves are the bewitching gateways to an undersea world of corals, gorgons, multicolor fish, and dolphins; given the richness of its wildlife and its proximity to the mainland, it's a pleasant surprise to find that most of the park's islands are largely overlooked by outsiders. This is not to say that foreigners are anything new here: Napoléon (1769–1821) spent a glamorous exile on lush Elba in 1814–15, and Alexandre Dumas's *Le Comte de Monte-Cristo* (*The Count of Monte Cristo*) was inspired by the tiny island of Montecristo, now a strictly protected wildlife refuge. But the islands are, thankfully, still a trip off the beaten path. Giglio and its little sister Giannutri, between Montecristo and Monte Argentario at the south of the island chain, are rocky retreats for nature lovers and beach bums. Even less touristed are remote Capraia, frequented mostly by sailors, and the former prison colony of Pianosa, whose last notorious inmates were released only a few years ago, leaving a massive, empty *carcere* (prison) and a landscape untouched by tourism.

Of the islands, only Elba and Giglio are well equipped for visitors, with excellent hotels and restaurants and easy transportation from the mainland. Capraia has a few hotels, Giannutri has basic facilities for those who really want to get away from it all, and Pianosa makes a good day trip from Elba. Montecristo can be visited in very limited and strictly controlled groups—all the better to preserve this, the most pristine part of the Tuscan sea.

Elba

③ *Portoferraio: 22 km (14 mi) by sea southwest of Piombino, 183 km (114 mi) southwest of Florence.*

Elba is the Tuscan archipelago's largest island, but it resembles its rocky Italian sisters less than it does nearby verdant Corsica, thanks to a network of underground springs that keep the island lush and green. It's this combination of semitropical vegetation and dramatic mountain scenery—unusual in the Mediterranean—that has made Elba so prized for so long, and the island's uniqueness continues to draw boatloads of visitors throughout the warm months.

Lively **Portoferraio,** the main ferry port where Victor Hugo (1802–85) spent his boyhood, makes a good base. Head right when you get off the ferry to get to the *centro storico* (historical center), fortified in the 16th century by the Medici Grand Duke Cosimo I (1519–74). Most of the pretty, multicolor buildings that line the old harbor date from the 18th and 19th centuries, when the boats in the port were full of mineral exports rather than tourists. The **Museo Archeologico** (⊠ Calata Buccari, Portoferraio, ☎ 0565/944024) reconstructs the island's ancient history through a display of Etruscan and Roman artifacts recovered from shipwrecks. It's open September–May, Monday–Saturday 9:30–noon and 3–6; June–July, Monday–Saturday 9:30–7; and August, Monday–Saturday 9–1 and 3–midnight. Admission is €2.

Napoléon was famously exiled on Elba, in 1814–15, during which time he built the **Palazzina dei Mulini** (⊠ Piazzale Napoleone 1, Portoferraio, ☎ 0565/915846) out of two windmills. It still contains furniture from the period and can be visited April–September, Monday and Wednesday–Saturday 9–7 and Sunday 9–1, and the rest of the year, Monday and Wednesday–Saturday 9–4 and Sunday 9–1. The €5 admission includes Napoléon's other residence on Elba.

A couple of miles outside Portoferraio, the **Villa San Martino** (⊠ Località San Martino, ☎ 0565/914688) was Napoléon's country residence. Its classical facade was added later by a Russian prince. The villa is open April–September, Tuesday–Saturday 9–7 and Sunday 9–1, and October–March, Tuesday–Saturday 9–4, and Sunday 9–1. Admission is €5 and includes the Palazzina Napoleonica dei Mulini.

On the south side of the island, **Marina di Campo** is a classic summer vacationer's town, with a long sandy beach and a charming, laid-back marina full of bars, restaurants, and shops. The splendid **Porto Azzurro** really is noticeably *azzurro* (sky blue) and is worth a stop for a walk and a gelato along the rows of yachts harbored there. The island's quietest town is old-fashioned **Rio Marina,** with a pebble beach, an old mine, a leafy public park, and ferry service to Piombino.

Elba's most celebrated beaches are the sandy stretches at **Biodola, Procchio,** and Marina di Campo, but the entire island—and particularly the westernmost section, encircling Monte Capanne—is ringed with beautiful coastline. Indeed, it seems that every sleepy town has its own perfect tiny beach. Try **Cavoli** and **Fetovaia** any time but July and August, when all the car-accessible beaches on the island are packed (there are also some accessible only by boat, such as the black-sand beach of **Punta Nera**). Off the coast, the slopes of Monte Capanne are crossed by a twisting road that offers magnificent vistas at every turn; the tiny towns of **Poggio** and **Marciano** have enchanting little piazzas full of flowers and trees. You can hike to the top of Monte Capanne, or take an unusual open-basket cable car from just above Poggio. A car is very useful for getting around the island, but public ATL buses (☎ 0565/914392) stop at most towns several times a day; contact the tourist office (☞ Visitor Information *in* Arezzo, Cortona, and Southern Tuscany A to Z) for timetables.

OFF THE
BEATEN PATH

PIANOSA – For years, visitors who came here didn't have a choice; the flat, undeveloped island was the site of a maximum-security prison that hosted some of Italy's most notorious Mafiosi. Now "Italy's Alcatraz" is no more, and only the caretakers of the nature preserve here—which includes Roman ruins, early Christian catacombs, and a swimming area at Cala Giovanna—remain. Visitor services are still being developed, so come prepared with a bag lunch and plenty of water. There are plans to open the prison to visitors in a few years. For now, however, the number of visitors even allowed on the island is limited, so be sure to reserve in advance. Toremar ferries (☎ 0565/31100) to the island leave from Porto Azzurro, on Elba.

MONTECRISTO – The most famous prisoner here was fictional: Alexandre Dumas's legendary Count. Today the island is a strictly protected nature preserve, home to wild Montecristo goats and vipers, peregrine falcons, and rare Corsican seagulls who make their home amid the island's rosemary bushes and, presumably, squabble for shade under the island's two trees. Visits to Montecristo mostly are limited to scientific-research trips. The Ministero delle Politiche Agricole, Corpo Forestale (ministry for agricultural policy; ☎ 0566/40019) authorizes Montecristo visits.

Dining and Lodging

$$–$$$$ ✕ **La Canocchia.** In the center of Rio Marina on the eastern shore of Elba is this airy, 40-seat place across from a public garden. Seafood takes center stage here. Specialties include ravioli *scampi e asparagi o calamari* (stuffed with shrimp or squid, in light asparagus sauce) and various saffron-perfumed catches of the day. The *frittura di paranza* (fried fish) are crisp and light, and the *involtini di pescespada* (swordfish rolls) also shouldn't be missed. Book ahead in summer, as it can get very crowded. ✉ *Via Palestro 3, Rio Marina,* ☎ *0565/962432. MC, V. Closed Mon. and Nov.–mid-Feb.*

$$–$$$ ✕ **Trattoria da Lido.** In the historic center of Portoferraio, at the beginning of the road to the old Medici walls, this bustling, casual restaurant serves commendable *gnocchetti di pesce* (bite-size potato-and-fish dumplings) with a white cream sauce and fresh *pesce all'elbana* (whitefish baked with vegetables and potatoes). ✉ *Salita del Falcone 2, Portoferraio,* ☎ *0565/914650. AE, DC, MC, V. Closed mid-Dec.–mid-Feb.*

$$ ✕ **Il Cantuccio.** The simple, rustic style of this small restaurant, a stand-
★ out in sometimes touristy Marina di Campo, is a welcome change of pace. If the long menu seems daunting, give your eyes a rest and admire the list of specials, which often includes such local delicacies as spaghetti *alle uova di pesce* (with sea-bream caviar). The staff is friendly and well informed, particularly about wine; shady outdoor tables on

a back street keep diners cool on warm nights. ✉ *Via Largo Garibaldi 2, Marina di Campo,* ☎ *0565/976775. AE, DC, MC, V.*

$–$$ ✕ **Il Mare.** Just a few steps from Rio Marina's calm and pretty port—
★ and an easy stop on your way to or from the ferry—this friendly restaurant serves up homemade pastas and fresh seafood with a dash of style. The young chef puts her creative spin on the classics, coming up with such delights as homemade vegetable gnocchi with scampi in a butter and saffron sauce. The *semifreddi* (literally, "half cold"; chilled or partially frozen desserts) are particularly good here. ✉ *Via del Pozzo 13 (across port from ferry dock), Rio Marina,* ☎ *0565/962117. V.*

$$$$ ☷ **Hermitage.** This heavenly bayside hotel on Elba, 8 km (5 mi) from Portoferraio, includes a low-slung central building with guest rooms as well as little cottages, each with six to eight rooms, all surrounded by lush grounds. The hotel bar and restaurant are on a private, white, sandy beach, near the large pool. During high season, half-board is mandatory. ✉ *Biodola, 57037,* ☎ *0565/936911,* FAX *0565/969984,* WEB *www.elba4star.it. 110 rooms. 2 restaurants, 6-hole golf course, 9 tennis courts, 3 pools, beach, soccer, volleyball, 3 bars, children's programs, meeting room, Internet, some pets allowed. AE, DC, MC, V. Closed Nov.–Apr. MAP.*

$$$$ ☷ **Hotel Riva del Sole.** Steps from the beach and a short walk to the
★ center of lively Marina di Campo lies this bright, pleasantly appointed hotel, which caters to a loyal Italian and German clientele. Breezy rooms, some with terraces, offer cool relief from the hot sun; marble bathrooms are an elegant touch. On warm nights, the scent of oleander growing next to the hotel will truly give you sweet dreams. ✉ *Viale degli Eroi 11, Marina di Campo 57034,* ☎ *0565/976316,* FAX *0565/976778. 53 rooms, 4 suites. Restaurant, cable TV, minibars, bar, baby-sitting, laundry service, Internet, free parking. AE, DC, MC, V. Closed Nov.–Apr. EP.*

$$$$ ☷ **Park Hotel Napoleone.** This late-19th-century villa, in a park next to Napoléon's Villa San Martino, has sumptuous interiors. It's 5 km (3 mi) outside the center of Portoferraio and 5 km (3 mi) from the sandy beach of Biodola. The rather high price reflects the fact that breakfast and dinner are included. Buses run often from the hotel to the port in Portoferraio. ✉ *Località San Martino, Portoferraio 57037,* ☎ *0565/918502,* FAX *0565/917836. 64 rooms. Minibars, cable TV, 2 tennis courts, 2 pools, mountain bikes, baby-sitting, dry cleaning, laundry service, Internet, free parking, some pets allowed. DC, MC, V. Closed Nov.–Easter. MAP.*

$$$ ☷ **Hotel Rio.** Convenient to ferries and Rio Marina's charming town center and gravel beach, this comfortable, modern hotel has pretty sea views. A nice bonus: your beach chair and umbrella are free with your room. Five rooms have terraces with sea views. ✉ *Via Palestro 31, Rio Marina 57038,* ☎ *0565/924225,* FAX *0565/924162. 32 rooms. Restaurant, minibars, refrigerators, baby-sitting, laundry services, Internet, free parking, some pets allowed; no air-conditioning in some rooms. AE, DC, MC, V. Closed Oct.–Mar. CP, EP.*

Outdoor Activities and Sports

There are numerous places to rent bikes, scooters, motorcycles, or cars on Elba. **Baby Rent** (✉ Piazza del Popolo 9, Portoferraio, ☎ no phone; Via Mascagni, Marina di Campo, ☎ 0565/977281 or 0330/777904) rents, among other things, BMW convertibles for touring the island in style. **BW's Rent** (✉ Via Manganaro 23, Portoferraio, ☎ 0565/930491 or 0347/7371790) has everything from mopeds to Yamaha touring bikes, as well as a few small cars. **Chiappi** (✉ Calata Italia 30, ☎ 0565/916779) rents Honda and Yamaha scooters, but if you have problems finding a hotel, keep in mind that they also rent a seven-bed camper. **Spaziomare** (✉ Via Vittorio Veneto, Porto Azzurro, ☎ 0565/95112 or 0348/6017862) has motorboats available for half- and full-day rentals and sailboats to rent by the week. Adventurous types can rent sea kayaks and mountain bikes from **Il Viottolo** (✉ Via Pietri 6, Marina di Campo, ☎ 0565/978005), which also organizes three-day guided excursions on land and sea.

Capraia

34 *50 km (31 mi) by sea northwest of Elba, 165 km (103 mi) southwest of Siena, 233 km (145 mi) southwest of Florence.*

Only a handful of people actually live on the island of Capraia, which is frequented mainly by sailors. It's a rocky and hilly unspoiled national park, with only one sandy beach, **Cala della Mortola,** on the northern end of the island; the rest of the coast is a succession of cliffs and deep green coves with pretty rock formations. Ferries from Livorno pull in at the town of **Capraia Isola,** dominated by the Fortezza di San Giorgio up above. Nearby, an archway leads to an area that was once a prison. Capraia's clear waters and undersea life draw raves from scuba divers. **Capraia Diving Service** (✉ Via Assunzione 64, ☎ 0586/905137) can help with scuba-diving equipment and boats. The **Cooperativa Parco Naturale Isola di Capraia** (✉ Via Assunzione 42, ☎ FAX 0586/905071) can help with villa rentals and ferry schedules.

Giglio

35 *20 km (12½ mi) west of Porto Santo Stefano (Monte Argentario), 138½ km (86 mi) southwest of Siena, 206½ km (129 mi) south of Florence.*

Rocky, romantic Isola del Giglio (Island of the Lily) is just an hour by ferry from Porto Santo Stefano but a world away from the mainland's hustle. The island's three towns—**Giglio Porto,** the charming harbor where the ferry arrives; **Giglio Castello,** a walled village at Giglio's highest point; and **Giglio Campese,** a modern town on the west side of the island—are connected by one long, meandering road. But to really explore Giglio, you'll need a good pair of hiking boots. A network of rugged trails climbs up the steep hills through clusters of wild rosemary and tiny daffodils, and once you leave town, chances are your only company will be the goats who thrive on Giglio's sun-baked hills.

The island's main attraction, however, is at sea level—a sparkling array of lush coves and tiny beaches, most accessible only by foot or boat. With the exception of Giglio Campese, where the sandy beach is as popular in summer as any mainland resort, most of the little island's coastline is untouched, leaving plenty of room for peaceful sunning for those willing to go off the beaten path.

Lodging

$$$ ☷ **Hotel Arenella.** This hotel is on the mountain road leading away from Giglio Porto, 3 km (2 mi) out of town but unfortunately not on the bus route to Giglio Castello—to get here you need a car, or the hotel will send one to pick you up at the ferry. The hotel is isolated and quiet, crowned above the sea with great views, and has a private beach reachable by a steep 60-ft walk down. Rooms in the main building are larger and nicer and include suites and rooms for families; more ordinary double rooms are in a smaller building, but they have verandas. Ask for a sea view. The stucco hotel was built and furnished in the 1970s, and rooms are in modest style with stone floors and simple wood furniture. ✉ *Località Arenella, Giglio Porto 58013,* ☎ *0564/809340,*

FAX *0564/809443,* WEB *www.albergoarenella.it. 27 rooms. Internet, laundry service; no air-conditioning in some rooms. AE, MC, V. Closed Nov.–Easter. MAP.*

$$$ ⌨ **Pardini's Hermitage.** Reachable only by boat or by an arduous
★   hour's hike, this tiny, ultraprivate hotel is the refuge of a world-traveling Giglian dedicated to preserving the island's natural past. Flowering gardens and terraces for dining spill down a rocky cliff to private beaches below; on the hill above the main house, the owners raise purebred donkeys on which you can ride over the mountain and goats that produce fresh yogurt and cheese for breakfast. Free from noise but for the lapping of waves on the rocks, the Hermitage is a tranquil retreat. ✉ *Località Cala degli Alberi, Giglio 58013,* ☎ *0564/809034,* FAX *0564/809177,* WEB *www.finalserv.it/hermitage. 12 rooms. Laundry service, cable TV, Internet, some pets allowed; no air-conditioning, no TV in some rooms. No credit cards. Closed Oct. and Mar. MAP, FAP.*

Outdoor Activities and Sports

HIKING

For day-trippers, the best hike is the 1,350-ft ascent from Giglio Porto to Giglio Castello. It's a 4 km (2½ mi) trek that takes about an hour and affords marvelous views of the island's east coast. Frequent bus service to and from Castello allows the option of walking just one way. The rest of the island's trails are reasonably well marked but rough enough that it's not advisable to try them at night. Pick up maps at the **Pro Loco** tourist office (☞ Visitor Information *in* Arezzo, Cortona, and Southern Tuscany A to Z).

WATER SPORTS

Dimensione Mare (✉ Via Thaon de Revel 28, Giglio Porto, ☎ 0564/809096) offers a variety of scuba courses and can help arrange dives. Rent motorboats for exploring the island's innumerable coves through **Giglio Noleggio** (✉ Giglio Porto (on the port), ☎ 0347/0954480). You can charter your own snorkeling or beach excursion and let someone else do the driving through **Marco Bartoletti** (✉ Ctr. Santa Maria 18, ☎ 0564/806125 or 0336/535054).

AREZZO, CORTONA, AND SOUTHERN TUSCANY A TO Z

To research prices, get advice from other travelers, and book travel arrangements, visit www.fodors.com.

AIRPORTS

The airports nearest to the region are Rome's Fiumicino (officially Aeroporto Leonardo da Vinci), Pisa's Galileo Galilei, and Florence's Peretola (officially Aeroporto A. Vespucci). Pisa has a train directly to its airport.

You can fly direct from Rome, Milan, and some other European cities to Elba's La Pila airport.
➤ AIRPORT INFORMATION: **Aeroporto A. Vespucci** (known as Peretola; ☎ 055/3061700). **Aeroporto Galileo Galilei** (☎ 050/500707, WEB www.pisa-airport.com). **Aeroporto Leonardo da Vinci** (known as Fiumicino; ☎ 06/6594420, WEB www.adr.it). **La Pila** (✉ Marina di Campo, ☎ 0565/976011).

BOAT AND FERRY TRAVEL

Boat services link the Tuscan islands with the mainland. Passenger and car ferries leave from Piombino and Livorno for Elba. From Piombino, Moby Lines travels to Porto Azzurro and Portoferraio on Elba. Toremar runs ferries between Capraia and Livorno, Pianosa and Elba's Porto Azzurro, and Giglio and Giannutri and Porto Santo Stefano. Prices can differ drastically, so comparison shop before buying your tickets; check both counters, or call both offices, before booking.

➤ BOAT AND FERRY INFORMATION: **Moby Lines** (✉ Piazzale Premuda, Piombino, ☎ 0565/221212, WEB www.mobylines.it). **Toremar** (WEB www.toremar.it; ✉ Piazzale Premuda 13/14, Piombino, ☎ 0565/31100; ✉ Porto Mediceo, Livorno, ☎ 0586/896113; ✉ Piazzale A. Candi, Porto Santo Stefano, ☎ 0564/810803).

BUS TRAVEL

Although tortuous roads and roundabout routes make bus travel in southern Tuscany terribly slow, it is a reliable way to get where you're going if you don't have a car; beware that schedules tend to be very spotty. Plan your trip carefully with the aid of local tourist offices; they can help with hard-to-find bus stops and ever-changing timetables, and they're more likely to have English-speaking staff than bus stations. Main bus stations in the region are in Arezzo and Cortona, but most towns in the region have bus service even if they don't have actual bus stations. Buses from Rome and Florence travel to many towns in the area. Call SITA in Florence or Rama in Grosseto for complete route information.

➤ BUS INFORMATION: **Rama** (☎ 055/214 721). **SITA** (☎ 055/214721 in Florence, WEB www.sita-on-line.it).

CAR RENTAL

➤ RENTAL AGENCY: **Avis** (✉ Piazza della Repubblica 1/a, Arezzo, ☎ 0575/354232, WEB www.avis.com).

CAR TRAVEL

The A1 Autostrada del Sole, which runs from Florence to Rome, passes close to Arezzo; Cortona is just off the highway linking Perugia to the A1. You can reach Pienza and the Val d'Orcia easily from the A1 or from the Siena–Rome route, which passes through San Quirico d'Orcia. There is also a good road (S223) linking Siena and Grosseto. From Genoa or the northern Tuscan coast, you can drive down the coastal highway (A12), which is being extended south, to reach the coastal towns and islands.

The best way to travel within the region, making it possible to explore tiny hill towns and country restaurants, is by car. But the roads are better north–south than east–west, so allow time for excessively winding roads when heading east or west. Sometimes it's faster to go a little out of your way and get on one of the bigger north–south routes.

EMERGENCIES

Dial 113 for Police or Fire assistance, and dial 118 for an ambulance or if you have a medical emergency. Pharmacies in major towns take turns staying open 24 hours; all pharmacies have a notice posted outside with the name and address of the nearest one open.

➤ HOSPITALS: **Arezzo** (✉ Via Nenni Pietro 20, ☎ 0575/351623). **Chianciano** (✉ Via dello Stadio 5, ☎ 0578/321015).

TRAIN TRAVEL

Train service (via the state railway, or FS) is frequent between Florence and Arezzo and between Siena and Chiusi or Buonconvento, where you can change to buses for smaller towns. The coast is also well served by trains from Genoa and Livorno to Piombino (where you can get a ferry to Elba) and Grosseto. Between Arezzo and the coast, train service is scarce or nonexistent, and there aren't many good train routes among towns in southern Tuscany; it's best to use buses or cars to get around locally.

➤ TRAIN INFORMATION: **Ferrovia dello Stato** (FS; ☎ 848/888088 toll-free within Italy, WEB www.fs-on-line.it or www.trenitalita.it).

VISITOR INFORMATION

Tourist offices (called, variously, Ufficio Turistico, APT, AAST, and Pro Loco) are generally open from 9–12:30 and 3:30–6 or 7.

➤ TOURIST INFORMATION: **Arezzo** (✉ Piazza della Repubblica 22, ☎ 0575/377678). **Capraia** (contact Elba office: ✉ Calata Italia 26, Porto-ferraio, ☎ 0565/914671). **Castiglione della Pescaia** (✉ Piazza Garibaldi, ☎ 0564/933678, FAX 0564/933954). **Chianciano Terme** (✉ via G. Sabatini 7, ☎ 0578/63538, FAX 0578/64623). **Cortona** (✉ Via Nazionale 42, ☎ 0575/630352, WEB wwwcortonantiquari.it). **Elba** (✉ Calata Italia 26, Portoferraio, ☎ 0565/914671, WEB www.aptelba.it). **Giglio** (✉ on the port, ☎ 0564/809400). **Massa Marittima** (✉ via Norma Parenti 22, ☎ 0566/902756, FAX 0566/940095). **Monte Amiata** (✉ Via Mentana 97, La Piazzetta, Abbadia San Salvatore, ☎ 0577/778608, FAX 0577/779013). **Monte Argentario** (✉ Corso Umberto 55/a, Porto Santo Stefano, ☎ 0564/814208, WEB www.regione.toscana.it). **Parco Nazionale dell'Arcipelago Toscano** (✉ Via Guerrazzi 1, Portoferraio, ☎ 0565/919411, FAX 0565/919420, WEB www.islepark.it). **Pienza** (✉ Piazza Pio II, ☎ 0578/749071). **Pitigliano** (✉ Via Roma 6, ☎ FAX 0564/614433). **San Quirico d'Orcia** (✉ Via Dante Alighieri 33, ☎ 0577/897211).

8 PERUGIA AND NORTHERN UMBRIA

Majestic art, architecture, and landscapes come together in perfect harmony in the land of Perugino and his pupil Raphael. After the simple geometry of Tuscan architecture, the palaces of Perugia and Urbino, in the nearby Marches region, appear more grandiose. This corner of the world is a fantasy land, where you can almost picture dukes and duchesses and costumed revelers at every turn.

PERUGIA IS A LIVELY CITY, majestic, handsome, and wealthy. Students from local universities keep the streets buzzing with music and activity year-round, and an important jazz festival every July adds to the mix. With its glamorous designer shops, refined cafés, and grandiose architecture, Perugia doesn't try to hide its affluence.

Updated by
Peter Blackman

It is the capital of a region rich in history, art, tradition, and breathtaking landscapes. The northern end of Umbria is squeezed between eastern Tuscany—notably Arezzo and Cortona—and the Marches, where the Renaissance architecture of the Palazzo Ducale in Urbino sets the stage. The landscapes are those depicted by the Renaissance master Perugino in his paintings: hills with a few sparse trees, flat land, and lakes.

Gubbio climbs straight up a mountain, filling the bottom half with its houses and churches. Every May, costumed runners ascend to the top, to the church of Sant'Ubaldo, during the bizarre Festa dei Ceri. From Gubbio, you can take side trips to Urbino or up to the Republic of San Marino, which claims to be the oldest and smallest independent state in the world.

In Etruscan times, Perugia and Gubbio were among the last to bow to Roman rule but were eventually conquered by the Romans in the 3rd century BC. Attesting to its importance in Roman times, Gubbio has a Roman theater that could seat about 12,000 spectators. Perugia was caught in the middle of a power struggle between two Roman rulers and was burned, sacked, and destroyed in 140 BC. The city was slowly built back up and during the medieval period gave its allegiance to the popes.

After winning a war with Assisi in 1202, Perugia flourished. Churches and government buildings were erected, and the university was founded in 1308. In the 15th century, noble families became more powerful and the Baglioni family briefly ruled the city, but it quickly returned to the Papal States. In 1540 the Perugians rebelled against a tax on salt imposed by Pope Paul III (1468–1549), winning the so-called Salt War, but the Pope's son, Pier Luigi Farnese (1503–47), quickly reconquered the area. Perugia didn't become independent of the church's rule until 1860, when the troops of Victor Emmanuel II of Savoy (1820–78) conquered it and unified the entire Italian peninsula.

Gubbio, Perugia's neighbor to the north, followed a different path. Its destiny, intertwined with that of Urbino, was ruled by the Montefeltro and Della Rovere families of Urbino during the Renaissance. Like Perugia, in 1631 it fell under the rule of the Papal States and didn't become independent until the unification of Italy, in 1848.

Pleasures and Pastimes

Dining

Northern Umbria is crossed by the Apennine mountains, the slopes of which curve into graceful, hilly landscapes. Called the "green heart of Italy," the terrain is hardly rugged, but Umbrians are in close touch with nature and its bounty—thus the cuisine of the northern part of Umbria is hearty. First courses such as pasta, rice, and soups (and, in this region especially, lentils) are often laden with rich *tartufi neri o bianchi,* black or white truffles, while the second courses are generally meat-based. The local pasta specialty, a thick, homemade spaghetti, goes by two names, *stringozzi* (also spelled *strangozzi*) and *ombrichelli,* and most often is served *al tartufo,* with a sauce of truffles. In addition, Umbria is known to produce excellent olive oils.

A meal of fresh fish pulled from Lago Trasimeno (Lake Trasimeno) is enough to warrant a detour on your way from Tuscany to Perugia. Otherwise, some area restaurants offer fresh seafood (largely in response to consumer demand), but it's prepared according to traditional Italian methods as there are no real Umbrian seafood dishes. Once you leave Umbria and head to the coastal Marches region, however, seafood becomes more available. One characteristic dish from Ancona, *brodetto,* is a savory fish soup chock-full of the latest catch from the Adriatic. Ascoli Piceno, inland, can take credit for a particular gastronomic specialty worth noting: olive *ascolane,* stuffed green olives rolled in breading, deep fried, and served as an appetizer. Want to try a local drink? Ascoli Piceno is known for the anisette it produces.

CATEGORY	COST*
$$$$	over €18
$$$	€13–€18
$$	€8–€13
$	under €8

Prices are for a second course (secondo piatto).

Lodging

Virtually every historic town in Umbria has some kind of hotel, no matter how small the place may be. But be sure to book ahead—traveling to Perugia or Urbino without reservations during the high season is a chancy proposition. Northern Umbria also abounds with *agriturismi,* literally "agritourist" accommodations. These are countryside lodgings, often in restored farmhouses, with guest rooms ranging in service from bed-and-breakfast-type accommodations to fully equipped apartments. Many such lodgings have excellent restaurants on the premises, and Italian law requires that at least 70% of what is served at agriturismi is cultivated and prepared on the property. In this way, you are assured of high-quality, honest, local meals. Note that some proprietors prefer that you book a stay of at least one week, although the length of stay required varies with each location and season; still, depending on availability, the owners will do their best to accommodate your request. For further information about agritourist locations in Umbria, *see* Agritourist Agencies *in* Perugia and Northern Umbria A to Z.

CATEGORY	COST*
$$$$	over €175
$$$	€125–€175
$$	€75–€125
$	under €75

All prices are for two people in a standard double room, including tax and service.

Shopping

Pottery and wine are the two most celebrated Umbrian exports, but if you like to cook, don't overlook the opportunity to take home a bottle of wonderful Umbrian olive oil.

If you would like to learn about local wine practices, Torgiano, south of Perugia, is the best-known Umbrian center for wine-making; you can see the process, partake in tastings, and purchase local wines.

If you are looking for ceramics, train your eye by taking notice of the various types of pottery that you see around. Ceramics are sold throughout the region and are easy to find in cities such as Deruta and Perugia.

Sports and Outdoor Activities

Umbria abounds with opportunities for the sportive traveler, and many agriturismi offer the opportunity to go horseback riding, mountain biking, golfing, or hiking, or even to practice archery.

Your tour through Umbria will keep you off the coastal regions, but you can stop at one of the communities that surround Lago Trasimeno and take a dip, go boating, or just relax. The lake, in Umbria but very close to the border with Tuscany, possesses the traits of both regions. Often overlooked by the foreign traveler, Italy's lake areas can be quite astonishing. And Trasimeno is well organized for the sport aficionado: visitors can swim, windsurf, and play volleyball. Swimming in the lake is quite safe; the communities of Castiglione del Lago, Lido di Trasimeno, Tuoro sul Trasimeno, Toricella, and Monte del Lago, as well as two of the islands on the lake—Isola Maggiore and Isola Pavese—have bathing establishments with lounge chairs, cabanas, and, in most places, windsurfing equipment and canoes for rent. Passignano sul Trasimeno, however, has mostly ports and rocky beaches, so public bathing facilities aren't available.

Exploring Perugia and Northern Umbria

The steep hills and deep valleys that make Umbria so picturesque also make it difficult to explore. Driving routes must be chosen carefully to avoid tortuous mountain roads, and major towns aren't necessarily linked to each other by train, bus, or highway. But Perugia is a convenient base from which to explore the region, and you can get around fairly quickly by car. You might want to combine your trip with a southern Tuscany itinerary that includes Arezzo and Cortona or with visits to Assisi, Spoleto, and Southern Umbria. You can reasonably visit the area around Perugia, see Gubbio and Città di Castello, and take a side trip to Urbino in four days. You would be shortchanging a trip to this region if you skipped Urbino (in the adjoining Marches region) and its storybook palace.

Great Itineraries

Covering distances in this area can take longer than it might look on the map because of the winding mountain roads. Between sightseeing, you might want to set aside extra time for lounging near Lago Trasimeno or shopping for pottery in Deruta. But if you're in the area, try not to skip Perugia or Urbino.

Numbers in the text correspond to numbers in the margin and on the Northern Umbria and the Marches and the Perugia maps.

IF YOU HAVE 2 DAYS

Spend a day in ⛰ **Perugia** ①–⑫ and stay overnight. The next day, visit **Gubbio** ㉒ in the morning and **Urbino** ㉓ in the afternoon. On your way to or from Perugia, stop at **Lago Trasimeno** ⑯–⑰, where a meal of fresh fish is highly recommended.

IF YOU HAVE 5 DAYS

Spend your first day exploring ⛰ **Perugia** ①–⑫ and stay overnight. The next day, visit **Torgiano** ⑬ and **Deruta** ⑭, and then head around **Lago Trasimeno** to **Castiglione del Lago** ⑰. If you're interested in art, an alternative route is via **Fontignano** ⑳, **Panicale** ⑲, and **Città della Pieve** ⑱ to see Perugino's works. Return to your hotel in Perugia for the second night. On the third day, visit **Città di Castello** ㉑ and then ⛰ **Gubbio** ㉒, where you can spend the next two nights. The morning of Day 4, take a day-long side trip to **Urbino** ㉓. You can spend Day 5 exploring more of the Marches: **Ancona** ㉕, **Loreto** ㉖, and **Ascoli Piceno** ㉗.

When to Tour Perugia and Northern Umbria

Northern Umbria is fairly free of the great masses of visitors that descend upon the other regions, even in summer, when you might welcome the lush greenness of these interior tracts. In August much of the local population shifts to Adriatic resorts such as Rimini and Parco del

Conero for vacation. The forested Umbrian hills also ensure a stunning autumnal landscape and an explosion of greenery in the spring. In both spring and fall, the visitor count is especially low and the temperature usually moderate, but keep in mind that April and November may be rainy.

The predominantly hilly terrain of Northern Umbria means that winters can be bitterly cold, and snow is common. Because many destinations here are hilltop towns, including Perugia itself, you should be prepared for harsh conditions and possible hazardous driving if you're traveling at this time of year. Regarding cuisine, however, the winter is possibly the best time in Umbria: January through April is the season to sample the truffles for which the area is famous (though, of course, truffles are dried and can be had at any time of year), and wild mushrooms are picked from October to December.

PERUGIA

Perugia, the largest and richest of Umbria's cities, owes its elegance to the 3,000 years of history concentrated in a town that, neither too big nor too small, was clearly designed to fit the human scale. Thanks to Perugia's position on a series of hills, the medieval city remains almost completely intact. It is the best-preserved hill town of its size, and few other places in Italy better illustrate the model of the self-contained city-state that so shaped the course of Italian history.

Exploring Perugia

The best approach to the city is by train. The area around the station doesn't attest to the rest of Perugia's elegance, but buses that run directly to Piazza d'Italia, the heart of the old town, are frequent. If you are driving to Perugia and your hotel doesn't have parking facilities, leave your car in one of the parking lots near the station and take the bus or the escalator; the latter passes through fascinating subterranean excavations of the Roman foundations of the city and leads to the town center.

A Good Walk

Start in Piazza d'Italia and stroll down **Corso Vannucci** ① to the **Duomo** ②, in Piazza IV Novembre. On this piazza is the original entrance to the mass of buildings that makes up the **Palazzo dei Priori** ③, Perugia's city hall, which also houses the Sala dei Notari. The entrances to the **Collegio del Cambio** ④, the **Galleria Nazionale d'Umbria** ⑤, and the **Collegio della Mercanzia** ⑥, all also housed in the palazzo, are strung along Corso Vannucci. For another museum visit, detour back to Piazza d'Italia, and then walk down Corso Cavour (to your left) to the **Museo Archeologico Nazionale** ⑦. Return to Piazza IV Novembre, breaking for lunch or an espresso at a café. Walk down Via dei Priori; on your left you'll pass the Sant'Agata church, which has Gothic archways and 14th-century frescoes. Continuing down the hill, you'll reach another church, the baroque **San Filippo Neri** ⑧, in Piazza Ferri. Farther down the street, past the escalator, note the **Torre degli Sciri** ⑨, the only tower of its time to survive in its original state. Walk around the tower to the Oratorio della Confraternità di San Francesco, another example of baroque architecture. After you pass the medieval city gateway, the Porta Trasimena, on your left, head to the right down Via San Francesco to the church of San Francesco al Prato. The *prato* (lawn) is a grassy square where students often lounge in nice weather. From the lawn, you can see the small **Oratorio di San Bernardino** ⑩, connected to San Francesco by an archway that spans the entrance to a

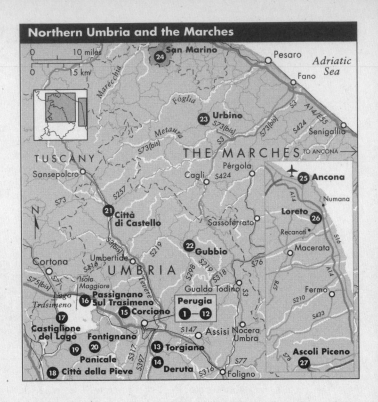

Northern Umbria and the Marches

former convent, now the Accademia delle Belle Arti (Academy of Fine Arts), with a museum that contains Antonio Canova's (1757–1822) plaster casts. Walk up the hill along Via del Poggio, turn right on Via Armonica, and walk along the Etruscan walls to Piazza Cavallotti. Turn left on Via Cesare Battisti, past a 13th-century aqueduct, and at the end of the street you'll find the **Arco di Augusto** ⑪, next to Perugia's Università per Stranieri (University for Foreigners). Down some steps to your right, wind around to Piazza Michelotti, take a left on Via dell'Aquila, and you arrive at the church of **San Severo** ⑫.

TIMING
A thorough walk through Perugia takes about an hour; if you're stopping at all sites along this walk, you should plan on a full day with a stop for lunch.

Sights to See

⑪ **Arco di Augusto** (Arch of Augustus). Dating from the 3rd century BC, this arch was the entrance to the Etruscan and Roman acropolis. In the same square is the Università per Stranieri (University for Foreigners). ⊠ *Piazza Fortebraccio.*

★ ④ **Collegio del Cambio** (Bankers' Guild Hall). These elaborate rooms, on the ground floor of the ☞ **Palazzo dei Priori,** served as the meeting hall and chapel of the guild of bankers and money changers. The walls were frescoed from 1496 to 1500 by the most important Perugian painter of the Renaissance, Pietro Vannucci, who is better known as Perugino. The iconography prevalent in the works includes common religious themes, such as the Nativity and the Transfiguration (on the end walls), as well as figures intended to inspire the businessmen who congregated here. On the left wall are female figures representing the virtues, beneath them the heroes and sages of antiquity. On the right wall are the prophets and sibyls—said to have been painted in part by

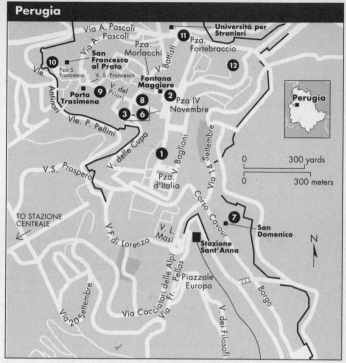

Perugino's most famous pupil, Raffaello Sanzio (1483–1520), or Raphael. (His hand, experts say, is most apparent in the figure of Fortitude.) On one of the pilasters is a remarkably honest self-portrait of Perugino, surmounted by a Latin inscription. The *cappella* (chapel) of San Giovanni Battista has frescoes painted by Giannicola di Paolo, another student of the Umbrian master Perugino. ⊠ *Corso Vannucci 25,* ☎ *075/5728599.* ▨ *€2.60 (includes the Collegio della Mercanzia).* ☉ *Mar.–Oct., Mon.–Sat. 9–12:30 and 2:30–5:30, Sun. 9–12:30; Nov.– Feb., Tues.–Sat. 8–2, Sun. 9–12:30 (Dec. 20–Jan. 6 museum follows Mar.–Oct. schedule).*

❻ Collegio della Mercanzia (Merchant's Meeting Hall). This room of carved wood, two doors away from the ☞ **Palazzo dei Priori** entrance for the Collegio del Cambio, dates back to the 1300s and was the original meeting room for merchants (especially fabric traders). Trading didn't actually take place here, but merchants met to haggle and set market prices and to standardize trade practices. ⊠ *Corso Vannucci 15,* ☎ *075/ 5730366.* ▨ *€2.60 (includes the Collegio del Cambio).* ☉ *Mar.–Oct., Mon.–Sat. 9–1 and 2:30–5:30, Sun. 9–1; Nov.–Feb., Tues.–Sun. 8–2.*

❶ Corso Vannucci. A string of elegantly connected *palazzi* (palaces) expresses the artistic nature of this city center, the heart of which is concentrated on Corso Vannucci. Stately and broad, the pedestrian-only street runs from Piazza d'Italia to Piazza IV Novembre and is the best place to soak in the uncomplicated beauty of the surroundings. Take time to appreciate the look of the bars and shops that line the street. Along the way, the entrances to many of Perugia's side streets will tempt you to wander off and explore. But don't stray too far as evening falls, when Corso Vannucci fills with Perugians out for their evening *passeggiata,* a pleasant pre-dinner stroll that may include a pause for an aperitif at one of the many bars that line the street.

You can enjoy the lively comings and goings on Corso Vannucci from
the vantage point of the **Bar Sandri** (✉ Corso Vannucci 32, ☎ 075/
5724112). The 19th-century bar has wood paneling and ceiling frescoes that date from 1860 as well as red-vested waiters. Sandri makes its
own chocolates, pastries, and ice creams and offers *tavola pronta,* a
daily selection of fast first and second courses, to its lunch crowd.

❷ **Duomo.** Severe yet mystical, the Duomo, also called the Cathedral of
San Lorenzo, is most famous as being the home of the wedding ring
of the Virgin Mary, stolen by the Perugians in 1488 from the nearby
town of Chiusi. The ring, kept high up in a red-curtained vault in the
chapel immediately to the left of the entrance, is the size of a large ban-
gle and kept under lock—15 locks, actually—and key all year except
July 30 and the second-to-last Sunday in January. The first date commemorates the day the ring was brought to Perugia, the second Mary's
wedding anniversary. The cathedral itself dates from the Middle Ages
and has many additions from the 15th and 16th centuries. The most
visually interesting element is the altar to the Madonna of Thanks; an
elegant fresco on a column at the right of the entrance depicts *La
Madonna delle Grazie* and is surrounded by prayer benches decorated
with handwritten notes to the Holy Mother. Around the column are
small amulets—symbols of thanks from believers who prayed for miracles and received help. Additionally, there are elaborately carved
choir stalls, executed by Giovanni Battista Bastone in 1520. The altarpiece (1484), an early masterpiece by Luca Signorelli (circa 1450–
1523), shows the Madonna with St. John the Baptist, St. Onophrius,
and St. Lawrence. Note that sections of the church may be closed to
visitors during religious services.

The **Museo Capitolare** displays a large array of precious objects associated with the cathedral, including vestments, vessels, manuscripts, and
gold work. Outside the Duomo is the elaborate **Fontana Maggiore,** which
dates from 1278 and was realized by Nicola and Giovanni Pisano. It
is adorned with zodiac figures and symbols of the seven arts. ✉ *Piazza IV Novembre,* ☎ *075/5723832.* 💷 *Duomo free, Museo Capitolare €4.* ☉ *Duomo daily 7–1 and 4–5:30; Museo Capitolare daily
10–1 and 4–5:30.*

❺ **Galleria Nazionale d'Umbria.** The region's most comprehensive art
gallery is housed on the fourth floor of the ☞ **Palazzo dei Priori.** Enhanced by skillfully lit displays and computers that allow you to focus
on the works' details and background information, the collection includes work by native artists—most notably Pinturcchio (1454–1513)
and Perugino (circa 1450–1523)—and others of the Umbrian and Tuscan schools, among them Gentile da Fabriano (1370–1427), Duccio
(circa 1255–1318), Fra Angelico (1387–1455), Fiorenzo di Lorenzo
(1445–1525), and Piero della Francesca (1420–92). In addition to
housing paintings, the gallery has frescoes, sculptures, and some superb examples of crucifixes from the 13th and 14th centuries; other
rooms are dedicated to Perugia itself, showing how the medieval city
evolved. ✉ *Corso Vannucci 19, Piazza IV Novembre,* ☎ *075/5741427,*
WEB *www.gallerianazionaleumbria.it.* 💷 *€6.50.* ☉ *Daily (except first
Mon. each month), 8:30–7:30; last admission ½ hr before closing.*

❼ **Museo Archeologico Nazionale.** The museum, next to the imposing
church of San Domenico, contains an excellent collection of Etruscan
artifacts from throughout the region. Perugia was a flourishing
Etruscan site long before it fell under Roman domination in 310 BC.
Other than the collection here, little remains of Perugia's mysterious
ancestors, although the Arco di Augusto, in Piazza Fortebraccio, the

northern entrance to the city, is of Etruscan origin. ⊠ *Piazza G. Bruno 10,* ☎ *075/5727141,* WEB *www.archeopg.arti.beniculturali.it/ museo/default.htm.* 🎫 €4. ☉ *Daily 8–7.*

★ ⑩ **Oratorio di San Bernardino.** Agostino di Duccio (circa 1418–81) designed this lovely little Renaissance church with a pink-and-blue lacy stone facade in 1457–61, to honor the memory of St. Bernard, who often preached in Perugia and became one of the city's most important saints. ⊠ *Piazza San Francesco,* ☎ *075/5733957.* 🎫 *Free.* ☉ *Daily 8–12:30 and 3:30–6.*

★ ③ **Palazzo dei Priori** (Palace of Priors). Actually a series of elegant, connected buildings, the palazzo serves as Perugia's city hall and houses three of the city's museums. The buildings string along Corso Vannucci and wrap around the Piazza IV Novembre, where the original entrance is located. The steps here lead to the **Sala dei Notari** (Notaries' Hall). Other entrances lead to the ☞ **Galleria Nazionale d'Umbria,** the ☞ **Collegio del Cambio,** and the ☞ **Collegio della Mercanzia.** The Sala dei Notari, which dates back to the 13th century and was the original meeting place of the town merchants, had become the seat of the notaries by the second half of the 15th century. Wood beams and an interesting array of frescoes attributed to Maestro di Farneto embellish the room. Coats of arms and crests line the back and right lateral walls; you can spot some famous figures from *Aesop's Fables* on the left wall, including the wolf and the crane, the bull and the lion, and the wolf and the cow. The palazzo facade is adorned with symbols of Perugia's pride and past power: the griffin is the city symbol and the lion denotes Perugia's allegiance to the Guelph (or papal) cause. The two bronze figures support heavy chains that, according to local legend, came from the gates of Siena, which fell to Perugian forces in 1358. ⊠ *Piazza IV Novembre.* 🎫 *Free.* ☉ *June–Sept., Tues.–Sun. 9–1 and 3–7.*

⑧ **San Filippo Neri.** With its grandiose facade dating from 1663, this church is an interesting piece of baroque architecture. Inside are frescoes by various 18th-century artists, as well as a 1662 altarpiece by Pietro da Cortona (1596–1669) depicting the conception of Mary. ⊠ *Piazza Ferri,* ☎ *075/5725472.* 🎫 *Free.* ☉ *Daily 7:30–noon and 4–7.*

⑫ **San Severo.** The only Raphael fresco in Perugia, painted in 1505–08, resides in this little church. The lower part (six saints) was added in 1521 by Raphael's teacher, Perugino. The admission ticket allows you also to visit the **Etruscan well** in Piazza Piccinino, behind the church. ⊠ *Piazza Raffaello,* ☎ *075/5733864.* 🎫 €2. ☉ *Oct.–Mar., weekdays 10:30–1:30 and 2:30–4:30, weekends 10:30–1:30 and 2:30–5:30; Apr.–Sept., daily 10–1:30 and 2:30–6:30.*

⑨ **Torre degli Sciri** (Sciri Tower). The tower, which dates to the 12th to 13th centuries, is the only one of its time still standing in Perugia. At a height of 151 ft, it proclaimed to the neighborhood the wealth of the family that built it. ⊠ *Via dei Priori.*

OFF THE BEATEN PATH

LA CITTÀ DELLA DOMENICA – The younger set might enjoy a day at this theme park, the only attraction in Umbria most directly aimed at children and families. The playground is in the town of Montepulito, 8 km (5 mi) west of Perugia on the secondary road that leads to Corciano. The 500 acres of parkland can be toured by a train that runs through the park grounds and that leads visitors on a tour through fairy-tale landscapes including Snow White's House, the Witches' Wood, Tarzan's parrot jungle, a zoo, an Indian camp, and Swan Lake. There is also a reptile house, an aquarium, a medieval museum, an exhibit of shells from around the world, and game rooms, as well as several restaurants. From

November until Easter, only the aquarium and reptile house are open. ⊠ *Via Col di Tenda 140, Località Montepulito, 8 km (5 mi) west of Perugia,* ☎ *075/5054941.* 🎫 *€9 (€10 Sun. and holidays).* ⊘ *Easter–mid-Sept., daily 10–7; mid-Sept.–Oct., weekends 10–7; Nov.–Easter (aquarium and reptile house only), Sat. 2–7, Sun. 10–7.*

Dining and Lodging

$$–$$$$ ✕ **Da Giancarlo.** Giancarlo himself is likely to greet you at this typical Umbrian restaurant. The main room has the original vaulted ceilings common in Perugia. Although the cuisine is local, hours here accommodate the traveler who may like to eat earlier than Italian diners. Giancarlo says he's known for his lentils, which he makes into wonderful soups or serves as side dishes, and also recommends the grilled Chianina, a handsome cut of beef from this prize breed of cattle raised to the west of Lago Trasimeno. Another house special is the *penne alla Norcina,* tubular pasta with spicy cream sauce and sausage. ⊠ *Via dei Priori 36,* ☎ *075/5724314. AE, MC, V. Closed Fri. and last 2 wks in Aug.*

$$–$$$$ ✕ **Ristorante Altro Mondo.** Home-cooked food is the specialty every day at this unpretentious restaurant. To please their customers, the owners include many fresh seasonal seafood dishes on the menu, but they are best known for Umbrian dishes such as *torello alla Ghiotta* ("glutton's dish"), a veal steak prepared with a sauce of porcini mushrooms and liver pâté. The salad of arugula with paper-thin slices of raw artichoke is wonderful. Local wine is served by the bottle or carafe. ⊠ *Via Caporali 11,* ☎ *075/5726157. AE, DC, MC, V. Closed Sun., last 2 wks of Aug., and 1 wk in Dec.*

$$$ ✕ **La Taverna.** Medieval steps lead to this rustic restaurant on two levels, where lots of wine bottles and artful clutter heighten the tavern atmosphere. Regional specialties as well as better-known Italian dishes form the menu. Good choices include *chitarrini* (extra-thick spaghetti) with either *funghi* (mushrooms) or tartufi, and grilled meats. ⊠ *Via delle Streghe 8, next to the Teatro Pavone, off Corso Vannucci,* ☎ *075/5724128. Reservations essential. AE, DC, MC, V. Closed Mon.*

$$–$$$ ✕ **Il Falchetto.** With exceptional food at reasonable prices, this is Perugia's best restaurant bargain. The owners aren't big on change and instead insist on keeping things sure and steady here. The service is smart but relaxed, and there are two medieval dining rooms, with an open kitchen so the chef is on view. The *falchetti* (homemade gnocchi with spinach and ricotta cheese, baked and served hot in a terra-cotta pot) are a house specialty. ⊠ *Via Bartolo 20,* ☎ *075/5731775. AE, DC, MC, V. Closed Mon. and last 2 wks in Jan.*

$$ ✕ **La Rosetta.** The restaurant, in the hotel of the same name, is a peaceful, elegant spot. In winter you dine inside under medieval vaults; in summer, in the cool courtyard. The food is simple but reliable and flawlessly served. Specialties of the house include *zuppa di lenticchie di Castelluccio* (a hearty soup made with Umbrian lentils) and *umbrecelli,* a thick hand-rolled noodle, served *all'arrabbiata* (with a spicy tomato sauce). Or consider the *scalloppine di Perugina,* a dish of Umbrian-style chicken livers. ⊠ *Piazza d'Italia 19,* ☎ *075/5720841. Reservations essential. AE, DC, MC, V. Closed Mon.*

$$$$ 🏨 **Hotel Brufani Palace.** Although completely modernized, the hotel reflects the romantic aspect of Perugia's past. Windows open out onto sweeping views of the green hills and valleys of Umbria below, or over artistic scenes of Perugia's elegant rooftops. Rich furnishings and fabrics that take hints from Umbria's traditional color scheme of blue, yellow, and rust dress the rooms to match the warmth and romance of the countryside outside. An American-style bar opens onto a pleasant

piazza, perfect for a refreshing drink after a day of sightseeing. The warm staff is on hand to help you with any request you might have. ✉ *Piazza Italia 12, 06121,* ☎ *075/5732541,* FAX *075/5720210,* WEB *www.brufanipalace.com. 63 rooms, 31 suites. Restaurant, room TVs, pool, gym, bar, meeting rooms, parking (fee). AE, DC, MC, V.*

$$$ 🏨 **Locanda della Posta.** From its faux-marble moldings, paneled doors,
★   and tile bouquets in the baths to the suede-upholstered elevator and fabric-covered walls, this luxuriously decorated small hotel in the center of Perugia's historic district is a delight to behold. Architectural details of the 18th-century palazzo are beautiful, and views from windows and balconies offer scenic rooftop glimpses of Umbria. ✉ *Corso Vannucci 97, 06121,* ☎ *075/5728925,* FAX *075/5732562. 38 rooms, 1 suite. Minibars, room TVs, bar, parking (fee). AE, DC, MC, V.*

$$ 🏨 **Hotel Fortuna.** The elegant decor in the large rooms of this friendly hotel complements the frescoes, which date to the 1700s. Some rooms have balconies. The building itself, just out of sight of Corso Vannucci, dates to the 1300s. ✉ *Via Bonazzi 19, 06123,* ☎ *075/5722845,* FAX *075/5735040,* WEB *www.umbriahotels.com. 33 rooms, 1 suite. Cable TV, in-room hot tubs (some), bar, meeting rooms, parking (fee); no air-conditioning in some rooms. DC, MC, V.*

$ 🏨 **Hotel Priori.** On an alley leading off Corso Vannucci, this unpretentious hotel has spacious and cheerful rooms with modern furnishings. Breakfast is served on the terrace in spring and summer. ✉ *Via dei Priori, 06123,* ☎ *075/5723378,* FAX *075/5723213,* WEB *www.perugia.com/hotelpriori. 49 rooms, 2 suites. Bar, parking (fee); no air-conditioning in some rooms, no TV in some rooms. MC, V. CP.*

$ 🏨 **Rosalba.** Rooms are basic and scrupulously clean at this bright and friendly lodging choice on the fringes of Perugia's historic center; the ones at the back enjoy a view. A loft-style suite has a ladder that leads to the upstairs beds (up to four guests can share the suite). Although somewhat out of the way, the hotel is minutes from Corso Vannucci by virtue of the nearby escalator stop. ✉ *Via del Circo 7, 06100,* ☎ *075/5728285,* FAX *075/5720626. 11 rooms, 1 suite. Free parking; no room TVs. No credit cards.*

Nightlife and the Arts

Viva Perugia is a good source of information about what's going on in town. The monthly, sold at newsstands, has a section in English.

Music Festivals

Summer sees two music festivals in Perugia. The **Umbria Jazz Festival** (☎ 075/5732432, FAX 075/572256, WEB www.umbriajazz.com) is held for 10 days in July. Information on the festival is available year-round; tickets are available for purchase, with a credit card, starting at the end of April. The **Sagra Musicale Umbra** (Umbrian Music Festival; ☎ 075/5721374, WEB www.sagramusicaleumbra.com), held from mid-August to mid-September, celebrates sacred music and choral symphonies. In Perugia, you can obtain information about music festivals at the **Perugia Tourist Office** (☎ 075/5736458 or 075/5723327), on Piazza IV Novembre.

Shopping

Shopping is easy in Perugia. A simple walk down any of the main streets, including Corso Vannucci, Via dei Priori, Via Oberdan, and Via S. Ercolano, takes you past many well-known Italian designer-clothing and specialty shops.

The most typical thing to buy in Perugia is some Perugina chocolate, which you can find almost anywhere. The most well-known chocolates made by Perugina are the chocolate-and-hazelnut-filled nibbles called Baci (literally, "kisses"). They're wrapped in silver paper that includes a sliver of paper, like the fortune in a fortune cookie, with multilingual romantic sentiments or sayings.

Perugians take their chocolate seriously: next to the Umbria Jazz Festival, the **Eurochocolate Festival** (WEB www.eurochocolate.perugia.it), the third week in October, is Perugia's—and Umbria's—biggest event. Perugia turns into a veritable chocolate walk as the city transforms itself, even changing the names of famous avenues and piazzas to reflect the theme. Corso Vannucci becomes Morso Vannucci (a *morso* is a bite); Piazza della Reppubblica becomes Piazza della Tazza (a *tazza* is a cup); Via Mazzini becomes Chocostreet, where international chocolate makers display their best products; and Piazza Gianduiotti displays a mega *gianduiotto,* a sculptured hazelnut–chocolate affair that passersby can sample.

Fans of Italian gastronomic specialties might like to stop by the **Casa del Parmigiano Reggiano** (✉ Via dei Priori 9, ☎ 075/5725369) to buy some of the best local bounty: rich green Umbrian olive oils, dried salami, cheeses, wines, cookies, and Umbrian lentils. Looking for Italian shoes? **Castagner** (✉ Via Calderini 3, ☎ 075/5723236) sells such well-heeled Italian brands as Hogan, Tod's, and Fratelli Rosetti. **Fabbri Antonio** (✉ Via Oberdan 13, ☎ 075/5726609) offers high-quality, traditional Umbrian fabrics—with their yellow, blue, and rust color schemes—off the bolt. **Fragile** (✉ Via dei Priori 70, ☎ 075/5736120) makes and sells colorful hand-crafted wood pieces, including fanciful decorations for children's bedrooms, or for the frivolous at heart. **Il Telaio** (✉ Via Rocchi 19, ☎ 075/5726603) sells woven traditional Umbrian fabrics. The name of the shop translates literally as "The Loom," but Il Telaio also stocks a nice selection of Umbrian and Deruta pottery.

AROUND PERUGIA

A simple drive or train ride through the curving terrain that surrounds Perugia may make you feel as if you have traveled back to a time when life was gentler and less complex and land was respected for its beauty and the life it sustains. Hilltop towns, churches that peek out from behind screens of trees, fields of poppies and vineyards, expanses of green where animals contentedly graze—one pastoral scene after another passes before your eyes. South of Perugia, Torgiano is the center of Umbrian wine production and Deruta is the Umbrian ceramics center. A short distance east of Perugia you encounter the serene lake district of Trasimeno. The sleepy port of Passignano sul Trasimeno is on the northeast part of the lake. Around Magione, also on the east side of the lake, the land once again becomes hilly and lush.

Torgiano

⑬ *16 km (10 mi) southeast of Perugia, 27 km (17 mi) southwest of Assisi.*

Wine aficionados are certain to want to visit this home to the winery **Cantine Lungarotti,** best known for delicious Rubesco Lungarotti, San Giorgio, and chardonnay. ✉ *Via Mario Angeloni 12,* ☎ *075/9880348.* ☉ *Tours by appointment only, weekdays 8–1 and 3–6.*

The fascinating **Museo del Vino** (Wine Museum) has a large collection of ancient wine vessels, presses, documents, and tools that tell the story of viticulture in Umbria and beyond. The museum traces the history of wine in all its uses—for drinking at the table, as medicine, and in mythology. Next door to the Museo del Vino, the **Osteria del Museo** (☎ FAX 075/9880069) is a local representative for the Lungarotti winery. You can taste and buy the winery's reds and whites here. ✉ *Corso Vittorio Emanuele 11,* ☎ *075/9880200.* 🎫 *€2.60.* ☉ *Apr.–Oct., daily 9–1 and 3–7; Nov.–Mar., daily 9–1 and 3–6.*

Dining and Lodging

$$$$ ✕🏨 **Le Tre Vaselle.** Four charming stone buildings, linked under-
★ ground, house this hotel in the center of Torgiano. Its rooms are spacious, especially the most expensive suites, some of which have fireplaces. The floors are of typical Tuscan red-clay tiles; ceilings have wood beams. Olive groves surround the outdoor pool; a current pool and a whirlpool are indoors. Le Melagrane, the restaurant—a comfortable affair with red tablecloths, wood-beam ceilings, and fireplaces—offers exquisite local specialties. The *tagliata di manzo,* for example, consists of quickly seared slices of steak served with balsamic–red grape sauce produced on the property. In summer, you can dine alfresco on a terrace between two of the hotel buildings. ✉ *Via Garibaldi 48, 06089,* ☎ *075/9880447,* FAX *075/9880214,* WEB *www.3vaselle.it. 47 rooms, 13 suites. Restaurant, room TVs, 1 indoor and 1 outdoor pool, sauna, gym, bar, meeting rooms, parking (fee). AE, DC, MC, V. CP.*

Deruta

14 *7 km (4½ mi) south of Torgiano, 19 km (11 mi) southeast of Perugia.*

The 14th-century medieval hill town is most famous for the ceramic craftsmanship for which it has been esteemed since the 16th century. A drive through the countryside to visit the ceramics factories surrounding Deruta is a good way to spend a morning, but be sure to stop in the town itself. Notable sights in Deruta include the **Museo Regionale della Ceramica** (Regional Ceramics Museum), part of which extends into the adjacent 14th-century former convent of San Francesco. Half the museum is a historic exposition of Deruta ceramics, with panels in Italian and English explaining the history, artistic techniques, and production processes. The museum also holds the country's largest collection of modern Italian ceramics. Nearly 8,000 pieces are displayed in the museum altogether, and the most notable are the Renaissance vessels using the lustro technique, a craft that originated in Arabic and Middle Eastern cultures some 500 years before coming into use in Italy in the late 1400s. Lustro, as the name sounds, gives the ceramics a rich effect, which is accomplished with the use of crushed precious materials, such as gold, silver, and other rare stones and metals. ✉ *Largo San Francesco,* ☎ *075/9711000,* WEB *www.sistemamuseo.it.* 🎫 *€3.* ☉ *Apr.–June, daily 10:30–1 and 3–6; July–Sept., daily 10–1 and 3:30–7; Oct.–Mar., Wed.–Mon. 10:30–1 and 2:30–5.*

Pinacoteca Comunale, the community museum, is housed in the **Palazzo Comunale** (town hall) and displays religious paintings from the surrounding area. The museum's most important works are those painted by the Umbrian master Niccolò di Liberatore (circa 1430–1502), known as L'Alunno, and a fresco attributed to Perugino. (At this writing, the museum is closed for restoration. All inquiries should be directed to the Museo Regionale della Ceramica.) ✉ *Piazza Consoli 13,* ☎ *075/9711000 (Museo Regionale della Ceramica).*

Lodging

$$ 🏨 **Antica Fattoria del Colle.** Two structures from the early 1800s make up this pleasant agritourist lodging, which includes furnishings of the same era. The friendly owners (who speak English) make your stay relaxing and peaceful. ✉ *Colle delle Forche 6, 06053,* ☎ FAX *075/972201,*

WEB *www.anticafattoriadelcolle.it. 5 rooms, 2 apartments. Restaurant, pool, archery, mountain bikes; no air-conditioning, no room TVs. No credit cards. Closed Jan. 15–Mar. 15. MAP.*

$-$$ ⊡ **Melody.** The plain, comfortable, modern hotel just outside the cen-
★ ter of Deruta has a reasonably priced restaurant and a big parking area surrounded by pine trees. Rooms are commodious, some with carpeting; the newer ones have nice wood floors and wood furniture. All rooms have balconies, but those in the back are quiet and have pleasant views of the surrounding hills. ⊠ *SS3 bis (on the south side of Deruta), 06053,* ☎ *075/9711186,* FAX *075/9711018. 53 rooms. Restaurant, room TVs, bar, meeting rooms; no air-conditioning in some rooms. AE, DC, MC, V. CP, EP.*

Shopping

Deruta is home to more than 70 ceramics workshops and boutiques. They offer a range of ceramics, including extra pieces from commissions for well-known British and North American tableware manufacturers. If you ask, most shop owners will take you to see where they actually throw, bake, and paint their wares. A drive along Via Tiberina Nord reveals one ceramics factory after the next. **Ceramiche El Frate** (⊠ Piazza dei Consoli 29, ☎ 075/9711435) sells unusual tiles and jugs. Innovative patterns and colors brighten the traditional forms created by **Ceramiche Sberna** (⊠ Via Tiberina 146, ☎ 075/9710206); the meticulously hand-crafted and painted ceramics are on display in its factory showroom. **Fabbrica Maioliche Tradizionali** (⊠ Via Tiberina Nord 37, ☎ 075/9711220) is open for visits weekdays 8:30–1 and 2:30–4:30 and also operates one of the largest shops in the area. **Fratelli Mari** (⊠ Via Circonvallazione Nord 1, ☎ 075/9710400, WEB www.mari-deruta. it), one of the oldest ceramics manufacturers in Deruta, produces a variety of ceramic pieces that ranges in style from the steadfastly classical to the ultramodern. **Maioliche Cynthia** (⊠ Via Umberto I 1, ☎ 075/9711255), in Deruta's central Piazza dei Consoli, specializes in reproductions of antique designs and offers a good selection. Four generations of the Veschini family have operated **Maioliche Fidia** (⊠ Piazza Consoli 25, ☎ 075/972121, WEB www.fidiaderuta.com), which produces elegant and highly crafted ceramics to traditional designs. The factory is in the valley below town. Ceramics manufacturer **Maioliche Figli Calzuola** (⊠ Via Tiberina Nord 50, ☎ 075/9711244) specializes in classically designed pieces in a great variety of shapes and sizes. Traditional patterns are the focus at **Maioliche Fima di Picchiotti Piero** (⊠ Via Tiberina Nord 111, ☎ 075/9711285).

Corciano

🔟 *21 km (13 mi) northeast of Deruta, 13 km (8 mi) northwest of Perugia, 97 km (60 mi) east of Siena.*

Corciano is a nicely preserved medieval hilltop village, with a view of the valley that stretches as far as Lago Trasimeno. At the **Museo della Casa Contadina** (Farmhouse Museum; ⊠ Via Tarracone, ☎ no phone), you can see what a typical Corciano home was like before the industrial era. Check with the city hall (☎ 075/5188254) for hours. Usually you can see the museum, which is free, on request. The **Chiesa di Santa Maria Assunta** (Church of the Assumption of Santa Maria) displays Perugino's *L'Assunta* (*The Assumption*), painted in 1513.

Lago Trasimeno

Passignano sul Trasimeno: 16 km (10 mi) northwest of Corciano, 30 km (18 mi) northwest of Perugia. Castiglione del Lago: 22 km (13 mi) southwest of Passignano, 52 km (31 mi) west of Perugia.

⑯ **Passignano sul Trasimeno** is a picturesque town on the northern shore of Lago Trasimeno, complete with castle ruins and medieval walls. Beaches here are mostly rocky and public bathing facilities aren't available, so this isn't the best spot for swimming. In the western-shore community of **Castiglione del Lago,** evidence of Etruscan origins, castle ruins, **⑰** and medieval city walls lend a mysterious, elegant air. The **Palazzo della Corgna** (✉ Piazza A. Gramsci 1, ☎ no phone) is worth a visit for its Renaissance frescoes. The palace is open daily April through October 10–1 and 3–7 but only 10–4 on weekends during the rest of the year; admission is €1.50. The city hall (☎ 075/96581) has additional information.

In both towns you can sail, windsurf, or take a ferry to **Isola Maggiore,** a small island on the lake that has a pleasant little fishing town with houses dating from the 15th century and a church from the 14th. The local men fish and the women still craft lace.

Dining and Lodging

$–$$$ ✗ **Cacciatori–Da Luciano.** Fresh fish here comes straight from the lake and is exceptional. But the entire menu is sumptuous, with delectable *antipasti* (starters), and a wide range of meat and seafood courses and fine wines. Ask for a table near the windows overlooking the lake. ✉ *Via Nazionale 11, Passignano sul Trasimeno,* ☎ *075/827210. Reservations essential. AE, DC, MC, V. Closed Wed.*

$$ ✗⌂ **Kursaal.** Every room in this pink two-story hotel has a balcony, and most rooms have views of the lake. Not far from the lake is the pool, and hotel guests have access to a private beach and a garden. The restaurant ($$–$$$$), on Lago Trasimeno, has a veranda that's especially nice in summer. The dishes featuring fish from the lake and seafood, including *pasta al sapore di lago con tinca affumicata* (pasta with smoked tench, a soft-finned freshwater fish related to carp), shine. Reservations for the restaurant, which is closed Monday, are essential. ✉ *Via Europa 24 (1 km/½ mi east of the center of Passignano sul Trasimeno), Passignano sul Trasimeno 06065,* ☎ *075/828085,* FAX *075/827182,* WEB *www.kursaalhotel.net. 16 rooms, 2 suites. Restaurant, room TVs, pool, beach; no air-conditioning in some rooms. MC, V. Closed Nov.–Mar. CP.*

$ ✗⌂ **Locanda del Galluzzo.** The hilltop agriturismo sits 2,145 ft above lake level and offers beautiful water and countryside views amid absolute quiet. You can stroll in the olive groves around the pool. Accommodations here—rooms and apartments—are simple with dark wood furniture. The restaurant ($–$$) turns out delicious meals, and in summer you can dine on a veranda under a pergola. Fish isn't served here; the menu is typically Umbrian, with rich dishes such as *papardelle al capriolo* (flat noodles in venison sauce) and *cinghiale alle olive nere* (roast boar with black olives). ✉ *Via Castel Rigone 12/a, Località Trecine (5 km/3 mi east of Passignano sul Trasimeno), Passignano sul Trasimeno 06060,* ☎ FAX *075/845352,* WEB *www.perugiaonline. com/locandadelgalluzzo. 4 rooms, 6 apartments. Restaurant, kitchens (some), room TVs, pool, bar; no air-conditioning, no room phones. DC, MC, V. CP.*

$$ ⌂ **Albergo Sauro.** You can reach this quiet lakefront hotel on tiny Isola Maggiore by ferry from either Castiglione del Lago or Passignano sul Trasimeno. Its rooms are rustic, but guests may relax on the beach, sit in the garden, or wander down to the boat dock. The hotel owner catches carp and other fish for his private stock and for the restaurant here. ✉ *Isola Maggiore 06060,* ☎ *075/826168,* FAX *075/825130. 10 rooms, 2 suites. Restaurant, room TVs. DC, MC, V. Closed Nov.–Feb. CP.*

ON THE PERUGINO TRAIL

Studying under Verrocchio (1435–88), native Umbrian Pietro Vannucci (circa 1450–1523), known as Il Perugino, developed his artistic career in Florence and then Rome, where he helped paint the Cappella Sistina (Sistine Chapel). He outlived his star pupil, Raphael Sanzio (1483–1520), a native of Urbino. Visiting Perugino's major works in the area around Perugia is a way to reconstruct the evolution of his career and also a way to see how much the artist was affected by—and re-created—the environment in which he grew up. If you follow a Perugino itinerary, remember that the Collegio del Cambio in Perugia is a must.

Città della Pieve

⑱ *26 km (16 mi) south of Castiglione del Lago, 43 km (26 mi) south-west of Perugia.*

Perugino was born in this small Etruscan town of plain redbrick build-ings, flat-top towers, and churches, so it makes sense that the churches here are chock-full of his frescoes, some in better condition than others. (Also worth a peek for their Perugino frescoes are the churches of Santa Maria dei Servi and San Pietro, outside the city walls near the hospi-tal; follow signs.)

Perugino's *Baptism of Christ* and *Madonna in Glory* in the 17th-cen-tury **Duomo** (⊠ Piazza Plebiscito, ☎ no phone), originally a Roman structure that was transformed via baroque and Gothic renovations, are examples of the artist's later works.

In **Santa Maria dei Bianchi,** the *Adoration of the Magi,* painted in 1504, is particularly well restored. It depicts the Nativity scene in perfect Re-naissance court style on a spring day, with the Perugian countryside in the background. At a time when Leonardo da Vinci (1452–1519) and Michelangelo (1475–1564) were exploring new scientific and re-ligious territory, Perugino reaffirmed a classical, humanistic Renaissance style. ⊠ *Via Vannucci,* ☎ *075/8299696.* ⊡ *Free.* ◔ *Mon.–Sat. 10:30–12:30 and 3:30–6, Sun. 10–1 and 3–6.*

Panicale

⑲ *21 km (13 mi) northeast of Città della Pieve, 34 km (20 mi) southwest of Perugia.*

The small town of Panicale, with a population of just over 5,000, sits on a low hill about 8 km (5 mi) inland from Lago Trasimeno. The town has preserved some of its original medieval walls and gateways and is known in the area for its handcrafted lace and needlework. On the drive from Città della Pieve to Panicale, a wide open view of Lago Trasi-meno appears, showing the islands on the lake and the mountains on its far shore.

Once you've reached Panicale, head for the church of **San Sebastiano,** where Perugino painted his famous fresco the *Martyrdom of St. Se-bastian.* Although it was executed in 1505, only one year later than the *Adoration of the Magi* in Città della Pieve, it is much more abstract and geometric. The painting is almost dreamlike, with St. Sebastian on a strange classical terrace and God appearing fatherlike above. The landscape in the background, however, is the same Perugian country-side found in the *Adoration of the Magi.* ⊠ *Outside the city walls, off Piazza Vittoria,* ☎ *0758/37602.* ⊡ *Free.* ◔ *Daily 10–noon and 4–6.*

Fontignano

ⓩ *12 km (7 mi) east of Panicale, 22 km (13 mi) southwest of Perugia.*

Fontignano, on a conical hill about 10 km (6 mi) from Lago Trasimeno, is famous as the place where Perugino died (in 1523). In this once-fortified medieval town, only the ruins of a lone turret mark the spot where the castle once stood.

A year before he died of the plague, Perugino painted the almost naive-looking *Madonna and Child* in the **Chiesa dell' Annunziata** (Church of the Virgin Mary Annunciate), which is open daily 7 AM–8 PM.

NORTH TOWARD URBINO

The trip north from Perugia to Città di Castello and Gubbio, and across to Urbino, passes through rugged, mountainous terrain. Città di Castello can be combined with San Sepolcro in an itinerary, possibly also including Arezzo.

Città di Castello

㉑ *54 km (32 mi) north of Perugia, 42 km (26 mi) east of Arezzo.*

The noble-looking town is still surrounded in part by 16th-century walls. At its center is the Piazza Matteotti, dominated by the 14th-century **Palazzo del Podestà,** which today houses Città di Castello's administrative offices and courts.

The **Duomo** dates from the 6th century but was renovated between 1466 and 1529; in the 17th century it received an unfinished baroque facelift. ⊠ *Piazza del Duomo,* ☎ *0758/521647.* 🎟 *Free.* ☉ *Daily 10–noon and 4–6.*

The **Palazzo Albizzini** is home to the **Fondazione Palazzo Albizzini "Collezione Burri,"** which displays some 130 works by the artist Alberto Burri (1915–95), perhaps the town's most famous native son. Trained as a doctor, Burri began painting while held in a World War II detention camp in the United States. The collection reflects his work as one of Italy's most important proponents of Art Informel ("unformed" art, sometimes referred to as Lyrical Abstraction) in the 1950s and 1960s. ⊠ *Via Albizzini 1,* ☎ *0758/554649.* 🎟 *€5.* ☉ *Tues.–Sat. 9–12:30 and 2:30–6, Sun. 9–1.*

Inside the 16th-century **Palazzo Vitelli alla Cannoniera,** built by Antonio da Sangallo the Younger (1483–1546) with a facade by Giorgio Vasari (1511–74), is the **Pinacoteca Comunale,** second only to Perugia's art gallery for Umbrian painting. It houses paintings by Raphael (including *The Creation of Eve*), Luca Signorelli (1441–1523), and Ghirlandaio (1449–94). ⊠ *Via della Cannoniera 22/a,* ☎ *0758/ 5206565.* 🎟 *€5.* ☉ *Apr.–Oct., Tues.–Sun. 10–1 and 2:30–6:30; Nov.– Mar., Tues.–Sun. 10–12:30 and 3:00–5:30.*

Dining and Lodging

$$$ ✕ **Il Postale di Marco e Barbara.** Friendly owners Marco and Barbara
★ turned an old bus depot into this stellar restaurant, creating a pleasant environment while retaining elements such as old wood beams in the ceiling and an antique gas pump outside. Every two weeks the kitchen invents recipes with the freshest local vegetables, fish, and meat. Artistic and tasty antipasti might be bite-size marinated veal with sprouts and lemon cream, or little tarts of mussels and vegetables. Entrées include roast quail with cherry tomatoes and beans as well as many delicious fish and seafood choices. Throughout the year, you can order

a *degustazione* (tasting) menu; the chef chooses your two antipasti, first, and second courses. ⊠ *Via De Cesare 8,* ☎ *075/8521356. Reservations essential. AE, DC, MC, V. Closed Mon. No lunch Sat.*

$-$$ ⌐ **Le Mura.** Built in the early 1990s, this hotel just inside the old city walls is modern and has a friendly and efficient staff. Guest rooms are bright and comfortable, with functional furnishings. A good buffet breakfast awaits you in the morning. ⊠ *Via Borgo Farinario 24/26, 06012,* ☎ *075/8521070,* FAX *075/8521350,* WEB *www.hotellemura.it. 35 rooms. Restaurant, room TVs, bar, meeting rooms, parking (fee). AE, DC, MC, V. CP.*

Nightlife and the Arts

Chamber music lovers should consider the **Festival delle Nazioni di Musica da Camera** (Chamber Music Festival of the Nations; ☎ 075/8521142, FAX 075/8552461), a two-week chamber music festival held between August and September in Città di Castello. For information year-round, contact the festival office or the town's tourist office (☎ 075/8554922).

Gubbio

❷   *35 km (22 mi) southeast of Città di Castello, 39 km (24 mi) northeast of Perugia, 92 km (57 mi) east of Arezzo.*

There is something otherworldly about this jewel of a medieval town tucked away in a mountainous corner of Umbria. Even at the height of summer, the cool serenity and quiet of Gubbio's streets remain intact. The town is perched on the slopes of Monte Ingino, and the streets are dramatically steep. Gubbio's relatively isolated position has kept it free of hordes of high-season visitors, and most of the year the city lives up to its Italian nickname, La Città del Silenzio, City of Silence. Just don't come looking for peace and quiet during the fast and furious festivals in May. Parking in the central Piazza dei Quaranta Martiri—named for 40 hostages murdered by the Nazis in 1944—is easy and secure, and it is wise to leave your car in the piazza and explore the narrow streets on foot.

The **Duomo,** on a narrow street on the highest tier of the town, dates from the 13th century, with some baroque additions—in particular, a lavishly decorated bishop's chapel. ⊠ *Via Ducale,* ☎ *no phone.* ⌐ *Free.* ☉ *Daily 8–12:45 and 3–7:30.*

★   The striking Piazza Grande is dominated by the medieval **Palazzo dei Consoli,** attributed to a local architect known as Gattapone—a man still much admired by today's residents (hotels, restaurants, and bars have been named after him), though studies have suggested that the palazzo was in fact the work of another architect, Angelo da Orvieto. In the Middle Ages the Parliament of Gubbio met in this palace, which has become a symbol of the town.

The Palazzo dei Consoli houses a small museum, famous chiefly for the Tavole Eugubine, seven bronze tablets written in the ancient Umbrian language, employing Etruscan and Latin characters and providing the best key to understanding this obscure tongue. Also in the museum is a fascinating miscellany of coins, medieval arms, paintings, and majolica and earthenware pots, not to mention exhilarating views over Gubbio's roofscape and beyond from the lofty loggia. For a few days at the beginning of May, the palace also displays the famous *ceri,* the ceremonial pillars at the center of Gubbio's annual festivities. ⊠ *Piazza Grande,* ☎ *075/9274298,* WEB *www.comune. gubbio.pg.it.* ⌐ €4. ☉ *Apr.–Oct., daily 10–1 and 3–6; Nov.–Mar., daily 10–1 and 2–5.*

ST. UBALDO WINS AGAIN

EVERY MAY 15—the eve of the day celebrating Gubbio's patron saint, St. Ubaldo—the townspeople gather for the **Festa dei Ceri** (www.festadeiceri.it), as they have since 1160. The day is rich in song and revelry, but the main event is a race during which teams of men in colorful costumes haul three enormous wooden pillars called *ceri* at breakneck speed to the top of Monte Ingino and the Basilica of St. Ubaldo. What makes the task so difficult? Each of the pillars weighs about 880 lbs and is carried vertically (with the aid of special frames).

The ceri, which are topped with statues of St. Ubaldo, St. George, and St. Anthony during the Corsa dei Ceri (Race of the Ceri), reside in the basilica. On the first Sunday in May, however, they're transported (in the horizontal position) in a procession to the Palazzo dei Consoli, where they're displayed ahead of the festival.

"Running" with the pillars is a serious matter and locals vie for the honor of being one of the bearers, called *ceraioli*. (Family tradition often dictates participation.) Teams accomplish the arduous task while surrounded by throngs of townspeople and visitors who come to absorb some of the fascinating, mystical emotion that defines the "race." Don't place any bets, though—the pillar capped with St. Ubaldo always wins.

The **Palazzo Ducale** is a scaled-down copy of the Palazzo Ducale in Urbino. (Gubbio was once the possession of that city's ruling family, the Montefeltro.) Gubbio's palazzo contains a small museum and a courtyard. Some of the public rooms offer magnificent views. ⊠ *Via Ducale,* ☎ *075/9275872.* ◻ €2.50. ☼ *Tues.–Sun. 8:30–7:30.*

Just outside the city walls at the eastern end of town (follow Corso Garibaldi or Via XX Settembre to the end) is a **funicular** (☼ July–Aug., daily 8:30–7:30; Sept.–June, Thurs.–Tues. 10–1:15 and 2:30–5; ◻ €2.60, round-trip €3.35) that provides a bracing ride to the top of Monte Ingino. At the top of Monte Ingino is the **Basilica di Sant' Ubaldo** (☎ 075/9273872), repository of Gubbio's famous ceri—three 16-ft-tall pillars crowned with statues of Sts. Ubaldo, George, and Anthony. The pillars are transported to the Palazzo dei Consoli on the first Sunday of May, in preparation for the Festa dei Ceri. The basilica is open daily 9–noon and 4–7 and admission is free.

Dining and Lodging

$$$–$$$$ ✕ **Fornace di Mastro Giorgio.** The building dates back to the 1300s, and its original stone-and-wood structure has been kept intact. (In the 1400s, the space housed a ceramics factory important in Gubbio.) The menu, with seasonal changes, includes traditional but creative fare: *gnochetti al finocchio selvatico,* potato dumplings with wild fennel; *agnolotti al tartufo nero,* ravioli-type pasta with black truffles; and *filetto alle prugne,* filet mignon with prune sauce. ⊠ *Via Mastro Giorgio 2,* ☎ *075/9221836. AE, DC, MC, V. Closed Tues. No lunch Wed.*

$$–$$$ ✕ **Grotta dell'Angelo.** The rustic trattoria is in the lower part of the old town, near the main square and tourist information office. The menu features simple local specialties, including *capocollo* (a type of salami), *stringozzi* (very thick spaghetti), and lasagna *tartufata* (with truffles). The few outdoor tables are in high demand in summer. The restaurant also offers a few small, basically furnished guest rooms, which should be booked ahead. ⊠ *Via Gioia 47,* ☎ *075/9273438. Reservations essential. AE, DC, MC, V. Closed Tues. and Jan. 10–31.*

$$–$$$ ✕ **Taverna del Lupo.** The "Tavern of the Wolf" is one of the city's best
★ *taverne,* and one of the largest—it seats 150 people and can get a bit hectic during the high season. Lasagna made in the Gubbian fashion, with ham and truffles, is the best pasta. The desserts here are excellent and the wine cellar extensive. ⊠ *Via G. Ansidei 21,* ☎ *075/9274368. Reservations essential. AE, DC, MC, V. Closed Mon. Oct.–Apr.*

$$ ✕ **Bosone Garden.** As the stone arches inside indicate, this was once the stables of the palace that now houses the Hotel Bosone. The menu includes a two-mushroom salad with truffles, risotto *alla porcina* (with porcini mushrooms, sausage, and truffles), and leg of pork. The garden, open in summer, seats 200. ⊠ *Via XX Settembre 22,* ☎ *075/ 9220688. AE, DC, MC, V. Closed Wed. Oct.–May and 2 wks in Jan.*

$$–$$$$ ☷ **Hotel Bosone Palace.** In the center of town, this old-style hotel occupies the Palazzo Raffaelli. Standard rooms, which vary in size, are comfortable and have heavy wooden furniture. Antiques furnish the two large suites, which, like the hotel's small and delightful breakfast room, have elaborately frescoed ceilings. Ask for a room looking out over the valley, as the street side can be noisy at times. ⊠ *Via XX Settembre 22, 06024,* ☎ *075/9220688,* ℻ *075/9220552. 28 rooms, 2 suites. Minibars, room TVs, bar; no air-conditioning. AE, DC, MC, V. Closed Jan.*

$$–$$$ ☷ **Castello Cortevecchio.** The energetic owners of this truly special agriturismo have plenty organized for you. Eleven apartments are available in the 19th-century castle; a number of houses on the grounds provide additional apartments, rooms, and suites. The castle sits amid a 40-acre wooded park with a pool, stables (replete with an English riding instructor and lodging for your horse), tennis courts, and a small soccer field. During truffle season, the owners take guests truffle hunting with specially trained dogs. Guest rooms are simple but elegant, with furnishings in wood and marble, beamed ceilings, and clay-tile floors. A one-week minimum stay is required in summer, but don't let this deter you: the owners say they do their best to accommodate guests interested in staying here. ⊠ *Località Nogna, 06020,* ☎ *075/9241017,* ℻ *075/9241079,* ⅏ *www.castellocortevecchio.it. 10 rooms, 18 apartments, 4 suites. Restaurant, room TVs, pool, 2 tennis courts, mountain bikes, boccie, horseback riding, soccer, bar; no air-conditioning. AE, DC, MC, V. Closed mid-Jan.–Feb. 10.*

$$ ☷ **Hotel Gattapone.** The views from this spiffy, family-run hotel in the center of Gubbio are of a sea of rooftops. Rooms are a good size, modern, and comfortable; some have well-preserved wood beams on the ceilings. ⊠ *Via Ansidei 6, 06024,* ☎ *075/9272489,* ℻ *075/9272417,* ⅏ *www.mencarelligroup.com. 16 rooms, 2 suites. Room TVs, bar; no air-conditioning. AE, DC, MC, V. Closed Jan.*

Outdoor Activities and Sports

☺ Gubbio's costumed **Palio della Balestra** (crossbow tournament), which takes place on the last Sunday in May, began in the 12th century as a competition between Gubbio and Sansepolcro. Details on the historical pageant are available from the Gubbio tourist office (⊠ Piazza Oderisi 6, ☎ 075/9220693).

THE MARCHES
Including San Marino

An excursion from Umbria into the Marches region allows you to see a part of Italy rarely visited by foreigners. Not as wealthy as Tuscany or Umbria, the Marches has a diverse landscape of mountains and beaches, and marvelous views. Like that of neighbors to the west, Le Marche's patchwork of rolling hills is stitched with grapevines and olive trees, bearing luscious wine and olive oil.

Traveling here isn't as easy as in Umbria or Tuscany. Beyond the narrow coastal plain and away from major towns, the roads are steep and twisting. Efficient bus service connects the coastal town of Pésaro to Urbino. Train travel in the region is slow, however, and stops are limited—although you can reach Ascoli Piceno by rail.

San Marino, perched high on the upper slopes of Monte Titano, is best reached from Rimini, on the southern coast of Emilia-Romagna. A main highway connects the two; regular bus service to San Marino is available from Rimini's train station, airport, and city center.

Urbino

㉓ *75 km (45 mi) north of Gubbio, 116 km (73 mi) northeast of Perugia, 230 km (144 mi) east of Florence.*

Majestic Urbino, atop a steep hill with a skyline of towers and domes, is something of a surprise to come upon—it's oddly remote. And yet it was once a center of learning and culture almost without rival in western Europe. The town looks much as it did in the glory days of the 15th century, a cluster of warm brick and pale stone buildings, all topped with russet-color tile roofs. The focal point is the immense and beautiful Palazzo Ducale.

The city is home to the small but prestigious Università di Urbino—one of the oldest in the world—and during school term the streets are lively and filled with students. Urbino is very much a college town, with the usual array of bookshops, record stores, bars, and coffeehouses. In summer, the Italian student population is replaced by foreigners who come to study Italian language and arts at several prestigious private fine-arts academies.

Urbino's fame rests on the reputation of three of its native sons: Duke Federico da Montefeltro (1422–82), the enlightened warrior-patron who built the Palazzo Ducale; Raffaello Sanzio (1483–1520), or Raphael, one of the most influential painters in history and an embodiment of the spirit of the Renaissance; and the architect Donato Bramante (1444–1514), who translated the philosophy of the Renaissance into buildings of grace and beauty. Unfortunately there is little work by either Bramante or Raphael in the city, but the duke's influence can still be felt strongly.

The **Casa di Raffaello** (House of Raphael) really is the house in which the painter was born and where he took his first steps in painting, under the direction of his artist father. There is some debate about the fresco of the Madonna here; some say it's by Raphael, whereas others attribute it to the father—with Raphael's mother and the young painter himself standing in as models for the Madonna and Child. ✉ *Via Raffaello 57,* ☎ *0722/320105.* 🎫 *€3.* ⏰ *Mon.–Sat. 9–2, Sun. 10–1.*

★ The **Palazzo Ducale** (Ducal Palace) holds the place of honor in the city, and in no other palace of its era are the principles of the Renaissance stated quite so clearly. If the Renaissance was, in ideal form, a celebration of the nobility of man and his works, of the light and purity of the soul, then there is no place in Italy, the birthplace of the Renaissance, where these tenets are better illustrated. From the moment you enter the peaceful courtyard, you know you're in a place of grace and beauty, the harmony of the building reflecting the high ideals of the men who built it. Today the palace houses the **Galleria Nazionale delle Marche** (National Museum of the Marches), with a superb collection of paintings, sculpture, and other objets d'art, well arranged and lit. Some works were originally the possessions of the Montefeltro family; others were brought to the museum from churches and palaces throughout the region. Masterworks in the collection include Paolo Uccello's *Profanation of the Host,* Titian's *Resurrection* and *Last Supper,* and Piero della Francesca's *Madonna of Senigallia.* But the gallery's highlight is Piero's enigmatic work long known as *The Flagellation of Christ.* Much has been written about this painting, and few experts agree on its meaning. Legend had it that the three figures in the foreground represent a murdered member of the Montefeltro family (the barefoot young man) and his two killers. However, Sir John Pope-Hennessy—the preeminent scholar of Italian Renaissance art—argues that they represent the arcane subject of the vision of St. Lawrence. Academic debates notwithstanding, the experts agree that the work is one of the painter's masterpieces. Piero himself thought so: it is one of the few works he signed (on the lowest step supporting the throne). ⊠ *Piazza Duca Federico,* ☎ 0722/2760, WEB *www.comune.urbino.ps.it.* ⌑ €4. ☉ *Tues.–Sun. 8:30–7:15 (10 PM Apr.–Oct.), Mon. 8:30–2; ticket office closes 90 mins before Palazzo.*

Dining and Lodging

$$–$$$$ ✕ **La Vecchia Fornarina.** The two small rooms of this trattoria not far from Urbino's central Piazza della Repubblica are often filled to capacity. The trattoria specializes in meaty country fare, such as *vitello alle noci* (veal cooked with walnuts) or *ai porcini* (with mushrooms), but also offers a good range of pasta dishes. ⊠ *Via Mazzini 14,* ☎ 0722/320007. *Reservations essential. AE, DC, MC, V.*

$$–$$$$ ✕ **Vecchia Urbino.** In the center of town is this simple yet elegant wood-paneled restaurant with views of the hills. Recommended pasta dishes include *vincisgrassi,* a meat lasagna named after an Austrian captain who brought the recipe to Urbino more than 100 years ago, and spaghetti *alla Vecchia Urbino,* with bacon and pecorino cheese. A particularly good second course is the *coniglio al coccio* (literally, rabbit in earthenware); the rabbit is cooked in milk on the stovetop in an earthenware casserole and then baked. ⊠ *Via dei Vasari 3/5,* ☎ 0722/4447. *AE, DC, MC, V. Closed Tues.*

$$–$$$ ⌂ **Hotel Bonconte.** This classic hotel, dating from the beginning of the 20th century, is just inside the city walls and close to the Palazzo Ducale. Rooms are pleasant and include some antiques and upholstered pieces; those at the front of the hotel have views of the valley below Urbino, although they also face the street. A terrace in the tranquil garden to the rear of the hotel adjoins the cozy breakfast room and bar. ⊠ *Via delle Mura 28, 61029,* ☎ 0722/2463, FAX 0722/4782, WEB *www.viphotels.it/ita/hotel_bonconte.htm. 23 rooms, 2 suites. Room TVs, bar, meeting rooms. AE, DC, MC, V.*

$ ⌂ **Hotel San Giovanni.** A renovated medieval building in the old town houses this hotel. Guest rooms are simple, clean, and comfortable, with a wonderful view from Rooms 24 to 30. A handy restaurant–pizzeria is below. ⊠ *Via Barocci 13, 61029,* ☎ 0722/2827, FAX 0722/329055. *33 rooms, 17 with bath. No air-conditioning, no room TVs. No credit cards. Closed July and Christmas wk.*

San Marino

24 *45 km (28 mi) northwest of Urbino, 168 km (104 mi) northeast of Florence.*

The town of San Marino is the capital of the Republic of San Marino, which measures 61 square km (23 square mi) and is landlocked on all sides by Italy. Legend has it that San Marino was founded in the 4th century AD by a humble stonecutter named Marino who settled here with a small community of Christians to escape persecution by pagan emperor Diocletian. Over the millennia, largely because of the logistical and strategic nightmares associated with attacking a fortified rock, the *republicca* was more or less left alone by Italy's various conquerors, and it continues to this day as a politically independent state. But don't worry about changing money, showing passports, learning telephone codes, and the like; San Marino is, for all practical purposes, Italy.

The state consists of nine municipalities, known as the San Marino castles (or *castelli*), each run by a council called the Consiglio del Castello. Most of the republic's 26,000 residents live not in the medieval cliff town but rather along the more modern and accessible streets below the rock.

Tourist stores, tacky hotels and restaurants, and gun shops line the tangle of cobblestone streets in the town of San Marino, which climbs the side of Monte Titano. However, the views of the stunning green countryside far below more than justify a visit—the 3,300-ft-plus precipices of sheer rock make jaws drop and acrophobes quiver—and the town's *tre castelli* (three castles) are medieval architectural wonders and engineering curiosities. Starting in the center of town, you can walk castle-to-castle along a paved cliff-top ridge and take in the spectacular views of Romagna and the Adriatic Sea. The walks make for a good day's exercise. The longest—and windiest—hike is the one between the second and third castles. Even if you arrive after castle visiting hours (8–8, shorter hours in winter), the ridge walk is worthwhile.

The **Castello della Guaita** (☎ 0549/991369) dates to the 10th century. The 13th-century **Castello della Cesta** (☎ 0549/991295) contains a museum of ancient weapons. It was built on a cliff 2,421 ft above sea level and offers great views. The 14th-century **Castello Montale,** the most remote of San Marino's castles, is closed to the public.

A must-see in San Marino is the **Piazza della Libertà,** whose battlemented and clock-topped Palazzo Pubblico is guarded by San Marino's real-life soldiers in their green uniforms. At the **Ferrari Museum** (Maranello Rosso, V. III Settembre 3, ☎ 0549/900824), you can gaze at the automotive toys of the wealthy. (Park at the border crossing.)

Shopping

Peer into the shops along the old town's winding streets and you're likely to notice that the republic is famous for its crossbows—and more: shopping for fireworks, firearms, and other items illegal for sale elsewhere is a popular activity here. Indeed, San Marino's legislation is looser than Italy's, and the republic is a tax haven that resembles a large duty-free shopping center. In addition to shops selling products with known brand names, plenty of stores are stocked with imitations, from perfumes to cheap stereos with labels like Panaphonic. All this may change, however; the Italian government has begun to tire of its lax little neighbor and has been stepping up border controls and pressure on San Marino to change.

Ancona

❷⑤ *87 km (54 mi) southeast of Urbino, 139 km (87 mi) northeast of Perugia, 262 km (164 mi) east of Florence.*

Ancona was probably once a lovely city. It's on an elbow-shape bluff (hence its name; *ankon* is Greek for "elbow") that juts out into the Adriatic. But Ancona was the object of serious aerial bombing during World War II—it was, and is, an important port city—and was reduced to rubble. The city was rebuilt in the unfortunate postwar poured-concrete style, practical and inexpensive but not aesthetically pleasing. Unless you're waiting for one of the many ferries to Albania, Croatia, Greece, or Turkey, there is little reason to visit the city—with a few exceptions. The 2nd-century **Arco di Traiano** (Trajan's Arch) is worth a look, and the **Duomo San Ciriaco** and the **Loggia dei Mercanti** offer a glimpse of the architecture of Ancona's past. The city's importance as a port means it's well served by trains, which can make it a good base for an excursion to Loreto or to Ascoli Piceno, farther south along the Adriatic coast.

Dining and Lodging

$$–$$$ ✕ **La Moretta.** In summer, this family-run trattoria offers outside dining on the central Piazza del Plebiscito, which has a fine view of the baroque church of San Domenico. Among the specialties here are *stoccafisso all'Anconetana* (stockfish baked with capers, anchovies, potatoes, and tomatoes) and the famous brodetto fish stew. ✉ *Piazza del Plebiscito 52,* ☎ *071/202317. AE, DC, MC, V. Closed Sun., Jan. 1–10, and Aug. 13–18.*

$$$ 🏨 **Grand Hotel Palace.** Classic and elegant, this hotel in the center of Ancona near the port is considered one of the best lodgings in town. Wood furniture and lovely fabrics dress the place, which dates to the 1600s. Thoughtful extras include slippers, bath salts, and shaving kits. The breakfast room, on the top floor, offers a panoramic view. ✉ *Lungomare Vanvitelli 24, 60100,* ☎ *071/201813,* ℻ *071/2074832. 39 rooms, 1 suite. Restaurant, room TVs, gym, bar, meeting rooms, parking (fee). AE, DC, MC, V. Closed Dec. 23–Jan. 1.*

Loreto

❷⑥ *31 km (19 mi) south of Ancona, 118 km (73 mi) southeast of Urbino.*

Loreto is famous for one of the best-loved shrines in the world, that of the **Santuario della Santa Casa** (House of the Virgin Mary), within
★ the **Basilica della Santa Casa.** Legend has it that angels moved the house from Nazareth, where the Virgin Mary was living at the time of the Annunciation, to this hilltop in 1295. The reason for this sudden and divinely inspired move was that Nazareth had fallen into the hands of Muslim invaders, whom the angelic hosts viewed as not suitable to lord over this important shrine. Excavations made at the behest of the Church have shown that the house did once stand elsewhere and was brought to the hilltop—by either crusaders or a family named Angeli—around the time the angels (*angeli*) are said to have done the job.

The house itself consists of three rough stone walls contained within an elaborate marble tabernacle. Built around this centerpiece is the giant basilica of the Holy House, which dominates the town. Millions of visitors come to the site every year (particularly at Easter and on the Feast of the Holy House, December 10), and the little town of Loreto can become uncomfortably crowded with pilgrims. Many great Italian architects, including Bramante, Antonio da Sangallo the Younger (1483–

1546), Giuliano da Sangallo (circa 1445–1516), and Sansovino (1467–1529), contributed to the design of the basilica. It was begun in the Gothic style in 1468 and continued in Renaissance style through the late Renaissance. The bell tower is by Luigi Vanvitelli (1700–73). Inside the church are a great many mediocre 19th- and 20th-century paintings but also some fine works by Renaissance masters such as Luca Signorelli and Melozzo da Forlì.

If you're a nervous air traveler you can take comfort in the fact that the Holy Virgin of Loreto is the patron of air travelers and that Pope John Paul II has composed a prayer for a safe flight—available in the church in a half dozen languages. ⊠ *Piazza della Madonna,* ☎ *071/ 970104,* WEB *www.santuarioloreto.it.* ☉ *June–Sept., daily 6:45 AM–8 PM; Oct.–May, daily 6:45 AM–7 PM (Santuario della Santa Casa closed daily 12:30–2:30).*

Ascoli Piceno

㉗ *88 km (55 mi) south of Loreto, 105 km (65 mi) south of Ancona.*

Ascoli Piceno isn't a hill town but sits in a valley ringed by steep hills and cut by the fast-racing Tronto River. With almost 60,000 residents, it's one of the most important towns in the region; in Roman times it was one of central Italy's most important market towns. Despite the growth Ascoli Piceno saw during the Middle Ages and at other times, the streets in the town center continue to reflect the grid pattern of the ancient Roman city. You'll even find the word *rua,* from the Latin *ruga,* used for "street" instead of the Italian *via.* Now largely closed to vehicular traffic, the city center is a great place to explore on foot.

★ The heart of the town is the majestic **Piazza del Popolo,** dominated by the Gothic church of **San Francesco** and the **Palazzo del Popolo,** a 13th-century town hall that contains a graceful Renaissance courtyard. The square itself functions as the living room of the entire city. At dusk each evening the piazza is packed with people strolling and exchanging news and gossip—the sweetly antiquated ritual called the *passeggiata,* done all over the country.

☾ Ascoli Piceno's **Giostra della Quintana** (Joust of the Quintana) takes place on the first Sunday in August. Children love this medieval-style joust and the processions of richly caparisoned horses that wind through the streets of the old town. The Ascoli tourist office (⊠ Piazza del Popolo 1, ☎ 0736/253045) has details.

Dining and Lodging

$$–$$$ ✕ **Ristorante Tornasacco.** The owners of this place, one of Ascoli Piceno's oldest restaurants, pride themselves on meaty local specialties such as *olive ascolane* (olives stuffed with minced meat, breaded and deep-fried), *maccheroncini alla contadina* (homemade short pasta in a lamb, pork, and veal sauce), and *bistecca di toro* (bull steak). *Piazza del Popolo 36,* ☎ *0736/254151. AE, DC, MC, V. Closed Fri., July 15–31, and Dec. 23–28.*

$$ ⊡ **Il Pennile.** A grove of olive trees surrounds this small, family-run hotel just outside the old city center and a short walk from the train station. Guest rooms are soberly decorated and functional, but offer good views of the city. *Via G. Spalvieri, 63100,* ☎ *0736/41645,* FAX *0736/342755. 28 rooms. Room TVs. AE, DC, MC, V.*

PERUGIA AND NORTHERN UMBRIA A TO Z

To research prices, get advice from other travelers, and book travel arrangements, visit www.fodors.com.

AGRITOURIST AGENCIES

➤ AGENTS: **Agriturist, Umbria** (✉ Via San Bartolomeo 79, Perugia 06087, ☎ 075/5997289, WEB www.agriturist.it). **Turismo Verde** (✉ Via Maria Angeloni 1, Perugia 06125, ☎ 075/5002953, FAX 075/5002956, WEB www.turismoverde.it).

AIRPORTS

Central Italy's closest major airports are Rome's Fiumicino (officially Aeroporto Leonardo da Vinci), Pisa's Galileo Galilei, and Florence's Peretola (officially Aeroporto A. Vespucci). Tiny Aeroporto Sant'Egidio, 12 km (7 mi) east of Perugia, has flights to and from Milan, Rome (Ciampino), and Palermo.

➤ AIRPORT INFORMATION: **Aeroporto A. Vespucci** (known as Peretola; ☎ 055/3061700). **Aeroporto Galileo Galilei** (☎ 050/500707, WEB www.pisa-airport.com). **Aeroporto Leonardo da Vinci** (known as Fiumicino; ☎ 06/6594420, WEB www.adr.it). **Aeroporto Sant'Egidio** (☎ 075/592141, WEB www.airport.umbria.it).

BUS TRAVEL

Perugia is served by the Sulga Line with daily departures from Rome's Stazione Tiburtina and from Piazza Adua in Florence. Connections between Rome, Spoleto, and the Marches are provided by the associated bus companies Bucci & Soget.

Local bus service between all the major and minor towns of Umbria is good. Some of the routes in rural areas, especially in the Marches, are designed to serve as many places as possible and are, therefore, quite roundabout and slow. Schedules change often, so consult with local tourist offices before setting out.

➤ BUS LINES: **Bucci & Soget** (☎ 0721/32401, WEB www.mediaworks.it/bucci.htm). **Sulga Line** (☎ 075/5009641, WEB www.sulga.it).

CAR RENTALS

➤ AGENCIES: **Avis** (WEB www.avis.com; ✉ Aeroporto Sant'Egidio, Perugia, ☎ 075/6929796; ✉ Stazione Ferroviaria Fontivegge, Piazza Vittorio Veneto 7, Perugia, ☎ 075/5000395; ✉ Via Piero della Francesca 20, Città di Castello, ☎ 075/8558534). **Hertz** (WEB www.hertz.com; ✉ Piazza Vittorio Veneto 4, Perugia, ☎ 075/5002439; ✉ Aeroporto Sant'Egidio, Via Aeroporto, Perugia, ☎ 075/5002439).

CAR TRAVEL

Umbria has a good road network. Highway 75 bis links Perugia to Tuscany (to Siena via S326 and E76) and to the Florence–Rome Autostrada del Sole (A1), Italy's main north–south highway; S75 bis also goes right by Lago Trasimeno. However, travel through the mountains to Urbino can be a bit treacherous because of the winding roads; plan for plenty of travel time.

The A14 superhighway travels southeast from Bologna and follows the Adriatic coast through the entire length of the Marches; branches lead to Urbino, Ancona, Loreto, and Ascoli Piceno. SS San Marino, a state highway, takes you to the Republic of San Marino from Rimini.

EMERGENCIES

If you have ongoing medical concerns, it's a good idea to make sure someone is on duty all night where you're staying—not a given in Umbria, less so in the Marches. As elsewhere in Italy, every pharmacy in Umbria and the Marches bears a sign at the door listing area pharmacies open in off-hours. Perugia, Gubbio, and Urbino all have at least one so-called "night" pharmacy, but out in the countryside you may need a car to get to one.

➤ EMERGENCY SERVICES: **Ambulance** (☎ 118). **Fire department** (☎ 115). **Police** (☎ 113).

TRAIN TRAVEL

Several direct daily trains link Florence and Perugia. Otherwise, a change between the Florence–Chiusi–Rome line and the Perugia line is required at Terontola. The Florence–Chiusi train stops at Castiglione del Lago, on Lago Trasimeno, and sometimes at Città della Pieve as well. Daily direct service between Perugia and Rome is available, but this service isn't frequent and a change at Foligno, from the main Rome–Ancona line, is often required. Main rail lines, with fast Intercity and Eurocity trains, link Ancona with Bologna and Rome. A small, privately owned railway, Ferrovia Centrale Umbra, runs south from Città di Castello to Terni via Perugia. Gubbio and San Marino have no train service.

➤ TRAIN LINES: **Ferrovia Centrale Umbra** (☎ 075/5729121). **Ferrovia dello Stato** (Italian State Railway; ☎ 848/888088 toll-free in Italy, WEB www.fs-on-line.it).

VISITOR INFORMATION

Umbria's regional tourism bureau is in Perugia.

➤ TOURIST INFORMATION: **Ancona** (✉ Via Thaon de Revel 4, ☎ 071/358991, WEB www.comune.ancona.it). **Ascoli Piceno** (✉ Piazza del Popolo 1, ☎ 0736/257288, WEB www.ascolipiceno.com). **Assisi** (✉ Piazza del Comune 12, ☎ 075/812534, WEB www.comune.assisi.pg.it). **Città della Pieve** (✉ Piazza Matteotti 4, ☎ 075/8299375). **Città di Castello** (✉ Piazza Fanti, ☎ 075/8554922). **Deruta** (✉ Piazza dei Consoli 4, ☎ 075/9711559). **Gubbio** (✉ Piazza Oderisi 6, ☎ 075/9220693). **Lago Trasimeno** (✉ Piazza Mazzini 10, Castiglione del Lago, ☎ 075/9652484). **Perugia** (✉ Piazza IV Novembre 3, ☎ 075/5736458 or 075/5723327, WEB www.comune.perugia.it). **San Marino** (✉ Contrada Omagnano 20, ☎ 0549/882412, WEB www.sanmarinosite.com). **Umbria** (✉ Corso Vannucci 30, Perugia, ☎ 075/5041). **Urbino** (✉ Piazza Duca Federico 35, ☎ 0722/2613, WEB www.comune.orvieto.tr.it).

9 ASSISI, SPOLETO, AND SOUTHERN UMBRIA

Legends linger in smiling Umbria, ethereal birthplace of the saints. Here awaits a host of treasures, with Assisi's Basilica di San Francesco and Orvieto's legendary cathedral the jewels in the artistic crown. Southern Umbria's wealth of hill towns, connected by sinuous roads lined with olive groves and vineyards, proves that central Italy doesn't begin and end with Tuscany.

Updated by
Peter Blackman

IN DISCOVERING THE PEACE AND TRANQUILLITY of the green Umbrian plains, we're really just following in the footsteps of the centuries of pilgrims who paid homage to one of Italy's most important religious figures, St. Francis of Assisi. Francis's hometown is the area's centerpiece, often overflowing with tour buses and crowds but nonetheless worth a visit if only to see the famous Basilica di San Francesco. A repository of some of Western art's most important paintings, the basilica is itself a showpiece of art—and art restoration. Farther down the Valle Umbra is a succession of lovely hill towns: Spello, Montefalco, and Trevi—easy-living hamlets well worth a stroll or lazy lunch. At the end of the valley is the medieval town of Spoleto, which puts on the Festival dei Due Mondi, a world-famous arts extravaganza. And there's plenty more to see beyond: east takes you through lush, mountainous terrain toward food-mad Norcia; to the west are the shadowy walled towns of Narni and Amelia as well as stunning Orvieto and Todi.

Given its size, Southern Umbria has an almost unfair concentration of enchanting towns, splendid vistas, and rich local culture—all waiting to be discovered. And while these towns don't offer the vast wealth of art and architecture you will find in Florence or Rome, this actually works in your favor; individual towns can be experienced whole, the way people live in them today, rather than as a forced march through a series of museums and churches. In Southern Umbria, art and history come in small bites, with plenty of good meals and relaxing walks in between.

Pleasures and Pastimes

Dining
The food of Southern Umbria is typically hearty and straightforward, with a stick-to-the-ribs quality that sees hardworking farmers and artisans through a long day's work and helps them make the steep climb home at night. You are never far from a rotisserie grill or fireplace, or a bowl of hot *ciriole* (roughly shaped thick spaghetti, often made in-house) or *stringozzi* (pasta slightly thinner than ciriole, also spelled *strangozzi*) laced with a light tomato or meat sauce. Truffles are the local delicacy, and you'll find the extravagantly flavored fungus shaved over pasta, pounded into sauces, or used to perfume meat—try it all, and you'll see what the fuss is about. The tiny town of Norcia deserves special mention for its cured pork-meat products, famous throughout Italy, yet difficult to find once you leave town; they go wonderfully well with the bread of the region, which is often made without salt. The nearby town of Castelluccio is renowned for its tiny, tender, and tasty lentils. Umbria is landlocked, but fish from the lakes and streams do have a role in local cooking—a famous dish is the *carpa in porchetta,* made with giant 40-pound carps that are dressed and roasted like suckling pigs.

Umbrian olive oil, essential to the local cuisine, is every bit as good as the more famous Tuscan olive oils (and less expensive). The basic cheese of the region is a soft pecorino (sheep's-milk cheese). It's often flavored with truffles or herbs and either eaten as a spread or stirred into hot pasta. Cheeses from neighboring Tuscany and Lazio also make their way to the Umbrian table. The monasteries and convents throughout the region produce various multicolor *rosolii* (sweet liqueurs) and digestive bitters, sold in all types of gift bottles. Desserts are strictly local, usually made with fruit, nuts, honey, and spices.

Wine making is nothing new to Umbria, where Sagrantino di Montefalco and Orvieto Classico are among Italy's oldest varieties, but mass commercialization has left them with middling reputations and decisively overshadowed by Tuscan varieties. Renewed attention in the region to top-quality wine making has produced such full-bodied winners as Rubesco and Torre di Giano, definitely worth seeking out.

CATEGORY	COST*
$$$$	over €18
$$$	€13–€18
$$	€8–€13
$	under €8

Prices are for a second course (secondo piatto).

Lodging

The main towns in Southern Umbria generally have one or two hotels in a high price category, and a few smaller, basic hotels in the inexpensive-to-moderate ($–$$) range, often family run. Since the early 1990s, some old villas and monasteries have been converted into small, first-class hotels. These tend to be out in the countryside, but the splendor of the settings often outweighs the problem of getting into town. If you plan to stay in the area for a few days or more, consider a cottage or apartment in the countryside (*agriturismo*); these offer excellent value and an interesting alternative to the usual hotels. Reservations are always advisable, and essential if you plan to visit Spoleto during the Festival dei Due Mondi (late June to early July) or Assisi from Easter through October.

CATEGORY	COST*
$$$$	over €175
$$$	€125–€175
$$	€75–€125
$	under €75

All prices are for two people in a standard double room, including tax and service.

St. Francis

Born to a noblewoman and a well-to-do merchant in 1181, Francis led a troubled youth and spent a year in prison. Although he planned on a career in the military, after a long illness he heard the voice of God, publicly renounced his father's wealth, and began a life of austerity. His mystical approach to poverty, asceticism, and the beauty of man and nature struck a responsive cord in the medieval mind, and he quickly attracted a vast number of followers. Without actively seeking power, he became very influential and changed the history of the Catholic Church. In 1209, his order was recognized by Pope Innocent III (circa 1161–1216), and St. Francis later traveled throughout the Mediterranean to spread the word of God. He was the first saint to receive the stigmata (wounds on the hands, feet, and sides, corresponding to those of Christ on the cross). He died on October 4, 1226, in the Porziuncola, the secluded chapel in the woods where he had first preached the virtue of poverty to his disciples.

The Franciscans are the largest of all Catholic orders. Among the clergy at Assisi, you can identify the saint's followers by their simple, coarse brown habits bound by sashes of knotted rope. St. Francis was made the patron saint of Italy in 1939 and is remembered as the gentle man who spoke to the birds. His *Canticle to the Creatures,* one of the first written examples of the Italian vernacular, is still taught in schools today.

Exploring Southern Umbria

The main towns in the region are easily accessible from Rome and Florence by road or rail, and despite the hilly terrain, getting around

TRUFFLE TROUBLE

UMBRIA IS RICH WITH TRUFFLES—more are found here than any-where else in Italy, and those not consumed fresh are pro-cessed into pastes or flavored oils. The primary truffle areas are around Spoleto (signs warning against unlicensed truf-fle hunting are posted at the base of the Ponte delle Torri) and the hills around the tiny town of Norcia, which holds a truffle festival every February. But even though truffles grow locally, the rare delicacy can cost a small fortune, up to $200 for a quarter pound (fortunately, a little goes a long way).

At such a price, there is great competition among the nearly 10,000 registered truffle hunters in the province, who use specially trained dogs to sniff them out among the roots of several trees, including oak and ilex. Although there have been incidents of truffle-hunting dogs being poisoned and of inferior varieties being imported from China, you can be reasonably assured that the truffle shaved onto your pasta has been unearthed locally.

The kind of truffle you taste will depend on the season: in summer, there's the *scorzone* (rough-skinned, dark gray-brown); the fall rains bring out the *bianchetto* (a small, smoother dirty-white variety); and the prized *tartufo nero* (black truffle) appears from December through March. Out of season, restaurants rely on preserved truffles (in olive oil, vacuum-sealed, frozen, or ground into a paste).

Southern Umbria is actually a snap. The main highways run southeast from Perugia through or near the main towns, which are almost all linked by fairly frequent train and bus service. Distances are relatively short from one town to the next, and Assisi and Spoleto are the most sensible bases from which to explore the rest of the region. A car is a must.

Numbers in the text correspond to numbers in the margin and on the Assisi, Spoleto, and Southern Umbria; Assisi; Spoleto; and Orvieto maps.

Great Itineraries

Southern Umbria is particularly well suited to touring in a limited time, as you can easily hop from one town to the next with a minimum of distance or difficulty. Alternatively, any of the towns, with the exception of Norcia to the east, can be covered in day trips from Perugia.

IF YOU HAVE 5 DAYS

Begin in ⊞ **Assisi** ①–⑥ with the Basilica di San Francesco, seeing the town's other major sites, including the tiny Museo Civico and fortress. Using Assisi as a base, spend the following day visiting some of the delightful hill towns in the Valle Umbra to the south, such as ⊞ **Spello** ⑦ or **Montefalco** ⑩. Devote the third day to good walks through the narrow streets of ⊞ **Spoleto** ⑫–㉑, including a walk across the Ponte delle Torri and around the pretty Monteluco. After spending the night in Spoleto, go east to **Norcia** ㉒ for a day hike and a sampling of the

Assisi, Spoleto, and Southern Umbria

savory local sausage before returning to Spoleto for the night, or head south to the towns of **Narni** ㉖ and **Amelia** ㉗. On Day 5 visit quaint **Todi** ㉙ and the legendary Duomo and museums in nearby **Orvieto** ㉚–㊱.

IF YOU HAVE 7 OR 8 DAYS

Use 🏨 **Assisi** ①–⑥ or nearby 🏨 **Spello** ⑦ as your base for the first three nights. Spend the first day discovering Assisi. The following day, make your way through the Franciscan sites outside the walls, like Eremo delle Carceri and the church of San Damiano, leaving time to explore Spello and **Foligno** ⑧. The third day can be spent visiting the other small and charming hill towns of the Valle Umbra. On the fourth day head south to 🏨 **Spoleto** ⑫–㉑. The following day, go east to **Norcia** ㉒ for a day's outing, being sure to try the sausage before returning to Spoleto for the night. The sixth day could be spent between the towns of **Terni** ㉕, **Narni** ㉖, and **Amelia** ㉗, or at the waterfalls at Marmore and lovely Lake Piediluco, before heading to **Todi** ㉙. On the final day, visit Todi and the Duomo and museums in nearby **Orvieto** ㉚–㊱.

When to Tour Southern Umbria

The forested hills of Southern Umbria ensure beguiling colors in the fall and an explosion of greenery and flowers in the spring. Keep in mind that winter can be cold, and that many hotels and restaurants close for some portion of it. Book accommodations far in advance if you are planning to visit Spoleto in June or July during the Festival dei Due Mondi. It's always a good idea to reserve in advance in Assisi, but the city is especially crowded during Christmas, Easter, the Festa di San Francesco (October 4), and the Calendimaggio festival (early May).

ASSISI

The legacy of St. Francis, founder of the Franciscan monastic order, pervades the rose-colored hills of Assisi. Each year, several million pilgrims come here to pay homage to the man who made God accessible to so many. But not even the constant flood of visitors to this town of just 3,000 residents can spoil the singular beauty of this significant religious center, the home of some of the Western tradition's most important works of art. The hill on which Assisi sits rises dramatically from the flat plain, and the town is dominated by a medieval castle on the mount's top. On the lower slopes of the hill is the massive Basilica di San Francesco, rising majestically on graceful arched supports.

Like most other towns in the region, Assisi began as an Umbri settlement in the 7th century BC and was conquered by the Romans 400 years later. The town was Christianized by St. Rufino, its patron saint, in AD 238, but it is the spirit of St. Francis, patron saint of Italy and founder of the Franciscan monastic order, that is felt throughout its narrow medieval streets. The famous 13th-century basilica built in his honor was decorated by the greatest artists of the period. Assisi is pristinely medieval in architecture and appearance, due in large part to relative neglect from the 16th century until 1926, when the celebration of the 700th anniversary of St. Francis's death brought more than 2 million visitors. Since then, Assisi has become one of the most important pilgrimage destinations in the Christian world.

A series of earthquakes in the fall of 1997 devastated Umbria and Le Marche, rendering countless homes uninhabitable and causing the partial collapse of a ceiling in the Basilica di San Francesco, frescoed with some of the great masterpieces of Giotto and Cimabue. It was feared that the frescoes, reduced to rubble, were beyond repair, but an ongoing and massive effort by art restorers and volunteers is saving some of them. The Upper Basilica, closed for more than two years, has reopened (albeit with blank spaces in the ceiling where the frescoes used to be). A few of Assisi's medieval stone buildings are still propped up by scaffolds, but extensive work has restored most of the town to its former state.

Exploring Assisi

Assisi lies on the Terontola–Foligno rail line, with almost hourly connections to Perugia and direct trains to Rome and Florence several times a day. The train station is 4 km (2½ mi) from town, with bus service about every half hour. Assisi is easily reached from the A1 Motorway (Rome–Florence) and the S75b highway. The walled town is closed to outside traffic, so cars must be left in the parking lots at Porta San Pietro (the gate just below Porta San Francesco), near Porta Nuova, or beneath Piazza Matteotti. It's a short but sometimes steep walk into the center of town; frequent minibuses (buy tickets from a newsstand or tobacconist) make the rounds for weary pilgrims.

A Good Walk

Much of your visit to Assisi will likely be spent visiting its churches and walking its narrow cobblestone streets. Make your first stop the **Basilica di San Francesco** ①, seeing both the Lower and Upper basilicas. Via San Francesco leads uphill from the Basilica di San Francesco, past souvenir and antiques shops, residential buildings, and the temporary home of the **Pinacoteca Comunale** ②. Up ahead is Piazza del Comune, the town square built in the Middle Ages over Roman remains, which can be viewed through the adjacent **Museo Civico** ③. On

Assisi

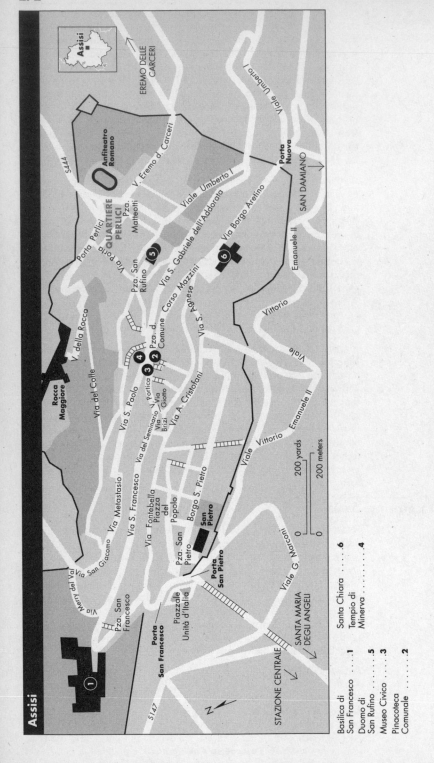

Basilica di
San Francesco **1**
Duomo di
San Rufino **5**
Museo Civico **3**
Pinacoteca
Comunale **2**

Santa Chiara **6**
Tempio di
Minerva **4**

the left side of the square is the graceful, if architecturally incongruous, **Tempio di Minerva** ④, among the best-preserved Roman-era facades in Italy. From the piazza, Via di San Rufino leads up to the **Duomo di San Rufino** ⑤, which houses the remains of the town's "other" saint, the martyred 3rd-century bishop who brought Christianity to Assisi. To the side is the small Museo Capitolare, with detached frescoes and artifacts from the church; admission includes a visit to the 11th-century crypt. Double back to Piazza del Comune and follow Corso Mazzini to **Santa Chiara** ⑥; then continue through Porta Nuova to the church of San Damiano, a 1½-km (1-mi) walk outside the walls. Also of interest outside the walls are the Eremo delle Carceri, east of the center along Via Santuario delle Carceri, and the church of Santa Maria degli Angeli, near the train station.

TIMING

Although the itinerary can be done in as little as a half day, it is a shame to be in a rush in a place as peaceful as Assisi, and a full day is recommended. An especially pleasant way to work up an appetite for dinner is to take part in the *passeggiata* (evening stroll) along the long streets (Via Fontebella, Via San Francesco) that cross the hill, where you can catch glimpses of the valley below and plenty of local color.

Sights to See

★ ❶ **Basilica di San Francesco.** Construction on the basilica was begun by followers of St. Francis in 1228, two years after his death. They finished what is now the Lower Basilica in just a few years. Less than half a century later, Franciscan leaders from Northern Europe crossed the Alps and arrived in Assisi. They built a second church right on top of the first; with soaring arches and stained glass, its Gothic style is a stark contrast to the dark and somber, Romanesque-Lombard Lower Basilica. The two levels are brought together by a 13th-century campanile (bell tower) and a Romanesque facade. Inside, the walls and ceilings are decorated with masterpieces by the greatest artists of the period.

At first, the grandeur of the basilica might seem at odds with the tenets of the Franciscan order, expressed in the credo "Carry nothing for the journey, neither purse nor bag nor bread nor money." But it is important to consider the essential role this church served for pilgrims as far back as the 14th century. Great works of art and lavish decoration were seen as an homage to saintliness, intended to elevate—as well as disquiet—the soul.

The **Upper Basilica,** which has drawn pilgrims, was devastated in the earthquakes of 1997. Portions of its vaulted ceiling collapsed over the entrance and the altar, killing four people and reducing ceiling frescoes by Giotto and his teacher, Cimabue, virtually to dust. Although it was feared that the frescoes could never be reconstructed, art restorers have used specially designed computers to piece some sections back together. It is hoped that in the future some of the frescoes will be back on display. For now, the ceiling is patched with white plaster.

Fortunately, Giotto's 28-panel fresco cycle, the *Life of St. Francis,* survived the earthquakes virtually unscathed. Giotto is often considered the first true Renaissance painter, and the innovations of his work, basic as they may seem to modern eyes, were in his time revolutionary. The roundness, depth, and weight of his figures, his knowing use of perspective, and the three-dimensionality of his painted space set the artistic stage for later masters, including Michelangelo, Leonardo, and Raphael.

View the panels of this landmark work from left to right, starting in the transept; the narration closely follows the biography of the saint given by St. Bonaventure. Although St. Francis's days were mostly filled with miracles and mystic visions, Giotto doesn't dwell much on the myth of the fragile, pure, and holy poor man. Instead, he portrays a powerful, good friar who worked actively and with deep commitment for his community. Giotto's St. Francis is a robust man busy meeting people in front of real buildings and trees; rather than floating through the clouds, the saint has his feet set firmly on the ground.

The first four episodes are a prelude to the fifth, in which St. Francis renounces his worldly goods. Episodes 6 to 20 depict St. Francis's miraculous works; look for *The Sermon to the Birds,* a touching image that sums up the gentle spirit of the saint. Its airy, light depiction of nature is in contrast to *St. Francis Appearing before Pope Innocent III in a Dream,* in which the pope dreams of a humble monk who will steady the church. In the panel next to the one of the sleeping pope, you see a strong St. Francis supporting a church that seems on the verge of tumbling down. Other famous scenes include *St. Francis Appearing to His Companions in a Flaming Chariot*; *St. Francis Proposing Trial by Fire before the Sultan*; and *St. Francis Chasing the Devils from Arezzo.* The 19th and 20th panels solemnly illustrate St. Francis receiving the stigmata, followed by his death and funeral. Aside from a depiction of St. Clare mourning her friend, the last eight episodes refer to the canonization of St. Francis (panel 24) and the miracles he performed after his death.

In the transept of the Upper Basilica are frescoes (in poor condition) by Cimabue (circa 1240–1302). Note the inlaid choir, a 16th-century masterpiece of 105 stalls that are decorated with episodes from the lives of famous Franciscan friars, and the 13th-century stained-glass windows (also used in the lower church), among the oldest in existence.

Around the left side of the facade and beneath a Renaissance porch is the entrance to the **Lower Basilica.** The low ceilings and dimly lit interior contrast sharply with the soaring, airy space above, but it seems an appropriate shrine for the tomb of St. Francis, beneath the main altar. Stairs at the sides of the nave lead down to the crypt. The saint's body was once visible through a window but was hidden away in the 15th century when rival towns threatened to steal it. The simple stone coffin was hidden so well, in fact, that in 1818 it took excavators 52 days to recover it; it was then reinterred in the center of the crypt, with the tombs of his four closest disciples placed at the corners.

The frescoes on the four sections of the cross-vaulting above the main altar are attributed to a student of Giotto. They represent allegories of the Franciscan virtues (*Poverty, Chastity,* and *Obedience*) and *The Triumph of St. Francis.* In the right transept is Cimabue's *Madonna and Child Enthroned, with Four Angels and St. Francis,* which may look familiar—it features one of the best-known images of the saint. Just below are the tombs of five of St. Francis's early followers, with their portraits by Pietro Lorenzetti (circa 1280–1348) on the wall above. By the same artist, in the left transept, is a moving group of frescoes that depicts the *Passion of Christ* with particular expressiveness and tension.

Also worth a look is the **Cappella di San Martino** (first on the left of the nave), with frescoes of the *Life of St. Martin* (1322) by Sienese master Simone Martini (circa 1284–1344). The cycle begins at the lower left, with the famous scene of St. Martin sharing his cloak with Christ, who is disguised as a poor man (he is barefoot, in torn garments, and covering himself from the cold). The scenes continue with the saint's knighthood and his renunciation of the sword. The frescoes along the walls on either side of the nave, by an unknown artist, present the lives of Christ and St. Francis and served as inspiration to Giotto's more fa- mous *Life of St. Francis* cycle in the Upper Basilica. The **Cappella della Maddalena** (last chapel in the right nave) contains frescoes of the life of St. Mary Magdalen by Giotto and assistants.

Steps lead up from the transepts of the lower church to the **Cloister,** where a well-stocked shop sells souvenirs and books and other items related to Saint Francis and Assisi. A small door leads from the Clois- ter to the **Treasury,** where precious religious objects belonging to the church, such as carved crucifixes, ivories, and tapestries, are on dis- play. Admission to the Treasury is free but donations are accepted. The basilica is run by monks, who give informal tours in English; call ahead to make sure someone is available. In addition to normal ser- vices, there are special celebrations throughout the year. On October 4, the anniversary of St. Francis's death, a ceremony is held in which olive oil is offered to the saint for the lamp that burns above his tomb. Masses are sung during Easter week, and special ceremonies during Lent re-create the lives of St. Francis and Jesus. Note: The dress code here (no bare shoulders or bare knees) is strictly enforced. ⊠ *Piazza di San Francesco,* ☎ *075/819001.* ☒ *Free.* ☉ *Lower Basilica, Easter– Oct, daily 6–6:50PM; Nov.–Easter, daily 6–5:50. Upper Basilica, Easter– Oct., daily 8:30–6:50; Nov.–Easter, daily 8:30–5:50.*

❺ **Duomo di San Rufino.** Sts. Francis and Clare were among those bap- tized in Assisi's Duomo, which was the principal church in town until the 12th century. The baptismal font has since been redecorated, but it is possible to see the crypt of St. Rufino, the martyred 3rd-century bishop who brought Christianity to Assisi. Admission to the crypt in- cludes a look at the small **Museo Capitolare,** where there are detached frescoes and artifacts. ⊠ *Piazza San Rufino,* ☎ *075/812283.* ☒ *Crypt and Museo Capitolare €2.07.* ☉ *Duomo, daily 7–noon and 2–sunset; Crypt and Museo, Mid-Mar.–mid-Oct., daily 10–1 and 2–5; mid-Oct.– mid-Mar., daily 10:30–1 and 3–6.*

OFF THE BEATEN PATH

EREMO DELLE CARCERI – Just 4 km (2½ mi) east of Assisi is a monastery set in dense wood against Monte Subasio. The "Hermitage of Prisons" was the place where St. Francis and his followers went to "imprison" them- selves in prayer. The only site in Assisi that remains essentially unchanged since St. Francis's times, the church and monastery are the kinds of oases of tranquillity that St. Francis would have appreciated. The walk out from town is very pleasant, and many trails lead from here across the wooded hillside of Monte Subasio (now a protected forest), with beautiful vistas across the Umbrian countryside. True to their Franciscan heritage, the fri- ars here are entirely dependent on alms from visitors. ⊠ *Via Rufino C., Eremo delle Carceri,* ☎ *075/812301.* ☒ *Donations accepted.* ☉ *Nov.– Mar., daily 6:30–5; Apr.–Oct., daily 6:30–7.*

❸ **Museo Civico.** Lest you forget that Assisi didn't begin and end with St. Francis, have a look at this one-room museum's trove of ancient Roman and Umbrian artifacts. The collection, housed in the crypt of a former church, is all the more interesting for its incongruity in this medieval- Renaissance town. Down a hallway to the right is an excavated ancient gallery, under Piazza del Comune; once thought to be the remains of the Roman-era forum, it is now believed to have been a sacred site, which jibes with its position in front of the Tempio di Minerva. ⊠ *Via Por- tica 2,* ☎ *075/813053.* ☒ *€2.50.* ☉ *Mid-Mar.–mid-Oct., daily 10–1 and 2–6; mid-Oct.–mid-Mar., daily 10–1 and 2–5.*

❷ **Pinacoteca Comunale.** The city art gallery was housed in the six-cen- tury-old city hall building at Palazzo dei Priori until damage from the

1997 earthquakes forced the building to close. After years of hopeful waiting, the collection of early paintings by Umbrian masters was reopened in this temporary location. ⊠ *Palazzo Vallemani, Via San Francesco 12,* ☎ *075/812033.* ☑ *€2.20.* ☺ *Mid-Mar.–Oct., daily 10–1 and 2–6; Nov.–mid-Mar., daily 10–1 and 2–5.*

Rocca Maggiore. Even if there isn't much to see inside this 14th-century fortress, the views are well worth the walk up to the peak, day or night. On the way, pass through the Quartiere Perlici, a little neighborhood with narrow streets that follow a symmetrical Roman layout; in one part the houses and street trace the elliptical plan of the 1st-century Anfiteatro Romano (Roman Amphitheater) that stood on the site. Although the Rocca largely escaped damage during the 1997 earthquakes, it was struck by lightning in 2000 that caused the collapse of a small section of wall at the entrance. ⊠ *At the end of Via della Rocca,* ☎ *075/815292.* ☑ *€1.70.* ☺ *Daily 10–sunset.*

OFF THE BEATEN PATH
SAN DAMIANO – Pleasantly situated in an olive grove, this church seems much more in keeping with the spirit of St. Francis and his followers than the great basilica across town, and for all its austerity, its history is closely tied to that of the city's saints. St. Francis composed his *Canticle of the Creatures* here, and it was here that a crucifix (now in Santa Chiara) spoke to him: "*Vade, Francisce, et repara domum meam*" ("Go, Francis, and repair my house"). Francis took the command literally: he not only set out to reform the church, but he also had the building restored. St. Clare, after taking the Franciscan vows, lived out her life in the convent of this church, attracting a wide following and fame for her piety. In a Papal Bull in 1253, Pope Innocent IV (died 1254) confirmed her order, the Poor Clares; she died the next day. Shortly before her death, she reported having "seen" masses held in the Basilica di San Francesco. For this reason she was designated the patron saint of television in the 1950s. ⊠ *Località San Damiano, 1½ km (1 mi) south, outside the walls of Assisi,* ☎ *075/812273.* ☑ *Free.* ☺ *Daily 10–noon and 2–6.*

❻ **Santa Chiara.** The lovely, wide piazza in front of this church is reason enough to stop by, its panoramic view over the Umbrian plains framed by the red- and white-striped facade of the church itself. Santa Chiara is dedicated to St. Clare, one of the earliest and most fervent of St. Francis's followers and the founder of the order of the Poor Ladies, or Poor Clares, which was based on the Franciscan monastic order. The church contains Clare's body, and in the **Cappella del Crocifisso** (on the right) is the cross that spoke to St. Francis. A heavily veiled nun of the Poor Clares order usually is stationed before the cross in adoration of the image. ⊠ *Piazza Santa Chiara,* ☎ *075/812282.* ☑ *Free.* ☺ *Daily 7–noon and 2–sunset.*

OFF THE BEATEN PATH
SANTA MARIA DEGLI ANGELI – Down by the train station, 8 km (5 mi) south of Assisi, this hulking Baroque church, restored in the 19th century, was built over the **Porziuncola**, St. Francis's little chapel in the forest. The shrine is much venerated: it was in the adjacent **Cappella Transito**, then a humble cell, that St. Francis died on the bare earth, wearing a borrowed tunic. ⊠ *Località Santa Maria degli Angeli,* ☎ *075/80511.* ☑ *Free.* ☺ *Daily 6:15 AM–8 PM.*

❹ **Tempio di Minerva.** Dating from the time of the emperor Augustus (27 BC–AD 14), this structure was used as a monastery and prison before being converted into a church in the 16th century. The expectations raised by the perfect classical facade are not met by the interior, which was subjected to a thorough Baroque assault in the 17th century. ⊠ *Piazza del Comune,* ☎ *no phone.* 🎫 *Free.* ☉ *Daily 7–noon and 2:30–sunset.*

Dining and Lodging

Assisi is not a late-night town, so don't plan on any midnight snacks. What you can count on is the ubiquitous stringozzi, as well as the local specialty *piccione all'assisana* (roasted pigeon with olives and liver). The locals eat *torta al testo* (a dense flatbread, often stuffed with vegetables or cheese) with their meals. Assisi doesn't have any bakeries (the bread comes from surrounding towns), but there are several pastry shops, featuring, of course, *pane di San Francesco* (an egg bread sweetened with raisins and sugar) and *rocciata di Assisi* (the local version of strudel, filled with apples, nuts, raisins, and dried fruit). A tantalizing display of these tasty treats fills the shop window of **Bottega del Pasticcere** (⊠ Via Portica 9, ☎ 075/812392). For something sweet on your way to visit the church of Santa Chiara, try **Fratelli Sensi** (⊠ Corso Mazzini 14, ☎ 075/812529).

Advance room reservations are absolutely essential if you are visiting Assisi between Easter and October or over Christmas, especially since hotels in the town itself are the first to fill up. Latecomers are often left to choose from those in the modern town of Santa Maria degli Angeli, 8 km (5 mi) away; if you have a car, Spello might be a more pleasant option.

Until the early 1980s, pilgrim hostels outnumbered ordinary hotels in Assisi, and they present an intriguing alternative to conventional lodgings. Usually called *conventi* or *ostelli* (convents or hostels) because they're run by private convents, churches, or Catholic organizations, they have rooms that are on the spartan side. However, you are virtually assured of a peaceful stay. Check with the tourist office for a list.

$$$ ✕ **San Francesco.** Here's your chance to dine in front of the Basilica di San Francesco, although you'll certainly do better than bread and water. The cuisine is the fanciest in town, with creative Umbrian dishes based on local ingredients and aromatic herbs. The menu changes periodically but might include dishes like *gnocchi alla melanzana* (eggplant gnocchi) and *oca stufata di finocchio selvaggio* (goose stuffed with wild fennel). ⊠ *Via di San Francesco 52,* ☎ *075/812329. AE, DC, MC, V. Closed Wed.*

$–$$ ✕ **La Buca di San Francesco.** One of Assisi's busiest restaurants, La Buca has a cozy dining room in the cellar and additional seating in the garden. The restaurant belongs to an association that prides itself on authentic regional cooking, and the wine list is among the best in town. The *filetto al rubesco* (fillet steak cooked in a heady red wine) is a specialty of the house. ⊠ *Via Brizi 1,* ☎ *075/812204. Reservations essential. AE, DC, MC, V. Closed Mon. and July.*

$–$$ ✕ **La Fortezza.** Parts of the walls of this modern, family-run restaurant were built by the Romans. The service is personable and the kitchen is reliable. A particular standout is *anatra al finocchio selvatico* (duck cooked with wild fennel). La Fortezza also has seven simple, clean guest rooms available. ⊠ *Vicolo della Fortezza 2/b,* ☎ *075/812418,* WEB *www.lafortezzahotel.com. Reservations essential. AE, DC, MC, V. Closed Thurs. and Feb.*

$–$$ ✕ **La Pallotta.** The women do the cooking and the men serve the food
★ in this cozy, honest family-run trattoria, which may very well be the best place to eat in town. All the local dishes are excellently prepared and reasonably priced—try the *menu degustazione* (tasting menu) or

the stringozzi *alla pallotta* (with a pesto of olives and mushrooms). The interior is cozy, with a fireplace and stone walls. ✉ *Vicolo della Volta Pinta,* ☎ *075/812649. AE, DC, MC, V. Closed Tues. and 2 wks in Jan.–Feb.*

$–$$ ✕ **La Stalla.** A kilometer or two (½–1 mi) outside Assisi proper, this onetime stable is now a simple, rustic restaurant. In summer, self-service lunch and dinner are eaten outside under a trellis shaded with vines and flowers. The kitchen turns out hearty country fare, with meats grilled in the fireplace at the center of the room. ✉ *Via Santuario delle Carceri 8,* ☎ *075/812317. No credit cards. Closed Mon. Oct.–June.*

$ ✕ **Osteria Piazzetta dell'Erba.** A great change of pace in a town with
★ more than its fair share of stodgy tourist eateries, this is an excellent place to come for an informal meal or light snack. There are two different *primi piatti* (first courses) on offer every day, along with various salads and a good selection of toppings to go with the ever-present torta al testo. The "imported" goat cheese is from Sardinia and is a delicious surprise. There are tables outside in the summer. ✉ *Via San Gabriele dell'Addolorata 15b,* ☎ *075/815352. AE, DC, MC, V. Closed Mon. and 3 wks in Jan.*

$$$$ · 🏨 **Fontebella.** Between Piazza del Popolo and the Basilica di San Francesco, the Fontebella has spacious lounges and comfortable rooms (with rather small bathrooms), decorated with cheerful tapestries. The breakfast is especially ample, the welcome warm. ✉ *Via Fontebella 25, 06081,* ☎ *075/812883,* 📠 *075/812941,* 🌐 *www.fontebella.com. 43 rooms, 3 suites. Restaurant, bar, parking (fee). AE, DC, MC, V. CP.*

$$$$ 🏨 **Hotel Subasio.** A little rough around the edges, but by far the fanciest hotel in town, the Subasio is a stone's throw from the Basilica di San Francesco. Housed in a converted monastery, some of the rooms remain a little cell-like, but others are very spacious and furnished with antiques. Most rooms have views of the valley, as do the comfortable old-fashioned sitting rooms, flowered terraces, and lovely garden. ✉ *Via Frate Elia 2, 06081,* ☎ *075/812206,* 📠 *075/816691. 54 rooms, 8 suites. Restaurant, bar. AE, DC, MC, V. CP.*

$$$$ 🏨 **Le Silve.** Not exactly the sort of hermitage in the forest that St. Francis had in mind, Le Silve is a well-restored medieval manor house in the Subasio reserve, just 8 km (5 mi) out of town. All rooms vary in the way they are furnished, but they are always well appointed. Common areas have fireplaces and antiques. The restaurant serves traditional Umbrian fare. ✉ *Località Armenzano, 06081,* ☎ *075/8019000,* 📠 *075/8019005. 15 rooms. Restaurant, pool, horseback riding. AE, DC, MC, V. CP.*

$$–$$$ 🏨 **San Francesco.** You can't beat the location—some of the rooms look out onto the facade of the Basilica di San Francesco, opposite the hotel. Rooms are rather basic, but with nice touches like slippers and a good-night piece of chocolate. The first-rate breakfast includes homemade desserts, fruit, savory tarts, and fresh ricotta. ✉ *Via di San Francesco 48, 06082,* ☎ *075/812281,* 📠 *075/816237,* 🌐 *www. hotelsanfrancescoassisi.it. 44 rooms. Restaurant, bar. AE, DC, MC, V. CP.*

$$ 🏨 **Hotel Umbra.** This 16th-century town house, now a family-run
★ hotel, is in a tranquil part of the city near Piazza del Comune. The rooms, all different and simply appointed, are arranged as small apartments, each with a tiny living room and terrace. In the warm season breakfast is served under the arbor on the patio. The restaurant in the garden serves regional cuisine. ✉ *Via degli Archi 6, 06081,* ☎ *075/ 812240,* 📠 *075/813653,* 🌐 *www.hotelumbra.it. 25 rooms. Restaurant, minibars, bar. AE, DC, MC, V. Closed early Jan.–mid-Mar. CP.*

$ ⊞ **La Pallotta.** Just above a great family-run restaurant of the same name,
★   this hotel is one of the best in its category. The beds are firm, and some
of the rooms look out across the rooftops of town, but the real attraction
is the reading room in the *torretta* (small tower), where there's a 360-
degree view. There is no breakfast, but a self-service bar is available.
⊠ *Via San Rufino 6, 06081,* ☎ *075/812649,* ☎ FAX *075/812307,* WEB
www.pallottaassisi.it. 8 rooms. AE, DC, MC, V.

Performing Arts and Festivals

Concerts are occasionally held in Assisi's various churches; check with
the tourist office or look for signs around town. All the major Catholic
holidays are celebrated with particular enthusiasm. **Calendimaggio,** a
three-day medieval pageant, begins the first Thursday after May 1. It
includes a procession in medieval costume and the singing of madri-
gals to celebrate spring. **Corpus Domini** (the ninth Sunday after Easter)
is celebrated with an *infiorata,* during which the streets are decorated
with flower petals. In the **Festa del Perdono** (Forgiveness Day) on August 1 and 2, crowds of pilgrims walk to the church of Santa Maria
degli Angeli to ask for forgiveness. **St. Clare,** the founder of the order
of Poor Clares, is remembered on her feast day, August 11, with solemn
masses. The last Sunday in August brings celebrations in honor of St.
Rufino, which include processions in historical dress and the **Palio della
Balestra,** a crossbow competition. The high point of the festival year
comes every October 4, with the **Festa di San Francesco,** commemorating the anniversary of St. Francis's death.

Shopping

If you're in the market for a St. Francis cigarette lighter, you've come
to the right place. In addition to the mountains of kitsch emblazoned
with the saint's image, from key chains to Franciscan sandals to tiny
blessed olive trees, Assisi is also well known for white-and-blue *ricamo a punto,* a traditional style of embroidery kept alive by religious institutions over the centuries. A good shop for *ricamo* items
is **Rossi** (⊠ Via Frate Elia 1, ☎ 075/812555). If you will not be passing through Deruta, near Perugia, Assisi has a number of shops that
sell ceramics from the town. You can also pick up Umbrian truffles
and all their aromatic and costly derivatives in Assisi's *alimentari* and
gift shops.

FROM ASSISI TO SPOLETO
Through the Valle Umbra

The main road (SS75) runs straight down the Valle Umbra from Assisi to Spoleto, but you'll do well to stop and smell the flowers in the
towns that line the valley. These sleepy medieval gems each have their
own characteristics but are uniform in the handsomeness of their historic centers. The artistic treasures hidden in their quiet streets would
merit museums anywhere else—here, they're just part of the scenery.

Spello

❼   *12 km (7 mi) southeast of Assisi, 33 km (21 mi) north of Spoleto.*

Although it's half the size of Assisi and has more than twice as many
inhabitants, chances are you'll find Spello relatively empty, perhaps a
welcome relief from where you have just been. Only a few minutes from
Assisi by car or train, this hill town at the edge of Mt. Subasio makes

an excellent base from which to explore the surrounding towns. But Spello has its own appeal, too, with first-rate frescoes by Pinturicchio (1454–1513) and fine Roman ruins.

The Romans called the town Hispellum, and traces remain of their walls, gates, amphitheater, and theater. The town is 1 km (½ mi) from the train station, and buses run every 30 minutes for Porta Consolare, the dilapidated Roman gate at the south end of town and the best place to enter.

From Porta Consolare continue up the steep main street that begins as Via Consolare and changes names several times as it crosses the little town, following the original Roman (main street). As it curves around, notice the winding medieval alleyways to the right and the more uniform Roman-era blocks to the left. Just up ahead is the basilica of **Santa Maria Maggiore,** with vivid frescoes by Pinturicchio in the Cappella Baglioni (1501). Striking in their rich colors, finely dressed figures, and complex symbolism, the *Nativity, Dispute at the Temple* (on the far left side is a portrait of Troilo Baglioni, the prior who commissioned the work), and *Annunciation* (with a self-portrait on the far right) were painted after the artist had already won great acclaim for his work on the Palazzi Vaticani in Rome and are among his finest works. Two pillars on either side of the apse are decorated with frescoes by Perugino (circa 1450–1523), the other great Umbrian artist of the 16th century. ⊠ *Piazza Matteotti 18,* ☎ *0742/301792.* ☒ *Free.* ☉ *May–Sept., daily 8–12:30 and 2:30–7; Oct.–Apr., daily 8–12:30 and 2:30–6.*

The **Pinacoteca Civica,** inside **Palazzo dei Canonici,** holds a rich assortment of art that once adorned the basilica, including several unusual wooden statues that were carried during Easter processions in centuries past. ⊠ *Palazzo dei Canonici, Piazza Matteotti,* ☎ *0742/301497.* ☒ *€2.60.* ☉ *Apr.–Sept., Tues.–Sun. 10:30–1 and 3–6:30; Oct.–Mar., Tues.–Sun. 10–12:30 and 3–5.*

The Gothic church of **Sant' Andrea** has a painting of the *Madonna and Child with Saints* by Pinturicchio, as well as the mummified remains of the church's namesake, who was an early follower of St. Francis. ⊠ *Via Cavour,* ☎ *no phone.* ☒ *Free.* ☉ *May–Sept., daily 8–12:30 and 2:30–7; Oct.–Apr., daily 8–12:30 and 2:30–6.*

Piazza della Repubblica sits at the center of town, with the 13th-century **Vecchio Palazzo Comunale,** one of the oldest town halls in the region, and the small **Museo Emilio Greco** (☎ 0742/30001) inside. Leave some time for strolling around town and stopping at the *belvedere* (panoramic overlook) at the top of Via Torre del Belvedere, with the remains of the Roman amphitheater just below and the surrounding towns in the distance.

OFF THE
BEATEN PATH

VILLA FIDELIA – The road out of town leads past the crumbling remains of the 1st-century AD Anfiteatro Romano (closed to visitors) on the left and the pleasant 12th-century church of San Claudio (also closed to visitors) on the right. Up ahead is Villa Fidelia, an 18th-century mansion modeled on Villa Madama in Rome and surrounded by a beautiful garden. It now holds the small, eclectic **Collezione Straka-Coppa,** set amid the antique furnishings of the villa. You'll find paintings and manifestos from the Italian Futurist movement on the ground floor, an assemblage of early painting on the second floor, and various contemporary pieces on display throughout. The villa occasionally hosts concerts with international artists; ask at local area tourist offices for details. ⊠ *Via Centrale Umbra 70,* ☎ *0742/651726.* ☒ *€2.60.* ☉ *Apr.–June and Sept., Thurs.–Sun. 10:30–1 and 3–6; July–Aug., daily 10:30–1 and 4–7; Oct.–Mar., weekends 10:30–1 and 2:30–5:30.*

Dining and Lodging

$–$$$ ✕ **La Cantina.** As its name implies, this place on the main street is the place to come for wines from all over the country. The menu has many pasta dishes with refreshing seasonal dressings, such as wild asparagus (in spring) or artichokes (in fall and winter). Although the specialty of the house is grilled meat (the prized Tuscan Chianina beef and baby lamb chops), you might be tempted by the pigeon casserole or roasted baby pork. For dessert there's homemade *rocciata* (strudel). ⊠ *Via Cavour 2,* ☎ *0742/651775. AE, DC, MC, V. Closed Wed.*

$–$$ ✕ **Il Cacciatore.** This trattoria run by several generations of the Cruciani family won't win awards for its looks (if weather permits, try the view from the terrace), but the food might be enough to make you check in to the family's adjacent inn and have another meal. The pasta is rolled fresh every day; try the *pappardelle con sugo d'oca* (ribbons of pasta dressed in goose sauce) or tagliatelle with peas and prosciutto; then select from grilled and roasted meats and truffles (in season). Round off your meal with a homemade dessert. ⊠ *Via Giulia 42,* ☎ *0742/ 651141,* ☎ 𝖥𝖠𝖷 *0742/301603. MC, V. Closed Mon., 3 wks in Nov., and 2 wks in July. Lunch Tues., Sat., Sun.*

$$ ✕▥ **La Bastiglia.** This tidy, cozy hotel is a renovated grain mill, but you'll find no grist lying around here. The comfortable sitting rooms and bedrooms are done in soft, light colors with a mix of antique and modern pieces. Rooms on the top floor have views. A separate building with seven additional rooms is surrounded by a cheerful garden. Breakfast includes (appropriately) homemade bread. The terrace looks out onto the green and tranquil valley behind Spello and is used by the hotel's elegant restaurant ($$$$), which serves refined and unusual adaptations of traditional recipes. The menu, which changes with the seasons, has included such dishes as *costoletto di agnello in crosta di pistacchi* (rib of lamb baked in a crust of pistachio nuts) followed by the *rocciata di ananas con sorbetto di peperoncino* (pineapple strudel with a hot-pepper sorbet). ⊠ *Piazza Valle Gloria 17, 06038,* ☎ *0742/651277,* 𝖥𝖠𝖷 *0742/301159,* 𝖶𝖤𝖡 *www.labastiglia.com. 31 rooms, 2 suites. Restaurant, pool, bar. AE, DC, MC, V. Closed early Jan.–early Feb. and late July. CP.*

Festivals

If you happen to be in the area, don't miss thc infiorata on **Corpus Domini** (the ninth Sunday after Easter). The streets of Spello are strewn with flower petals, which are arranged in vast canvases depicting religious subjects. The **Festa dell'Olio,** on the last Sunday of Carnevale, is a celebration of the area's olives and their oil. Streetside booths offer tastings of all kinds of local delicacies during the festival.

Shopping

Spello is a good place to find excellent Umbrian olive oil, carved olive wood, and a variety of hemp (*canapa*) crafts. Try **Frantoio Cianetti** (⊠ Via Bulgarella 10, ☎ 0742/652781), for their own brand of cold-pressed, extra-virgin olive oil. **Angelo Passeri** (⊠ Via Giulia 18, ☎ 0330/ 282104) is a specialist in olive wood carvings and produces works in an amazing variety of forms. At **Le Ali di Paldina** (⊠ Via Sant'Angelo 26, ☎ no phone), you'll find a great variety of woven hemp handicrafts.

Foligno

❽ *5 km (3 mi) southeast of Spello, 18 km (11 mi) southeast of Assisi, 28 km (17 mi) north of Spoleto.*

The third-largest town in Umbria, Foligno has been an important commercial center since the 14th century. It's known for ceramics, miniatures, ironwork, carving, and embroidery (some small workshops can still be found around town). This made the city a target for heavy Allied bombing in World War II; postwar reconstruction and flourishing light industry now obscure much of what must have once been a charming town.

The town also suffered some of the worst damage wrought by the 1997 earthquakes, losing among other things the 14th-century bell tower of the Palazzo Comunale (city hall). Still, the historic center, which retains the old Roman street grid and a medieval feel, has several churches worthy of a stop. Stroll along Via delle Conce and Via dei Molini for views onto the canals. The main shopping street is Corso Cavour.

Find your way to Piazza della Repubblica, the central square in the old part of town. The two-faced 12th-century **Duomo** shows its better side to the piazza—with the elaborate geometric patterns of Cosmati mosaics lining the doorway and fantastic carvings of animals all around. The other facade, renovated in the early years of the 20th century, is around the corner. The interior got a thorough dressing-up in the 18th century. The two busts in the sacristy are attributed to Bernini. ⊠ *Piazza della Repubblica.* ⊞ *Free.* ⊙ *Daily 9–noon.*

The facade of **Palazzo Trinci** is neoclassical, but inside the mostly Gothic interior is an early-15th-century fresco cycle of the personification of the liberal arts by Benozzo Gozzoli (1420–97). The building houses the **Museo Archeologico,** with Roman-era relics found in the area, and the **Pinacoteca Civica,** with works by local painters who made Foligno an important art center in the Renaissance. ⊠ *Piazza della Repubblica,* ☎ *0742/357989.* ⊞ *€5.* ⊙ *Tues.–Sun. 10–7.*

At the other end of town from the Palazzo Trinci, straight down Via Mazzini, is the Romanesque church of **Santa Maria Infraportas.** There are several cycles of votive frescoes in its three naves and 12th-century frescoes in the Byzantine style in the **Cappella dell'Assunta.** ⊠ *Piazza San Domenico,* ☎ *0742/2350517.* ⊞ *Free.* ⊙ *Daily 8–12:30 and 3:30–7.*

Dining and Lodging

$–$$ ✕ **Il Bacco Felice.** Probably the only smoke-free *enoteca* (wine bar) in the entire country, Happy Bacchus is just perfect for a light meal and a glass of wine. The owner personally selects not only the prosciutto and cheeses but even the bread, brought from the best bakeries in the valley. Hot vegetable soups (lentil, fava, barley) and rabbit casseroles are tasty standards here. ⊠ *Via Garibaldi 73–75,* ☎ *0742/341019. AE, DC, MC, V. Closed Mon.*

$$ ▥ **Le Mura.** In the center of town, this quiet hotel has well-appointed rooms and cozy corners to read or sip a cup of tea. The restaurant has a good reputation even among locals, and breakfast includes freshly baked cakes. ⊠ *Via Mentana 25,* ☎ *0742/357344,* ℻ *075/353327,* WEB *www.albergolemura.it. 26 rooms, 3 suites. Restaurant, bar, Internet, meeting rooms, parking (fee). AE, D, MC, V. CP.*

$–$$ ▥ **Villa Roncalli.** You won't have to put up with the creaking and squealing of old floors and fixtures in this late-16th-century villa on the outskirts of town. The 10 rooms have terra-cotta floors and modern furniture. An ample buffet breakfast with homemade bread, jams, and cakes makes it hard to leave. ⊠ *Località Sant'Eraclio, Via Roma 25,* ☎ *0742/391091,* ℻ *0742/391001. 10 rooms. Restaurant, pool, bar; no air-conditioning in some rooms. AE, DC, MC, V. Closed most of Jan. and last 3 weeks in Aug. CP.*

Festivals

The **Giostra della Quintana** is a joust held in the stadium among the town's 10 neighborhoods, with the participants and several hundred cheering locals in traditional 17th-century dress. It's held twice yearly, at night on July 1 and during the day on the second Sunday in September.

Bevagna

❾ *9 km (5½ mi) west of Foligno, 27 km (17 mi) south of Assisi.*

Built on the Via Flaminia, an important consular road, Bevagna was a prosperous Roman outpost (they called it Mevania) until the road was diverted and the town dried up. As a result, Bevagna shows more evidence of its Roman past than other towns that were successively built up and torn down over the centuries by various conquering forces.

Enter through **Porta Foligno** and walk along the main road, Corso Matteotti, which follows the old path of the Via Flaminia. Just to the right, a pretty group of trees traces the elliptical bowl where the amphitheater once stood. Via Crescimbeni curves off to the right toward another Roman-era gate, leading to more Roman ruins: on the right, the church of **San Francesco** is built over the remains of a 2nd-century AD temple. Down Via di Porta Guelfa is what's left of the baths, mostly a wonderful **marine mosaic** visible from a walkway that passes over it.

Uncharacteristically, medieval Bevagna was built next to, rather than on top of, Roman Mevania, which may explain the relative dearth of recognizable remains. The **Museo Archeologico** has a small collection of relics, supplemented by a Roman house and some scattered ruins outside the city walls. ⊠ *Palazzo del Municipio, Corso Matteotti 70,* ☎ *0742/360031.* ☑ *€2.60.* ☉ *Sept.–May, Tues.–Sun. 10:30–1 and 2:30–5; June–Aug., Tues.–Sun. 10:30–1 and 4–7.*

At the center of town, the asymmetrical, medieval **Piazza Silvestri** is bordered by three Romanesque churches (two of which are closed indefinitely as of this writing). Begun in 1195, the church of **San Silvestro** (⊠ Piazza Silvestri, ☎ 0742/361147), at the southeastern end of Piazza Silvestri, is a particularly fine example of Umbrian Romanesque architecture. A rather plain facade hides the dark interior, where the apse is raised above the level of the nave to reveal the crypt below—a feature typical of the time. The church (free) is open daily 10:30–noon and 4–7.

If you come through in off-hours, ask downstairs at the Pro Loco tourist office to visit the exquisite **Teatro Torti,** a 19th-century theater built inside the Gothic **Palazzo dei Consoli.** Cast-iron decorations adorn the fronts of the seating boxes, and there are frescoes in the entrance, bar, and foyer. ⊠ *Piazza Silvestri,* ☎ *0742/361667.* ☑ *Donations accepted.* ☉ *Mon.–Sat. 9:30–12:30 and 3–7.*

Shopping

A few shops on the **Via di Porta Mulini,** just off Piazza Silvestri, still carry on the art of rope making: a holdover from when hemp and flax were mainstays of the local economy. At the end of June, the town holds the **Mercato delle Gaite,** a medieval market with arts and crafts and vendors in traditional dress.

Montefalco

❿ *6 km (4 mi) southeast of Bevagna, 34 km (21 mi) south of Assisi.*

Nicknamed the "balcony of Umbria" for its high, spectacular vantage point over the valley, Montefalco began as an important Roman settlement. It owes its current name—Falcon's Mount—to Emperor Frederick II (1194–1250). A greater fan of falconry than Roman architecture, he destroyed the ancient town. Aside from a few fragments incorporated in a private house just off Borgo Garibaldi, no traces remain of the old Roman center. However, Montefalco has more than its fair share of interesting art and architecture and is well worth the drive up the hill.

The 14th-century **Porta Sant'Agostino** is one of five gates that open in the medieval walls. From there, Corso Goffredo Mameli (the main street) heads straight toward the 13th- to 14th-century Gothic church of Sant'Agostino, which is closed indefinitely. At the end of the Corso is the **Piazza del Comune,** surrounded by several Renaissance buildings, including the 15th-century **Palazzo Comunale.** Ask the custodian to let you into the tower, from which you get the falcon's-eye view of Southern Umbria; on a clear day you can see nearly 20 mi, as far as Perugia to the north and Lake Piediluco to the south.

Montefalco's artistic highlight is the 14th-century **San Francesco,** a church turned museum that enshrines the masterworks of some of the region's finest Renaissance artists. In tribute to the Franciscan order and the religious significance of the region, the 16th-century artist Perugino painted a Nativity scene in an Umbrian setting; Benozzo Gozzoli decorated the church apse with medallions bearing portraits of eminent Franciscans. The highly original and vivid fresco cycle of the *Life of St. Francis* that he completed here in 1452 compares favorably with those by Giotto in Assisi. The small **Pinacoteca,** upstairs, contains religious paintings and altarpieces by local artists. In the basement, there is a small collection of sculpture and fragments from various periods. Note that the cost of admission may vary when special exhibitions are displayed. ⊠ *Via Ringhiera Umbra,* ☎ *0742/379598.* 🎫 *€5.* ☉ *Nov.–Feb., Tues.–Sun. 10:30–1 and 2:30–5; Mar.–May and Sept.–Oct., daily 10:30–1 and 2–6; June–Aug., daily 10:30–1 and 3–7:30.*

If you like Gozzoli's work, there's more in the **Convento di San Fortunato,** although it's in less pristine condition than that in San Francesco. The convent is a 15-minute walk outside the town walls: look for *Madonna with Saints and Angels* in the lunette over the doorway of the cloister chapel (left side) and the fresco of San Fortunato on the altar. Tiberio d'Assisi's *Life of St. Francis* (1512) is also in the cloister chapel. ⊠ *Follow signs,* ☎ *no phone.* 🎫 *Free.* ☉ *Daily 9–12:30 and 3–6.*

Festivals

The local wine, Sagrantino di Montefalco, is celebrated twice yearly—in its nascent stage during September's **Festa dell'Uva** (Grape Festival) and in its full rosy glory during the springtime **Settimana Enologica** (Wine Week). For the former, the area's grape farmers turn out for a parade through the streets and a tasting of past years' labors in the Piazza del Comune. The latter skips the marching band and gets straight to the tasting, with local wine producers offering *rosso* (red), *secco* (dry white), and *passito* Sagrantino, a dessert wine. Details on these and other regional wine festivals can be obtained from the **Centro Agro-Alimentare dell'Umbria** (☎ 0742/344214, 🆆🅴🅱 www.umbriadoc.com).

Shopping

Sagrantino di Montefalco, the strong, full-bodied red wine, is much appreciated by connoisseurs but not well known outside the region. Among the various types, the most interesting is the *passito,* made with grapes that have been picked and left to dry to half their original volume. The high concentration of sugar yields a sweet, complex flavor that might remind you of good sherry. Adanti, Caprai, and Paolo Bea are among the well-known producers.

Trevi

⑪ *5 km (3 mi) southeast of Spello, 16 km (10 mi) southeast of Assisi.*

If you aren't in a hurry to get to Spoleto, Trevi—no relation to the famous fountain in Rome, which takes its name from the three streets
(*tre vie*) that once met in front of it—makes a pleasant stop. It's an
especially well-preserved town. Although Trevi has no Roman ruins
to hunt down, the small **Raccolta d'Arte San Francesco** contains a good
little collection of paintings by local artists, including Lo Spagna
(circa 1450–1528) and Perugino. ⊠ *Convento di San Francesco,
Largo Don Bosco,* ☎ *0742/381628.* ⊡ *€2.60.* ☉ *Apr.–May and
Sept., Tues.–Sun. 10:30–1 and 2:30–6; June–July, Tues.–Sun. 10:30–
1 and 3:30–7; Aug., daily 10:30–1 and 3–7:30; Oct.–Mar., Fri.–Sun.
10:30–1 and 2:30–5.*

The best works in town, as usual, are in the local churches. **San Martino** (for entry, ring the bell at the monastery next door) and **Madonna
delle Lacrime** (ring the bell at the convent next door) are pleasantly set
1 km (½ mi) north and south of the town, respectively, along the main
road that leads up the steep hill from the highway below. The latter,
the Church of Madonna of the Tears, has works by Lo Spagna and Perugino; over the altar is a portrait of the Madonna that is said to have
been seen miraculously crying, giving the church its name.

OFF THE
BEATEN PATH

TEMPIETTO E FONTI DEL CLITUNNO – South of Trevi is the so-called Tempietto ("little temple") del Clitunno, an early-Christian church built from bits
and pieces of Roman temples in the area. The badly worn frescoes,
some of the earliest in the region, date from the 7th century. Farther
down the road are the Fonti del Clitunno, springs named after a Roman
river god, that were famous in the ancient world. (The remains of the
Roman-era Tempio del Clitunno are also nearby.) The waters flow from
fissures in the rocks and collect in a shallow pond before passing on to
an artificial basin. The springs were created when the Romans diverted
several rivers upstream, and were used until the 19th century to supply
water to run the mills in the nearby town of Pissignano. ⊠ *About 2 km
(1 mi) south of Trevi.* ⊡ *Free.* ☉ *Apr.–Oct., daily 9–8; Nov.–Mar.,
daily 9–2.*

Dining

$$ ✕ **Taverna del Pescatore.** The unpromising location of this "fisherman's
★ tavern"—right next to the busy Via Flaminia—belies idyllic tranquil-
lity often found inside. Once seated on the terrace, with the clear
stream of the Clitunno River flowing just beyond your wineglass,
you'll forget all about the highway. Sit back, listen for the birds in the
trees, and keep an eye out for the fresh fish in the river, on which the
menu is based each day. Preparations are clean and simple and at
times wonderfully eclectic: one springtime favorite is stringozzi with
wild asparagus tips, trout fillet, and tiny, fresh tomatoes. The wine list
is long but not expensive. ⊠ *Statale Flaminia Km 139,* ☎ *0742/
780920. AE, DC, MC, V. Closed Wed. Sept.–July, and 2 wks in Jan.*

SPOLETO

For most of the year, Spoleto is one more in a pleasant succession of
sleepy hill towns, puttering away atop its mount. But for three weeks
every summer, the town dusts off its cobblestones and shifts into high
gear for a turn in the spotlight: the Festival dei Due Mondi (Festival
of Two Worlds), a world-class extravaganza of theater, opera, music,
painting, and sculpture. As the world's top artists vie for honors,

throngs of art aficionados vie for hotel rooms. If you plan to spend the night in Spoleto during the festival, make sure you have confirmed hotel reservations, or you may find yourself scrambling at sunset.

But there is also good reason to visit Spoleto during the rest of the year. A solid collection of Roman and medieval attractions and superb natural surroundings make it one of Umbria's most inviting towns. Spoleto also makes a good base from which to explore all of Southern Umbria: Assisi, Orvieto, and the towns in between are all within easy reach.

Umbri tribes were the first to settle here, probably taking advantage of the protection provided by the steep and narrow gorge that runs along the back side of Spoleto's hill. As usual, the Romans were not far behind, fortifying the city walls and building an aqueduct across the gorge, which serves as a foundation to Spoleto's breathtaking Ponte delle Torri. By all accounts an important city, Spoletum (as it was called in Latin) turned away Hannibal in the 2nd century BC. Ancient churches set in silvery olive groves below either side of town testify to Spoleto's importance in the early Christian period, when it ruled over a sizable independent duchy. In the 14th century, the town fell under church control, and La Rocca was built at its summit to enforce papal rule.

Exploring Spoleto

The walled city is set on a slanting hillside, with the most interesting sections clustered toward the upper portion. Parking options inside the walls include Piazza Campello (just below the Rocca), Via del Trivio, Piazza della Vittoria, and Piazza San Domenico. Also, several well-marked larger lots are just outside Porta San Matteo and near the train station. If you arrive by train, you can walk 1 km (½ mi) from the station to Piazza Garibaldi and the entrance to the lower town. There are good bus connections from the train station to Piazza della Libertà, near the upper part of the old town, where you'll find the visitor information office. Like most other towns made up of narrow, winding streets, Spoleto is best explored on foot, but do bear in mind that much of the city is on a steep slope, necessitating lots of stairs. Several pedestrian walkways cut across Corso Mazzini, which zigzags up the hill. A €2.60 combination ticket allows you entry to the Pinacoteca Comunale, Casa Romana, and Galleria d'Arte Moderna.

A Good Walk

Begin your day at Piazza della Libertà, with a visit to the adjacent **Teatro Romano** ⑫ and Museo Archeologico (enter on Via Apollinare). From the ancient ruins it's a short jump to the **Galleria d'Arte Moderna** ⑬, a five-room collection with paintings and small sculpture that has won awards in past festivals. Return to Piazza della Libertà, walk up Via Brignone to Piazza Fontana, and go left on Via Arco di Druso, through the **Arco di Druso** ⑭. Up ahead is Piazza del Mercato, built over the ancient Foro Romano and today the site of a small daily open-air produce market. Take the street that leads up out of the piazza and make a quick left onto Via Visiale, crossed by several arches. On the right is the entrance to the **Casa Romana** ⑮. Continue along Via Visiale and then turn right onto Via Saffi. Just ahead on the left is Palazzo Arcivescovile, with the church of **Sant'Eufemia** ⑯ in the courtyard and a small museum. Via Saffi continues uphill to Via dell'Arringo, which descends to **Piazza del Duomo** ⑰. The **Duomo** ⑱ stands against a backdrop of hill and sky with **La Rocca** ⑲ towering overhead. After lunch, proceed from the Duomo up to Piazza Campello and take Via del Ponte,

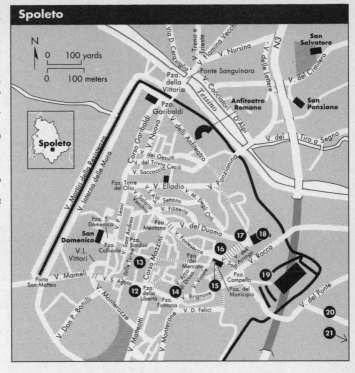

which loops around the base of La Rocca, passing the magnificent **Ponte delle Torri** ⑳. Walk across the bridge, and either circle back around La Rocca or continue along the shady paths of Monteluco and down to the church of **San Pietro** ㉑. From there, return the way you came or cross the highway and take Via Monterone back up into town.

TIMING

Spoleto is small, and its noteworthy sights are clustered in the upper part of town; allow a full day for a thorough exploration, including time to stroll around town and across the Ponte delle Torri. Note that the Casa Romana is closed on Monday.

Sights to See

⑭ **Arco di Druso** (Arch of Drusus). Built in AD 23 by the Senate of Spoleto to honor the Roman general Drusus (circa 13 BC–AD 23), son of the emperor Tiberius, this arch once marked the entrance to the Foro Romano (Roman Forum). Excavations to the side reveal the original street level. ⊠ *Piazza del Mercato.*

⑮ **Casa Romana.** Spoleto became a Roman colony in the 3rd century BC, but the best excavated remains date to the 1st century AD. Excavated in the late 9th century, the Casa Romana was not your typical Roman residence—according to an inscription, it belonged to Vespasia Polla, the mother of Emperor Vespasian. The rooms, arranged around a large central atrium built over an *impluvium* (rain cistern), are decorated with intricate mosaics that are still mostly intact. There was once a sizable garden surrounded by a peristyle, which faced the valley. ⊠ *Palazzo del Municipio, Via Visiale 9,* ☎ *0743/224656.* ⌨ *€4.15 combination ticket includes the Galleria Civica d'Arte Moderna.* ⊘ *Oct. 16–Mar. 15, Tues.–Sun. daily 10–1 and 2:30–5; May 16–Oct. 14, daily 10:30–1 and 3–6:30.*

★ ⑱ **Duomo.** The cathedral's facade consists of a rather dour 12th-century Romanesque background, lightened up by the addition of a Renaissance loggia, eight rose windows, and an early-13th-century gold mosaic of the Benedictory Christ. A stunning contrast in styles, it is one of the finest in the region. The original pavement dates from an earlier church that was destroyed by Frederick I (circa 1123–90). Above the entrance wall is Bernini's bust of Pope Urban VIII (1568–1644), who had the rest of the church redecorated in 17th-century Baroque; fortunately he didn't touch the 15th-century frescoes in the apse by Fra Filippo Lippi (circa 1406–69). Have some coins on hand so that you can illuminate the immaculately restored masterpieces, which tell the story of the life of the Virgin—the *Annunciation, Nativity,* and the *Death of Mary.* The *Coronation of the Virgin,* adorning the half dome, is the literal and figurative high point. Portraits of Lippi and his assistants are on the right side of the central panel. The Florentine artist died shortly after completing the work, and his tomb—designed by his son, Filippino Lippi (circa 1457–1504)—lies in the church's right transept. Another fresco cycle, including work by Pinturicchio, can be seen in the **Cappella Eroli** off the right aisle. In the left nave, not far from the entrance, is the well-restored 12th-century crucifix by Alberto Sozio, the earliest known example of this kind of work, with a painting on parchment attached to a wood cross. To the right of the presbytery is the Cappella della Santissima Icona (Chapel of the Most Holy Icon), which contains a small Byzantine painting of a Madonna given to the town by Frederick Barbarossa as a peace offering in 1185 (following his destruction of the cathedral and town three decades earlier). ✉ *Piazza del Duomo,* ☎ *0743/44307.* ☜ *Free.* ☉ *Mar.–Oct., daily 7:30–12:30 and 3–6; Nov.–Feb., daily 7:30–12:30 and 3–5.*

⑬ **Galleria d'Arte Moderna.** This five-room gallery contains the winning paintings and sculptures from the first 13 years of the festival, including the original preparatory sketches for Alexander Calder's (1898–1976) *Teodelapio* (1962): the actual sculpture is near the train station. There are also several more-recent pieces by contemporary Italian artists, such as Alberto Burri and Arnaldo Pomodoro. ✉ *Palazzo Rosari-Spada, Corso Mazzini, Vicolo III,* ☎ *0743/45940.* ☜ *€4.15 combination ticket includes the Casa Romana.* ☉ *Tues.–Sun. 10–1 and 3–6.*

★ ⑲ **La Rocca.** Built in the mid-14th century for Cardinal Egidio Albornoz, this massive fortress served as a seat for the local pontifical governors, a tangible sign of the restoration of the papacy's power in the area. Several popes spent time here, as did Lucrezia Borgia (1480–1519). The plan is long and rectangular, with six towers and two fine courtyards inside. The Gubbio-born architect Gattapone (14th century) used the ruins of a Roman acropolis as a foundation and took materials from many Roman-era sites, including the Teatro Romano. Until 1982, the Rocca was used as a high security prison, but in 1999, the building was reborn as a cultural complex, housing performance and exhibition spaces and a museum of the town's medieval history. ✉ *Via del Ponte,* ☎ *0743/223055.* ☜ *€5.* ☉ *Mid-Mar.–mid-June and mid-Sept.–mid-Oct, weekdays 10–noon and 3–7, weekends 10–7; mid-June–mid-Sept., weekdays 10–8, weekends 10–9; Nov.–mid-Mar., weekdays 2:30–5, weekends 10–5. Visits are accompanied by a guide and begin on the hour; the last visit begins one hour before closing time.*

⑰ **Piazza del Duomo.** The piazza is stage-set perfect, a sunny square bordered by fine buildings, including the Duomo and the small Teatro Caio Melisso, one of the first theaters built in Italy.

★ ⑳ **Ponte delle Torri** (Bridge of the Towers). Standing massive and graceful through the deep gorge that separates Spoleto from Monteluco, this 14th-century bridge is one of Umbria's most-photographed monuments, and justifiably so. The 750-ft-long bridge was built by Gattapone over the foundations of a Roman-era aqueduct and soars 262 ft above the forested gorge at its highest point—higher than the dome of St. Peter's in Rome. Sweeping postcard views over the valley and a pleasant sense of vertigo make a walk across the bridge a must, particularly on a starry night. ⊠ *Take Via Saffi (off Piazza del Duomo) to Via del Ponte.*

㉑ San Pietro. A walk to the church of San Pietro, at the foot of Monteluco, is a pleasant excursion from town, either across the Ponte delle Torri and down the path to the right or out Porta Monterone and across the highway. The church was rebuilt in the 13th century over earlier Christian, Roman, and Umbri holy sites. It is rarely open, but the real attractions here are the puzzling decorations on the facade, among the best Romanesque carvings in the region. Beneath the tympanum is an empty square frame, which presumably once held a mosaic, flanked by reliefs of Sts. Andrew and Peter, with a bull beneath each. Paired reliefs in the panels around the doors represent allegories of work and the eternal life, and typical Christian scenes. The fates of the just and the sinner were written on the church wall: the former being saved by St. Peter, with the devil held at bay, the latter being abandoned by the Archangel Michael to a pair of demons. ⊠ *Beginning of the Strada di Monteluco, 1 km (½ mi) south of town center,* ☎ *0743/44882 custodian.* ⊠ *Free.* ⊙ *Hrs vary; call custodian.*

....

OFF THE
BEATEN PATH **SAN SALVATORE** – The church and cemetery of San Salvatore seem very much forgotten, ensconced in solitude and cypress trees on a peaceful hillside with the motorway rumbling below. One of the oldest churches in the world, it was built in the 4th century, largely of Roman-era materials. The highlight is the facade, with three exquisite marble doorways and windows, one of the earliest and best preserved in Umbria; it dates from a restoration in the 9th century and has hardly been touched since. Inside is a 9th-century cross, studded in gems. On the way back from San Salvatore, have a look at **San Ponziano** (⊠ 250 yards down Via del Cimitero, open daily 10–1 and 2:30–5, or ring next door for the custodian); it has a crypt containing the remains of the church's namesake, the patron saint of Spoleto. Walking back to town, you'll pass **Ponte Sanguinario** (⊠ Piazza della Vittoria), named for the waters that flowed red with blood during the games in the Anfiteatro Romano just upstream. The amphitheater is now part of the local military barracks; its stones were stripped away and used to build La Rocca. ⊠ *Via della Basilica di San Salvatore, just out of town on the Via Flaminia.* ⊙ *Nov.– Feb., daily 7–5; Mar.–Apr. and Sept.–Oct., daily 7–6; May–Aug., daily 7–7.*

....

⑯ Sant'Eufemia. Set in the courtyard of the archbishop's palace with a partial view of the Duomo over the back wall, this austere ancient church dates from the 12th century. Built on the site of a Roman-era *insula* (city block), the plain Romanesque interior has a Cosmati mosaic altar and frescoes on the pillars. An interesting feature is the gallery above the nave where female worshipers were required to sit—a holdover from the Eastern Church and one of the few such galleries in this part of Italy. Admission to the church also includes a visit to the **Museo Diocesano d'Arte Sacra**, which has a collection rivaling that of the nearby Pinacoteca. ⊠ *Via Saffi, between Piazza del Duomo and Piazza del Mercato,* ☎ *0743/231022.* ⊠ *€3.* ⊙ *Church and Museum, April–Sept., Mon.–Sat. 10–1:30 and 4–7, Sun. 10:30–1 and 3–6; Oct.–Mar., Mon. and Wed.–Sat. 10–12:30 and 3–6, Sun. 11–5.*

⑫ **Teatro Romano.** This small 1st-century Roman theater was used as a quarry for building materials for centuries, so the most intact portion is the hallway that passes under the *cavea* (stands). The rest was heavily restored in the early 1950s and serves as a venue for Spoleto's festival. The theater was the site of a gruesome episode in Spoleto's history: during the medieval struggle between Guelph (papal) and Ghibelline (imperial) factions for control of central and northern Italy, Spoleto took the side of the Holy Roman Emperor. And woe to those who disagreed—400 Guelph supporters were massacred in the theater, their bodies burned in an enormous pyre. In the end, the Guelphs were triumphant, and Spoleto was incorporated into the states of the Church in 1354. Through a door in the west portico of the adjoining building is the **Museo Archeologico,** with assorted artifacts found in the theater and around the town. The collection contains mostly busts and devotional epigrams found around the theater, although one room holds Umbrian and pre-Roman pieces. The highlight is the stone tablet inscribed on both sides with the *Lex Spoletina* (Spoleto Law). Dating from 315 BC, this legal document prohibited the desecration of the woods sacred to Jupiter on the slopes of nearby Monteluco. All violators were required to pacify the god by sacrificing an ox, those who were found to have broken the law with malicious intent paid an additional fine. The area was later frequented by St. Francis of Assisi. ⊠ *Via Apollinare, off Piazza della Libertà,* ☎ *0743/223277.* 🎫 *€2.* ☉ *Daily 8:30–7:30.*

Dining and Lodging

Truffles found in the vicinity are served locally with abandon and shipped all over the country. Dishes like stringozzi *alla spoletina* (with tomato, parsley, garlic, and hot red-pepper flakes) and the delicious *crescionda* (a flanlike dessert, with a base of crushed almond cookies) stay closer to home. Much harder to find is the tangy mix of wild greens that make up the *insalata di campo,* a freshly picked seasonal assortment of dandelion leaves, wild arugula, fennel, borage, and sometimes edible flowers.

Although Spoleto's restaurants for the most part reflect the mass tourism of the Festival dei Due Mondi year-round, the hotel scene is a little better, with a good selection of midsize hotels and small, family-run inns. Because Spoleto is known for outdoor sports and hiking, there are also many *agriturismi* (agritourist farms), with accommodation that ranges from the rustic to the downright luxurious. Wherever you plan to stay, if you're coming to stay during the festival, book your room well in advance and be prepared for the high rates that accompany high demand.

$$–$$$$ ✕ **Il Panciolle.** In the heart of Spoleto's medieval quarter, this restaurant has one of the most pleasant settings you could wish for. Dining outside in summer, in a small piazza filled with lime trees, is a treat. Specialties include stringozzi with mushroom sauce and *agnello scottadito* (grilled lamb chops). Seven guest rooms are also available. ⊠ *Vicolo degli Eroi 1,* ☎ *0743/45598. Reservations essential. AE, DC, MC, V. Closed Wed. and last 2 wks in Nov.*

$$–$$$ ✕ **Apollinare.** Low wooden ceilings and candlelight make Apollinare the most romantic restaurant in Spoleto. The menu takes a slightly sophisticated, innovative approach to local cooking, with good-size portions; here the usual stringozzi are served with cherry tomatoes, mint, and a touch of red pepper. Try the *caramella* (light puff pastry roll filled with local cheese, served on a Parmesan fondue). In late spring and summer there is dining under a pergola on the piazza.

⊠ *Via Sant'Agata 14,* ☎ *0743/223256. AE, D, MC, V. Closed Tues. Nov.–Mar.*

$$–$$$ ✕ **Il Tartufo.** As the name suggests, this is Spoleto's shrine to the truffle, a restaurant that prides itself on using only the finest seasonal truffles available (and the best-quality preserved truffles when there are no fresh truffles to be found). Preparations vary, from the traditional and simple (stringozzi *al tartufo*—with truffles) to the creative and elaborate (pheasant breast stuffed with truffles and potatoes, served on a bed of wild asparagus). There is also a nontruffle menu if you'd rather forgo the fungus. Don't miss the original Roman brick floor in the cellar dining room. ⊠ *Piazza Garibaldi 24,* ☎ *0743/40236. Reservations essential. AE, DC, MC, V. Closed Mon. and last 2 wks in July. No dinner Sun.*

$–$$ ✕ **Il Pentagramma.** If it weren't for the festival, chances are the menu wouldn't group first courses as "symphonies" and grilled dishes as "ballets," but the food is in good voice just the same and the bill won't sound like a requiem. Try the *tortelli ai carciofi e noci* (artichoke-filled pasta in a hazelnut sauce) and *agnello al tartufo* (lamb in a truffle sauce). If you happen by in springtime, ask about the insalatina di campo, composed of wild herbs. ⊠ *Via Martani 4,* ☎ *0743/223141. DC, MC, V. Closed Mon. No dinner Sun.*

$ ✕ **Pecchiarda.** If you're wondering where the Spoletini go to eat, here's
★ your answer. There's barely a sign out front, and the menu, supplemented as it is by innumerable daily specials, is beside the point, but that's part of the (very informal) experience. Ask your waiter what's new in the kitchen and you'll soon find your table graced with treats like *bruschetta al tartufo* (truffle toast), *lenticchie rosse* (stewed red lentils), and tasty *involtini di vitello* (veal rolls)—everything so good you'll wish you lived here so you could come every day. The excellent crescionda goes well with home-distilled grappa. Overexcited kids can burn off steam in the enclosed garden, visible from the glassed-in dining rooms. ⊠ *Vicolo San Giovanni 1,* ☎ *0743/ 221009. D, MC, V.*

$$$–$$$$ ▦ **Hotel Gattapone.** Lucky Gattapone—this small, secluded hotel sits
★ on the edge of the gorge separating the Rocca from Monteluco, overlooking the Ponte delle Torri. Wake up to wonderful views of the ancient bridge and the wooded slopes of Monteluco, and go for a morning walk around the Via del Ponte, which circles the base of the Rocca above. Interiors are done in modern style that's understated and tasteful, with beautiful wooden floors and comfortable leather furniture. ⊠ *Via del Ponte 6, 06049,* ☎ *0743/223447,* ℻ *0743/223448,* WEB *www. hotelgattapone.it. 8 rooms, 8 suites. In-room safes, bar, meeting rooms, free parking. AE, DC, MC, V. CP.*

$$$ ▦ **Hotel dei Duchi.** This excellent, well-run hotel is a favorite among performers in the festival. It's in the center of town, near the Roman amphitheater. Some rooms have fine views of the city. ⊠ *Viale Matteotti 4, 06049,* ☎ *0743/44541,* ℻ *0743/44543,* WEB *www.hoteldeiduchi. com. 47 rooms, 2 suites. Restaurant, bar, meeting rooms, free parking. AE, DC, MC, V. CP.*

$$$ ▦ **Hotel San Luca.** The elegant San Luca is Spoleto's finest hotel, thanks
★ to the commendable attention it pays to details. Spacious rooms (some accessible for people who use wheelchairs) are decorated with hand-painted friezes, firm beds are laid with linen sheets, and the hotel's rose garden provides a sweet-smelling backdrop for your afternoon nap. An ample breakfast buffet, including homemade cakes, is served in a pretty room facing the central courtyard, while afternoon tea can be sipped in oversize armchairs in front of the fireplace. Service is cordial and prices are surprisingly modest. ⊠ *Via Interna delle Mura 21, 06049,* ☎ *0743/*

223399, FAX 0743/223800, WEB *www.hotelsanluca.com. 33 rooms, 2 suites. Bar, Internet, parking (fee). AE, DC, MC, V. CP.*

$-$$ 🏨 **Nuovo Clitunno.** A renovated 18th-century building houses this pleasant hotel, a five-minute walk from the town center. Some rooms have lovely wood-beamed ceilings, wrought-iron beds, and Oriental carpets; others have a mixture of period as well as less charming, modern furniture. ⊠ *Piazza Sordini 6, 06049,* ☎ *0743/223340,* FAX *0743/222663. 40 rooms. Restaurant, bar, meeting rooms. AE, DC, MC, V. CP.*

$ 🏨 **Aurora.** This simple little hotel, right on Piazza della Libertà, is run by the owners of the Apollinare restaurant, which is downstairs. The rooms are basic and clean. ⊠ *Via Apollinare 3, 06049,* ☎ *0743/ 220315,* FAX *0743/221885. 22 rooms, 1 suite. Bar; no air-conditioning in some rooms. AE, DC, MC, V. CP.*

$ 🏨 **Azienda Agrituristica Bartoli.** Just 13 km (8 mi) southeast of Spoleto, this agriturismo offers simple rooms with private baths in a converted farmhouse, with common kitchen and TV rooms. There is also an apartment that sleeps six. Rooms look out onto the green valleys below Monte di Patrico. Rent by the night or the week, with half- or full-board. There are ample hiking trails in the area, and horses are available with or without guides. ⊠ *Località Patrico, 06049,* ☎ *0743/ 220058,* WEB *www.agriturismobartoli.it. 11 rooms. Horseback riding; no air-conditioning. No credit cards. MAP.*

Performing Arts and Festivals

In 1958, composer Gian Carlo Menotti chose Spoleto for the first **Festival dei Due Mondi** (Festival of Two Worlds), a gathering of artists, performers, and musicians intended to bring together the "new" and "old" worlds of America and Europe (there was once a corresponding festival in Charleston, South Carolina, but it is no longer connected to Spoleto's festival). The annual event (late June–early July) soon became one of the most important cultural happenings in Europe, attracting big names in all branches of the arts—particularly music, opera, and theater—and drawing thousands of visitors. With so much activity, the small town gives itself over entirely to the festival—events are staged in every possible venue, from church cloisters to the Roman Theater; street performers abound; and prices rise considerably. The closing concert (always free) takes place on the Piazza del Duomo.

At any other time of year, you will notice the changes brought by the festival—Spoleto is far more cosmopolitan than other towns in the region, its people more welcoming—and undoubtedly you will see traces of past festivals: old promotional posters hung in virtually all the shops and hotels, and modern sculptures left to the city in its art gallery and on permanent display outdoors. These include Alexander Calder's enormous bronze *Teodelapio* sculpture in front of the train station, Anna Mahler's *Sitting* in Piazza della Signoria, and *Geodesic Dome* by Buckminster Fuller (1895–1983) in the Parco della Passeggiata. Tickets for all performances should be ordered in advance from the **festival box office** (⊠ Piazza Duomo 8, ☎ 0743/220320; 800/565600 toll-free in Italy, WEB www.spoletofestival.it), which has full program information starting in February.

In addition to the festival, Spoleto hosts a prestigious vocal competition at the Teatro Lirico Sperimentale Adriano Belli from mid-August to mid-September. Check with the visitor information office about other special concerts, exhibitions, and cultural events.

Outdoor Activities and Sports

Biking

The pretty countryside around Spoleto is well suited for bicycling, with terrain that ranges from flat country roads to steep mountain paths. The Spoleto tourist office publishes an excellent pamphlet, *In Bicicletta nello Spoletino* (*Bicycling Around the Spoleto Area*), which details routes, distances, and levels of difficulty in Italian and English. Bicycles can be rented at **Scocchetti Cicli** (⊠ Via Marconi 82, ☎ 0743/44728), open Monday through Saturday 9–1 and 3:30–8 (call ahead to reserve).

Hiking

Pick up a map of local roads and trails from the tourist office and head out for a stroll in the country or a hike up the mountainside. Trails on Monteluco (just across the Ponte delle Torri) wind steeply through thick woods, passing caves and hermitages abandoned by spiritual seekers who have lived in this traditionally sacred forest since the time of St. Francis.

Horseback Riding

Horses can be rented with English-speaking guides at the **Centro Ippico La Somma** (⊠ Frazione Aiacugigli-Montebibico, about 15 km [9 mi] south of Spoleto, ☎ 0743/54370), open daily 9:30–noon and 3:30–7.

Shopping

Spoleto's main shopping street begins as **Via Fontesecca** (near Piazza del Mercato) and continues down the hill, changing names several times. **Aracne** (⊠ Vicolo Primo di Corso Mazzini 2, ☎ 0743/46085) specializes in fine lace and embroidery. **Mobilia** (⊠ Via Filitteria 3, ☎ 0743/45720) is one of many antiques shops. Spoleto's tiny open-air **produce market,** open Monday through Saturday 8–1:30, is held in Piazza del Mercato, near the Arco di Druso. The second Sunday of every month sees the **Mercato delle Brisciole,** with antiques and crafts vendors taking over the streets of Spoleto's historic center. Down the road in Pissignano, the region's best **antiques fair** is held the first Sunday of each month.

En Route The road east from Spoleto (S395) goes 19 km (12 mi) to the Nera river, then turns north and becomes S209. As you climb higher, the olive groves that produce Spoleto's fine oil give way to chestnut trees and forests populated by wolves, porcupines, and owls. When you reach Cerreto di Spoleto, take the long way around to the S320, passing Triponzo, for the best views. Most minor roads are not in the best of shape, but they reward you with dramatic mountain scenery.

SPOLETO ENVIRONS AND NORCIA

Spoleto is the obvious starting point for a visit to the eastern edges of Umbria, as few roads cut across the rugged mountainous terrain that quickly rises from the Valle Umbra. Roads narrow and the towns get smaller and farther apart as you break out off the well-traveled path between Assisi and Spoleto, but great rewards await. Spring is the best time of year to venture east from Spoleto, as the climate and wildflowers are at their finest. The main attractions are Norcia, a town famous for its culinary delights, and the road you take to get there, full of breathtaking views across unspoiled verdant mountain landscapes. To the east of Norcia, and extending into the Marches, is the Parco Nazionale dei Monti Sibillini, one of Italy's best nature reserves.

No less inviting is the Valnerina (Valley of the Nera River), which has its own protected nature area and stunning scenery. Lest any part of Italy be without an interesting church, the Abbazia di San Pietro della Valle sits like a gem amid the lush greenery of the valley.

Norcia

🄪 *48 km (31 mi) east of Spoleto, 99 km (62 mi) southeast of Perugia.*

For most Italians, Norcia is synonymous with legendary sausages and prosciutto and the great tradition of butchers who produce them. In fact, from Rome to Rimini a *norcineria* is a place where sausages are made and sold, and a *norcino* is a pork butcher. (Under the circumstances, it is no wonder that the locals call themselves *nursiani*.) There is, however, more to Norcia than pork products—here you'll also find the finest truffles in Umbria, a solid tradition of cheese making, plenty of delicious baked goods, and chocolate. If all this weren't enough to put Norcia on the map, it is also the birthplace of St. Benedict (San Benedetto), the founder of Christianity's first monastic order, and the town is surrounded by stupendous, lush mountainous terrain.

If you arrive on a full stomach, head for the local sights, which are clustered around Piazza San Benedetto. The 14th-century church of **San Benedetto** was built over the purported birthplace of the saint and his twin sister, St. Scolastica. Both are represented in statues set into the facade, which in turn must have been constructed over the remains of a Roman house, visible in the church crypt. Don't miss the fascinating set of nine medieval stone vessels, once used to measure grain, that are attached to the right flank of the building. ⊠ *Piazza San Benedetto,* ☎ *0743/817125.* 🎟 *Free.* ☉ *Daily 8:30–12:30 and 3:30–6:30.*

Off to the side of San Benedetto, the **Duomo** (⊠ Piazza San Benedetto) bears the scars of repeated redecoration necessitated by frequent earthquakes over the centuries (the locals now adhere to strict building codes and height limitations). The superb **Castellina,** the sturdy papal palace, holds the **Museo Civico,** which offers more than the usual drab collection of local work. The Della Robbia terra-cotta of the Madonna, a rare example in this region of the work of the masterful Florentine family, and a 13th-century *Deposition,* made up of several wooden statues, are worth the admission alone. ⊠ *Piazza San Benedetto,* ☎ *0743/ 817030.* 🎟 *€2.60.* ☉ *Oct.–May, Tues.–Sun. 10–12:30 and 3:30–6; June–Sept., Tues.–Sun. 10–1 and 4–7.*

At the **Mostra Permanente della Civiltà Contadina,** a museum, you can have a good look at clothes, tools, and personal items from the local farming community. ⊠ *Piazza Sergio Forti 9,* ☎ *075/802145.* 🎟 *Donations accepted.* ☉ *Weekends 8–1 and 3–6.*

Dining and Lodging

$$ ✕🏨 **Granaro del Monte.** This is a typical Norcia restaurant ($–$$$$), so the menu includes a feast of pork prepared every which way, famous lentils from nearby Castelluccio, and mushrooms and truffles from the local forests. The owners also run a simple but comfortable hotel next door, the Grotta Azzurra. ⊠ *Via Cesare Battisti 7, 06046,* ☎ *0743/ 816513,* 🌐 *www.bianconi.com. AE, DC, MC, V.*

Parco Nazionale dei Monti Sibillini

🄫 *About 46 km (29 mi) east of Spoleto.*

Norcia lies within the boundaries of the Parco Nazionale dei Monti Sibillini, an unspoiled mountainous ridge that straddles the border between Umbria and the Marches region. Just south of town is **San Pellegrino,** source of one of the country's most famous mineral waters. The main road that winds its way through the mountains, eventually crossing the border into Le Marche, passes through **Castelluccio,** a pretty town known nationwide for its lentils. You're not here for the towns, though, but for the park, which, weather permitting, offers some of the country's best hiking and other outdoor activities. A good resource are the maps issued by the Club Alpino Italiano (CAI), available at newsstands.

The **Cooperativa Monte Patino** (☎ 0743/817487 for reservations), open weekdays 9:30–1:30 and 3:30–6, offers guided tours in English, including excursions to villages and isolated churches and hiking in the Parco dei Sibillini. A full-day food-shopping tour called "Sentiero Sapori" (Flavor Trail; ☎ €7.75) focuses on visits to artisanal workshops and cheese and sausage producers. If you prefer to travel without a guide, try the **Casa del Parco** (✉ Via Solferino 22, Norcia, ☎ 0743/817090; ✉ Via Santa Caterina, Preci Alto, ☎ 0743/937000). Both offices, open daily 9:30–12:30 and 3–6, have free maps and brochures about the Umbrian side of the national park.

Lodging

$ ☷ **Rifugio Perugia.** You won't have a private room in this *rifugio di montagna* (mountain refuge)—in fact you'll have to share with three more people. But if you like the coziness and the getting together over a last bottle of wine typical of these high inns, do join in and get the seat near the guy with the guitar. You don't need to pack tuna fish and chocolate for your day's excursion, since the Perugia has a restaurant done up in wood and stone. Rates of €16.00 a person includes sheets and bath towels. ✉ *Località Canapine, about 22 km (14 mi) southeast of Norcia,* ☎ *0743/823019, 368/646189, or 335/7010781. 35 beds. Restaurant. AE, D, MC, V. Closed Nov.–Easter.*

Abbazia di San Pietro in Valle

㉔ *35 km (22 mi) southeast of Spoleto, 44 km (27 mi) southwest of Norcia.*

It's hard to believe that this remote building once served as one of the region's centers of Christianity, but the remnants of one of the fortresses that once protected it, still visible in the distance, testify to its earlier importance. Capitals in the apse and a 1st-century BC altar near the back door seem to suggest that the 8th-century abbey was built over the ruins of a Roman temple. Sacked by the Saracens, the abbey was rebuilt in the 12th century. At that time the perfectly graceful cloister and Lombard-style campanile were added, as were the stunning frescoes in the side naves that illustrate scenes from the Old and New Testaments. The unknown artist who painted them preceded Giotto by more than 100 years in his attempt to break away from rigid Byzantine models. The frescoes have been restored, and the best-preserved scenes overflow with realistic and vivid details that bring the stories to life. The skillful use of light and shadow can be considered as an early, tentative step toward the techniques of perspective that were developed in the Renaissance. The main altar is a rare 8th-century artifact with unusual reliefs, which include representations of the lord who commissioned the piece and the artist himself, called Ursus. To the right is a handsome Roman sarcophagus containing the bones of Duke Faroald II of Spoleto, who built the abbey after having a vision of St. Peter. ✉ *S209,* ☎ *0744/780316.* ☷ *Donations accepted.* ☉ *Oct.–Apr., daily 10:15–12:30 and 2–5; May–Sept., daily 10:15–12:30 and 2–6. If it's closed, ring at the custodian's house, about 1 km (½ mi) south of the abbey.*

En Route   You can take the secondary road that goes southeast to Monteleone di Spoleto, cutting across the main mountain ridge and climbing toward Mt. Coscerno (5,527 ft). The road continues to Cascia, an unremarkable town where the only attraction is a famous (modern) sanctuary dedicated to St. Rita of Cascia, the powerful protector of all women in serious trouble. The road proceeds along the path of the Corno and Sordo rivers, leading up toward Norcia.

Dining

$$–$$$$ ✕ **Piermarini.** In the tiny town of Ferentillo, 4 km (1½ mi) south of the Abbazia di San Pietro in Valle, this is a great place to have your Umbrian truffle experience, especially in winter (truffle season). Traditional, no-nonsense dishes highlight the precious fungus: truffles are often served with eggs, which bring out their full flavor without obscuring it. Second courses are excellent as well and include the usual grilled meats plus kid, lamb, and roasted pork. There is a pleasant garden for outside dining in good weather. ✉ *Via Ancaiano 23, Ferentillo (18½ km [11 mi] northeast of Terni, 31 km [19 mi] southeast of Spoleto),* ☎ *0744/ 780714. AE, D, MC, V. Closed Mon. and 1 wk in Jan.*

Shopping

Local cheeses, salami, and truffle products are on plentiful, redolent display at **Norcineria Ercole Ulivucci** (✉ Via Mazzini 4, ☎ 0743/ 816661), closed Monday in even years, Tuesday in odd years. As its name implies, **Norcineria Fratelli Ansuini** (✉ Via Anicia 105, ☎ 0743/ 816643), closed Tuesday, stocks a full range of the local pork products. Pick up some cheese (or truffles, in season) at the **Boutique del Pecoraro** (✉ Via San Benedetto 7, ☎ 0743/816453). Well worth a visit is **Tartufi Moscatelli** (✉ Corso Sertorio 42, ☎ 0743/817388), renowned for its truffles. For cakes and pastries, head to the shop at **No. 13 Corso Sertorio** (☎ 0744/816623), closed Sunday.

SOUTHERN UMBRIA

It's a short drive from Spoleto to Terni, but tempting diversions along the way include one of central Italy's finest abbeys and the refreshing Lake Piediluco. Hold your breath while river rafting at the foot of the tallest falls in Europe, and then recover while driving through olive groves to sleepy Amelia—Umbria's oldest town—before stepping into the medieval past of Todi. Finish off your visit to the province in Orvieto, with its unforgettable Duomo and wine that's pleased locals for 3,000 years.

Terni

 33 km (21 mi) southwest of Spoleto, 70 km (45 mi) southeast of Orvieto.

Although a convenient jumping-off point for Lake Piediluco and the Marmore Falls, there's not much to attract you to Terni. The town was heavily bombed by the allies in World War II because of its weapons and metals industry—not the kind of place you would associate with St. Valentine, who was martyred here in AD 273. Although a church just outside of town marks his burial place, his heart was removed and taken to Venice, that most romantic of cities. If you happen to find yourself here, Terni is not bereft of art, and the local **Pinacoteca** has Benozzo Gozzoli's *The Marriage of St. Catherine,* as well as several noteworthy modern paintings. ✉ *Via Frattini 55,* ☎ *0744/59421.* ✍ *€3.62.* ☉ *Tues.–Sun. 10–1 and 4–7.*

Just a few blocks from the Pinacoteca is the round church of **San Salvatore,** open daily 9–noon and 4–6. It was once thought to have been a Roman temple on account of its dome and oculus, a circular hole in the dome meant to represent the all-seeing eye of heaven.

....
OFF THE
BEATEN PATH

CASCATA DELLE MARMORE – East of Terni the road leads 10 km (6 mi) to the waterfalls at Marmore, which at 541 ft are the highest falls in Europe. They were created by the Romans in the 3rd century BC to prevent flooding in the nearby agricultural plains. Nowadays the waters are often diverted to provide hydroelectric power for Terni reducing the roaring falls to an unimpressive trickle, so check with the information office at the falls (☎ 0744/62982) or with Terni's tourist office before heading here. On summer evenings, when the falls are in full spate, the cascading water is floodlit to striking effect.

LAGO DI PIEDILUCO – The road east from Terni continues to Lake Piediluco, a nice spot to rest and get your feet wet. The lake is the prettiest in the region, surrounded by steep, forested hillsides. There are facilities for boat and canoe rental, as well as waterskiing and sailing.

Outdoor Activities and Sports

Rapids near the Cascata delle Marmore make for good water rafting for all skill levels; inquire at the **Centro Rafting Le Marmore** (⊠ Belvedere Inferiore, ☎ 0330/753420 or 0337/729154), open daily mid-March–October. Rafting is available to those between the ages of 15 and 55 and weighing less than 220 pounds. A descent, with a brief class beforehand, takes about two hours.

Narni

❷❻ *13 km (8 mi) southwest of Terni, 46 km (29 mi) southeast of Orvieto.*

Once a bustling and important town at a major crossroads of the Via Flaminia, Narni is now a quiet backwater with only the wind and the occasional tourist invading its quiet hilltop streets. Modern development is kept at bay (and out of sight) in the new town of Narni Scalo, below. This means that you will find the old part safely preserved behind, and, in the case of Narni's subterranean Roman ruins, beneath, the town's sturdy walls. For a look at Narni underground, contact the **Associazione Culturale Subterranea** (☎ 0744/722292) to set up a tour in English (⊠ €3.60).

The **Duomo** originally had three naves, but a fourth nave was added to the right of the church to incorporate a 6th-century shrine of San Giovenale, the patron saint of the town. As a result the Via Flaminia passes through the church. A 9th-century mosaic over the shrine is partially visible. ⊠ *Piazza Cavour,* ☎ *0744/722610.* ⊠ *Free.* ☉ *Daily 8–12:30 and 3–7.*

Piazza Garibaldi, the town's main square, is built over the **Lacus,** a large late-medieval cistern with vaulting and remains of the Roman-era stone pavement. The town's big artistic attraction is an altarpiece by Domenico Ghirlandaio (1449–94), *The Coronation of the Virgin,* in the Sala del Consiglio of the **Palazzo Comunale.** Opposite the altarpiece is a loggia by Gattapone. ⊠ *Piazza dei Priori,* ☎ *0744/715362.* ☉ *Daily 9–1 and 3–5.*

For centuries Narni was protected from invasion by its lofty perch above the Nera River and by its imposing **Rocca** (fortress). Built by Cardinal Albornoz in the 14th century, little now remains of the interior decoration of the castle, but the architecture and the views make the walk uphill worthwhile. ⊠ *Via del Monte,* ☎ *0744/715362.* ⊠ *Free.* ☉ *Apr.–Sept., Fri–Sun. 10–7; Oct.–Mar., call ahead for hrs.*

The 12th-century church of **Santa Maria Impensole** is well worth a visit for its finely carved facade. Under the church, excavations have revealed an 8th-century church with three naves and two aisles, built over a Roman temple that was converted into a crypt for the church above. There are also two Roman cisterns, one of them in especially good condition. ⊠ *Via Mazzini,* ☎ *0744/715362.* ⊠ *Free.* ☉ *Daily 9:30–12:30 and 4:30–6:30.*

The **Monastero di San Domenico,** once a monastery, is now the town library. Around the back, underneath the monastery, an entrance leads to a Romanesque church with frescoes from the 13th to 15th centuries. In the adjacent remains of a Roman building with a cistern is a cell used during the Inquisition. On its walls is graffiti left by prisoners. ⊠ *Via Mazzini,* ☎ *0744/747203.* 🎫 *Free.* ☉ *Weekdays 9–noon.*

Dining

$–$$$$ ✕ **Il Cavallino.** When it comes to eating out, many Narniani head 3 km (2 mi) out of town for first-rate home-style cooking in this trattoria run by the third generation of the Bussetti family. There are always lots of pastas to choose from and truffle in season. The specialty of the house is *palombaccio alla leccarda* (roasted pigeon). ⊠ *Via Flamina Romana 220,* ☎ *0744/761020. AE, D, MC, V. Closed Tues., last two weeks in July, and Dec. 20–26.*

Festivals

The town celebrates May's **Festa di San Giovenale** with two weeks of special festivities that culminate in the **Corsa all'Anello**: a ring is strung up across Via Maggiore and contestants from the town's neighborhoods try to put a lance through it.

Amelia

㉗ *50 km (31 mi) southeast of Orvieto.*

Amelia has the distinction of being the oldest town in the region, with archaeological evidence going back as far as 1100 BC. The little town's main attraction, the bulky **walls** that still surround it, shows that the Umbri knew a thing or two about fortifications—the walls are more than 20 ft thick at some points. Admire the town walls from a path that leads from Porta Romana around the perimeter of the town, or walk up the main road to the brick **Duomo,** open daily 10–1 and 4–6:30, at the top of the town. The interior, redone in the 19th century, is decorated with two Turkish flags won in the Battle of Lepanto. Although it now serves as its bell tower, the unusual **Torre Civica** (1050) predates the Duomo, its 12 sides thought to represent the signs of the zodiac or the Twelve Apostles. There are fine views from the top of the hill.

En Route The road northwest (S205) passes first through **Lugnano in Teverina,** with its important Collegiata di Santa Maria Assunta. The facade is the region's best piece of Romanesque architecture. The interior is mostly undecorated, apart from a handsome Cosmati mosaic floor, which has complex geometric patterns. Just a couple of miles ahead is the town of **Alviano,** where an important nature reserve, good for bird-watching, has been established at the nearby lake. The road continues through Baschi, westward (13 km [8 mi]) toward Orvieto, and east (28 km [17 mi]) to Todi.

Dining

$$ ✕ **Il Carleni.** This pleasant restaurant in the center of Amelia offers very good value, as well as special menus for children and vegetarians, a particular rarity in Umbria. The cuisine is Italian with some French influence (the owner's wife is French), and the seasonal menu may include tasty specialties such as pasta with eggplant and ricotta cheese or with truffles. There's also a pleasant garden for outside dining. ⊠ *Via P. Carleni 21,* ☎ *0744/983925. AE, D, MC, V. Closed Tues.*

Giove

㉘ *12½ km (8 mi) southwest of Amelia, 9½ km (6 mi) south of Lugnano in Teverina, 24 km (15 mi) west of Terni.*

The little town of Giove was named for the Roman god Jupiter (Jove) and a famous temple in his honor that once stood here. Just outside the town is a convent with a Madonna by Perugino. The town has an interesting 16th-century **Palazzo Ducale** (✉ Piazza XXIV Maggio, ☎ 0744/992928), open by appointment, with 365 windows (one for each of the days of the year) and a peculiar spiral ramp large enough to allow horse-driven carts to enter the building through the front door and reach the upper floors. The road continues to **Attigliano,** where the modern church of San Lorenzo the Martyr gives an idea of how all the churches in the region might look had they been built in the previous century.

Todi

🟡 *34 km (22 mi) south of Perugia, 34 km (22 mi) east of Orvieto.*

As you stand on Piazza del Popolo, looking out onto the Tiber Valley below, it's easy to see how Todi is often described as Umbria's prettiest hill town. Legend has it that the town was founded by the Umbri, who followed an eagle who had stolen a tablecloth to this lofty perch. They liked it so much that they settled here for good. The eagle is now perched on the insignia of the medieval palaces in the main piazza. But historical evidence suggests that the Umbri didn't find an empty nest; Iron Age remains dating from 2700 BC make it the oldest settled area in the region. The usual Etruscan to Roman progression continued, and Todi rose to prominence in the 13th century, when it ruled over the *comune* (township) that included Amelia and Terni. Aside from the view and charm of the streets, there are also two small but worthwhile museums. Todi is best reached by car, as the town's two train stations are way down the hill and connected to the town by infrequent bus service.

Built above the Roman Forum, **Piazza del Popolo** is Todi's high point, a model of spatial harmony with stunning views onto the surrounding countryside. In the best medieval tradition, the square was conceived to house both the temporal and spiritual centers of power.

On one end of the Piazza del Popolo is the 12th-century Romanesque–Gothic **Duomo,** with a simple facade enriched by a finely carved rose window. There's not much to draw you inside, as Ferraù da Faenza's copy of Michelangelo's *Last Judgment* only serves to illustrate the gap between the two artists. The severe, solid mass of the Duomo is mirrored by the Palazzo dei Priori across the way. ✉ *Piazza del Popolo,* ☎ *075/8943041.* 🎫 *Church free; crypt €1.* 🕐 *May–Sept., daily 8:30–12:30 and 2:30–6:30; Oct.–Apr., daily 8:30–4:30.*

A staircase on the Piazza del Popolo leads to the Palazzo del Popolo and the entrance to the **Museo Etrusco-Romano and Pinacoteca.** The first room is devoted to the history of Todi; the collection includes religious garments, local coins, Roman relics, Etruscan pottery, and more-recent ceramics from Deruta. The highlight of the Pinacoteca is the *Coronation of the Virgin* by Lo Spagna. ✉ *Palazzo del Popolo, Piazza del Popolo,* ☎ *075/8944148.* 🎫 *€3.10.* 🕐 *Oct.–Feb., Tues.–Sun. 10:30–1 and 2–4:30; Mar. and Sept., Tues.–Sun. 10:30–1 and 2–5; Apr., daily 10:30–1 and 2:30–6; May–Aug., Tues.–Sun. 10:30–1 and 4:30–6.*

Via di Santa Prassede heads down to the northern part of town; although called the *borgo nuovo* (new quarter), it includes two 14th-century churches and many well-preserved old buildings. Piazza del Popolo is thought to have been built over the remains of the town's Roman Forum, but the only ancient ruins visible are the so-called **Nicchioni** (large niches) that make up one side of Piazza del Mercato Vecchio, now used as a parking lot. Follow the signs from Corso Cavour. From the Nicchioni, continue down to the **Fontana di Scarnabecco,** a good stop for a sip of cool spring water. Benches are nearby.

Near Piazza Jacopone is the **Chiesa di San Fortunato.** Had the church been completed, it might have looked like a small version of the Duomo in Orvieto. But the project was never realized (legend has it that Lorenzo Maitani [circa 1275–1330] was given the job but was murdered by the jealous Orvietani to ensure that no other Duomo could rival their own). Aside from the carved doorway and captivating angels attributed to Jacopo della Quercia (circa 1371–1438), the church remains more impressive for its sheer mass than its makeup. The whitewashed interior is remarkably free of any Gothic atmosphere. Under the main altar is the crypt of the local saint Jacopone da Todi (circa 1230–1306), who was no stranger to sin when he experienced an extreme conversion, becoming so stringently ascetic that at first even the Franciscans didn't accept him. ⊠ *Piazza Umberti I,* ☎ *no phone.* 🎫 *Free.* ⊙ *Oct.–Mar., Mon. 9:30–12:30, Tues.–Sun. 9:30–12:30 and 3–5; Apr.–Sept., Mon. 9:30–12:30, Tues.–Sun. 9:30–12:30 and 3–7.*

The lane to the left of the Chiesa di San Fortunato exit leads to a public garden, where you'll find a few benches and all that's left of the Rocca, the papal fortress. Follow the signs for the winding path that descends to an unexpected Renaissance treasure, the church of **Santa Maria della Consolazione.** Thought to have been inspired by designs by Bramante, it was begun in 1508 but not finished for another hundred years. The perfect symmetry it has is heightened by an almost neoclassical purity of form and proportions. ⊠ *Piazza della Consolazione,* ☎ *075/8943120.* 🎫 *Free.* ⊙ *Apr.–Sept., daily 9–1 and 3–6; Oct.–Mar., daily 10–noon.*

Dining and Lodging

$$–$$$ ✕ **Ristorante Umbria.** Todi's most popular restaurant for more than four decades, Umbria is a reliable address for sturdy country food that can be enjoyed from a terrace with a wonderful view. There's always a hearty soup simmering away, as well as game, homemade pasta with truffles, and the specialty of the house, *palombaccio alla ghiotta* (roasted pigeon). ⊠ *Via San Bonaventura 13,* ☎ *075/8942737 or 075/8942390. AE, DC, MC, V. Closed Tues. and July.*

$$ ✕ **La Mulinella.** If it weren't for all the other tables around, you'd think you were a guest at the home of Signora Irma, who has been making bread and pasta for 35 years. If you intend to go on to *secondi* (second courses), beware of the primi piatti, which include dishes such as *tacchino farcito d'uva* (turkey stuffed with grapes) or stewed wild boar. Portions are enough for three and the waiters fear the wrath of Irma if they don't bring back an empty serving platter. So share a dish of her light-as-a-feather *gnocchetti* or tagliatelle in a goose sauce, and save room for the simple desserts. ⊠ *Località Pontenaia 29,* ☎ *075/ 8944779. MC, V. Closed Wed.*

$$ 🏠 **Fattoria di Vibio.** A cluster of old stone farmhouses set on a ridge
★ north of Todi has been converted into this gracious and relaxed country compound, with painter's views of the vineyards and valleys below. Hike the country roads or relax poolside in summer; you can while the evening away at candlelit tables outside on the lawn or, on chilly nights, in front of the ample stone fireplace. For families or extended stays, the two independent cottages, with maid service and full use of hotel facilities, are a good deal. ⊠ *Località Buchella, Doglio, Montecastello di Vibio 06057 (12 km [7 mi] northwest of Todi),* ☎ *075/ 8749607,* 🖷 *075/8780014,* 🌐 *www.fattoriadivibio.com. 10 rooms, 3 suites, 2 cottages. Dining room, pool, mountain bikes, paddle tennis, bar, Internet; no air-conditioning. AE, DC, MC, V. Closed Dec.– Feb., bookings of 1 wk or more only July–Aug. MAP.*

$$ ⛨ **Tenuta di Canonica.** Exposed stone walls, high beamed ceilings, and terra-cotta tiles are set off by cool colors and handsome lighting in this brick farmhouse 5 km (3 mi) northwest of Todi in the Tiber Valley. Guest rooms, which have access to a working ancient well, are filled with family antiques, Oriental rugs, candelabra, and fresh fruit and flowers. You can hike or horseback ride among the olive groves, orchards, and forest on the grounds, which also include two apartments that each sleep two to three people. ✉ *Località La Canonica, 75–76, follow signs to Titignano and Cordigliano, 06059,* ☎ *075/8947545,* 🅵🅰🆇 *075/ 8947581,* 🆆🅴🅱 *www.tenutadicanonica.com. 11 rooms, 2 apartments. Dining room, pool, library; no air-conditioning. No credit cards.*

Shopping

Todi is full of little shops, a surprising number of them selling fresh fruit. The local sweet, available in most pastry shops, is *panpolenta* (a coffee cake made with corn flour and ground almonds). Local ceramics are available from several boutiques along Corso Cavour. The town also hosts one of Italy's most important annual antiques fairs (usually two weeks around Easter). For the dates and venue, contact the tourist office.

ORVIETO

The natural defenses of an enormous plateau rising 1,000 ft above the flat valley proved very attractive to settlers in central Italy as far back as the Bronze Age, making Orvieto among the oldest cities in the region. The Etruscans developed the town considerably, carving a network of 1,200 wells and storage caves out of the soft tufa (volcanic stone) of the mount on which the city was built. By 283 BC, the Romans had attacked, sacked, and destroyed the city, by then known as Volsinii Veteres. Perhaps they were attracted by the golden Orvieto Classico made from grapes grown in the rich volcanic soil of the valley below—a wine the town is still famous for today.

Charlemagne (742–814) changed the name to Urbs Vetus, from which the modern name derives. The town rose steadily as an independent commune in the late Middle Ages, with construction beginning on the Duomo after the Miracle at Bolsena took place in 1263. When the Guelphs won decisively over the Ghibellines in the 14th century, Orvieto passed under the control of the papacy and was subsequently used by the popes as a refuge from enemies or the summer heat of Rome.

In addition to wine and some of the best restaurants in the region, Orvieto has much to offer: the much-celebrated Duomo, with Italy's finest Gothic facade, is worth the trip alone. Inside are masterful frescoes, stunningly restored, by Luca Signorelli (circa 1450–1523), perhaps the most underrated in the entire country. A couple of good museums and some excavations round out the sights.

The festival highlight of the year is the Festa della Palombella on Pentecost Sunday (the seventh Sunday after Easter). In this unique take on a fireworks show, a tabernacle with images of the Madonna and the Apostles is set up on the steps in front of the central doorway of the Duomo. A white dove attached to a cable strung across the piazza slides down and ignites the fireworks.

A more traditional celebration is the Festa del Corpus Domini (the ninth Sunday after Easter), begun by Pope Urban IV in 1264, which may have its origin in the Miracle at Bolsena, the same event the Duomo was built to commemorate. Each year Bolsena's miraculous, blood-stained *corporale* (square linen cloth) is taken out of the chapel and led around town in a solemn procession, preceded by a rich court in sumptuous period costumes. Between Christmas and the first days of January, the Umbria Jazz Festival comes to Orvieto. Plan on big crowds, high-season rates in the hotels, and plenty of music flowing through the streets.

Exploring Orvieto

Orvieto is well connected by train to Rome, Florence, and Perugia. It's also adjacent to the A1 superstrada that runs between Florence and Rome. Parking areas in the upper town tend to be crowded. There is ample parking in the lower town, near the railway station, and on the other side of town in Campo della Fiera (at the end of SS71).

In the 19th century, the steep grade led the Orvietani to build an ingenious funicular that runs from the train station up the side of the hill and through the fortress to Piazzale Cahen. It runs every 20 minutes, daily 7:15 AM–8:30 PM, and costs 80 European cents. Although the workings have been modernized, there are a few pictures in each station of the old cog railcars, which were once run hydraulically. Keep your funicular ticket, as it will get you a discount on admission to the Museo Claudio Faina.

Bus 1 makes the same trip from 8 AM to 11 PM. From Piazzale Cahen, bus A runs to Piazza del Duomo in town center. A *biglietto unico* (single ticket) is a great deal; for €12.50, you get admission to the four major sights in town—Cappella di San Brizio (at the Duomo), Museo Claudio Faina, Torre del Moro, and Orvieto Underground—plus a combination bus–funicular pass or five hours of free parking.

A Good Walk

Piazzale Cahen, where there's a large parking lot and the funicular station, is a good place to begin. A quick walk around **La Rocca** will give you an idea of just how far you have come from the valley floor. The fortress is now a public garden with great views from its battlements. Nearby are the **Pozzo di San Patrizio** ㉚ and the ruins of an Etruscan Temple. Cross Piazzale Cahen and walk up Corso Cavour, which cuts through to the center of town. Only about halfway up, as the streets narrow and plaster and stucco are replaced by stone, does Orvieto begin to resemble the other hill towns in the region. Off to the right, Via San Leonardo leads to Piazza del Popolo, where there's a good little market on Thursday and Saturday mornings, as well as Orvieto's most handsome civic building, the 13th-century Romanesque-Gothic **Palazzo del Popolo** ㉛.

Return to the Corso and take Via del Duomo to the left, which leads past several gift shops selling local ceramics and curves toward Piazza del Duomo. The spires of the **Duomo** ㉜ just come into view, along with a glimpse of the marvelous multicolored facade that extends skyward, an effect that is heightened once you arrive at the piazza. Stop in at the nearby tourist office for tickets to the Duomo's Cappella di San Brizio to marvel at the fresco cycle by Luca Signorelli. Around the corner is the **Museo Archeologico** ㉝, with a disappointingly sparse collection that is poorly maintained—only a must for hard-core Etruscan fans, who by now will probably have seen much better relics elsewhere. In the part of the building at the far right that juts out is the **Museo Emilio Greco** ㉞, housing a worthwhile collection of bronze sculptures and sketches by the contemporary Sicilian sculptor, who made the doors of the Duomo. The **Museo Claudio Faina** ㉟, directly across from the entrance to the Duomo, has a beautifully arranged collection of Etruscan sculpture and jewelry; it's worth the admission price just for

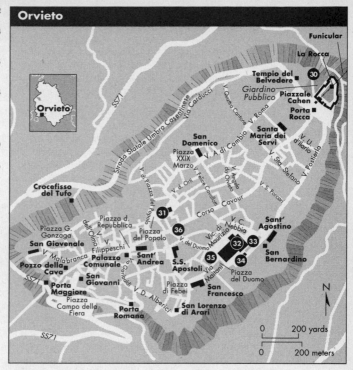

Orvieto

the views of the facade of the Duomo from the second-floor hallway.
Back on the Corso is the 14th-century **Torre del Moro** ㊱, with a bell
at the top with the 24 symbols of the arts practiced in Orvieto. With
all the activity focused around Piazza del Duomo, you're likely to find
the rest of Orvieto relatively quiet, except during the *passeggiata*
(evening stroll), which is particularly thick along the Corso in the
evenings. Before you leave Orvieto, don't miss the chance to have a
look at the carved-out bowels of its mighty tufa mount.

TIMING

The main sights in town can be seen in a full day; allow plenty of time
for the Duomo and the Cappella di San Brizio, although a day and a
half might do just as well, especially because Orvieto has several great
restaurants. Thursday and Saturday are especially good for the market in Piazza del Popolo.

Sights to See

OFF THE
BEATEN PATH

CROCEFISSO DEL TUFO – This 6th century BC Etruscan necropolis, about 2
km (1 mi) down Viale Crispi, doesn't have the frescoes that other Etruscan tombs are famous for, and the relics that were buried within have
long since been taken away (mostly to the Museo Claudio Faino). But
the walk here is pleasant, and it can be interesting to see the type of site
from which nearly all our knowledge of Etruscans comes; like the Egyp-
tians, they equipped the dead with everyday items to ease their journey
to the next world. Names of the deceased are carved into the stone ar-
chitraves above tomb chambers. The relative lack of pictorial decoration
and the standard size of these tombs have led some to speculate that
these were not tombs of aristocratic families or warriors. ⊠ 1½ km (1
mi) from Piazzale Cahen, down Viale F. Crispi (SS71), ☎ 0763/
343611. ⊠ €2.00. ⊙ Daily 8:30–dusk.

★ **Duomo.** Orvieto's Duomo is, quite simply, stunning. In a country with so many churches to marvel at, hyperbole should be reserved for a select few—this is one of them. Your first glimpse of the facade will likely be a partial view, perhaps of the gray spires against the sky or the gold mosaics shimmering in the light. Even when you get to the center of the piazza, you'll find that it's too shallow to allow the monumental facade to be taken in with a single glance.

Before completion, the Duomo passed into the hands of dozens of architects, artists, and artisans, but the die had essentially been cast. For a building designed by committee, the results are surprisingly harmonious and balanced. It is thought that Arnolfo di Cambio (circa 1245–1302), the famous builder of the Duomo in Florence, was given the initial commission. But the project was soon taken over by Lorenzo Maitani (circa 1275–1330), who consolidated the structure and designed the facade. Maitani also made the bas-relief panels between the doorways, which graphically tell the story of the Creation (on the left) and the Last Judgment (on the right). The lower registers, now protected by Plexiglas, succeed in conveying the horror of hell as few other works of art manage to do, an effect made all the more powerful by the worn gray marble.

Above are bronze statues of an eagle, lion, angel, and bull. Representing the four evangelists, they were also done by Maitani. The bare lunette above the central doorway marks the place of the bronze and marble *Maestà* (1325), which was removed for restoration (at this writing, the decision to return the statue to its original location after restoration or to move it into the cathedral museum has not yet been made). Gold mosaics, framed by finely detailed Gothic decoration, lead up to a sensational rose window by mid-14th-century artist Orcagna. The mosaics were remade in the 17th and 18th centuries.

The origins of the church itself go back to the Miracle at Bolsena. In 1263, a young priest who questioned the miracle of transubstantiation (in which the communional bread and wine become the blood and flesh of Christ) was saying mass at nearby Lago di Bolsena. His doubts were put to rest, however, when a wafer he had just blessed suddenly started to drip blood, staining the linen covering the altar. The cloth and the host were taken to the pope, who proclaimed a miracle and a year later provided for a new religious holiday—the Feast of Corpus Domini. Thirty years later, construction began on a *duomo* to celebrate the miracle and house the stained altar cloth.

Step inside the vast and rather empty interior, and head straight to the transept. To the left is the **Cappella del Corporale,** where the square linen cloth (corporale) is kept in a golden reliquary that's modeled on the cathedral and inlaid with enamel scenes of the miracle. The cloth is removed for public viewing on Easter and on Corpus Domini (the ninth Sunday after Easter). On the right wall is the miracle scene as imagined by mid-14th-century artist Ugolino di Prete Ilario; opposite are scenes of past miracles involving the Eucharist. Also in the chapel is 14th-century artist Lippo Memmi's *Madonna dei Raccomandati,* showing groups of pious men and women gathered for protection beneath the outspread cloak of the Virgin Mary. Much modified, especially during the 19th century, restoration work has revealed the rich tones of the painting's original colors.

In the right transept is the **Cappella di San Brizio,** or Cappella Nuova. In this chapel is one of Italy's greatest fresco cycles, notable for its influence on Michelangelo's *Last Judgment,* as well as for the extraordinary beauty of the figuration. Along with Giotto's frescoes in Assisi, these are the most important paintings in Umbria. The frescoes have emerged from restoration with colors that are nothing short of shocking in their brilliance, made all the more powerful by the relatively short distance from which they are viewed.

Several great masters, including Benozzo Gozzoli and Fra Angelico, were called to decorate the chapel, but none got very far, and what is admired today is almost entirely the work of Luca Signorelli, who painted here between 1499 and 1504. The choice of the Last Judgment as a subject can be linked to apocalyptic predictions concerning the year 1500. General confidence had been very badly shaken by the invasion of Italy in 1494 by the King of France, Charles VIII (1470–98). It is believed that the preachings of the Dominican friar Girolamo Savonarola (1452–1498)—eventually burnt at the stake for heresy—provided Signorelli with a model for the Antichrist of the frescoes.

The story begins on the left wall with *Sermon of the Antichrist,* in which Christians are martyred in the background as Signorelli and Fra Angelico (1387–1455) look on from the left side. On the archway over the entrance wall, the story continues with the scene of the *End of the World,* closely tied to the description in the New Testament: the young and old flee in fear, tumbling out of the scene as the sun darkens, the stars fall from the sky, earthquakes bring buildings to the ground, and demons appear, breathing fire and blood. In *Resurrection of the Body* on the right wall, two angels summon skeletons from the ground to be recomposed for Judgment Day. The notable absence of children and the elderly suggests that Signorelli followed the interpretation that the dead would be resurrected in perfect health and to age 33, the same age as Christ when he was crucified, a notion that undoubtedly appealed to the classical ideals of the perfection of man. Here we see Signorelli's tremendous fascination with the male body, a hallmark of the Renaissance; but rather than dozens of different figures, it seems that the artist has painted a single perfected human form, seen from a thousand angles and iterated across a glorious scene in a fugue of flesh and bones. Michelangelo (1475–1564) was an admirer, while Leonardo (1452–1519) thought otherwise, complaining that the figures' bulky musculature looked like a "sack full of nuts." The following scene, *Casting out of the Damned,* is an impressive tangle of bodies and demons flying above, picking up sinners and dropping them into the gates of hell. On the wall behind the altar, the *Angels Drive the Sinners to Hell and Guide the Elect to Paradise* are scenes heavily influenced by the imagery in Dante's (1265–1321) *The Divine Comedy.* The cycle finishes on the left wall with a majestic final scene of the *Blessed Entering Heaven* as they are serenaded by angels on the rise. In this case the bodies reinforce the classical pairing of goodness and beauty.

As if the fresco cycle did not do enough to link the contemporary with the classical, Signorelli chose to decorate the lower registers with medallions of great classical personages such as Homer (circa 9th–8th centuries BC), Virgil (70–19 BC), and Horace (65–8 BC) and show the link to his day by including Dante and other great Italian thinkers. ✉ *Piazza del Duomo,* ☎ 0763/342477. 🎫 *Cappella di San Brizio €3.* 🕐 *Nov.–Feb., daily 7:30–12:45 and 2:30–5:15; Mar. and Oct., daily 7:30–12:45 and 2:30–6:15; Apr.–Sept., daily 7:30–12:45 and 2:30–7:15.*

NEED A BREAK? Orvieto has plenty of spots to grab a quick bite—a boon in off-hours, when restaurants are closed and sightseers get peckish. **Gastronomia Carraro** (✉ Corso Cavour 101, ☎ 0763/342870), closed Sunday, has an excellent selection of local cheeses and sausages. The **Pasticceria Montanucci** (✉ Corso Cavour 21, ☎ 0763/341261) offers a seemingly endless selection of chocolates and candies. For a snack or coffee on tables outside, check out **Bar Sant'Andrea** (⊠ Piazza della Repubblica, ☎ 0763/343285). Across the piazza is the odd-looking 12-side bell tower of the church of Sant'Andrea. Wonderful gelato in large scoops is to be had at **L'Archetto** (⊠ Piazza del Duomo 14, ☎ 0763/341034), its outdoor tables shaded by ivy. It's closed mid-December through February.

③ **Museo Archeologico.** With its Etruscan roots, one might expect that Orvieto would have a first-rate archaeological museum, but it seems that the best relics and enthusiasm for displaying them were put into the Museo Claudio Faina, the private collection housed in front of the Duomo. Greek vases and some interesting relics found in excavations nearby, including pieces of soldiers' armor, have been set out in four rooms of one of the 13th-century papal palaces that stand next to the Duomo, but the items are poorly presented, with incomplete descriptions. If you do go, ask the sleepy staff to turn the lights on in the two reconstructed Etruscan tombs with detached frescoes from the Necropolis of Settecamini. ⊠ *Piazza del Duomo,* ☎ *0763/341039.* 🎟 €2.00. ☉ *Daily 8:30–7.*

★ ③ **Museo Claudio Faina.** This superb private collection, beautifully arranged and presented, goes far beyond the usual museum offerings of a scattering of local remains. The collection is particularly rich in Greek- and Etruscan-era pottery, from large Attic amphorae (6th–4th century BC) to Attic black-and-red figure pieces to Etruscan *bucchero* (dark, reddish clay) vases. The collection shows how the Etruscans were slowly influenced by Greek culture, first importing their pottery, then crafting pottery themselves, and eventually taking on the Greek notion of gods of the afterworld—as shown in several pots found nearby with the figure of Vanth, a winged Etruscan goddess. Other interesting pieces in the collection include a 6th-century sarcophagus with traces of polychromatic decoration, gold jewelry, masks, and a substantial display of Roman-era coins. Don't miss the view of the facade of the Duomo from the hallway windows on the second floor. ⊠ *Piazza del Duomo 29,* ☎ *0763/341511.* 🎟 €4.20; €2.50 with funicular or bus ticket. ☉ Apr.–Sept., daily 9:30–6; Oct.–Mar., Tues.–Sun. 10–5.

③ **Museo Emilio Greco.** Another medieval building built by a pope on leave here from Rome, 13th-century Palazzo Soliano was for many years the location of the Museo dell'Opera del Duomo, a fine collection that includes works by Signorelli and other notable names like Simone Martini, Pisano, and Arnolfo di Cambio. But the art treasures have been locked away during an interminable restoration. Meanwhile, the ground floor has been made into the Museo Emilio Greco, a good-looking space filled with sculpture and sketches that the prolific Sicilian artist Emilio Greco (born 1913)—who also made the doors for the Duomo in the 1960s—donated to the city. ⊠ *Piazza del Duomo, Palazzo Soliano,* ☎ *0763/344605.* 🎟 €2.50; €4.50 combination ticket, including the Pozzo di San Patrizio. ☉ Apr.–Sept., Mon.–Fri. 10:30–1 and 2–6:30, weekends 10:30–1 and 2:30–7; Oct.–Mar., daily 10:30–1 and 2–5:30.

OFF THE
BEATEN PATH

ORVIETO UNDERGROUND – More than just about any other town, Orvieto has grown from its own foundations—if one were to remove from present-day Orvieto all the building materials that were dug up from below, there would hardly be a building left standing. The Etruscans, the Romans, and those who followed dug into the tufa (the same soft volcanic rock from which catacombs were made) and over the centuries created more than 1,000 separate cisterns, caves, secret passages, storage areas, and production areas for wine and olive oil. Some of the tufa they removed was used as building blocks for the city that exists today and some was partly ground into *pozzolana,* which was made into mortar. The most thorough tour of the Orvieto underground (in English, about an hour long) is run daily at 11 AM and 4 PM out of the Orvieto **tourist office**; admission is €5.20. If you are short on time but still want a look at what it was like down there, head for the **Pozzo della Cava** (✉ Via della Cava 28, ☎ 0763/342373), open Wednesday through Monday 8–dusk; admission is €1.70.

③① **Palazzo del Popolo.** Built in tufa and basaltic rock, this was once the town hall. Restoration work in the late 1980s revealed the remains of an Etruscan temple underneath, and it now holds the conference center and the state archives. ✉ *Piazza del Popolo.*

③⓪ **Pozzo di San Patrizio** (St. Patrick's Well). When Pope Clement VII (1478–1534) took shelter in Orvieto during the Sack of Rome in 1527, he saw the need to ensure a safe water supply in the event that Orvieto were to come under siege. Many wells and cisterns were built, and the pope commissioned one of the great architects of the day, Antonio da Sangallo the Younger (1493–1546), to build the well adjacent to the Rocca. After nearly a decade of digging, water was found at a depth of 203 ft. The pope had since died, but the well was finished as planned, with two one-way spiral stairways that allowed donkey-driven carts to descend to the water level and then climb back out without running into one another. Windows open onto the shaft, providing natural light in the stairwells. There are 248 steps down to the bottom, but you'll probably get the idea after just a few. About the name: somebody once likened the well to St. Patrick's Well in Ireland. The name stuck, and in Italian the phrase *"pozzo di san patrizio"* has come to represent an inexhaustible source of wealth. ✉ *Via Sangallo, off Piazza Cahen,* ☎ *0763/343768.* ▦ *€3.50; €4.50 combination ticket, including the Museo Emilio Greco.* ☉ *Apr.–Sept., Mon.–Fri. 10–7, weekends 9:30–7:30; Oct.–Mar., daily 10–5:15; ticket office closes 15 mins before closing time.*

③⑥ **Torre del Moro.** Perhaps the extraordinary attention lavished on the Duomo left the locals indifferent about the tower in the center of their town; it's hard to imagine a simpler, duller affair. It took on a little more character in the 19th century, when the large, white-faced clock was added along with the fine 14th-century bell, marked with the symbols of the 24 arts-and-crafts guilds then operating in the city. The views, however, are worth the climb. ✉ *Corso Cavour at Via del Duomo,* ☎ *0763/344567.* ▦ *€2.50.* ☉ *May–Aug., daily 10–8; Mar.–Apr. and Sept.–Oct., daily 10–7; Nov.–Feb., daily 10–1 and 2:30–5.*

Dining and Lodging

$$–$$$ ✕ **Le Grotte del Funaro.** This restaurant is within a series of caves in-
★ side the volcanic rock beneath Orvieto. Once you have negotiated the steep steps, typical Umbrian specialties such as tagliatelle *al vino rosso* (with red-wine sauce) and grilled beef with truffles await. Sample the fine Orvieto wines, either the whites or the lesser-known reds. ✉ *Via Ripa Serancia 41,* ☎ *0763/343276,* ᴡᴇʙ *www.ristoranti-orvieto.it. Reservations essential. AE, DC, MC, V. Closed Mon. and 1 week in July.*

$$–$$$ ✕ **Maurizio.** In the heart of Orvieto, just opposite the cathedral, this
★ warm and welcoming restaurant gets its share of tourists and has a local clientele as well. The unusual interior makes use of wood sculptures by Orvieto craftsman Michelangeli. The menu offers hearty soups and homemade pastas such as *tronchetti* (a pasta roll with spinach and ri-

cotta filling). ✉ *Via del Duomo 78,* ☎ *0763/341114. Reservations essential in summer. AE, MC, V. Closed Tues.*

$$$$ 🛏 **Hotel La Badia.** This is one of the best-known country hotels in Umbria. The 12th-century building, a former abbey, is set in rolling parkland that provides wonderful views of the valley and the town of Orvieto in the distance. The rooms are elegantly appointed with antique furnishings, parquet flooring and well-equipped bathrooms. ✉ *Località La Badia, 4 km (2½ mi) south of Orvieto, 05018,* ☎ *0763/ 301959,* FAX *0763/305396,* WEB *www.labadiahotel.it. 21 rooms, 7 suites. Restaurant, 2 tennis courts, pool, bar, meeting rooms. AE, MC, V. Closed Jan–Feb.*

$$$ 🛏 **Hotel Maitani.** In a 17th-century Baroque palazzo, this hotel has rather ugly public rooms and no restaurant. On the other hand, parquet and marble grace the floors and there's a deluxe roof terrace. The rooms are old-fashioned but comfortable. ✉ *Via Maitani 5, 05018,* ☎ *0763/ 342011,* FAX *0763/342012,* WEB *www.argoweb.it/hotelmaitani. 31 rooms, 8 suites. Bar. AE, DC, MC, V. Closed Jan. and Dec. 24–25.*

$–$$ 🛏 **Grand Hotel Reale.** The best feature of this hotel is its location in the center of Orvieto, across a square that hosts a lively market. Facing the impressive Gothic–Romanesque Palazzo del Popolo, rooms are spacious and adequately furnished, with a traditional accent. ✉ *Piazza del Popolo 25, 05018,* ☎ *0763/341247,* FAX *0763/341247. 32 rooms. Bar, breakfast room. MC, V. CP.*

Enoteche

Orvieto has been known for white wine since its beginnings. There is evidence that the Etruscans grew grapes in the rich volcanic soil in the valley below and then fermented their wine in the cool caverns dug out of the tufa atop the hill. The Romans made special efforts to bring the local wine, which they blended with water and spices, down to Rome. Things had not changed by the early 16th century, when Signorelli was paid in part with wine for his work on the Cappella di San Brizio.

Today, wine (along with tourism) is an essential part of the local economy. Although it is the best-known wine in the region, it is no longer one of Italy's best. However, it is pleasantly drinkable and light, and chances are that the Orvieto Classico you find in the town itself will be better than those exported in large quantities. You will also have the chance to taste different types of Orvieto, from the well-known dry Orvieto Classico to the less-commercialized *abboccato* (semisweet) and the intensely flavored, sweeter *muffato*.

Begin your tastings at these *enoteche* (wine bars), *cantine* (cellars or wine shops), and *vinerie* (wineries). At **Cantina Foresi** (✉ Piazza del Duomo 2, ☎ 0763/341611), closed Tuesday, November through February, hundreds of bottles are stored in the cool earth of the cellar. The few outdoor tables are a great place for a light snack while sipping. In addition to wine served all day long, **L'Asino d'Oro** (✉ Vicolo del Popolo 1, ☎ 0763/344406), closed October through March, serves lunch and dinner, with a different soup and first course every day and plenty of cold snacks between meals. At **La Bottega del Buon Vino** (✉ Via della Cava 26, ☎ 0763/342373), closed Tuesday, a window in the floor looks down into the caves.

Many area wine producers create excellent variations of the standard Orvieto Classico wine. Close to town is **Azienda Agricola Palazzone** (✉ Località Rocca Ripesana, 5 km [3 mi] from Orvieto, ☎ 0763/ 344166), where Muffa Nobile, Grechetto, and Orvieto Classico Superior may be sampled. **Castello della Sala** (✉ Località Sala, 20 km [12 mi] north of Orvieto, ☎ 0763/86051), owned by the Antinori group, produces white wines of high quality. Housed in a 14th-century castle, this is an especially interesting place to try out some of Orvieto's new-style wines—Cervaro della Sala, Grechetto, and Chardonnay—all aged in oak barrels.

Festivals

If you're in Orvieto on Pentecost Sunday (the seventh Sunday after Easter), don't miss the **Festa della Palombella.** The fireworks show in front of the Duomo is set off with a dove.

Shopping

Ceramics

As do other towns in the region, Orvieto has its fair share of pottery resellers, along with a few genuine shops selling Orvietan-style pottery, bright-white vessels with hand-painted motifs. **La Torreta** (⊠ Corso Cavour 283, ☎ 0763/340248) has a kiln right in the shop and will custom paint something for you on the spot. The copies of ancient ceramics that were made by **L'Arte del Vasaio** (⊠ Via Pedota 3, ☎ 0763/342022) were good enough to fool the curators of a famous museum, who displayed them as the real thing.

Embroidery and Lace

Established in 1907 to provide work to impoverished women, the tradition of lace-making, or *Ars Wetana,* has flourished in Orvieto. Using designs inspired by the reliefs on the facade of the Duomo, the patterns of Orvietan lace are unique and distinctive. Specializing in *merletto* (lace) products, **Duranti** (⊠ Corso Cavour 107, ☎ no phone) maintains the high standards set by one of the sustainers of the tradition during the last century, Eleonora Duranti. The Moretti family has long been associated with lace-making in Orvieto. Their products can be admired at **Ditta Moretti Merletti** (⊠ Via Duomo 55, ☎ 0763/41714).

Liqueurs

Gli Svizzeri Drogheria (⊠ Corso Cavour 35, ☎ 0763/341233) makes its own digestives and bitters, as well as *rosolio* (a sweet liqueur, mildly alcoholic) flavored with almond.

Market

The best times to experience an outdoor market in Orvieto are Thursday and Saturday morning, when a small but good market bustles at **Piazza del Popolo.** You'll find a few stalls selling crafts, but mostly vegetable stands and an assortment of clothing, housewares, and junk.

Woodwork

Orvieto is a center for woodworking, particularly fine inlays and veneers. Corso Cavour is lined with a number of artisan woodworking shops, the best known being the **Michelangeli family studio** (⊠ Via Gualverio Michelangeli 3, at Corso Cavour, ☎ 0763/342377). The imaginatively designed objects range in size from a giant *armadio* (wardrobe) to a simple wooden spoon.

ASSISI, SPOLETO, AND SOUTHERN UMBRIA A TO Z

To research prices, get advice from other travelers, and book travel arrangements, visit www.fodors.com.

AIR TRAVEL

There are no direct international flights into Perugia's Aeroporto Sant' Egidio, the only major airport in the region, and connections to do-

mestic services are required if you wish to travel all the way by air to Umbria. Flights to Perugia are operated by Alitalia from Milan's Malpensa airport, by Meridiana from Florence's Amerigo Vespucci Airport at Peretola, and by Air Vallée from Rome's Leonardo da Vinci at Fiumicino. Because only Alitalia offers a daily service, arrival through Milan is much more convenient than through either Florence or Rome.
➤ CARRIERS: **Alitalia** (☎ 848/865641, WEB www.alitalia.it). **Meridiana** (☎ 119/111333, WEB www.meridiana.it). **Air Vallée** (☎ 0165/303303, WEB www.airvallee.com).

AIRPORTS
The closest major airports are Rome's Fiumicino (officially Aeroporto Leonardo da Vinci), Pisa's Galileo Galilei, and Florence's Peretola (officially Aeroporto A. Vespucci). Tiny Aeroporto Sant'Egidio, 12 km (7 mi) east of Perugia, has flights to and from Milan, Florence, and Rome.
➤ AIRPORT INFORMATION: **Aeroporto A. Vespucci** (known as Peretola; ☎ 055/3061700). **Aeroporto Galileo Galilei** (☎ 050/500707, WEB www.pisa-airport.com). **Aeroporto Leonardo da Vinci** (known as Fiumicino; ☎ 06/6594420, WEB www.adr.it). **Aeroporto Sant'Egidio** (☎ 075/592141, WEB www.airport.umbria.it).

BUS TRAVEL
A number of private bus lines operate within the region and offer service to and from major cities in Tuscany and Lazio. Perugia's Sulga line runs between Rome's international airport and Perugia. The Sienese company SENA makes city connections between Tuscany, Umbria, and Lazio, and Florence, Siena, Perugia, Orvieto, and Rome. Spoletina operates buses both within the city of Spoleto and between a number of the main towns of the region, including Perugia, Assisi, Norcia, Terni, and Foligno.
➤ BUS LINES: **SENA** (✉ Piazza Gramsci, Siena, ☎ 0577/283203, WEB www.sena.it). **Spoletina** (✉ SS Flaminia Km. 127.7, Spoleto, ☎ 0743/212208). **Sulga** (✉ Strada dei Cappucinelli 4/d, Perugia, ☎ 075/5009641, WEB www.sulga.it).

CAR RENTALS
If you don't arrive in the area with a rental car from a major airport or town elsewhere in Italy, the best place to pick up a rental vehicle is probably Orvieto, accessible by train and by bus from both Florence and Rome.
➤ AGENCIES: **Avis** (✉ Via XX Settembre 80/d, Terni, ☎ 0744/287170, WEB www.avis.com). **Europcar Italia** (✉ Lungonera Savoia 12/c, Terni, ☎ 0744/282652). **Hertz** (WEB www.hertz.com; ✉ Via 7 Martiri 32/f, Orvieto, ☎ 0763/301303; ✉ Via Cerquiglia 144, Spoleto, ☎ 0743/46703).

CAR TRAVEL
The region is easily reached from the Rome–Florence autostrada (A1), which has exits at Orvieto and Perugia. The main highways within the region run south from Perugia (E45) to Todi and Terni or southeast from Perugia to Assisi, Spello, Foligno, and Spoleto (via S75) and Terni (via S3). Orvieto lies above the Rome–Florence autostrada (A1) and is also connected to Todi by a country road (79 bis).

EMERGENCIES
In an emergency, dial **113** for paramedics, police, or the fire department.

Pharmacies take turns staying open late or on Sunday; for the latest information, consult the list posted outside each pharmacy, or ask at the local tourist office.

LANGUAGE

English is fairly commonly spoken in the major tourist towns of Perugia, Assisi, Spoleto, and Orvieto. Elsewhere in the area it's more important to know at least a few phrases of Italian.

LODGING

APARTMENT AND VILLA RENTALS

➤ LOCAL AGENTS: **Home in Italy** (✉ Via Adelaide 50/c, Perugia, 06128, ☎ 075/5057865, FAX 075/5006127, WEB www.homeinitaly.com).

BED-AND-BREAKFASTS

➤ RESERVATION SERVICES: **Tandem** (✉ Piazza Mazzini, Trevi, 06038, ☎ 0742/780066, WEB www.bedandbreakfastumbria.it).

OUTDOOR ACTIVITIES AND SPORTS

Magnificent scenery makes Umbria a great place to enjoy the outdoors. The region offers excellent hiking, mountaineering, rock climbing, and horseback riding, and most tourist offices have maps of nearby trails and itineraries of walks and climbs to suit all ages and abilities.

Lago di Piediluco (Lake Piediluco) is a safe, clean place to swim, and there is river rafting in the Valnerina, in the Nera River, below the waterfalls at Marmore. Southern Umbria has several famous *terme* (thermal springs), which have long been visited by travelers for their soothing, curative powers.

➤ HIKING AND CLIMBING: **Club Alpino Italiano** (CAI; ☎ 075/220433).
➤ THERMAL SPRINGS: **Terme Amerino** (✉ Via San Francesco 1, Acquasparta 05021, between Terni and Todi, ☎ 0744/943921); closed Nov.–Apr. **Terme di San Gemini** (✉ SS3 [Tiberina] Km 21, San Gemini, near Terni, ☎ 0744/630426); closed Oct.–Apr. **Terme di Santo Raggio** (✉ Via P. A. Giorgi 6, near Assisi, ☎ 075/816064); closed Nov.–mid-May.

TOURS

Fully licensed English-speaking guides are available for groups or for individuals in many towns throughout Umbria. Full- and half-day tours may be booked with fixed rates through the regional Association of Tourist Guides.

➤ CONTACT: **Associazione Guide Turistiche dell'Umbria** (Umbrian Association of Tourist Guides; ☎ 075/815228).

TRAIN TRAVEL

Although three train lines connect most of the towns, the stations are often a couple of miles from the towns themselves. Slow trains on the Rome–Ancona line make stops in Narni-Amelia, Terni, Spoleto, Trevi, and Foligno, while the Terontola–Foligno line connects Foligno, Spello, Assisi, and Perugia. Slow trains on the Rome–Florence line stop in Orvieto. Ferrovia dello Stato, the Italian state railway, has information about train schedules and fares, including a pre-booking service.

➤ TRAIN STATIONS: **Ferrovia dello Stato** (FS; ☎ 848/888088 toll-free within Italy, WEB www.fs-on-line.it or www.trenitalia.it).

TRAVEL AGENCIES

➤ AGENCIES: **Agenzia Jazz Viaggi e Vacanze** (✉ Piazza della Libertà 11, Spoleto, ☎ 0743/221818). **Agenzia Stoppini** (✉ Corso Mazzini 31, Assisi, ☎ 075/812597). **Orvietur Viaggi e Turismo** (✉ Via Duomo 23, Orvieto, ☎ 0763/341555).

VISITOR INFORMATION

➤ TOURIST INFORMATION: **Assisi** (✉ Piazza del Comune 12, ☎ 075/812534). **Bevagna** (✉ Piazza Silvestri, ☎ 0742/361667). **Foligno** (✉ Porta Romana 126, ☎ 0742/354459). **Montefalco** (✉ Via Ringhiera

Umbra, ☎ 0742/379598). **Narni** (✉ Piazza del Popolo 18, ☎ 0744/715362). **Orvieto** (✉ Piazza del Duomo 24, ☎ 0763/341772). **Spello** (✉ Piazza Matteotti 3, ☎ 0742/301009). **Spoleto** (✉ Piazza della Libertà 7, ☎ 0743/238920). **Terni** (✉ Viale C. Battisti 7/a, ☎ 0744/423047). **Todi** (✉ Piazza Umberto I, ☎ 075/8945416).

10 BACKGROUND AND ESSENTIALS

Portrait of Florence, Tuscany, and Umbria

Artistically Speaking: A Glossary

Books and Movies

Chronology

Vocabulary

THE ARTLESS ART OF ITALIAN COOKING

YOU ARE STAYING WITH friends in their villa in a windswept olive orchard above Florence. After a day in town—a morning at the Palazzo Pitti, afternoon in the Brancacci Chapel—you have returned to rest. In the garden, you find your hostess lifting heavy tomatoes into a basket, the acrid smell of their skins wafting up in the gentle September heat. You pick basil and tug figs from a tree that warms its back against the 14th-century kitchen wall. Inside, you watch your hostess rinse greens in the quarried stone sink. The tomatoes are still sun-warm when she scoops them, chopped, into a blender with the basil and a stream of olive oil; she pours the mixture into a faience bowl over steaming pasta. You eat at the kitchen table, pour wine from a crockery pitcher, and wipe your bowl with torn chunks of flour-flecked bread. Over the greens your hostess drizzles more olive oil and a bit of rock salt pinched from an open bowl. The figs melt in your mouth like chocolate. A scalding syrup of Arabic coffee streams from the *macchinetta,* and you're ready for a midnight survey of the olive groves.

Simple, earthy, at once wholesome and sensual, as sophisticated in its purity as the most complex cuisine, as inspired in its aesthetics as the art and architecture of its culture, Italian cooking strikes a chord that resonates today as it did in the Medici courts. Its enduring appeal can be traced to an ancient principle: respect for the essence of the thing itself—nothing more, nothing less. Like Michelangelo freeing the prisoners that dwelt within the stone—innate, organic—an Italian chef seems intuitively to seek out the crux of the thing he is about to cook and flatter it, subtly, with the purest of complements. To lay a translucent sheet of prosciutto—earthy, gamey, faintly redolent of brine—across the juicy pulchritude of a melon wedge is a stroke of insight into the nature of two ingredients as profound as the imaginings of Galileo.

Considering the pizzas, lasagnas, and red-drenched spaghetti that still pass for Italian food in many places abroad, it's no surprise that visitors to Italy are often struck by the austerity of the true Italian dishes put before them. The pasta is only lightly accented, not drowning in an industrial ladle-full of strong, soupy sauce. And while there may have been a parade of vegetable *antipasti,* the salad itself bears no resemblance to the smorgasbord of Anglo-American salad bars—it's a simple mix of greens, a drizzle of oil, a spritz, perhaps, of red-wine vinegar. If you've just come from Germanic countries, you'll notice a lack of Maggi, the bottled brown "flavor enhancer" that singes the tongue with monosodium glutamate, on the table. If you've come from Belgium, you'll miss the sauceboat of Hollandaise. And if you've come from France, you may shrug dismissively at the isolated ingredients you're served, saying as other Frenchmen before you, "But this is not really a true *cuisine. . . ."*

Ah, but it is. Shunning the complexities of heavy French sauces and avoiding the elaborate farce, Italian cuisine—having unloaded the aspirations of *alta cucina* onto its northern neighbors when Catherine de' Medici moved (chefs and all) to Paris—stands alone, proud, puristic, unaffected.

The Italians' pride comes in part from a confidence in their raw ingredients, an earthiness that informs the appreciation of every citizen-connoisseur, from the roughest peasant in workers' blue to the vintner in shoulder-tied cashmere: they are in touch with land and sea. In the country, your host can tell you the source of every ingredient on the table, from the neighbor's potted goose to the porcini gathered in the beech grove yesterday. In the city, the market replaces the country network, and aggressive shopping will trace the genealogy of every mushroom, every artichoke, every wooden scoop of olives. And in balconies overhanging the seashore, the squid floating in their rich, blue-black ink were bought from a fisherman on the beach at dawn.

Careening in your rental car down the western coast, clinging to the waterfront through sea-shanty villages that cantilever over the roaring surf, you feel a morning lag: your breakfast of *latte macchiato* and sugary *cornetto* has worn away. A real espresso would hit the spot; you hurtle down a web of switchbacks and pull into a seaside inn. You sip aromatic coffee and watch the waves. An hour passes in reverie—an aperitif, perhaps? Another hour over the Martini rosso, and you give in to the impulse, adjourning to the dining room. The odor of wood smoke drifts from the kitchen. A nutty risotto with a blush of tomato precedes a vast platter—austere, unembellished—of smoke-grilled fish, still sizzling, lightly brushed with oil, and glittering with rock salt. At the table beside yours, when the platter arrives, the woman rises and fillets the fish dexterously, serving her husband and sons.

There's a wholesomeness in the way Italians eat that is charming and contagious. If American foodies pick and kvetch and French gastronomes worship, Italians plunge into their meal with frank joy, earnest appreciation, and ebullient conversation. Yet they do not overindulge: portions are light, the drinking gentle, late suppers spartan with concern for digestion uppermost. It's as if the voice of Mamma still whispers moderation in their ear. They may, on the other hand, take disproportionate pleasure in watching guests eat, in surrounding them with congenial company, in pouncing on the bill. (This wholesome spirit even carries into the very bars: unlike the dark, louche atmosphere of Anglo lounges and pubs, in Italy you'll drink your *amaro* in a fluorescent-lit coffee bar without a whiff of sin in the air.)

Yet for all their straightforwardness, Italians are utterly at ease with their heritage, steeped from birth in the art and architecture that surrounds them. Without a hint of the grandiose, they'll construct a still life of figs and Bosc pears worthy of Caravaggio; a butcher will drape iridescent pheasants and quail, heads dangling, with the panache of a couturier. Consider the artless beauty of ruby-raw beef on an emerald bed of arugula, named for the preferred colors of the Venetian painter Carpaccio; pure

white porcelain on damask; a mosaic of olives and pimientos in blown glass; a flash of folkloric pottery on a polished plank of oak.

In fact, it must be said: a large part of the pleasure of Italian dining is dining in Italy. We have all eaten in Italian restaurants elsewhere. The food can be superb, the ingredients authentic, the pottery and linens imported by hand. Yet who can conjure the blood-red ocher crumbling to gold on a Roman wall, the indigo and pastel hues of fishing boats rocking in a marina, the snow flurry of sugar papers on a café floor? These impart the essence that—as much as the basil on your *bruschetta*—flavors your Italian dining experience.

Inside the great walls of Lucca, you are lunching—slowly, copiously, and at length—in the shade of a vaulted portico. Strips of roasted eggplant and pepper steeped in garlic and oil; tortelloni stuffed with squab in a pool of butter and sage; roasted veal laced with green peppercorns; blackberries in thick cream. The bottle of Brunello di Montalcino, alas, is drained. It has been a perfect morning, walking the ramparts, and you have found the perfect restaurant: a Raphaelesque perspective of arcades and archways, pillars, porches, and loges spreads before you. The shadows and lines are strong in the afternoon sun; you admire from your seat in the cross breeze. It's only slowly that you realize that this Merchant/Ivory moment has a sound track, so organic to the scene you hadn't noticed—but now you feel goose bumps rising on your neck. It is Puccini: a young woman is singing, beautifully, from a groined arcade across the square, accompanied by a portable tape player.

". . . Ma quando vien lo sgelo . . . il primo sole è mio . . ."

Your coffee goes cold, untouched until the song, the moment, are over—and, in all its multifaceted magnificence, your Italian meal as well.

— Nancy Coons

ARTISTICALLY SPEAKING: A GLOSSARY

The eloquence of the world's greatest masterpieces can be deafening, and Italy's treasures—their message made manifest in marble, pigment, and precious metals—instill a spirit of awe. The privilege of enjoying this bounty of the ages can be enhanced by a familiarity with the terms of art-speak. Here is a limited glossary. Many of these Italian words are now part of the basic art-history vocabulary.

Acanthus: Sculptural ornamentation from antiquity; it's based on the foliage of the acanthus plant.

Apse: A semicircular terminus found behind the altar in a church.

Atrium: The courtyard in front of the entrance to an ancient Roman villa or an early church.

Badia: Abbey.

Baldacchino: A canopy—often made of stone—above a church altar, supported by columns.

Baptistery: A separate structure or area in a church where rites of baptism are held.

Baroque: A 17th-century European art movement in which dramatic, elaborate ornamentation was used to stir viewers' emotions. The most famous Italian baroque artists were Carracci and Bernini.

Basilica: A rectangular Roman public building divided into aisles by rows of columns. Many early churches were built on the basilican plan, but the term is also applied to some churches without specific reference to architecture.

Belvedere: Usually a lookout point for vistas; the word means "beautiful view."

Campanile: A bell tower of a church.

Capital: The crowning section of a column, usually decorated with Doric, Ionic, or Corinthian ornament.

Chiaroscuro: Literally "light/dark;" used to describe the distribution of light and shade in a painting, either with a marked contrast or a muted tonal gradation.

Cinquecento: Literally, "five hundred," used in Italian to refer to the 16th century.

Contrapposto: A dramatic pose of a sculpted figure in which the upper portion of the body is placed in opposition to the lower portion.

Cortile: Courtyard.

Cupola: Dome.

Duomo: Cathedral.

Fresco: A wall-painting technique, used in Roman times and again in the early Renaissance, in which pigment was applied to wet plaster.

Gothic: Medieval architectural and ornamental style featuring pointed arches, high interior vaulting, and flying buttresses to emphasize height and, symbolically, an ascension to heaven.

Grotesques: Decorations of fanciful human and animal forms, embellished with flowers; first used in Nero's Golden House and rediscovered during the Renaissance.

Loggia: Roofed balcony or gallery.

Maestà: The Virgin and Child enthroned in majesty often surrounded by angels, saints, or prophets.

Mannerism: Style of the mid-16th century, in which artists—such as Pontormo and Rosso Fiorentino—sought to replace the warm, humanizing ideals of Leonardo and Raphael with super-elegant, emotionally cold forms. Portraits in the Mannerist style feature lively colors and often strangely contorted bodies.

Nave: The central aisle of a church.

Palazzo: A palace, or more generally, any large building.

Perspective: The illusion of three-dimensional space that was obtained in the early 15th century with the discovery that all parallel lines running in one direction meet at a single point on the horizon known as the vanishing point.

Piano nobile: The main floor of a palace (the first floor above ground level).

Pietà: Literally "piety"; refers to an image of the Virgin Mary holding the crucified body of Christ on her lap.

Polyptych: A painting—often an altarpiece—on multiple wooden panels that are joined.

Predella: A series of small paintings found below the main section of an altarpiece.

Putti: Cherubs, cupids, or other images of infant boys in painting.

Quattrocento: Literally "four hundred"; refers to the 15th century.

Renaissance: Major school of Italian art, literature, and philosophy (14th century–16th century) that fused innovations in realism with the rediscovery of the great heritage of classical antiquity. After Giotto introduced a new naturalism into painting in the early 14th century, Florentine artists of the early and mid-15th century, such as Masaccio and Fra Filippo Lippi, paved the way for the later 15th-century realism of Botticelli and Ghirlandaio. The movement particularly flourished in Florence and Venice, but most other Italian cities were participants as well. Some scholars believe that the movement culminated in Rome with the High Renaissance (circa 1490–1520) and the masterpieces of Leonardo, Raphael, and Michelangelo.

Rococo: Light, dainty 18th-century art and architectural style created in reaction to heavy baroque. Tiepolo is the leading painter of the rococo style.

Romanesque: Architectural style of the 11th and 12th centuries that reworked ancient Roman forms, particularly barrel and groin vaults. Stark, severe, and magisterial, Romanesque basilicas are among Italy's most awe-inspiring churches.

Sacra conversazione: A "holy conversation" wherein saints act as intercessor to the Madonna and Child.

Tondo: Circular painting or sculpture.

Triptych: A three-panel painting executed on wood.

Trompe l'oeil: An artistic technique employed to "fool the eye" into believing that the object or scene depicted is actually real.

Veduta: A painting of a city or landscape as viewed from afar, popular in the 18th century.

BOOKS AND MOVIES

Books

The musings of some well-known travelers who visited Tuscany and Umbria when travel was as much ordeal as vacation make for entertaining reading. Many keen observations by Henry James's *Italian Hours* (offered in many editions, including *Traveling in Italy with Henry James: Essays*) and D.H. Lawrence's *Etruscan Places* still hold true, and their experiences put modern travel into an interesting perspective.

For background, *The Italians,* by Luigi Barzini, is a comprehensive, lively analysis of the Italian national character, still worthy reading although published in 1964. More-recent reflections on Italian life include *Italian Days*, by Barbara Grizzuti Harrison, and *That Fine Italian Hand,* by Paul Hofmann, for many years *New York Times* bureau chief in Rome. For a general historical and art-history framework, Harry Hearder's *Italy, a Short History* cuts right to the chase, with 2,000 years covered in fewer than 300 pages, and Michael Levey's clear and concise treatments of the Renaissance, *Early Renaissance* and *High Renaissance,* are good places to begin. The history of the Renaissance, the great artists and political figures and turbulent power struggles throughout the region, make great reading when told by Christopher Hibbert, in *The House of Medici: Its Rise and Fall.* Two wonderfully written and beautifully illustrated volumes on that most vaunted of artistic periods are John T. Paoletti and Gary M. Radke's *Art in Renaissance Italy* and Evelyn Welch's eloquent *Art and Society in Italy 1350–1500. The Civilization of the Renaissance in Italy,* by 19th-century Swiss historian Jacob Burckhardt, is the classic study of the culture and politics of the time.

You can learn about the Renaissance from those who actually lived it in *The Autobiography of Benvenuto Cellini,* Giorgio Vasari's *Lives of the Artists,* and Machiavelli's *The Prince,* and some recent studies of famous Renaissance and baroque figures offer fine opportunities to enter into lives lived centuries ago. Ross King's highly anecdotal *Brunelleschi's Dome* tells in detail about the making of Florence's fabled cupola. R.W.B. Lewis fleshes out the details of perhaps Italy's most famous poet in *Dante*; also worth a look in the Penguin Lives series is Sherwin Nuland's *Leonardo da Vinci.* A more scholarly, but eminently readable, biography is *Leon Battista Alberti: Master Builder of the Italian Renaissance* by Princeton Renaissance historian Anthony Grafton. Although the title is somewhat of a misnomer (as it's more about father than daughter), Dava Sobel's *Galileo's Daughter* artfully brings to life the brilliant astronomer and his devotion to his family, particularly his first-born, Suor Maria Celeste.

Novels and historical fiction often impart a greater sense of a place than straight history books: George Eliot reconstructs 15th-century Florentine life in *Romola*; Irving Stone's best-selling *The Agony and the Ecstasy* romanticizes the life of Michelangelo but paints an enduring picture of Renaissance Florence; Umberto Eco's *The Name of the Rose* is a gripping murder mystery that will leave you with tremendous insight into monastic life in Italy. Lovers of detective stories are likely to be highly entertained by the antics of Aurelio Zen, Michael Dibdin's bumbling detective. It's best to read them in order, as he builds on characters and situations; each novel is set in an Italian city. The series commences in Perugia with *Ratking.* Florence is the setting for two of Magdalen Nabb's entertaining thrillers: *Death in Autumn* and *Death of a Dutchman.*

Some English-speaking visitors have chosen to settle in Italy long-term, and the resulting expatriate memoirs make up their own literary subgenre. In *A Tuscan Childhood,* Kinta Beevor lovingly recounts growing up in a castle near Carrara between the two world wars. Those with a yen to buy a dilapidated farmhouse and restore it can check out the experience of Frances Mayes in *Under the Tuscan Sun: At Home in Italy* (as well as in *Bella Tuscany* and *In Tuscany*). Matthew Spender's *Within Tuscany: Reflections on a Time and Place* and Lisa St. Aubin de Terán's *A Valley in Italy: The Many Seasons of a Villa in Umbria* are both rewarding reads. Tim Parks's *Italian Neighbors* tells with candor and good humor of the contemporary expatriate life in Verona.

If you truly want to understand the Italian psyche, learn about the national passion for *calcio* (soccer). Tim Parks made his own soccer odyssey with the Verona club and recorded his experiences in *A Season with Verona.*

For glimpses of the Tuscan landscape, pick up Harold Acton's *Great Houses of Tuscany: The Tuscan Villas* or Carey More's *Views from a Tuscan Vineyard.* The glories of historic Italian gardens are caught in the ravishing photographs of Judith Chatfield's *Gardens of the Italian Lakes* and Ethne Clark's *Gardens of Tuscany.* In the pages of Fodor's *Escape to Tuscany,* the region is brought to life via stunning photographs and wonderful prose depicting such special experiences as staying at the convent where *The English Patient* was filmed and ballooning over Chianti's vineyards.

Although every year there are more and more cookbooks on Italian food, Waverley Root's *Food of Italy,* published in 1977, is still a handy (if not infallible) reference. Faith Heller Wilinger's *Eating in Italy* helps to guide you to the good food and restaurants, and Burton Anderson's *Best Italian Wines* helps guide you through wine lists.

Movies

You'll recognize the idyllic scenery of central Italy in numerous English-language films, including the Academy Award–winning *The English Patient* (1996), Kenneth Branagh's *Much Ado About Nothing* (1993), and Bernardo Bertolucci's *Stealing Beauty* (1996). Indispensable and not at all dated are Merchant/Ivory's *A Room with a View* (1986) and *Enchanted April* (1991), which depicts the awakening spirits of four English women who have rented a villa in Tuscany. The scenes of Florence are a good reason to see *Up at the Villa* (2000), a slow-moving story about a young English widow in Italy at the start of World War II. *Tea with Mussolini* (1999) is Franco Zeffirelli's love letter to a group of Anglophone women who helped raise a character very much like the director himself in pre–World War II Tuscany.

FLORENCE, TUSCANY, AND UMBRIA AT A GLANCE

ca. 1000 BC   Etruscans arrive in central Italy.

ca. 800 BC   Rise of Etruscan city-states.

510 BC   Foundation of the Roman republic; expulsion of Etruscans from Roman territory.

ca. 350 BC   Rome extends rule to Tuscia (Tuscany), the land of the Etruscans.

ca. 220 BC   Umbria, the land of the Umbri and later Etruscans, comes under Roman sway.

133 BC   Rome rules entire Mediterranean Basin except Egypt.

49 BC   Julius Caesar conquers Gaul.

46 BC   Julian calendar is introduced; it remains in use until AD 1582.

44 BC   Julius Caesar is assassinated.

27 BC   Rome's Imperial Age begins; Octavian (now named Augustus) becomes the first emperor and is later deified. The Augustan Age is celebrated in the works of Virgil (70 BC–AD 19), Ovid (43 BC–AD 17), Livy (59 BC–AD 17), and Horace (65–8 BC).

14 AD   Augustus dies.

65   Emperor Nero begins the persecution of Christians in the empire; Sts. Peter and Paul are executed.

117   The Roman Empire reaches its apogee.

165   A smallpox epidemic ravages the Empire.

ca. 150–200   Christianity gains a foothold within the Empire, with the theological writings of Clement, Tertullian, and Origen.

212   Roman citizenship is conferred on all nonslaves in the Empire.

238   The first wave of Germanic invasions penetrates Italy.

293   Diocletian reorganizes the Empire into West and East.

313   The Edict of Milan grants toleration of Christianity within the Empire.

410   Rome is sacked by Visigoths.

476   The last Roman Emperor, Romulus Augustus, is deposed. The Empire of Rome falls.

552   Eastern Emperor Justinian (527–565) recovers control of Italy.

570   Lombards gain control of much of Italy, including Rome.

590   Papal power expands under Gregory the Great.

ca. 600–750   Lucca is chief city of Tuscany.

774   Frankish ruler Charlemagne (742–814) invades Italy under papal authority and is crowned Holy Roman Emperor by Pope Leo III (800).

ca. 800–900   The breakup of Charlemagne's (Carolingian) realm leads to the rise of Italian city-states.

1077 Pope Gregory VII leads the Holy See into conflict with the Germanic Holy Roman Empire.

1152–90 Frederick I (Barbarossa) is crowned Holy Roman Emperor (1155); punitive expeditions by his forces (Ghibellines) are countered by the Guelphs, creators of the powerful Papal States in central Italy. Guelph-Ghibelline conflict becomes a feature of medieval life.

ca. 1200 Lucca appears strongest of Tuscan cities. Religious revival in Umbria centers on activities of St. Francis of Assisi and the foundation of the Franciscan order. Umbria takes the lead in art and architecture, attracting Pisano, Cimabue, Giotto, Simone Martini, and Lorenzetti.

1250 Florence takes the cultural and financial lead.

1262 Florentine bankers issue Europe's first bills of exchange.

1264 Charles I of Anjou invades Italy, intervening in the continuing Guelph-Ghibelline conflict.

1290–1375 Tuscan literary giants Dante Alighieri (1265–1321), Francesco Petrarch (1304–74), and Giovanni Boccaccio (1313–75) give written imprimatur to modern Italian language.

1309 The pope moves to Avignon in France, under the protection of French kings.

1376 The pope returns to Rome, but rival Avignonese popes stand in opposition, creating the Great Schism until 1417.

ca. 1380–1420 Umbrian cities ruled by *condottieri*.

1402 The last German intervention into Italy is repulsed by the Lombards.

1443 Brunelleschi's (1377–1446) cupola is completed on Florence's Duomo.

1469–92 Lorenzo "Il Magnifico" (1449–92), the Medici patron of the arts, rules in Florence.

1498 Girolamo Savonarola (1452–98), the austere Dominican friar, is executed for heresy after leading Florence into a drive for moral purification, typified by his burning of books and decorations in the "bonfire of vanities."

1504 Michelangelo's (1475–1564) *David* is unveiled in Florence's Piazza della Signoria.

1513 Machiavelli's (1469–1527) *The Prince* is published.

1521 The Pope excommunicates Martin Luther (1483–1546) of Germany, precipitating the Protestant Reformation.

1540 Pope Paul III consolidates rule of Umbria with other Papal States.

1545–63 The Council of Trent formulates the Catholic response to the Reformation.

ca. 1700 Opera develops as an art form in Italy.

1720–90 The Great Age of the Grand Tour: Northern Europeans visit Italy and start the vogue for classical studies. Among the famous visitors are Edward Gibbon (1758), Jacques-Louis David (1775), and Johann Wolfgang von Goethe (1786).

1796 Napoléon begins his Italian campaigns, annexing Rome and imprisoning Pope Pius VI four years later.

1801 Tuscany is made kingdom of Etruria within French domain.

1807–09 Tuscany is a French *département*; Umbria is annexed (1808) to French empire as département of Trasimeno.

1815 Austria controls much of Italy after Napoléon's downfall.

1848 Revolutionary troops under Risorgimento (Unification) leaders Giuseppe Mazzini (1805–72) and Giuseppe Garibaldi (1807–82) establish a republic in Rome.

1849 French troops crush rebellion and restore Pope Pius IX.

1860 Garibaldi and his "Thousand" defeat the Bourbon rulers in Sicily and Naples.

1861 Tuscany and Umbria join Kingdom of Sardinia, which becomes Kingdom of Italy.

1870 Rome is finally captured by Risorgimento troops and is declared capital of Italy by King Vittorio Emanuele II.

1900 King Umberto I is assassinated by an anarchist; he is succeeded by King Vittorio Emanuele III.

1915 Italy enters World War I on the side of the Allies.

1922 Fascist "black shirts" under Benito Mussolini (1883–1945) march on Rome; Mussolini becomes prime minister and later "Il Duce" (head of Italy).

1929 The Lateran Treaty: Mussolini recognizes Vatican City as a sovereign state, and the Church recognizes Rome as the capital of Italy.

1940–44 In World War II, Italy fights with the Axis powers until its capitulation (1943), when Mussolini flees Rome. Italian partisans and Allied troops from the landings at Anzio (January 1944) win victory at Cassino (March 1944) and force the eventual withdrawal of German troops from Italy.

1957 The Treaty of Rome is signed, and Italy becomes a founding member of the European Economic Community.

1966 November flood damages many of Florence's artistic treasures.

1968–79 The growth of left-wing activities leads to the formation of the Red Brigades and provokes right-wing reactions. Bombings and kidnapings culminate in the abduction and murder of Prime Minister Aldo Moro (1916–78).

1992 The Christian Democrat Party, in power throughout the postwar period, loses its hold on a relative majority in Parliament.

1993 Italians vote for sweeping reforms after the Tangentopoli (Bribe City) scandal exposes widespread political corruption, including politicians' collusion with organized crime. A bomb outside the Galleria degli Uffizi in Florence kills five but spares the museum's most precious artwork; authorities blame the Cosa Nostra, flexing its muscles in the face of a crackdown.

1994 A center-right coalition wins in spring elections, and media magnate Silvio Berlusconi becomes premier—only to be deposed within a year. Italian politics seem to be evolving into the equivalent of a two-party system.

1995 Newly appointed Lamberto Dini takes hold of the government's rudder and, as president of the Council of Ministers, institutes major reforms and replaces old-line politicians.

1996 A league of center-left parties wins national elections and puts together a government coalition that sees the Democratic Party of the Left (PDS), the former Communist party, into power for the first time in Italy.

1997 Political stability and an austerity program put Italy on track toward the European Monetary Union and adoption of the single European currency. A series of earthquakes hits the mountainous interior of central Italy, severely damaging villages and some historic towns. In Assisi, portions of the vault of the Basilica di San Francesco crumble, destroying frescoes by Cimabue.

1998 Romano Prodi's center-left government, widely praised for its economic policies and lack of scandals, is brought down by a no-confidence vote in October, when the Reformed-Communist Party (PCI) withdraws its support for Prodi. The center-left regroups and forms a new government under Massimo D'Alema, leader of the former Communist Party, who in large part continues Prodi's policies.

1999 Rome continues preparations for the Giubileo (Holy Year) celebrations in 2000 with an array of public-works projects.

2000 The Jubilee of the third millennium is proclaimed by Pope John Paul II. Millions of pilgrims flock to religious sites througout the country.

2001 Media mogul Silvio Berlusconi is elected prime minister for the second time.

2002 The lira is supplanted by the euro as the currency of the land.

WORDS AND PHRASES

English	Italian	Pronunciation

Basics

English	Italian	Pronunciation
Yes/no	Sí/No	see/no
Please	Per favore	pear fa-**vo**-ray
Yes, please	Sí grazie	see **grah**-tsee-ay
Thank you	Grazie	**grah**-tsee-ay
You're welcome	Prego	**pray**-go
Excuse me, sorry	Scusi	**skoo**-zee
Sorry!	Mi dispiace!	mee dis-spee-**ah**-chay
Good morning/afternoon	Buongiorno	bwohn-**jor**-no
Good evening	Buona sera	**bwoh**-na **say**-ra
Good-bye	Arrivederci	a-ree-vah-**dare**-chee
Mr. (Sir)	Signore	see-**nyo**-ray
Mrs. (Ma'am)	Signora	see-**nyo**-ra
Miss	Signorina	see-nyo-**ree**-na
Pleased to meet you	Piacere	pee-ah-**chair**-ray
How are you?	Come sta?	**ko**-may **stah**
Very well, thanks	Bene, grazie	**ben**-ay **grah**-tsee-ay
And you?	E lei?	ay **lay**-ee
Hello (phone)	Pronto?	**proan**-to

Numbers

English	Italian	Pronunciation
one	uno	**oo**-no
two	due	**doo**-ay
three	tre	tray
four	quattro	**kwah**-tro
five	cinque	**cheen**-kway
six	sei	say
seven	sette	**set**-ay
eight	otto	**oh**-to
nine	nove	**no**-vay
ten	dieci	dee-**eh**-chee
eleven	undici	**oon**-dee-chee
twelve	dodici	**doe**-dee-chee
thirteen	tredici	**tray**-dee-chee
fourteen	quattordici	kwa-**tore**-dee-chee
fifteen	quindici	**kwin**-dee-chee
sixteen	sedici	**say**-dee-chee
seventeen	diciassette	dee-cha-**set**-ay
eighteen	diciotto	dee-**cho**-to
nineteen	diciannove	dee-cha-**no**-vay

twenty	venti	**vain**-tee
twenty-one	ventuno	vain-**too**-no
twenty-two	ventidue	vain-tee-**doo**-ay
thirty	trenta	**train**-ta
forty	quaranta	kwa-**rahn**-ta
fifty	cinquanta	cheen-**kwahn**-ta
sixty	sessanta	seh-**sahn**-ta
seventy	settanta	seh-**tahn**-ta
eighty	ottanta	o-**tahn**-ta
ninety	novanta	no-**vahn**-ta
one hundred	cento	**chen**-to
one thousand	mille	**mee**-lay
ten thousand	diecimila	dee-eh-chee-**mee**-la

Useful Phrases

Do you speak English?	Parla inglese?	**par**-la een-**glay**-zay
I don't speak Italian	Non parlo italiano	non **par**-lo ee-tal-**yah**-no
I don't understand	Non capisco	non ka-**peess**-ko
Can you please repeat?	Può ripetere?	pwo ree-**pet**-ay-ray
Slowly!	Lentamente!	**len**-ta-men-tay
I don't know	Non lo so	non lo **so**
I'm American/ British	Sono americano(a) Sono inglese	**so**-no a-may-ree-**kah**-no(a) **so**-no een-**glay**-zay
What's your name?	Come si chiama?	**ko**-may see kee-**ah**-ma
My name is . . .	Mi chiamo . . .	mee kee-**ah**-mo
What time is it?	Che ore sono?	kay **o**-ray **so**-no
How?	Come?	**ko**-may
When?	Quando?	**kwan**-doe
Yesterday/today/ tomorrow	Ieri/oggi/domani	**yer**-ee/**o**-jee/ do-**mah**-nee
This morning/ afternoon	Stamattina/Oggi pomeriggio	sta-ma-**tee**-na/**o**-jee po-mer-**ee**-jo
Tonight	Stasera	sta-**ser**-a
What?	Che cosa?	kay **ko**-za
What is it?	Che cos'è?	kay ko-**zay**
Why?	Perché?	pear-**kay**
Who?	Chi?	kee
Where is . . .	Dov'è . . .	doe-**veh**
the bus stop?	la fermata dell'autobus?	la fer-**mah**-ta del ow-toe-**booss**
the train station?	la stazione?	la sta-tsee-**oh**-nay
the subway station?	la metropolitana?	la may-tro-po-lee-**tah**-na
the terminal?	il terminale?	eel ter-mee-**nah**-lay
the post office?	l'ufficio postale?	loo-**fee**-cho po-**stah**-lay

the bank?	la banca?	la **bahn**-ka
the . . . hotel?	l'hotel . . . ?	lo-**tel**
the store?	il negozio?	eel nay-**go**-tsee-o
the cashier?	la cassa?	la **kah**-sa
the . . . museum?	il museo . . . ?	eel moo-**zay**-o
the hospital?	l'ospedale?	lo-spay-**dah**-lay
the first aid station?	il pronto soccorso?	eel **pron**-to so-**kor**-so
the elevator?	l'ascensore?	la-shen-**so**-ray
a telephone?	un telefono?	oon tay-**lay**-fo-no
Where are the restrooms?	Dov'è il bagno?	do-**vay** eel **bahn**-yo
Here/there	Qui/là	kwee/la
Left/right	A sinistra/a destra	a see-**neess**-tra/a **des**-tra
Straight ahead	Avanti dritto	a-**vahn**-tee **dree**-to
Is it near/far?	È vicino/lontano?	ay vee-**chee**-no/lon-**tah**-no
I'd like . . .	Vorrei . . .	vo-**ray**
a room	una camera	**oo**-na **kah**-may-ra
the key	la chiave	la kee-**ah**-vay
a newspaper	un giornale	oon jor-**nah**-lay
a stamp	un francobollo	oon frahn-ko-**bo**-lo
I'd like to buy . . .	Vorrei comprare . . .	vo-**ray** kom-**prah**-ray
a cigar	un sigaro	oon see-**gah**-ro
cigarettes	delle sigarette	**day**-lay see-ga-**ret**-ay
some matches	dei fiammiferi	**day**-ee **fee**-ah-**mee**-fer-ee
some soap	una saponetta	**oo**-na sa-po-**net**-a
a city plan	una pianta della città	**oo**-na **pyahn**-ta day-la chee-**tah**
a road map of . . .	una carta stradale di . . .	**oo**-na **cart**-a stra-**dah**-lay dee
a country map	una carta geografica	**oo**-na **cart**-a jay-o-**grah**-fee-ka
a magazine	una rivista	**oo**-na ree-**veess**-ta
envelopes	delle buste	**day**-lay **booss**-tay
writing paper	della carta da lettere	**day**-la **cart**-a da **let**-air-ay
a postcard	una cartolina	**oo**-na car-toe-**lee**-na
a guidebook	una guida turistica	**oo**-na **gwee**-da too-**reess**-tee-ka
How much is it?	Quanto costa?	**kwahn**-toe **coast**-a
It's expensive/cheap	È caro/economico	ay **car**-o/ay-ko-no-mee-ko
A little/a lot	Poco/tanto	**po**-ko/**tahn**-to
More/less	Più/meno	pee-**oo**/**may**-no
Enough/too (much)	Abbastanza/troppo	a-bas-**tahn**-sa/**tro**-po
I am sick	Sto male	sto **mah**-lay
Call a doctor	Chiama un dottore	kee-**ah**-mah oon doe-**toe**-ray
Help!	Aiuto!	a-**yoo**-toe
Stop!	Alt!	ahlt

| Fire! | Al fuoco! | ahl **fwo**-ko |
| Caution/Look out! | Attenzione! | a-ten-**syon**-ay |

Dining Out

A bottle of . . .	Una bottiglia di . . .	**oo**-na bo-**tee**-lee-ah dee
A cup of . . .	Una tazza di . . .	**oo**-na **tah**-tsa dee
A glass of . . .	Un bicchiere di . . .	oon bee-key-**air**-ay dee
Bill/check	Il conto	eel **cone**-toe
Bread	Il pane	eel **pah**-nay
Breakfast	La prima colazione	la **pree**-ma ko-la-**tsee**-oh-nay
Cocktail/aperitif	L'aperitivo	la-pay-ree-**tee**-vo
Dinner	La cena	la **chen**-a
Fixed-price menu	Menù a prezzo fisso	may-**noo** a **pret**-so **fee**-so
Fork	La forchetta	la for-**ket**-a
I am diabetic	Ho il diabete	o eel dee-a-**bay**-tay
I am vegetarian	Sono vegetariano/a	**so**-no vay-jay-ta-ree-**ah**-no/a
I'd like . . .	Vorrei . . .	vo-**ray**
I'd like to order	Vorrei ordinare	vo-**ay** or-dee-**nah**-ray
Is service included?	Il servizio è incluso?	eel ser-**vee**-tzee-o ay een-**kloo**-zo
It's good/bad	È buono/cattivo	ay **bwo**-no/ka-**tee**-vo
It's hot/cold	È caldo/freddo	ay **kahl**-doe/**fred**-o
Knife	Il coltello	eel kol-**tel**-o
Lunch	Il pranzo	eel **prahnt**-so
Menu	Il menù	eel may-**noo**
Napkin	Il tovagliolo	eel toe-va-lee-**oh**-lo
Please give me . . .	Mi dia . . .	mee **dee**-a
Salt	Il sale	eel **sah**-lay
Spoon	Il cucchiaio	eel koo-kee-**ah**-yo
Sugar	Lo zucchero	lo **tsoo**-ker-o
Waiter/Waitress	Cameriere/cameriera	ka-mare-**yer**-ay/ka-mare-**yer**-a
Wine list	La lista dei vini	la **lee**-sta **day**-ee **vee**-nee

INDEX

Fodor's Key to the Guides

America's guidebook leader publishes guides for every kind of traveler. Check out our many series and find your perfect match.

Fodor's Gold Guides
America's favorite travel-guide series offers the most detailed insider reviews of hotels, restaurants, and attractions in all price ranges, plus great background information, smart tips, and useful maps.

Fodor's Road Guide USA
Big guides for a big country—the most comprehensive guides to America's roads, packed with places to stay, eat, and play across the U.S.A. Just right for road warriors, family vacationers, and cross-country trekkers.

COMPASS AMERICAN GUIDES
Stunning guides from top local writers and photographers, with gorgeous photos, literary excerpts, and colorful anecdotes. A must-have for culture mavens, history buffs, and new residents.

Fodor's CITYPACKS
Concise city coverage with a foldout map. The right choice for urban travelers who want everything under one cover.

Fodor's EXPLORING GUIDES
Hundreds of color photos bring your destination to life. Lively stories lend insight into the culture, history, and people.

Fodor's POCKET GUIDES
For travelers who need only the essentials. The best of Fodor's in pocket-size packages for just $9.95.

Fodor's To Go
Credit-card–size, magnetized color microguides that fit in the palm of your hand—perfect for "stealth" travelers or as gifts.

Fodor's FLASHMAPS
Every resident's map guide. 60 easy-to-follow maps of public transit, parks, museums, zip codes, and more.

Fodor's CITYGUIDES
Sourcebooks for living in the city: Thousands of in-the-know listings for restaurants, shops, sports, nightlife, and other city resources.

Fodor's AROUND THE CITY WITH KIDS
68 great ideas for family days, recommended by resident parents. Perfect for exploring in your own backyard or on the road.

Fodor's ESCAPES
Fill your trip with once-in-a-lifetime experiences, from ballooning in Chianti to overnighting in the Moroccan desert. These full-color dream books point the way.

Fodor's FYI
Get tips from the pros on planning the perfect trip. Learn how to pack, fly hassle-free, plan a honeymoon or cruise, stay healthy on the road, and travel with your baby.

Fodor's Languages for Travelers
Practice the local language before hitting the road. Available in phrase books, cassette sets, and CD sets.

Karen Brown's Guides
Engaging guides to the most charming inns and B&Bs in the U.S.A. and Europe, with easy-to-follow inn-to-inn itineraries.

Baedeker's Guides
Comprehensive guides, trusted since 1829, packed with A–Z reviews and star ratings.

At bookstores everywhere.   www.fodors.com/books